from Ady
AND Sarah
ISRAEL 1991

ISRAEL
ROOTS & ROUTES

"The Zion concept of the Jewish people can be called a national concept.... This national concept was named after a place and not... after a people, which indicates that it is not so much a question of a particular people as such but of its association with a particular land, its native land."

Martin Buber

ISRAEL
ROOTS & ROUTES

A NATION LIVING IN ITS LANDSCAPE

EDITED BY IRIT ZAHARONI

דרך ארץ

עם חי בנופיו

בעריכת עירית זהרוני

DESIGN: **AMRAM PRAT**
TRANSLATION: **RACHEL ROWEN**

Production Manager: Yitzhak Kempler
Maps: Dalia Egozi
ISBN 965-05-0479-6
Typesetting: Aliyah Press Ltd.
Prepared for Publication: Dorit Bar-Adon, Michal Ḥay
Layout: Ruth Eilat
Montage: Yosef Yisrael, Kav-Or, Giv'atayim
Plates: Kav-Or, Giv'atayim
Printing: Peli Printing Works Ltd.
First Edition – 1990

preface

This book lays before the reader pictures of the Land of Israel and sagas of its various landscapes, telling of the land, its past and present existence.

A homeland is, first of all, its soil, rocks and stones, flowers and trees, mountains and valleys; it is the landscape in which the roots of the people are sunk, in which its spiritual and cultural essence took shape.

The way to love of the homeland lies in the fragrance of its flowers, through its thickets, over the face of its hard, unwelcoming rocks, up the side of its bald mountains. The aim of this book is not simply to convey information but to forge deep ties to the land and to its landscapes, to all that these express and tell travelers in these landscapes.

For some, the lovely scene and good feeling conveyed by simply spending time in them suffices. Others attain a higher level, seeking to understand the life that was interwoven with these landscapes. There is no contradiction between knowledge and aesthetic appreciation; the latter draws on the former and is reinforced by it.

When I was a child my father used to take us with him on hikes through the Jezreel Valley and the hills encompassing it. We used to stand on the heights of Mount Carmel, or Mount Gilboa', or Giv'at ha-Moreh, and drink in the wide open view. Then father would begin describing some event from the past: as if by the touch of a wand, the figure of Elijah would emerge before our eyes, girding his loins and running before Ahab's chariot; or the figure of Saul, returning downcast from 'En dor; the figure of Gideon, under cover of night, sneaking up to the Midianite camp. The past became immediate, alive, and we grieved over the death of Saul and his sons, or trembled in fear at the sight of Barak, son of Abinoam leading his people to war against Sisera.

Birds, stones, and flowers were more than a mere assemblage of animals, minerals, or vegetables; they were a source of aesthetic pleasure, a moving experience, and thus also an object of love.

From these hikes we came to understand that dry facts and an intellectual approach are not enough. A deeper appreciation, a tangible, immediate bond, a feeling of belonging to and loving the land, the people and its spiritual heritage, cannot be fully attained without a sense of identifying, without experiencing true, deep emotion.

In this book we share with the reader something of the great treasure which our father gave us through his unique love of the land and his special way of teaching us to know and love our land. We also incorporate in the book something of the small amount of written material which he left after him, in order to enrich the lives of others.

Long years of history and spiritual creativity, unparalleled by other nations or lands, have united the Land of Israel and the people of Israel. The history of the Jewish people, rooted in the landscapes of the Land of Israel, is not simply a remote tale of yore, for this story of the past nurtures our thoughts and deeds and has an impact on our life in the present.

Through its long years of exile the Jewish people kept the Land of Israel close to its heart, scenes of the land shimmering through the pages of the Book of Books which accompanied us along our way. When we had the good fortune to renew a Jewish state in our ancient homeland, we returned to direct contact with its landscapes once again and were able to know our land, experiencing it through all our senses. Long years of severance from the land cannot be wiped out in the blink of an eye. Renewing the immediate, organic bonds with the landscapes and with the events and spiritual creativity that these landscapes brought forth is a lengthy and difficult process.

One of the goals of this book is to draw young and old closer to the scenes of our land and the heritage of our people. To this end, articles written in a popular style have been contributed by scholars, educators, and guides who share a love of the Land of Israel and a desire to study it and convey their knowledge to others.

This volume, an anthology of articles subtitled "A Nation Living in its Landscape", is arranged under four headings, symbolically named after the gates of Jerusalem in the time of the Bible:

A. "Our Feet are Standing Within thy Gates, O Jerusalem" – a fitting way to begin, with sketches of the city at various periods.

B. "The Gate of My People" – landscapes which tell the sagas of the history of the Jewish people.

C. "The Gate Between the Two Walls" – sites around the Land of Israel representing different eras and events in chronological order.

D. "The New Gate" – stories of the Land of Israel reborn, legend and deed intertwined.

We wish the reader an enjoyable and rewarding experience as he peruses the pages of this book and, with new inspiration, traverses the routes of the Land of Israel.

Irit Zaharoni

table of contents

The New Gate
The Land of Israel Reborn

Our feet are standing
within thy gates,
O Jerusalem

Psalms 122:2

and david called it the city of david

Second Samuel 5:9

Menachem Zaharoni

david conquers jebusite jerusalem and defeats the philistines on the outskirts of the city

David, from Beth-lehem in the tribe of Judah, was the youngest of Jesse's sons. This young man **"was ruddy, and withal of beautiful eyes, and goodly to look upon"** (I Samuel 16:12). From his earliest days he was brave, inquisitive, and ambitious. He was yet a lad when he left his father's sheep for the vale of Elah, to see the battle of the Philistines against the Israelites. On the battlefield he dared challenge the Philistine giant Goliath to a duel, the giant heavily armed from head to foot and himself only equipped with a shepherd's sling. For killing Goliath he won the reward of becoming the king's son-in-law, husband of Saul's daughter, Michal. The people's love of young heroes was the king's downfall. **"And it came to pass as they came, when David returned from the slaughter of the Philistine, that the women came out of all the cities of Israel, singing and dancing, to meet king Saul, with timbrels, with joy, and with three-stringed instruments. And the women sang one to another in their play, and said: Saul hath slain his thousands, and David his ten thousands. And Saul was very wroth... and Saul eyed** [or viewed with ill-will, i.e. hated] **David from that day and forward"** (I Samuel 18:6-9). Jealousy is only human, and Saul was suspicious that his young heroic son-in-law, beloved of the people, would steal the crown from his royal line. Saul's fears grew to the point of obsession. He conspired against David, hoping to kill him. Thus persecuted, David gathered round himself a host of bold but embittered men, rejected by society and enamored of their young leader. At first David's men sought refuge in the outlying settlements of the Judean Desert and later in the strongholds of En Gedi (in the cleft hills resembling fortresses around En Gedi). The long arm of Saul reached him even there, compelling David and his men to go over to the land of their people's enemy, the Philistines. David, pursued by Saul, an enemy of the Philistines, was well received by Achish, the Philistine king of Gath, with the understanding that he would serve the Philistines' ends. Nevertheless, they did not trust David's loyalty and did not take him with them upon setting out to fight Saul on Mount Gilboa.

1

When Israel was routed on Mount Gilboa, David and his troops fled from the Philistines' territory to Hebron, the major city of the tribe of Judah. At first David was crowned king over the tribe of Judah alone; but as the civil war drew to a close, with almost all of the house of Saul annihilated, he was made king over all Israel.

To rid himself of the yoke of the Philistines, David immediately launched into military action. First he conquered the Jebusite city of Jerusalem, which lay in the highlands separating the tribe of Judah to the south from the tribe of Benjamin to the north, in order to create territorial continuity between the lands of the two tribes. Then he began his battle against the Philistines.

The Philistines had come to the Land of Israel in the 12th century b.c.e., about a hundred years after Joshua's conquests. They settled along the southern coastal strip of the land and from there tried to subjugate the entire land. Although they were a minority in comparison to the Israelites, they were excellent warriors and had a stable political regime and strong military organization.

"And when the Philistines heard that David was anointed king over Israel, all the Philistines went up to seek David" (II Samuel

1 *En-Rogel (Bir Aiyub) viewed from the southwest (Thompson, 1880).*

2 *The northern part of the City of David, below the wall of the Temple Mount, rising steeply over the Qidron Valley.*

3 *En-Rogel, a spring which served as an important source of water for Jerusalem, today enclosed in a building.*

4 *A section of the Jebusite wall, discovered in Kathleen Kenyon's excavations at the foot of the City of David, on the east.*

2

4

3

5:17). This was the beginning of the struggle between the Philistines and David at Baal-Perazim in Emeq Refa'im (the Valley of Rephaim; the modern-day vicinity of the train station in Jerusalem). In short order David decisively defeated the Philistines, so that they ceased being a major factor in the history of the Land of Israel. He confined them to the borders of their territory along the southern coastal plain and apparently also subjugated them. David created an Israelite empire extending from the upper Euphrates in Syria to the eastern estuary of the Nile in Egypt, and from the desert in eastern Transjordan to the shores of the Mediterranean.

The Philistines never inhabited more than a small part of the Land of Israel. The name Palestine (Lat. *Palaestina*) is based on a historical deception, resulting from an act of hostility towards

Israel. After the defeat of Bar Kokhba, the Roman emperor Hadrian sought to root out the name Israel from his land, which at that time was known by all as Judah (Lat. *Judea*). Hence he gave the Land of Israel the name Palaestina, after the Philistines, even though by Hadrian's time the Philistines virtually no longer existed. Christianity, because of its hostility towards the Jews, tried to accustom all the nations of the world to this name, and thus it became the accepted nomenclature, replacing the names Land of Israel and Judah.

the route

A. Baal-Perazim – conjectured to be the area between the Serpents' Pool (Sultan's Pool), southeast of Mishkenot Sha'ananim, and Giv'at Hananya (Abu-Tor).
B. Descent to the floor of the Hinnom Valley and walk along the stream bed until its effluent into the Qidron (Kidron)
C. Ascent to the right, to the road leading to Government House, and observation of the view towards the City of David, from a point on the road opposite En-Rogel (Bir Aiyub, or the well of Job).
D. Return by the road through the Qidron Valley, walking along it as far as the Giḥon Spring.
E. Ascent along the path to the Jebusite wall, unearthed in Kathleen Kenyon's archaeological excavations.

a. baal-perazim

The Philistines were aware that King David posed an even greater threat to their control of the land than had Saul, and that it was best to take action against him before he became too strong. **"All the Philistines went up to seek David; and David heard of it, and went down to the hold** [Heb. *mezudah* or

1

1 *Descent to the Giḥon Spring (C. Geikie, 1903).*

2 *Baal-Perazim: conjectured to be the region between the Serpents' Pool (Sultan's Pool) and the vicinity of Mishkenot Sha'ananim and Giv'at Hananya (Abu-Tor). On this site David defeated the Philistines who came to fight him after he captured the fortress of Zion.*

fortress]" (i.e. the fortress of Zion, or Jerusalem; II Samuel 5:17).

A deft partisan fighter, David knew that he could only overcome the highly organized Philistine army by stratagem. In going to his stronghold in Jerusalem he lured the Philistines to Emeq Refa'im. From their cities in the coastal plain the Philistines ascended to the highlands and proceeded towards Jerusalem along the path of the Sorek river and the Refa'im brook which feeds into it, corresponding to the modern-day route of the railroad to Jerusalem. Let us pause a moment to imagine how the Valley of Refa'im must have looked in those days. Having amply deep soil, the bottom of the valley was entirely covered with fields of grain. Rockier terrain, covered by a dense low thicket consisting mostly of shrub-like mastic trees (*bekha'im* or mulberry trees, in the language of the Bible), lined its sides.

The Philistines assumed that David had taken up a fortified position in Jerusalem, and therefore did not take precautions as they went. David, however, lay in ambush for them in Baal-Perazim. Charging suddenly out of the Hinnom Valley, he and his men must have caught the Philistines by surprise and caused them high casualties.

The Philistines could not give up their plans to destroy David's growing power while they still had time. Before long they returned again to Jerusalem. Being an experienced warrior, David knew he could not succeed at the same stratagem twice, for this time the Philistines would be more cautious. As the Bible recounts: **"And the Philistines came up yet again, and spread themselves in the valley of Rephaim. And when David inquired of the Lord, He said: 'Thou shalt not go up** [from the valley of Hinnom], **make a circuit behind them, and come upon them over against the bakha trees. And it shall be, when thou hearest the sound of marching in the tops of the bakha trees, that then thou shalt bestir thyself; for then is the Lord gone out before thee to smite the host of the Philistines' "** (II Samuel 5:22-24).

Thus David's fighters hid among the mastic trees. They discerned the Philistines' approach by the rustling of the mastic trees which they heard as the Philistine fighters advanced. David's men let the enemy pass by and then attacked from the

and david called it the city of david

1 *The Valley of Hinnom, named after the Hinnom family through whose land the watercourse ran. The name Gehenna evolved after the cruel cult of Molech practiced there.*

1

rear, dealing the Philistines a blow before they had time to prepare for battle.

an episode from the life of david and his troops, awaiting the philistine advance

First Chronicles 11:15-19 reads: "**and the host of the Philistines were encamped in the valley of Rephaim** [apparently in the vicinity of Beit Ṣafafa, where the deep canyon opens into the valley]; **And David was then in the stronghold, and the garrison of the Philistines was then in Beth-lehem.**" David found himself close to the beloved city of his birth, which he had not visited for years. Nevertheless, he was unable to reach it (although it was only some 6 km. south of his position), because it was under enemy control. In a moment of longing he murmured to himself: "**Oh that one would give me water to drink of the well of Beth-lehem, which is by the gate,**" for the water of one's youth has a special flavor. David's men, who heeded every word on his lips, took up the challenge: "**And the three** [three of David's brave men who were always prepared to risk their lives for his sake] **broke through the host of the Philistines, and drew water out of the well of Beth-lehem, that was by the gate, and took it, and brought it to David; but David would not drink thereof, but poured it out unto the Lord, and said: 'My God forbid it me, that I should do this; shall I drink the blood of these men that have put their lives in jeopardy? for with the jeopardy of their lives they brought it.'** "

This episode gives an inkling of the relations between David and his men and testifies to David's charismatic personality and leadership which won him the hearts of his fighters.

b. walking through the hinnom valley

The stream is named after the family of Hinnom, in whose inheritance it lay. Today the left (northern) slope of the valley is covered with the ruins of the upper city, which stood above it, on Mount Zion. Picturesque boulders lay revealed along the southern slope. In the winter, after a heavy rain, the stream bed fills with torrents of water, coming from the nearby watershed. The incline from the watershed is considerable, and hence the water flows with great force towards the Qidron and from there to the Dead Sea.

According to Joshua's allocation of the tribal inheritances, this stream formed a section of the boundary between the territory of Judah to the south and of Benjamin to the north.

At a later period, in the time of the split monarchy, the worship of Molech, a cruel semitic deity to whom children were sacrificed, penetrated into Judah from neighboring lands. This worship was practiced in an area called the Topheth, in the

sites from jerusalem of the first and late second temple periods located on a modern map

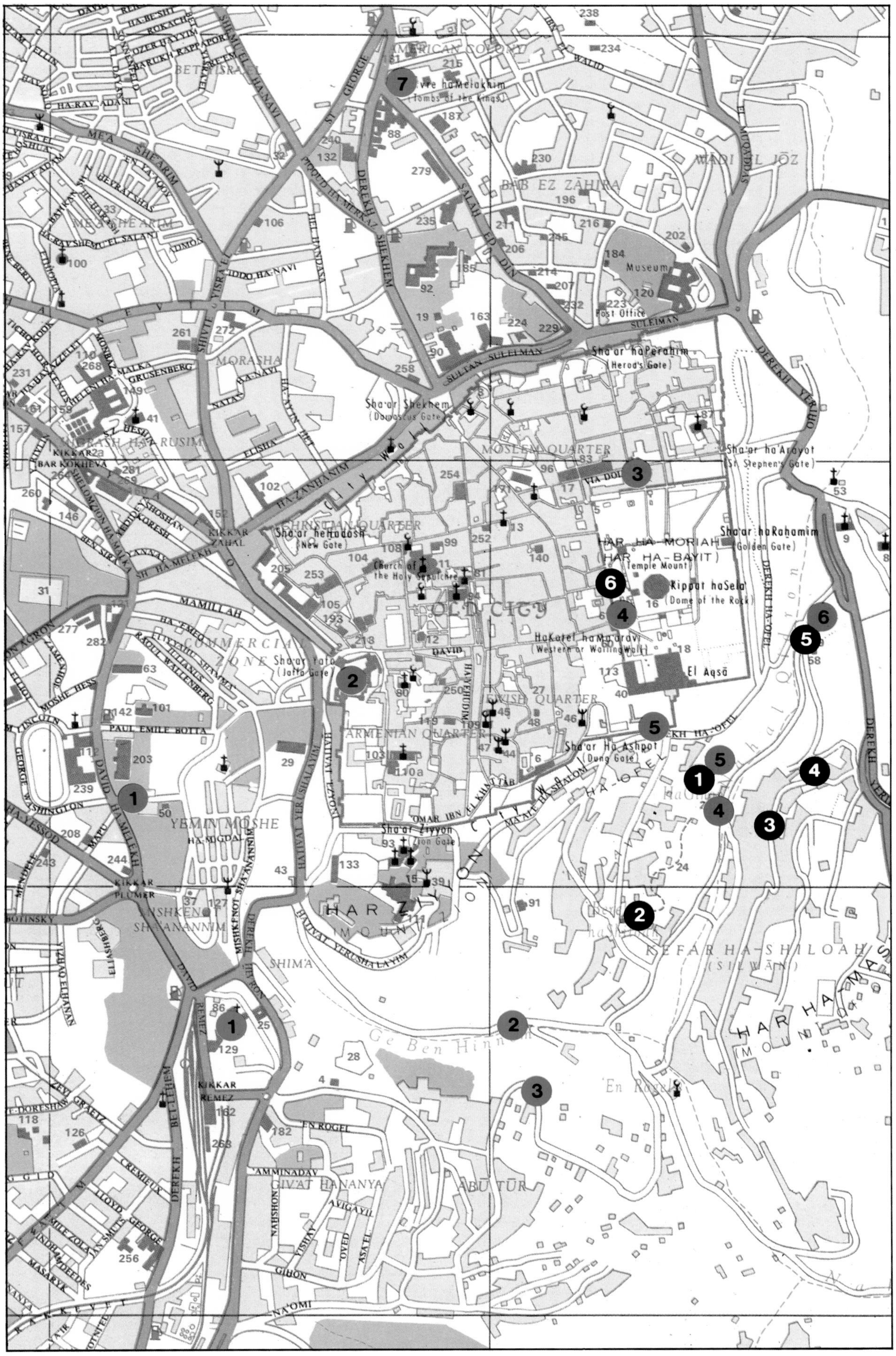

a. Jerusalem of David

1. Baal-Perazim.
2. Hinnom Valley.
3. Observation poin overlooking the City of David and 'En-Rogel.
4. Giḥon spring.
5. Jebusite wall.

b. Jerusalem of Hezekiah

1. Refortified Jebusite wall.
2. Pool of Shiloah (Siloam).
3. Tomb of "... yahu, who is over the household."
4. "Tomb of Pharaoh's Daughter."
5. Tomb of the Ḥezir Family
6. The Upper Pool, today the Cotton Merchants' Market and the esh-Shifa baths.

c. Jerusalem of the late Second Temple period

1. Herod's Family Tomb.
2. The Citadel ("Tower of David").
3. Antonia Fortress (present-day Sisters of Zion Convent and the Omariyya School).
4. Wilson's Arch and the Western Wall.
5. Excavations at the Western Wall.
6. "Absalom's Monument," Tomb of the Ḥezir Family, and "Tomb of Zechariah."
7. "Tombs of the Kings" (of the Adiabene royal family).

Hinnom Valley. The prophets fought irately against this barbaric worship, but did not succeed in eradicating it until the time of King Josiah.

The name Valley of Hinnom (Gai Hinnom) gave birth to the proper noun Gehenna, the place where in afterlife the evil are condemned to suffer eternal fire.

Above the right hand slope of the end of the Hinnom Valley there are ancient catacombs from the Second Temple period, as well as a Greek-Orthodox monastery, Aceldama (Field of Blood), which in Christian tradition was the proselytes' burial ground which Judas Iscariot purchased with the 30 pieces of silver he received for betraying Jesus.

c. the road above en-rogel

Today En-Rogel is enclosed in an ancient building, and is no longer a spring, but a deep well. During an earthquake in Uzziah's reign, according to Josephus, a landslide on the hill above it covered the spring. Since it was an important source of water for Jerusalem, Uzziah dug through the debris of the landslide and built a well. During a rainy winter the well fills with water and overflows like a spring. Today En-Rogel is surrounded by an orchard of fig and mulberry trees and small irrigated fields. During the period of the Bible this was the site of the "King's Gardens."

The tel of the City of David stands out to the north, greyish in hue, due to the color of its ruins. It is shaped like a triangle with its base near the wall of the Temple Mount (this section was called the Ophel in the biblical period), and its apex not far from us, near the Pool of Shiloaḥ (Siloam).

The City of David was built on a hill which archaeologists refer to as the eastern ridge. This ridge was skirted by two watercourses, on the east the Qidron, and on the west the Gai, which flowed along the foot of Mount Zion (referred to by archaeologists as the western ridge). In time the Gai (the Tyropoeon Valley of the Second Temple period) became silted up by ruins and debris, making it difficult to detect the valley on the landscape today.

1

1 *Area G of the excavations in the City of David. The remains of Canaanite-Jebusite Jerusalem appear in the lower left of the photograph. Above them are the walls of the House of Aḥi'el, an Israelite residence from the end of the First Temple period. Standing out in the center and above is a terraced stone structure, part of the city's citadel from the time of David and Solomon. In the upper left is a square tower, part of Jerusalem's defenses in the Second Temple period. The City of David was excavated under the direction of Prof. Yigal Shiloh.*

2 *The hill on which the City of David lay, with the Temple Mount above it. East of the hill (to the right in the photograph) is Naḥal Qidron, running between the City of David and the village of Shiloaḥ (Silwan). The hillside of the City of David is strewn with pale-colored piles of earth, removed in the 1982 excavations. Since 1978 remains of the past have been unearthed on the hill of the City of David, and an archaeological park has been opened on the site.*

As David and his men came out of the Hinnom Valley, they must have seen, rising before their eyes, the towering walls which encompassed the city about two thirds of the way down the slope.

d. the giḥon spring

What did David see as he stood by the Giḥon?

In the time of David the bed of the Qidron was about 10 meters lower than the present-day ground level, for over the years it has been silted up by ruins and debris.

The spring emanated from a small cavity in the rock, near the western ridge. The steep incline of the western slope rose above the spring. (The Giḥon no longer appears as a spring today, since it flows to the Pool of Shiloaḥ by way of Hezekiah's tunnel, which we shall walk through later.)

The Giḥon is a karstic* spring which functions intermittently, with water bursting forth from it for 30 to 40 minutes, once every 8 to 10 hours (in a wet winter every 4 to 6 hours), after which the flow comes almost to a complete halt, until the next eruption. Hence its name Giḥon, from the Hebrew root *giḥ,* meaning sudden eruption.

In David's day the Giḥon lay outside the walls of Jerusalem. To assure the city water in time of siege the Jebusites cut a deep shaft in the area within the walls and connected it by a tunnel to the spring. This shaft they called *ẓinor.*

e. the jebusite wall

Let us climb up the path behind the building over the Giḥon to the section of the Jebusite wall discovered in the excavations of the English archaeologist, Kathleen Kenyon.

Only four and a half meters remain of the original height of the

---

*Karstic – adjective form of karst, an area of limestone formations, characterized by sinks, ravines and underground streams.

2

wall, which was two and a half meters thick. It was built on the steep bedrock of the hillside, about 1800 b.c.e., in the Middle Bronze (Canaanite) period (the time of the patriarchs). Repairs were made in the wall during the period of the kings of Judah. In David's day the foot of the wall was 18 meters above the floor of the Qidron Valley. Since the slope beneath it was steep, the wall towered high and invincible. The weapons of David's time were no match for it. The battering-ram had not yet been invented; the prevalent weapons were for the most part contact arms (swords, lances, and spears); and the bow and arrow was ineffective at long range. No wonder the Jebusites felt secure behind the walls of their city. Let us stretch our fancy and imagine the conversation that may have taken place between David and his men, down in the Qidron Valley, and Araunah king of Jerusalem and his entourage, atop the city wall. We can hear Araunah taunting David: **" 'Except thou take away the blind and the lame, thou shalt not come in hither'; thinking: 'David cannot come in hither.' "** (II Samuel 5:6). Or, as we might say today: "I don't give two hoots for you and your brave men. Our city wall is so high and invincible, that it can even be defended by the blind and the lame." David made no reply. Nor did his men. All heads were turned towards the summit of the wall, which seemed to touch the sky. They knew that Araunah was right, that they could not succeed in taking the city by force. Yet David's sharp eyes did not overlook the shaft through which the Jebusites drew their water.

At that moment an idea struck David, and he appealed to the honor and ambition of his men: **"And David said on that day: 'Whosoever smiteth the Jebusites, and getteth up to the gutter' "** (Heb. *ẓinor;* in other words, whoever enters the City of David by way of the water shaft; II Samuel 5:8). Or, according to another version: **"Whosoever smiteth the Jebusites first shall be chief and captain"** (I Chronicles 11:6). The daring man to do so immediately came forth: Joab, the son of Zeruiah (sister of David's father Jesse), **"and was made chief"** (*ibid.*). In the stealth of night, when the Jebusites were not on their guard, never having imagined such a thing was possible, Joab climbed the shaft, penetrated the city, and opened its gates to David's men. Jerusalem was conquered without shedding a drop of blood. The Jebusites continued to live in the city and soon assimilated with the Jews.

Thenceforth Jerusalem was called by a new name: the City of David.

Neither David nor Joab ever imagined, as they were conquering Jerusalem, what an historic deed it was, an act which would affect mankind throughout history. Before David's time Jerusalem was simply a Canaanite city, albeit quite an important one. With its conquest by David it became the capital of the empire which he built. Solomon sanctified it in the religion of Israel by building the Temple there. The holiness of Jerusalem was transmitted from Judaism to Christianity and Islam, the religions which emerged from it, and thus the sanctity of Jerusalem become an important factor in the general history of mankind and of the Jewish people.

jerusalem in the time of hezekiah

Menachem Zaharoni

After the death of Solomon (930 b.c.e.) his realm split into two kingdoms: that of the Ten Tribes, which in time came to be called Samaria, and that of Judah. Judah continued to be ruled by kings from the house of David. Both kingdoms, vanquished by the world empires of those days, suffered greatly at their hands. In 721 b.c.e. Sargon II, King of Assyria, laid waste the kingdom of Samaria and exiled part of its inhabitants. Judah, for the while, was spared destruction and exile by accepting Assyrian subjugation. Samaria was partitioned into Assyrian provinces.

After the death of King Sargon of Assyria and the ascent of Sennacherib to the throne (705 b.c.e.), the mighty Assyrian kingdom seethed with wave upon wave of fierce revolt. For a number of years, until Sennacherib put down the revolts closer to home, Judah had respite. Hopes began to rise: if only Assyria might fall; the Assyrian provinces in Samaria remained undefended, and the time had come to heal the breach from the days of Jeroboam and unite all the Land of Israel under the rule of the house of David, as in the time of David and Solomon. The way to accomplish this had to be on the strength of the Temple in Jerusalem.

Hezekiah purified the Temple and planned a joint celebration of the Passover feast for all the Children of Israel. Messengers were speedily dispatched to regions of the Land of Israel still inhabited by the Children of Israel to invite them to celebrate the festival. **"And there assembled at Jerusalem much people to keep the feast of unleavened bread in the second month, a very great congregation"** (II Chronicles 30:13). **"And all the congregation of Judah, with the priests and the Levites, and all the congregation that came out of Israel, and the strangers that came out of the land of Israel, and that dwelt in Judah, rejoiced. So there was great joy in Jerusalem; for since the time of Solomon the son of David king of Israel there was not the like in Jerusalem"** (*ibid.,* 30:25-26).

The religious fervor roused the people to make reforms: **"And they arose and took away the altars that were in Jerusalem, and all the altars for incense took they away, and cast them into the brook Kidron"** (*ibid.,* 30:14); **"Now when all this was finished, all Israel that were present went out to the cities of Judah, and broke in pieces the pillars, and hewed down the Asherim, and broke down the high places and the altars out of all Judah and Benjamin, in Ephraim also and Manasseh, until they had destroyed them all"** (*ibid.,* 31:1). The Qidron, as we read, received its share in all this. No wonder, therefore, that the bed of this river rose some 10 meters or more over the years.

1

Then, in the midst of these hopeful days, Sennacherib found himself free to come to Judah and suppress the revolt there and in the neighboring states. In a world which then too was divided between East (Assyria) and West (Egypt), Hezekiah had a certain hope of victory, if only the uprising were organized properly. Hezekiah energetically set about forming a defense alliance of Israel's neighbors and assumed its leadership. He turned to Egypt and received a promise of aid. Shebna "who is over the house," apparently the highest general, surely was the vital spirit of the revolt and won broad popular support. After years of suppression and humiliation the people found pleasure in seeing the emissaries of Ekron bringing Padi their king to Jerusalem, bound in fetters, because he had opposed the revolt. This must have taken place at a time when the allies were

1. *The Pool of Shiloaḥ (photograph from 1862).*

2. *The monument which the Arabs call the "Tomb of Pharaoh's Daughter," a typical catacomb from the First Temple period, is situated in the village of Shiloaḥ, the burial ground of the Jerusalem aristocracy during that period.*

3. *The present-day Pool of Shiloaḥ is the lower pool from the time of Hezekiah.*

4. *Suq Kutnin (the cotton merchants' market) with its "health baths" (hammam esh-Shifa), near which the upper pool apparently was located.*

2

3

4

gathered in conference, and aroused tremendous excitement among the residents of Jerusalem: **"What aileth thee now, that thou art wholly gone up to the housetops, thou that art full of uproar, a tumultuous city, a joyous town?"** (Isaiah 22:1-2). It was on the rooftops of the City of David which we see before us that this took place, and we can easily reconstruct the scene in our mind's eye. The only person not swept along in the general wave of enthusiasm was the prophet Isaiah. He foresaw with clarity the tragic unravelling of events, since he had a correct assessment of the forces operating in the arena and knew well the ways of the enemy: **"Thy slain are not slain with the sword, nor dead in battle,"** he shouted at his beloved city. **"All thy rulers are fled together, without the bow they are bound; all that are found of thee are bound together, they are fled afar off. Therefore said I: 'Look away from me, I will weep bitterly; strain not to comfort me, for the destruction of the daughter of my people'** " (Isaiah 22:2-4). In his mind's eye the prophet saw the horrors of the siege, the starvation and thirst, and the exile which would follow them. The prophet directed his bitter wrath against the central figure planning the revolt, the general Shebna. Perhaps it was on this very spot, where we now stand, that the prophet thundered at him: **"What hast thou here, and whom hast thou here, that thou hast hewed thee out here a sepulchre, thou that hewest thee out a sepulchre on high, and gravest a habitation for thyself in the rock? Behold, the Lord will hurl thee up and down with a man's throw; yea, He will wind thee round and round; He will violently roll and toss thee like a ball into a large country; there shalt thou die"** (*ibid.*, 22:16-18).

The prophet underscored his contempt for the man by choosing the words, **"Go, get thee unto this steward** [Heb. *sokhen],* **even unto Shebna, who is over the house"** (*ibid.*, 22:15). *Sokhen* is the Phoenician word for general. It appears that Shebna was a foreigner, perhaps of Phoenician extraction; for, in naming him, the Bible does not mention the name of his father, and the grave which he hewed was not the grave of his forefathers. A lone man in Jerusalem, he was buried with his maidservant.

the route

A. The Jebusite wall which Hezekiah repaired.
B. Through Hezekiah's tunnel (the Shiloaḥ water conduit), extending from the Giḥon spring to the Pool of Shiloaḥ.
C. The Tomb of Pharaoh's Daughter and the burial ground of the Jerusalem aristocracy from the First Temple period.
D. The sepulchre of "...yahu, who was over the household."
E. The Tomb of the Ḥezir Family.
F. *Suq Kutnin* (the cotton merchants' market) and the esh-Shifa baths – the conjectured location of the upper pool.

a. the jebusite wall, repaired by hezekiah

The Jebusite wall still stood in the time of Hezekiah but was dilapidated and in need of repair and reinforcement. The

1. *Jerusalem of the Monarchy*

2. *Irrigated land in the area called by the Arabs Birket Ḥamra.*

Panorama overleaf: View of the City of David, the Qidron Valley, and the "King's Gardens." The City of David stood on the hill west of the Qidron (on the left in the photo).

Across from it, on the site of the present-day village of Shiloaḥ, was the "City of the Dead," the burial ground of the Jerusalem nobility of the First Temple period.

jerusalem in the time of the monarchy

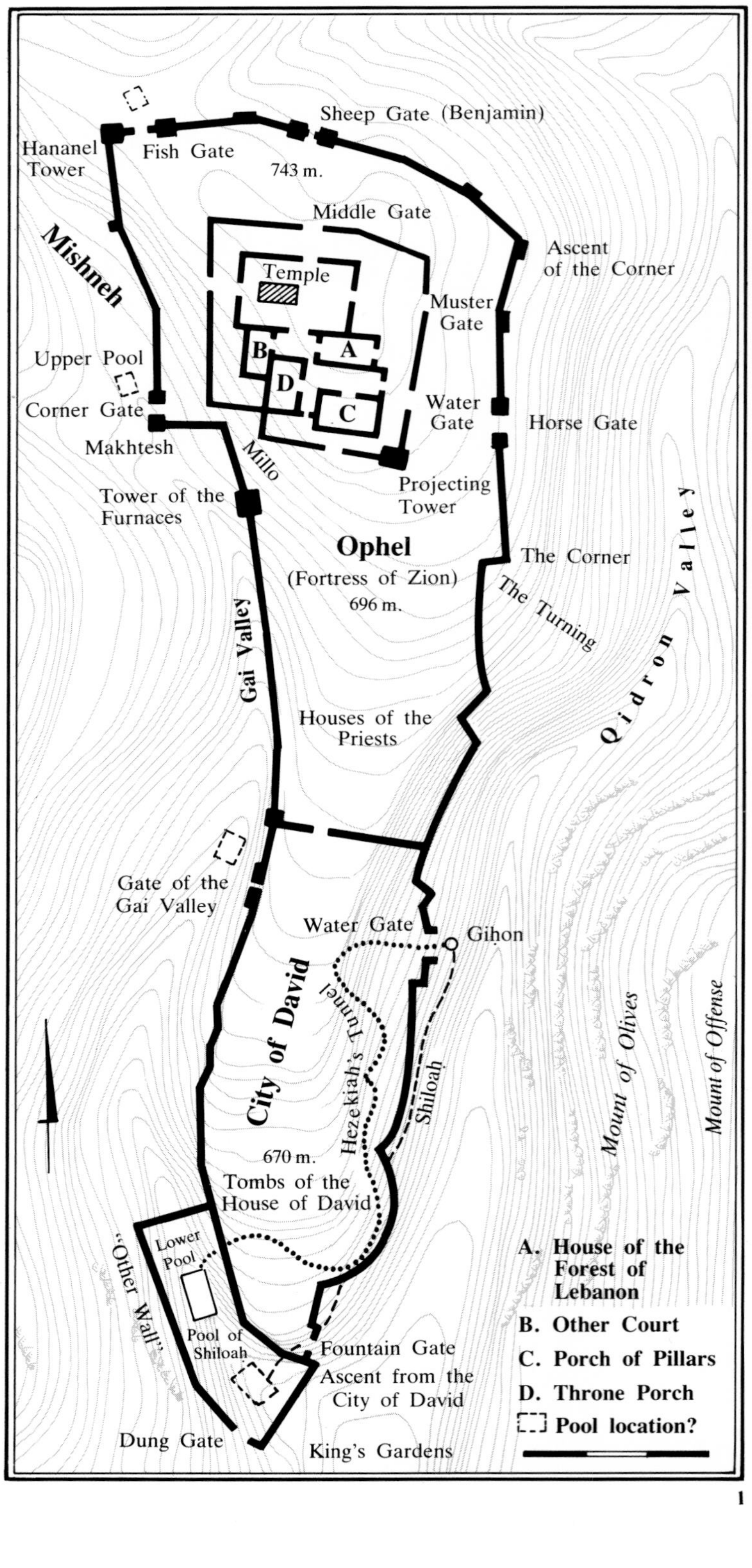

1

2

archaeologist Kathleen Kenyon, who excavated the site, discovered that in the eighth century b.c.e. the wall had been extended to a height of 5 meters. Various repairs can be discerned in the wall, some from the period of Hezekiah and his generals, who keenly appreciated the gravity of the situation and made feverish preparations for war. **"And he** [Hezekiah] **took courage, and built up all the wall that was broken down, and raised it up to the towers, and another wall without** [i.e., he built an additional wall opposite the weak sections of wall], **and strengthened Millo in the city of David"** (II Chronicles 32:5). The Millo, the terraced section of the City of David, was originally a sloping hillside. To enable the construction of houses on it, the slope was leveled out into terraces, perhaps as early as the Jebusite period, by filling it with stones and dirt. Due to the rains of the Jerusalem winter, however, this fill of dirt and stones (Heb. *millui)* from time to time would slide down towards the city walls and by its pressure would put them in danger of fissure and collapse. Therefore in the time of Hezekiah it was essential to reinforce the Millo.

The extensive repairs required a large supply of stone, which in an hour of emergency could not be supplied by quarrying. Therefore old building materials were used. To this end, every house not deemed essential was broken apart: **"And ye numbered the houses of Jerusalem, and ye broke down the houses to fortify the wall"** (Isaiah 22:10). Executing the many projects at maximum speed required scrupulous organization and a massive volunteer effort. Once more it became imperative to strengthen the people's spirit, for the great might of the Assyrian army was well known and its tyranny famous. Memory of the atrocities which had befallen the Ten Tribes was still fresh in the hearts of the inhabitants of Judah. **"And** [Hezekiah] **made weapons and shields in abundance. And he set captains of war over the people, and gathered them together to him in the broad place at the gate of the city, and spoke encouragingly to them, saying: 'Be strong and of good courage, be not afraid nor dismayed for the king of Assyria, nor for all the multitude that is with him; for there is a Greater with us than with him; with him is an arm of flesh; but with us is the Lord our God to help us, and to fight our battles.' And the people rested themselves upon the words of Hezekiah king of Judah"** (II Chronicles 32:5-8). The gate at the end of the city street may have been close to the place where we are standing. The remains of the wall from the Bronze Age belong to the gate leading out to the Giḥon spring. Reason would dictate that the "Water Gate," the gate of the new wall,

was located somewhere in close proximity.

Across the Qidron Valley we see a rock face with the remains of caves in it lining the bank of the river and above this cliff we see the houses of the village of Silwan. The modern village of Silwan (Shiloaḥ) now stands on what was once a burial ground for the Jerusalem nobility. It was in this cemetery that Shebna, too, hewed himself a sepulchre.

b. hezekiah's tunnel, from the giḥon spring to the pool of shiloaḥ

Guaranteeing a supply of running water was the paramount problem of Jerusalem. The city's springs, the Giḥon and En-Rogel, were situated outside the walls and during a siege would provide water to quench the thirst of the foe, to the great anguish of the besieged, hopelessly beholding the sight of water they could not reach. "[Hezekiah] **took counsel with his princes and his mighty men to stop the waters of the fountains which were without the city; and they helped him. So there was gathered much people together, and they stopped all the fountains, and the brook that flowed through the midst of the land** [apparently Solomon's Shiloaḥ conduit], **saying: 'Why should the kings of Assyria come, and find much water?'** " (II Chronicles 32:3-4). Denying the enemy water was only half a solution, for during a siege one also had to see to drinking water for the besieged. Jerusalem did have some cisterns and pools, but they did not hold sufficient water to withstand a protracted siege. The solution was to cut a conduit through the hill in order to channel the water of the Giḥon to a point inside the walls. The general line of the tunnel was obvious. The water could only be directed towards the lower pool and the Pool of Shiloaḥ on the south of the City of David. Channeling the water directly to the west would have necessitated quarrying enormous reservoirs to a depth of 50 meters or more, a task beyond the technical capabilities of the times. On the south of the City of David, however, the conduit could come out of the hill into the open, and reservoirs had already been hewn there by previous generations. The Pool of Shiloaḥ, the southernmost one, had apparently been hewn in the time of Solomon, and it was there that the Shiloaḥ conduit terminated. **"This same Hezekiah also**

1 *The "Ḥamra Pool," the Shiloaḥ Pool of Hezekiah's time (photo from 1870).*

stopped the upper spring of the waters of Gihon, and brought them straight down on the west [actually, southwest] **side of the city of David''** (*ibid.,* v. 30).

There was little time to spare; hence tunneling was begun at both ends of the conduit's course. Although the distance between either end is 320 meters as the crow flies, the excavators quickly realized the tunnel would have to be much longer. Cutting through the white limestone of which the Temple was built, a stone of medium hardness, was easy for them; but when they reached dolomite, an extremely hard stone, they had to make a detour. Hence the tunnel was cut no wider than a single man and followed a very sinuous course.

How did the borers manage to find the right course, working from both ends? They might, after all, have failed to meet!

It turns out that there was some flow of water along the entire course of the tunnel even before it was cut through and that this is what guided the borers. Nevertheless, considering the surveying techniques of the times, the meeting of the two parties seems a remarkable feat. Necessity must have imparted a rare sense of direction to the tunnelers.

Work on the tunnel was begun with great enthusiasm. At the Giḥon end they bored to a height of more than 3 meters and at the end near the lower pool they reached as high as 5 meters. Shortly, however, as boring became more difficult and as tension rose due to the approach of the enemy, the dimensions of the tunnel were reduced to no more than a man's height, and at certain places even less. It was a question of life and death, which would happen first: completion of the tunnel or the enemy's arrival in Jerusalem. The closer the enemy came to Jerusalem, the more anxious the borers became. The walls of the tunnel bear witness to this in the errors that were made and in the poorer quality of the boring. Something of the great dread which lay over the inhabitants of Jerusalem and which dictated the pace of work on the tunnel can be sensed in the words of Isaiah: **''He** [the enemy] **is come to Aiath, he is passed through Migron; at Michmas he layeth up his baggage. They are gone over the pass; they have taken up their lodging at Geba. Ramah trembleth; Gibeath-shaul is fled. Cry thou with a shrill voice, O daughter of Gallim! Hearken, O Laish! O thou poor Anathoth! Madmenah is in mad flight; the inhabitants of Gebim flee to cover. This very day shall he halt at Nob** [apparently the village Isawiya, south of the amphitheatre on Mount Scopus], **shaking his hand at the mount of the daugther of Zion, the hill of Jerusalem''** (Isaiah 10:28-32). The enemy approached from the north, from Samaria, by way of the watershed, for each city named here is south of the preceding one. These verses reverberate with the panic instilled by the rate of the enemy's advance and the cataclysmic reports reaching Jerusalem. The verses are short, like the short breath of the couriers bringing the tidings.

Who can imagine how the hearts of the borers must have pounded in the depths of the earth? How their suspense must have risen as they approached the meeting point! At last the blows of pick-axes and the voices of excited borers became audible through the stone separating them. The race against time was becoming fateful – perhaps deliverance was at hand! The hands of the borers trembled. For sheer excitement they could not find the correct direction to hew, since the sounds misled them (because, as the Shiloaḥ Inscription said, "there was a split in the rock"), making it seem that they were approaching from different angles. Wild attempts were made to hew every which way. A start would be made in one direction, then abandoned for another. Only three cubits (approx. 1.5 meters) separated one set of tunnelers from the other, yet the time it took to bore through must have seemed to them an eternity. At last came the great moment. The tunnelers met and

2

2. *Inside view of the Shiloaḥ tunnel, hewn between the Giḥon spring and the present-day Pool of Shiloaḥ. Marks of the borers' axes can be seen in the rock of the tunnel's walls.*

1. *The Shiloaḥ Inscription, testimony to a superhuman effort, frozen for all time.*

2 *Hezekiah's Tunnel, hewn in the rock in order to channel the water of the Giḥon Spring to the Pool of Shiloaḥ, south of the City of David. Designed to assure drinking water to Jerusalem's residents in time of siege, it was built by King Hezekiah on the eve of Sennacherib's campaign to conquer Judah (701 b.c.e.).*

the shiloaḥ inscription

This is the story of the boring through: whilst [the tunnellers lifted] the pick each towards his fellow and whilst three cubits [yet remained] to be bored [through, there was heard] the voice of a man calling his fellow, for there was a split in the rock on the right hand and on [the left hand]. And on the day of the boring through, the tunnellers struck, each in the direction of his fellows, pick and against pick. And the water started to flow from the source to the pool, twelve hundred cubits. A hundred cubits was the height of the rock above the head of the tunnellers.

1

there was a great sense of relief. The water flowed quietly, for over a course of 533 meters ("twelve hundred cubits") the level dropped only slightly more than two meters. The sound of the water was reassuring and seemed to promise deliverance.

Walking through the tunnel it is easy to tell where the tunnelers met, for the great excitement and the moods oscillating between hope and despair are engraved in the rock. The many false starts testify to this. Our ancestors were not accustomed to glorify their deeds with monuments or pretentious inscriptions, yet the emotions of the borers of Hezekiah's tunnel at the triumphant moment of meeting had to be expressed. This was done in a modest inscription which rings with an echo of the great feat. Hewn into the wall of the tunnel, near its egress to the pool, as if there had been a desire to conceal it for generations long to come, the inscription reads:

The present-day Pool of Shiloaḥ was then called the "lower pool." What was then known as the Pool of Shiloaḥ was located further to the south, in what is today cultivated land whose Arab name, Birket (Pool of) el-Ḥamra, indicates there had once been a pool there in the past. Through the years the lower pool has undergone a variety of transformations and repairs, the last of which, in 1879, determined its present shape. The dimensions of the original pool, as revealed in archaeological excavation, were 1.5 x 6 x 26 meters. Its capacity was too small to impound all the water of the Giḥon. The overflow continued through a channel to the nearby Pool of Shiloaḥ. This channel is now visible next to the rock on the right side of the way leading from the Qidron road to the present-day Pool of Shiloaḥ, and the overflow of the pool flows through it towards the "King's Gardens," the nearby garden in the Qidron Valley. In the time of Hezekiah both pools were walled in on all sides, on the east by the western wall of the City of David, running midway down the slope the length of the Gai Valley, and on the west by the "Other Wall." Additional sections of wall connected these two walls on the north and south. Thus the water in the pools was beyond reach of the enemy and available to the besieged.

c. the tomb of pharaoh's daughter and the tombs of the jerusalem nobility of the first temple period

Let us follow the path which ascends from the Qidron Valley, near the Tomb of Zechariah, to the edge of the village of Shiloaḥ. About 300 meters south-southwest of Zechariah's Tomb, on a scarp overlooking the Qidron, is the Tomb of Pharaoh's Daughter.

We are now standing in the area which served as the burial ground of the Jerusalem nobility during the First Temple period. The monument which the Arabs call the "Tomb of Pharaoh's Daughter" is a typical burial tomb of the period. A monolith, a building hewn from a single block of stone, it stands in an open area, surrounded on three sides by the rock from which it was cut. The fourth side of the tomb is connected most of the way up to the scarp of the tomb's facade, which rises 4 meters high and overlooks the Qidron. A concave Egyptian cornice, in the prevailing style of the land of Israel and neighboring lands in the time of the First Temple, projects near the ceiling of the structure. An examination of the current roof indicates that it had once been crowned by a four-sided pyramid of hewn stone. The top of the entrance to the tomb is flanked by two small rectangles. The left one bears the end of an ancient Hebrew inscription with only the letter *resh* and a fragment of the preceding letter preserved, so that today the inscription cannot be deciphered. It turns out that over the existing entrance there once had been a long narrow panel bearing an inscription which ran over slightly on the left side. At a later period the entrance was made taller by removing the panel, leaving only the end of the inscription. This tomb, very well preserved, is a fine exemplar of tombs from the seventh century b.c.e., including the time of Hezekiah.

Now we are standing across from the Ophel. The full length of the ancient site of the City of David lies before us. From here we can take in the surroundings of Hezekiah's Jerusalem. On our right, scattered over the foot of the Mount of Olives, are tombstones of the Jewish cemetery where Jews are buried to this day, continuing the tradition of the ancient cemetery here. To the right of the Qidron is the city of the living, to its left the city of the dead. We may pause a moment and marvel at this unique people which from its earliest days has been bound heart and soul to its holy city, ever striving with all its might to live there, and which, for three thousand years, has also brought its dead to rest in a certain spot opposite its eternal city, with but brief interruptions imposed upon it by force of arms.

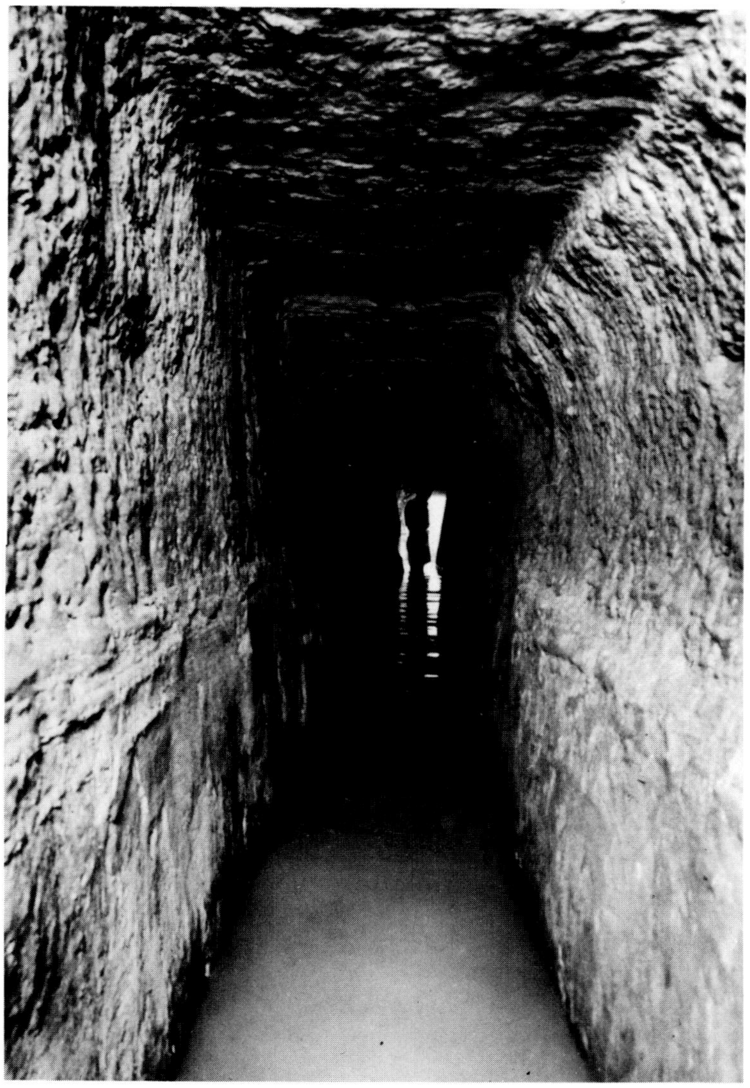

2

d. the sepulchre of "...yahu who is over the house," presumably that of "shebna (shebnayahu) who is over the house"

Let us continue along the main road of the village of Shiloaḥ, about 60 meters. We pass the openings of some ancient tombs and reach a square, rock-hewn tomb with a facade facing northwest and measuring some 8 meters long by 4 meters high. Above the tomb is a residential building forming a sort of second storey. We can also make out the facade by its opening with a niche to the right of it. Access to the residential building is by way of steps hewn into the northern side of the tomb.

At first glance we can discern that above the niche and opening there once were some panels which have since been removed (by the archaeologist Clermont-Ganneau, who transferred them to the British Museum). These panels bore two inscriptions, one of which has been deciphered by Nahman Avigad. Inserting (in parentheses) the letters obliterated by the ravages of time, it read: **"This is the (burial ...) yahu who is over the house. There is no silver or gold here, (but) only (his bones) and the bones of his**

maidservant with him. Cursed is the man who doth open this."

Research has shown that the letters of this inscription are similar to those in the Shiloaḥ Inscription from the time of Hezekiah. Chapter 22 of Isaiah mentions "Shebna who is over the house," Hezekiah's leading general. The name Shebna also appears in Scripture in the longer form, Shebnayahu. Thus it may be that the letters "yahu" are the latter part of this name. Scientifically we must admit that the archaeological data are insufficient to identify the person buried here with the Shebna mentioned in Isaiah. Nevertheless, there is something to be learned here. In Isaiah we read that Shebna hewed himself a sepulchre into the rock, i.e., in the burial ground where we are now standing. If this is not the tomb of that same Shebna, then his tomb must surely be somewhere in the vicinity and must be similar to this one. Thus, on this spot, we may reconstruct the dramatic encounter between the prophet and the general. Here Isaiah pronounced his words of wrath: **"What hast thou here, and whom hast thou here, that thou hast hewed thee out here a sepulchre, thou that hewest thee out a sepulchre on high, and gravest a habitation for thyself in the rock?"** (Isaiah 22:16).

1 *The domed rooftops above the esh-Shifa baths. The Upper Pool, which collected rainwater from the Gai and the rivulet which feeds in from the west at this point, was apparently located near these baths. The pool is mentioned in the Books of Isaiah and Kings. After conquering the fortified cities of Judah, Sennacherib, king of Assyria, sent "Tartan and Rab-saris and Rab-shakeh from Lachish to king Hezekiah with a great army unto Jerusalem. And they went up and came to Jerusalem. And ... they came and stood by the conduit of the upper pool, which is in the highway of the fullers' field" (II Kings 18:17).*

e. reconstructing the view of hezekiah's jerusalem from the tomb of the ḥezir family

Let us go down from the village of Shiloaḥ to the floor of the Qidron Valley, and from there climb up to the tomb with the columns on its facade. This is the Tomb of the Sons of Ḥezir, a priestly family from the end of the Second Temple period.

To reconstruct the environs of Hezekiah's Jerusalem we have to pretend not to see most of the buildings before us. The ancient memorials of the Monument of Absalom, the Tomb of the Ḥezir Family, and the Tomb of Zechariah did not yet exist, for they are from the Second Temple period. The bed of the Qidron was at least ten meters lower, and its right hand bank rose more westerly. The left bank was especially steep. Then, just as now, rising over the bank was a rock scarp into which and from which sepulchres were hewn. This was the burial ground of Jerusalem's nobility, generals, and priests. Today the houses of the village of Shiloaḥ stand here, yet amidst them several ancient tombs are still visible. Here and there burial caves gape open right under the houses. Across from us, above the right hand bank of the Qidron, is the Temple Mount. At that time Solomon's Temple stood there.

The area of the Temple covered only a small part of the walled Temple court of today. A wall starting approximately from the present-day Iron Gate and running as far as the Golden Gate, which of course did not exist then, enclosed the platform on the north. South of the Temple and north of the Ophel were the magnificent palace buildings, including the "house of the forest of Lebanon," built by Solomon **"the length thereof a hundred cubits** [50 meters], **and the breadth thereof fifty cubits** [25 meters], **and the height thereof thirty cubits** [15 meters], **upon four rows of cedar pillars, with cedar beams upon the pillars"** (I Kings 7:2).

The houses of the priests were in the center of the City of David, and south of them, stacked one above the other on east-west terraces (the *Millo,* according to Kenyon), were the houses of Jerusalem's residents.* Their type of structure is known to us from excavations of strata at Megiddo dating to the 8th century b.c.e.

The Temple court and the city were surrounded by a wall. Neither the Herodian wall nor, to be sure, that of Suleiman existed yet. Let us envision the eastern wall of that time. It consisted of various segments built in different periods. Rising above the wall at certain intervals were square towers, positions for the defenders of the city. The towers protruded from the wall so that the defenders could obtain a good view of the area between one tower and the next without leaving any "blind spots" (see the Lachish reliefs at the Hebrew University, or the reconstruction of the siege on the wall at Lachish in *The Art of Warfare in Biblical Lands,* by Yigael Yadin, pp. 436-437). Excavations have revealed sections of this wall, including a section of stone wall running somewhat south of the southeastern corner of the present-day wall of the Temple Mount. To the west, above the building over the Giḥon, in the distance we can see the remains of a wall which, according to Kenyon, was built in the eight century b.c.e. on the foundations of the Middle Bronze Age wall. The western ridge (Mount Zion and the present-day Jewish Quarter) rises west of the City of David (located on the eastern ridge).

During the time of Hezekiah Jerusalem had already expanded beyond the City of David to the western ridge (the Upper City of

*The walls built of new stone, visible in the distance on the east of the ridge of the City of David, are retaining walls built by Kenyon to prevent the terraces revealed in the excavation from collapsing.

the Second Temple period). Between the western ridge and the City of David lay the Gai Valley, a watercourse which over the years became silted up with ruins and debris.

From the Giḥon southward the course of the Qidron was verdured with gardens. It was there that the Shiloaḥ flowed (**"the waters of Shiloah that go softly,"** Isaiah 8:6) – a water conduit hewn in the rock of the Qidron Valley during the time of Solomon. (It was discovered in excavations and filled in; today a road passes over it). It watered the gardens planted by the king in the Qidron Valley, especially in the wider part of the valley at the confluence of the Hinnom Valley and around En-Rogel (the King's Gardens). Even today this area abounds in fruit trees, primarily figs.

f. the upper pool, today suq kutnin* and the esh-shifa baths

Leaving the area of the Western Wall through Wilson's Arch, we reach el-Wad Street (Simtat ha-Gai), at the end of which, on the right, is the Suq Kutnin (Cotton Merchants' Market) and the Ḥammam esh-Shifa, a bath-house. Somewhere near this bath-house, apparently, was once the site of the upper pool, which collected the water of the Gai and the western confluent which feeds in at this spot. Over the years the pool became blocked, yet rainwater continues to drain towards it. Evidence of this is the pseudo-spring located beneath the bath-house.

After capturing the fortified cities of Judah, Sennacherib sent **"Rab-shakeh from Lachish to Jerusalem unto king Hezekiah with a great army. And he stood by the conduit of the upper pool in the highway of the fullers' field"** (Isaiah 36:2). Hezekiah's generals, **"Eliakim the son of Hilkiah, who was over the household, and Shebnah the scribe, and Joah the son of Asaph the recorder"** (II Kings 18:18), came out to speak with him from the top of the wall, across from the palace buildings. Thus, the emissary of the Assyrian king reached the king of Judah, but for obvious reasons was kept outside the walls.

Isaiah's prophesy only came to pass in part. Shebna was only deposed from his high office and transferred to a secondary post, and his office given, as the prophet demanded, to Eliakim son of Hilkiah. Facing great trouble, the people and the government joined hands, and this time the prophet concurred.

Let us imagine the wall with its towers and, standing on the wall in stony silence, the soldiers defending it, and the figures of the generals, leaning over slightly towards the Assyrian general who stood with his entourage at the foot of the wall. The long speech of Rabshakeh, who spoke in the language of the Jews (Hebrew), most likely through an interpreter, is relayed in chapter 36 of Isaiah and chapter 18 of II Kings. It was a strange dialogue, one side doing the talking and the other mostly remaining silent: **"But the people** [the generals and the soldiers

1

guarding the wall] **held their peace, and answered him not a word; for the king's commandment was, saying: 'Answer him not' "** (II Kings 18:36). The Assyrian demanded not only surrender but also that the people prepare to go into exile, according to the dictates of Assyrian politics, which called for exchange of populations in order to prevent rebellion in conquered lands. The reasons he gave the Jews to accept his demands were weighty: relying on Egypt was like leaning on a broken reed; Judah was weak and defeated, and its army untrained: **"Now therefore, I pray thee, make a wager with my master the king of Assyria, and I will give thee two thousand horses, if thou be able on thy part to set riders upon them"** (*ibid.,* v. 23). The Lord would not help, he argued (according to the crude conception of an idolater!), for Hezekiah had destroyed his shrines and altars. Severe starvation and thirst lay in store for the besieged, and they would have **"to eat their own dung, and to drink their own water"** (*ibid.,* v. 27).

The generals of Judah naively requested the spokesman of the enemy to speak Aramaic, the *lingua franca* of the time, **"and speak not with us in the Jews' language, in the ears of the people that are on the wall"** (*ibid.,* v. 26). However Rabshakeh was well schooled in psychological warfare: **"But Rab-shakeh said unto them: 'Hath my master sent me to thy master, and to thee, to speak these words? hath he not sent me to the men that sit on**

*Suq Kutnin, the Cotton Merchants' Market, a Mameluke covered market, is an impressive building. The Jerusalem Municipality cleaned and renovated it, and set up shops there.

1. *In Hezekiah's time the overflow of the Giḥon ran from the lower pool (present-day Pool of Shiloaḥ) through a conduit (to the right of the guardrail) into the Pool of Shiloaḥ (present-day Ḥamra Pool).*

2 *Rahat: a public fountain typical of the Mameluke and Ottoman periods, built by the ruler or a wealthy man, in the city or on its outskirts, to provide free drinking water to travelers.*

3 *The gateway to* Suq Kutnin, *the Cotton Merchants' Market, built by the Mameluke emir, Tankiz, ruler of Damascus, in 1336-1337.*

2

3

the wall, to eat their own dung, and drink their own water with you?' Then Rab-shakeh stood, and cried with a loud voice in the Jews' language" (*ibid.*, v. 27-28.).

How must the men on the wall have felt?

The war came to an end, miraculously, with the fall of Sennacherib; yet Hezekiah's tunnel undoubtedly contributed to the marvelous deliverance. At least the people in Jerusalem did not suffer from thirst during the siege, and thus an important factor which breaks the spirit of the beleaguered in time of siege was absent. Jerusalem was not captured. The fate of destruction had been spared it and was postponed for over a hundred years. When the Ten Tribes went into exile they were not yet equipped with the spiritual capacity which would separate them from the gentiles and hence became quickly assimilated. In the intervening hundred and thirty-five years from the fall of Samaria to the destruction of Jerusalem the great prophets lived and preached, and the major works of the Bible were created; Jewish monotheism took shape and gathered strength, producing its first edifying fruits in the heroic stand of the people of Judah against Sennacherib's siege. When Judah went into exile, the people carried with them spiritual values which preserved them from assimilation and made a great contribution to shaping world civilization. And to think, that all this might have come out differently, had it not been for the timely completion of Hezekiah's tunnel!

Had Jerusalem fallen and been destroyed by Sennacherib, he would undoubtedly have exiled its people, as Rab-shakeh had said, and the Jews would have assimilated into the population in their place of exile, just as the Ten Tribes had. Without the Judaism of the Second Temple, Christianity would not have arisen, nor Islam; and the course of world history would have been entirely different.

It is strange to think that all this may have depended on the completion of Hezekiah's tunnel and that completing the tunnel depended on a handful of borers and the superhuman effort which they made, an effort which has been frozen for all time in the walls of Hezekiah's tunnel.

From the Hebrew pamphlet, "Tours in Jerusalem of the First and Second Temple," published by the Chief Education Officer – Section for Teaching about Israel, May 1979.

jerusalem in the late second temple period

Menachem Zaharoni

At the close of the Second Temple period Jerusalem was one of the world's most famous and beautiful cities. It spread over an area of about two square kilometers and was entirely enclosed by walls. Its main quarters as well were set off by walls as a result of the way the city developed. When a new quarter was built outside the city, the wall enclosing the city's former limits remained. On the east the city bordered the Qidron Valley, on the south and west the Hinnom Valley. These valleys provided the city natural defense to the south and east but also prevented the city from expanding on these sides. On the north there was not a single river valley providing natural defense; hence the city grew in this direction.

In terms of defense, the north was Jerusalem's vulnerable side; and that is how we are to understand Jeremiah 1:14, **"Out of the north the evil shall break forth."** At the close of the Second Temple period the northernmost suburb of Jerusalem, Bezetha, was enclosed by the Third Wall, which ran along the line of the present-day Russian Compound, Hanevi'im (Prophets) Street, and eastward to the Qidron Valley. At this point the wall turned south, meeting the wall of the Temple Mount. Construction of the wall was begun by King Agrippa I, but Emperor Claudius halted its construction for fear of rebellion. It had to be hastily completed during the Great Revolt and hence was not as strong as had been planned.

The Second Temple (the first having been destroyed by Nebuchadnezzar in 586 b.c.e.), built by Herod the Great,* its construction continuing until the very outbreak of the Jewish Revolt, was Jerusalem's pride and glory. The wealthy lived in the Upper City (in the area of the present-day Jewish and Armenian quarters, as well as the area of Mount Zion), and the poorer residents lived in the Lower City, along the slope descending from Mount Zion towards the Tyropoeon (Cheesemakers' Valley, called the Gai in the biblical period) and the City of David.

*King of Judah from 37 - 4 b.c.e.

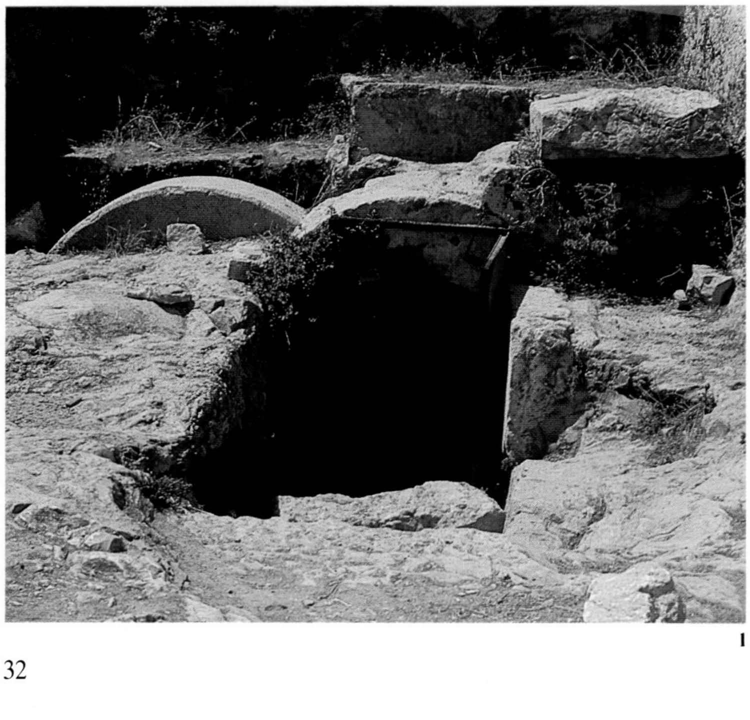

1 *Tomb of Herod's Family. The entrance was sealed by a rolling stone to prevent the tomb from being pillaged.*

2 *The Triple Gate in the southern retaining wall of the Temple Mount is now blocked. West of it is the Double Gate. Both groups of gates comprised the Hulda Gates of the Second Temple.*

The city appears to have had about 100,000 residents, but during the festivals its population used to increase two-fold or more. Then the city would hum with crowds and the babble of different tongues spoken by Jewish pilgrims from all lands of the Diaspora.

The day the Romans deposed Archelaus from the office of Ethnarch, Jerusalem ceased to be the official capital of Judah. The Roman Procurator resided in Caesarea and only rarely came to Jerusalem. For the Jewish people in the land and outside it, however, Jerusalem remained the eternal capital and the Temple the object of yearning of Jewish hearts the world over.

The great builder and architect of Jerusalem was King Herod the Great. The remains of his buildings are impressive to this day.

To acquaint ourselves with Jerusalem of the end of the Second Temple period we shall visit a number of sites of remains from that time.

the route

1. The Tomb of Herod's Family – behind the King David Hotel (view of Jerusalem in the eyes of a contemporary of the Destruction).
2. The Tower of David (reconstructing the line of the city walls).
3. The Convent of the Sisters of Zion and the Omariyya School (site of the Antonia Fortress which protected the northern side of the Temple Mount; view of the Temple Mount from the roof of the Omariyya School).
4. Wilson's Arch and the Western Wall – the bridge between the Upper City and the Temple.
5. Excavations at the Western Wall (a Jerusalem street from the late Second Temple period; Robinson's Arch and the pier across from it; the Steps of Hulda and the gates to the Temple court; the stone that fell from the top of the wall on the day of Jerusalem's destruction and to this day remains where it landed, near the southwestern corner of the wall of the Temple Mount);
6. Part of Jerusalem's "City of the Dead," near the Qidron Valley: the Tomb of Zechariah, the Tomb of the Ḥezir Family, and the Monument of Absalom; and the slope of the Mount of Olives, around the Dominus Flevit Church.

7. The Tombs of Queen Helena of Adiabene, on Salaḥ ed-Din Street (Jerusalem as bringing the world a spiritual message).

the tomb of herod's family

Behind the King David Hotel is an ancient and magnificent mausoleum identified, according to Flavius Josephus, as the tomb of the house of Herod (see *The Jewish War,* Book V, 3:2). This was apparently the burial place of Mariamne I (the Hasmonean), beloved wife of Herod whom, in a moment of jealous anger, he had executed. "But rage quickly gave way to remorse, and as anger died down love was rekindled. So hot was the flame of his desire that he could not believe her dead, but in his sickness of mind talked to her as if still alive" (*The Jewish War,* Book V, 3:2; trans. G. A. Williamson, Penguin edition, p. 81).

As we face east, we see the wall of the Old City, which roughly corresponds to Herod's wall. The Tower of David and two other lofty towers which stood next to it were part of the city's fortifications. Herod's palace lay south of these towers, on the other side of the wall, spreading over the area which today houses the buildings of the Police Department and the new Armenian Theological Seminary. Through the many chambers and courtyards of his palace, which, in Roman style, abounded in fountains and baths, the sick king used to run about at night and shout at his beloved queen, whom he murdered with his own hands.

Water for the palace was supplied by three large pools: Mamilla Pool; the Serpents' Pool (Sultan's Pool), southeast of us, across from the modern neighborhoods of Yemin Moshe and Mishkenot Sha'ananim; and the Towers' Pool, now surrounded by houses in the Christian Quarter Road of the Old City. The Mamilla Pool and Serpents' Pool collected the runoff water of the upper Hinnom Valley. The Towers' Pool was fed by an aqueduct running from the Mamilla Pool. Today the Serpents' Pool is part of a park around the Old City of Jerusalem, and the bottom of the pool is a pleasant manicured lawn.

Herod could see his wife's tomb from every tower in the wall or palace. Several steps led down to the tomb's entrance, which had a finely hewn, large heavy rolling stone, used to seal the tomb in order to prevent it from being pillaged. To clean the tomb, one entered through an opening in the roof at the southern end.

The tomb consisted of a set of chambers in the shape of a cross, their walls covered with rectangular stone panels, impressive in their superior workmanship and finish to this day. The ornamented sarcophagi discovered here were transferred to

2

the building of the Greek Orthodox Patriarchate in the Old City, which holds title to the land around the catacomb. North of the catacomb we can see the foundations of a structure built of large ashlars, apparently the monument marking the tomb.

the tower of david

The Tower of David is actually Phasael's Tower, built by Herod in memory of his beloved brother, who preferred to commit suicide rather than betray Herod. The minaret, which stands out from afar and which we are familiar with from the many drawings of the Tower of David, is nothing other than part of a later mosque. The ancient tower, preserved only to part of its height, can only be seen from inside the Old City, from the square next to the steps leading to the tower's court.

Only the section of the tower built of Herodian masonry* is from the time of Herod. The lower eight courses were built slanting outwards in order to reinforce the base of the tower. Above them eight more courses of Herodian ashlars have survived. (The courses above these are from later periods.) At the end of the Second Temple period the height of the tower was 45 meters. The Tower of Hippicus (a friend of Herod's), somewhat lower than Phasael's Tower, stood northeast of it, and the Tower of Mariamne, the most beautiful and lowest of the towers, stood to the southeast.

The First Wall, built before Herod, ran east from the Tower of Hippicus, following the modern-day David Street and Street of the Chain. When Jerusalem expanded to the north, a new wall had to be built to encompass the added areas; this was the Second Wall. From this vicinity the wall turned northward, leaving the Towers' Pool (see above), which supplied water to Herod's palace, outside the wall, and continuing north towards the Damascus Gate (Shechem Gate). (The Towers' Pool is known today by the Jews of Jerusalem as Hezekiah's Pool and by the Christians as the Pool of the Patriarch. It is surrounded by houses but may be seen from the balcony of an Arab cafe located on the second storey of a building on the west side of the Christian Quarter Road.) The courses of Herodian stone discovered beneath the Damascus Gate are apparently part of this wall. From there the wall turned east and then south, meeting the northwestern tower of the Antonia, the fortress defending the north of the Temple Mount. In time Jerusalem expanded north of the Second Wall, as well, and the suburb of Bezetha (probably *Bet Zayit*) came into being. Agrippa I attempted to enclose this area, too, by the Third Wall, which ran from the Tower of David to the Russian Compound (the site of the Tower of Psephinus) and from there followed the course of the present-day Nevi'im (Prophets') Street, passing north of the Rockefeller Museum as far as the Qidron River, then south along the bank of the Qidron to meet the wall of the Temple Mount.

Work on the construction of the Third Wall ceased by orders of Emperor Claudius, Agrippa's "friend," who suspected him of rebellious intentions, leaving the wall to be hastily completed during the Great Revolt. Remains of the Third Wall can be seen today near Nablus Road, corner of St. George Street.

The Tower of David stood at the weak point in the intersection of the city walls (only the first and the second of which stood in Herod's day). Here Herod erected his three fortified towers in a triangular formation. Inside the courtyard of the Tower of David we can see remains of buildings from many periods, for the city's citadel always stood on this site. However, let us focus on the excavations of Herod's palace and the Hasmonean wall. The upper foundations discovered in the excavations inside the courtyard belong to Herod's palace. Beneath them we see the foundations of Hasmonean buildings (running in a different direction from the Herodian foundations).

The Hasmonean wall reveals remains of the construction work of various Hasmonean rulers. This wall joins the Tower of Phasael, showing distinctly the constrast between the impressive Herodian construction and the simple Hasmonean construction.

The name, Tower of David, appears to have evolved from

*Herodian masonry is recognized by the double draft around its edge, the outer one wider and the inner narrower, framing a slightly protruding, flatly tooled rectangular center.

1

2

1 A model of Jerusalem at the end of the Second Temple period, located on the grounds of the Holyland Hotel.

2 A reconstruction of Herod's three towers, built at the weak point in the intersection of the city walls (right to left): the Tower of Phasael, of Mariamne, and of Hippicus. Shown in the model of Jerusalem in the Second Temple period (Holyland Hotel).

the name of the quarter at the close of the Second Temple period, as we may infer from the words of Josephus: **"It [Jerusalem] was built on two hills facing each other... Of these hills the one occupied by the Upper City was much the higher and straighter along its length; being so strong it was called the 'Stronghold of King David,' the father of Solomon who built the first Temple"** (*The Jewish War,* Book V, 4:1).

the antonia fortress

A citadel, known as the Birah (the castle) and designed to defend the north of the Temple Mount, stood on this spot since the time of Nehemiah. This fortress existed through the Hasmonean period, as well. Herod rebuilt it with different intentions and called it the Antonia, after his "friend" Marc Antony, a member of the Triumvirate. Under Herod and the Roman procurators foreign soldiers were stationed here to keep an eye on the activities in the courtyards of the Temple, to prevent any uprisings by the masses of people who used to assemble there on the festivals. At times, however, uprisings were actually caused by misunderstandings between the pilgrims and the foreign soldiers. The Roman soldiers of many nationalities, stationed in the Antonia, thought the customs of the Jewish pilgrims strange and ludicrous, and out of a sovereign's sense of superiority sometimes caused provocations by taunting and ridiculing the Jews.

Herod's fortress occupied the site of the present-day Sisters of Zion Convent, the Chapel of Flagellation to its east, and the Omariyya School across from it. Lofty towers soared at each of its four corners. The two eastern towers were 35 meters tall, and the two western ones 25 meters. A model of the Antonia Fortress and a topographical map of Jerusalem including the fortress can be seen in the small museum of the Sisters of Zion Convent. The chief remains of the Antonia – remains of the soldiers' quarters, courtyards, and a pool – are inside this convent. To the north the Antonia bordered on Bezetha. The Second Wall adjoined the fortress at its northwestern tower. To make the fortress self-sufficient, enabling it to withstand a siege without outside help, Herod built two large reservoirs inside it (the Struthion Pool), connected to one another and fed by water from Lacus Legerii, a pool northwest of the Damascus Gate.

The pools are exceedingly impressive to this day. (They may be reached by way of an opening off the hallway in front of the convent's museum.)

The room adjoining the museum is built over the courtyard of the Antonia, which is paved with large stones. Some of these stones, worn from years of traffic, are grooved across their width to provide sure footing for the horses which passed through here at one time. The continuation of the courtyard lies on the other side, in the Chapel of Flagellation. Various games apparently played by the soldiers, as well as a star of David, are engraved in the floor. A niche in the courtyard pavement provides a glance at one of the Struthion pools.

Part of the victory arch built in honor of Emperor Hadrian after he quashed the Bar Kokhba Revolt can be seen in the convent's basilica, which is called Ecce Homo –"Behold the Man" (John 19:5). This, in Christian tradition, was where the Roman procurator Pontius Pilate held the trial of Jesus, surrounded by Jews who came to view the proceedings. According to the New Testament, Pilate found no fault in Jesus. Barabbas, a zealot accused of insurgence, was also on trial along with Jesus. As was the custom, Pilate was about to set one of the prisoners free in honor of the feast of Passover, and the Jews called for Barabbas to be released, whereas Jesus – "Behold the man" or "This is the man" – they demanded be crucified. In ridicule, the Roman soldiers dressed him in royal purple, placed a crown of thorns on his head, and at Pilate's behest hung a plaque on him which read, "King of the Jews."

Jesus was led to his crucifixion at Golgotha, along the road thus called the Via Dolorossa, i.e. the Way of Affliction. The events which took place according to Christian tradition at various stations along the Via Dolorossa, also known as the Way of the Cross, are described in the Latin inscriptions on the buildings along the right side of the road.

Scholars actually are not sure the trial of Jesus really took place in the Antonia. Most are of the opinion that it took place in Herod's palace, the seat of the Roman procurator on his visits to Jerusalem.

2

a view of the temple platform

With permission from the school's administration, one can climb to the roof of the Omariyya School which offers a breathtaking view of the entire Temple platform, with all its buildings and mosques.

Proceeding from the generally accepted view that the Holy of Holies (the interior and most sanctified place in the Temple) was located on the site of the present-day Foundation Stone in the Dome of the Rock, we may use a map to help reconstruct the appearance of the Temple platform and the Temple itself before its destruction.

The balustrade was a low wall which even non-Jews, i.e. people who did not observe the laws of ritual cleanliness, were allowed to approach. Latin and Greek inscriptions cautioning gentiles not to enter within ran the length of this balustrade. One of the Greek inscriptions, accidentally discovered on the Temple Mount, is now in the Rockefeller Museum. The Women's Court, open to both men and women, served for assemblies of the people. The Court of the Israelites was restricted to men bringing sacrifices.

wilson's arch and the view around the western wall

From the Via Dolorosa let us leave the Old City by way of the Lion's Gate and walk along the Moslem cemetery which runs the

3

1 *The Tombs of the Kings: the catacombs of the royal house of Adiabene, whose members converted to Judaism in the first century c.e.*

2 *Robinson's Arch: Visitors to the Second Temple used to climb the stairs leading from the street level to the top of the pier, then cross the bridge which passed over the arch and enter the Temple courtyard.*

3 *The Tombs of the Royal House of Adiabene: the broad steps pictured are hewn into the rock and descend to a forecourt in front of the catacombs.*

length of the eastern wall, in which some ancient Herodian segments have survived. We pass the Golden Gate, built in the Byzantine period and, entering the city through the Dung Gate, reach the vicinity of the Western Wall.

The Gai Valley separated the Upper City from the Lower City in the south of Jerusalem and the Upper City from the Temple Mount in the central part of the city. The Wailing Wall (also called the Western Wall or the *Kotel*) is part of the western wall of the Temple platform. Herod blocked off the Gai, which ran roughly along the line of the western wall of the Temple Mount, and filled it in with earth, thus enlarging the area of the Temple platform. This may have become feasible because the Gai was no longer necessary for drainage, its water having been blocked further up and impounded into Lacus Legerii and the pools of Struthion, Bethesda, and Israel, on the north side of the Temple Mount. (The Pool of Israel was filled in during the British Mandate.)

Even after the Gai was filled in, a deep depression remained between the Upper City and the wall of the Temple platform, just as in our day. Wilson's Arch, to the north of the Western Wall, connected the Upper City with the Temple court. Beneath it were many halls whose function remains obscure. A synagogue now occupies the large, foremost hall next to the Western Wall.

Beside the Western Wall we can see the open shafts excavated by the British archaeologist Charles Warren in an attempt to reach the foundations of the wall. The wall beneath the floor level of the hall is built of huge Herodian ashlars, to a depth of 18.5 meters. The sides of the stones found above ground level are hewn in Herodian fashion (a flatly tooled center surrounded by a narrow margin and then a wider margin). The width of the arch over the hall is 13.40 meters, and its maximum height 22 meters. A maze of halls, some small, some large, apparently built in different periods, opens off the room of the synagogue.

The two aqueducts which carried water from Ein Arub to Jerusalem and the Temple, at the end of the Second Temple period, passed over Wilson's Arch.

the excavations at the western wall

To reconstruct how this area looked before the Destruction we shall tour the excavations at the Western Wall, focusing on the lowest stratum of the various occupational levels which these excavations have unearthed.

We shall begin our tour with the northwestern section of the dig. At the end of the Second Temple period a long road, extending as far as the Pool of Shiloaḥ, passed near the Western Wall. The excavations revealed large, heavy paving stones – the Herodian paving of this road. A drain ditch has survived along the western edge of the road. This road once bustled with Jerusalem residents and pilgrims on their way to celebrate the festivals at the Temple.

A stone arch, called Robinson's Arch after the American archaeologist who discovered it, can be seen protruding near the southwest corner of the wall. Across from it, further to the west, excavations have revealed a massive support structure, or pier, which was part of a roughly square building, magnificently

1

constructed of large ashlars. Stairs once led from the street level to the top of this pier, which then connected to Robinson's Arch. Visitors to the Temple would climb these, then cross along the viaduct over the arch and enter the Temple courtyard.

A royal portico, two storeys tall, extended the width of the southern part of the Temple platform. This was a roofed structure on columns, without walls, apparently designed for the royal family and the Jerusalem nobility to sit under and gaze at the Temple worship and festivities. The main vestibule to the Temple courts was reached through the Hulda Gate, in the southern wall of the Temple platform. Let us proceed rapidly through the excavations, starting at the soutwest corner, past the remains of a large Umayyad (early Arab) building partially constructed of huge Herodian ashlars taken from the mounds of debris of the Temple Mount wall. Proceeding through the entrance adjacent to the Crusader structure which protrudes from the wall, we reach the Hulda steps, discovered in the excavations and partially reconstructed. These steps were climbed by celebrants approaching the Temple court from the north side of the City of David. To force the pilgrims to proceed slowly and reverently, the steps were not built of equal depth. Each broad step was succeeded by a narrow one. Above the steps we see some blocked gates (the easternmost, the Single Gate, did not yet exist in the time of the Second Temple and was opened by the Crusaders).

South of the Al-Aqsa Mosque, recognized by its silver dome, we see the Double Gate. Today it is partially covered by a Crusader building. East of it is the Triple Gate. Masses of people once streamed to the Temple through the Double Gate and the Triple Gate – the Hulda Gates of the Second Temple period. First they would enter the subterranean halls, known today as "Solomon's Stables," which Herod built in the fill, enlarging the Temple platform and preventing excessive pressure on the walls. From these halls they would ascend stairs to the Temple courtyard. The procession was very orderly, with people entering through the Triple Gate and exiting through the Double Gate. Mourners, however, proceeded in the opposite direction, entering through the Double Gate and exiting through the Triple gate, so that the people coming towards them would console them.

A babble of different tongues could be heard on the Steps of Hulda in those days. Jews from all over the Diaspora would come here in holy reverence. Here the caravans of people bringing first fruits were greeted; and here the spiritual leaders of the people stood and delivered their messages to the Jewish communities of the Diaspora and various parts of Israel, so that their words would be carried to their destination by the pilgrims celebrating the festivals. It is said that Rabban Gamaliel the

Elder stood on the steps of the Temple Mount and instructed his scribe to write letters to the Jewish communities regarding the intercalation of the year.

Psalm 122 conveys a sense of the deep emotion the celebrants must have felt as they ascended the Steps of Hulda:

A Song of Ascents; of David.
I rejoiced when they said unto me:
'Let us go unto the house of the Lord.'
Our feet are standing
Within thy gates, O Jerusalem;
Jerusalem, that art builded
As a city that is compact together;
Whither the tribes went up, even the tribes of the Lord,
As a testimony unto Israel,
To give thanks unto the name of the Lord.
For there were set thrones for judgment,
The thrones of the house of David.
Pray for the peace of Jerusalem;
May they prosper that love thee.
Peace be within thy walls,
And prosperity within thy palaces.
For my brethren and companions' sakes,
I will now say: 'Peace be within thee.'
For the sake of the house of the Lord our God
I will seek thy good.

From the Steps of Hulda we return to the southwest corner of the wall. Excavations here have uncoverd a stone that fell from the top of the wall surrounding the Temple Mount, on the Tenth of Av, the day the Temple was destroyed. It remained where it landed, mute testimony to the tragedy of our people which transpired here nearly two thousand years ago, in 70 c.e., and which shaped the course of our history as one of exile, suffering, and persecution. A large number of coins minted in the last year of the revolt were found around the stone. They were simply cast, unwanted, from the top of the wall by soldiers, despairing at the sight of their holy Temple going up in flames.

the city of the dead

Let us follow the road which leads from the Dung Gate to the Qidron Valley and then turn left. Soon some ancient monuments of tombs hewn into the rock rise before our eyes.

The City of the Dead was hewn into the rocks south and east of Jerusalem. Few burial places were hewn close to the city, on the west, to avoid bad odors being spread over the city by the westerly wind. The southernmost tomb was popularly called the "Tomb of Zechariah." The entire structure is cut out of the stone

1 *Second Temple period monuments in the Qidron Valley: the Tomb of Zechariah (right) and the Tomb of the Ḥezir Family.*

2 *The Steps of Hulda, climbed by pilgrims approaching the Temple courtyard from the north side of the City of David. Part of the Double Gate can be seen at the juncture of the two walls.*

2

jerusalem in the late second temple period

1. *Tower of Phasael*
2. *Tower of Hippicus*
3. *Tower of Mariamne*
4. *Towers' Pool*
5. *The Hidden Gate*
6. *Herod's Palace*
7. *Upper City Market*
8. *Hananiah's Palace*
9. *Chamber of Hewn Stone*
10. *Theatre*
11. *Palace of the Priest Caiaphas*
12. *Fullers' Quarter*
13. *"Tomb of David"*
14. *Wilson's Arch*
15. *Robinson's Arch*
16. *Hippodrome*
17. *Pool of Hezekiah*
18. *Pool of Shiloaḥ*
19. *Essenes' Gate*
20. *Synagogue*
21. *Palace of Helena of Adiabene*
22. *Monument of Hulda the Prophetess*
23. *Gates of Hulda the Prophetess*
24. *Tadi Gate*
25. *"Birket Isra'il" Pool of Israel*
26. *Pool of Bethesda*
27. *Monument of Alexander Yannai (Jannaeus)*
28. *Women's Tower*
29. *Tower of Psephinus*
30. *Monument of John Hyrcanus*

jerusalem in the time of the second temple

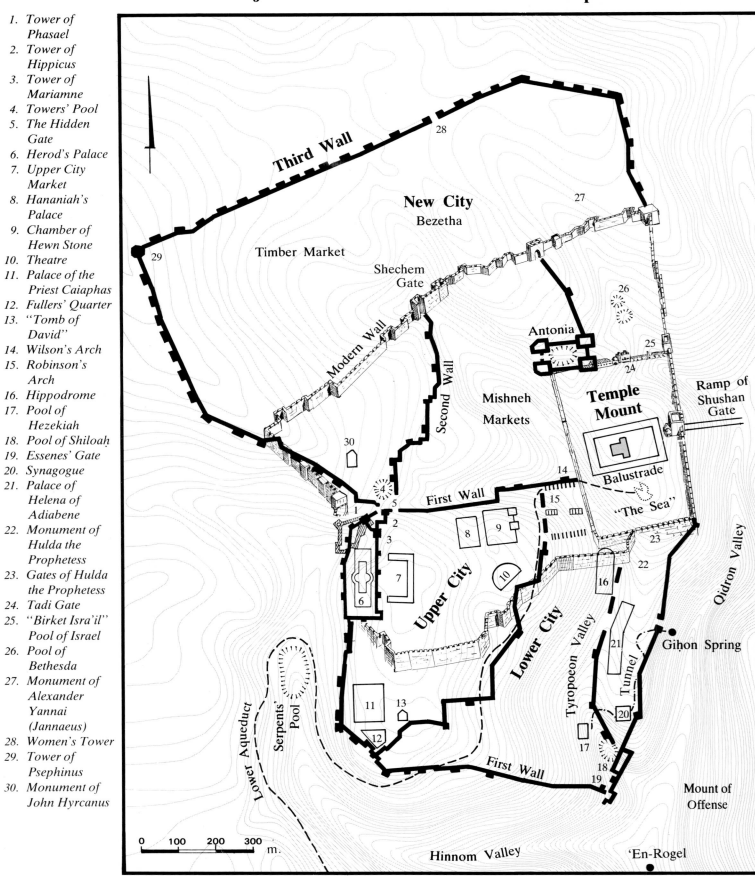

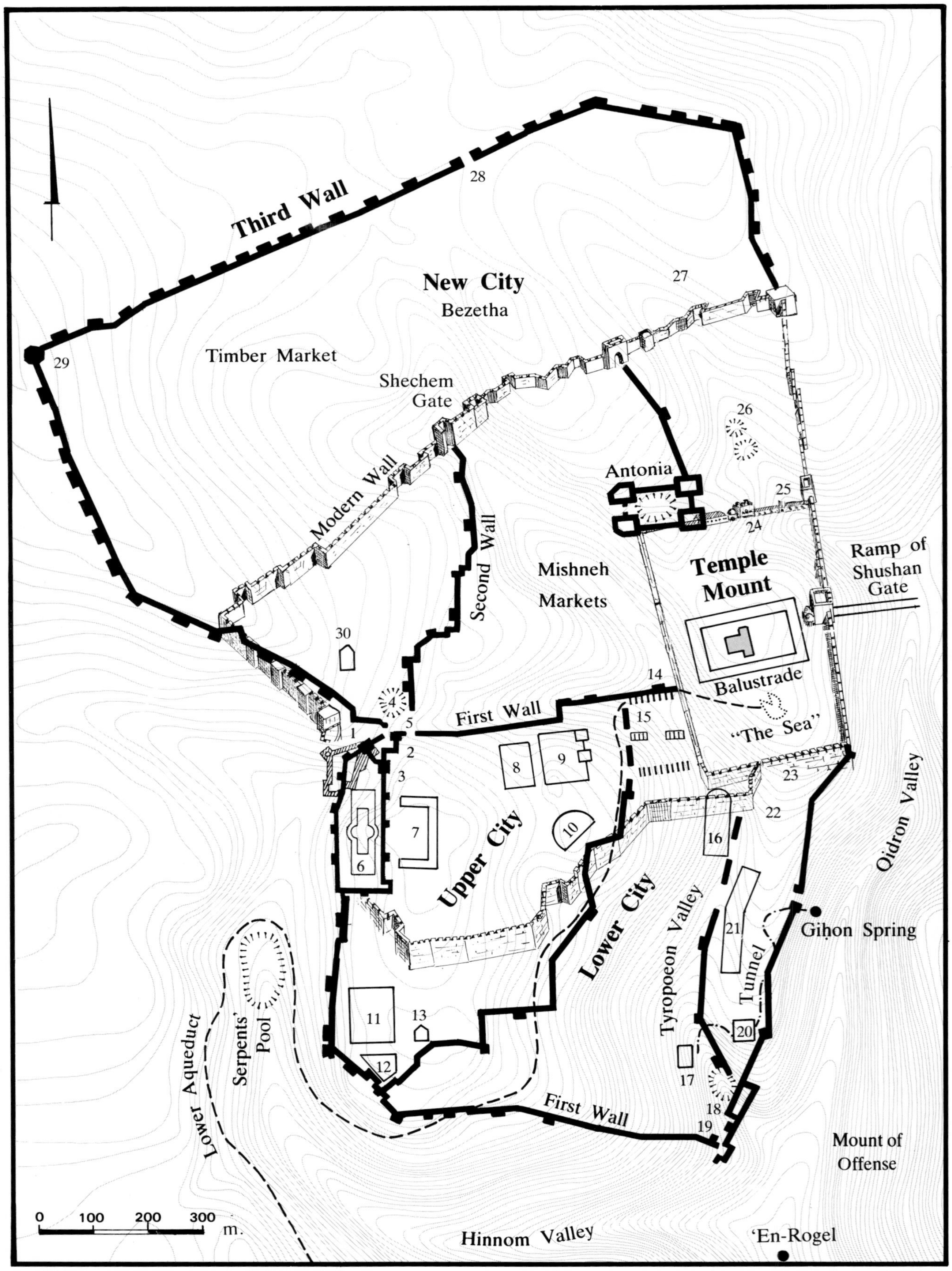

1

2 A model of Jerusalem in the Second Temple period, viewed from southwest to northeast. The houses of the Upper City are in the foreground, with the southern and western walls of the Temple platform behind them. Robinson's Arch and the staircases leading to it are near where the two walls meet. Further along the Western Wall we see Wilson's Arch, which provided access from the Upper City to the Temple court. The four towers of the Antonia Fortress, which commanded the Temple Mount from the north, can be seen rising above the wall of the Temple platform, to its left.

3 The plan of the Temple according to Avi-Yonah. Information on the structure of the Second Temple may be gleaned from: a) the Mishnah, especially tractates Middot and Tamid, and, to a lesser extent, the Talmud and Midrash; b) the writings of Josephus; c) archaeological findings on the Temple Mount and its vicinity.

4 The Temple Mount as reconstructed in the model of Jerusalem in the Second Temple period (at the Holyland Hotel). The Temple is in the center and the royal portico in the background. Between the portico and the Temple is the entrance to the underground passageways leading from the Gates of Hulda.

2

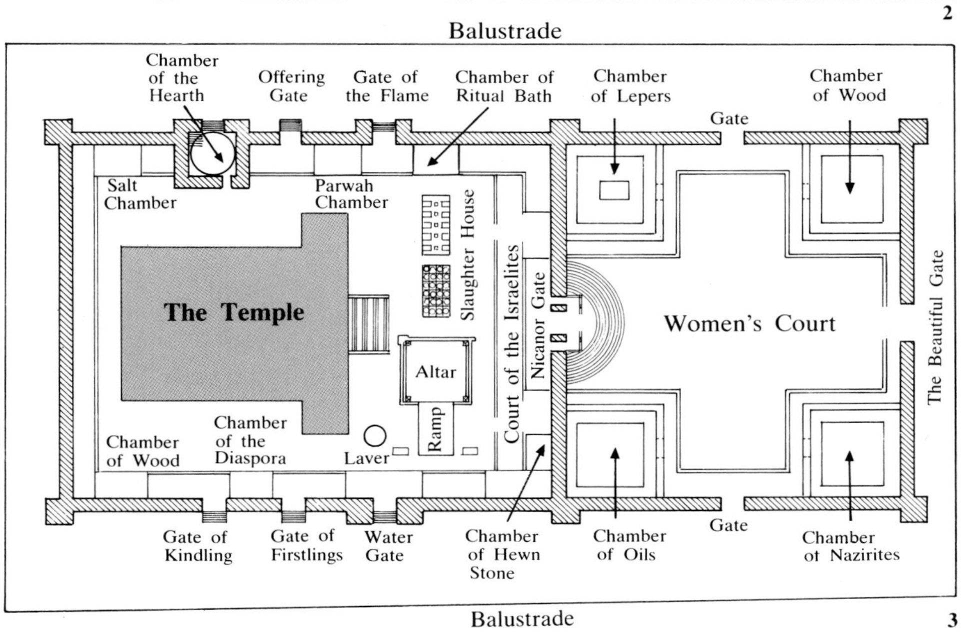

3

4

on the site. Its roof is a square-based pyramid 4.7 meters high. The part beneath the pyramid is 7.5 meters tall. Pilasters with Ionic capitals are carved on all four sides of the structure. At the base of the facade is a small chamber, hardly large enough to bury a person. For this reason it is believed that the "Tomb of Zechariah" is actually only the memorial monument of the neighboring Tomb of the Ḥezir Family. This monument appears to have been built at the end of the Hasmonean period and probably belonged to a member of Jerusalem's nobility.

The Tomb of the Ḥezir Family is taller than the "Tomb of Zechariah" and has two Doric columns on the facade. On the lintel over the front entrance is a Hebrew inscription in Assyrian letters, which reads: **"This is the burial and monument of Eleazar, Haniah, Joezer, Judah, Simeon, Johanan sons of Joseph son of Oved, Joseph and Eleazar son of Haniah, Priests from the sons of Ḥezir."** The Ḥezir priestly family is mentioned in I Chronicles 24:15. They were the 17th of 24 shifts of priests serving in the Temple.

The facade leads to a catacomb, popularly called "Bet Ḥofshit" or "a house set apart" (i.e., for leper's residence; II Kings 15:5) and believed to have been the place where King Uzziah dwelled after he was smitten with leprosy. Its inscription, however, reveals its true identity. It was apparently hewn in the beginning of the Hasmonean period.

The best known site here is "Absalom's Monument," erroneously attributed to Absalom son of David. Actually this is a tomb from the beginning of the first century of the Common Era, as may be judged by its mixed Hellenistic-Egyptian style, resembling the Nabatean tombs in Petra, which date from the same period.

Looking at Absalom's Monument from bottom to top, we can make out four sections: 1) the plinth; 2) a square chamber hewn into the rock (a monolith with a hole on the south side, made by monks who lived in the chamber in the Middle Ages);
3) a square structure consisting of several courses of large stones rimmed by a course of smaller stones, with a square opening in the southern wall, through which the coffin was inserted;
4) a round structure with a cylindrical body and conical roof. The conical roof is capped by a stone carved in the form of a lotus flower, with six petals, today partially broken, reaching up to the sky.

1

2

Behind Absalom's Monument we can see another catacomb, popularly called the Cave of Jehoshaphat. Over its entrance there is a pediment ornamented with an arabesque of acanthus leaves and grape vines, as well as various carvings of fruits and lily flowers. This catacomb dates to the same period as Absalom's Monument, i.e., the early part of the first century c.e.

The burial ground of the common folk of Jerusalem during the Second Temple period was located north of these memorial monuments, along the side of the Mount of Olives, in the vicinity of the small and strange looking Dominus Flevit Church (the brown building with white stripes which stands out above the Church of Gethsemane). Thus far nearly1000 ossuaries have been discovered here, many of them with Hebrew, Aramaic, or Greek inscriptions. The soft chalky stone made it possible to dig catacombs here cheaply.

the tombs of the house of adiabene

This catacomb is located on Salaḥ ed-Din Street, corner of Nablus Road. It was purchased in the 19th century by a Jewish

1 *A sculpted ossuary. Ossuaries were used in secondary burial as receptacles for bones of the dead.*

2 *Absalom's Monument, a burial monument from the Second Temple period, in the Qidron Valley.*

3 *One of the large twin Struthion Pools, hewn by Herod in the Antonia to enable the fortress to withstand a siege. The Antonia defended the northern approach to the Temple Mount. The pools were fed by water from Lacus Legerii, a reservoir north-west of Damascus Gate.*

family from France and was donated to the French government. The first archaeologists to excavate here believed that they had discovered the tombs of the House of David (see the sign in French and Hebrew over the front of the catacomb). Later, however, it became clear beyond a shadow of doubt that this was the burial place of the royal house of Adiabene (today a region in northern Iraq), whose members converted to Judaism in the first century c.e.

Queen Helena, whose Hebrew-Aramaic name may have been Ẓidan, the name discovered on one of the sarcophagi which was removed from the catacomb and transferred to the Louvre in Paris, came to Jerusalem and specifically built herself a palace in the City of David and not in the Upper City, where Jerusalem's higher classes lived. She did much philanthropic work for the poor of Jerusalem, especially in years of drought. Helena and her son Monobaz donated precious gifts to the Temple, and Monobaz even participated in the Great Revolt and was taken captive by the Romans.

This tomb is very impressive, even today. First one descends to its forecourt by way of stairs cut into the rock. Rainwater was carried from the stairs to cisterns, most likely used for ritual purification, by way of channels hewn along the stairs. On the left side of the forecourt there is an entrance to a large court hewn entirely into rock. At the far end of the court we can see the opening of the tomb, with a frieze above it, showing a cluster of grapes flanked by acanthus leaves and palm fronds, the carvings badly damaged by the ravages of time. The lintel of the facade was once supported by two columns. Three pyramids, according to Josephus, stood above the structure; the remains of one have been discovered in excavations.

The entrance to the catacomb, which consisted of two stories, is to the left of the facade. The heavy rolling stone used to seal the entrance to the tomb still lies next to it. To the right of the facade we can see a round depression which apparently housed the mechanical apparatus used to move the rolling stone from a distance. Popular tradition erroneously attributed this catacomb to Kalba Savua, Rabbi Akiva's wealthy father-in-law.

The tomb is testimony to the great spiritual influence which the Jewish religion had on the peoples of the world in the first century of the Common Era. Roman-Hellenistic society was in a state of perturbation and seeking new meaning in life. Many found an answer in the Jewish faith; some adopted it fully, while others raised their children in its spirit but themselves did not take the last step of entering the faith, due to the difficulties in observing the commandments. It was among the latter, who were known as "God-fearing people," that Paul preached in the name of a religion close to Judaism and, in order to win more converts to Christianity, absolved them from practicing the Jewish commandments.

3

From the Hebrew pamphlet, "Tours in Jerusalem of the First and Second Temple," published by the Chief Education Officer – Section for Teaching about Israel, May 1979.

jerusalem: a city of walls

Zvi Ilan

City walls in general, and those of Jerusalem in particular, are an expression of the development of a city throughout its history. If you can identify and locate the walls, you can determine how far the city extended at each stage of its development. With such information at your disposal you can determine whether the city was large or small at a given moment in its history; i.e., whether the city was flourishing or declining. The very fact of building a wall indicates that the city had a sufficiently strong central government to undertake works whose aim was to ward off any potential enemy. A wealth of information about the walls of Jerusalem, a city continuously inhabited for thousands of years, can be derived from archaeological findings and from written sources, such as the Bible and the works of Josephus.

the walls of zion

Passing by the southeastern corner of the Temple Mount, an area of excavations can be seen south of the road. This was the site of the City of David, the city captured by the Israelites from the Jebusites about 1000 b.c.e. The city, dating back two thousand years earlier, was built on this location largely due to the proximity of the Giḥon Spring which provided water for its inhabitants.

One of the sections of wall found in the excavations dates to the twentieth century b.c.e. A thousand years later we hear again of the walls of Jerusalem, or "the fortress of Zion," which belonged to the Jebusites who inhabited the city. This was such a strong wall that a special reward had to be offered to the person who succeeded in penetrating it and in killing a Jebusite. The Jebusites, using psychological warfare, stationed blind and lame men on the walls in order to put a curse on the enemy so that should he succeed in penetrating the wall he would be smitten with blindness and lameness (II Samuel 5:8).

Joab son of Zeruiah, one of David's heroic fighters, was the first to volunteer to penetrate the city and, after succeeding, was appointed chief general (I Chronicles 11:4-6). He must have penetrated the city by way of the *ẓinor* mentioned in the Bible, possibly a tunnel connecting the city to the Giḥon Spring, or perhaps through Warren's shaft, discovered in recent excavations.

Under David, and especially under his son Solomon, the narrow confines of the Jebusite city were broken through. The royal buildings were built north of the old wall which had been breached, in the region of the *Millo.* This region is the site of the excavations south of the Temple Mount. B. Mazar conjectures that a structure having a large foundation fill, which he discovered there, is the biblical *Millo* (from a Semitic root meaning "filling"). This new section, called *Ophel,* was enclosed by a well constructed wall (II Chronicles 27:3).

King Uzziah undertook serious work to strengthen the walls of Jerusalem. He made **"engines, invented by skilful men, to be on the towers and upon the corners, wherewith to shoot arrows and great stones"** (II Chronicles 26:15) and equipped the defenders of the walls with superior personal arms. In Yigael Yadin's opinion, this text refers to some sort of defense galleries on the towers which enabled the defenders to use their weapons effectively while being protected from the arrows of the enemy.

A tremendous project to reinforce the walls of Jerusalem, whose full extent we can only now appreciate, was undertaken in the time of Hezekiah, who faced the tangible threat of the Assyrians under the leadership of King Sennacherib. He reinforced the breached wall and built an additional wall with towers, brought the water of the Giḥon Spring into the city, and also walled in the Pool of Shiloaḥ (II Chronicles 32:2-5).

The Bible helps us thus far; henceforward archaeology comes to our assistance. In this instance, as in many others, its discoveries account for the great interest in archaeology in Israel, for they shed marvelous light on the verses of Scripture, without which we would not understand the full significance of the text. To begin with, in the previous century an inscription dedicated to the conclusion of the tunneling work of Hezekiah's men was discovered in the Shiloaḥ conduit. Just within the past few years an extremely broad wall and, next to one of its

1

2

3

1 *A gate and ancient stone courses of the wall east of Damascus Gate and below it. This is the Hadrianic gate to Aelia Capitolina, the Roman name which Hadrian gave Jerusalem after suppressing the Bar Kokhba Rebellion.*

2 *The Golden Gate, a blocked up double gate in the eastern wall of the Temple Mount. In front of it is a Moslem cemetery.*

3 *Two tombstones next to Jaffa Gate, believed to be the graves of the architects of Suleiman's wall. Legend has it that the Sultan had them beheaded after they completed their work, so that they could not build walls of equal beauty in other cities.*

1

1 The southeastern corner of the wall. The lower courses of stone are Herodian construction.

2 The city's citadel, which remained in the same location for thousands of years. This is where Herod built his three towers, named after Hippicus, Phasael, and Mariamne. Left of it is Jaffa Gate. The gate was erected in 1536 by Suleiman the Magnificent, upon completion of the wall. The entrance between the gate and the citadel was broken open in 1898 in honor of a visit paid by the Kaiser of Germany, Wilhelm II, to enable his carriage to enter the city.

sections, a tower were discovered in the heart of the Jewish Quarter. The wall was built on top of an earlier house. We have seen that the City of David was situated on the eastern ridge; but we now know that the city wall continues much further west! What this means is that the city expanded that far and even further. Now we can understand what the prophet Isaiah said about breaking apart houses to build the wall. Unwalled quarters, called the *Mishneh* and the *Makhtesh,* which appear to have been settled at least in part by refugees from Samaria, which had been conquered by the Assyrians, sprung up beyond the ancient walls of the city. Urgencies of the war caused Hezekiah's men to build the wall along a certain line, even though that left a handful of sparsely scattered houses outside the wall. These houses were knocked down in order to create a clear firing area in front of the wall, so as to deny the enemy a covered approach close to the wall (Isaiah 22:9-11). Indeed, in his excavations, N. Avigad discovered arrows which had been shot towards the wall from without.

The walls of Jerusalem were broken apart by Nebuzaradan and the Babylonian army, after Nebuchadnezzar conquered the city and destroyed the Temple (II Kings 25:8-11).

A marvelous description of the repairs of the broken walls of Jerusalem is presented in the Book of Nehemiah. In view of the foe besieging Judah round about, construction work was done simultaneously with defense: guarding by night, working by day "every one with one of his hands wrought in the work, and with the other held his weapon" (Nehemiah 4:11). This was a repair job hastily executed along many parts of the wall simultaneously. The Book of Nehemiah presents a most unusual list, a sort of "census of the guard" of the defense system for the walls and gates of Jerusalem, which was based on territorial and occupational considerations. Sections of the wall were built by the inhabitants of a given city, who were regularly responsible for the defense of their section. The rebuilt city was relatively small, measuring only 120 dunams (as compared with 500 dunams in the time of Hezekiah, 130 dunams in the time of Solomon, and 44 dunams under David).

the three walls

Thus far the Bible was our sole written source on the walls. Henceforth, for the later periods, Josephus is our source. His works give a marvelous picture, describing how one wall after another was added for the defense of Jerusalem as the city and its defense needs grew, to the north in particular.

From the Hellenistic period (which we also call the Hasmonean period) on, there is a clear trend towards urban growth over considerable expanses of territory. Jerusalem thus spread over the entire western hill, as far as the vicinity of the Tower of David, Jerusalem's citadel. One of the Hasmonean kings enclosed the entire city with a wall which Josephus calls the First Wall. Its northern line ran from the Tower of David (near the modern Jaffa Gate), east to the Temple Mount, at Wilson's Arch, north of the area used for prayer at the Western Wall.

Several dozen years later the Second Wall was built, encompassing all of the northern part of the city and including most of the area of the Old City of today. The north of the city remained the problem, for the new residential quarters had expanded in that direction; the enemy was destined to come from there (**"out of the north the evil shall break forth"** – Jeremiah 1:14); and that side had no obstacle to stand in the enemy's way, whereas the city's other sides were defended naturally by deep valleys.

2

Therefore the last Hasmonean king, Agrippa I, decided to build the Third Wall. This wall was erected approximately half a kilometer north of the present northern wall of the city, in the area between the large gas station presently located near Salaḥ ed-Din Street, and the American School of Oriental Research. The Roman procurators demanded that Agrippa cease construction of the wall because they knew its construction was intended against them. Hence it was only with the outbreak of the Jewish Revolt, in 66 c.e., that the Jews managed to complete the wall in great haste. At that time the city had reached its largest expanse – 1800 dunams. The three walls did not succeed in withstanding the well trained Roman army and its siege engines, and after breaching the walls the Romans entered the city and burned the Second Temple.

Discovering remains of the wall was, and still remains today, a fascinating challenge for archaeologists. Since the city is densely built up, the various sections of the wall must be reconstructed on the basis of incidental findings and fragmentary excavations. Therefore scholars still disagree over one or another detail with respect to the line of the entire wall. Jerusalem's walls during subsequent periods were less extensive, about the size of the city today. It was a more or less square city, in the Greco-Roman tradition of city planning, with gates to the north, south, east, and west: Damascus Gate, David (Zion) Gate, Jaffa Gate and the Lions' (St. Stephen's) Gate.

The Moslems reinforced the city's walls in anticipation of the Crusader onslaught in 1099 c.e. The inhabitants were supposed to defend the section of wall nearest their own homes. At that time the Jewish Quarter was on the northeast of the city (around Herod's Gate, opposite the present-day Rockefeller Museum). The Jews fought valiantly to defend the section of wall in their quarter, but to no avail. The Crusaders attacking them, commanded by Godfrey of Bouillon, succeeded in breaching the Jewish section of the wall and joined forces with their compatriots, who had breached the wall in two other places.

Later, when Jerusalem was once more returned to the Moslems, the walls were repaired. About 120 meters east of Zion Gate a gate tower has been discovered in the wall. According to an inscription found on the site it was built by Sultan al-Malik al-Muazzam in 1212 c.e. Seven years later, however, facing a possible Crusader attack, this sultan decided to embark on a scorched earth policy and destroyed all the walls of Jerusalem. In the same vicinity wells for water and the foundations of ancient buildings, now incorporated in the park around the city walls and accompanied by explanatory plaques, were also discovered.

sultan suleiman the magnificent

Jerusalem remained without walls for over 300 years. After the Ottoman Turkish conquest Suleiman the Magnificent set about rebuilding the walls. He erected them along the line of the previous walls, and, like the earlier walls, they did not include Mt. Zion. He used stones from the ancient walls, easily reconized by their fine marginal draft, characteristic of Herodian masonry. It should be noted that the sultan was assisted in financing the construction work by a Jew, Abraham Castro, the Egyptian minister of finance. In the north, as well, the foundations of the wall followed the line of the ancient wall, which had been built on a natural rock outcropping, as may be seen to this day.

Remains of the wall of Aelia Capitolina, the name the Romans gave Jerusalem after their suppression of the Bar Kokhba Revolt in 134 c.e., are located near Damascus Gate, beneath the level of Suleiman's wall.

Near Jaffa Gate are two ancient tombstones. To whom do they belong? According to legend this is where the two architects of Suleiman's wall were buried. After the enterprise was completed Suleiman had them executed to prevent their building walls rivaling the beauty of Jerusalem's walls in any other city.

The walls stood untouched for over 200 years. In 1889 an opening was broken through them in order to build the New Gate on the northwest of the Old City, to provide convenient access between the Christian Quarter and Christian institutions in the new city. Another entrance to provide a way into town was opened in the walls in 1898 in honor of the arrival of the German Kaiser, Wilhelm II. The deep trench separating the Jaffa Gate from David's Citadel was filled in to lay the road which passes over it to this day. From 1948 until 1967 the road was blocked. The Jordanians built a thick concrete wall the width of the road and even blocked up the Jaffa Gate.

During the War of Independence, Jews living in the Land of Israel made several attempts to breach the walls to reach their besieged brethren in the Jewish Quarter, blasting through the wall and tunneling under it. The Palmaḥ succeeded in one of its attempts to penetrate Zion Gate, but lacked sufficient strength to take full advantage of its success. The bullet-shot gate was shut once more and again separated the Jews of Israel from the Jewish Quarter and the Old City as a whole, until 1967.

The wall of the Old City is an architectural treasure unique among the many archaeological and historical sites of Jerusalem. This fine and complete *chef d'oeuvre,* built by Suleiman the Magnificent, is the last in a series of walls and fortifications, successively built, destroyed and rebuilt since the city was first established on the hill overlooking the Giḥon Spring.

The city wall remained standing under Suleiman's successors, the Ottoman sultans who ruled Jerusalem and the Land of Israel. For lack of maintenance, however, it began to show the ravages of time, particularly in its upper portions, where its crenellation was knocked down or fell, and its stones became eroded. The wall, which on the eve of the British conquest of the Land of Israel looked rather dilapidated, was restored by the Mandatory authorities.

After the Israeli War of Independence the wall suffered again, this time at the hands of the Jordanian army, which built positions on many sections of the wall, erecting cement walls and dismantling unwanted stones from the wall in the process.

The wall again came into its own as a result of the Six Day War and the reunification of Jerusalem. Israel's leaders invested great energy and resources in restoring and caring for the wall and have recently seen the fruition of their many years of hard labor. In addition to restoring the wall to its former glory, a promenade has been opened on top of the wall itself, and verdant archaeological gardens have been planned and executed at its foot. Now it is possible to walk on the wall and look at the sites of Jerusalem, inside and out of the Old City, from above.

1 *Suleiman's wall, built on a rock outcropping on the north side of the city.*

2 *The courtyard of the citadel: remains of a wall from the Hasmonean period, perhaps from the time of Jonathan (153-143 b.c.e.).*

1

2

breaking out of the walls

Yehoshua Ben-Arieh

Let us turn the clock back to 1855 and begin our tour at the Citadel, the "Tower of David," beside the Jaffa Gate. Here we can look west, beyond the wall of the Old City. Imagine everything we see today as not existing. All the buildings and roads have not yet come into being. In front of us is a bare hill covered with rocks and thorns. The emptiness surrounding Jerusalem can be felt by the fact that every evening the gates of the city are shut and locked until the next morning; no one comes or goes, for fear of bandits who are likely to attack anyone who dares venture forth at night. If we were to look from atop the wall in any other direction – north, east, or south – the sight would be the same. Further on in our tour we shall have to exercise our imagination time and again in order to reconstruct the scenery in which the pioneering settlements of Jews beyond the city walls were founded. Only in this way shall we have any conception of the courage of those members of the Old *Yishuv* (pre-Zionist community, before 1880), who, in the eyes of many, have been labeled *galut* (exile) Jewry, but who dared leave the haven of the city walls and dwell in houses and quarters in the desolation surrounding the city.

We began our tour in 1855 because that year marks a turning point. Sir Moses Montefiore, visiting the country for the fourth time, purchased a plot of land on the hill west of the Hinnom Valley, facing Jaffa Gate and across from the Sultan's Pool. That is where we shall set out for now. Let us head south to Ḥativat Yerushalayim (Jerusalem Brigade) Street, cross the wadi to Hebron Road, and climb up the hill facing it to the houses of Mishkenot Sha'ananim, which we can recognize from afar by the unusual form of their crenellated parapets. Another landmark is the windmill on the hill above the houses. Here, where the two buildings of Mishkenot Sha'ananim and the windmill stand, Jewish settlement beyond the walls began.

mishkenot sha'ananim – montefiore cares for the poor

We begin our tour at the windmill. Above the entrance to the mill we see the emblem of the Montefiore family, decorated with three flags and the word Jerusalem above them. This emblem also appears on Montefiore's carriage, in the adjacent building, which bears the following inscription: "In his indefatigable efforts to assist his Jewish brethren, Sir Moses Montefiore, often accompanied by his wife Judith, visited the Land of Israel, Egypt, Morocco, Turkey, Russia, Romania, and other lands of Europe. He visited the Land of Israel seven times. Generally he journeyed overland in carriages, the primary mode of land transportation in those times. This carriage was used by Sir Moses Montefiore on some of his journeys."

Montefiore appreciated the plight of Jerusalem's Jews from his earliest visits and realized that it was imperative to improve their sanitary conditions and to create sources of livelihood for them.

On the plot which he purchased here he planned to build them 20 apartments and a windmill to provide a livelihood for those who settled here.

Montefiore sent all the equipment for the mill from England. It was brought to Jerusalem on camelback, for there was as yet no road for carts from the port of Jaffa to Jerusalem. The windmill was erected in 1857, some distance from the place where the houses were subsequently built. At first the mill was operated by millers sent from England and in the course of time was handed over to a Jew. When steam powered mills were built in the city the mill was shut down and its equipment abandoned.

Incidentally, Montefiore also brought the building materials for Mishkenot Sha'ananim from England. The mark of the factory in Ramsgate, which manufactured the decorated pillars supporting the roof of the balcony running the length of the building, can be made out on the pillars. In addition, an iron hand-pump was installed next to the well which was dug in the yard. This, the first pump in the country, was considered one of the marvels of technology, and many Jerusalem residents came here to witness with their own eyes how water could be drawn from a well without using a rope and bucket.

Montefiore was assisted in building the neighborhood by a bequest from Judah Touro, a rich Jew from New Orleans; hence it is also sometimes called the "Court of Judah Touro." About twenty housing units were built here, each consisting of two rooms, a kitchen, and a storeroom. In addition, two synagogues, one for the Ashkenazim and one for the

1 *Mishkenot Sha'ananim, the first quarter outside the Old City wall. The crenellated edge of the roof of the quarter's houses mirrors the wall of the Old City. Drain pipes along the walls carried rainwater off the roof to the wells in the courtyard.*

2 *A courtyard in the Maghrebi quarter, Maḥaneh Yisrael, the first quarter built outside the Old City by the residents of Jerusalem themselves.*

Sephardim, a ritual bath, a public oven, and a well were also built here. For security the residences were designed as two buildings, one above the other, and were enclosed by a high stone wall. The walls of the houses are very thick, and the windows and doors all face the same direction – towards the Old City. The doors were covered with strips of iron, and the windows closed with iron railings, also brought over from England. The parapet was crenellated, perhaps for easier defense, perhaps to mirror the design of the Old City wall.

Montefiore intended the apartments which he built in Mishkenot Sha'ananim for the poor and for Talmud students from the Old City. According to the original plan the tenants were supposed to switch around every three years, in order to give all the city's poor a chance to enjoy the good living conditions and farming work available here. However when the construction work was concluded in 1860, it proved difficult to find families willing to settle in the place, for fear of the robbers at night and because of its remoteness from the center of the Jewish community. Therefore, apparently, it was decided to give the houses as irrevocable property to those who agreed to live there and even to allot them a stipend.

The people who settled in Mishkenot Sha'ananim accepted the by-laws of the community, which, among other things, required them to maintain cleanliness in their houses and in the public areas of the community. Indeed, when an epidemic of cholera which claimed many lives broke out in Jerusalem in 1866, not a soul among the inhabitants of Mishkenot Sha'ananim

was struck by the disease. This was due not only to the cleanliness of the houses and the yards, but primarily to the sanitation of the water which we shall discuss on the last location in our tour of Mishkenot Sha'ananim.

Let us walk down from the open area near the windmill, passing the taller of the small houses of Mishkenot Sha'ananim, and stop between the two houses. Beneath us we can see the dogtoothed roof of the larger house and can easily make out the drains which channeled the rainwater from the roof to the wells. This clean water saved the lives of the residents of Mishkenot Sha'ananim during the plague; and it was this deliverance which, once it became known to the residents of the Old City, greatly encouraged people to move beyond the walls. It became clear to the residents of the Old City of Jerusalem that living outside the wall was not only not dangerous, but even promised better health. Perhaps this was the reason that immediately after the plague, in 1866, land for a second quarter was purchased, and two years later for a third, thus beginning the wave of Jewish exodus beyond the walls.

maḥaneh yisrael – the forgotten pioneers

The second quarter founded outside the walls was Maḥaneh Yisrael. We leave Mishkenot Sha'ananim and turn onto King David Street, pass the King David hotel, walk down towards Mamilla and, halfway down the slope, turn left into Ben-Simeon Street, which forms a shortcut to the building of the Ministry of Commerce and Industry on Agron Street. The neighborhood of Maḥaneh Yisrael (Camp of Israel), or more correctly what remains of it, can be seen on the left side of the street, several dozen meters in front of the building of the Fast Hotel, which houses the aforementioned offices. The quarter is marked by two large and handsome stone arches which look as if they do not belong to the disintegrating buildings behind them.

The land of the neighborhood was purchased in 1867 by R. David Ben-Simeon, the rabbi of the Maghrebi Jews in Jerusalem, for the members of his community. The Maghrebis (Jews from the Maghreb, North Africa) built some twenty houses here and a synagogue called Ẓuf Dvash, after their rabbi's famous book of the same name. Later ten more houses were added. Insofar as Mishkenot Sha'ananim was built by outside initiative, we may say that Maḥaneh Yisrael was the first community to be built outside the walls by the residents of Jerusalem themselves. This is also the first quarter belonging to a specific community of Jews, more of which were established later on. The founder of the quarter passed away shortly after it was founded, leaving his community without a leader; thus this settlement effort dropped from the history of the new city.

The surviving buildings of the original houses of Maḥaneh Yisrael, along the street bearing the name of the neighborhood's founder and along Maghrebi Alley which runs parallel to it and branches off of Agron Street, testify to their age. The technology of building with concrete or supporting roofs on steel girders was not yet known, so the roofs and windows were built using arches.

naḥalat shivah – the first cooperative

The third quarter built outside the wall was Naḥalat Shivah (The Inheritance of Seven), which also may lay claim to being a first: the first of the "cooperative quarters," many more of which were founded in its wake. These were quarters established by a cooperative of settlers, who purchased the land and built the houses (or at least the first ones) jointly. Naḥalat Shivah was built in 1869 by a group of seven people from distinguished families of old Jerusalem, who established a cooperative to purchase land outside the wall and erect residential buildings on it. The cooperative and the quarter were both named after the number of its members.

From Maḥaneh Yisrael we exit to Agron Street, turn left on Queen Helena Street, and left again on Ben-Sira Street, which takes us to Bet Agron (Agron House) and Bet ha-Mehandess (Engineer's House). The parking lot next to these buildings borders on Naḥalat Shivah, which lies between the parking lot and Jaffa Street, from Joseph Rivlin Street to Joel Moses Salomon Street, both of which are named after founders of Naḥalat Shivah.

Why did the founders buy precisely this plot of land? There were three reasons, the first of which has to do, strangely enough, with the Suez Canal. The inauguration of the canal, in November 1869, changed the eastern basin of the Mediterranean from an inland sea into an international maritime route. The great powers began to take an interest in the regions around the canal, including the Land of Israel. Thus it was not religious sentiment alone which motivated the Kaiser of Austria and the Crown Prince of Prussia to visit the Land of Israel on their way back from the inauguration ceremony to their own lands. The Kaiser's visit, however, was not only a ceremonial and political act, but also an important act in terms of settlement of the land. In honor of his visit the Turkish authorities paved the road from Jaffa to Jerusalem and made it suitable for the passage of carriages, thus essentially ushering in the era of wheeled transit in the Land of Israel.

The last section of this route is Jaffa Road in Jerusalem, which rapidly became the vital artery of the new city. The location of the designated plot for building Naḥalat Shivah on this road gave the settlers additional convenience and security. Another contributing factor was the proximity to the Russian Compound where, in the sixties, the Russian Orthodox Church had built a complex of buildings for the many pilgrims who came to the city every year. The third reason was that the plot was situated on the side of a hill, providing convenient water drainage.

The settlers, who wished to preserve the principle of equality among them, ran into a difficulty: the upper, northern part of the jointly owned plot bordered on Jaffa Road and therefore had many advantages; whereas the southern part was both low and near the Moslem cemetery and hence of lesser value. In order not to disadvantage any one of their group, the seven divided the plot into seven parallel strips running from north to south, so that each member received a lot equivalent to that of his fellow in size and in quality. The members of the group collected money in a joint fund and, after buying the land, began building the

1 *Naḥalat Shivah, a cooperative quarter, built by the resources of the residents themselves.*

2 *A window ornamented with a Star of David, in Naḥalat Shivah.*

3 *A well and hand-pump in Bet David, a quarter consisting of a single house.*

houses. When the first two houses were completed, lots were cast to determine who would move into them. In this manner they continued to collect funds and build until they had built houses for them all. They decided that when construction of the seven houses was completed there would be another lottery, which alone would determine the final ownership of the houses; and that, if necessary, the settlers would change houses in accordance with the outcome of this lottery.

As we have said, this was the first "cooperative quarter." It is interesting how these Jews, members of the Old *Yishuv*, arrived at the notion of a cooperative, which later was to find expression in Israel in many forms. The cooperative did not exist solely for the purpose of building the houses, but also for organizing life in the quarter. Whoever wished to come and live here was accepted as a member of the cooperative and had to abide by all its by-laws, which had to do with electing a governing body, collecting taxes for maintenance of public services, and so on.

Let us proceed through the heart of the neighborhood, along the alley of steps on Naḥalat Shivah Street, towards Jaffa Road. The settlers of Naḥalat Shivah were undecided on the question of how wide to make the streets in their quarter and finally decided to follow the prevalent practice, making them wide enough for a laden camel to pass. New residents were taken into the community over the years, as the founders sold off parts of their lots, and narrower alleys leading to the houses came into being. Doorways to the houses were designed by the founders according to the accepted practice of the times, in such a manner that they would not be directly facing one another, in keeping with the rules of modesty. The synagogue of the neighborhood, which bears a sign noting that it was the first synagogue outside the walls, is located on Naḥalat Shivah Street. Actually the synagogues in Mishkenot Sha'ananim and Maḥaneh Yisrael predated it, but they went to ruin over the years.

Most of the houses of this neighborhood have survived. At one time a plan was proposed to demolish the entire neighborhood and build a shopping center on the site, but it has since been shelved. Only the northeastern corner of the quarter was changed and replaced by a large office building, Bet Yo'el, named in memory of Joel Moses Solomon, as the memorial plaque on its doorway indicates.

1 *Me'ah She'arim, built as a modern neighborhood. Its founders passed by-laws forbidding rental to "anyone who is not recognized as an observant member of the faith of Israel."*

1

bet david – a neighborhood in one house

Let us exit from Naḥalat Shivah to Jaffa Road, turn towards Zion Square, and from there to Rav Agan Street, which takes us to Rav Kook Street. On the corner of Ticho Street, a small street leading to the house where the noted opthalmologist, Abraham Albert Ticho, lived and where, until recently, his widow, the artist Anna Ticho, also lived, there is a house over whose doorway is a sign reading, "Ha-Vaad ha-Kelali Knesset-Israel" (The General Committee, Congregation of Israel). This house is essentially an entire neighborhood: Bet David (David House), the fourth quarter established beyond the walls.

The impetus for establishing this quarter came in the wake of the great progress made by Naḥalat Shivah. Towards the end of the Jewish year 5632 (1872), a rich Jew named David Reise, who was physically weak, already approaching the end of his days, settled in Naḥalat Shivah. On *Rosh Ha-Shanah* in 1872, he was inspired by the sermon of R. Joseph Rivlin, one of the leaders of Naḥalat Shivah, who, expounding the verse **"Enlarge the place of thy tent"** (Isaiah 54:2), called for enlargement of the quarter. When he was called up to the Torah, David Reise donated the sum of money necessary to build David House, to provide housing for the city's poor.

If we enter the building, on the wall facing us we can see an inscription which tells about the building of the quarter. **"By the grace of God, blessed be He, in this house and its walls I give them a monument and a good name, better than sons and daughters; an everlasting name I shall give it, which shall never be wiped out."** There is a special significance to the beginning of this inscription; many of the magnanimous men who donated money for constructing the sacred quarters and buildings of Jerusalem were childless – David Reise, R. Moses Wittenberg, who built the quarter of Battei Wittenberg, and Moses Montefiore. In building neighborhoods they erected themselves a "monument and good name, better than sons and daughters."

David Reise built the lower storey of the building, and another storey was added later on. One of the wings on this floor houses the offices of the General Committee of Knesset-Israel, a body, also established in the 1860's, which was intended as an umbrella organization for the *Kolels* (groups devoting themselves to Torah study and living on outside support), which collected money in various countries of the Diaspora and distributed it in Jerusalem, generally to Jews who had immigrated from the same country. Over the years dozens of *Kolels* arose in Jerusalem, each one constituting a community unto itself. In the 60's of the previous century, when there were about 10,000 Jews living in Jerusalem, the number of *Kolels* reached 25. The General Committee, which had originally been intended to unify the *Kolels,* in time became a sort of *Kolel* itself. It dealt with raising

2 *The Montefiore coat of arms, above the entrance to the windmill in Mishkenot Sha'ananim. Montefiore was the first to promote and establish a Jewish quarter outside the walls of the Old City.*

funds and distributing them and also built a number of residential quarters, known as "Knesset Quarters." The body exists to this day, and its offices are housed here.

By the way, when Rav Kook, who was Rabbi of Jaffa, came to Jerusalem, he was given an apartment here in Bet David, where he lived until a special apartment was built for him; thus the street next to it is called Rav Kook Street.

me'ah she'arim – guardians of the walls

Let us proceed north along Rav Kook Street, cross Nevi'im (Prophets) Street to Ethiopia Street, and from there continue to Zalman Bahran Street, which forms the continuation of Ethiopia Street on the north side of Salant Street. On our right, one hundred and fifty meters ahead of us, we come to Me'ah She'arim. Avraham mi-Slonim Street forms the southern boundary of the quarter, and here its original form has been preserved. Once again, we must remember that this quarter was built in a remote and isolated spot. For security reasons the houses were built so that their outer facades formed a continuous wall, with several archways leading to a large inner court. Let us walk along the wall, peer into the basement floor rooms, which are characterized by the use of arches in their construction, and then enter the gate into the quarter. Over the years houses were built in the courtyard, causing it to lose much of its original character. In the center of the quarter there is a building which houses educational institutions for all ages, ranging from a Talmud Torah (religious school) for three- and four-year-old schoolchildren to a *yeshivah*.

Me'ah She'arim was founded in 1874, about a year after Bet David. This, too, was a "cooperative community," founded by a group of some 150 residents of the Old City who sought to build themselves comfortable housing at a reasonable price. The founders had no capital, since most of them lived on *ḥalukkah* funds (philanthropy from the Diaspora handed out to the poor of the Land of Israel). Perhaps this is why they bought a plot far from the main thoroughfare, Jaffa Road, where land was dear. The decision to build the quarter was taken on the Sabbath when the weekly Scriptural portion of *Toledot* is read, where it is said of the patriarch Isaac, **"And Isaac sowed in that land, and found in the same year a hundredfold** [Heb. *me'ah she'arim*]; **and the Lord blessed him"** (Gen. 26:12). Hence the name of the quarter.

The quarter was planned by Conrad Schick, a German architect and resident of Jerusalem, who lived not far from here, near Bet David. The land was registered in the name of a wealthy merchant, Ben-Zion Leon, a British subject, and the British consul assisted in signing the contracts for building the houses and digging the wells. First the houses along the northern boundary of the quarter, which is Me'ah She'arim Street of today, were built, next the two wings were built, and lastly the southern side was completed.

The quarter's by-laws provide an important source of information on the character of the quarter. Management of the quarter was entrusted to a committee of seven. Special concern was given to the cleanliness of the neighborhood, a related issue to the problem of water supply. When the quarter was being built three public wells were dug, and the committee urged the owners of the houses to dig private wells in their own houses. Rainwater from the roof, and even from the yards and streets, was channeled into the wells. Hence we can understand the strictness about sanitation in the markets, which is mentioned in the by-laws together with cleanliness and maintenance of the gutters, "so that the water will go into the wells clean."

Me'ah She'arim became the quarter of those holding the most extreme religious views in the territory outside the walls. This is even reflected in the by-laws of the community, which forbade renting an apartment to a Jew who was among those "who break the words of our Sages" and which stated, "It is forbidden to rent an apartment to anyone who is not recognized as an observant member of the faith of Israel," i.e., they did not hold every Jew to be suitable for, nor deserving of, membership in the community. In order to prevent the character of the community from changing, the founders stipulated that the by-laws be for all time and that they never be changed.

Today the *Neturei Karta* (Guardians of the City), an extremist ultra-orthodox group which does not recognize the State of Israel out of the belief that one must wait for Divine redemption through the Messiah and not anticipate His coming, is centered in and around Me'ah She'arim.

kerem avraham – the work of consul finn

Let us continue westward down Me'ah She'arim Street and follow its continuation, Malkhei Yisrael (Kings of Israel) Street, which brings us to Amos Street, turning off to the right. Next we turn left onto Ovadiah Street, and at number 22 we see a sorry sight for anyone who holds dear the history of modern Jerusalem. Before us is an old abandoned house which once served as a building for the Gadna (Israel's youth movement for training 13- to 18- year-olds in defense and national service) but now stands vacant and even untended.

To appreciate its place in the history of the city we must go back to 1853. In that year this site was purchased by the British consul, James Finn. Finn and his wife were sympathetic to the Jews of Jerusalem and supportive of them. In order to provide the Jews of the city creative employment, they purchased this place, which in Arabic was called *Kerem al-Halil* (The Vineyard of Abraham the Patriarch), built this house, dug many wells for water and planted crops – "industrial crops" as they were then called. The Crimean War at that time had drastically decreased the influx of charity (*Ḥalukkah* money) to Jerusalem and the condition of the Jews in the city had become exceedingly grave. Finn employed several hundred Jews here, building the house, digging wells, and planting vineyards.

Finn's motives were a subject of controversy. Some accused him of missionary intentions. Montefiore even lodged a complaint against him to Queen Victoria, who recalled him to England after 16 years of office in Jerusalem. Then several of Jerusalem's rabbis, remembering the great service he had done the city's Jews, became indignant and sent the Queen of England a letter requesting the consul's return.

The house at 22 Ovadiah Street is the earliest house built outside the walls of Jerusalem which still stands to this day. Although it is not what may be called a Jewish quarter, it was built by Jews and for the sake of Jews. Hence when plans to sell the area and build a housing project here, which would have demolished the house in the process, became known, a loud cry of protest arose and the plan was buried. This house surely ought to be a museum of the history of Jerusalem of the middle of the last century.

We shall enter the house by the main door, above which is an inscription reading, "Fear of God Brings Benefit to All." One can also enter through the back entrance, which bears the inscription, "Our Father that art in Heaven," perhaps in evidence of the missionary intentions of the person who erected the house. The eastern room on the ground floor has a stairway leading down to a cave. If we go down the steps we shall find ourselves in a columbarium – a cave with dozens of little niches, resembling dovecots, in its walls. It is not clear how the niches were used or what they were intended for, although there are many conjectures on the subject. This, however, belongs to the history of a period several hundred years earlier than the period being discussed.

'even-yisrael – a preserved quarter

We digressed from our story of the pioneering quarters of Jerusalem and now shall return to it. The next quarter, which was founded shortly after Me'ah She'arim, is 'Even-Yisrael (Stone of Israel). It is located between Jaffa Road and Agrippa Street, near the eastern end of the latter. This was also a cooperative community and was also built in the form of a courtyard surrounded by apartments. Here, however, unlike many other quarters, the courtyard did not become filled with later buildings. Thus, as we enter it from Agrippa Street, we find ourselves in a square which has become a public park. The houses of the quarter have changed their appearance, yet their original shape can still be discerned. One of the houses, now a bookstore with books about Israel, has been restored and reconstructed by the owners. We can walk through its rooms and see its arched ceilings, and can go down the stairs to the basement. If only all the houses in the quarter were renovated in this way.

The name of the quarter comes from Jacob's blessing to his son Joseph: **"From the shepherd, the Stone (*'Even*) of Israel."** Founded in 1875, it was settled by a group of Jerusalem's intellectuals who wanted to move away from Naḥalat Shivah, which had become commercialized. Among the people who lived here were Yeḥiel Michael Pines (author, pioneer of the Hebrew-speaking movement, and exponent of religious Zionism), and his sons-in-law, David Yellin (a key figure in the development of Hebrew as a spoken language) and Yosef Meyuḥas (a writer and educator, and leader of the Sephardic

1

1 The inner courtyard of 'Even Yisrael. In contrast to many other quarters, this quarter's courtyard did not become built up, and is now a public park.

Panorama overleaf: Mishkenot Sha'ananim, the first neighborhood outside the Old City, founded by Moses Montefiore in 1860. He built houses and a flour mill to provide a means of livelihood for the Jews who moved out of the Old City and settled here.

community). Pines' daughter, Ita Yellin, described life in the quarter in her memoirs. There was a large well for water, which exists to this day, in the center of the quarter. Most of the families lived in two-room apartments. In front of each apartment was a small yard, part of which was a kitchen and part a roofed corner serving as a dining room. One of the rooms had a doorway in the floor leading to the cellar, where the family stored coal, wine, sesame seed oil, and other things they themselves made in the course of the year.

mishkenot yisrael – "six hundred thousand"

Further to the west, down Agrippa Street, we come to Mishkenot Yisrael (Dwellings of Israel), founded in the same year as 'Even Yisrael. The successful ventures of the many new quarters attracted a large number of energetic and enterprising people living in the Jewish community of the Old City. Many of them began joining the builders and men of action and contributed to further building up Jerusalem. Thus numerous companies for purchasing land and building houses were founded. Businessmen became caught up in a wave of messianism and viewed building up Jerusalem as an important step on the way to the promised Redemption. All the letters, by-laws and founding papers of that era open and conclude with verses from the Prophets about the End of Days and the Redemption of Israel.

Enthusiastic speeches in this vein were delivered at the founding meeting of the cooperative of Mishkenot Yisrael. An answer was given to the question of how much Jerusalem had to be built and the exiles ingathered in order to hasten Redemption: "According to our teacher the Vilna Gaon, and his disciples, the founders of the *yishuv*, the number is six hundred thousand people within the gates of Jerusalem." We must point out that the population of the entire Jewish community of the Land of Israel only reached this figure more than seventy years later, on the eve of the establishment of the state.

This quarter, too, was built as a square courtyard; but over the years buildings were added inside it, and only its external appearance has been preserved along the streets surrounding it. The bakery of the quarter and the synagogue next to it, with its adjoining ritual bath, have been restored in the center of the quarter.

kiryah ne'emanah – a quarter later abandoned

The same year in which 'Even-Yisrael and Mishkenot Yisrael were built, work was begun on another quarter, near Damascus Gate, called Kiryah Ne'emanah (Faithful City). The promoters of the quarter were a group of Jerusalem hassidim, followers of Nisan Bak. The quarter was named after him and called the Nisan Bak Houses. Hassidic families settled on the site, but for various reasons only half the number of houses planned were actually built. Later, a quarter for Jews from Aleppo, Iraq, and Persia was built on the remaining land, as well as a quarter for Kurdistani Jews, called Eshel Avraham (Abraham's Tamarisk).

Kiryah Ne'emanah and its neighboring quarters were not destined to serve as a base for further development of Jewish

Jerusalem. These quarters suffered sorely in the 1929 riots.* Many people were killed or wounded, and the quarter plundered. Many buildings were destroyed and burned, including the three synagogues in the area. The Jews left and their houses were taken over by Arabs.

The buildings of Kiryah Ne'emanah are located at the eastern end of Nevi'im St., across from the large parking-lot northwest of Damascus Gate. Today the area looks like an Arab quarter in every respect, although here and there the signs of *mezuzot* can be discerned on the doorways, evidence of its Jewish past.

bet yaakov – a market and central bus station

The last of the pioneering quarters is Bet Yaakov, located west of Maḥaneh Yehuda, between Jaffa Road and Ha-Dekel St. It was founded in 1877 and called Bet Yaakov (House of Jacob), since its founders had planned to build 70 houses, one for each of the "seventy souls of the house of Jacob," but only fifteen members of the group built their houses on the site. At the time it was built, it was the quarter furthest from the Old City. One source describes it as follows: "The surroundings were a desolate desert, nothing but crags and boulders." The founders of the quarter took advantage of its location at the entrance to the city and built a marketplace there, where the residents of the neighboring villages sold their produce. The market square was also the last station of the carriage service from Jaffa Gate and the central station for carriages from Jerusalem to Jaffa. In modern times the market has moved a bit further east, to the Maḥaneh Yehuda quarter, while the Central Bus Station is now about a kilometer to the west. Today the houses of this quarter have been swallowed up in the buildings of Jaffa Road. The original roofs of the early buildings can still be discerned from their backyards and testify to their having been built before the era of steel and cement construction.

the new direction – agricultural settlement

The year Bet Yaakov was founded, 1877, also witnessed the beginning of a crisis in settling the new city of Jerusalem. Two years earlier two important visits were paid to the city. One was another visit by Sir Moses Montefiore, who was filled with admiration as he toured the new quarters. This encouraged the leaders of the quarters to work towards establishing a Jewish community of "six hundred thousand within the gates of Jerusalem." Fund raising began abroad and work was initiated to purchase extensive tracts of land west of the city. However the second visit, which also took place in 1875, reveals that efforts to check this development began at the same time. A commission of inquiry was sent by the Committee of Community Emissaries in England to ascertain the condition of the *yishuv,* the Jewish settlement in the Land of Israel. A conversation which took place between Dr. Asher, one of the commission's leaders, and Joseph Rivlin is indicative of its approach. When the commission visited Mishkenot Yisrael, Rivlin laid his plans to purchase large tracts of land in the area and build new quarters before its members. Dr. Asher responded in the following words: "Suppose you succeed in building thousands of houses and in settling the thousands of families which you say will immigrate to Zion in them – it is easy to foresee that this will be but another large camp of do-nothings and *schnorrers,* who will throw themselves on the mercy of Jews outside of the Land of

*In the 1929 riots the Arabs attacked the Jewish communities of the Land of Israel, killing 133 Jews and wounding over 300. Dozens of Jewish settlements were attacked and Jewish property lost. The Mandate authorities proved weak and ineffectual at subduing the riots.

Israel. And you, the leaders of the *Kolels,* will have added on another ample pasture for increasing the cries to our brethren, the Children of Israel, the merciful sons of merciful fathers, that they send you money to save another few thousand families from hunger."

The difficulty of providing sources of livelihood for the Jews in the Land of Israel, particularly in Jerusalem, became increasingly formidable. Thus the shift towards establishing agricultural settlements was not incidental in the least. Even the quarters that were built outside the walls of the Old City set aside plots for farming, and several of the champions of construction beyond the walls, such as Joel Moses Salomon and David Gutmann, were later among the founders of the first agricultural *moshavah* (colony), Petaḥ Tikva. It may be said that establishing the new quarters and building agricultural settlements were two processes which occurred both concurrently and successively. The actual construction of the quarters was accomplished earlier, since the first agricultural endeavors came to nought. The exodus beyond the walls was accompanied by expectations of developing productive sources of livelihood, although it quickly became apparent that establishing the quarters did not contribute to this end. When, in 1877, the influx of money for construction was curtailed and in addition the economic situation in the country as a whole had deteriorated because of successive years of drought, a crisis erupted in construction of new quarters. This crisis, and the founding of Petaḥ Tikva in 1878, were related events.

Nevertheless, agricultural settlement, which encountered tremendous difficulties, did not provide a solution for the crowds of Jerusalem. The straits of the population in the Old City led to a renewal in the construction of living quarters outside the walls in 1882, which was also the year in which the *Bilu* pioneers (a group of Russian Jews who formed the nucleus of the First Aliyah) and immigrants from Yemen came to Israel.

Landscapes Tell of their Past

the dothan valley

Irit Zaharoni

If you should happen to drive from 'Afula to Jenin on a February day, you will be captivated by the rolling fields of the Jezreel Valley, a checkerboard of green and brown squares as far as the horizon. The green foothills of Mt. Gilboa', speckled with the first wildflowers of the season, to your left, and facing you, the hills of Samaria, glistening white with the blossom of thousands of almond trees.

If you pass by here in summer, on the road which wends its way along the crest of the hills of Samaria, through the tribal land of Benjamin, approaching Jerusalem, you will see fields of grain ready for harvest, golden in the sun, and cotton fields in their fresh green. Mt. Gilboa' lies to your left, withered and dusty, even its olive groves appear wearied by the heat. Only the gardens of Jenin (the biblical Bet ha-Gan or "garden-house"), with their pomegranate and citrus trees and towering date palms, provide a fresh retreat from the oppressive surroundings, sweltering in the summer heat.

Before entering the town we pass a small brook, dry most of the year. If you have not seen the torrents of water which fill it in the rainy season, you will find it hard to believe that this is actually the Kishon, **"that ancient brook"** (Judges 5:21), which swept away Sisera and his army.

We pass through Jenin and enter the mountain pass between the Dothan Valley and the Jezreel Valley, the biblical "ascent of Gur." Samaria is characterized by a series of internal valleys, connected by mountain passes. Many of these passes form natural bottlenecks, restricting the passage of vehicles. The Jordanian-made anti-tank barricade testifies to this.

Two kilometers south of Jenin, west of the road, is a large tel, resting all its weight on the road. This is biblical Ibleam, identified with Kh.Bal'ama.

The Bible writes more about the Kingdom of Judah than about Israel. However, after the two royal houses became one, with the marriage of Joram the son of Jehoshaphat, King of Judah, to Athaliah, daughter of Ahab and Jezebel, their fate was bound together for a time.

During the reign of Joram, son of Ahab, Israel was still at war with the Arameans. Israel's failures in the war led Jehu, the commander of Joram's forces, to revolt against his king. When Joram was recuperating in Jezreel, the summer capital of the kings of Israel, from wounds he had received in the battle of Ramoth-Gilead, King Ahaziah set out from Jerusalem to visit his wounded uncle; and of course he followed the route along the mountain ridge from Jerusalem to Shechem, as far as Bet ha-Gan (Jenin), and from there through the valley to Jezreel. When the rebel leader Jehu defeated Joram, Ahaziah beat a fast retreat: **"he fled by the way of the garden-house. And Jehu followed after him, and said: 'Smite him also in the chariot'; [and they smote him] at the ascent of Gur, which is by Ibleam..."** (II Kings 9:27), to do away with all surviving contenders to the throne from the line of Ahab.

A man-made entrance to a cave can be seen right at the roadside, and on its far side, a spring. This is Ibleam's ancient

waterworks. As in Megiddo, an underground passage carried water from the spring, whose Arabic name is 'Ein Najar or 'Ein Sinjil, to the city.

Ibleam and Bet ha-Gan (Jenin) lay at either side of the mountain pass connecting the Dothan and Jezreel valleys, on the most convenient route to the heart of the Kingdom of Samaria and its capital. These two cities undoubtedly were under siege a number of times in their history. Hence it was important for the Israelite residents of Ibleam to assure themselves a supply of water in time of siege via an underground passage with one opening in the city and the other at the spring, concealed from enemy eyes.

Further along the road, as the hills to our right and left level out, a broad valley opens before us. This is the Valley of Dothan, a tranquil, pastoral scene. A green orchard, the gurgle of water through an irrigation channel, and the blurping of a distant pump recall bygone days, when sounds such as these once echoed through orchards the entire length of the Coastal Plain.

This idyllic scene is shattered by the sight of a tank, its gun awry, which suddenly appears before us. This is Qabatiya Junction, with its memorial to the soldiers from the artillery corps who fell in battle here, during the Six Day War.

1

1 *"And he [Joseph] said: 'I seek my brethren. Tell me, I pray thee, where they are feeding the flock.' And the man said: 'They are departed hence; for I heard them say: Let us go to Dothan.' And Joseph went after his brethren, and found them in Dothan" (Gen. 37:16-17). This tel, like many historical sites in Israel, has retained its ancient name.*

2 *The capture of Qabatiya Junction, on June 7, 1967, brought the artillery battle in the Dothan Valley to a close. A memorial to the fallen soldiers of the brigade which broke through here from the direction of Yamun and Ya'bad was built at the junction.*

Names engraved on a memorial, a tank, quiet. It is difficult to turn in our imagination to the storm of battle, the thunder of artillery, the smell of dust and fire, of killed and wounded, in summer ... June 1967.

battles in an idyllic landscape

Fire on the settlements in the Jezreel Valley began at dawn. Shells shrieked through the air and the fields of grain waiting to be harvested went up in flames. The entire southern end of the Jezreel Valley was ablaze; a heavy cloud of smoke lay over

2

everything. Towards the afternoon the flames died down, and with them the shelling. At nightfall the brigade passed through the smoldering fields of the valley and traversed the olive groves on the hills on the way to the Dothan Valley. In this tranquil setting, between ancient olive trees and golden fields of grain, only a burnt tank and names engraved in stone remain to recall the bloody battles which once raged here.

The road branches to the left, towards Tubas, perhaps the biblical Thebez, and on to the Jordan Valley. Continuing several kilometers southward, on our left we see a large tel, in profile resembling a truncated cone. This tel, like many historical sites in Israel, has preserved its ancient Hebrew name (*Tel Duthan* in Arabic), testimony to the great historical impact of our people on the land, for all time. This is the city of Dothan.

This city undoubtedly owed its importance to its key location, at the juncture of the north-south road along the ridge of the mountains and the east-west road connecting the Via Maris with the hills of Gilead. The biblical story of selling Joseph brings this fact to life.

Dothan is associated in our heritage with two stories. Better known is the story of Joseph being sold by his brothers; lesser known is the story of the siege which the Arameans laid to Dothan because the city was obstructing the progress of the Aramean army on its way to conquer Samaria, the capital of Israel.

elisha mocks the arameans

The Bible tells us that the Arameans laid siege to Dothan in order to capture the prophet Elisha, who had apprised the king of Israel of the ambushes which the Arameans were laying for him.

"Now the king of Aram warred against Israel; and he took counsel with his servants, saying: 'In such and such a place shall be my camp.' And the man of God sent unto the king of Israel, saying: 'Beware that thou pass not such a place; for thither the Arameans are coming down.' And the king of Israel sent to the place which the man of God told him and warned him of; and he guarded himself there, not once nor twice. And the heart of the king of Aram was sore troubled for this thing; and he called his servants, and said unto them: 'Will ye not tell me which of us is for the king of Israel?' And one of his servants said: 'Nay, my lord, O king; but Elisha, the prophet that is in Israel, telleth the king of Israel the words that thou speakest in thy bed-chamber.' And he said: 'Go and see where he is, that I may send and fetch him.' And it was told him, saying: 'Behold, he is in Dothan.' Therefore sent he thither horses, and chariots, and a great host; and they came by night, and compassed the city about" (II Kings 6:8-14).

Elisha mocked the Arameans, first striking them blind, then, when they were seeking the way to Dothan, telling them, **"This is not the way, neither is this the city; follow me, and I will bring you to the man whom ye seek.' And he led them to Samaria"** (*ibid.,* v. 19). To the Aramean's great astonishment, upon regaining their sight, they found themselves captive in the very capital of the Kingdom of Israel.

"behold, this dreamer cometh"

Approaching the tel, we can make out a well built of stone. Glancing inside it, we discover that the well is empty – it has no water in it.

This surely sounds familiar! Indeed these are the very words spoken of the well Joseph was thrown into: **"And they took him, and cast him into the pit – and the pit was empty, there was no water in it"** (Gen. 37:24).

Again we are overcome by that strange feeling which one experiences when standing in the spot where a great event once

1 *A view of the valley from Tel Dothan.*

2 *The ancient tunnel whose opening can be seen on the west side of the road from Qabatiya Junction to Jenin is part of the waterworks of the biblical city of Ibleam, located on the site of Tel Bal'ama, above the tunnel.*

took place. In the very setting where the tragic saga of the sale of Joseph took place, we almost feel as if the plot were unraveling itself again, before our very eyes. The landscape is the same as two thousand years ago; as we see the peasant plowing his field, the shepherds and their flocks, the caravan of camels crossing the valley, for a moment it seems that even the human landscape has not changed at all.

The story takes place in the Middle Bronze Age (2200-1600 b.c.e.). Jacob and his family were living in the Hebron Valley. In summer, when pasture in this valley became sparse, Joseph's brothers wandered, as was the way of shepherds, to seek better pastures to the north. In the mountains of Shechem, and even more so in Samaria, the hills remain green far longer. The brothers did not find sufficient pasture for their sheep around Shechem and therefore wandered further north, to the Dothan Valley, perhaps to let their sheep feed in the broad fields of post-harvest stubble. Joseph, after learning in Shechem where his brothers had gone, set out after them. **"And a certain man found him, and, behold, he was wandering in the field. And the man asked him, saying: 'What seekest thou?' And he said: 'I seek my brethren. Tell me, I pray thee, where they are feeding the flock.' And the man said: 'They are departed hence; for I heard**

them say: Let us go to Dothan.' And Joseph went after his brethren, and found them in Dothan" (Gen. 37:15-17).

Around Dothan one can see afar and easily notice anyone coming through the mountain-pass into the valley: **"And** [the brothers] **saw him** [Joseph] **afar off, and before he came near unto them, they conspired against him to slay him. And they said one to another: 'Behold, this dreamer cometh. Come now therefore, and let us slay him, and cast him into one of the pits, and we will say** [to our father]: **an evil beast hath devoured him; and we shall see what will become of his dreams!"** (*ibid.*, vv. 18-20).

Reuben, however, the eldest and head of the family in the father's absence, displayed greater responsibility than his brothers. He was well aware that he would not be able to allay his brothers' fury with rational and moral arguments in such a moment of anger and pent up hostility. Therefore **"Reuben heard it, and delivered him out of their hand; and said: 'Let us not take his life ... cast him into this pit that is in the wilderness** [pasture], **but lay no hand upon him"** (*Ibid.*, vv. 21-22). Thus Joseph was thrown into the well. The Bible passes over Joseph's reaction to this treatment in silence. Did he break down? Did he bewail the bitter end of belied dreams? As is its way, Scripture leaves it to our imagination to construe Joseph's turbulent emotions, telling us only that Reuben parted from his brothers, surely so that they would not discover his undisclosed plan to rescue Joseph from the pit and return him to his father.

" and...the child is not"

The road, however, lay on the caravan route from Gilead. The brothers had the equanimity to sit by the road **"to eat bread; and they lifted up their eyes and looked, and, behold, a caravan of Ishmaelites** [nomadic tribes who also engaged in trade] **came from Gilead, with their camels bearing spicery and balm and ladanum, going to carry it down to Egypt"** (Gen. 37:25). This was a caravan of traders who supplied precious spices grown in this land to the Egyptian nobility and royalty, the greatest consumers of spices in that era. **"And Judah said unto his brethren: 'What profit is it if we slay our brother and conceal his blood? Come, and let us sell him to the Ishmaelites, and let not our hand be upon him; for he is our brother, our flesh.' And his brethren hearkened unto him..."** (*ibid.*, vv. 26-27); in other words, they agreed to what he proposed. (Perhaps there is a deeper significance behind the biblical narrator putting these words into Judah's mouth. Perhaps they are meant to echo the relations of Judah and the kingdom of Judah to the house of Joseph and the kingdom of the Ten Tribes, relations which for many years were colored by emotions of love and hate alike.)

Joseph was sold to the Midianites and disappeared with the caravan into the distance, either along the Dothan Valley or along the mountain road. Now the story returns to Reuben, the responsible eldest son, who was wandering agitatedly through the fields, waiting for nightfall, to rescue his brother from the pit. One glance into the pit ... and **"the child is not."** Dumbfounded and despairing, he could no longer hide his intentions from his brothers: **"and he rent his clothes. And he returned unto his brethren, and said: 'The child is not; and as for me, whither shall I go?' "** (*ibid.*, v. 29-30).

The end of the story is well known, yet it is precisely this end that has sparked the imagination of greater and lesser creative men for generations: with shaking knees the brothers return to their father in Hebron, bearing in their hands Joseph's accursed tunic of many colors, drenched in the blood of a kid.

The drama comes to a climax: the brothers stood before their father, guilefully putting on pretences: **"This have we found. Know now whether it is thy son's coat or not!"** (*ibid.*, v. 32).

The father, dreading the worst, fell over the blood-soaked tunic and cried: **"It is my son's coat; an evil beast hath devoured him; Joseph is without doubt torn in pieces!"** (*ibid.*, v. 33).

What must have run through Joseph's mind as he rode, hands tied, on camelback, rhythmically plodding through the desert sands, on his way to the greatest land of servitude in the world at that time, we leave the reader to imagine.

1 *A memorial to the soldiers who fell in the heroic battle of Qabatiya Junction. When the Six-Day War broke out, the Northern Command was deployed along the Syrian and Jordanian fronts. In the morning of the first day the Jordanians fired heavily on the area of the Ramat David airfield. Around noon orders were issued to attack the Jordanian front in order to capture the Jordanian part of the Umm el-Fahm hills which was a threat to our airfield, to encircle Jenin, and to open an axis for a possible advance on Shechem. Our forces captured the villages along the ridge west of Jenin, penetrated the Dothan Valley, and took Jenin. Then 60 Jordanian tanks were reported advancing along a road intersecting the Shechem–Jenin road in the Dothan Valley. Our brigade left Jenin to return to the Dothan Valley. Meanwhile a battalion of Jordanian Patton tanks had reached Qabatiya Junction and was advancing towards Jenin. As night fell the forces massed opposite each other, our brigade in the Dothan Valley, the Jordanian tanks on the hills of Qabatiya, commanding the valley from the south. After three or four hours' battle the remaining enemy forces retreated towards Tubas (biblical Thebez), which was already in our hands.*

נפלו בקרבות במלחמת ששת הימים
5.6.67-11.6.67
בין כ"ו באייר תשכ"ז-ג' בסיון תשכ"ז
אביחר יעקב
ביטמן רמי
גינסברג עודד
גולן יהודה
לוי יובל
אבנון מנשה
אגר שאול
אסייג דוד
בן-עמי אלישע
ברזלי אורי
הר-נוי יורם
בורגין יוסף
גזז יהודה
וורונקר יהודה
אבוטבול מחלוף
אילוז מרדכי
אלאלוף אפרים
בורשטיין עוזי
זיתון ויקטור
ירמיהו אלברט
ינקולוביץ ישראל (סורין)
וקסלר ינקו
חקון יעקב
לוין יצחק
מימון משה
רופפה יצחק
שטראוס דן
כהן זכריה
שלימק דוד
שרפברג גיורא
לנצנר בנימין
לבין משה
לבני יעקב
לוי ארמונד
נוביק יקותיאל
סופר אריה
פלד עוזי
קרפל איתן
תירוש אבי
חיימוביץ יעקב
ינקוביץ מנחם
כהן שמעון
לבפלד יצחק
מדחפיאן רפאל
מירס ברונו
נחשוני גדעון
עטייה אברהם ברכה
פוכטונגר אמיר (אהרן מאיר)
חדד אברהם
סופר יעקב
רזי יעקב

1

landscapes tell of their past

The sites mentioned in the story of each landscape are marked in bold on the map, each story in its own color.

● the dothan valley

1 Bet ha-gan – Garden-house (Jenin)
2 Ibleam (Kh. Bal'ama)
3 Dothan (Tel Duthan)

● the battle of deborah and barak against sisera

1 Ḥaẓor (Tel Ḥaẓor)
2 Harosheth-goiim (Allonim-Shefar'am Forest)
3 Kedesh-naphtali (Kh. Kadis, Mount Poriyya)
4 Mount Tabor
5 Megiddo (Tel Megiddo)
6 Taanach (Tel Ta'anakh)
7 Elon-bezaanannim (Miẓpe Elot)
8 Meroz (Mazar, Mount Giborim)

○ gideon's war on the midianites

1 Chisloth-tabor (Iksal)
2 Ophrah (Tayyiba, Ramot Issachar?)
3 Ophrah (Kh. Tayyiba, Mount Amir?)
4 'En-ḥarod (Ḥarod Spring)
5 Gibeath-moreh (Giv'at ha-Moreh)
6 Mount Gilead (Mount Saul?)
7 Beth-shittah (Bet ha-Shitta)
8 Abel-meholah (Meḥola)
9 Adam (Damiya) and Succoth (Tel Deir 'Allah)

● saul's last stand

1 Shunem (Sulam)
2 "The fountain which is in Jezreel" (at the foot of Tel Jezreel)
3 'En-dor (Tel Ẓafẓafot)
4 Mount Gilboa' – Mount Saul
5 Beth-shan (Tel Bet She'an)
6 Jabesh-gilead (north of Ḥalawa)

● the great revolt revisited

1 Caesarea
2 Narbata (Ma'anit?)
3 Narbata (Kh. Ḥammam?)
4 Acre
5 Cabul (Kabul)
6 Sepphoris or Ẓippori
7 Mount 'Aẓmon
8 Siḥni (Sakhnin)
9 'Arav ('Arraba)
10 Galilean Be'er-Sheba (Kh. Seb'a)
11 Ẓalmin (Kh. Ẓalmon)
12 Yodefat; Jotapata (Kh. Jifat)
13 Japhia (Yafa; Yafia')
14 Mount Tabor
15 Ḥammat and Tiberias
16 Migdal; Tarichaeae
17 Arbel Fortress (Arbel caves)
18 Safed
19 'Akhbera ('Akbara boulder)
20 Jamnith (Ḥ. Yavnit)
21 Meron
22 Gischala or Gush Ḥalav (Jish)
23 Soganaea (Yahudiyya?)
24 Seleucia (Deborah?; Dabbura?)
25 Gamala (Gamla)

HAR ZIV
HAR ADDIR
HAR BEN ZIMRA
HAR MERON
HAR PEQI'IN
HARE MERON
HAR HILLEL
HAR SHEZOR
HAR HA'ARI
HAR KENA'AN
Ma'alot Tarshiha
Jish
Dalton
Meron
Zefat
Rosh Pinna
Hazor HaGelilit
Mahanayim
Ayyelet HaShahar
Gesher Benot Ya'aqov
Mishmar HaYardén
Sedé Eli'ezer
HAR ELI'EZER
Yesud HaMa'ala
Gadot
Qazrin
HAR YOSIFON
Dabiya
Qusbiya
Taiyiba
Yahudiya
GIV'AT BAZAQ
Jurnaya
Parod
Amirim
Shefer
Ammi'ad
Almagor
Amnun
Karmi'el
HAR KAMMON
HAR QADDARIM
HAR HAZON
Maghar
HAR GILON
HAR HILLAZON
Sakhnin
Arraba
HAR NETOFA
Deir Hanna
HAR SHEKHANYA
Yodefat
Kaukab
HAR AZMON
Kafr Manda
Biq'at Bet Netofa
Rummana
'Uzeir
HAR TIR'AN
Tur'an
Bet Rimmon
Huqoq
Livnim
Ginnosar
Migdal
HAR RAVID
Eilabun
Hamam
Arbel
QARNE HITTIM
K. Hittim
Lavi
Mizpa
Hodayot
YAM KINNERET
(SEA OF GALILEE)
Teverya
(Tiberias)
Hammat
Menora
Rabbi Me'ir's Tomb
'En Gev
Kefar Haruv
Ne'ot Golan
Afiq
Ramot
Geshur
Giv'at Yo'av
Eli 'Al
HaOn
Ma'agan
Tel Qazir
Kh. et Tawafiq
Mukheiba
Hammat Gader
Kursi
Samar
Ibdar
Malka
Sham
Balad el Basha
Balad esh Sheikh
Balad el Mansura
Hatim
Umm Qeis
Kinneret
Deganya
Alummot
Yavne'el
Bet Zera'
Massada
Afiqim
Ashdot Ya'aqov
Menahemya
HAR YAVNE'EL
HAR ADAMI
Sede Ilan
Sharona
Poriyya
Kafr Kama
Kefar Tavor
HAR TAVOR
Shadmot Devora
Kefar Kisch
Nazerat
(Nazareth)
Nazerat 'Illit
Zippori
Kafr Kanna
HAR YONA
'Ein Mahil
Reina
Bet Qeshet
Dabburiya
Iksal
Migdal HaEmeq
Ginnegar
Sarid
Tel 'Adashim
Mizra'
Daverat
Kafr Misr
Tamra
Gazit
En Dor
Kefar Gid'on
Balfouriyya
'Afula
Nein
Dahi
GIV'AT HAMORE
Sulam
Merhavya
Na'ura
Taiyiba
RAMOT YISSAKHAR
Ramat Zevi
Moledet
Gesher
Naharayim
Bakura
Newe Ur
Yardena
Bet Yosef
Kh. Shuna
Ma'ad
Kafr Asad
Samma
Hawar
Saum
Jijjin
Qam
Kafr Rahta
Makhraba
Zabda
Haufa
Qumeim
Zahar
Jumha
Kafr 'An
Kafr Yuba
Mandah
Waqqas
Deir es Sa'na
Irkhim
Jenin
Samt
Sammu'
Zimal
Marhaba
Deir Abu Sa'id
Juffein
Kufr el Ma
Abu el Qein
Khanzira
Tibna
Kafr Rakib
Beit Idis
Zubiya
Hawi
Kufr 'Awan
Kufr Abil
Judeita
Irjan
Halawa
Ausara
Ba'un
Fara
Ishtafeina
Mihna
Ajlun
Yizre'el
Kefar Yehezqel
Geva'
En Harod
Tel Yosef
SHELUHAT ZEVA'IM
Bet HaShitta
Gid'ona
Avital
Addirim
Gadish
Devora
Mele'a
Nir Yafe
Perazon
Baraq
Ram On
Magén Sha'ul
Sandala
Mugeibila
Jalama
'Arabuna
Zububa
Ti'innik
Harithiya
Yamun
'Arrana
Deir Ghazala
Faqqu'a
HARE GILBOA'
Hefzi Bah
Bet Alfa
Nir Dawid
Sedé Nahum
Hamadya
Bet She'an
Mesillot
Ma'ale Gilboa
Reshafim
Sheluhot
Newe Etan
Ma'oz Hayyim
En HaNaziv
Kefar Ruppin
Rehov
Sedé Eliyyahu
Sedé Terumot
Jalbun
Deir Abu Da'if
Beit Qad
Jenin
Birqin
Kafr Qud
Kafr Dan
Kaddim
Gannim
'Emeq Dotan
Umm et Tut
Nahal Malkishua
Jalqamus
Mughaiyir
Qabatiya
Mirka
Tilfit
Tirat Zevi
Zababida
Jarba
Raba
HAR BEZEQ
Misilya
Zawiya
Kufeir
Bardala
Biq'at Bezeq
Mehola
Shadmot Mehola
Anza
Sanur
Meithalun
Aqqaba
Nahal 'Irit
Tayasir
JEBEL
Ghor el Arba'in
Ghor Fara
HA GALIL
GOLAN
GILAD
YIZRE'EL
Dismantled Railway

events of the bible come alive in the jezreel valley

the view from giv‘at ha-moreh

Menachem Zaharoni

The lookout on top of Giv‘at ha-Moreh (biblical Gibeath-moreh) provides a panoramic view of the area which we shall scan, starting from the north and proceeding counterclockwise.

North-north east we see the crest of Mt. Tabor (588 m. above sea level) and across from us, to the northwest, the hills of Nazareth. The Valley of Chesulloth, a branch of the Jezreel Valley, lies between Mt. Tabor and Nazareth. On a clear winter day the distant mountains of Gilead can be discerned to the east and southeast, and the snow-covered peak of Mt. Hermon can be seen in the distance. Under the clear winter sky we can feel the psalmist's exhiliration as he sang, **"Tabor and Hermon rejoice in Thy name"** (Psalms 89:13).

At the western foothills of Mt. Tabor lies the large Moslem village of Daburiyya (pop. almost 4000) on the site of biblical Dobrath, a levitical city. During the Great Revolt against the Romans, Dobrath was one of the insurgent centers in the Jezreel Valley, and was noted by Eusebius as a large Jewish town at the beginning of the Byzantine Era.

The Moslem village of ‘Ein Mahil (pop. over 4000), perhaps the village of ‘En Tav from the time of the Talmud, lies further up the mountain, north of Daburiyya. The hill to the west of Daburiyya is Mt. Deborah (437 m.). Rising behind Mt. Deborah, we see Mt. Chesulloth (443 m.). Upper Nazareth covers its crest, and at its bottom is the Moslem village of Iksal (pop. over 3000), which stands on the site of biblical Chisloth-tabor.

West of Mt. Chesulloth we see a mountain which looks truncated. This is Mt. Kedumim (popularly called Jebel Qafza, meaning the "mountain of the jump," ht. 397 m.), which is associated with the life of Jesus. Nazareth lies on this hill. On Mt. Kedumim there is an important prehistoric cave, Kedumim Cave, in which Old Stone Age artifacts and skeletons of Neanderthal man have been discovered.

1

The Arab village of Yafa en-Naṣra (pop. over 6000, two-thirds Moslem, one-third Christian) lies on the western side of Nazareth, barely separated from the city. Yafa is identified with biblical Japhia, a city in the tribal territory of Zebulun: **"And it** [the border] **turned from Sarid** [Tel Sarid, next to *kibbutz* Sarid] **eastward toward the sunrising unto the border of Chisloth-tabor; and it went out to Dobrath, and went up to Japhia"** (Joshua 19:12). At the close of the Second Temple period Japhia was the largest village in the Galilee, whereas the neighboring village of Nazareth was hardly of any significance. Japhia was fortified by Josephus and conquered by Trajan after a difficult and bloody battle (during the Great Revolt, 66-70 c.e.) in which all its Jewish inhabitants were killed. An ancient Jewish synagogue, dating to the late Roman period, has been discovered in Japhia, in excavations near the village's churches.

The thriving immigrant town of Migdal ha-‘Emeq (founded in 1952 on the site of the abandoned village of Mujeidil, built on

Giv'at ha-Moreh provides a scenic view of the surrounding landscape of hill and dale. With a Bible in hand and giving free rein to our fancy to transcend the gap in time, we can discover the stage on which many events were played out in the history of our people.

1 *View from the summit of Giv'at ha-Moreh, near the tomb of Nabi Daḥi, towards Mt. Tabor and the Chesulloth Valley, a branch of the Jezreel Valley.*

2 *View from Giv'at ha-Moreh towards the Gilboa' and the Ḥarod Valley, the Jezreel Valley of the Bible.*

2

the ancient settlement of Migdal) lies to the west of Japhia. Below Migdal we see the Balfour Forest and at the foot of the forest, *kevutzat* Ginnegar.

Kibbutz Dovrat (founded 1946, by a Youth Aliyah group from Germany) lies in the valley, south of Iksal. South of Dovrat, at the base of Giv'at ha-Moreh, we see the Moslem village of Nein (talmudic Na'im), with a population of 600. It is holy to the Christians as the site of a miracle attributed to Jesus there.

Tel 'Adashim, a *moshav* founded in 1923, but which began as a settlement of *Ha-Shomer* in 1913, is located midway between Mt. Kedumim and 'Afula. West of Tel 'Adashim is *kibbutz* Mizra' (1923), and along the road is Kefar Gid'on (1923).

Looking to the west, we see the broad expanses of the Jezreel Valley, delimited on the west by the Carmel mountain range, and further to the south by the lower range of Ramat Menasheh (Plateau of Manasseh) and the somewhat higher Amir range (Umm el-Faḥm). The lake of Kefar Barukh stands out in the middle of the valley. On a clear day one can see west (and a trifle south) all the way to the tel of Megiddo. In the winter the area south of Megiddo, at the base of the Amir range and the adjoining hills of Samaria, becomes rather boggy due to the many springs in the vicinity and the rivulets which flow sluggishly into the Kishon.

The Gilboa', essentially a spur of the hills of Samaria, is the range which we see across from Giv'at ha-Moreh, to the south and south-east. The mountain which stands out at the northwestern end of the Gilboa' is Mt. Giborim (413 m.), and the village below it, Nurit. The spring of Ḥarod is hidden among the trees at the foothills of the Gilboa', below Nurit.

On the summit of Mt. Giborim is the abandoned village of Mazar, identified by some with the biblical site of Meroz: **" 'Curse ye Meroz', said the angel of the Lord, 'Curse ye bitterly the inhabitants thereof, because they came not to the help of the Lord, to the help of the Lord against the mighty** [*giborim*]**' "** (Song of Deborah, Judges 5:23).

Northwest of Mt. Giborim we see the hill of Jezreel on which the biblical city of Jezreel lay (where Ahab demanded possession of the vineyard of Naboth the Jezreelite, and, upon the latter's refusal, had him framed and stoned; I Kings, ch. 21), on the site of the abandoned village of Zar'in. Today *kibbutz* Jezreel stands on this site (1948). At the foot of the hill, slightly to the east, we see a cluster of trees which in the distance looks like a single tree. This is a small eucalyptus grove, planted by the spring in the Jezreel Valley: **"and the Israelites pitched by the fountain which is in Jezreel"** (I Samuel 29:1). North of the spring, at the foot of Giv'at ha-Moreh, is the Moslem village of Sulam (pop. 1000), identified with biblical Shunem. Between Sulam and 'Afula we see the *moshav* of Merḥavya (1922) and *kibbutz* Merḥavya (founded 1910 by *Ha-Shomer,* at which time it was called "The Cooperative." In 1924, after "The Cooperative" had been disbanded and another abortive attempt made to establish a *kibbutz,* the present *kibbutz* was established).

Ramot Issachar (the Heights of Issachar) extend eastward from Giv'at ha-Moreh. The Ḥarod Valley, the Jezreel Valley of the Bible, begins between Giv'at ha-Moreh and the Gilboa' mountains. From Giv'at ha-Moreh it is difficult to discern where the Ḥarod Valley becomes the plateau, Ramot Issachar, since the transition between the two is very gradual. On a clear day Tel Bet She'an can be seen at the northern end of the Bet She'an Valley, which is the continuation of the Ḥarod Valley.

events of the bible come alive in the jezreel valley

the battle of deborah*

Menachem Zaharoni

In the first quarter of the 12th century b.c.e. Egypt's hold on the Land of Israel weakened markedly and the Canaanite city-states grew stronger. The relatively new Israelite population, as yet weak and unorganized, dwelled almost entirely in small settlements and had not managed to build any fortified cities. Little wonder, therefore, that the Israelites were oppressed by the Canaanites. The name "Issachar," whose tribal territory (on the Heights of Issachar and in the Jezreel Valley) lay closest to the field of battle between Sisera and the Israelites, alludes to the tribe's subjugation. The name appears to be a compound of the words "*ish sakhar*" – a hireling. **"Issachar is a large-boned ass, couching down between the sheepfolds. For he saw a resting-place that it was good, and the land that it was pleasant; and he bowed his shoulder to bear, and became a servant under taskwork"** (Genesis 49:14-15). The image of sheepfolds perhaps refers specifically to the subjugation of the tribe of Issachar, which had settled in the Ḥarod Valley between the Gilboa' and Giv'at ha-Moreh, a land of pasture and sheepfolds.

The tribe of Issachar fought in the war against the Canaanites – **"As was Issachar, so was Barak; into the valley they rushed forth at his feet"** (Judges 5:15) – but, being the most subjugated tribe, it was not among the leaders in that war. Naphtali and Zebulun were the tribes which took the lead – **"Go and draw toward mount Tabor, and take with thee ten thousand men of the children of Naphtali and of the children of Zebulun"** (Judges 4:6) – spurred on by a woman from the more distant and free tribe of Ephraim: **"And she sat under the palm-tree of Deborah between Ramah and Beth-el in the hill-country of Ephraim; and the children of Israel came up to her for judgment"** (Judges 4:5).

The Israelite tribes suffered cruel and intolerable oppression at the hands of the Canaanites, worse than mere enslavement. **"In the days of Shamgar the son of Anath, in the days of Jael, the highways ceased, and the travellers walked through byways. The rulers ceased in Israel, they ceased"** (Judges 5:6). The Israelites ceased travelling on the main roads for fear of the Canaanites, and whoever had to travel somewhere went by a back way. Security was found only in the walled settlements; unfortified settlements were simply disbanded.

Ḥaẓor took the lead among the oppressors, **"for Hazor beforetime was the head of all those kingdoms"** (Joshua 11:10). Sisera, who commanded the army of Jabin king of Ḥaẓor, lived in Harosheth-goiim (Woods of the Nations), i.e. the southern Lower Galilee, a densely wooded region extending from the hills of Nazareth westward. The area is a woodland to this day, especially at its western end, the hills of Allonim – Tiv'on, which are forested with Tabor oaks.

awaiting the winter rains

The tribes of Israel were pitted against an alliance of Canaanite kings – **"Then fought the kings of Canaan"** (Song of Deborah, Judges 5:19) – capable of putting a huge "fleet" of 900 iron chariots in the field against a poorly equipped Israelite citizen army, fighting with primitive bows and arrows, and homemade swords and spears. Under normal conditions such an alliance would have had no difficulty beating the Israelites; therefore Deborah and Barak conducted the war by stratagem.

To begin with Barak called men from the tribes of Zebulun and Naphtali to his home town of Kedesh (the present-day Ḥurvat Qedesh, east of Poriyya, near Tiberias). Since Kedesh was accessible to the Canaanite chariots, making fighting conditions difficult for the Israelites if war were to erupt there, Barak and his men hastily moved to the steep Mt. Tabor, which the enemy chariots could not climb, and from where they could observe the enemy's manoeuvres.

From Giv'at ha-Moreh or from Mt. Giborim, the battlefield on which Sisera and Barak fought is spread out before us. The Canaanite chariots were most likely scattered among the chariot cities, such as Megiddo. **"And Sisera gathered together all his chariots, even nine hundred chariots of iron, and all the people**

*A narrative set on the landscape seen from Giv'at ha-Moreh and Mt. Giborim, "Mt. of the Mighty," so named after King Saul and his son Jonathan, who fell there.

Then fought the kings of Canaan, in Taanach by the waters of Megiddo... The brook Kishon swept them away, that ancient brook, the brook Kishon... *Judges 5:19-21.*

1

1 "The brook Kishon swept them away" *(Judges 5:21). The Kishon during a flood. The large area of the Kishon basin and the slow seepage of rainwater into the deep soil of the valley are what cause the river to overflow, inundating broad expanses of land and leaving behind muddy, boggy terrain.*

2 *The Kishon flowing innocuously. Throughout most of the year the Kishon is nothing more than a slowly trickling stream. In the summer many sections of the riverbed dry up entirely, and only a subterranean flow of water remains.*

that were with him, from Harosheth-goiim, unto the brook Kishon" (Judges 4:13). Both Megiddo and Taanach had Canaanite chariots stationed in them. (Megiddo was a chariot city in later times, as well, under Solomon and Ahab.)

The time was the beginning of winter, before the heavy rains which turn almost the entire valley into a bog, impassible by any vehicle. Indeed the region west of the Kishon, near Megiddo and Taanach, becomes boggy sooner than the land east of the Kishon. In order to prevent the rains from restricting the passage of their vehicles, the Canaanites transferred them to the right bank of the Kishon, to the area which in a normal winter does not become boggy until the middle of the season. The Canaanite chariots were thus deployed between the Zavdon brook (which passes by *moshav* Ram-On), beyond the tel of Taanach, as far as "the waters of Megiddo" along the Kishon River.

The Canaanites surely wanted to hasten their encounter with the Israelite fighters, trusting in the destructive force of their chariots; yet they could not dictate to Barak when he should descend from the mountain. Barak and Deborah, on the other hand, knew that the season of the year was working to their advantage and awaited the right moment for battle – the heavy winter rains. Heaven helped them, bringing the rains early that

2

year: **"They fought from heaven, the stars in their courses fought against Sisera. The brook Kishon swept them away, that ancient brook, the brook Kishon"** (Judges 5:20-21).

now is the day

Due to the nature of the soil, the surface run-off in the mainstream of the Kishon is very great. In a heavy rain the bed of the Kishon may be filled by the many rivulets which run down from the Gilboa' and the Plateau of Manasseh, at times becoming several hundred meters wide. Dashing their hopes, the region where the Canaanites had camped, east of the Kishon, also turned rapidly into a bog. The flooding put their chariots out of action, for the mud made the way impassible.

events of the bible come alive in the jezreel valley

1

1 *An oak on the edge of the Yavne'el Valley, above which is Mizpe Elot (Elot observation point), probably the site of Elon-bezaanannim, where Jael, the wife of Heber the Kenite, lived. Sisera, fleeing from the battlefield, reached her tent: "Howbeit Sisera fled away on his feet to the tent of Jael the wife of Heber the Kenite; for there was peace between Jabin the king of Hazor and the house of Heber the Kenite" (Judges 4:17).*

2 *'En Qedesh, at the foot of Tel Qedesh, on the eastern slope of Mount Poriyya. Kedesh was the birthplace of Barak the son of Abinoam.*

3 *"Then fought the kings of Canaan, in Taanach by the waters of Megiddo" (Judges 5:19). Tel Ta'anakh, visible between the blossoming almond trees, is situated southeast of the Megiddo junction.*

4 *"So Barak went down from mount Tabor, and ten thousand men after him" (Judges 4:14). Mt. Tabor and the Chesulloth Valley lying below.*

2

The charioteers and fighters in the chariots surely numbered no more than two thousand men, whereas the force at Barak's command numbered ten thousand, all of them peasants accustomed to conditions of hardship. This was the moment Barak had awaited. **"And Deborah said unto Barak: 'Up; for this is the day in which the Lord hath delivered Sisera into thy hand; is not the Lord gone out before thee?' "** (Judges 4:14. Mt. Giborim offers a better view of the battlefield of Barak and Sisera.)

And so the foes clashed in hand-to-hand combat, the Israelites full of daring and assurance of divine assistance, the Canaanites panicky and demoralized. Neither the Canaanites nor their chariots could retreat westward to Megiddo or Taanach, within whose walls they might find refuge, since the Kishon had inundated the area, barring their passage.

3

1 *The Nazareth iris, one of the most beautiful and rare of Israel's wildflowers, grows on the crest of the southern slope of Giv'at ha-Moreh, east of Nabi Daḥi. There is another large concentration of the Nazareth iris on Mt. Yonah, near the village of 'Ein Mahil.*

2 *"The captain of whose host was Sisera, who dwelt in Harosheth-goiim" (Judges 4:2). Harosheth-goiim is generally thought to refer to the forest of Tabor oaks on the hills of Allonim – Shefar'am.*

3 *Restoration of an ivory tablet from Megiddo with carvings of Canaanite chariots from the early 13th century, b.c.e. Similar chariots were probably used in the time of the Judges. The artist captured the heat of attack and the swift charging of the horses. The arrow case and quiver attached to the side of the chariot indicate that a second warrior, not portrayed on the tablet, rode in each chariot.*

1

It is easy to imagine the scene of battle, the war-cries of the men and the rampage of horses harnessed to chariots. The only somewhat passable avenue of retreat open to the Canaanites lay north towards Harosheth-goiim, since one could not even cross the Kishon on foot without being swept away in its torrents. The Canaanites hoped to find refuge by hiding in the forests and perhaps reach the Canaanite cities, or even Ḥaẓor, under cover of the woods. That was what Sisera had in mind when he fled in the direction of Ḥaẓor. The rest of the story is well known. He met his death en route at the hands of Jael, the wife of Ḥeber the Kenite, who dwelled in Elon-bezaanannim by Kedesh-naphtali, or present-day Yavne'el. (Yavne'el is 17 km. northeast as the crow flies from Giv'at ha-Moreh.) **"For there was peace between Jabin the king of Hazor and the house of Heber the Kenite"** (Judges 4: 17).

Sisera probably had decided simply to take a sip of water to quench his thirst and then quickly continue to Ḥaẓor, where he would be out of danger. That, however, is not how things turned out. With his first draught of milk he realized his strength was drained and his eyes began to shut. Exhaustion overcame him. He lay down in the tent, and Jael covered him with a blanket. Nevertheless, he remained wary. **"And he said unto her: 'Stand in the door of the tent, and it shall be, when any man doth come and inquire of thee, and say: Is there any man here? that thou shalt say: No' "** (Judges 4:20).

Jael had a brief but difficult struggle with her conscience. The slumbering man was not exactly an enemy of her clan; yet he had enslaved and oppressed her kinsmen. The slumbering man, having entered the cover of her tent, was her guest, and hence she was responsible for his welfare. At that moment he was no longer a commander, but a poor and pathetic man. But what would her victorious relations say when they learned that she had helped save the life of their foe? How could her father's house continue to live amidst them? And so she made up her mind and did her deed.

As the fateful battle was developing and being fought, the people of Meroz sat by on Mt. Giborim, idly looking on. From atop the mountain they could make out nearly every stage of the battle, especially its end, as we ourselves shall see if we climb it for a view of the valley's expanses. The inhabitants of Meroz understood precisely the strategic balance: an enormous Canaanite army of chariots, on the one hand, pitted against a peasant army, equipped with farm tools and some light arms, on the other. Hence they could have had no doubts regarding the outcome of the battle and must have realized their brethren were marching to their death. Dwelling in a high, inaccessible, easily defended retreat, they did not feel this was their war. Thus they did not answer Barak's call, nor did they deign to participate in the fray. It was not for naught that Deborah cursed them: **" 'Curse ye Meroz', said the angel of the Lord, 'Curse ye bitterly the inhabitants thereof, because they came not to the help of the Lord, to the help of the Lord against the mighty' "** (Song of Deborah, Judges 5:23).

2

The Israelite victory had not yet decisively quashed the Canaanite alliance, yet it rooted the tribes more firmly in the land, increased their strength, weakened their enemies, and hastened the day the entire north of the country would become pure Israelite territory (under David).

3

events of the bible come alive in the jezreel valley

gideon fights the midianites

Menachem Zaharoni

In the course of its history any settled land bordering on the desert suffers incursions of nomadic desert tribes, especially during years of drought. These incursions generally occur in periods when the central rule over the land is weak, as was the case in this country during the reign of the Judges. The Canaanite city-states became much weaker after the war against Deborah (end of the 12th century b.c.e.), while the Israelite tribes were still only loosely organized. Thus there was no one to stop the nomadic incursions of Amalekites, Kedemites, and Midianites from the desert lands of the Transjordan into the sown land. Indeed, these nomads crossed the Jordan: **"And so it was, when Israel had sown, that the Midianites came up, and the Amalekites, and the children of the east** [Kedemites]; **they came up against them; and they encamped against them, and destroyed the produce of the earth, till thou come unto Gaza, and left no sustenance in Israel, neither sheep, nor ox, nor ass. For they came up with their cattle and their tents, and they came in as locusts for multitude; both they and their camels were without number; and they came into the land to destroy it. And Israel was brought very low because of Midian"** (Judges 6:3-6).

Sometimes the book of Judges does not bother to mention the names of all the invading tribes, noting only the most important, the Midianites. However, as is mentioned several times in the stories about Gideon, the Amalekites and Kedemites also took part in the invasion. The Midianites were headed by "kings," indicating a level of military and political organization which gave them added strength. Domestication of the camel, which occurred on a large scale during that period, made the nomads equally mobile in the desert as in a settled land. Hence they spread out over large expanses of the western part of the Land of Israel. The nomads fought on camelback with bows and arrows, lances and spears, making warfare against them very difficult for the Israelites, who, lacking camels, had but dismal prospects of victory.

The greatest concentration of nomads in the Jezreel Valley was in the Valley of Chesulloth, where Mt. Tabor protected their rear. This brought them into contact with Gideon's brothers, whom they killed. The Ḥarod Valley was too narrow for their numerous tents, and the gradual incline to Ramot Issachar (Heights of Issachar), a densely Israelite area, did not provide them security. The same could not be said of the Chesulloth Valley, which was bordered on the north by the steep hills of Nazareth, on the east by the Tabor, and on the west by Giv'at ha-Moreh. Yet this location also had a weak point, the transition from the valley to the hills of 'En Dor (biblical En-dor), which had to be closely guarded and defended. **"And the hand of Midian prevailed against Israel; and because of Midian the children of Israel made them the dens which are in the mountains, and the caves, and the strongholds"** (Judges 6:2).

2

who shall stand in the breach?

The Israelite tribes did not yet have any fixed organization, but in time of trouble a number of tribes would come into action, led by a savior who emerged and fought off their enemies. This time their savior was Gideon son of Joash, of the tribe of Manasseh, from Ophrah.* Issachar, the closest tribe, suffered from a long history of surrender and enslavement and could not take the initiative in leading a band of tribes in their fight for survival.

Since the nomads had harvested and trampled the fields, as was their custom on land not belonging to them, the Israelites had no option but to salvage what they could of the crop and

*Ophrah in Arabic means devil. The Arabs therefore replaced the name Ophrah by the name Tayyiba ("good"), thus changing the name of Ophrah at Baal-Hazor and Ophrah in the "Triangle." Some scholars believe the Ophrah of Gideon to be Tayyiba in Ramot Issachar, others locate it at the foot of Mt. Amir. The tribe of Manasseh was known to have had enclaves in the territory of Issachar.

And when Gideon was come, behold, there was a man telling a dream unto his fellow, and saying: "Behold, I dreamed a dream, and, lo, a cake of barley bread tumbled into the camp of Midian, and came unto the tent, and smote it that it fell,..." And his fellow answered and said: "This is nothing else save the sword of Gideon the son of Joash, a man of Israel: into his hand God hath delivered Midian, and all the host." *Judges 7:13-14.*

1

1 *"And so it was, when Israel had sown, that the Midianites came up, and the Amalekites, and the children of the east; they came up against them ... and destroyed the produce of the earth" (Judges 6:3-4). Fields of grain in the Jezreel Valley, with Mt. Tabor in the background.*

2 *"And the camp of Midian was beneath him in the valley" (Judges 7:8). The Midians encamped here, in the Valley of Chesulloth, surrounded by mountains on three sides.*

3 *View from above the cave of the Ḥarod Spring, towards Giv'at ha-Moreh and the Ḥarod Valley, the Jezreel Valley of the Bible.*

3

thresh it in secret. **"And the angel of the Lord came, and sat under the terebinth which was in Ophrah, that belonged unto Joash the Abiezrite; and his son Gideon was beating out wheat in the winepress, to hide it from the Midianites"** (Judges 6:11). There are many winepresses hewn into the rocks of Ramot Issachar and along the slopes of Giv'at ha-Moreh, such as those found in Kumey Hill, above the eastern quarters of *kibbutz* Tel Yosef. While thus threshing clandestinely, sensing the humiliation of it and the gravity of the situation, Gideon planned his military operation: **"But the spirit of the Lord clothed Gideon"** (Judges 6:34), not without emotional qualms, which the Bible expresses through the conversation, full of doubt, which takes place between Gideon and the angel.

Rumors of the resistance movement being stirred up by Gideon undoubtedly reached the nomads. One night, scouting with his assistant on the edge of the Midianite camp, Gideon overheard two Midianites interpreting a dream one of them had: **"And his fellow answered and said: 'This is nothing else save the sword of Gideon the son of Joash, a man of Israel: into his hand God hath delivered Midian, and all the host' "** (Judges 7:14). Therefore all Gideon's military operations had to be undertaken with the utmost secrecy and caution, particularly under cover of night.

The first to answer Gideon's call were from the clan of Abiezrites, to which he himself belonged: **"and he blew a horn; and Abiezer was gathered together after him"** (Judges 6:34). The main Midianite post was encamped at 'En Dor, a place which has remained a permanent testimony to the people's victory over their foe. The Midianites **"Who were destroyed at En-dor; they became as dung for the earth"** (Psalms 83:11). 'En Dor cannot be seen from Giv'at ha-Moreh even though it is only four kilometers away by air. Northeast of the peak, at the foot of Giv'at ha-Moreh, it is hidden from sight by the stony spurs of the hill which we see in the same direction. The historical site of 'En Dor has been identified with Tel Ẓafẓafot, near the abandoned village of Indur, and can be reached by driving along the side road which branches off the 'Afula-Tiberias road towards the Arab village of Tamra.

Gideon did not attack the Midianites from the western edge of Ramot Issachar. This, as we said, was the weak side of the nomad camp and hence was closely guarded. Gideon called his men to the Gilboa', apparently to the vicinity of Nurit: **"And the Lord said unto Gideon: 'The people are yet too many; bring them down unto the water' "** (Judges 7:4), for 'En Ḥarod (Ḥarod Spring) lies beneath the hill of Nurit.

The forces gathered at night, as we may deduce from the verse, **"Then Jerubbaal, who is Gideon, and all the people that were with him, rose up early, and pitched beside En-harod"** (Judges 7:1). Gideon and his men did not reach the spring until dawn. In the dark of night the Midianite watchmen could not observe the suspicious movement, especially since Giv'at ha-Moreh obstructed the view between the gathering forces and the Midianite camp in the Chesulloth Valley: **"And** [Gideon and his men] **pitched beside En-harod; and the camp of Midian was on the north side of them, by Gibeath-moreh, in the valley"** (Judges 7:1).

planning the battle and selecting warriors

The attack opened from the side the Midianites least expected – from the south. It was planned to the last detail. The vast number of warriors, some thirty-two thousand, who rallied initially to Gideon's call, was too many for a surprise night-time attack. Twenty-two thousand left straight off, as soon as Gideon set forth the boldness and danger of his plan. They chose to climb to a high spot from which they could look on at the battle without risking their lives. Of course the Gilead referred to in the verse, **"Whosoever is fearful and trembling, let him return and depart early from mount Gilead"** (Judges 7:3), is not the well-known mountains of Gilead. Judging by the geography, it seems the reference was to Mt. Saul (a hypothesis supported by the Arab name of the Ḥarod Spring – 'Ein Jalud), which provides the best view from the Gilboa' of events in the Chesulloth Valley.

A night-time operation such as Gideon's requires rigorous coordination in planning and execution, as well as restraint and good judgment. The plan of the operation, as we shall see later, was based primarily on the Midianites' psychological reaction and demoralization, and not on the mightiness of the attacking force. This being so, even the slightest error or mistiming would spell defeat for the attackers.

Reducing the number of men, no less than selecting the proper ones, was therefore of the utmost importance. The plan of attack testified to Gideon's wisdom and understanding of human behavior, no less than the method he used for selecting his three hundred warriors – stable, well-balanced men of restraint.

1

Parched and weary, Gideon's warriors descended to the spring below Nurit. Most of them immediately dropped to their knees, letting their arms fall to the ground, and became absorbed in quenching their great thirst. But not the cautious and conscientious: holding their weapons in one hand, they scooped up a few drops of water in the other, put it to their mouth, and lapped it like a dog: **"So he brought down the people unto the water; and the Lord said unto Gideon: 'Every one that lappeth of the water with his tongue as a dog lappeth, him shalt thou set by himself; likewise every one that boweth down upon his knees to drink.' And the number of them that lapped, putting their hand to their mouth, was three hundred men; but all the rest of the people bowed down upon their knees to drink water"** (Judges 7:5-6). For a night-time battle the three hundred who lapped the water were enough. It was with these men that he planned his attack. **"So they took the victuals of the people in their hand, and their horns; and he sent all the men of Israel every man unto his tent, but retained the three hundred men; and the camp of Midian was beneath him in the valley"** (Judges 7:8).

1 *"And they pitched beside En-ḥarod" (Judges 7:1). The cave at the foot of Mt. Gilboa', where the Ḥarod Spring emanates.*

2 *"But all the rest of the people bowed down upon their knees to drink water" (Judges 7:6). Those who fell hastily upon the water, letting go of their weapons, were disqualified.*

3 *"And the number of them that lapped, putting their hand to their mouth, was three hundred men" (Judges 7:6). The patient and self-controlled few were mindful of security and preparedness and hence were chosen to participate in the battle.*

That same night Gideon and his men shifted to the northeastern slope of Giv'at ha-Moreh, perhaps to where Upper 'Afula lies today. Everything was planned to the last detail, including updating reports on conditions on the night of attack and on enemy deployment at that very hour. In the dark of night Gideon and his assistant, Purah, stole up to the Midianite camp to ascertain the morale of the enemy. **"Now the Midianites and the Amalekites and all the children of the east lay along in the valley like locusts for multitude; and their camels were without number, as the sand which is upon the sea-shore for multitude"** (Judges 7:12). They listened to the conversations in the camp: **"And... behold, there was a man telling a dream unto his fellow, and saying: 'Behold, I dreamed a dream, and, lo, a cake of barley bread tumbled into the camp of Midian, and came unto the tent, and smote it that it fell, and turned it upside down, that the tent lay flat.' And his fellow answered and said: 'This is nothing else save the sword of Gideon the son of Joash, a man of Israel: into his hand God hath delivered Midian, and all the host' "** (Judges 7:13-14). The Midianites knew that danger lurked somewhere in the hill country, where Gideon and his fighters were hiding, and they anticipated it with dread; but Gideon, after his night patrol, took the dreams to be evidence of the Midianite fears and low morale and realized that bold scare tactics would completely destroy them. Thus, the decisive hour had come.

victory and pursuit

"And he [Gideon] **divided the three hundred men into three companies, and he put into the hands of all of them horns, and empty pitchers, with torches within the pitchers** [so that the light of the flames would not give away the fighters before it was time]. **And he said unto them: 'Look on me, and do likewise; and, behold, when I come to the outermost part of the camp, it shall be that, as I do, so shall ye do. When I blow the horn, I and all that are with me, then blow ye the horns also on every side of all the camp, and say** [the watchword]: **For the Lord and for Gideon!' "** (Judges 7:16-18). And so it was.

Gideon set the zero hour for the beginning of the middle watch, when the Midianite guards, awakened by their comrades from the first watch, were still half asleep and guarding laxly.

At Gideon's signal all his men broke their pitchers and blew their horns. The torch flames, which had been hidden in the pitchers, suddenly burst forth, spreading terror in the midst of the darkness. Taken utterly by surprise, the Midianites were thrown into great confusion. In the dark it was impossible to tell

2

3

1

1 *An Arab woman in the Hebron Hills, threshing wheat by beating it with a stick. Photo from Gustaf Dalman's turn of the century book. "And his son Gideon was beating out wheat in the winepress, to hide it from the Midianites" (Judges 6:11). Unable to thresh his wheat in the open, using a draft animal or threshing sledge on the threshing floor, Gideon beat it with a stick in the winepress, a narrow place hewn in the rock and thus more secluded.*

2 *The Jordan River is Israel's major watercourse. From the Sea of Galilee to the Dead Sea the Jordan Rift Valley has two terraces; the lower of which, where the river flows, is referred to in the Bible as the "thickets of the Jordan" (Zechariah 11:3), and is an area of dense vegetation and rich animal life. In ancient times the Jordan River was impassable, save at certain shallow points, the fords of the Jordan. During a war the army in pursuit would try to block the enemy's retreat by capturing the river fords, as did the tribe of Ephraim, blocking the way of the Midianites fleeing from Gideon (Judges 7:24).*

friend from foe, Israelite from Midianite. The seeds of fear germinating among the Midianites had grown into tremendous dread and confusion. Thus it was that **"the Lord set every man's sword against his fellow, even throughout all the host; and the host fled as far as Beth-shittah** [near the present-day *kibbutz* Bet ha-Shitta] **toward Zererah, as far as the border of Abel-meholah** [near Wadi Maliaḥ], **by Tabbath"** (Judges 7:22). The path of flight appears to have been the shortest route clear of Gideon's warriors, who chased the Midianites in hot pursuit, southeast via 'En Dor and Tamra, as far as the ascent to Ramot Naphtali, towards *kibbutz* Bet ha-Shitta. It is interesting that the Ẓaḥar Bedouin tribe took exactly the same route in fleeing from a British attack during the Mandate period, when a drought had brought them across the Jordan River, as far as the Chesulloth Valley. From the vicinity of Bet ha-Shitta the intruders fled across the Jordan River fords, to Beth-barah, near what is likely the city of Adam (Tel Damiya, near the Adam Bridge).

Three hundred fighters were enough for a partisan night-time operation, but not for pursuit of the enemy in flight. Therefore Gideon called up the Israelite tribes in the vicinity of the battle

2

and along the route of flight – men from the tribes of Naphtali, Asher, and Manasseh – to chase after the foe and put an end, once and for all, to the incursions from the desert. The tribe of Ephraim, whose northeastern settlements were close to the Jordan River crossings at the city of Adam, was called upon to seize the river ford, thus blocking the path of retreat. The Ephraimites succeeded in their mission and captured two of the Midianite officers, while Gideon himself continued the pursuit up the Jabbok River, without slackening the chase.

Hungry, tired, and weary, he and his fighters reached the vicinity of Succoth; but the inhabitants of Succoth* refused to risk giving them assistance: **"And the princes of Succoth said: 'Are the hands of Zebah and Zalmunna** [the kings of Midian] **now in thy power, that we should give bread unto thine army?' "** (Judges 8:6). As long as the Midianite rulers were alive in the desert, they believed the Midianites to have the upper hand. Gideon also understood this and therefore, making a superhuman effort, continued pursuing the Midianites way south, as far as Karkor in Wadi Sirḥan. Again Gideon used the element of surprise, a partisan weapon par excellence, in a place so remote the Midianites did not believe Gideon would reach it: **"And** [Gideon] **smote the host; for the host was secure"** (Judges 8:11). Killing the kings of Midian was not simply an act of revenge for their having killed Gideon's brothers; it was also an act which shattered the unity of the Midianites and crushed their organization.

On his return Gideon punished the people who had refused him aid at the crucial moment: **"And he caught a young man of the men of Succoth, and inquired of him; and he wrote down for him the princes of Succoth, and the elders thereof, seventy and seven men"** (Judges 8:14). Some people believe that "young man" simply meant a clerk. Whether "young man" should be taken literally or taken to mean clerk, this verse indicates that our forefathers knew how to write in the 12th century b.c.e., and if the person writing was a young lad, we are pleased to know that in that era even a young Israelite knew how to write. From the list given him, Gideon found the people responsible for refusing him aid and killed them.

epilogue

More than three thousand years later a man sat in a small tent at 'En Ḥarod, reading the story of Gideon's battle over and over. Sunk in the past, as if the intervening thousands of years had never been, his eyes gleamed with excitement. Captain Charles Orde Wingate did not view the Bible as a story of the past, but as part of the present which he was witnessing around him – the revival of the Jewish people on its own land. Gideon's fighters were one to him with the pioneers in the Jezreel Valley and the Galilee, who enlisted in "night squadrons" in order to protect their settlements and fight against Arab gangs (1936-1938). Gideon's understanding, his methods, and approach provided a guiding principle for this audacious and innovative British officer. Daring and originality led Wingate and his "night squadrons" to choose modes of operation which were surprisingly similar to those of Gideon, laying a very important foundation for the building of a Jewish military force in the Land of Israel.

*A good view of the tel on which Succoth was built in the Transjordan (Tel Deir Allah), can be seen from the hill on which the settlement of Argaman now stands. The tel is located near where the Jabbok comes out of the Mountains of Gilead.

events of the bible come alive in the jezreel valley

saul's last stand*

Menachem Zaharoni

Saul was crowned king over Israel because of the need to unify all the Israelite tribes in the war against their great foe, the Philistines. This man, who was taken from behind the plow and who never sought to be king, spent his entire life fighting external and internal enemies until his mental state suffered. Depressed, sick, and lacking self-confidence, he reached the scene of his last battle (c. 1006 b.c.e.).

why mount gilboa'?

At first glance it seems strange that the scene of this fray should have been between Mt. Gilboa' and Giv'at ha-Moreh, far both from the cities of Philistia and Saul's main base in the tribal territory of Benjamin. The explanation lies in a close analysis of the struggle between Saul and the Philistines. Saul had foiled the Philistine attempt to storm the Israelite highlands from the direction of the hills of Benjamin and along the roads leading to these hills and the hill country of Judah. Now the Philistines hoped to win a decisive victory over the Israelites by attacking the central part of the Israelite settlement from the rear, thus severing the highland region, solidly settled by the Israelites. Their plan was to strike a wedge between the northern and central tribes.

The Philistines' preparation for this decisive battle obviously had to take place in close proximity to their settlements. They decided to mass at Aphek (present-day Rosh ha-'Ayin, near the source of the Yarqon R.), an important crossing along the Via Maris, which they controlled. From here they must have proceeded by way of the 'Iron Valley and Megiddo to the vicinity of Shunem at the foot of Giv'at ha-Moreh. It was the Philistines who determined where the battle would be fought.

Saul and his army reached the region of Jezreel, a city originally founded by the Israelites, in the wake of the Philistine advance but not following the same route. Coming through the highlands, they assembled on the northwest side of Mt. Gilboa', which is essentially nothing more than a spur of the hills of Samaria. As was Saul's practice, they arrived in the night and, not to give themselves away to the enemy, clearly could not remain on the spur of Nurit. Therefore they descended to the

2

area around **"the fountain which is in Jezreel"** (I Samuel 29:1), today identified on the landscape by a cluster of trees which from a distance looks like a single tree (in actual fact a grove of eucalyptus trees, planted beside a spring most of whose water today is drained in pipes). The spring provided Saul's citizen army with water to quench their thirst, and the small valley in which it is located concealed him from the eyes of the Philistines (for one can not see what is happening in this valley from Shunem).

grasping at a straw

Saul's advantage over the Philistines always lay in the bold spirit of his army, their self-confidence, and the faith that they were fighting for survival and hence would win. At the sight of the highly organized Philistine army, well-trained and equipped with the best arms of those days, the last vestige of the sick and weary king's self-assurance was undermined. It was then that he did something contradictory to his entire way of life. Until then he had viewed necromancy as a delusion and a pagan practice, opposed to the worship of God: "And Saul had put away those that divined by a ghost or a familiar spirit out of the land" (I Samuel 28:3). Only exceptional weakness compelled him, grasping at a straw, to turn to a necromancer, surely out of a faint hope that he might receive some word of encouragement. Passing the edge of the Philistine camp on his way to 'En Dor, albeit in disguise and under cover of night, was an act of despair. We may assume that the king went roughly along the

*A story set against the view from Givat ha-Moreh.

Ye mountains of Gilboa, let there be no dew nor rain upon you, neither fields of choice fruits; for there the shield of the mighty was vilely cast away, the shield of Saul, not anointed with oil. *Second Samuel 1:21.*
How are the mighty fallen in the midst of the battle! *ibid., v. 25.*

1

1 *"And the men of Israel fled from before the Philistines, and fell down slain in mount Gilboa" (I Samuel 31:1). View from Mt. Giborim, overlooking the heights on which the last battle was fought. The small cluster of trees in the center of the photo is "the fountain which is in Jezreel" (ibid., 29:1).*

2 *Biblical En-dor, the home of the medium, has been identified with Tel Ẓafẓafot, near the abandoned Arab village of Indur (whose name retains the ancient name).*

3 *"Ye mountains of Gilboa, let there be no dew nor rain upon you." Despite this curse the mountain blossoms with an abundance of flowers, especially the Gilboa' iris.*

route of Kefar Yeḥezkel and Na'ura and from there to Tel Ẓafẓafot, which is identified with ancient En-dor. (Tel Ẓafẓafot cannot be seen from the top of Giv'at ha-Moreh, even though it is only four kilometers away as the crow flies, because it is hidden from view by the northeastern spur of Giv'at ha-Moreh at whose base it lies).

The medium immediately recognized the disguised king and decided to avenge herself on the king who had persecuted her all her life. Now her adversary was in her hands, dependent upon her kindness. She played her part well. Ostensibly surprised and pitying Saul, she actually made a mockery of him when he swore by the Lord, **"As the Lord liveth, there shall no punishment happen to thee for this thing"** (I Samuel 28:10). For she then proceeded to shake him to the core with the words of Samuel, who was ostensibly speaking from her throat. To strengthen Saul's belief that Samuel was indeed speaking through her, she described to the king, who saw nothing, the figure which she supposedly beheld: **"An old man cometh up; and he is covered with a robe"** (*ibid.,* v. 14) – a schematic depiction which any Israelite could have given even without having seen the prophet. However, having lost his soundness of mind, the frightened gullible king believed her and identified the figure described as the prophet Samuel, his adversary at the end of his days.

We have a full psychological account of Saul's actions. He bowed down before the imaginary figure, thus expressing his heart-break and submission before the spirit of the wrathful prophet, and whispered in a broken voice: **"I am sore distressed; for the Philistines make war against me, and God is departed from me"** (*ibid.,* v. 15). The figure of the prophet answered him mercilessly, through the medium, with all the spite of a vengeful woman: **"Moreover the Lord will deliver Israel

3

also with thee into the hand of the Philistines; and tomorrow shalt thou and thy sons be with me; the Lord will deliver the host of Israel also into the hand of the Philistines"** (*ibid.,* v. 19).

The prophet's words hit Saul like a sledge-hammer, and his reaction was quite predictable. **"Then Saul fell straightway his full length upon the earth, and was sore afraid, because of the words of Samuel; and there was no strength in him; for he had eaten no bread all the day, nor all the night"** (*ibid.,* v. 20). The medium, however, had not yet had enough revenge and continued her sport. The erstwhile persecuted woman's "pity" on the king, who revealed himself in all his weakness in his great hour of despair, is most cruel and intensifies his sense of downfall: **"Now therefore, I pray thee, hearken thou also unto the voice of thy handmaid, and let me set a morsel of bread before thee; and eat, that thou mayest have strength, when thou goest on thy way"** (*ibid.,* v. 22), perhaps adding to herself, "on thy way to doom."

The king refused. Helpless, he lay on the floor. Finally he gave in to her entreaties, perhaps because he had lost what little remained of his will-power.

"Then they rose up, and went away that night" (*ibid.*, v.25). Thus Saul returned to his camp with the certain knowledge that he was going to his defeat and ruin. In such a frame of mind there could be no hope of victory.

"for there the shield of the mighty was vilely cast away"

The battle broke at dawn. The attacking Philistine force moved towards the Israelite camp, and the despair and lack of confidence reigning among the Israelites soon turned into flight towards the Gilboa'. Everyone fled for his life, hiding out among the groves of the highlands. The king and his sons, however, fought valiantly. One by one Saul's sons fell in battle before the king's eyes. He was already seriously wounded when the Philistines surrounded him with their bows and arrows. He feared death less than Philistine brutality. Since his arms-bearer did not have the courage to stab him with his sword and kill him, the king fell on his own sword and died.

The outcome of the battle appeared at first to have sealed the fate of the nation: **"And when the men of Israel that were on the other side of the valley** [i.e. the Israelite towns in the hills on either side of the valley, on the Gilboa' and the Heights of Issachar], **and they that were beyond the Jordan, saw that the men of Israel fled, and that Saul and his sons were dead, they forsook the cities, and fled; and the Philistines came and dwelt in them"** (I Samuel 31:7).

repaying an ancient debt

By taking his own life Saul prevented the Philistines from torturing him while alive, but he did not prevent them from desecrating his corpse and those of his sons: **"And it came to pass on the morrow** [of the battle], **when the Philistines came to strip the slain, that they found Saul and his three sons fallen in mount Gilboa. And they cut off his head, and stripped off his armour, and sent into the land of the Philistines round about, to carry the tidings unto the house of their idols** [the shrines of their gods], **and to the people. And they put his armour in the house of Ashtaroth** [probably the temple from the period of Ramses III, discovered in excavations at Bet She'an]; **and they fastened his body to the wall of Beth-shan"** (I Samuel 31:8-10).

Hanging the enemy on the city wall for all to see, a practice common in the ancient world, was considered the greatest humiliation in those days, disgracing the vanquished even after death.

It is not clear why the inhabitants of Jabesh-gilead did not join Saul, to whom they owed their honor and their lives, in his war against the Philistines, especially since the battlefied was relatively close to them. If they did not risk their lives for Saul in his lifetime, they certainly did so for Saul's corpse and for the bodies of his sons.

Approximately 15 kilometers lie between the tel of Bet She'an and the Jabesh River, where it comes out of the hill country. The men of Jabesh-gilead covered this distance and back in the dark of night in order to remove the bodies of Saul and his sons from the wall of Bet She'an. While they were moving along the valley to the mountains, they were in danger of being discovered by the Philistines; but the night was sufficiently long for them to cover the distance there and back.

(From Giv'at ha-Moreh on a clear day one has a good view of the mountains of Gilead rising above the Jordan Rift Valley and can even make out Tel Bet She'an. However one cannot see the location of Jabesh-gilead, which lies somewhere near the Jabesh-gilead River. The bed of the river cuts deep into the mountains of Gilead and from atop the tel of Bet She'an can be discerned as a break between the mountains.)

The corpses were presumably hung opposite the house of Ashtaroth which, if it is indeed the temple from the time of Ramses III, means they were hung in the middle of the southern wall of Bet She'an, above the steepest slope of the tel. It seems reasonable that, due to the steepness of the location, this part of

1

1 *Mt. Saul overlooks the Ḥarod Valley, Giv'at ha-Moreh, and the hills of Nazareth.*

2 *Bet She'an as seen from the Gilboa'.*

3 *"And they took the body of Saul and the bodies of his sons from the wall of Beth-shan" (I Samuel 31:12). Tel Bet She'an.*

2

3

the wall was not guarded by the Philistines. Thus the men from Jabesh-gilead could accomplish their mission without being discovered: **"All the valiant men arose, and went all night, and took the body of Saul and the bodies of his sons from the wall of Beth-shan; and they came to Jabesh, and burnt them there. And they took their bones, and buried them under the tamarisk-tree in Jabesh, and fasted seven days"** (I Samuel 31:12-13).

what lay in store?

At that moment it seemed as if the Land of Israel would indeed become the land of Philistia, as the enemies of the Jews wished during a much later period when, perverting history, they gave the name Palaestina to the entire land. History, however, destined that it should be otherwise. Absurd as it may seem, the very man who would one day tip the balance decisively in favor of Israel was at the time in the service of the Philistines. Upon learning of Israel's defeat, for a brief moment he was severely shaken; then, lamenting in the heat of his anger, he gave vent to his great emotion: **"Ye mountains of Gilboa, let there be no dew nor rain upon you, neither fields of choice fruits; for there**

1 *"Now David [the second king of Israel] went to and fro from Saul [the first king] to feed his father's sheep at Beth-lehem" (I Samuel 17:15). Sheep and goat raising, a major branch of the economy in the ancient Near East, was a mainstay of the Israelites and their neighbors, especially in regions bordering on wooded lands and desert. Flocks provided milk and milk products, meat, goat's hair, wool, and leather.*

The end: "The sun has set and the battle is done, and by his own sword the king lies slain." from "The Wailing City" *by Nathan Alterman.*

1

the shield of the mighty was vilely cast away, the shield of Saul, not anointed with oil ... Saul and Jonathan, the lovely and the pleasant in their lives, even in their death they were not divided" (II Samuel 1:21-23).

Yet David was not a man to lament for long. He quickly embarked upon political and military action which in the end left the Philistines only their relatively small corner of land along the southwestern edge of the coastal plain and reduced them to a secondary factor in the history of the Land of Israel.

Although Israel suffered many a blow since Saul's crushing defeat, that defeat has become deeply engraved in the national consciousness. Was this due to the tragedy of his life, which has found expression in Saul Tchernichowsky's famous poem?

Why has Thou taken me from following after the flock
And placed me this day as chief over thy folk?
The Philistines encompass me, the deep shadow fills
me with dread
An evil spirit oppresses me even unto death.
O man of God, what will God answer me?
For He has turned aside from me,
What may I do? O say!

"At 'En-Dor"
translated by Yocheved Welber

Or was this due to the national and historical significance of his defeat, which has never lost its tangible reality?

scenes of the hasmonean revolt revisited
the birthplace of the hasmoneans

Menachem Zaharoni

A. By car and on foot – recommended route: Herzl Forest; Me'or Modi'im; "Tombs of the Hasmoneans" (Maccabees); Sheikh el-'Arbawi, Military Post 219; ford Naḥal Modi'in (Modi'in Brook) on foot and continue to Tel er-Ras (one hundred meters south of the sheikh's tomb, via the dirt path which descends to Naḥal Modi'in), visit el-Midya (cars may drive via Bet Neḥemya, Budrus, Qibya, and Ni'lin, and wait for the hikers at el-Midya, or may follow route B); drive through Ni'lin and Kharbata to Lower Bet Ḥoron (Beit Ghur et-Taḥta); Upper Bet Ḥoron (Beit Ghur el-Fauqa); Emmaus and Canada Park (*Park Ayyalon – Aijalon*); Latrun.
B. By car only – recommended route: Herzl Forest; Me'or Modi'im; "Tombs of the Hasmoneans"; Sheikh el-'Arbawi, Military Post 219; *moshav* Shillat, situated on the site of the Shilta military post; Kefar Rut (and right, via the dirt road to the Kharbata-Latrun road); via Kharbata and Ni'lin to el-Midya (Modi'in); Tel er-Ras; continue as in route A.

station 1: me'or modi'im

This is a cooperative *moshav* established by a group of religious Jews from the United States. No matter when you happen by, the sound of song and chant will greet you from the houses. Initially (1964) this was a religious Naḥal settlement, Mevo Modi'im.

The finds on this site include remains of mosaic floors, wells (sealed by heavy, round stones), and a press (consisting of a surface for treading, a press-stone, depressions for sediment, and conduits for channeling the grape juice) belonging to a Byzantine monastery. The monks apparently supported themselves growing grapes and olives, which probably also provided the livelihood of our ancestors in Modi'in in the time of the Maccabees.

station 2: "the tombs of the maccabees"

In front of us we see two rows of tombs hewn into the rock from west to east, ten tombs in the southern row and eleven in the northern one. Each tomb consists of a trench and two parallel chambers the size of a human body. The central trench is covered by a heavy stone. On some of the trenches the stone has been removed. The two chambers on either side, perhaps meant for a man and his wife, were used for burial. South of the rows of tombs is a small catacomb in which the graves are arranged in the same manner.

The Arabs called these tombs "Qubur el-Yahud" (tombs of the Jews) and the catacomb – "Qabr Sultan el-Yahud" (tomb of the king of the Jews). Students of the Herzlia Gymnasium and their teachers identified the tombs with the burial place of the Hasmoneans and inaugurated the custom, observed since 1910, of visiting these tombs during Hanukkah. The Hanukkah torch which is relayed by runners to Jerusalem has been lit on this spot since 1944. Nevertheless there is some uncertainty in attributing these tombs to the Hasmoneans, since they are more characteristic of the Roman than the Hellenistic period.

station 3: hill of sheikh el-'arbawi; military post 219

The site is marked by a characteristic, domed sheikh's tomb with a holy tree beside it. Looking eastward we see the Judean Mountains rising steeply above the Shefela (foothills), a hilly region ascending gradually to the east from the Coastal Plain. At the edge of the steep incline we can see the village of Deir Qaddis and north of it, a police station. From here we cannot see the hills of Beth-El, Gophna, and Bir Zeit which lie further to the east and are cleft by many gulches and deep river beds, abounding in caves which could provide shelter to those seeking refuge. We are standing at the northern tip of the Shefela, about two kilometers away from the watercourse of Naḥal Natuf

If all the heathen in the king's dominions listen to him and forsake each of them the religion of his forefathers, and choose to follow his commands instead, yet I and my sons and my brothers will live in accordance with the covenant of our forefathers. God forbid that we should abandon the Law and the ordinances. *First Book of Maccabees 2:19-21.*

1 *The village of el-Midya. The ancient name of Modi'in is preserved in the name of the modern Arab village. Hasmonean Modi'in was situated south of el-Midya, on Tel er-Ras. Modi'in is denoted on the Madaba Map as a building with two towers and one gate and next to it, in Greek, are the words: "Modi'in, today Mod'ita, whence came the Maccabees."*

which forms its northern boundary. The area is very rocky, full of Upper Cretaceous chalkstone covered by a hard crust of caliche or recrystallized chalkstone 1-2 meters thick. The soil between the rocks is poor and eroded. This area was the home of the Hasmoneans and the birthplace of the rebellion (beginning in 167 b.c.e.) which brought about the re-establishment of the kingdom of Judah in the historic boundaries of the Land of Israel.

Why did the revolt begin here of all places, and how? What did the Maccabees see when they cast their eyes westward? Of course the densely populated area east of the Mediterranean did not look the same then as now. Jaffa, however, could be seen from here. We can make out its location by using the Shalom Tower as a landmark. Closer to us we see smoke coming from the stacks of the cement factory in Ramla, next to Lod. Ramla was founded during the Arab period, but Lod existed in the time of the Maccabees. According to the Sages, Lod marks the end of the Shefela and the beginning of "the valley" or the Coastal Plain, which then too was intensively cultivated. Rabbi Joḥanan (one of the great sages of the Talmud) said: **"From Beth Ḥoron until Emmaus is hill country, from Emmaus to Lod – Shefela, and from Lod to the sea – valley"** (Jerusalem Talmud, *Shevi'it*).

The repatriates from the Babylonian exile (538 b.c.e.) naturally returned to the settlements from which they or their predecessors had been exiled and rejoined the few remaining Jews whom the Babylonians had not deported. We read in Scripture: **"The children of Lod, Hadid, and Ono** [returned], **seven hundred twenty and five** [in number]" (Ezra 2:33). Among those returning to the land of Benjamin were **"Hadid, Zeboim, Neballat** [Beit Naballa]; **Lod, and Ono, Ge-harashim"** (Nehemiah 11:34-35). **"And the sons of Elpaal: Eber, and Misham, and Shemed** [families of the tribe of Benjamin], **who built Ono, and Lod, with the towns thereof"** (I Chronicles 8:12).

Reestablishing themselves on the land of their ancestors was not easy. In the course of time the Persian rulers had given most of the coast to the Phoenicians in repayment for the services of their fleets in their maritime battles (the Persian Empire was a continental power with no fleet of its own and no experience in seafaring). Greek penetration into the Coastal Plain began before the conquest by Alexander the Great (332 b.c.e.) and increased thereafter, pushing the Jews further and further from fertile land into the barren highlands to lead a life of hardship during the Hellenistic period. The Jews around Modi'in overlooked the fertile coastal area with its wealthy, flourishing gentile communities, the area which had once been the land of their forefathers. Jaffa symbolized maritime trade and a life of well-being. The God of Israel had been expelled from there; Zeus and his pantheon now reigned there. We can easily appreciate how Mattathias and his five sons, Joḥanan, Simeon, Judah, Jonathan, and Eleazar, must have felt, what they dreamed of, and what they anticipated. The new situation compelled them to launch an offensive. The struggle of the Hasmonean brothers against the Greeks and the Syrians lasted for decades. Four of the sons fell in the fierce fighting, but Simeon (called Thassis) lived to see the independence of Judah and was elected "President of the League of the Jews," the supreme institution governing the independent state of Judah. Thus the dream of his youth was fulfilled, and the territory west of Modi'in returned to Jewish hands. He took Jaffa as well and made it Judea's port. When he enjoyed greater ease, according to the Book of Maccabees, he built a monument over his parents' tomb, consisting of seven pyramids (in memory of his father, mother, and five brothers), most likely where we are standing now. The sides of the pyramids were engraved with figures of arms and of various ships, an allusion to the dream of an outlet to the sea at Jaffa come true. According to legend, sailors on the high seas navigated their ships ashore by this monument which could be seen from afar. Nineteenth century excavations around the sheikh's tomb revealed the foundations of a large edifice, fragments of columns, and hewn stones.

station 4: on the left bank of naḥal modi'in

From Sheikh el-'Arbawi we turn east and approach the left bank of Naḥal Modi'in.

The watercourse of Naḥal Modi'in cuts deep into the hills, meandering northwest towards Naḥal Natuf into which it feeds. (Naḥal Natuf is a tributary of Naḥal Ayyalon (Aijalon), which in turn flows into the Yarqon River near Tel Aviv.) Across the brook, northeast of where we are standing, is a small Arab village called el-Midya, a distortion of the name Modi'in.

This poor Arab village (population less than 200) was founded here only 250 years ago on the site of the Modi'in of the Byzantine period. Ancient Modi'in – from the time of the Second Temple, the Mishnah and Talmud – lies to the south on the tel which stands out over the bank of the stream, known as Tel er-Ras by the Arabs. This was the home of the Hasmoneans, the town in which Mattathias and his five sons were born. The landscape is one of poor, barren hills. The natural woodland has been destroyed, leaving only some lone shrubs, primarily indigenous buckthorn, the remains of the woodland, rising here or there over the barren soil.

1 *"The Tombs of the Hasmoneans." There is some doubt whether this is truly the burial place of the Hasmoneans, since the graves are more characteristic of the Roman than the Hellenistic period.*

2 *The Roman road at the ascent of Bet Ḥoron.*
"These routes were marked on the map as Roman roads, but turned out to be mere goat tracks, quite impassable for wheels, and even for camels, without improvement. The only means of portage between villages in these hills was by donkeys, and any path up which a donkey could scramble was described by the local native as a good road. The Yeomanry Division sent back all vehicles, including guns, on the 18th, and the leading brigade of the 52nd Division next day found it equally impossible to get wheels forward." General A. P. Wavell, The Palestine Campaigns.

Isolated patches of cultivated land line the floor of the valley. Aside from these there is hardly any tillable soil here; therefore the fertile soil of the tel was used for planting. Thus the present Arab village lies beside the tel, on which olive trees and almond trees grow. Some grass which may be used for pasturing sheep grows among the rocks. Most likely our ancestors in Modi'in during the Hasmonean period also lived from pasturing sheep and growing olives and almonds. As was customary in every family at the time, the task of pasturing the family's flock was undoubtely placed in the hands of the sons. Sturdy young men,

1

accustomed to a hard life, they roamed the area, particularly towards the end of summer when the nearby pastures had been depleted, seeking good pasture for their flock further to the east and southeast, often on the slopes of Naḥal Modi'in. In this way they surely reached Bet Ḥoron, only eight kilometers in a direct line southeast of Modi'in, and Emmaus (called Ḥammat in Hebrew for the hot baths found there), directly south of their birthplace. They probably did not wander very far to the north because the Samaritans lived on the other side of Naḥal Natuf. Thus they became closely acquainted with their surroundings and in time used this knowledge of the terrain to deal crushing military defeats to their Greco-Syrian enemies. They were acquainted with the iron hand of these gentiles from youth; they had experienced personally the extortions of the Greco-Syrians.

historical setting of the maccabean* revolt

After the death of Alexander the Great (323 b.c.e.) his vast empire split into several domains, each seized by one of his generals. Seleucus ruled over Syria and Ptolemy over Egypt.

Initially the Land of Israel was ruled by the Ptolemies, but in 200 b.c.e. the Seleucid king Antiochus III (the Great) conquered the Land of Israel. Antiochus the Great treated the Jews with relative decency, but the same cannot be said of his son Antiochus IV (Epiphanes), who succeeded him. (Ephiphanes, the name which he chose, means "God made manifest" and testifies to his character.) Antiochus Epiphanes was cruel and perverse. The Syrians derisively called him "Epimanes" or "the wild man" in Greek. Relations between Ptolemaic Egypt and Seleucid Syria were almost constantly strained, both seeking to swallow up the neighboring land.

In 169 b.c.e Antiochus Epiphanes conquered part of northern Egypt and, on his return to Syria after the war, pillaged the golden implements of the Temple in Jerusalem. In 168 b.c.e. he fought Egypt again and succeeded in conquering it, but at orders from the Romans, then the strongest power in the ancient world, was forced to retreat. Embittered, Antiochus returned from Egypt. Meanwhile rumors of his death began to spread in Jerusalem. A revolt erupted, which Antiochus suppressed most cruelly, appearing in Jerusalem himself, slaughtering thousands of Jews and burning the most beautiful quarters of the city. In what remained of the city he settled many Greco-Syrian colonials.

2

Roman pressure threatened to crumble Epiphanes' kingdom. In order to strengthen it he attempted to impose Greek religion and culture on all the nations living in his realm. Hence he began religious persecution of the Jews, who were the least likely of all people to heed him and betray the faith of their forefathers. He forbade the Jews to keep the Sabbath, to circumcise their sons, and to observe other commandments. He turned the Temple into a shrine of the "god of the sky," identified with Zeus, the head of the Greek pantheon, whose worship was accompanied by licentiousness. The great historian, Theodor Mommsen, in his *History of Rome* effectively said the cult of the Syrian gods was in many instances nothing more than a branch of the Syrian brothel.

Spreading throughout the towns and villages of Judah, Antiochus' men commanded the Jews to worship the Greek gods and, among other things, also ordered them to sacrifice pigs on their altars to mark the change which had occurred in their culture and way of life. There were among the Jews some Hellenizers, who willingly accepted Antiochus' decrees. Most Jews, however, resisted, refusing to comply with the decrees. Antiochus' emissaries were afraid to enter the towns deep in the highlands, where there were very large concentrations of Jews. Therefore they started with the outlying villages, close to the gentile areas. Since Modi'in was very close to Gezer, the

*The name Maccabee occurs in the Books of the Maccabees, which survived only in Greek and Syriac translation. Modern scholars believe its origins to lie in the epithet "Judah the Maccabee," given Judah son of Mattathias (I Maccabees 2:4) because he struck at his people's enemies with a *maccavet,* a hammer-like implement. Other historical figures have been similarly dubbed, such as Charles Martel (the Hammer), for the same reason.

The name Maccabees does not appear in the Talmud or in midrashic literature, and the Hasmonean dynasty is referred to there as the Hasmonean House.

1

2

1 *Olive trees growing along the bed of Naḥal Modi'in. Olives are one of the subsistence crops in rocky hilly terrain.*

2 *A flock of sheep near Bet Ḥoron. Here our early ancestors as well as the Hasmoneans doubtless depended on herding sheep and cultivating olives and almonds for their livelihood. Roaming after the sheep, they became closely acquainted with their surroundings and in time used this knowledge to defeat their enemy on the battlefield.*

administrative center of the Hellenistic government during that period, Antiochus' men descended on the town. The Jews were congregated in the center of Modi'in, and the king's emissary called on Mattathias, the most respected member of the local Jewish community, to set an example to his brethren by sacrificing a pig on the altar, thus fulfilling the king's decree. Mattathias refused, saying: **"If all the heathen in the king's dominions listen to him and forsake each of them the religion of his forefathers, and choose to follow his commands instead, yet I and my sons and my brothers will live in accordance with the covenant of our forefathers. God forbid that we should abandon the Law and the ordinances"** (I Maccabees 2:19-21). Nevertheless, a Jew was found who was willing to obey the king and sacrifice a pig; for every generation has some individuals of this type. This sparked off the revolt. Mattathias killed both the Jew and the king's emissary. Clearly Mattathias and his sons could no longer remain in Modi'in for fear of vengeance by the Greek authorities: **"Then Mattathias cried out in a loud voice in the town and said, 'Let everybody who is zealous for the Law and stands by the covenant come out after me'"** (I Maccabees 2:26-28). Judah, Mattathias' third son, called the Maccabee, was his right hand man and after his father's death assumed leadership of the revolt.

station 5: tel er-ras, site of hasmonean modi'in, and the village of el-midya

Tel er-Ras lies on the other side of Naḥal Modi'in, rising steeply over the right bank of the riverbed. Potsherds discovered there indicate that it was inhabited since the First Temple period and only by chance did not happen to be mentioned in the Bible. The soil of the tel has the grey color of ruins and is rich in organic material. Relatively more fruit trees grow there than grow nearby. The potsherds which we come across on our way are from the First Temple period, of course, but there are also some Hellenistic, Roman and Byzantine sherds. Only Byzantine potsherds, however, were found in the village of el-Midya, which perhaps suggests that the mound of Tel er-Ras, which extends over seven acres, was abandoned during this period so that the land-hungry people could use its relatively fertile soil for growing fruit trees. Thus the village may have moved north to rockier terrain, to the site of the present-day village of el-Midya.

On top of the tel there is a large edifice hewn into the rock, with an extensive network of caves connected one to another. The exact nature of the building is not known but may be connected in some way with agricultural production.

The village of el-Midya has changed little since the Mandate period. Few new houses have been built in it because of lack of money. Changes have occurred since the Six Day War, perhaps far more than since the British conquest. The standard of living of el-Midya's inhabitants has risen greatly due to their working outside the village. An ancient subterranean olive press, which has been partially destroyed, is situated within the village.

3 An ancient underground olive press found in Midya. This, more than any other archaeological find, is evidence that Modi'in's economy depended on olive cultivation. The picture shows the circular basin in which the olives were crushed by rolling an upright press-stone over them.

3

(Take a flashlight with you if you wish to enter it.) More than any other archaeological remain, it is evidence that Modi'in's inhabitants depended in the past on olive groves for their livelihood. Today there are not many olive trees in the immediate surroundings of el-Midya, although they are plentiful along either side of the road from Qibya to Ni'lin (beginning about one kilometer northeast of el-Midya) and provide the basic livelihood of the latter villages. Ni'lin has a modern olive press. Olives, it must be understood, are one of the basic subsistence crops of farmers in the rocky highlands of the Land of Israel. When the Sages went from Tiberias to Sepphoris, R. Joḥanan, one of the great *amoraim* (Talmudic scholars) of the Land of Israel (third century b.c.e.), showed his disciple R. Ḥiyya bar-Abba his farm, which he sold in order to study Torah. This farm included fields of grain, olive plantations, and a vineyard (Exodus Rabbah 47). Olives ranked second among the crops of the Land of Israel. In rocky terrain such as the region of Modi'in they ranked first, since olive trees can strike roots even in stony soil: **"And He made him to suck honey out of the crag, and oil out of the flinty rock"** (Deuteronomy 32:13). The hillsides were probably planted with vineyards as well. Aside from the honey of wild bees, honey for the people of the Bible also referred to concentrated grape juice ("honey out of the crag") and the sweetness of dates.

early scenes of battle

Menachem Zaharoni

station 6: the maccabee victory at upper bet horon

Judah the Maccabee and his brothers, not having a large army at their disposal, had to resort to guerrilla warfare. Judah was a genius at partisan improvisation. He knew how to surprise the enemy by stratagem, to take advantage of the topography, and force him to fight where the size of his force was of no consequence. Judah had a pronounced advantage over the Greco-Syrians since he knew the regions of the battles well, while the Greeks did not know them at all. The battle against Seron at Bet Ḥoron illustrates the full import of his capabilities.

There is a Lower Bet Ḥoron and an Upper Bet Ḥoron (the Arab villages of Beit Ghur et-Taḥta and Beit Ghur el-Fauqa, respectively). Between the two villages, which are less than three kilometers apart as the crow flies, is a steep climb of 225 meters ("Ascent of Bet Ḥoron"). The road here winds back and forth over a narrow spur of mountain between deep valleys.

In order to pave the modern road the spur was broadened, but in ancient times the road here was extremely narrow. The Talmud describes the road as follows: **"If two camels try to climb the ascent at Beth Ḥoron at the same time, they both tumble down** [so narrow was the road that two camels could not climb it abreast], **but if they ascend one after the other, both can go up safely"** (Sanhedrin 32b). In Hasmonean times thick shrubbery covered the slopes down to the valleys.

Seron, the Syrian commander, ascended here with his army from the Greek-settled coastal plain into the highlands in order to attack Judah and his guerrillas and to wipe them out. The Greco-Syrians were not very familiar with the way but trusted their large, well-armed forces. But not Judah; his men were few and poorly armed, yet they were brave and knew the area well. Judah deployed his men along the Ascent of Bet Ḥoron, concealing them in the shrubbery.

South of the modern village of Beit Ghur el-Fauqa (the hill of Sheikh Abu Susa) the road became extremely narrow. Here there was a bend in the road which prevented travelers from seeing their fellows coming up behind and vice versa. It was here that Judah the Maccabee laid his ambush for the Greco-Syrian army. As the Greco-Syrian soldiers passed, possibly in single file, Judah's guerrillas stormed out of the ambush and attacked them. The Syrian soldiers, caught by surprise, fled in disarray back down the hill towards the Aijalon Valley (Ayyalon). In their flight they surely must have knocked one another into the abysses on either side of the road. Then Judah's fighters came out of their hiding places on either side of the road and slaughtered them. Judah the Maccabee's victory was complete and afforded his men an opportunity to equip themselves with arms taken as booty from the Greco-Syrians.

Bet Ḥoron is a site rich in historical events, worth reviewing in order to understand the ingenuity of Judah the Maccabee's military mind.

Since ancient times a road along the spur of the mountain, flanked by deep valleys, has run from the Aijalon Valley (Ayyalon) to the crest of the hill country and on to Jerusalem. Judah the Maccabee and Simeon bar-Giora, however, were the only ones to take advantage of the topography here in order to attack and win brilliant victories over the enemy.

This place is first mentioned in connection with the battle of the five Amorite kings against the inhabitants of Gibeon. Joshua came to the aid of his ally, and roundly defeated the Amorites. Naturally, since three of the kings ruled over city-states in the Shefela (Lachish, Eglon, and Jarmuth), they fled to the Shefela by way of Bet Ḥoron, only eight kilometers away from Gibeon (Joshua 10). The Philistines, too, followed exactly the same route of flight after being defeated by Saul and Jonathan at Michmas (I Samuel 14:31).

Neither the Philistines nor the Israelites knew how to use the topography of the area to their advantage. Perhaps Simeon bar-Giora recalled Judah the Maccabee's tactics here, and followed in his footsteps. The following was the situation in Roman times:

The Roman procurator in Syria, Cestius Gallus, suffered a crushing defeat here in 66 c.e. After failing in his mission to

1 *The vicinity of the ascent of Bet Ḥoron. The road from Lower Bet Ḥoron to Upper Bet Ḥoron rises steeply, wending back and forth along a narrow spur between two deep riverbeds. The spur was widened to pave the present road, but in ancient times the path was so narrow that the Talmud said, "If two camels try to climb the ascent at Bet Ḥoron at the same time, they both tumble down, but if they ascend one after the other, both can go up safely"* (Sanhedrin *32b). In Hasmonean times the hillsides were covered with scrub.*

suppress the revolt in Jerusalem, he retreated towards Bet Ḥoron, on his way back to Caesarea. **"In the wide spaces the Jews pressed them less vigorously, but when they were crowded together in the defiles of the descending road, one group got in front of them and barred their egress, others pushed the rearmost down into the ravine, and the main body lined the high ground overlooking the waist of the pass and showered missiles on the massed Romans. At this point the infantry were unable to defend themselves, and the danger to the cavalry was still greater; for they could not keep their formation and march down the road while being pelted, and the steep slope made it impossible for mounted men to charge the enemy; on both sides there were cliffs and ravines into which they fell to destruction. No one could find a way to flee or a means to defend himself; in their helplessness they turned to lamentation and despairing groans"** (*The Jewish War,* Book II, 19:8, Penguin edition, p.164). Possibly Simeon bar-Giora knew of Judah the Maccabee's strategy at this spot, and copied it, but Judah's feat was greater than Simeon's, and not only by virtue of being first. Simeon bar-Giora enjoyed military superiority over the Romans, whereas Judah won here with a small force fighting a large one.

Although Judah the Maccabee's battle at Bet Ḥoron was a partisan battle, it is nevertheless worth comparing it with the British battle here, which was part of their fight for Jerusalem, during World War I. The British advance through Bet Ḥoron was slow, in no small measure due to their lack of familiarity with the area. General A. P. Wavell, Chief of Staff of the British Expeditionary Force, describes their movement in his book, *The Palestine Campaigns,* thus: "On the 18th [of October], while the Australian Division was manoeuvring the Turks out of Latrun, the Yeomanry Division made good progress towards Lower Beth-horon (Beit Ghur el Taḥta). The 75th Division assembled towards Latrun, and the 52nd at Ramleh and Ludd. On the 19th the two infantry divisions plunged into the hills. Simultaneously winter set in, with heavy rain and a sudden fall in the temperature.... The routes taken by the 52nd Division and Yeomanry Division lay through the famous Vale of Aijalon, up and down which assaults on and sorties from the Judaean fortress have been many since the day when Joshua bade the sun stand still that he might complete his destruction of the Canaanites. These routes were marked on the map as Roman roads, but turned out to be mere goat tracks, quite impassable for wheels, and even for camels, without improvement. The only means of portage between villages in these hills was by donkeys, and any path up which a donkey could scramble was described by the local native as a good road. The Yeomanry Division sent back all vehicles, including guns, on the 18th, and the leading brigade of the 52nd Division next day found it equally impossible to get wheels forward. The hill sides are steep and rocky, often precipitous, and the wadis which wind between them are strewn with great boulders..." (pp. 159-160).

The point is not to tell how the British captured Jerusalem which, after much bloodshed, fell at long last on December 8, 1917, in a joint operation of troops closing in on the city from every side; it is to stress the consequences which lack of familiarity with the area had for a modern army in the early 20th century. There can be no doubt that planning a campaign on a mistaken assumption – that the Yeomanry Division and the 52nd Division could use cannons and motorized vehicles on "Roman roads" which turned out to be non-existent – prolonged the campaign and led to needless loss of life.

Route: From Beit Ghur el-Fauqa, via Beit Ghur et-Taḥta and Mevo Ḥoron (on the left, a new Jewish settlement, identifiable by its modern buildings), to Canada Park and Emmaus (about two kilometers northeast of Latrun).

station 7: canada park

After the Trappist monastery we come to Canada Park (*Park Ayyalon*), the first park in the country to be devoted to agricultural history. It has streams and cool shady corners. Vineyards, cultivated trees, and other plants characteristic of agriculture in the Land of Israel from the time of the Mishnah and Talmud grow here.

The path branching off to the right behind the Trappist Monastery, on the road to Bet Ḥoron, leads to the water conduit uncovered by archaeologists which channeled water to Emmaus. (Here it is worthwhile proceeding on foot.) The conduit, fed in part by water from a spring which is enclosed in an ancient building, illustrates how meagre sources of water can be put to use when efficiently channeled together. Among the archaeological findings worth seeing is a special olive press, of a type not common in Israel.

Ayyalon is an ancient biblical city, after which the valley was named. During the First Temple period it protected the road to Jerusalem, but in the Second Temple period it was supplanted by Emmaus. Biblical Aijalon (Ayyalon) is identified with the abandoned village of Yalu, east of the ruins of Emmaus. Southeast of the village is a very picturesque tel, Tel Qauqa. Biblical Aijalon is believed to have been built on this tel. Yalu is also the site of a Crusader stronghold, Fort Arnaldo.

In the Valley of Ayyalon Joshua defeated the five Amorite kings. He pursued them from Gibeon, by way of Bet Ḥoron, to the Valley of Ayyalon and further. During the battle Joshua cried excitedly: " **'Sun, stand thou still upon Gibeon; and thou, Moon, in the valley of Aijalon.' And the sun stood still, and the moon stayed, until the nation had avenged themselves of their enemies"** (Joshua 10: 12-13), so that he would have time to defeat the foe while it was yet daylight.

station 8: emmaus (ḥammat – ḥammata)

Emmaus, according to the Talmud, marked the beginning of the foothills, the Shefela (see R. Joḥanan's remark, above). In Hebrew it was called Ḥammat or Ḥammata, because of its hot baths. Volcanic geological findings in the area may indicate a hot spring nearby. At Emmaus Judah the Maccabee won his third victory over the Syrians (his first was won over Apollonius, ruler of Samaria, at the Ascent of Levonah, and his second at Bet Ḥoron).

The Syrians sent three commanders with a large army of about 40,000 infantry and 7,000 cavalry in order to wipe out Judah and his partisans, and avenge Seron's defeat. The most important of

the battle of bet ḥoron, 166 b.c.e.

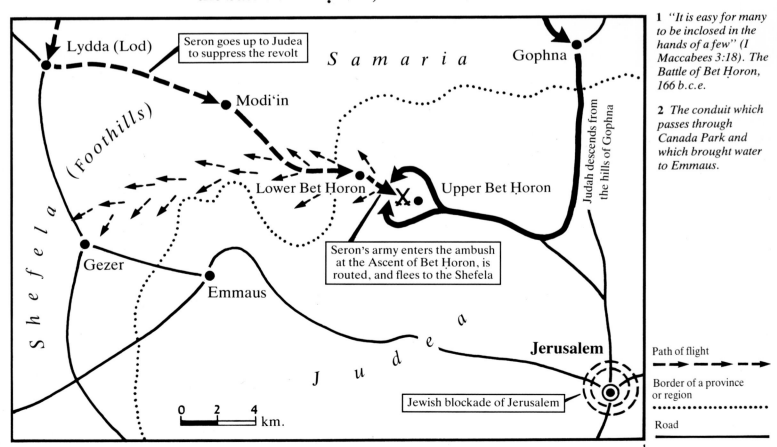

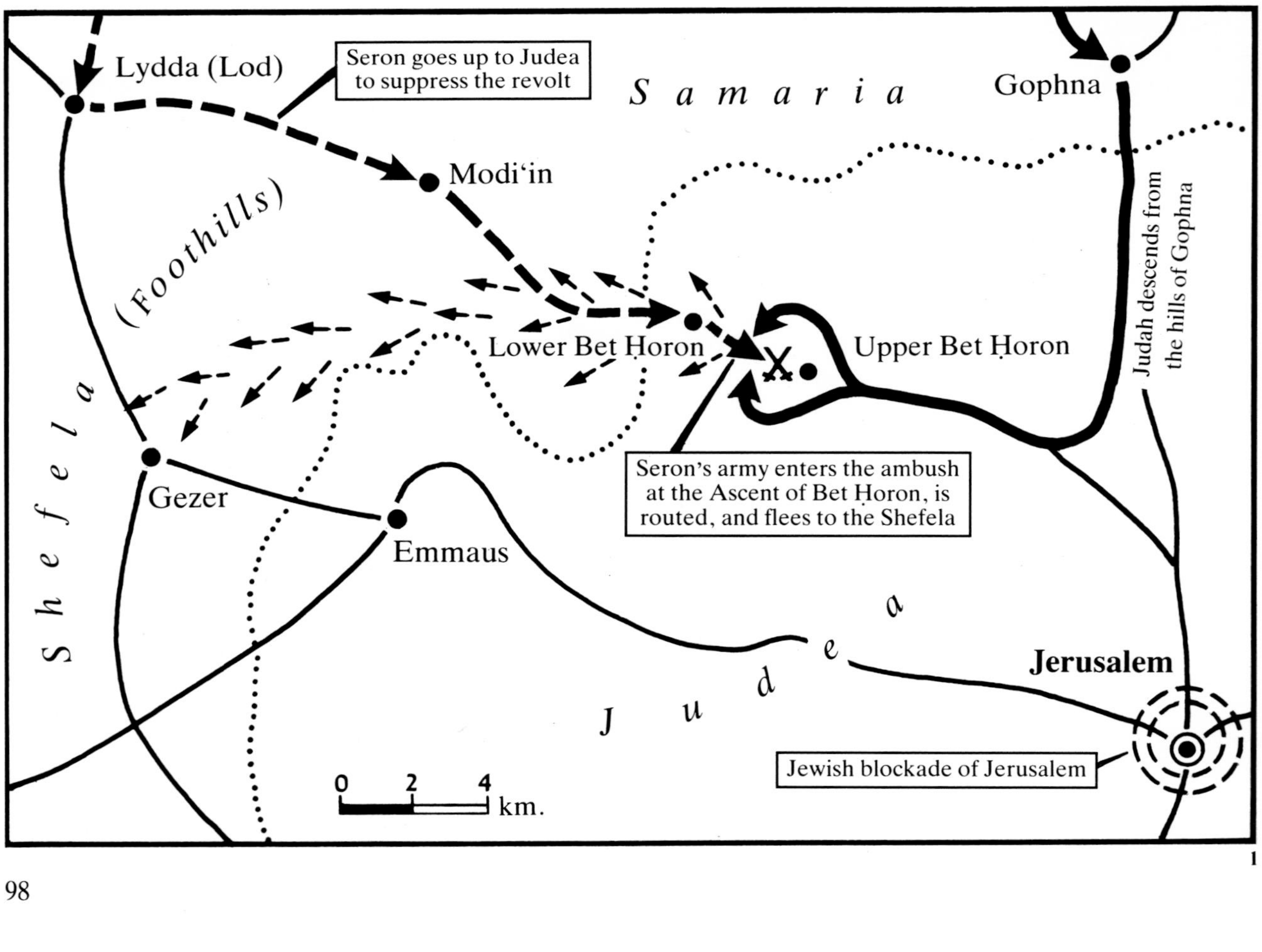

1 *"It is easy for many to be inclosed in the hands of a few" (I Maccabees 3:18). The Battle of Bet Ḥoron, 166 b.c.e.*

2 *The conduit which passes through Canada Park and which brought water to Emmaus.*

1

the commanders was Gorgias. This time the Syrian commanders were more cautious. To secure themselves against a Jewish surprise attack, the Syrians encamped near Emmaus, apparently in the enclosed valley, located north of the police station. Here, close to a Greek city, the Syrians thought they were safe. Moreover, here they could obtain water for their many soldiers (remember the conduit!). Judah the Maccabee's men amassed at Miẓpah (now Tel en-Naṣba, about 3 kilometers south of Ramallah). Here they held a service and ceremony to encourage the fighters, at the place where, according to Scripture (Deuteronomy 20:1-9), the Jews had gathered in the past, in biblical times, in their hour of need. (Miẓpah was the city of the prophet Samuel. It was also the center of operations of Gedaliah, governor of Judah, after Nebuchadnezzar's destruction of Jerusalem.) The Jews knew they were fighting for their lives, the lives of their children, and the survival of their people. Judah the Maccabee knew he could not remain in Miẓpah, for if he did so the Syrians would soon come in their

2

1 *Reconstruction of the water conduit in Canada Park (two views).*

2 *Canada Park (Park Ayyalon – Aijalon), devoted to the history of agricultural life, is covered with trees and vegetation characteristic of farming in the Land of Israel in the time of the Mishnah and Talmud. In the foreground is a unique kind of wine press, not commonly found in Israel.*

1

masses and surround him. First he spread rumors, which reached the Syrians, about his whereabouts. Then he and his men left Miẓpah in the night and headed south, then west. North of Jerusalem they turned onto the route to the Coastal Plain, via Biddu - Ma'ale ha-Ḥamisha and Deir Ayyub, towards the Aijalon Valley (Ayyalon).

While it was still dark, Judah and his men encamped at the place today called 'Ein Ḥilla, at the side of the Ayyalon Valley road, not far from the entrance to Sha'ar ha-Gai, where a eucalyptus grove grows today. When Gorgias heard that Judah the Maccabee was encamped at Miẓpah, he took 5,000 infantry and one thousand cavalry and ascended by way of Bet Ḥoron to Miẓpah. But alas, he searched for Judah and his men in vain. At daybreak the Jewish guerrillas attacked the Syrian camp at Emmaus from the south. This was during the morning watch and, feeling all too secure, the Syrians apparently were not guarding their camp. Half asleep, the sudden attack threw them into panic, and they took flight towards Gezer, the provincial capital of the Greek authorities. Judah and his men chased them as far as this city, but, knowing that Gorgias would soon come back to his camp, they quickly returned. Then they burned the Greco-Syrian camp and its smoke rose into the sky. In the morning Gorgias returned with his men, disappointed. He had not discovered Judah's fighters but, while at Upper Bet Ḥoron, he had seen the smoke rising from the Greco-Syrian camp, and as he drew closer, he discerned the Jewish partisans. Panic stricken, his men fled southwest, to a region inhabited by Greek-speaking people, foes of the Jews.

Judah's victory was complete. He looted the Greek camp and found a large quantity of arms and supplies for equipping his men.

Judah the Maccabee was the first famous partisan fighter in the history of mankind. A valiant military genius, he was also simple in his way of life and devoted with all his being to the Jewish people and his faith. He proved that a small force of men, fighting for their lives and their country and closely familiar with the terrain on which they are fighting, thus able to use the topography to their advantage, are capable of defeating an organized and far larger army.

The importance of Emmaus in the history of the land did not come to a close with the end of the Maccabean wars. It suffered greatly at the hands of the Romans. As is typical of this region, after the death of Herod (4 b.c.e.) a revolt led by a shepherd broke out here and was cruelly suppressed by the Roman general, Varus, who went so far as to set fire to the city. Easily accessible from the coast, en route to the highlands, the Romans chose it as a base for their legions both during the Great Revolt and during the Bar Kokhba Rebellion. (Tombstones of soldiers from the Fifth Legion have been discovered at Emmaus.) Since then it had a mixed population of Jews, Samaritans, and Syrians. The well-to-do of Emmaus knew how to live the good life. After the death of R. Joḥanan ben Zakkai, his teacher, R. Eleazar ben Arakh, is said to have **"joined his wife at Emmaus, a place of good water and beautiful aspect** [a textual variant renders "good water" as Demasit, a distortion of the Greek *dimusia* – hot baths] ... **and so good was the place that in the end**

1

2

1 *A Byzantine church with three apses, on the site of the churches at Emmaus. Later the Crusaders used the central apse of the Byzantine church as the apse of their church.*

2 *After Alexander the Great died, his empire in the Middle East split in two, the Seleucids ruling Syria and the Ptolemies ruling Egypt. The citizens of the Seleucid kingdom were not actually Greeks, but Syrians who had adopted the Hellenistic culture. Hence the terms Seleucids and Greco-Syrians.*

of his days he forgot all his learning" (Ecclesiastes Rabbah 7:15).

The Byzantines' harsh treatment of the principle inhabitants of Emmaus, Jews and Samaritans, led them to rebellion, an indication that during this period the Jewish and Samaritan populations were still an important factor in the region.

Emmaus is holy to Christianity, even though there is some doubt whether this is indeed the Emmaus where, according to the New Testament, Jesus was revealed to two of his disciples after his crucifixion. In time, the Christians supplanted both the Jews and the Samaritans, although not without difficulty, as the Jewish-Samaritan revolt in the Byzantine period demonstrates.

Remains of a church were evident here, even before any archaeological excavation. Excavations unearthed remains of five structures: 1) Structures hewn into the bedrock and foundations of walls from the Hasmonean period. 2) Remains of a villa from Mishnaic times (second century c.e.) – a rectangular building (18 x 17 m.), with a long room on its northern side and, in its northeastern corner, an almost square court. Continuing to the north it had a long colonnaded court. A mosaic floor with floral and geometric motifs was discovered in this building. 3) A Christian basilica, which the excavators believed to be third century c.e. (Archaeologists today challenge the date, since Christianity was still persecuted in the third century and did not operate in the open.) The basilica is divided into a nave and two side aisles by two rows of 13 columns, and ends on the east with three apses. This building has a mosaic floor portraying various animals. 4) A sixth century basilica. Beyond the nave is a parallel structure, divided into two parts. In its rear there is a four-columned baptistery with a trefoil font in the shape of a cross, hewn in the rock. Beside it is another basin for baptising children. Next to the baptistery is a deep well. Remains of a mosaic floor, with geometric patterns, a grape vine arabesque, and a floral border design, with a fragment of a Greek inscription containing the word "*episcopus,*" may be seen in the baptistery. 5) A 12th century Crusader church, one of the more prominent buildings. The Crusaders used the central Byzantine apse, mentioned above, for the apse of their church, adding a semi-circular room to it, with its main entrance from the west and two smaller entrances in the curve in front of the apse. The ceiling of the hall was supported by four pointed arches. Discoveries on the site include fragments of capitals, one of which is without doubt Samaritan and has a bilingual, Greek-Hebrew inscription in Samaritan script, reading: "Blessed be His name forever." In addition, Emmaus also has a Byzantine olive press.

1

station 9: the battles of latrun in 1948 and the six day war

The chain of historical events in the annals of the Jewish people continued here during the War of Independence, as well. In Latrun there is a police station, built by the British, which controlled an important crossroads on the way from the Shefela to Jerusalem, as well as the nearby pumping station for the water pipeline from Rosh ha-'Ayin to Jerusalem. In the War of Independence Latrun was a key position in the fight for Jerusalem: the *Haganah* and later the IDF attempted to send convoys to Jerusalem and keep the road to the city open, while the Arabs, who took over the police station and the surrounding area after the British evacuation (14 May, 1948), did all they could to block the way. On May 16 and 17 *Haganah* forces succeeded in seizing control of the police station and sent two convoys to Jerusalem via this route. However, because of pressure in other sectors, this important site was evacuated, and on the 18th of the month was captured by the Fourth Battalion of the Arab Legion. The Latrun junction remained blocked for 19 years. The situation in the beleaguered city of Jerusalem prompted the IDF to launch at least five attacks on Latrun, all of which were repulsed by the Arab Legion, which inflicted heavy losses on the IDF. The brigades which fought at Latrun include Palmaḥ Har'el, Giv'ati, Alexandroni, Yiftaḥ, and the "Seven" Brigade. The terms of the armistice with Jordan left the area of Latrun in the hands of the Arab Legion, creating a sort of enclave connected to the Arab rear by means of a single road, and a no-man's land between it and Israel. The pumping station in the no-man's land was blown up by the Arabs, in violation of the agreement, in order to deprive Jewish Jerusalem of water. The road junction also lay in no-man's land, and convoys were supposed to be allowed passage through it under United Nations supervision. In the first convoy to try to pass, however, several Israelis were killed, and the idea was dropped. Both sides tilled portions of the no-man's land, according to local arrangements. A number of shooting incidents occurred in the no-man's land over the years. In the Six Day War, Latrun and the junction near it fell into IDF hands without a battle.

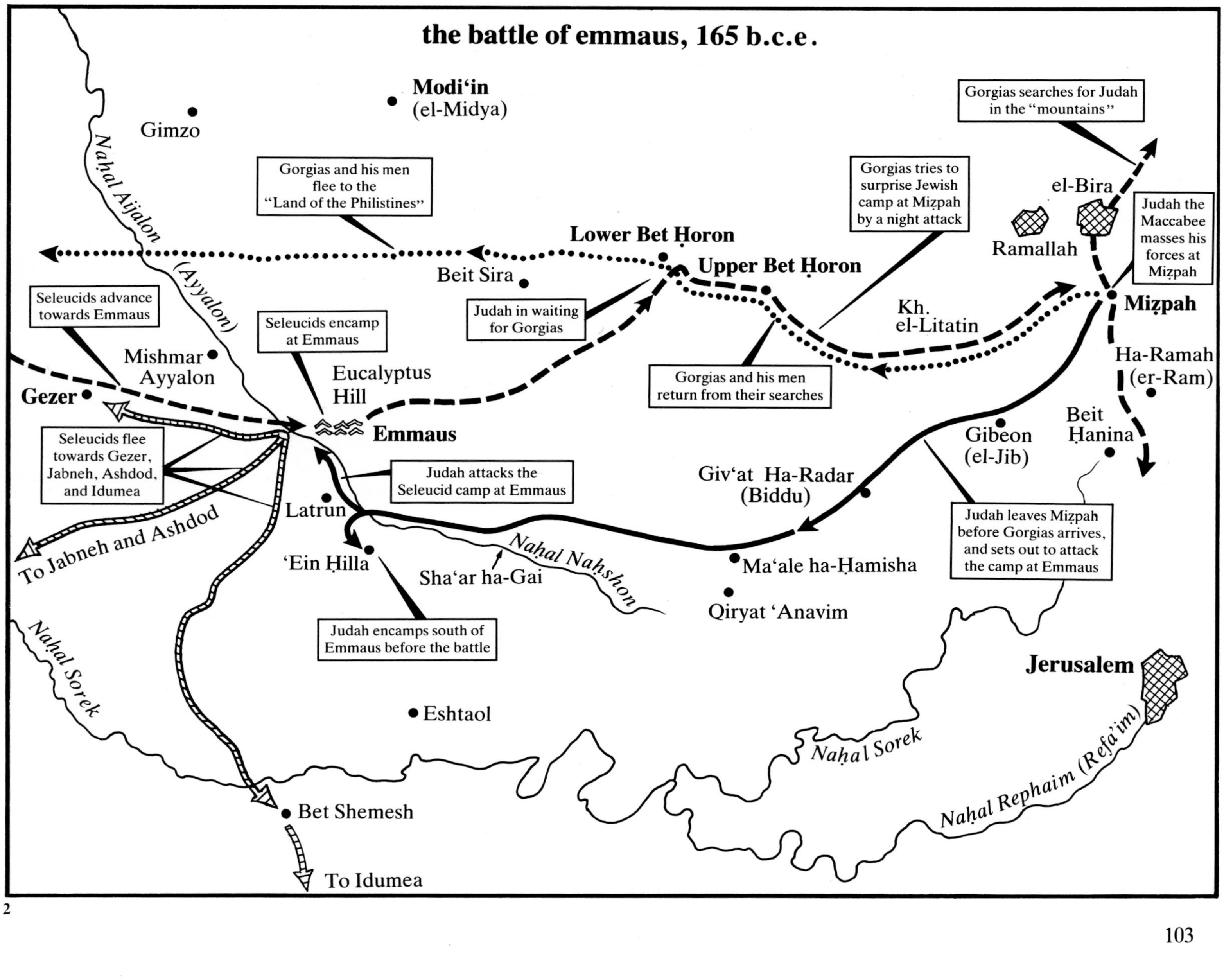

2

the great revolt revisited

and caesarea is flourishing

Menachem Zaharoni

"...as we thought it better to be destroyed at once than by little and little" (Josephus, *Jewish Antiquities*).

the background of the great revolt

The Great Revolt (66-70 c.e.) and the Bar Kokhba Rebellion (132-135 c.e.) determined the fate of the Jewish people for over 1800 years. The roots of these two events, fateful in their own time, date back to Pompey's conquest of Jerusalem (63 b.c.e.). The Romans, who had indirectly helped the Hasmoneans free themselves from the Seleucid yoke and, according to a contract engraved on brass tablets, were officially allies of Judea (see I Maccabees 8:22 and I Macabees 14:18), came back and subjugated the country. The quarrel between the Hasmonean brothers, Hyrcanus II and Aristobulus, simply gave Pompey a convenient opportunity to take over the country of the Jews; yet the Roman conquest would have occurred even without this pretext, albeit probably somewhat later.

After conquering Syria and Egypt, the two jewels in the crown of the Roman Empire, the Romans could not agree to an independent Judea, for a free Judea broke the territorial continuity between Egypt and Syria. A large fraction of the Jewish people actually welcomed this conquest, for they had wearied of the wars of Alexander Yannai (Jannaeus) and of his rule. Augury of the destruction in store lay not so much in the conquest itself as in the behavior of the conquerers when capturing the Temple Mount: **"Many of the priests, though they saw the enemy approaching sword in hand, quietly went on with the sacred rites and were cut down as they poured libations and offered incense, putting the service of God before their own preservation.... Among the disasters of that time nothing sent such a shudder through the nation as the exposure by aliens of the Holy Place, hitherto screened from all eyes. Pompey and his staff went into the Sanctuary, which no one was permitted to enter but the high priest, and saw what it contained.... Neither on this nor on any other of the sacred treasures did he lay a finger"** (Josephus, *The Jewish War,* Book I, 7:5-6; Penguin ed., p. 41).

Even those factions of the people who favored the conquest could foresee in this act what lay in store – a clash between two diametrically opposed worlds, with the Romans having a mighty military force at their command. Pompey wished to discover the secret of the Jewish religion, that which made the Jewish people unique among the nations of the world. The faith, practices and culture of the Jews were incomprehensible to the ancient world, especially to the Greeks, who had left the mark of their culture on the Roman Empire, and on Rome itself.

What did Pompey know about the Jews? What appreciation did he have of their religion and practices? The Romans' knowledge of the Jews came primarily from the Greek population of Alexandria, which oppressed Egypt's large Jewish population (about one million people). The struggle between the two groups, full of malice and libels, produced a perverted image of the Jewish religion. Despite the efforts of the Jews, who had also been bred in Hellenistic culture, the two cultures remained at opposite poles, with no bridge between them (see Josephus, *Against Apion*).

a nation "singularly prone to lust"

The Roman historian Tacitus, who lived during the period of the Destruction, summed up what the Romans knew of the Jews. According to him the Jews were a group of lepers who had been expelled from Egypt. Moses organized this expelled herd and

If someone tells you that Caesarea and Jerusalem have both been destroyed, do not believe him; if he says that both are flourishing, do not believe him; if he says that Caesarea has been laid waste and Jerusalem is flourishing, or that Jerusalem has been laid waste and Caesarea is flourishing, you may believe him. Megillah 6a .

1

1 *"Herod also built therein a theatre of stone; and on the south side of the harbour behind an amphitheatre also, capable of holding a vast number of men, and conveniently situated for a sea view"* (Antiquities, *Book XV, 9:6; Schocken ed., p. 245). On a small peninsula west of the theatre we can see the remains of Herod's palace: a large swimming pool surrounded by rooms.*

2 *The bay of Caesarea: the Crusader fortress and pier. The shadow which can be made out in the water beyond them, below the surface, is the mole of the ancient Herodian port. The area between the mosque and the restaurant once had access channels to the piers dug in it.*

led them through the desert, where, Tacitus writes, "Nothing, however, distressed them so much as the scarcity of water, and they had sunk ready to perish in all directions over the plain, when a herd of wild asses was seen to retire from their pasture to a rock shaded by trees. Moyses [Moses] followed them, and, guided by the appearance of a grassy spot, discovered an abundant spring of water. This furnished relief. After a continuous journey for six days, on the seventh they possessed themselves of a country, from which they expelled the inhabitants, and in which they founded a city and a temple.

Moyses, wishing to secure for the future his authority over the nation, gave them a novel form of worship, opposed to all that is practised by other men. Things sacred with us, with them have no sanctity, while they allow what with us is forbidden. In their holy place they have consecrated an image of the animal [the ass] by whose guidance they found deliverance from their long and thirsty wanderings. They slay the ram [sacred to the Egyptian god, Hammon], seemingly in derision of Hammon, and they sacrifice the ox, because the Egyptians worship it as Apis. They abstain from swine's flesh, in consideration of what

2

they suffered when they were infected by the leprosy to which this animal is liable. By their frequent fasts they still bear witness to the long hunger of former days, and the Jewish bread, made without leaven, is retained as a memorial of their hurried seizure of corn. We are told that the rest of the seventh day was adopted, because this day brought with it a termination of their toils [their wanderings in the desert]; after a while the charm of indolence beguiled them into giving up the seventh year [the sabbatical year] also to inaction....

This worship, however introduced, is upheld by its antiquity [antiquity of custom was held by the Romans to be an asset]; all their other customs, which are at once perverse and disgusting, owe their strength to their very badness. The most degraded out of other races, scorning their national beliefs [i.e., those Romans and Greeks who had abandoned paganism and converted to Judaism], brought to them their contributions and presents. This augmented the wealth of the Jews, as also did the fact, that among themselves they are inflexibly honest and ever ready to shew compassion, though they regard the rest of mankind with all the hatred of enemies. They sit apart at meals, they sleep apart, and though, as a nation, they are singularly prone to lust, they abstain from intercourse with foreign women; among themselves nothing is unlawful. Circumcision was adopted by them as a mark of difference from other men....

1

1 *Shadows of Caesarea's port, now underwater. The port which Herod built, large for its time, was neglected and, due to shifts in the surface of the earth, in time became submerged. Today marine archaeologists are working to uncover the port.*

2 *Herod built a "haven sheltered from the waves of the sea, in size not less than the Piraeus, and containing inside two stations for ships"* (Antiquities, *Book XV, 9:6; Schocken ed., p. 244). The basin which today serves as a swimming area was but part of the Herodian port.*

It is a crime among them to kill any newly-born infant.* They hold the souls of all who perish in battle or by the hands of the executioner [by the enemy] are immortal. Hence a passion for propagating their race and a contempt for death. They are wont to bury rather than to burn their dead, following in this the Egyptian custom; they bestow the same care on the dead, and they hold the same belief about the lower world. Quite different is their faith about things divine. The Egyptians worship many animals and images of monstrous form [idols with animal heads and human bodies]; **the Jews have purely mental conceptions of Deity, as one in essence. They call those profane who make representations of God in human shape out of perishable materials. They believe that Being to be supreme and eternal, neither capable of representation, nor of decay. They therefore do not allow any images to stand in their cities, much less in their temples. This flattery is not paid to their kings, nor this honour to our Emperors.** From the fact, however, that their priests used to chant to the music of flutes and cymbals, and to wear garlands of ivy, and that a golden vine was found in the temple, some have thought that they worshipped Father Liber, [the Roman god identified with Dionysus, the Greek god of wine], the conqueror of the East, though their institutions do not by any means harmonize with the theory; for Liber established a festive and cheerful worship, while the Jewish religion is tasteless and mean" (Tacitus, *The History,* Book V, 3-5; Modern Library ed., pp. 658-660).

a fateful encounter

Deifying the Caesars caused considerable friction between the Roman authorities and the Greek-speaking pagan population of the country, on the one hand, and the Jews, on the other. Until the Hadrianic decrees following the Bar Kokhba Revolt, however, the Romans did not apply religious coercion and even came to terms with the prohibition against gentiles entering the sanctified limits of the Temple.

* Roman custom and law permitted parents to kill their children up to ten days of age, and also permitted abortions.

Pompey's first act was to return the Greeks to the coastal cities of the Land of Israel, from which they had been expelled by the Hasmonean kings. Thenceforward the Jews became a minority in the coastal cities. King Herod, like the Romans, based his rule largely upon the Greek-speaking population, a group which was inevitably loyal to the government and a beneficiary of special privileges. Herod settled a Greek majority and a Jewish minority in Caesarea. Friction between the Jews and the Greek-speaking residents, who wished to deprive the Jews of civil rights in their own land, contributed significantly to the tension between the Jews and the Roman authorities, since the latter were inclined to favor the alien population in the Land of Israel (just as in Alexandria until the Destruction, in most instances, they protected the Jews against the ruling Greek majority). King Herod imposed his rule on the people with the aid of the Romans, shedding rivers of Jewish blood. The first and last Roman procurators, whose rule was briefly interrupted by the reign of Agrippa I, well-liked by the people, came from the class of Roman decurions and sometimes even of emancipated bondsmen, who had come to the country in order to enrich themselves as quickly as possible, by any available means, using the enormous force which lay at their disposal.

In addition to religious-cultural differences, extortion was a significant cause of Jewish rebelliousness. The tax burden was beyond bearing, for the Jewish nation of peasants not only paid heavy taxes to the central Roman government but also had to fill the pockets of the Roman procurators and other officials. The procurators did not balk at employing any means, sometimes even collaborating with robbers, to satisfy their greed. "**The kings** [of the Herodian dynasty]," writes the anti-Semitic Roman historian, Tacitus, "**were either dead or reduced to insignificance, when Claudius entrusted the province of Judaea to the Roman Knights or to his own freedmen, one of whom, Antonius Felix, indulging in every kind of barbarity and lust, exercised the power of a king** [being above the law, his will was law] **in the spirit of a slave.... Yet the endurance of the Jews lasted till Gessius Florus was procurator. In his time the war broke out**" (*The History,* Book V, 9-10; Modern Library ed., p. 663).

In *The Jewish War* Josephus commented on the procurators Albinus and Gessius Florus: "**Albinus... acted very differently, being guilty of every possible misdemeanour. Not content with official actions that meant widespread robbery and looting of private property, or with taxes that crippled the whole nation, he allowed those imprisoned for banditry by local courts or his own predecessors to be bought out by their relatives, and only the man who failed to pay was left in jail to serve his sentence... The result was that the victims kept their wrongs to themselves while those still immune, through fear of the same fate, flattered those they should have battered... Tyranny reigned everywhere; from then on the seeds of the coming destruction were being sown in the City.**

Such a man was Albinus, but his successor Gessius Florus made him appear an angel by comparison. Albinus for the most part did his mischief with secrecy and dissimulation; Gessius boasted of the wrongs he did to the nation and, as if sent as public executioner to punish condemned criminals, indulged in every kind of robbery and violence. When pitiable things happened, he showed himself the most heartless of men; when disgraceful things, the most disgusting... Making a profit out of individuals he considered poor sport: he stripped whole cities, ruined

2

complete communities, and virtually announced to the entire country that everyone might be a bandit if he chose, so long as he himself received a rake-off. The result of his avarice was that every district was denuded, and many people left their old homes and fled to foreign provinces" (*The Jewish War,* Book II, 14:1-2; Penguin ed., pp. 137-138).

Jewish lives were taken lightly during the time of the procurators; at the slightest sign of opposition or rebelliousness the procurators would stage a massacre, usually on the Temple Mount, at a time when masses of Jews were assembled there to celebrate the festivals. The condemned were hanged on crosses and left to die a slow and painful death. The Romans crucified not only Jesus, but also other saviors who emerged in large numbers due to the desperateness of the situation, on the one hand, and the hope for redemption, on the other.

Flavius Josephus – "Romanophile" – who, in the manner of a freed slave, took his family name from Emperor Vespasian and lived out the remainder of his days after the Destruction by the grace of the emperor and in his palace, tallies up the events of his day thus: "... for it was Florus who forced us to take up arms against the Romans, as we thought it better to be destroyed at once than by little and little" (*Antiquities*, Book XX, 11:1; Schocken ed., p. 526).

History is not an objective discipline. When dealing with nations in conflict, or with opposing world views, it cannot help but take a stand which identifies with one or the other side. Caesarea represents an extreme case of this conflict of world views. After prolonged close contact a fateful confrontation between the Jews and the Hellenistic world – a world shaped against the background of the *weltanschauung* of the Roman Empire – took place in this city. The hostile relations between the two ethnic groups – Jews and pagans – which began to develop here led, in the final analysis, to the greatest tragedy in Jewish history: the destruction of Jerusalem and the prolonged suffering of the Jewish people living in exile.

1

1 Kenishta de-Mardeta – *the remains of the synagogue in the Jewish quarter of Caesarea, on the slopes of Tel Sharshon. This is believed to be the synagogue over which the street fight between the Greeks and the Jews, which sparked off the Great Revolt, broke out.*

2 *Remains of Herod's palace, including a large swimming pool (35 x 18 m.) similar to the pools Herod built in his other palaces, as in Jericho, surrounded by magnificent rooms facing the pool, can be seen on the strip of land extending west of the theatre. Today only the eastern portion of the palace remains above water, yet even this part testifies to its regal splendor: the floors are tiled with mosaics; the middle of the mosaic of the central room displays a colorful carpet design of geometric shapes, in Roman style.*

touring roman caesarea

Touring the excavations at Caesarea enables us to comprehend and experience the historical clash which took place here between Judaism and the pagan world during the Roman era, not as a conflict of abstract ideas, but as events which happened to living human beings, oppressors and oppressed, scorners and scorned alike, men with beliefs and aspirations, wills and emotions. Visiting the excavations at Caesarea enables us to understand all this at first hand. Often one can point dramatically and with great accuracy to the sites in Caesarea where various fateful events in the history of Israel transpired. For example, touring the excavations of the Jewish quarter near the remains of Kenishta de-Mardeta, the "Synagogue of the Revolt," one can reconstruct most vividly that fateful Sabbath on which a brawl with the Greeks turned into the wholesale massacre of the Jews of Caesarea – the proximate cause of the outbreak of the Great Revolt.

Caesarea was built by Herod in 22 b.c.e., on the site of Straton's Tower, a small port town built in the Hellenistic period, apparently by 'Abd 'Ashtart, the Phoenician "king" of Sidon, a contemporary of Alexander the Great. The original name of the city was probably 'Ashtarton's Tower, which became distorted in Greek to Straton's Tower and in Hebrew to Sharshon's Tower. Sharshon's Tower stood on the shore, north of the moat protecting the northern Crusader wall, which still stands today. Tel Sharshon may be reached by a dirt path running north from the Crusader city's eastern gate, which leads to the excavations.

Tel Sharshon. Remains of a wall with a round tower in it have survived north of the tel. Some people believe this to be the wall of Herod's city. The high aqueduct which Herod built approaches this point from the north and passes over the remains of the wall.

Alexander Yannai conquered Sharshon's Tower, removed its gentile inhabitants and settled the town with Jews. Excavations

2

1

have shown that the Jewish quarter of Caesarea was located on the tel of Sharshon's Tower.

Kenishta de-Mardeta. Foundations of houses from the Hellenistic period and artifacts characteristic of this era were discovered on the rock of the tel. The foundations of a square building, with sides 9 meters long, were found above the Hellenistic remains. Its walls are as much as 1.2 meters thick and rise five courses high of cut stone. The potsherds and lamps discovered near it are Herodian and later. The fray which erupted between the Greeks and the Jews and which sparked off the conflagration of the Great Revolt in the Land of Israel is believed to have been fought on account of this synagogue, called in the Talmud *Kenishta de-Mardeta* or the "Synagogue of the Revolt."

There are a number of grounds for this view:

A. Several of the walls of this structure were incorporated in a fourth century c.e. building which is undoubtedly a synagogue. (A fragment of a Hebrew inscription listing the 24 shifts of priests who served in the Temple was found in it. Every synagogue for hundreds of years after the Destruction kept such inscriptions, thus expressing the hope that redemption might come at any moment and the priests would return to their holy service in the Temple. Part of a column with a relief of a six-branched candelabrum was also discovered here.)

B. Jews tended to build synagogues on the remains of earlier synagogues, as has been shown by excavations of synagogues throughout the country. Indeed, remains of synagogues from several periods have been found here.

C. The *Kenishta de-Mardeta,* according to the Talmud, was built on the shore. This building is indeed on the shore, across from the remains of the anchorage of Sharshon's Tower.

Thus we are now standing on the site where the most fateful chain of events in the history of the Jewish people began: the Great Revolt against Rome.

Let us leave Tel Sharshon and, returning through the eastern gate of the Crusader wall, enter the area of excavations.

The sewer system. Along the road leading west from the gate we can make out a sewer beneath the Herodian and post-Herodian paving. "Nay, the very subterranean vaults and cellars," wrote Josephus, "had as much care bestowed on them as the buildings above ground. Some of these vaults carried things at regular distances to the haven and to the sea; but one of them ran obliquely, and undergirt all the rest, that both the rain and sewage of the citizens were conveyed away with ease, and the sea itself at full tide entered the city, and washed it all clean" (*Antiquities,* Book XV, 9:6).

The acropolis. Walking along the street, whose remains are from the Crusader period, we soon reach a man-made hill which Herod's workmen created by building vaults and covering them with sandstone, described by Josephus as an "elevation." The center of Hellenistic and Roman cities generally had an acropolis, an elevated site for temples. Since the land here was flat, Herod created an artificial hill on which he built the "Augusteum," a shrine to Emperor Augustus, and a temple to the goddess of Rome. Niches which once held idols line the western wall of the Augusteum. The fragments of statues which we see here on the ground are from various periods of the Roman era. This was the center of life and ritual for Caesarea's non-Jewish inhabitants, in which the Jews of Caesarea could not take part because of religious proscriptions.

The port. The anchorage closest to shore of Caesarea's port, officially called Sebastus, after the Greek name of Augustus, was dredged west of the Augusteum. A promenade (see the sign on the acropolis) was built around the dock. South of the Augusteum we can still see the vaulted quarters (one of which has survived in its entirety) where the crews of the ships anchoring at Caesarea were housed. We must remember that sailors were slaves and, when they docked in a port, were put up in windowless buildings to prevent their escaping. During the Byzantine period the anchorage basin became filled with sand and ceased being used.

The main port was built in the sea. Josephus describes it as

1 During the Roman period large cities were founded in the Land of Israel. Local springs were inadequate to meet the demand for water in these heavily populated centers, especially in view of the numerous public and private baths that used vast amounts of water. From the Romans Herod learned to supply water from distant sources via aqueduct. He built this high aqueduct which brought water from the springs of Shumi, north of Binyamina, to Caesarea.

2 The ancient racecourse (hippodrome). "Bread and circuses" was the motto of life in Greco-Roman cities. In addition to its theatre, where shows were performed non-stop from morning to afternoon, Caesarea also had other places of entertainment. Horse races and chariot races were an integral part of the city's amusements.

3 This gem, a semiprecious stone with an engraved design, found in Caesarea, displays four horses pulling a racing chariot. Caesarea's hippodrome was one of the largest and most famous in the East. Racing scenes were a common motif on Roman coins and personal objects such as the signet ring shown here.

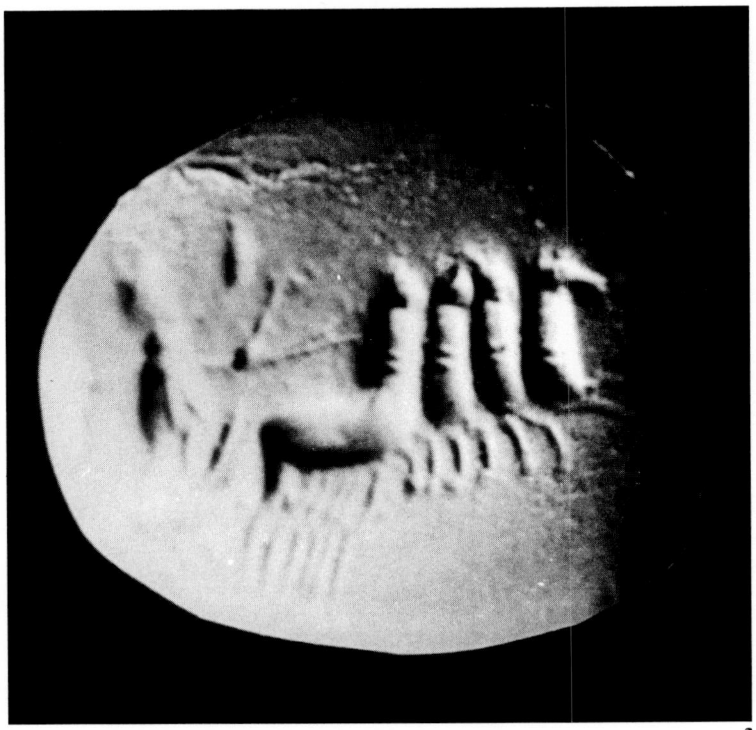

3

2

being "excellently constructed, which was the more remarkable from its being built in a place that of itself was not suitable for such a noble structure, but had to be brought to perfection by materials fetched from other places at very great expense...." (Indeed, there are many granite and marble columns lying on the shore, across from the restaurant. The granite was apparently imported from Aswan, Egypt, by way of the sea.) To rectify the inconvenience of having to ride at anchor out at sea, Herod also put down "huge stones of above fifty feet in length, and not less than eighteen in breadth, and nine in depth, twenty fathoms deep.... This mole which he built by the sea-side was two hundred feet long, and half of it was opposed to the force of the waves, so as to keep them off, and so was called break-water, and the other half had upon it a wall, with several towers at intervals..." (*Antiquities,* Book XV, 9:6; Schocken ed., p. 244). The southern breakwater extends from southeast to northwest, in the shape of a broad arch, to a length of about 600 meters. The northern breakwater extends 250 meters out to sea. The entrance to the port was from the northwest, since the dangerous winds were southwesterly. The entire area of the port was about 160 dunams (40 acres). The Crusader port, which today is used for bathing, covers only a fraction of the Herodian port, which extended much further north. Deep under the water, the piers' foundations have been discovered by American and Israeli archaeologists and divers.

The palace of Herod and his successors. Northwest of the theatre is a small peninsula which juts into the water. In its center there is a pool which after a storm at sea fills with salt water. The palace of Herod and his successors stood around this pool. East of the pool have been found mosaics, similar in style to the colorful floors discovered in Herod's palace on the banks of Wadi Qelt, near Jericho. The mosaics, which formed a colorful carpet of geometric designs, and the pool in the middle of the buildings are characteristic of Herod's palaces. In its day this pool was probably filled with sweet water. It is apparently to this palace that Agrippa I was carried after he had been poisoned by the Greeks at the theatre.

The theatre. "Herod also built therein a theatre of stone; and on the south side of the harbour behind an amphitheatre also, capable of holding a vast number of men, and conveniently situated for a sea view" (*Antiquities,* Book XV, 9:6; Schocken ed., p. 245). Josephus' comments on the amphitheatre essentially relate to the theatre. An amphitheatre is a round building lined with rows of seats, like the Colosseum in Rome. A theatre is a semicircular structure with seats situated above the orchestra (the circular place used by the Greek chorus) and *skene* (the proscenium, or stage, behind the orchestra). A theatre was discovered in the excavations. Aerial photographs have revealed the location of the amphitheatre, northeast of Caesarea, beyond the Crusader walls, although the site has not yet been excavated.

Herod was the first to build a theatre in the eastern realms of the Roman Empire. It appears that he viewed himself as an emissary of the Empire in matters of cultural life as well. The theatre which we see today is not entirely Herodian. Herod's theatre underwent repairs during the many years of its existence and was altered a number of times. Still its general plan and the pit which surrounds the orchestra are Herodian. "Bread and circuses" was the motto of life in Greco-Roman cities. Plays were shown in the theatre continuously, from morning to afternoon, and the audience coming to view them would bring themselves food for the entire day. Much Greek mythology was incorporated in the plays, which were accompanied by pagan rites. Therefore Jews who were true to their faith could not take part in them. Passing time at the theatre underscored the difference in way of life between Greeks and Jews. It was at the theatre that the Greeks poisoned the Jewish king Agrippa I, who had come to watch the amusements in his capacity as king of Judea and hence also sovereign of the Greeks in Caesarea.

The hippodrome. Life in a Roman-Hellenistic city called for diversions in addition to theatre performances; horse and chariot races were also indispensible. Caesarea's hippodrome, or stadium, is located several hundred meters east of the Crusader city, south of the road. Today the area is cultivated by *kibbutz* Sedot Yam. The hippodrome measured 460 meters from north to south, and 95 meters from east to west. Today a fragment of an obelisk and three segments of a granite cone lie in the center. The grooves in the cone were made later by Arabs who attempted to make it into grinding stones but could not succeed in cutting it. Another fragment of the obelisk was discovered elsewhere in the hippodrome, and according to calculations the complete obelisk once stood 27 meters tall. A low fence, called a *spina* or spine, generally bisected the hippodrome lengthwise. The obelisk and red granite cones stood at one end of this *spina* and were intended to startle the horses so that they would run faster. The races began at the northern end of the *spina* (today near the entrance to the hippodrome) and consisted of seven circuits around the *spina.* Seven balls would be placed on a high base at one end of the *spina,* and seven figurines of dolphins at the other. As each half-round was completed, one dolphin or one ball would be removed.

The spectators sat in seats built into the top of the steep slopes of the hippodrome, the length of its eastern and western sides. The rounded, southern end of the hippodrome was for the city's dignitaries. Excavations date the present hippodrome to the third century c.e. Yet it undoubtedly was preceded by a hippodrome built at Herod's behest, since Josephus mentions that at the inauguration of Caesarea there was "a great festival, and most sumptuous preparations were made at once for its dedication. For the king appointed contests in music and athletic exercises, and also got ready a great number of gladiators, and of beasts for like purpose: horse races also..." (*Antiquities,* Book XVI, 5:1; Schocken ed., pp. 280-281).

opposing worlds

Josephus mentions the hippodrome built by Herod in connection with an appalling event which occurred during the rule of Pontius Pilate, the procurator who executed Jesus. The former provocatively attempted to bring a bust of the emperor into Jerusalem. The Romans considered the emperor to be a god;

1 *Aerial view of Caesarea. Note the plan of the city, designed to provide its residents all that the Greco-Roman style of life in the city required. The historic confrontation between Judaism and the pagan world of the Roman era, so tangible in this city built by Herod, prompted the Sages' remark, "Caesarea and Jerusalem: if someone tells you that both have been destroyed, do not believe him; if he says that both are flourishing, do not believe him; if he says that Caesarea has been laid waste and Jerusalem is flourishing, or that Jerusalem has been laid waste and Caesarea is flourishing, you may believe him"* (Megillah *6a*).

1

thus this act was tantamount to introducing pagan gods into the Jews' holy city. The Jews came in vast numbers to Caesarea, the seat of the Roman procurator, which had become the capital of the Land of Israel after Herod's death, to beg the procurator not to defile their holy city. After hearing the Jews weeping for several days and rejecting their request, Pilate hid his soldiers in the hippodrome, so that when the Jews came once more to petition the procurator, he threatened to kill them if they did not cease entreating and weeping before him. The Jews responded that they were prepared to die if their holy city were defiled. The actual proof of their willingness to lay down their lives so astounded the procurator that he conceded and had the busts of the emperor removed from Jerusalem. This time the clash between these two worlds which did not understand one another ended with the Romans conceding. Incidentally, an inscription mentioning Pilate was found, out of place, in the excavations at the theatre. Today the stone on which the inscription is engraved stands next to the entrance to the theatre. This inscription is the only place where Pilate is mentioned, aside from the Gospels and the writings of Josephus.

While Jews may have been able to attend the races at the hippodrome, they could not participate in the "entertainment" in the amphitheatre. Here gladiator duels were held, and human blood was shed for the enjoyment of spectators. The amphitheatre was also used for executing people sentenced to death. (After the failure of the Bar Kokhba Rebellion, Rabbi Akiva was flayed to death in the amphitheatre of Caesarea.) According to Josephus, Herod also built an amphitheatre in Jerusalem, against the "laws of the forefathers," for, he wrote, the Jews could not tolerate killing and shedding blood, even of a criminal.

Thus in Caesarea two diametrically opposed worlds came face to face. Living beside one another led to friction. We must bear in mind that the Jews of Caesarea were wealthy and naturally were close in outlook to the hedonistic Hellenistic culture with its motto of "bread and circuses." The Greeks of Caesarea earned their living primarily from the army. Many of their sons served in the Roman forces, and during the riots and quarrels these Greeks naturally stood by their relatives.

Citizenship in Hellenist-Roman cities was conditional upon participating in the worship of the city's gods. The Jews could have no part in such worship; hence the Greeks tried to deprive them of their civil rights. The Jews claimed in response that Caesarea was a Jewish city since it had been built by a Jewish king. The Greeks replied that if Herod had wanted to build it as a Jewish city, he would not have built a temple to the gods in it. Given such polarization between the Greek populace of Caesarea and its wealthy Jewish residents, we can imagine the depth of antagonism which must have existed between the Greek population and the Roman officialdom – a privileged group, enjoying a high standard of living – on the one hand, and the Jewish masses – most of them peasants, oppressed and exploited by the Roman authorities and their Greek collaborators – on the other.

the course of the great revolt – 66 to 70 c.e.

The confrontation with the mighty Roman Empire, which brought on the greatest disaster in the annals of the Jewish people – the destruction of Jerusalem and the Temple – a major step in uprooting the Jews from their land, was caused by the polarity between the Romans' pagan world view, which deified the emperor and considered pagan rites an expression of loyalty to the empire, and the Jews' monotheistic world view, characterized in part by faith in redemption and the anxious awaiting of the coming of the Messiah. The direct causes of the revolt, however, were exploitation of the Jewish inhabitants of the land by the Roman procurators and use of wholesale slaughter to suppress the slightest sign of opposition to the Romans, if only in thought or in passively entertaining messianic hopes. In the last few decades before the Great Revolt any Jew could expect to die by a Roman's sword or by crucifixion, on the pretext of a riot. The Greek-speaking Syrian population, as well, added fuel to the fire. A privileged minority in the country, they hated the Jews and were the primary supporters of

1

1 *A relief found at Caesarea. In the center is a stone altar with offerings on it; on the left, a uniformed Roman soldier holding a case in his hand (for scrolls or jewelry?); and on the right, a nobleman wearing a toga and shoes.*

2

2 *Two enormous statues, undoubtedly not on their original sites but rather taken from some other location, were found flanking the gate of the central thoroughfare of Byzantine Caesarea, east of the Crusader city. The shorter the Roman emperors, the taller their statues, as evidenced by these two gigantic monuments. Since these figures are without heads (apparently having been beheaded by Arab conquerers, in whose religion idols are an abomination) we do not know which Roman emperors they represent. The statue shown here is made of white marble, the other of red porphyry.*

the Roman authorities. Almost the entire garrison stationed in Judea was raised from this group, and at the slightest sign of political unrest they would gleefully put down the Jewish masses with great bloodshed.

insurrection

The revolt began with the events at Caesarea – the seat of Roman rule over the Land of Israel since the abolition of Herod's dynasty – with the outrages perpetrated by the city's Syrian population against the Jews' holy objects and their mass slaughter of the Jews. (About 20,000 Jews were massacred; those who survived took the Torah scrolls and fled to Narbata, a Jewish city some 10 km. east of Caesarea.) Florus, the procurator, who supported the Greeks and sold the remaining Jews of Caesarea into slavery, further fanned the flame of revolt by pillaging the treasures of the Temple and massacring the Jews of Jerusalem, who had protested the events in Caesarea. Agrippa II, the Jewish king ruling the Golan, the Bashan, and a small part of the Galilee, tried to allay the people's wrath and almost succeeded; however, when he requested that the Jews also give in to Florus, open revolt ensued.

The revolt broke out at Masada and came to a close at Masada. Extremist Zealots for freedom, led by Menahem son of Judah the Galilean, the son of Hezekiah the Galilean, who had been executed by Herod and who founded the Zealot movement, took over Masada. Menahem wiped out the Roman garrison at Masada, seized the weapons in its depots, and returned to Jerusalem to assume leadership of the rebels (for the leadership of the revolt operated out of Jerusalem). A civil war erupted in Jerusalem between the city's aristocracy, who were generally doves, and the diverse supporters of the war. We must bear in mind that the Great Revolt also had characteristics of a social revolution. The most reliable fighters came from the poor, who were debtors to the land's wealthier inhabitants, and from the many landless, oppressed peasants and refugees from neighboring countries and outlying districts, who had fled to Jerusalem after the Syrian massacres of the Jewish population.

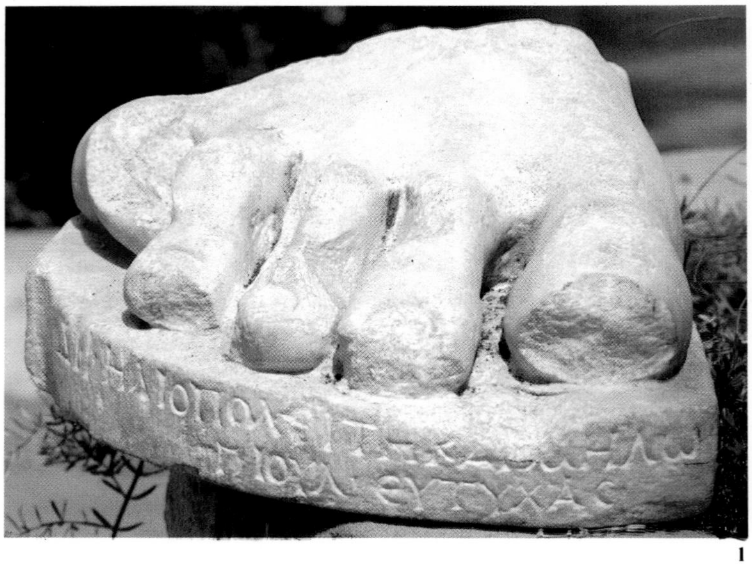

1

1 *On Mt. Carmel in ancient times there was a pagan oracle on the site of the present Carmelite Monastery. Vespasian, as was the Roman way, consulted the oracle before he set out to suppress the Jewish revolt. In the picture is a statue of a foot, found on Mt. Carmel, bearing a Greek inscription: "To Heliopolitan Zeus, god of the Carmel, from Gaius Eutychas of Caesarea."*

2 *Seleucia and Gamla are located on this map according to their former identifications – Gamla with al-Jamaliya, southeast of Wadi Ruqad, and Seleucia with an abandoned village off the Khushniyya-Yahudiyya road in the Golan. Today Gamla is identified with the hill between the fork of the Daliyyot and Gamla rivers. Seleucia is identified with the abandoned village of Dabbura.*

National leadership, initially in the hands of relatively moderate forces, emerged in Jerusalem. However the balance of power gradually shifted, placing extremists at the helm.

suppression of the revolt in the galilee

At first Cestius Gallus, the Roman procurator in Syria, tried to suppress the revolt with a Roman army which he brought from Syria and Greco-Syrian recruits from the coastal cities of the Land of Israel. He set up his base in Acre and from there turned to the Jewish border town of Cabul (the present-day Arab village of Kabul), bordering the plain of Acre and the Lower Galilee, and laid it to waste. Several villages in the Galilee surrendered without battle, foremost among them the city of Sepphoris (Ẓippori). Then he slaughtered the Zealots of the Galilee, who had fled from their villages and taken up fortifications on Mt. 'Aẓmon. En route to Jerusalem he laid waste the Jewish villages around Narbata* and Jaffa. His battle for Jerusalem ended in defeat, with the Jews destroying his army and pursuing him as far as Antipatris (Rosh ha-'Ayin).

Emperor Nero then chose Vespasian, a renowned and experienced general who had suppressed insurrections in Germany and had conquered Britain, to put down the Jewish revolt. Vespasian and his son Titus brought a large Roman army, sixty thousand strong, to the country. From Acre Vespasian set out to conquer the Jewish-settled Galilee, then under the command of Joseph son of Mattathias the Priest, later called Flavius Josephus. The main fortress obstructing his way to the Galilee was Yodefat. He approached it by way of the Siḥnin Valley, on his way capturing the Jewish village of Siḥni (today

---

* Narbata has recently been identified by the archaeologist Adam Zertal with Kh. Ḥammam, east of Baqa esh-Sharqiyya. Previously it had been identified by Benjamin Mazar with the site of the ruins near kibbutz Ma'anit.

vespasian's campaigns in the galilee, 67 c.e.

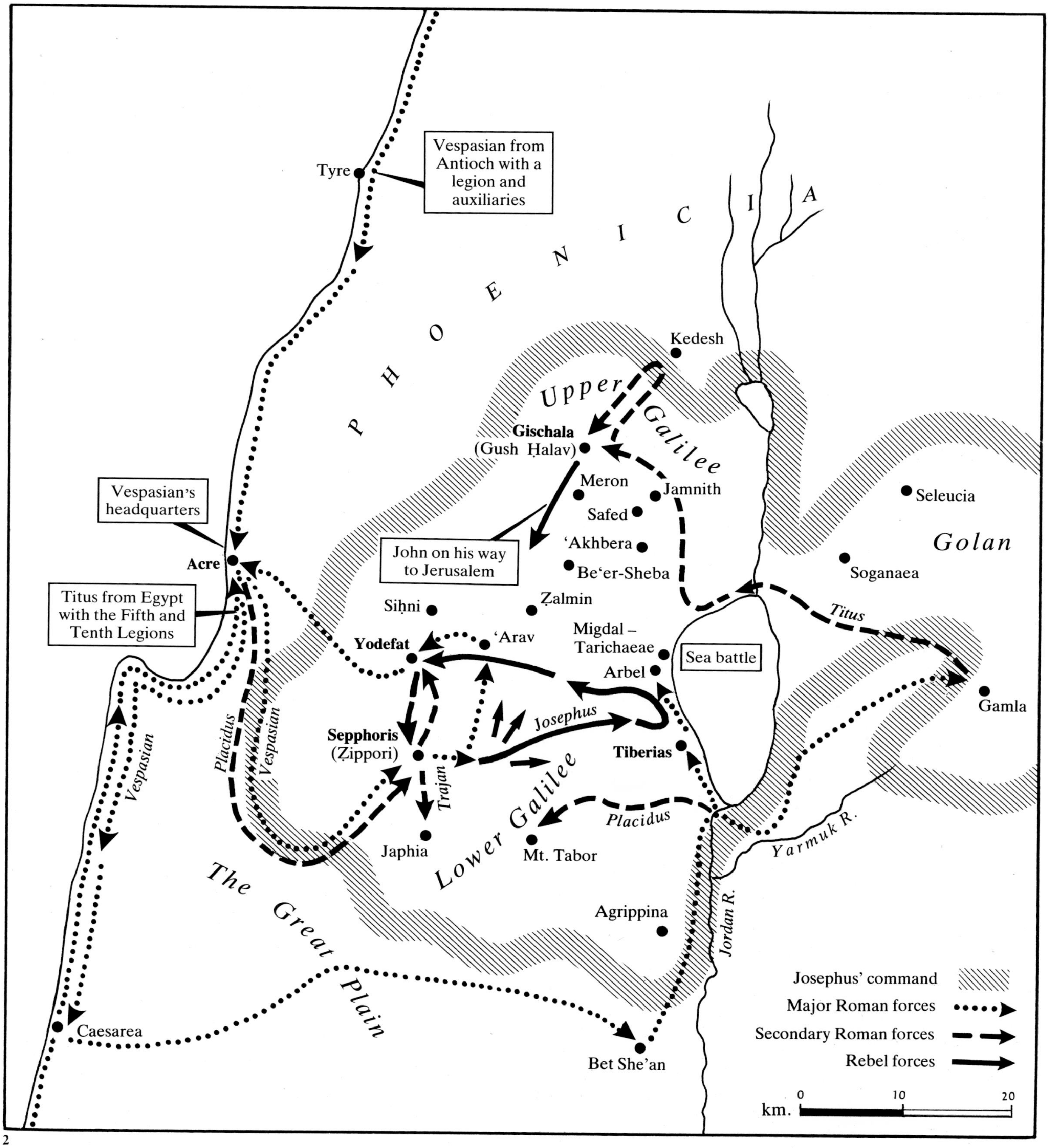
Vespasian from Antioch with a legion and auxiliaries
Tyre
PHOENICIA
Kedesh
Upper Galilee
Gischala
(Gush Ḥalav)
Meron
Jamnith
Safed
'Akhbera
Be'er-Sheba
Vespasian's headquarters
John on his way to Jerusalem
Acre
Titus from Egypt with the Fifth and Tenth Legions
Sihni
Ẓalmin
Yodefat
'Arav
Migdal – Tarichaeae
Arbel
Sea battle
Seleucia
Golan
Soganaea
Titus
Gamla
Sepphoris
(Ẓippori)
Josephus
Tiberias
Trajan
Placidus
Vespasian
Japhia
Lower Galilee
Mt. Tabor
Yarmuk R.
Jordan R.
The Great Plain
Agrippina
Caesarea
Bet She'an
Josephus' command
Major Roman forces
Secondary Roman forces
Rebel forces
km.
0
10
20

2

Arab Sakhnin) and 'Arav (today the Arab village 'Arraba, then a Jewish town mentioned in the Talmud in connection with the pious sage, Rabbi Ḥanina b. Dosa, who lived there). From 'Arav he moved his large army up the ridge of Yodefat, encamping above the city (at Kh. Jifat, near the present-day *moshav* of Yodefat). After fighting heroically and withstanding 47 days of siege in the brutal heat of summer, without water or salt, Yodefat fell to Vespasian. Josephus b. Mattathias, commander of the Galilee, then turned traitor to the Romans. As a prisoner of war he became Vespasian's slave, and when later freed he was given the name of Flavius, according to Roman law, after the surname of his former master, Vespasian. From then on he worked in the service of the Romans, agitating for surrender. While Yodefat was under siege, Roman generals were fighting the Jews elsewhere, as well. The general Trajan, father of the future Emperor Trajan, took Japhia (today the Arab village Yafa en-Naṣra, near Nazareth. In the vicinity of the churches of this village is the site of the ancient Jewish town of Japhia, during the Second Temple period the largest town in the Galilee. The Greek-Catholic church has a windowsill bearing a relief of a seven-branched candelabrum, taken from the synagogue and used in secondary construction. The synagogue was located above the Greek Orthodox church, on the site where remains of pillars and capitals have been found. Part of the mosaic floor from the Japhia synagogue is now housed in the Israel Museum in Jerusalem.) Jaffa, which the Jews had rebuilt, fell again after a bitter maritime battle. Most of the fighters in the fortress on Mt. Tabor were wiped out by stratagem, and the few who survived surrendered to the Romans when their supply of water ran out.

Tiberias, the second largest city in the Galilee, was split between a number of Jewish factions, Zealots and doves. After the defeat of the Jews in the western Lower Galilee the doves gained the upper hand, and the Zealots left the city, moving north to Tarichaea (Migdal). Tiberias surrendered without a battle. A fierce battle was waged over the highly fortified town of Tarichaea (Migdal), part of the battle being fought on the Sea of Galilee, which is said to have turned red from the blood of the slain. Tarichaea had many refugees, who fought the most desperately of all. The Romans cleverly brought about a split between some of the city residents and the refugees. After conquering Tarichaea, Vespasian broke his promise to spare all those who had fought. He gathered the refugees, who had set out unsuspectingly for Tiberias, into the hippodrome, slaughtered the weak among them, sent those who were fit for battle to Nero's army, and sold the rest into slavery. Henceforth the Jews in other places had no choice but to fight to the bitter end or to surrender immediately. After the battle of Tarichaea the remaining villages and towns of the Galilee surrendered, save for Gischala (or Gush Ḥalav, today the Maronite village Jish) in the Upper Galilee, under the leadership of John, and ancient Gamala (Gamla) in the Golan. Gamala was built on a rock scarp, surrounded by the deep gorges of Naḥal Gamla (to the north) and Naḥal Daliyyot (to the south). The Jews battled fiercely and bitterly at Gamla, heroically trying to defend the city, since it was the birthplace of the Zealot movement. The fighting became particularly bitter and heroic after the wall was breached and the scene of battle moved to the steep incline leading to the streets of the city. As on Masada, here too the wind worked to the benefit of the enemy: "But to ensure their [the Jews'] destruction they were struck full in the face by a miraculous tempest, which carried the Roman shafts up to them but checked and turned aside their own" (*The Jewish War,* Book IV, 1:10; Penguin ed., p. 218). Gamala predated Masada in mass suicide: about 4,000 fell at the hands of the Romans, and 5,000 "plunged to destruction" into the ravine surrounding the city.

John of Gischala (Johanan of Gush Ḥalav) stealthily escaped from his city to Jerusalem, and Gischala surrendered to the Romans.

By 67 c.e. the Galilee had been conquered. The Jewish Transjordan, as well, was conquered by the Romans. Vespasian himself led the force which took the districts of Lydda (Lod), Emmaus (near the Trappist Monastery in the Ayyalon Valley), and Timna. At Jericho his army joined the Roman forces returning from the conquest of the Transjordan.

Meanwhile Emperor Nero had been assassinated in Rome, and a struggle had erupted among the contenders to the throne, one of whom was Vespasian. Suppression of the revolt was suspended for a while, until the spring of 70 c.e. The Jews did not take advantage of this reprieve to reinforce themselves, but rather spent it fighting a bloody civil war in which one camp burned the other's stores of food. The Romans were glad to let

1

1 *A round tower in the wall of Sharshon's Tower.*

2 *A statue of one of the Muses, the nine goddesses of the arts in Greek mythology, in Caesarea's theatre. Statues of the Muses, especially the goddesses of poetry, music and drama, decorated theatres throughout the Roman Empire.*

the Jews fight one another and waited for them to exhaust their strength. Only after Titus had begun to lay siege to Jerusalem did the civil war cease.

the destruction of jerusalem

The siege of Jerusalem and destruction of the city lasted from early April, 70 c.e., to the first week in September of the same year. The attack on Jerusalem began from the north, at the natural weak point of the city (north of modern Damascus Gate, somewhat south of the Tombs of the Kings). The hastily constructed Third Wall, which encompassed Bezetha, the northern suburb of Jerusalem, fell first. Construction work on this wall, which Agrippa had initiated in a thorough manner, was halted by Emperor Claudius and was only resumed during the revolt. Next to be captured was the Antonia Fortress (on the site of the present-day Sisters of Zion Convent), which defended the Temple Mount from the north. In the beginning of the Hebrew month of Av (roughly corresponding to August) the Romans succeeded in overcoming the Jews' fierce resistance on the Temple Mount. On the 8th of Av the Romans set fire to the Temple. Upon consulting with his commanders (one of whom was the ex-Jew, Alexander Tiberius, nephew of the Jewish Hellenist philosopher, Philo of Alexandria), Titus, son of Vespasian, decided to burn the Temple in order to shatter the unity of the Jewish people and put an end to its insurrections.

The fighters who survived the battle on the Temple Mount retreated to the Upper City (from the modern Jewish Quarter to the Tower of David and south as far as present-day Mt. Zion). Simeon bar-Giora, who from the very outset had defended this part of the city, held out until the 8th day of the Hebrew month of Elul (roughly corresponding to September). In the Upper City the Jews fought from the sewers, just as they were to do some 1900 years later in the Warsaw Ghetto. Hunger, in the end, sealed the fate of the warriors. Masada held out three years longer, as did the fortress of Machaerus, east of the Dead Sea (its remains can be seen from north of the Dead Sea, near 'Enot Ẓuqim ('Ein Fashkha), on the foothills of the Mts. of Moab in Jordan).

The magnificent victory arch which Vespasian and Titus built in Rome to commemorate the suppression of the revolt, and which is almost completely intact to this day, testifies to the great importance which this victory had in the eyes of the Romans. Simeon bar-Giora, the leader of the revolt, was put to death during the victory procession by being thrown off the rock of Thermopylae in Rome. John of Gischala lived out his days in a narrow dungeon cell, and Flavius Josephus in the Emperor's palace. Flavius asserts that 1,100,000 Jews – about a fifth of the Jewish population of the Land of Israel – were slain in the revolt. Scholars believe this figure to be exaggerated, yet everyone agrees that the extent of the ruin and destruction was enormous. Jerusalem was laid waste and its Jewish community decimated; nevertheless the Jews remained an absolute majority in the Galilee, in the south of Mount Hebron, and in parts of the Shefela, the Judean foothills.

2

strongholds of the galilee

Menachem Zaharoni

Josephus, appointed commander of the Galilee, prepares for war.

"There are two Galilees, known as Upper and Lower, shut in by Phoenicia and Syria.... Small as they are, and encircled by such powerful foreign neighbours, the two Galilees have invariably held out against enemy attack; for the Galilaeans are fighters from the cradle and at all times numerous, and never has cowardice afflicted the men or a declining population the country" (*The Jewish War,* Book III, 3:1-2).

"Both parts of Galilee were assigned [by the government which was set up in Jerusalem upon the outbreak of the revolt] **to**

1 *The sages maintained that the fertile Siḥnin Valley lay in the tribal inheritance of Asher: "And He made him to suck honey out of the crag, and oil out of the flinty rock" (Deuteronomy 32:13) refers, they said in the homiletical literature, to Siḥnin and the neighboring villages. Old picturesque olive trees grow in the Siḥnin Valley to this day.*

2 *The Bet Netofa Valley, named after the ancient Jewish town of Bet Netofa which lay at its northeastern end (today Ḥurbat Bet Netofa, 2 km. west of 'Eilabun). In a rainy winter the eastern end of the valley becomes flooded and looks like a lake even in May.*

3 *Yodefat – the fortified hilltop encompassed by a wall, against the background of Mt. 'Azmon. The unfortified lower city, the main residential area, lay to the north, lower down the hill. Caves, some of which are large cisterns, can be made out on the hill, confirming Josephus' description of Yodefat's water sources.*

2

1

"From our hands nothing in the wide world has hitherto escaped; the Jews, we must admit, have not yet shown any sign of lying down under defeat. ...they face the dangers of war to defend the liberty of their country," Titus said, addressing his soldiers before battle (The Jewish War, Book III, 10:2; Penguin ed., pp. 208-209).

3

Josephus, son of Matthias, together with Gamala, the strongest city in that area" (*The Jewish War,* Book II, 20:4).

After appointing magistrates and making "rules for settling the internal problems of the cities [of the Galilee], he [Josephus] turned his attention to their safety from external foes. Realizing that the Romans would invade Galilee first, he fortified the most defensible positions, Jotapata [Yodefat], Bersabe [Galilean Be'er-sheba], Selame [Ẓalmon], Caphareccho, Japhia [Yafia'], and Sigoph [Segev?], Mt. Tabor, Tarichaeae [Migdal], and Tiberias, next fortifying the caverns near Lake Gennesareth [Kinneret] in Lower Galilee, and in Upper Galilee the rock called Acchabaron ['Akbara Boulder], Safed, Jamnith [Yavnit], and Meron. In Gaulonitis [Golan] he strengthened the defences of Seleucia, Soganaea, and Gamala. Only in Sepphoris [Ẓippori] were the citizens invited to build a wall on their own responsibility: Josephus saw that they had ample means and that their enthusiasm for the war needed no stimulus. In the same way Gischala [Gush Ḥalav] was fortified by John, son of Levi, on his own responsibility at the request of Josephus" (*The Jewish War,* Book II, 20:6).

"I built walls round Seleucia and Soganaea, two towns highly fortified by nature itself; likewise I fortified with walls the towns of the Upper Galilee that are situated in rocky terrain: Jabne [Jamnith, Yavnit], Meron and Acchabaron. I also fortified several cities in the Lower Galilee: Migdal [Tarichaeae], Tiberias and Sepphoris, and the towns of the Arbel caves, Be'er-sheba [in the Galilee], Selame, Jotapata, Capharecchо, Siḥni, Japhia [Yafia'] and Mt. Tabor" (*Josephus: Life,* ch. 37).

Joseph son of Matthias the priest (known to us as Josephus) took as his primary task the fortification of the major cities of the Galilee (Ẓippori, Tiberias, 'Arav and Migdal). The Zealots' strongholds, including those whose construction Josephus attributes to himself, were built in strategic spots where the topography made access difficult and provided a natural defense. Yet this had an inherent disadvantage, for the strongholds had no sources of water within them. Water was normally available in the river valleys nearby, but the residents of the strongholds now had to manage with rainwater collected in wells. Quite a number of fortresses were built to block transportation arteries which were either financially important to the Roman empire or provided access to centers of Jewish settlement in the Galilee.

When, after withstanding 40 days of siege, Yodefat finally fell, Josephus, commander of the revolt in the Galilee, defected to the Romans. Betrayed by their leader, his men put one another to death, rather than fall captive to the Romans. Although a prisoner of Vespasian, Flavius Josephus was well treated by him and, accompanying his army, appealed on behalf of the Romans to the Jewish fighters to surrender.

the great revolt revisited
gamla – a heroic stand

Shmaryahu Guttman

as told to benjamin gevirtzman

"... but Gamala had refused to surrender, relying on its inaccessibility.... Sloping down from a towering peak is a spur like a long shaggy neck, behind which rides a symmetrical hump, so that the outline resembles that of a camel [Heb. *gamal*]**; hence the name [Gamala].... On the face and both sides it is cut off by impassable ravines. Near the tail it is rather more accessible, where it is detached from the hill; but here too, by digging a trench across, the inhabitants made access very difficult. Built against the almost vertical flank the houses were piled on top of one another, and the town seemed to be hung in air and on the point of tumbling on top of itself from its very steepness. It faced south and its southern crest, which rose to an immense height, served as citadel, resting on an unwalled precipice that went straight down into the deepest ravine. There was a spring inside the wall at the far side of the town ..."** (*The Jewish War*, Book IV, 1:1; Penguin ed., p. 213).

Thus, in *The Jewish War,* Josephus describes Gamla (ancient Gamala), the city which fought Vespasian's huge army during the Great Revolt and succeeded in repulsing it, before ultimately being captured in a ruthless battle and destroyed.

For many years Gamla* was identified with the spot bearing the Arabic name Jamaliya, actually located in the Bashan, beyond the Ruqad Wadi, and not in the Golan. Then the archaeologist Shmaryahu Guttman came along and located it somewhere else altogether, on a mountain ridge northeast of the Sea of Galilee. Moreover, he even determined exactly where on that ridge the ruins of the city lay and gave instructions where to dig. Indeed, the ruins of the unusual synagogue, to be discussed later at greater length, were discovered precisely where he indicated.

Shmaryahu Guttman recounts:**

"After the Six Day War the Department of Antiquities requested me to make an archaeological survey of the Golan. The survey, which lasted on and off for an entire year, brought to light two extremely distinct periods of habitation in the Golan during ancient times: one during the Early Bronze age and the other during the period of the Second Temple and the Mishnah and Talmud, most of the findings being from the later period. Between these two periods there was a big gap, a period with no significant settlements and no significant distribution of population.

"The period of the Jews' war against the Romans has occupied me since my days in the youth movement. I spent much time thinking, reading, and doing research, and all my work on Masada stemmed from that. Thus, going up to the Golan, from the very outset I thought about Gamla. It was only natural for me to search for the town which had been at the center of the historic events of the revolt against the Romans. I was also intrigued by the great difference between Gamla and Masada, Gamla appearing on the scene at the beginning of the revolt, as a populated town, naturally fortified, and the site of one of the battles which were fought to the bitter end in this revolt; Masada appearing on the scene at the end of the revolt, as a fortress, protected only by a handful of Zealots.

"Just as I was once impelled to discover what had prompted the Romans to bring a mighty armed force into the desert to

1

* Gamla is in the Golan Heights, overlooking the Sea of Galilee.

** Shmaryahu Guttman relayed this account in April 1979. Since then further excavations have been completed.

conquer Masada, so too, I was driven by the challenge to find out why the Romans had sent such a mighty armed force against Gamla and why they had destroyed it with such venom, razing it to the very ground.

"I did not accept the claims of various scholars who located Gamla in the Bashan. I felt there was but one reason for this mistaken identification: the noted Roman historian, Pliny.

"Identification of Gamla hinged on the location of the city of Tarichaea, on the western shore of the Sea of Galilee. Josephus

1 *"Sloping down from a towering peak is a spur like a long shaggy neck, behind which rides a symmetrical hump, so that the outline resembles that of a camel; hence the name [Gamala].... On the face and both sides it is cut off by impassable ravines. Near the tail it is rather more accessible, where it is detached from the hill; but here too, by digging a trench across, the inhabitants made access very difficult"* (The Jewish War, *Book IV, 1:1*).

wrote that Gamla lay east of the Sea of Galilee, in the Golan, in a line with Tarichaea. Pliny wrote in his *Natural History* that Tarichaea lay south of Tiberias, while everything Josephus said indicated that the city lay north of Tiberias.

"I believe Pliny to have been completely wrong. What is more, he may well have relied only on hearsay evidence in distant Rome, whereas Josephus was the commander-in-chief of the Galilee, and his evidence was first hand."

three clues

"Early scholars, who held that Gamla was located in the Bashan, relied more on Pliny than on Josephus, and herein, apparently, lay their error. For Josephus is remarkably accurate in the details which he gives of geographic information, place descriptions, and accounts of battles. One simply needs to know how to read him. After all, Josephus was a Jew from the Land of Israel, a sage and a Jerusalem aristocrat of a priestly family; in other words, he was a man who knew his country well and was acquainted at first hand with the various towns of the Galilee, which he himself fortified in anticipation of the war against Rome. Since my research on Masada I have come to accept him as a reliable guide.

"Here I wish to say that I do not in the least accept his world outlook or his personal behavior during the war. Had I lived in his day and been in a position to do so, I would surely have gone so far as to order him executed for going over to the Roman side.

"Nor do I hold his military talent in the least regard. He was certainly a military historian, but I am not sure he had any ability as a general.

"However, let us return to identifying the site of Gamla.

"Josephus gives us three pieces of information which establish its location: a geographic description, a topographic description, and information describing its precise location in the general topography.

Let us examine them:

Geographic: east of the Sea of Galilee, on the Golan Heights, across from Tarichaea. If we can locate Tarichaea we can also find Gamla.

Topographic: Gamla is flanked by ravines on the south and north and a very steep slope on the west, and is accessible, although only with great difficulty, from the east.

Topographic situation: the city lies on the southern slope of the spur.

Thus, to begin with, we must locate Tarichaea. Pliny, as mentioned, said the city was south of Tiberias, but as I have said, I believe this to be an error. Josephus makes no mention of whether it was north or south of Tiberias. Indeed, Jewish sources do not mention the name Tarichaea at all. On the other hand, the name Migdal Nunaya (Migdal of the Fish), which does not appear at all in Josephus, is mentioned in connection with the same general area. Thus this Jewish name appears to correspond to the Hellenistic name Tarichaea, meaning literally, "place of the fish salters." This spot is identified today with Migdal, at the entrance to the Ginnesar Valley from the direction of Tiberias.

"In another of his books, *Life,* Josephus mentions Agrippa cutting off Gamla from the Galilee by stationing his army north of the Sea of Galilee. If indeed Gamla lay in the Bashan, as early scholars erroneously claimed, stationing an army where Josephus describes would have been senseless.

"This leads us to conclude that we must look elsewhere for Gamla.

"The suggestion which finally led me to the place where we identified Gamla was put forward by Yitzḥaki Gal, my assistant in the archaeological survey of the Golan. It was after we had completed our survey, as Yitzḥaki was dealing with matters of the terrain. One day he climbed a certain ridge in the Golan, looked around and decided this was where Gamla had stood.

"He called me, brought me to the village of Deir Qruḥ and directed my eyes west, towards Naḥal Daliyyot, which splits into a southern watercourse and a northern watercourse, with all of the Ginnesar Valley lying in the distance. What we beheld was a ridge lined by a northern ravine, a southern ravine, a steep precipice to the west, and a possible path descending east – exactly as Josephus described.

"The first question I confronted then as an archaeologist was whether there were any signs of habitation here. I looked closely at the slope and decided that the entire southern flank, on its eastern side, might possibly have been surrounded by a wall.

"We walked down to the site and immediately discovered that the south side of the ridge was covered with potsherds, a clear

1 *A corner in Gamla's synagogue. Only one segment of the corner column, in the heart-shape characteristic of Galilean synagogues, has survived.*

2 *Three rows of seats were built around the walls of the Gamla synagogue. The rows of pillars which divided the nave from the aisles flanking it can still be made out. The ravine of Naḥal Daliyyot dictated that the entrance to the synagogue face southwest and not, as customary, directly towards Jerusalem.*

1

sign of habitation. The northern flank, on the other hand, had not a single potsherd. Again, it was just as Josephus had written.

"Josephus mentioned that Gamla had been inhabited in two periods: one, when it was conquered by Alexander Yannai (Jannaeus) the Hasmonean, during the Hellenistic period, and the other during the Roman period, in the time of the Great Revolt. The potsherds, to our great satisfaction, matched these two periods exactly. They also made it clear to us that the settlement which existed here suddenly ceased in the first century c.e. (approximately during the Great Revolt) and was never rebuilt – again evidence that this could indeed have been Gamla.

" 'Whoever finds one Hasmonean coin will have made a great discovery,' I said at the time to my fellow workers. And the great discovery came about; during our first half hour there we came upon a Hasmonean coin.

"In the wake of all this I resolved to excavate the city. Neither the decision nor its execution were easy. I was under considerable pressure from various sides. To begin with there were intellectual pressures; many colleagues, archaeologists, did not believe I would find anything of importance here. Hence I was full of apprehension, lest what they said prove true. There was also a physical fear: a natural rock-slide of the 'crushing boulders' which had fallen from the top of the hill to the vicinity of the city posed a considerable safety hazard. There were also considerable difficulties with access to the site. The paucity of leading signs of ruins on the surface led to further difficulty. A major difficulty was lack of funds, due to the skepticism that this was indeed Gamla. People doubted whether it was really worth spending money on an archaeological excavation here.

"In the end we succeeded in solving the financial problem with the aid of several bodies: the Department of Antiquities, the JNF, crucial practical assistance from the IDF, without which we would not have been able to move, and the aid of Yeruḥam Gittleman, a Mexican Jew. The *kibbutzim* also helped us greatly: the United Kibbutz Movement contributed ... my own services and a car, and the *kibbutz* departments for studying Israel assisted greatly in the excavation work, along with many volunteers from the youth movements and from abroad."

beyond our wildest dreams

"The next step was to decide where to begin digging. The city extended over some 45 acres, an area of considerable size,

2

which can not be excavated all at once. Therefore I had to select a spot of particular interest, where excavating was likely to yield significant results.

"My point of departure, therefore, was the wall east of the city. I decided to dig at a certain point on either side of the wall, in order to reveal its original appearance. The wall, however, extended 320 meters from the summit to the foot of the hill. Where was one to begin? I spent many days reviewing the area, walking the length of the wall time and again, until I settled on a certain spot where I had found several stones which were more finely hewn than the rest and a fragment of a basalt column. From these stones I concluded that a magnificent building had once stood here. Indeed, shortly after we began excavating at this point, we discovered that it was a synagogue. This was far more than we had hoped for when we began excavating.

"This synagogue was one of the earliest unearthed in the Land of Israel. It was destroyed in the time of the Great Revolt, which means that it existed when the Temple was still standing.

"This find leads to extremely interesting conclusions regarding the role of the synagogue among the Jewish people. For if synagogues existed before the Destruction, and if alongside sacrificial worship in the Temple, Jews also had the custom of praying, reading and studying the Torah in the synagogue, then the synagogue may have been what preserved Jewish culture and religion after the destruction of the Temple, by continuing traditions which existed before the Destruction. This would indicate that there was no sudden change from centralized worship in the Temple to decentralized worship in synagogues scattered over the country.

"There is a further significance to this synagogue: it is the architectural prototype of later synagogues built in the Galilee and the Golan, for in them we see a continuation of its style. Thanks to it, we also see how synagogues developed: in Gamla people prayed facing the entrance, and the Torah scrolls were kept in a side room (sometimes in an ark which was kept there) from which they were brought into the prayer hall of the synagogue to be read. Some structural differences appear in later synagogues, allowing the Torah scrolls to be stored in the prayer hall itself; and later still, the Torah shrine becomes an organic part of the building, pre-planned in the design.

"Remains of a conduit channeling rainwater from the roof of the building were found next to the synagogue. We dug along the conduit and reached a *mikveh,* a ritual bath. This *mikveh* is different from the one discovered on Masada, and this season we plan to continue excavations around it in order to learn more about how it corresponds to the Jewish law regarding ritual baths.

"Bringing to light many details about the war in which the city fell is valuable in its own right. This may be the first time archaeological excavations enable us to describe how the Roman legions conquered a city.

"In this respect Gamla differs from Masada. In Masada we only see the preparations for war: camps, a rampart and a battery. No signs of the battle itself are visible there. In Gamla, on the other hand, signs of the actual deployment of forces, of

1

1 *"There the Jews inflicted heavy casualties on their attackers, rolling down rocks and hurling missiles of every kind.... But to ensure their destruction they [the Jews] were struck full in the face by a miraculous tempest, which carried the Roman shafts up to them but checked and turned aside their own. So violent was the blast that they could neither keep their feet on the narrow ledges, having no proper foothold, nor see the approaching enemy. Up came the Romans and hemmed them in: whether they resisted or tried to surrender their fate was the same..."* (The Jewish War, *Book IV, 1:10; Penguin ed., pp. 218-219).*

2 *Looking at this hill, Yitzhaki Gal of* kibbutz *Afiqim decided Gamla must be located here, for the site matched exactly the description given by Josephus.*

2

1 *"Built against the almost vertical flank the houses were piled on top of one another, and the town seemed to be hung in air and on the point of tumbling on top of itself from its very steepness" (*The Jewish War, *Book IV, 1:1). The houses of the city are revealed along the steep southern slope, each house providing a supporting terrace for the one above it. The synagogue is at the top of the slope, and remains of the wall are visible to the east.*

the city's attack and its defense, have been found. The sensation we experienced while digging there was expressed well by several of the participants: 'We are losing the dimension of time. We feel as if everything were happening now, as if we ourselves are actually in the war...'

"As I said, we excavated on both sides of the wall. The first find was an enormous quantity of slingstones, shot by the offense at the defense. This was the stage of softening up the

1

enemy. Many nails, used by the Romans to build ladders for climbing over the wall, were also discovered outside the wall. Inside the city arrowheads of two main kinds were discovered: arrows shot by bows, and larger arrows shot by catapults, either one after another or in salvos.

"These findings were analyzed meticulously. We found, for example, that the Romans had not shot the stones directly at the wall, but rather in a steep trajectory so that they would land on the defending forces from a great height, gaining speed in their fall and thus making their blow more destructive. The steep trajectory was also intended to deflect the attention of the defense from activities in front of the wall by making them look up in an attempt to avoid the falling stones, thus enabling the fighters at the foot of the wall to climb it unhindered.

"We also found that these stones were concentrated as far as possible at the points where the attackers breached the walls, and that the percentage of hits was very high: over 90%. After all, direct hits were imperative since such shot does not explode and, to be effective, had to strike its target directly. What this means is that the Roman marksmen were very adept and that they had scientists who could calculate with high precision the steep trajectory of the stones which they shot.

"With respect to the arrows, too, we took care to record exactly what direction they faced when they fell, what percentage of them hit, and what percentage missed and were bent by hitting a stone, for instance.

"All this enables us to analyze in great detail the techniques of warfare used by the three Roman legions that conquered Gamla. It reveals that the Romans used techniques of softening up the enemy and concentrating forces at the breach points.

"The information we are gathering is very important to the study of the history of warfare and will undoubtedly contribute to our knowledge in this field.

"Other interesting findings relating to the war have also emerged. For example, Josephus writes about a tower in the wall, under which the Romans tunneled, causing it to collapse. And indeed, at the top of the cliff, at the end of the wall, we found the foundations of a tower which had collapsed.

"Aside from our important research in this field, we embarked on another, new field of inquiry. We climbed up to the part of the city which was not in the face of the battle when the Romans broke into it. This part was very wealthy, with high level construction, proving that Gamla, which served as a district capital, was a flourishing settlement. The architecture here is reminiscent of the capital, Jerusalem, in the same period. We found fragments of frescoes, like those in Herod's palaces, and interior columns and arches, like those in Jerusalem's houses. The topography of the city, however, required its builders to use techniques which we have not encountered elsewhere. We still do not know how one house related to the next, nor how the streets ran here. It seems that the architecture and city-planning employed by the builders of this town assumed a unique form, like a "beehive" hung on the edge of a precipice.

"It should be mentioned that the city was thoroughly and methodically plundered. Excavation of the area not damaged in the war revealed buildings which remained intact after the conquest but were completely empty. Not a thing was found in them, for everything they had once contained had been taken by the enemy conqueror.

"What led the Romans to attack Gamla with such force and afterwards to empty it of all its inhabitants?

"To answer this question we must recall the history of the Great Revolt, which broke out in 66 c.e. After the eruption of the revolt the Romans sent a large army under Cestius to conquer Jerusalem. This army came as far as the very walls of Jerusalem, and conquest of the city lay within its reach, since many of Jerusalem's inhabitants were willing to open the city gates to Cestius. Yet, for some reason (which even Josephus does not explain persuasively), Cestius did not conquer the city and his entire force fled in disgrace, the Zealots attacking from the rear the entire course of his retreat.

"This defeat must have sorely hurt Roman pride. But it was not merely a question of honor. The Romans feared lest this Jewish victory stir up insurgency in other states neighboring the Land of Israel. And yet another fear was that the Jews of Parthia, who were a considerable factor in that country, one of Rome's enemies at the time, would assist the Jews of the Land of Israel in their war against Rome in order to tie up the Roman army and prevent it from acting with a free hand in the war against the Parthians."

2

2 *Gamla's synagogue, after partial restoration (viewed eastward toward Naḥal Daliyyot and the path ascending to Gamla). Built as a rectangular hall (33 by 50 feet), a row of columns once stood near either of the long sides. The walls were lined with rows of benches, four on the northeast, three along each of the two longer sides, and two on the southwest, flanking the entrance. The congregation sat on these benches, generally facing the entrance and toward Jerusalem. Above the rows of seats is a level raised area with another bench on it, apparently the women's gallery. In plan the synagogue resembled the assembly hall of the Greco-Roman* boule, *the legislative council that ran the economic, social and cultural life of the* polis. *The Jews in the Roman world adopted this plan for places of prayer and gathering before the destruction of the Second Temple.*

gamla's end

"All these facts led the Roman leadership to discuss the matter in depth and to decide on a more strong-armed policy, including systematic renewed conquest of the entire Land of Israel. To this end a large Roman army, several legions strong, was dispatched to the Land of Israel under the command of Vespasian, who had already won a reputation in his wars on Spain and England. This army, later placed under Vespasian's son Titus, set out for the Land of Israel and conquered city after city, until it finally captured Jerusalem and destroyed the Temple.

"The fact that the Jews did not have a regular trained army made the Romans' work easier. Nevertheless, freedom-loving Jews in every village and town banded together and fought the Romans with great drive and determination. Yet nowhere could they withstand the mighty military prowess of the Romans on their own.

"Gamla itself provides a good example.

"When Vespasian reached Gamla's wall he succeeded in breaching it in his very first onslaught. The Jews, however, managed to turn the tables. The Romans penetrated full force into the city, with Vespasian at their lead, and began to press into the narrow passages between the houses. Seemingly retreating from the enemy, the Jewish fighters decided to move further up towards the crest. When the Romans had worked themselves well into the narrow alleys of the city, the Jews suddenly turned round and stormed the enemy, fiercely descending on them from above.

"Here we see how a regular army may be well trained in certain battle arrays; however, when it encounters an unusual situation it finds itself at a loss and is likely to be routed by a much smaller force. And so it was that, seeing the Jews descending on them down the slope, the Romans lost their heads. Those in the fore turned round to flee, but the new forces pouring in through the breaches in the wall, unaware of what was happening, pushed them back uphill. Terrible bedlam resulted. Many Romans fell off the rooftops and were killed. Others were trapped one after another in the alleys between the houses and were killed. Many Roman soldiers had fallen before their comrades understood what was happening. Those left alive turned about and fled from the city.

"Vespasian himself was one of the last to leave the city, fighting valiantly against the Jews as he retreated step by step, until he was outside the wall.

"Had a Jewish force been marshalled at this point to attack the depressed and defeated Romans, the course of history might not have been radically altered, but the story of this battle would have ended differently. The Jews, however, did not have any such force. Thus the Romans returned to their camp and, after a rallying speach by Vespasian (a fine example of what to say to a routed army), were willing to lick their wounds and return to the fray.

"This time, however, the Romans had learned a lesson. In the second offensive, which came a while later, only about 200 cavalry and infantry, commanded by Titus, penetrated the city, under heavy cover of stone shot.

"The outcome of this battle was not like Masada. There all the inhabitants and fighters took their own lives. Here the story ended differently. Most of the city's residents apparently succeeded in escaping down the steep western slope, while the commander of the city, Joseph son of the midwife, gathered all his soldiers and fought in hand-to-hand combat with the enemy, until the last of the Jewish fighters fell in battle.

"Thus the proud city of Gamla met its end."

Catapult: an arrow launcher with a range several times that of a normal archer.

Ballista: a kind of mortar for launching heavy ballistic stones in a steep trajectory and over a great distance.

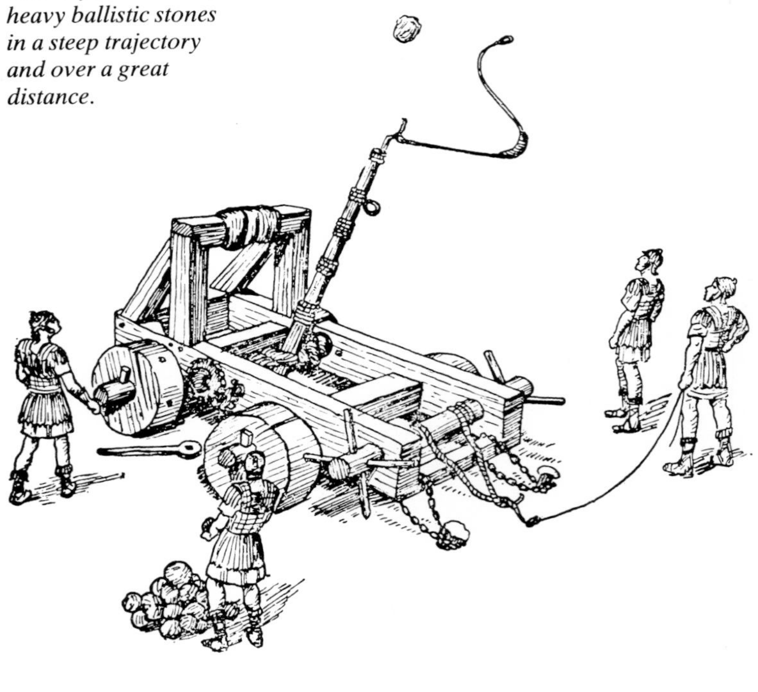

Battering-ram: a beam with a heavy iron head, used to batter defense walls and undermine their foundations. So named after the custom of shaping the end like a horned ram's head.

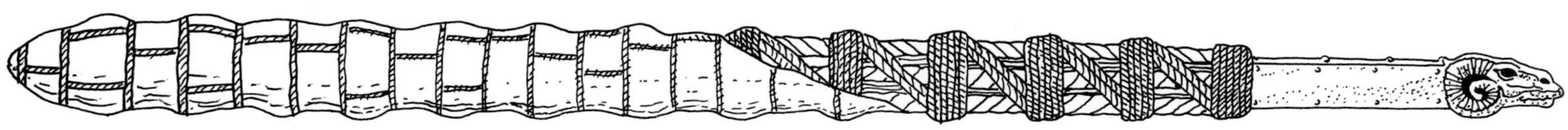

how the romans were repulsed at gamla

Josephus describes the battle in which the Romans breached Gamla's walls, and were repulsed by the defenders of the city.

Vespasian set out from Ammathus [Ḥammat], where he had been encamped before Tiberias, and marched to Gamala. Unable to put an unbroken ring of men round the town because of its situation, he posted sentries wherever he could and occupied the hill that overlooked it. When the legions had fortified their camps in the usual way on its slopes, he began to construct platforms at the tail end. In the eastern part of the ridge where rose the highest of the towers the construction was done by the Fifteenth Legion, the Fifth worked opposite the middle of the town, and the filling in of the trenches and ravines was undertaken by the Tenth...

With so many skilled hands the platforms were soon finished and the engines brought up. Chares and Joseph, the most effective leaders in the town, lined up their armed forces, ... and led them out on to the wall. For a time they beat back those who were bringing up the engines, but becoming the target for the catapults and stone-throwers they withdrew into the town. Then the Romans brought up the Rams at three points, and battering their way through the wall poured in through the breaches with a great blare of trumpets and din of weapons, and shouting themselves hoarse flung themselves upon the defenders of the town. They for a time stood firm against the first waves of attackers, and offering strenuous resistance prevented the Romans from advancing further. But under heavy pressure from all directions they withdrew to the upper parts of the town, and as the enemy pursued them they swung round and counter-attacked vigorously. Swept down the slope and jammed inextricably in the narrow alleys, the Romans suffered fearful casualties. Unable either to resist those above them or to force their way through the advancing mass of their companions, they climbed on to the roofs of the houses where they rested against the slope. Crowded with men and unequal to the weight these quickly collapsed. As one fell it knocked down many of those underneath, and so on to the bottom. The effect on the Romans was devastating. Completely at a loss, even when they saw the roofs falling in they jumped on to them. Many were buried under the debris, many while trying to escape found one limb or another pinned down, still more were choked by the dust. Seeing in this the hand of God and indifferent to their own losses, the men of Gamala pressed their attack, driving the enemy on to the roofs as they stumbled in the steep, narrow ways, and with a rain of weapons from above dispatching those who fell. The debris furnished them with any number of great stones, and the bodies of the enemy with cold steel: they wrenched the swords from the fallen and used them to finish off those who were slow to die. Many as the houses were actually falling flung themselves to their death. Not even those who fled found it easy to get away; for unacquainted with the roads and choked with the dust they could not even recognize their friends, but in utter confusion attacked each other. At last after long search they found the outlets and escaped from the town.

Vespasian, keeping as close as he could to his struggling soldiers, and deeply moved by the sight of the town falling in ruins about his army, had forgotten his own safety, and without realizing it had gradually reached the highest level of the town, where he found himself in the utmost peril and almost alone.

The Jewish War, Book IV, 1:3-5 (Penguin ed., pp. 214-215).

the great revolt revisited
masada shall not fall again

Mike Livneh

What has made Masada more famous than any other tourist attraction of its type? What is so special about this site?

Everything. The diamond-shaped hill with sheer sides and a top flat as a table; the marvelously well preserved antiquities, skillfully uncovered with awesome care and preserved with an investment of means, know-how and reverence; the fascinating story of the defenders of Masada, besieged by the Romans; the mood of the surrounding desert landscape, an ancient landscape barely touched by the modern world.

the history of masada

Four main periods have left their mark on Masada:

The Hasmoneans, who first built the fortress of Masada, were here between 100 and 60 b.c.e. They built a palace, a water-storage system and roads.

Herod, King of Israel from 40 b.c.e. to 4 c.e., undertook vast construction projects throughout the entire land, but especially at Masada. Most of what we see today on Masada was built by Herod; everything built before him appears to have been either renovated or torn down to the ground and rebuilt by him. Hence it is difficult to establish which structures on Masada were built by the Hasmoneans and which by Herod. Josephus Flavius (Joseph b. Mattathias) attributes the wall, the northern palace, the water system, the storerooms and more all to Herod.

The Great Revolt. A great number of Zealots lived on Masada from 66 to 74 c.e. Even after crowding into the existing buildings, magnificent palace halls, or narrow barracks and casemates, housing was insufficient. Hence the Zealots built themselves additional abodes in the form of humble, narrow rooms whose thin walls were built of small, unhewn stones cemented together with large quantities of plaster. Such rooms were mostly built in clusters which can hardly be called buildings or even houses and were frequently erected adjacent to an existing structure such as a wall, palace, or barracks.

Although these humble abodes are a far cry from Herod's magnificent palaces, they are more precious to us than all the treasures of kings and are not to be disparaged, for they represent the rebels whose heroism we admire. It is the story of the rebels' fight against Rome which we hope to bring alive for you in your visit to Masada.

In the Byzantine period Masada was inhabited by Christian monks who wished to lead a life of seclusion in the desert. They dwelled in caves and unused cisterns and built themselves a fine church. The Byzantine period forms a chapter of its own in the history of Masada.

natural defenses and man-made fortifications

Nature endowed Masada with excellent defenses. On the border of two geographical regions – the Judean Desert and the Dead Sea rift – deep wadis and abysses encompass it. It is remote

"Silva... seeing the rest of the country reduced to impotence and only one fortress still holding out, marched against it with all available forces. The fortress was Masada, occupied by the Sicarii under the command of an influential man called Eleazar..."
(The Jewish War, Book VII, 8:1; Penguin ed., p. 357).

from sizeable inhabited areas and is not accessible by roads suitable for the passage of large, cumbersome armies, but only by narrow paths along the ridge of the mountain, apparently built especially to reach Masada.

Two main paths, paved with great labor, expertise and talent, built according to the well-developed tradition of using retaining walls to make paths along steep inclines, led up the mountain itself. The eastern ascent, called the Snake Path, is well preserved and restored, and is in use to this day. The original western ascent, partially covered by the Romans' siege ramp, was probably similar to the route ascending Masada from the west today. A third, well-paved path connected the western ascent to the Roman Camp D, north of Masada; and a fourth path, the water route, ascended from Masada's cisterns to the northern end of the plateau. All of these paths were suitable for laden animals to pass. A worse path, passable only by men, and at that with difficulty, ascended Masada from the west, at its southern corner, from the direction of the Roman Camp G, to the southern gate.

Herod the Great (nearly 100 years before the Great Revolt) added mighty fortifications to the natural defenses of Masada, whose only weak points were the tops of the paths leading up the mountain, making the fortress impregnable. A wall originally five meters high was built around the entire mountain, at the weak points as well as where the rock face was utterly impassable. Here and there we can discern this wall rising above a vertical rock face 80 meters high. This was a casemate wall 1,400 meters long and built of two parallel sections, the outer 1.40 meters thick and the inner one meter thick, with four meters between them. Perpendicular walls divided the interior space into chambers (called casemates) varying from five to 35 meters in length. Each casemate could be entered from the inner wall, from Masada. The entire space between the walls was roofed, creating a covered area of close to 2.25 acres. Thus the wall may be viewed as one enormous building. Towers were built on the wall at intervals of approximately 40 meters.

The wall had four gates, one to each path. In contrast to the usual design of gates, the gates of Masada were not particularly strong or well fortified and were built no stronger than the rest of the wall.

The natural and man-made defenses of Masada were well described by Josephus 1800 years ago:

"A rock with a very large perimeter and lofty all the way along is on every side broken off by deep ravines. Their bottom is out of

1 *Storerooms for food, provisions, and arms. On the left, before excavation; on the right, after restoration. Before the day of canning or refrigeration, the dry air of the Judean desert provided a way of preserving food. The storerooms built by Herod on Masada are described by Josephus: "The provisions stored inside were even more astonishing in their abundance and diversity, and in their perfect preservation. The stores included a great quantity of corn – more than enough to last for many years – and quantities of wine and oil..."* (The Jewish War, *Book VII, 8:4; Penguin ed., p. 400).*

sight, and from it rise sheer cliffs on which no animal can get a foothold except in two places where the rock can with great difficulty be climbed. One of these paths comes from the Dead Sea to the east, the other from the west – an easier route.... Later King Herod devoted great care to the improvement of the place. The entire summit, measuring 3/4 mile round, he enclosed within a limestone wall 18 feet high and 12 wide, in which he erected 37 towers 75 feet high: from these one could pass through a ring of chambers right round the inside of the wall.... So strong had the fortress's defences against enemy attack been made both by nature and by human effort" (*The Jewish War,* Book VII, 5:5; Penguin ed., pp. 399-400).

water and supplies

Herod knew that Masada could not be taken by storm and that the enemy's only chance of forcing a surrender was by starvation and thirst. He set about countering this problem with the enterprise, technological know-how, and large scale undertaking characteristic of his works. As Josephus recounts:

"At every spot where people lived, whether on the plateau, round the palace, or before the wall, he had cut out in the rock numbers of great tanks to hold water, ensuring a supply as great as where spring water can be used.... The provisions stored inside were even more astonishing in their abundance and diversity, and in their perfect preservation. The stores included a great quantity of corn – more than enough to last for many years – and quantities of wine and oil, with pulse of all varieties and dates in great heaps.... There was found too a quantity of weapons of every kind, stored there by the king, and enough for 10,000 men, as well as unwrought iron and bronze and a store of lead" (*The Jewish War,* Book VII, 8:3-4; Penguin ed., pp. 399-400).

In modern terms we might say that Masada served as an emergency supply depot. Bearing in mind that the ancients could not preserve food by means of refrigeration, freezing, canning, and the like, we realize that Masada's location in the Judean Desert with its exceptionally dry climate, which made it possible to store food and munitions for many years, was a distinct advantage. Storehouses cover a large area of Masada. "Private" storerooms were also discovered in various houses and palaces on the mountain. Even the casemates could be used as storerooms.

Masada's waterworks fall into two categories: one for water storage and the other for water usage.

The water storage system was built of three parts: one collected rainwater which fell on the top of the plateau, on the ground and the roofs of the houses, and channeled it to cisterns which had been dug on the mountain. This is the oldest system and the simplest one technologically. Presumably every drop of rain which fell on Masada found its way to one of the cisterns (save for what the ground absorbed). This system was renovated later by Byzantine monks and can be seen in the form in which they left it to this day.

A second system collected the water which flowed into Naḥal Ha'armon (the Palace Wadi, north of Masada), around Roman Camps E and F, and channeled it in a conduit to Masada's lower row of cisterns, hewn in the northern end of Masada's western cliff. This system appears to have gathered more water than the first system.

A third water system was fed by the water of Naḥal Masada (south of Masada). This is a large brook which gathers water

2

1

2 *Storage jars after restoration. They can be dated with certainty between Herod's time and the fall of Masada in 73 c.e. Several of them bear Hebrew inscriptions, in ink or charcoal, indicating their owners' names: "Samuel bar Ezra" and the like.*

3 *Supplying water to Masada was one of Herod's prodigious works. In the aerial views of Masada (pp. 140-141 and 142-143) are what look like two rows of dark holes, one above the other. These are huge cisterns hewn in the rock, each with a capacity of 140,000 cubic feet, yielding a total capacity of close to 1,400,000 cubic feet. To fill these cisterns Herod's engineers built dams in the small wadis to the north and south of Masada, and from them they laid open channels to the two rows of cisterns, on the assumption that when it rained the water would be stopped by the dams and would flow downhill along the aqueducts and into the cisterns. The water was then carried up in jars from the lower cisterns to another set of rock-hewn cisterns on top of Masada. In the picture: a huge cistern on top of Masada, with a sunbeam streaming through the hole by which the cistern was filled. The staircase is on the right. (Photo by Prof. Yigael Yadin)*

3

from an extensive drainage basin and, after a rain, gushes with large quantities of water. A dam built in this brook deflected the water to a large conduit planned and constructed with superior hydrological and technological know-how. The conduit channeled water to Masada's upper row of cisterns, which apparently were the ones referred to in Josephus' remark about Herod **"ensuring a supply** [of water] **as great as where spring water can be used"** (*The Jewish War,* Book VII, 8:3; Penguin ed., p. 399).

The installations for water usage were shockingly wasteful, as if Masada indeed had a supply of spring water. Every abode had its jug of water for drinking, cooking, and washing dishes. In addition there were many waterworks for bathing and for beauty: ritual baths and bathhouses, and two pools, one for swimming, the other perhaps for landscaping, or for swimming, too, or for watering gardens.

1 *Aerial view of Masada from the north.*

2 *Remains of the lower terrace of the northern palace before excavation. (Photo by Prof. Yigael Yadin) The rock outcropping at this point is extremely narrow, at most a few yards wide. To create a flat artificial area on which to build, Herod's engineers constructed huge supporting walls, up to eighty feet high, on the edge of the abyss. Excavators of the lower terrace had to be rope-tied for safety.*

scene of a battle

Prof. A. Schulten, thought to be the greatest expert on the Roman army, desired his entire life to excavate Masada and study the site of the famous battle whose every detail he knew from reading the works of Josephus. However, living in the beginning of our century, he faced many obstacles. It was thirty years after his first plans for an expedition before he finally set out with a small research team to explore Masada. He pitched his tent at the foot of the mountain and, for a month, set out daily to study the camps of the Roman army which had besieged Masada. His research contributed vastly to our knowledge of the battle of Masada, particularly from the Roman side. The Jewish side has been studied at length, especially by Israeli archaeologists Shmaryahu Guttman, Yoḥanan Aharoni, Yigael Yadin, Ehud Neẓer, and many others. Most of the story is told us in the writings of a contemporary Jewish historian, Flavius Josephus.

After the Roman army had quelled the freedom fight of the Jews of the Land of Israel (70 c.e.), conquered all the Jewish fortresses and killed hundreds of thousands of soldiers and civilians, one last fortress remained in the hands of the Jews – Masada. Nearly a thousand people – families and single individuals, soldiers and civilians, men and women, young and old – were gathered here and refused to surrender to the Romans.

The Roman army, which had overcome its foes throughout the world and established Roman hegemony everywhere, could not suffer rebels to exist even in a lone, remote fortress. Thus it was that the Roman legions with their superior organization, vast experience, talented and ambitious commanders and equally motivated soldiers, and with their technological edge over the Jews in expensive, sophisticated and advanced war engines, set out to conquer Masada.

The Romans knew well what difficulties lay in store and prepared in advance for a massive campaign. First they assured themselves a supply of food and water. To do so they had to pave wide roads to their supply bases at 'Ein 'Aneva to the north

1

2

and, it appears, to the shore of the Dead Sea to the east. Next they built eight encampments around Masada, so well constructed that they stand to this day, over 1900 years later. (Hikers wishing to go off the beaten track and study Masada in closer detail might consider looking at Roman Camp A which has been excavated and partially reconstructed, or Roman Camp B which is particularly large and interesting, but regrettably has been littered with heaps of sightseers' trash.) Then the Romans laid siege to the fortress and built a siege-wall measuring close to five kilometers round the mountain to prevent the besieged from escaping, forming contact with the outside world, or receiving food and supplies from outside. Only after all this did they prepare to breach the fortress itself.

The plateau of Masada plunges to precipitous depths on all sides. The formidable eastern rock face is 320 meters high. A spur connects the rock of Masada with the mountains of the Judean Desert, making the western approach slightly more accessible; here the cliff is only 150 meters high. On this spur the Romans built a huge ramp rising at an angle to a height of 100 meters. The ramp, a wooden frame onto which soil was poured and pressed in place, has survived in the arid desert climate to this day. The soil, well fastened to it, has withstood the erosion of rain, and the wooden frame, sometimes showing through the dirt, has not been affected by rot. We can imagine how Masada's defenders must have felt as they saw the ramp rising before their eyes and tried to roll stones down on the foe, shoot arrows at them, or throw burning torches in an attempt to set fire to the wooden frame of the ramp. And facing them, we can imagine, the experienced Romans, prepared for any stratagem with a counter-stratagem, chasing the Jews off the wall with a storm of arrows and missiles from their sophisticated war engines, leaving a depression at the top of the ramp to halt the cascade of rocks which was hurled down on them, covering the wood of the ramp with mud so that it would not catch fire and, above all, with enormous perseverance, bringing basket upon basket of earth to complete the ramp.

On the ramp, 50 meters from the table-top of Masada, the Romans built a solid square platform of carefully hewn stone which reached another 25 meters up. On this they placed their war engines: a battering ram which stood directly across from the wall itself; and a firing tower clad with iron to foil attempts at setting it ablaze and rising 30 meters high so that the Romans, with their superior arms, could stand on it and drive the defenders off the wall and thus allow their battering ram to operate unobstructed. We can easily imagine the fierce battle which raged as the siege engines were put in place – the Jews with their topographical advantage, and the Romans with their advantages of superior armaments and experience in warfare.

When the Romans finally breached the stone wall of Masada, they discovered that the Jews in the meantime had built another wall opposite the same spot – a wall of earth, invincible to battering rams which can break rigid stone walls but are ineffectual against walls of yielding material. To prevent the earth from being easily scattered, the Jews poured it over a wooden frame (just as the Romans did in building their ramp). The Romans now set upon the wall with their torches. The wood rapidly caught fire and a dramatic scene, which we shall describe in the words of Josephus himself, ensued:

"Being made mostly of wood it soon caught fire: owing to its loose construction the whole thickness was soon ablaze and a mass of flame shot up. Just as the fire broke out a gust of wind from the north alarmed the Romans: it blew back the flame from above and drove it in their faces, and as their engines seemed on the point of being consumed in the blaze they were plunged into despair. [Engines such as theirs are not built overnight. Had they been burned, it would have taken the Romans weeks to build new ones and set them in position. In the meanwhile summer, which was more difficult for the besiegers than the besieged, would have come.] **Then all of a sudden as if by divine providence the wind swung to the south, and blowing strongly in the reverse direction carried and flung the flames against the wall, turning it into one solid blazing mass. God was indeed on the side of the Romans, who returned to camp full of delight, intending to assail the enemy early next day..."** (*The Jewish War,* Book VII, 8:5; Penguin ed., p. 360).

josephus and his works – an aside

Since we all know how the story of Masada ends, it is pardonable for us to interrupt our narration at this dramatic moment and turn to another equally fascinating subject – the figure of Josephus and his works.

The narrative which we just quoted is full of suspense: at first the Romans are in danger and the Jews, it seems, are about to be saved and gain the upper hand; then the situation reverses itself, the Romans are saved and the Jews ruined. However it was neither the heroism of the Jews which endangered the Romans, nor the heroism of the Romans which defeated the Jews; rather, according to the view emphatically expressed by Josephus, it was "as if by divine providence": at first God helps the Jews, and then He shifts to help their enemies.

This remark is not incidental. Such an approach is found throughout *The Jewish War.* Whether this was Josephus' way of expressing his faith, or whether it was a literary technique to increase the reader's suspense, as in the tradition of Greek tragedy, is unclear. Considering what we know about Josephus, his character, his education, his style as a writer and historian, either interpretation is equally plausible.

Be that as it may, his approach had an important, almost absurd impact. The Greco-Roman culture of which Josephus was a part produced hundreds of thousands of books. Even though printing had not yet been invented and every book had to be copied by hand, many books were written and copied, and became widely distributed and known to the public. Other histories aside from the works of Josephus existed on the war between the Romans and the Jews. Josephus, aware that his audience may have read other books on the same subject, was therefore obliged to take care not to fall into lies, exaggerations, or distortions. Wherever he made an assertion different from that of his contemporaries, he tried to prove himself correct and his colleagues in error; and wherever he did

1

*The northern palace was Herod's villa. "He built a palace, too, on the western slope, below the fortifications on the crest and inclining in a northerly direction..., the supporting pillars cut from a single block in every case, the partition walls and floors of the rooms paved with stones of many hues" (*The Jewish War, *Book VII, 8:3; Penguin ed., p. 399). The northern palace is built on three rock tiers. The upper terrace, a narrow continuation of the plateau, is the most elevated point on Masada; the middle terrace, with remains of a circular building, lies 60 feet below; and the lower terrace, with remains of a square structure and pillars, 45 feet further down.*

1 *Remains of frescoes on the lower terrace of the palace. The pillars were not made of a single stone; rather, they were assembled of several drums of soft stone, plastered in a grooved pattern to resemble gigantic carved pillars.*

2 *The middle terrace of Herod's palace, from the upper terrace.*

3 *The lower terrace. The view of the Dead Sea and the marly badlands at the foot of Masada was an integral part of the effect achieved by the architect in selecting the site for the palace.*

2

3

1 *Aerial view of Masada to help identify the sites in the picture on the next two pages.*

"A rock with a very large perimeter and lofty all the way along is on every side broken off by deep ravines. Their bottom is out of sight, and from it rise sheer cliffs on which no animal can get a foothold except in two places where the rock can with great difficulty be climbed. One of these paths comes from the Dead Sea to the east, the other from the west – an easier route." (The Jewish War, *Book VII, 8:3; Penguin edition, p. 399)*

not challenge the distortions of his fellows, presumably his account agreed with theirs. Insofar as the works of his contemporaries have not survived, there is further ground for trusting Josephus' accuracy. It is not because we must rely on him that we use him as a reliable source, but because he knew he had to defend himself against his critics, and heaven forbid that he write anything which would leave him open to charges of inaccuracy.

Modern scholarship since the middle of the past century has been inclined to cast doubt on the veracity of ancient sources. This is particularly true of biblical scholarship, but also applies to the study of Josephus. Nevertheless, the further Israeli archaeology advances, and the more the facts which Josephus presents in his works can be checked in the field, the more we must admire him for his accuracy of detail. Many things which scholars suspected were exaggerated or even impossible have proven true (although sometimes they are indeed wondrous almost beyond belief, such as the construction works undertaken by Herod and by the Hasmoneans).

Christianity, born several decades before the Jews' revolt against Rome, initially tried to establish itself among the Jews. When it encountered failure among the Jews, Christianity turned to the pagans. There it caught on slowly at first and did not emerge victorious until several centuries later, by which time it had become obvious that Christianity could succeed in polemics against the pagan world but not in philosophical battles against Judaism. It was then that Christianity seized upon the works of Josephus as an excellent weapon in that battle. In him they had a reliable witness, himself a Jew, who several decades after the advent of Jesus, after the Jews had refused to accept his gospel, clearly proved that God had removed His grace from the Jews and transferred it to another group. Ostensibly this proved the merit of Christianity.

Absurd as it may seem, it was their appreciation of Josephus that preserved his important works. When the Christians were burning hundreds of thousands of books, destroying much of the culture of the ancient world, they vigilantly cherished the works of Josephus that they might use them as an ideological weapon in their fight against Judaism. Educated, literate men sat in remote monasteries the world over and painstakingly copied these books; and thus it is that they have survived.

With this background we can continue, for the rest of the story is strange and dreadful, and requires us to weigh Josephus's credibility.

1

Mt. Eleazar
Roman Camp H
Wadi Masada
Casemate wall
Western palace
Storerooms
Synagogue
Wadi Masada
Silva's ramp
Upper cisterns
Lower cisterns
Roman Camp E
Palace Ravine
Roman Camp F (Silva's camp)

the great revolt revisited

The prevalent view among scholars today – a view which I advocate – is that Josephus undoubtedly did not receive a precise transcript of the speech delivered by Eleazar the son of Yair, the leader of Masada, but did receive general information on the content and impact of what Eleazar had said. The details Josephus could fill in on the basis of his familiarity with the cultural and political background of the Zealot leader and his general views and character, which were well known to him.

1 *The bitter end. Among the most thrilling findings on Masada was a woman's plaited hair, found beside a leather sandal in a small bathhouse in Herod's palace.*

2 *Parchment scrolls, written over two thousand years ago, in square Hebrew script, were discovered on Masada. They include sections of the Pentateuch, Prophets (Ezekiel) and Writings (Psalms).*

utter contempt for death

After breaching Masada's defenses, the Romans reinforced their guard on the siege wall and alerted the guards against attempts by the besieged to escape. Fleeing, however, was far from Eleazar's mind, nor did he think of allowing his men to flee. When he saw that the wall had been breached, that the emergency wall had been burned, and that there was no way to ward off defeat, he envisioned what the Romans would do to him and his men, to their women and children, once they gained the upper hand; and he resolved to die, himself and all those with him, for he believed that to be the proper action under the circumstances. He assembled all the people on Masada – nine hundred and sixty men, women and children – and addressed words of warning to them, a speech both pathetic and stirring, to convince them that death was the correct way out of their predicament. He concluded: **"Let our wives die unabused, our children without knowledge of slavery: after that, let us do each other an ungrudging kindness, preserving our freedom as a glorious winding-sheet"** (*The Jewish War,* Book VII, 8:6; Penguin ed., p. 361).

This frightful idea, however, was hard for people to accept. Therefore Eleazar continued his appeal, describing what awaited them should they fall into Romans hands, and how much more terrible that would be than death itself. Indeed his powerful remarks swayed the people to do that which was most dreadful of all. Each man slaughtered his beloved family with his own hands, feeling he was doing them an act of kindness, saving them from an even more ghastly fate. Next, ten men were chosen by lots to kill the rest. Lastly, these then cast lots to choose one who would kill the other nine, then set fire to the king's palace and kill himself as well.

The next day the Romans came to capture the fortress and instead of being greeted by the din of battle they met deathly silence. At first they suspected a trap. But upon finding the corpses, they felt no glory of victory. On the contrary, their victory had been stolen from them. **"When they came upon the rows of dead bodies, they did not exult over them as enemies but admired the nobility of their resolve, and the way in which so many had shown in carrying it out without a tremor an utter contempt of death"** (*The Jewish War,* Book VII, 9:2; Penguin ed., p. 367).

1

the symbol of devotion to a meaningful life

The story of Masada is a powerfully stirring saga. The remains of the fortress, the Roman camps, the ramp and the surrounding landscape add a dimension of credibility and immediacy, setting this saga apart from other tragedies described in works of literature or history.

Masada has become the symbol of unconquerable tenacity, the symbol of a people who remain invincible, even when humbled, oppressed, down-trodden and routed on the battlefield; the symbol of defense without retreat, for there is nowhere to retreat. **It was never the suicide of the people on Masada that the Jewish people championed, but rather their lives. Masada symbolizes devotion to a life with meaning. The defenders of Masada fought against the brutal force of the Roman Empire not only for their lives, but also for the survival of the values of the Jewish people. They preserved the embers which continued to glow for generations, until they blazed once more, as a torch lighting the way for the modern Zionist movement.**

The lives of the defenders of Masada, more so than their deaths, are an expression of the command not to retreat before the enemy advancing against us with greater numbers and strength, but to stand firm and staunchly defend the values of our people with infinite courage and devotion.

2

daily life

What do we know about the day to day life of Masada's defenders? Closely examining every detail Josephus wrote, we discover that he spoke at length about the mountain itself, its fortifications, how Herod prepared it for its purpose, including building a water-supply system and putting aside enormous emergency stores of food and arms, and about the building of Herod's palace, and the place of the site in the history of Herod and his dynasty. Yet when it comes to details about the people living there during the Great Revolt, Josephus is extremely terse. He mentions only that they arrived there and conquered the fortress from the Romans by stratagem, in the beginning of the revolt (66 or 67 c.e.); and, in characteristic style, describes the last battle (73 or 74 c.e.) in great detail. On all that transpired in the interim – during the long years, the many days, the countless hours – Josephus says hardly a word.

Actually this is not surprising in the least. Consider what history students are likely to learn about us and our era, some 2000 years from now (or what an educated person in Belgium or Costa Rica knows about us today): that we fought a protracted war against our neighbors (he certainly will not distinguish six different wars, as we do, but will see it all as one long war, lasting several decades), that we established a state for the Jewish people after a prolonged period of exile. He will not know that there was a student strike, that we had nursery schools, that we had a national lottery, that our main forms of entertainment were soccer, basketball, tennis, and public songfests; that the most popular authors were Agnon, Amos Oz, and Ruth Sirkis; that the Finance Minister called for curtailment of government spending, and all sorts of other important facts which fill our daily lives.

One of the objectives of the archaeological expeditions excavating Masada was to learn more about the daily lives of the people there. Archaeologists did not come to Masada to verify the words which Josephus put into the mouth of Eleazar, the Zealot leader of Masada, nor did they unearth a pile of 960 skeletons.

They did discover that for the most part people on Masada lived in a family setting, not in barracks. They lived as refugees who straggled there with a few possessions, bringing along the traditional way of life in their home, and found their refuge different from their abandoned home. Families which had been accustomed to live in a house of many small rooms, in Masada received "housing" in half the reception room of the king's palace. These were perhaps very grand and magnificent accomodations, but certainly not very comfortable. They adapted their new abode to resemble the home from which they had fled, or at least make it answer their needs, by building dividers and various fixtures, such as a place to cook and an oven to bake bread, a storeroom for grain and a corner for their water jug, by cutting a hole in the wall for light and air and by making a niche for storing their clothes and various possessions. Not everyone could bake his own bread. Some families bought bread from a bakery, as is attested by the rooms discovered on Masada with a number of ovens and other installations related to the preparation of dough. In one such room even bags of salt were discovered, and in another a pile of coins near the door.

The coins discovered on Masada are very informative. They attest, among other things, that Masada was not besieged and severed from its surroundings all five years of the revolt, but in fact maintained reciprocal relations with the rest of the rebels. Excavation has done away with the picture of *sicarii* stranded on an isolated island, which some people indirectly, and erroneously, inferred from the writings of Josephus. Over the years a varied collection of Jews from diverse classes and sects – urban and rural, Pharisees and Essenes (as attested by unique scrolls attributed to this sect), rich and poor, single men and families – gathered here.

The image of life under perennial emergency conditions, or in unceasing preparation for battle, has also proven false. Women living on Masada took painstaking care of their looks, anointed their skin and wore cosmetics. In addition to cooking they engaged in weaving and presumably in many other occupations which have not left material remains, ranging from various domestic skills to the education of their children, and perhaps even participated in circles of Torah study and general education.

To maintain a normal day-to-day existence, the rebels on Masada needed workshops. Excavations, interestingly, have revealed that the rebels' workshops were frequently located in the towers of the wall. Where the Herodian and Hasmonean workshops were located, we do not know. Several of the rebels' workshops have been reconstructed and are open to the public.

The people on Masada did not view their unnatural circumstances as an excuse for not performing religious commandments. They zealously followed the Jewish way of life, performing its precepts. Whether they faced a shortage of provisions or had food in abundance, they assiduously set aside the commanded donations and tithes, as is attested by the jugs uncovered in excavation, bearing inscriptions such as "priestly tithe", "suitable for consecrated, holy use", "holy", the letter *tet* (signifying *tevel* – untithed produce), the letter *taf* (signifying *terumah* – heave offering), and the like.

They also adhered meticulously to all the commandments regarding personal purity. Ritual baths discovered by archaeologists on Masada have been examined by rabbis, who have confirmed that they fully meet the ritual requirements. One *mikveh* (ritual bath) did not suffice; the rebels appear to have had a *mikveh* in every housing area on Masada. It seems only reasonable to assume that they also kept other commandments which have not left material remains that could be unearthed in excavations.

The rebels on Masada enlarged the synagogue which they found there and assembled in the building. What exactly they did in the synagogue is by no means clear, since the structure of prayer and religious ritual as we know it appears to have taken shape at a later period. They also built a *beit midrash* (house of study) upon their arrival in Masada. The rebels brought books with them, remains of which have been discovered in excavation. Most, of course, were books of Scripture, although some were Apocrypha (The Wisdom of Ben Sira), and some actually sectarian scrolls such as the "Song of the Sabbath

1

2

1 Ovens in a Zealot dwelling in the casemate wall. When the rebels came to Masada they found the existing dwellings unsuitable, both in number and character, for they had been planned for King Herod and his family, who led a different way of life from the many rebels on Masada. Thus the Zealots lived in existing houses which they adapted to their needs, casemate rooms, and apartments which they built themselves.

2 Vats and installations apparently related to leather tanning, found in one of the towers of the Zealot wall. The rebels lived on Masada for a number of years, leading a normal daily life. Workshops were an integral part of their existence.

3 Unearthing the large cooking stove in the palace kitchen (photo by Prof. Yigael Yadin).

3

Sacrifices." This scroll, unique to the Essene sect, is evidence that the people on Masada were not all of "one kind," as Josephus intimates in his simplistic description, but that the rebels who gathered here came from a variety of backgrounds.

On the face of it, one might not expect to find a rich spiritual life in a camp of besieged rebels. However when we consider a large community of people cut off by force of circumstance from their usual occupations such as farming, trading, priestly service, etc., we realize that these people surely had much free time at their disposal. Hence it is very likely that spiritual and cultural life flourished on Masada far beyond the intimations given us by material findings.

far more than restoration

The story of Masada was masterfully told by Josephus. The story of the archaeological excavation led by Yigael Yadin was recounted in detail by Yadin himself in his books and lectures throughout Israel and abroad. However the story of the restoration work on Masada, although worth publicizing, has not been fully told. It was executed with great reverence for the task and the responsibility entailed, and with consideration for visitors to the site. The work included conventional preservation and reinforcement, as well as altogether different undertakings such as safety precautions and preparation of an explanatory booklet.

What does restoration include and why is it necessary? Masada is more than an archaeological site, a subject of scientific study. It is also a national monument, a place visited by a broad and varied public, a stage for reconstructing a chapter of history. For the site to fulfill all its functions properly a series of operations had to be performed:

Reinforcing walls. Walls which had survived because the earth covered them became in danger of collapse as they were exposed to the air in the process of excavating. Moreover, mischievous sightseers (such as children or photographers) often climb on walls at archaeological sites. These people are likely to cause double harm, injuring themselves and causing an ancient wall to collapse. Therefore all the walls at Masada were reinforced with concrete. The task, however, was done with such talent and good taste that the sightseer is not aware of it.

Reinforcing mosaics. Mosaics are made with the awareness that people will walk on them, yet over the years they too may suffer. Since the durability of a mosaic depends on its foundation, how can it be reinforced? First a cloth is glued to the surface, then the foundation is loosened from below, leaving the stones of the mosaic glued to the fabric in their original design. Next a new foundation of high quality concrete is cast and the mosaic re-set as before. Finally the glue binding the cloth to the stones is dissolved. Reinforcing the edges is most important because disintegration is most likely to resume there.

1

Reinforcing plaster. "First aid" for plaster, which for years had been protected by heaps of dirt and now was suddenly exposed, was administered by injecting thin plastic glue into the plaster and reinforcing edges with concrete. In the long run, however, the plaster can only hold up if it receives treatment similar to that described above for mosaics. All the frescoes preserved at Masada were removed from their location, flown to Jerusalem where they were painstakingly treated using complicated procedures in air-conditioned laboratories, had new foundations built for them, and then were returned, one square at a time, and affixed to their original locations. To our great dismay, every section of plaster which was uncovered in the excavations and did not undergo this lengthy, complicated and costly procedure has disintegrated in the interim.

Ovens are built of earth and after being uncovered are prone to disappear very quickly. Even identifying them in the course of excavating is far from simple. Where less experienced archaeologists dug, the ovens were damaged in the very process of excavating. The ovens, too, were injected with glue, although this has not solved the problem of their disintegrating. The only ovens which are well preserved today are those that were completely destroyed and rebuilt of concrete by skilled masons, not only following the same plan as the original ovens, but also reproducing the color and texture of the originals – something the masons learned to do after many trials.

The benches in the synagogue are also restored or "counterfeited" as described above. To begin with, the plaster was removed from most of the benches, leaving only one original corner. Everywhere else the benches were covered with concrete which was mixed to a color and texture resembling the original plaster. In time the plaster which had been left in the original corner completely disintegrated, and there, too, a sham had to be made. Today sightseers can sit on the original benches of the ancient synagogue on Masada, albeit on new plaster built to imitate the original, and sense a spiritual and physical closeness to the people of Masada of 1800 years ago, without being afraid of damaging the site.

Providing access for sightseers. Paths, handrails, lookouts, and safety precautions have been set up for most of Masada, while attempting to detract as little as possible from the character and spirit of the site. In line with this approach, the signs on Masada were put up in shades of brown (as opposed to the more usual blue) and, as far as possible, the roofs which had to be built to protect special findings were concealed, as were the lavatories and other functional installations. Despite strong pressure to do otherwise, the upper terminal of the cable car was built below the summit of Masada so that it would not be visible from the top of the plateau, even though this meant that thousands of visitors must climb exhausting stairs from the terminal to the summit.

Black lines. All the "shams" were executed with far more integrity than at any other archaeological site in the world.

1 Many important and impressive finds were discovered while sifting the earth.

2 Moshe Yoffe restores a section of the northern wall. Since the work was at the edge of an abyss, safety measures were essential. The middle terrace of the palace and Roman Camp D, at the foot of Masada, appear in the background.

Wherever a wall was built up, a clear black line marks off the original segment from the restored one. This was done even though there was no question, at least in most cases, as to the faithfulness of the restoration to the original building.

All these works were executed with painstaking attention to detail and masterful professional talent by a group of devoted masons under the leadership of the master mason Moshe Yoffe from Sheikh Abreik, near ancient Bet She'arim, and the able assistance of J. Gasko from the National Parks Authority. Restoration policy was set by a public committee headed by Yigael Yadin, in which the archaeologist and architect Ehud Neẓer was the motive force, and of which I was privileged to have been a member.

The restoration work covered many other areas such as removing unsightly mounds of earth and stones which had accumulated in the course of the excavation, preparing a pamphlet for tourists, planning and constructing the cable car, and other plans which have not yet been executed such as displaying movable findings, building a museum on the site (Yehudah Almog's vision), preparing a sound and light show, and more. It is good to know that not everything has been accomplished and that there is still room for people with initiative to make improvements.

When you visit Masada next, bear all of this in mind and your deeper understanding and appreciation will enhance your enjoyment and enrich your experience.

moshe yoffe, head of the restoration team on masada

Moshe recounts: "When we climbed Masada, we found the mountain covered with heaps of stone, which apparently had fallen from the walls during an earthquake and were now strewn among the ruins at their feet. Since Masada had not been inhabited after its destruction and no one had used these stones in secondary construction, we knew that all the stones on the site were part of the ancient buildings."

Moshe, born in a Byelorussian village in 1903, migrated with his family to the Crimea during the First World War. At the age of 17 he came to the Land of Israel with his brother and joined the Labor Corps, in which he worked paving the Tiberias-Migdal road. He spent long days hammering away at stones, producing two and a half cubic yards of gravel per day. Subsequently, he was a fisherman in the Sea of Galilee, worked in a quarry, and was a guard in vineyards. Later the Yoffe brothers established a small construction company in Haifa, learning their trade from the Arabs and a local Yemenite Jew, who was an excellent builder.

Meanwhile, in Russia, where there was wide-spread starvation, Yoffe's mother died of typhus, leaving his father to care for three small children. After working day and night to save up the necessary money, in 1923 Moshe and his brother finally managed to bring the rest of their family to the Land of Israel.

In 1929 the group of builders went to visit the watchman, Alexander Zeid (later murdered by an Arab) on the hill of Sheikh Abreik, the site of the Bet She'arim antiquities. The place was desolate, without a settlement for miles around. Thrilled by an abandoned ruin which he spied there, Moshe decided to build his home on the site. In time he married and raised a family, continuing all the while to live in the same isolated spot, open to the threat of Arab attack.

"In Bet She'arim," Moshe recounts, "in 1936, I acquired my first experience in restoration. Being a builder by profession helped me understand the rules of ancient construction. I began reinforcing places in danger of collapse, rebuilding arches which had fallen, etc. Later I worked on antiquities at Shivta and Avdat in the Negev, the Crusader castle of Belvoir, Caesarea, Mamshit, and the Chalcolithic temple at 'En Gedi. Only afterwards did I come to Masada."

2

following up

Ilan Zaharoni

The failure of the Great Revolt and the destruction of Jerusalem brought disaster upon the Jewish people. Ruin, slaughter and exile opened gaping wounds in the body of the nation. Yet, however serious these may have been, they were not the factors which endangered its future and survival. Because Judaism was unique in the inseparability of its faith from its national identity, the destruction of the Temple was precisely what most jeopardized our national survival. Jerusalem and the Temple were the heart of the nation, the point around which its life revolved. The loss of this center raised many questions and sowed confusion and uncertainty.

Establishing a center at Jabneh and reinstating the Sanhedrin and other institutions under the leadership of Rabban Joḥanan ben Zakkai assured Jewish continuity. The rapidity with which the settlements in the foothills of Judea and in the Galilee were restored indicates that the extent of the holocaust was not as great as described by Josephus.

The Bar Kokhba Rebellion (132-135), which was carefully planned and initially reaped great success, ended with far graver consequences. The Jewish settlements in Judea became sorely depleted and the Galilee, which apparently took little part in this rebellion, became the center of rehabilitation and renewal of Jewish life.

Despite oppressive decrees, starvation, and poverty, the Sanhedrin and the patriarchate were re-established in the Galilee, and the codification of Jewish law, assuring answers to questions of the hour and the continuation of normal Jewish life, was resumed.

Sixty-five years after the fall of Betar and after the terrible ravage and ruin which the land had suffered, Jewish life in the Land of Israel reached its fullest flowering, with the patriarchate of Rabbi Judah ha-Nasi and the compilation of the Mishnah (200 c.e.). Thenceforth began the decline of the entire Jewish community in the country, including the Galilee. When in 425 c.e. Rabban Gamaliel passed away without leaving any descendants, the Romans abrogated the institution of the patriarchate and the Sanhedrin at Tiberias. Little by little spiritual leadership shifted from the Land of Israel to the Babylonian exile, whose *amoraim* (third-sixth century Jewish scholars whose work comprises the Talmud) in the Talmudic academies of Sura, Nehardea, and Pumbedita assumed the crown.

The Jewish communities in the Galilee, although somewhat depleted, continued to exist and even benefited from the economic prosperity of the Byzantine period. Nevertheless the inhabitants of the Jewish villages in the Galilee, and elsewhere in Israel, occasionally came upon unbearable economic hardship. Evidence of this is provided in the Talmud, which calls tax collectors "pillagers," and rates agriculture as the lowliest of occupations. These difficulties stemmed in no small measure from the rise of the rival Christian faith and the increase in the number of powerful people among its adherents.

The rebellion of the Jews of Sepphoris (Ẓippori) under the leadership of Patricius, in the fourth century, which spread to Tiberias and Lod, is indicative of the recognition of Jewish strength in the Galilee, on the one hand, and of the attempt to limit their freedom and oppress them, on the other. The many ruins of synagogues, mostly in the Galilee, are also silent testimony to the Jewish settlements of that period.

Even after the Moslem conquest Tiberias continued to be a center for Jews in the Land of Israel and the Diaspora. Although the center moved to Jerusalem in the 10th century, the majority of Jewish villages were still located in the Galilee.

1

Documents found in the Cairo *genizah* (11th cent.) mention the names of the Galilean villages: Dalton, Gush-Ḥalav, ‘Akhbera, Safed, Evlayim (I‘billin), Kefar Ḥananya, Kefar Mandi (today the Arab town of Kafr Manda in the Bet Netofa Valley), and Sepphoris. Aside from these places there were other Jewish villages not mentioned in *genizah* documents.

The Galilee, more than any other region, has been continuously inhabited by Jews. Kafr Kanna (today an Arab village), near Nazareth, was the home of dozens of Jewish families in the 15th and 16th centuries, as were Kefar Ḥananya, Shefar‘am (today Arab) and other villages in the region of Safed and Acre.

The remarkable story of the Jews of Peqi‘in, where Jewish settlement has existed continuously, symbolizes the tenacity with which the Jews of the Galilee held on to their land. Joseph Zeynati, a member of one of these families, refused to abandon his village and flee, even with the onslaught of Syrian forces in 1948. The stoutheartedness of this rawboned Jew so astounded colonel Shishaqli that, at the last moment, he decided not to execute him, but rather to chase this proud Jew over to the Jewish line.

Our people is once more sovereign in its land, but millions of Jews in the Diaspora have yet to return and build their homes in their land, the Land of Israel.

1 *The relief on the Arch of Titus, the victory arch built in Rome, depicting the parade carrying off the vessels of the Temple, among them the golden candelabrum plundered by the Romans.*

2 Judaea Capta – *a coin minted by Vespasian, celebrating his victory over Judea in 71 c.e., after the destruction of Jerusalem. The palm tree and the weeping woman at its feet represent vanquished Judea; the soldier, the victorious Roman army.*

2

silent witness to a jewish golan

Zvi Ma'oz

Remains of monumental synagogues bear witness to the strength and prosperity of Jewish settlement even in outlying regions of the Land of Israel. At times they are the only evidence of past settlements where there is no record in written historical sources.

Since 1885 ruins of synagogues have been discovered in the central and western parts of the Golan Heights, the Lower Golan as this area was designated in ancient times. Thus far such remains have been discovered on 25 sites, and more discoveries are yet to be made.

Archaeologists try to make these silent ruins talk, to extract information from them which can help us understand and reconstruct the unknown success story of the Jews of the Golan.

When did Jewish settlement here begin? On what was its economy based? What accounts for the dense settlement pattern in such a small area? What was the origin of the architectural style of these synagogues? Do we know anything of the social and spiritual character of the settlement? When and why were the agricultural villages abandoned? Where did their inhabitants go?

We do not have answers to all of these questions. Much of the story remains a mystery, and new enigmas are spurs to further research. Nevertheless we shall try to answer some of these questions with our present knowledge.

how is an ancient jewish settlement identified?

We set out for the fields and ruins scattered over the plateau, preferably in early winter when the vegetation is still low, and look for ornamented stones. The first places to check are the abandoned Syrian villages. Sometimes ashlars (large stones cut in precise rectangles, with flatly tooled sides) are incorporated into the walls of houses. This level of stonecutting and construction is not typical of Syrian buildings, thus we know that these stones were stolen from an ancient ruin nearby or even from right beneath the Syrian village.

Ancient stones and potsherds lying on the ground tell us that we are on an ancient site. Next we must determine whether Jews lived here. Fortunately for us, from the fourth century c.e. on, with the growing struggle between Christians and Jews, both sides began to employ artistic symbols to identify themselves. The *menorah* (candelabrum) was the Jewish symbol *par excellence* and appeared only among the Jews. If we find symbols of a *menorah* in a ruin, it is a sure sign we are dealing with a Jewish village. Aside from the emblem of the *menorah,* Hebrew or Aramaic inscriptions also help identify Jewish habitation (since the Christians wrote primarily in Greek).

Synagogue art has developed a repertoire of motifs which, while not used exclusively by Jews, are characteristic of Jewish art. Examples of such are reliefs of lions, eagles and bull heads, meandering grape vine motifs, wreaths, etc.

An ancient public building, should we chance upon it, can be

identified by hewn stones found *in situ* or by columns and capitals strewn around it. The building's plan and the direction of its façade also indicate the religious affiliation of the community which the structure served: if a pre-Islamic public building is oriented south, towards Jerusalem, it is almost surely a synagogue, since churches were always oriented east. These findings and clues enable us to identify conclusively many ruins in the Golan as Jewish villages. Marking our findings on a map, we can define the area of Jewish settlement in the Golan as bordered by the streams of Naḥal Gilbon on the north and Naḥal Samakh on the south, the Jordan River and the Sea of Galilee on the west, and the Ramat Magshimim – Dabiya – Kafr Nafakh road on the east. It turns out that hardly any churches, motifs of crosses, or pagan idols have been discovered in this area; hence we may conclude that it was inhabited exclusively by Jews. Henceforth, any obvious remains, even if less definitive than those constituting the criteria used thus far, can establish the existence of synagogues in this area: a few hewn stones, a fragment of a capital and an ornamented stone will suffice to identify a synagogue and to mark another Jewish village on the map. Later we shall return to the results of our survey and an

1 *The synagogue at 'En Nashut on the west bank of Upper Naḥal Meshushim, north of Qaṣrin. Only the column in the corner where the local "rich man" sat, facing the Torah shrine, was ornamented with a menorah and a unique capital.*

analysis of the map; but now we must address ourselves to the geographic question of what distinguished the Jewish settled region of the Golan from other parts of the Golan.

a land of grain and land of pasture

A century ago Gottlieb Schumacher, one of the first to study the Golan, noted that the Golan was divided, according to local peasants and bedouins, into two regions: the land where grains were grown and the land used for pasturing. Arable land spreads over the southern Golan Heights, from the Yarmouk River in the south to Naḥal Samakh and Mt. Peres in the north. The soil here is level, deep and fertile, and the rainfall adequate (400 mm. annually). The area is coverd with fields of grain and fruit plantations. The edges of the basalt plateau abound in springs, near which permanent settlements have existed since the beginning of history. In Schumacher's day this region had large farming villages, each numbering dozens or even hundreds of houses. Today, too, the principal agricultural area and 15 of the 25 new settlements in the Golan Heights are in this region.

The pasture land lies in the upper, northern part of the Golan Heights. North of Naḥal Samakh there is little arable land. Schumacher calls this part of the plateau the "stony Joulan," its fields strewn with rocks and boulders where nothing grows but wild grass and a park-like forest of Tabor oaks. Therefore, during the thousands of years preceding Jewish settlement in the Golan, this area was inhabited mostly by shepherds and nomads. Many archaeological remains from thousands of years back have been discovered in the central Golan: enclosures fortified by huge stone walls and thousands of dolmens – gigantic stone tombs. All of this, however, testifies to the presence of pastoral semi-nomadic tribes who subsisted on herding and who did not build themselves permanent settlements. Even a hundred years ago, according to Schumacher, the central Golan had only a few small permanent settlements, and most of the area was taken up by bedouin tribes.

Considering this background, it is most surprising that the central region of the plateau, the pasture land, was where the Jewish villages were in ancient times and that these were permanent agricultural settlements. In order to understand the contradiction between the geography of the area and the distribution of the Jewish population, let us go to one of the villages, Ḥurbat Kanaf. Excavations here have uncovered some clues as to how the story began.

ḥurbat kanaf

We were not the first to find Ḥurbat Kanaf. The site was discovered by Laurence Oliphant, an Englishman and supporter of Zionism, who lived in the village of 'Isfiya on Mt. Carmel. Oliphant, acquainted with the hardship suffered by the Jews of Eastern Europe at the end of the last century, aspired to survey the Golan Heights and prospect the area in order to settle masses of European Jews there. In December 1885 he set out from Tiberias to tour the region northeast of the Sea of Galilee. His bedouin guides led him from ruin to ruin, and in many he discovered and identified the remains of ancient synagogues. Thus, he already determined that this region, northeast of the Sea of Galilee, had been settled by Jews in ancient times. The bedouins also took him to Ḥurbat Kanaf, which lay atop a spur overlooking the Sea of Galilee from 530 meters above the lake and about 3.5 km. east of the shore (south of the modern settlement of Ma'ale Gamla). On the summit he found a large structure with a vaulted roof built of stone and concrete. The structure had been built by the Effendi of Damascus as a granary for vassal bedouins who lived in huts and tents around the storehouse.

West of this structure Oliphant discovered stones decorated "in Jewish style" and an inscription in Hebrew characters. He did not understand the inscription, yet it sufficed for him to determine that a Jewish village and synagogue once stood here. In 1932 Ḥurbat Kanaf was visited by a team of archaeologists from the Hebrew University of Jerusalem, led by E. L. Sukenik. They discerned ancient courses of hewn stone in the lower part of the storehouse walls. Adjacent to the long side of the building, outside it, they noticed ancient paving and conjectured that the storehouse had been built over a synagogue and that the paving was the remains of the court of the synagogue.

Upon our first visit to Ḥurbat Kanaf, enchanted by this isolated and lofty site, overlooking Lake Kinneret and the Galilee and surrounded by open landscape where gazelles roamed as in days of yore, we decided to excavate it.

We were attracted to the site no less by its spectacular location and view than by the obvious remains of the structure on it: the Syrian village, built on the site in the 50's, had mercilessly plundered parts of a synagogue. In the houses near the granary we found parts of a magnificent gateway, columns and capitals, all used as stones to build the walls – what we call "secondary use" of building materials. Almost all the data necessary to reconstruct the synagogue lay scattered nearby, available without even having to excavate. However we lacked two essential details: the plan of the interior of the hall and the layout of the columns, and even more important, the date of construction, without which the entire finding would have no historical significance. These things could be discovered only by archaeological excavation.

Therefore in April 1978 we set out on an expedition organized by the Golan Field School of the Society for the Protection of Nature in Qaẓrin. The excavating was done by youth interested in archaeology and guides from the field school (who may also lay claim to much of the credit for other findings concerning the study of ancient synagogues, having also excavated the synagogue at 'En Nashut and done the recent surveys).

The results of the excavation can be seen in the reconstruction of the synagogue – an edifice built of hewn stone, with an ornamented gate on the west and a secondary entrance on the north. Above the main entrance is an Aramaic inscription preserving the name of the generous donor, which translates as follows: **"This is the lintel; may he who made it, Yose son of Ḥalfo son of Ḥonio, be well remembered."** The interior of the hall is divided by two rows of columns supporting an upper gallery on either side of the central nave and a triangular roof. Among the attached semi-capitals we found one with a three-branched *menorah* engraved on it. The date of the building was established by coins discovered in its foundation. These are small coins which fell, or perhaps even were deposited, during the construction of the building. The latest coin dates to 491 c.e. Thus we established that the building was erected in the early sixth century.

"the people of the land of tob"

North of the synagogue, beneath the paving we found a stratum with foundations of a structure built on bedrock – the stratum of the beginning of the settlement. Potsherds, locally made as well as imported, clearly indicate that the beginnings of settlement at

1

2

1 *The lintel which once stood over the entrance of the synagogue discovered in Taiyiba.*

2 *Relief of a lion's head from the synagogue at Ḥurbat Bet Lavih (Wakhshara).*

3 *Conjectured reconstruction of the synagogue at Kanaf, after Z̤. Ma'oz, B. Wool, and L. Rittmayer, 1980.*

4 *A frieze with a foliage scroll, from the façade of the synagogue at Dikke.*

5 *The ornate capital with a menorah relief, from the synagogue at 'En Nashut.*

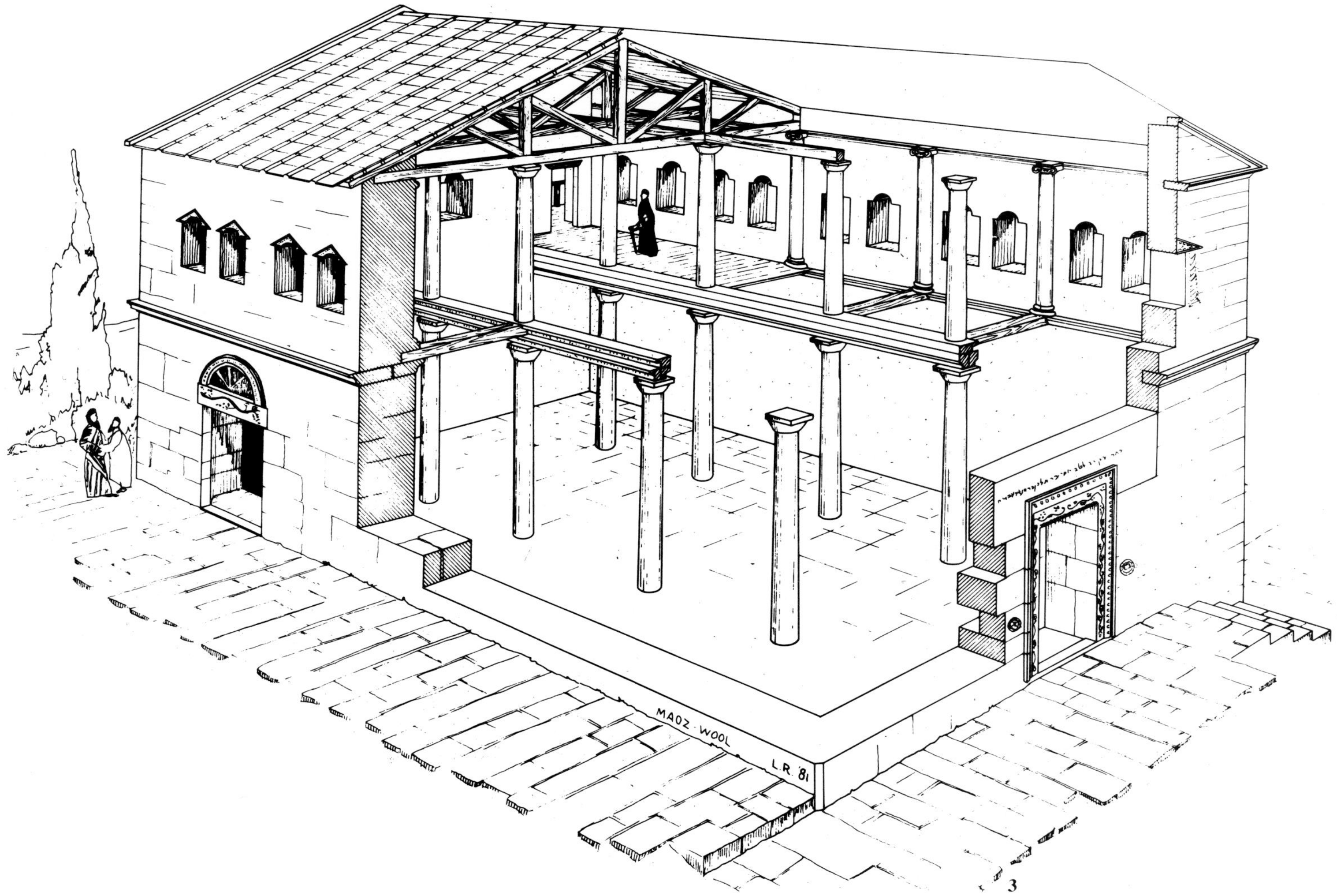

3

4

Kanaf date to the middle of the second century b.c.e. (This is the earliest stratum uncovered to date in the Jewish sites such as Gamla, Qaẓrin, and 'En Nashut, being excavated in the Golan today.) This early structure seems to be a fortified watchtower erected by the Seleucids sometime during the second quarter of the second century b.c.e. The tower appears to have been destroyed by the Hasmonean king Alexander Yannai (Jannaeus) in 81 b.c.e. in his campaign to conquer the Central Golan (Josephus, *Antiquities* XIII 335). Over the ruins of the Hellenistic tower another stratum was revealed, consisting of a series of rectangular rooms, perhaps soldiers' barracks. Signs of

5

prolonged occupation in the century that followed (first century c.e.), such as raising of floors in some rooms, were detected.

Judging by potsherds and stains of ashes found on the floors, the destruction of this stratum occurred during the Great Revolt in 67 c.e. Thus, based on excavations at Kanaf, we concluded that Jews began to settle the region in the first century b.c.e., following Yannai's conquest. Whence did they come? Why precisely then and not earlier or later? What made it possible for them to settle here? To answer these questions let us examine some historical works and the history of the Land of Israel.

It is possible that the Jews dwelling in the Transjordan since biblical times did not go into exile with the destruction of the kingdom of Israel. The Books of the Maccabees refer to the Jews of the northern Transjordan as "Tobians," men from the Land of Tob (Hebrew for "Land of Good"). A rural agricultural area, Tob lay in the region of the eastern tributaries of the Yarmouk in the northern Gilead and southern Bashan. A large rural population of Aramean descent lived between Bozra (in the north of modern Jordan) and Naveh (Nawa in modern Syria), in and around the Jewish villages, the Jewish population being only a sparse and weak minority in the region. From the second century b.c.e. on, the Greco-Hellenistic authorities of the Ptolemaic and Seleucid regimes founded *poleis,* city-states with Greek institutions and culture, inhabited by discharged Greek soldiers and local hellenized Syrians. Thus the Decapolis cities of Bozra, Gadara, Hippos (Susita), Raphon, and Karnaim, which became sworn enemies of the Jews for years to come, were founded in and around the Jewish "Land of Tob." The first confrontation between these Hellenistic cities and the Jews of this region occurred as a retaliation against the initial success of the Hasmonean revolt in Judea. In 164 b.c.e. the inhabitants of these cities fell upon the Jewish villages in an attempt to destroy them, and the Jewish villagers fled for their lives to the fortress of Dethema, whose exact location is unknown. Judah the Maccabee rushed to their rescue, leading a force of 8,000 men. In a swift surprise action Judah succeeded in burning and destroying the gentile towns and villages of Bozra, Caspin, Alema, Raphon, and Karnaim, all places on the borders of the Land of Tob. He rescued the beleaguered Jews in the fort of Dethema and led them – men, women, and children – in a convoy to Judea.

It seems that at this stage of the Hasmonean revolt Judah was not able to maintain his rule over an area so remote from his base; hence his main objective was to save Jewish lives. This battle is the earliest historical evidence of Jewish settlement in the northern Transjordan during the Second Temple period (II Maccabees, 12).

1 *The Qaṣrin synagogue from the time of the Mishnah and Talmud. Built of ashlars, as many as six or seven courses of some walls have survived. The building had a magnificent entrance on the north, its lintel decorated with a wreath design flanked by a pomegranate and a jug. Carved stones with designs of five- and seven-branched candelabra were found on the site, some of them used in secondary construction of Arab buildings in the area.*

2 *Remains of an olive press in the Golan Heights. The press-stone was rotated in a circular basin to crush and pulverize the olives, the first step in extracting oil.*

In the background the snowy Mount Hermon.

an agricultural revolution

During the Hellenistic period, as these struggles and battles were going on, the Land of Israel began to flourish and enjoy a hitherto unknown level of prosperity. "Modern" and highly

2

organized rule brought the Land of Israel an "agricultural revolution" which included production planning and regional specialization, organized marketing by regular overland and maritime trade routes, and a world-wide financial system. The agricultural boom, spurred by new markets and the development of new technologies such as aqueducts for irrigation and new mechanical devices for processing production, led to an increase in the population and expansion of settlement. Regions which had hitherto been arid deserts, such as the Jordan Rift Valley, became blossoming gardens.

The second most important technological innovation, ranking next after the aqueduct, was the olive press. It was this that opened the way for the development of agriculture and settlement in mountainous regions lacking tillable land. The olive press was an industrial installation for extracting olive oil in vast quantities compared to the level of home production known until then in the Land of Israel. Olives grow only along a narrow strip (50 km.) surrounding the Mediterranean in the countries of the Near East, Europe, and Egypt. This product, much in demand for food, bathing, medicinal uses, and providing light, became the primary economic base for new settlements in the Upper Galilee and the central Golan. Thanks to the olive, the "pasture land" of the Golan Heights became the "land of olives," and by the mid-second century it had acquired permanent settlements.

"hezekiah, brigand leader"

This new rural settlement was accompanied by the establishment of fortified Seleucid administrative centers in locations offering excellent natural defense. Thus the forts of Gamala and Seleucia, which we shall encounter again in our story as Zealot fortresses in the revolt against the Romans, were built in the Golan. As the Seleucid kingdom began to crumble, the Hasmonean state waxed stronger, and the Jewish sovereigns expanded their rule over wider areas of the Land of Israel, conquering large regions and converting the inhabitants to Judaism. Judah Aristobulus conquered the Galilee, and the great conqueror, Alexander Yannai, annexed the southern and central Golan to the Hasmonean state (83-81 b.c.e.). Henceforth Jewish settlement also received governmental backing and encouragement. The Roman conquest (63 b.c.e.) put an end, at least temporarily, to Jewish rule. By 23 b.c.e., however, the Golan was back under the sovereignty of the great Jewish ruler, Herod. Under Herod, Jewish settlement began to flourish and expanded throughout all of the Bashan and the Hauran as part of the regime's defense policy of military settlement.

Talmudic sources attest to this expansion, describing the boundaries of the Land of Israel on the east as bordering on Damascus and Bozra, and Jewish legal codes have preserved records of Jewish villages within these boundaries, in the environs of Naveh and Susita (Tosefta, *Shevi'it* 4-10).

Even then this growth and prosperity showed signs of disaster. With the fall of the Hasmoneans and the advent of Roman rule,

1

2

1 The ruins of Jewish Deborah and the Syrian village of Dabura, built alongside it and in whose houses stones taken from the ruins of the Jewish town were found.

2 Remains of an olive press at 'En Nashut. In the foreground is the circular basin used to crush the olives by means of a press-stone which rotates, crushing and pulverizing the olives. In the background, the base of the press, on which hemp bags containing the pulverized olives were placed and the oil extracted by applying pressure with a screw.

3 An ancient lintel found in a wall of the mosque in the Syrian village of Dabura. Short-toed eagles carved in relief at either end are shown holding snakes, which twist into a Herculean knot, in their beaks. Between the eagles there is an inscription in Hebrew (although Aramaic was the prevalent language at that time): "This is the House of Study of Rabbi Eleazar ha-Kappar" – a prominent disciple of Rabbi Judah ha-Nasi.

the Zealot movement of opposition to foreign rule was born. It first appeared in the Golan: "Hezekiah the Brigand Leader" was captured by Herod when the latter was governor of the Galilee, for he had raided settlements in the direction of Damascus, capital of the Roman province. After Hezekiah was killed, his sons and grandsons kept the flame of rebellion burning and fanned it into a huge conflagration in the great war against the Romans in 66 c.e. The revolt centered in the Lower Golan, a wild region cut by deep ravines and adjacent to the Galilee. The fortress towns of Gamala, Seleucia and Soganaea revolted and were fortified by the rebels, with Josephus commanding the revolt in the Galilee. After the arrival of the Roman legions only part of the Golan continued the rebellion. Soganaea and Seleucia surrendered without battle, perhaps thus sparing themselves destruction. The rebels and their supporters took up a position in Gamala, the birthplace of Hezekiah and his son Judah, founder of the Zealot movement. After eight months of siege and two attacks by the Roman legions, Gamala fell in an heroic last stand. Its defenders and inhabitants were killed or committed suicide, and the city was destroyed.

renewed growth in the byzantine era

For the two hundred years following Roman suppression of the Great Revolt, Jewish villages in the Golan step down from the stage of history. They are not mentioned in the Mishnah or the Talmud and are not reflected in any archaeological strata discovered to date. It seems that habitation in this area suffered severely, and that the population shrank drastically. Judging by the coins found in the Kanaf and 'En Nashut excavations, renewed growth only began in the second half of the fourth century c.e., under Byzantine rule over the Land of Israel. The most striking manifestation of this renewed growth is the construction of synagogues in the fifth and sixth centuries c.e., whose remains are being revealed today.

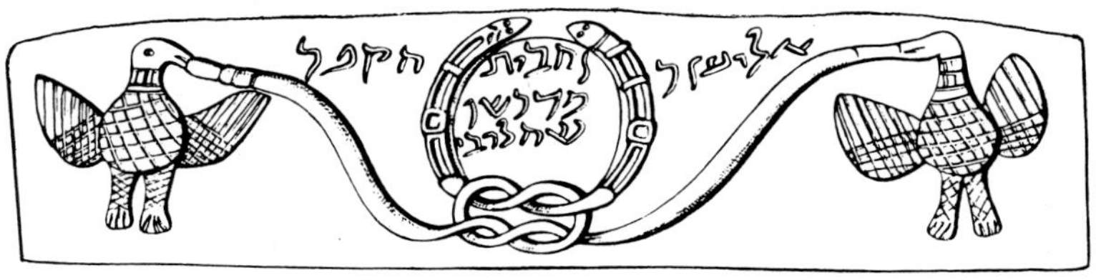

3

Before describing these remains let us look at the distribution of settlement and the layout of a typical village.

The map of distribution of villages in the Lower Golan presents a picture of very dense settlement. For example, within a radius of no more than two to four kilometers surrounding the ancient village of Qaṣrin lay the villages of Quṣbiya, 'Assaliya, Faḥura, 'En Nashut and Aḥmadiya. In a square of 10 by 10 km. northeast of the Sea of Galilee we counted no fewer than 15 Jewish villages. The large number of settlements would seem to indicate a large population, yet when we examined the size of the villages by the number of yards and ruins of buildings visible in aerial photographs (see the aerial photos of Ḥ. Deborah (Dabbura) and Yahudiya), we realized they were quite small. One must remember that not all the structures visible in an aerial photograph of a ruin or an abandoned Syrian village are residential buildings. Some are storehouses, pens, etc. In order to assess the population one must count the number of organized farming units surrounding a courtyard. After examining many villages we found that most had only about 7-15 courtyards and that only a few larger villages had up to 30 or 40 households. Taking a mean figure for the number of people per household (say five), we come up with villages whose population numbered several dozen, or at most a few hundred, people.

A more significant fact, however, is that the number of heads of households or economic units in the large villages was no more than 30 or 40. From this we conclude that the inhabitants of this area must have been quite wealthy farmers (even by modern standards) to afford to build such magnificent synagogues.

the worth of water

Why did the Jews of the Golan settle in dozens of small villages, rather than concentrate themselves in a number of larger villages? The answer became clear when we checked a map of the springs and sources of water in the area. There are indeed many springs, yet each provides only a small amount of water and apparently could not meet the demand of more than a handful of families together with their flocks and herds. Thus there was no alternative to settling in numerous villages close to these small springs.

The situation of the spring determines the way the village is laid out. In the northern part of the Lower Golan the springs tend to issue at the foot of terraced topography, on the front of the basalt flow. Here we find villages built on the incline of the terrace in such a way as to be sparing of level agricultural land. The synagogue, however, is generally located at the top of the slope (as in 'Assaliya, Aḥmadiya, Dabiya, and other villages).

The northern part of the central Golan also has streams which flow the year round. Here some of the villages are built on the plain adjoining the cliff over the stream and obtain their water supply from the springs along the cliffs of the canyon or by an aqueduct coming out of the stream (Dabura, Zumeimra, Zawitan, Jarabe, Rafid, Dikke, and others). In villages built on the plain the synagogue is generally located in the center of the built up area of the village. In the southern part of our region the springs generally appear above chalk and limestone strata exposed in the riverbanks, and on the edges of the plateau. Hence the villages here are generally found on a terraced slope of the riverbank or along the cliff side of the plateau (Kanaf, Khawkha, and others). The most convenient and best site in the village is always selected for the synagogue.

builders' trademarks

Taking a closer look at synagogue remains in the Golan we see that the style of their construction is very definite and uniform. The structures, two stories high and topped by a triangular roof, are built of closely fit ashlars laid without any cementing material. The facade with a triangular pediment is decorated with various reliefs, the emphasis generally being placed on the frame of the entrance and the lintel, displaying carvings of animals and symbols. The outward appearance of the synagogue is somewhat reminiscent of an eastern Roman temple. Indeed the architecture belongs to the Roman-Byzantine style of building in the East. The interior of the synagogue, however, is altogether different from a temple. A spacious hall is designed for seating the congregation. Its ceiling is supported by rows of columns also supporting balconies around the sides of the nave. Stone benches line the walls, and a Torah shrine made of wood stands on a raised stone platform in the wall facing Jerusalem.

1

Not all the synagogue façades face the same direction: some are oriented south, as in the Galilee, and some west, as in the Transjordan. Both directions appear to have been customary during that period, although we do not know why one or another particular direction was chosen.

Within the category of synagogues in the Golan, which is altogether different from the style of third century Galilean synagogues (Capernaum, Bar'am, Meron, and others), we may distinguish two subgroupings which differ in their geographical distribution and apparently also in date. The first group, built in the fifth century c.e. (especially in the latter half), has been found at 'En Nashut, Dikke, Rafid, Khawkha and Ḥurbat Bet Lavih. Stylistically this group resembles the synagogue in Korazim, west of the Jordan River. Its characteristic features include square pedestals which support the columns, friezes of foliage reliefs, and windows ornamented with reliefs of geometric designs and miniature animal motifs (lions, eagles, and birds).

The second group, built in the sixth century c.e., is typified by the synagogue at Qaṣrin. Thus far synagogues of this style have been discovered at 'Assaliya, Yahudiya, and Quṣbiya. The construction is simpler than that of the Korazim group and is marked by a specific type of ornamented entrance, characteristic bases and capitals, and a large relieving arch surmounting the main entrance.

Aside from these two groups of builders, we can also distinguish stylistic trademarks of individual builders who worked in a number of places such as Kanaf and Deir 'Aziz, where they left identifying signs. There is also a style of very simple, unornamented synagogues such as those of Ṣalabe and Dardara.

Analyzing the art of construction and sculpture in the Golan yields an impression of architectural creativity and innovation unique to the Golan in the Byzantine era, less influenced by the western Land of Israel than by the style of the eastern town of Naveh, the large Jewish center in the southern Bashan.

inscriptions speak to us

Analyzing the architecture and art of synagogues gives us something of the sources of influence, creative talent, and internal development in this region, but it is inscriptions found in the synagogues and the villages that provide us first hand information about the people, from the inhabitants of the villages themselves. The inscriptions appear in Aramaic, Hebrew, and occasionally in Greek. The use of Hebrew, the holy tongue, and Greek, the language of the rulers, indicates a high level of education in the villages of the Golan. A tombstone inscription, **"Rabbi Abbun, may he rest in dignity,"** found in Qaṣrin, testifies to the presence of rabbis and Torah scholars in the villages. An inscription of rare importance was discovered in Dabura: **"This is the House of Study of Rabbi Eleazar ha-Kappar."** This may have been the central House of Study, the "local university" of those days, for the Golan region. Another inscription informs us of a post in the village society aside from rabbi: the *ḥazzan,* today cantor of the synagogue but at that time an administrative official of the institution. The person who held this post donated a column to the synagogue in the village of Fiq and immortalized his name on the column, **"I, Judah the ḥazzan."** We already indicated that the farmers in the Golan – olive growers – were wealthy. We know the names of several such prosperous men who helped build synagogues, their names being inscribed on various parts of the building. Thus the entrance to the Kanaf synagogue preserves the name **"Yose son of Ḥalfo son of Ḥonio."** We know of an **'Uzi** from Qaṣrin who donated the **"ravu'ah"** (a courtyard for public feasts) and a certain **Eleazar bar Rabba** from Dabura who gave **"the columns above the beams and the dome."** The wealthy donor from 'En Nashut, not content with immortalizing his name in an inscription, saw to it that the corner in which he sat in the synagogue, opposite the Torah shrine, was more decorated

talmudic period synagogues in the golan heights

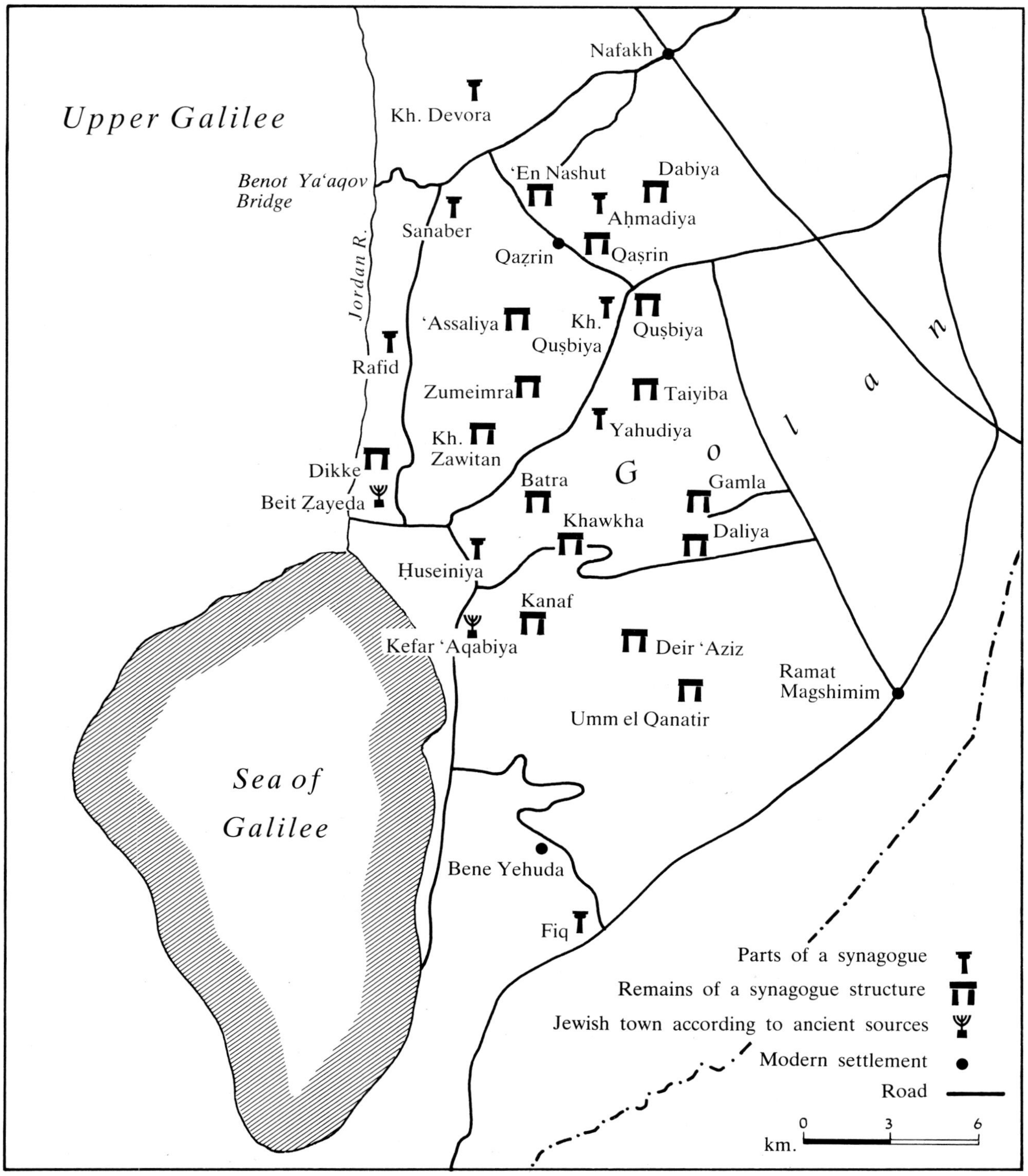

1 *The village of Yahudiya, built on a spur between two watercourses. Remains of a synagogue from the Talmudic period were discovered in the village.*

On the next two pages:

1 *Qaṣrin – from an ancient synagogue to a new settlement.*

than the rest of the building. Only the column next to his seat had a pedestal ornamented with a *menorah*. The capital of this column is the only one of its kind in the country (see photograph). Above these was a stone beam ornamented with wreath designs and bearing the name of this wealthy man, **"Abun bar Yose."** We know that the son of this man of means died at a young age, since the cover of his coffin, discovered on a hill near 'En Nashut, is inscribed **"Simeon bar Abun, of 26 years,"** indicating that he died and was buried at the age of 26.

A rare discovery in one of the houses in Kanaf provides a glimpse of the private life of a woman in the Golan in ancient times: an amulet made of a thin piece of bronze, six cm. wide, rolled in the shape of a cigarette, and probably kept in a leather case worn around the neck. This amulet, skillfully opened by David Shenhav of the Israel Museum and deciphered by Joseph Naveh of the Hebrew University, is written in Aramaic and translates as follows: **"Good amulette that heals Yaita, daughter of Maryan, from fever and chills and the evil eye, abracascas ya... el el... qqq... ẓẓẓ..., chase the fever and the chills, the spirits and demons, out of the body of Yaita, daughter of Maryan, in the name of Ehye asher ehye (I am that I am), Amen Amen Selah, good amulette that chases the fever and the chills out of Yaita, daughter of Maryan, in the name of Kariel, Kasiel, Zariel in the name of qqq... Michael, Azriel..."**

This amulet, discovered in the archaeological excavations at Kanaf, gives us an intimation of the woes and the mystic world of women in the Golan during that period.

from village to city

When did rural habitation in the Lower Golan cease, and why were the villages abandoned? Contemporary research can not yet provide conclusive answers to these questions. Coins dating as late as the end of the sixth century c.e. have been found at 'En Nashut. Coins of Emperor Focas from the early seventh century were disovered in a hoard of coins beneath the Torah shrine in the Qaṣrin synagogue. This hoard is connected with a stage of new construction and renovation in the Qaṣrin synagogue. The synagogue was destroyed by an earthquake in 746 c.e. We conjecture that the troubled times at the turn of the sixth to the seventh century led to the abandonment of the villages, apparently because of the neglect of internal security and because of bedouin raids into the Golan, and indirectly because of the reliance of the Golan villages on an intricate system of olive oil production and marketing abroad.

The Arab rulers had no interest in preserving this system. Maritime commerce came to a halt, and overland haulage became dangerous. Thus the farmers of the Golan lost the market for their produce and villages based mainly on this crop could not hold out. All the villages of the Golan, Jewish and Christian alike, were abandoned (save for Qaṣrin and the villages in the south, whose livelihood was more diversified, based on grain, fruit, and vegetable cultivation). The Jewish population migrated to cities bordering on the Golan: Damascus, Banias, Naveh, and Tiberias.

From documents in the Cairo *genizah* we know that a Jewish community existed in Banias as late as the 11th century, and we also know of Jews from Naveh and Damascus up to the Crusader conquest. Tiberias, the capital of the region, served as an important Jewish center, with many Jewish farming villages

1

around it, until it was destroyed by the great earthquake in 1033 and the massacre of the Jews by the Crusaders in the early 12th century. All these urban communities were situated in the Land of Israel, yet economically they were modeled after Diaspora communities and not dependent on agriculture. In contrast the farming community which existed in the Lower Golan for about 800 years, from Hasmonean times until the Islamic period, was the bastion of a strong, indigenous, and even wealthy Jewish population, with a special cultural and artistic heritage of which only intimations remain in the silent basalt stones.

The Gate between the Two Walls

Jeremiah 52:7

Sites Tell of the Past

the cult site on mount ‘ebal

Adam Zertal

a stone mound on the northeastern ridge

Archaeological surveys are no easy task. They involve combing an area on foot, day after day, month after month, in order to map and register all sites in the area. All the historical sites known to us were discovered because of ancient traditions handed down from generation to generation, or by accident, or as a result of systematic archaeological survey. Over the millenia, sites have been forsaken and cities abandoned and destroyed, and their names have often fallen into oblivion. Many a time an archaeologist faces the difficult riddle of discovering the name of a lost city or identifying the people who inhabited it.

We began a systematic survey of Mt. ‘Ebal (a large mountainous bloc north of Shechem, 940 meters above sea level, making it the highest mountain in the region of central and northern Samaria) in the winter of 1980. We knew, at that time, that the hill country of Samaria must conceal countless historical discoveries. In early 1978 a small team from Tel Aviv University, succeeded by a group from Haifa University, began an archaeological survey of the biblical allotment of the tribe of Manasseh in the hill country, an area extending from the Jezreel Valley on the north to Shechem and Naḥal Qanah on the south, and from the River Jordan on the east to the Via Maris on the west. It soon became clear that Samaria was a blank spot on the map of the Land of Israel. Few studies in depth have been made of the area, and a search for substantial reference material is bound to be disappointing. There are two reasons for this neglect. Firstly, the three great monotheistic religions did not view Samaria as a holy region for pilgrimage. Judaism sanctified Judea and Jerusalem and, during the Second Temple period, also the Galilee. Christianity attributed sanctity to the Galilee, where Jesus was active, and to Jerusalem. For Islam, only Jerusalem was sacred. The sites of the land were generally first publicized by pilgrims' writings, but this area was not of particular interest to them. Secondly, for the past two hundred years Samaria has been the center of Arab nationalism and of the Arabs' struggle against both Ottoman and British rule, and few scholars have dared penetrate into its hills. It seems that Samaria is the only place left where survey techniques can still reveal large and important sites, hitherto unknown. That is how we discovered King Solomon's town of Arubboth, the zealot city of Narbata. This method of systematic survey is what brought us to the mound of stones on the ridge of Mt. ‘Ebal.

The mountain is an inclined area descending steeply to the south towards the valley of Shechem. Eastward it slopes down in four broad "steps," today mostly covered with olive groves and field crops. Most of the mountain is bald and rocky, and is built of hard, Eocene chalk. On a clear day, from its summit you can see westward all the way to the Mediterranean, southward to the mountains surrounding Jerusalem, eastward to a glorious view of Mt. Gilead, northward to the snow-capped Mt. Hermon.

1 *Reconstruction of the altar of the Second Temple in Jerusalem, as it is described in tractate* Middot *of the Mishnah. The reconstruction includes all the parts discovered in the altar on Mt. ‘Ebal: a central platform, a surround, a major ramp, and a secondary ramp leading to the surround.*

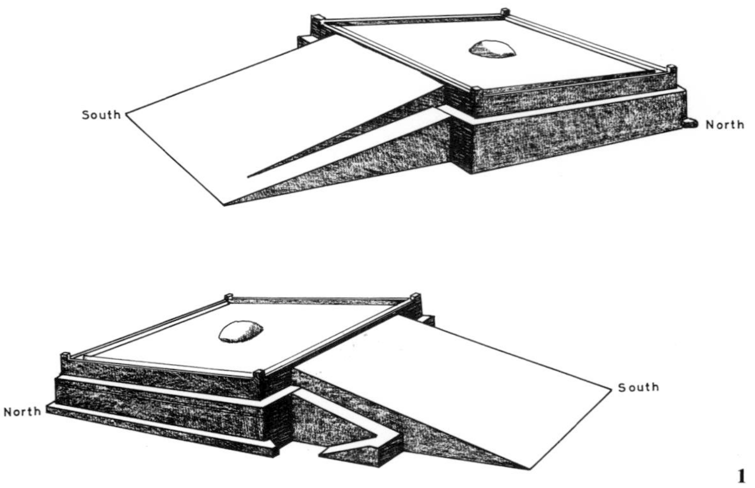

1

On the northern side of the second "step" from the summit, on an extended spur, we discovered a large pile of stones, almost 80 feet in diameter and 10 feet high. The mound was situated in the center of an eliptical area enclosed by a narrow stone wall. Thousands of sherds were scattered inside this area, silent testimony to what had transpired on the site. Classification of the pottery immediately led us to one of the most fascinating periods in archaeological and biblical research in Israel: the period of the Israelite settlement in the Land of Canaan (13th-12th century b.c.e.). Of no less interest was the fact that nowhere else on the mountain, whose area extends over 4,500 acres, were any other biblical sites, either Canaanite or Israelite, discovered. At the time the site was discovered, we did not dream of what we would find there in the end. We believed – this was the hypothesis underlying our scientific inquiry – that we were dealing with a small settlement site, perhaps a farmhouse or a fortified tower.

a mysterious structure filled with ashes and burned bones

For decades the period of the Israelite settlement has been one of the most controversial periods in archaeological research, and justifiably so. On the one hand, the books of Joshua and Judges present us a rich, multi-faceted saga, full of vicissitudes, about the conquest and settlement of the land, about inter-relations

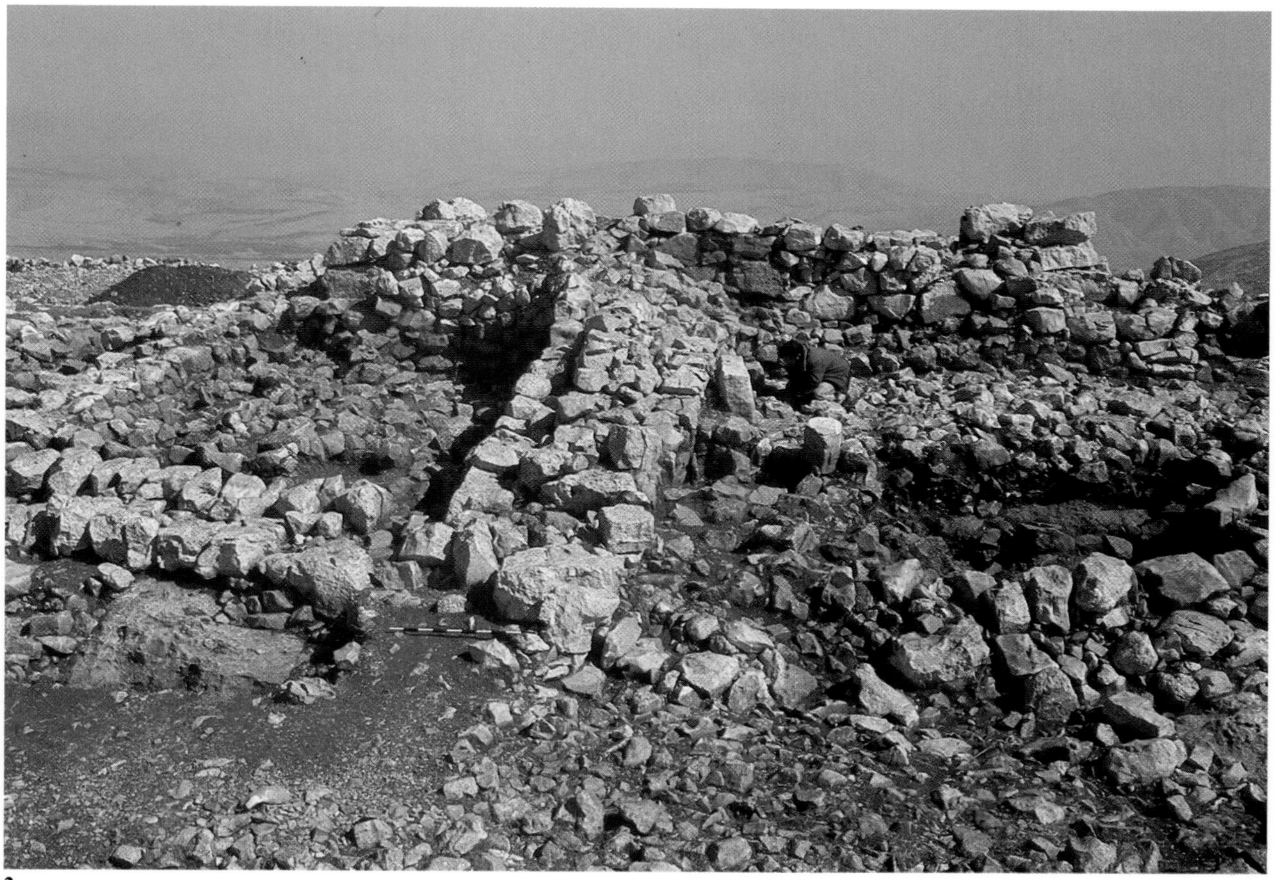

2

2 The burnt offering altar on Mt. 'Ebal (near Shechem – Nablus), viewed from the southwest. The elevated platform, preserved almost to its entire original height of approximately 10 feet, can be seen in the rear. Leading to this structure is a double ramp; the wider one, on the right, was for the High Priest to ascend the platform, bearing in his hands the animal sacrifice to be burned. The smaller ramp (the row of stones to the left) leads to a ledge that surrounds the platform of the altar on three sides. The priest used to stand on this ledge when he recited his prayers, performed the ritual of spattering the sacrificed animal's blood on the altar, and supervised the burning of the sacrifice. Paved courts were discovered on either side of the ramp, and gift offering installations were uncovered in the courts.

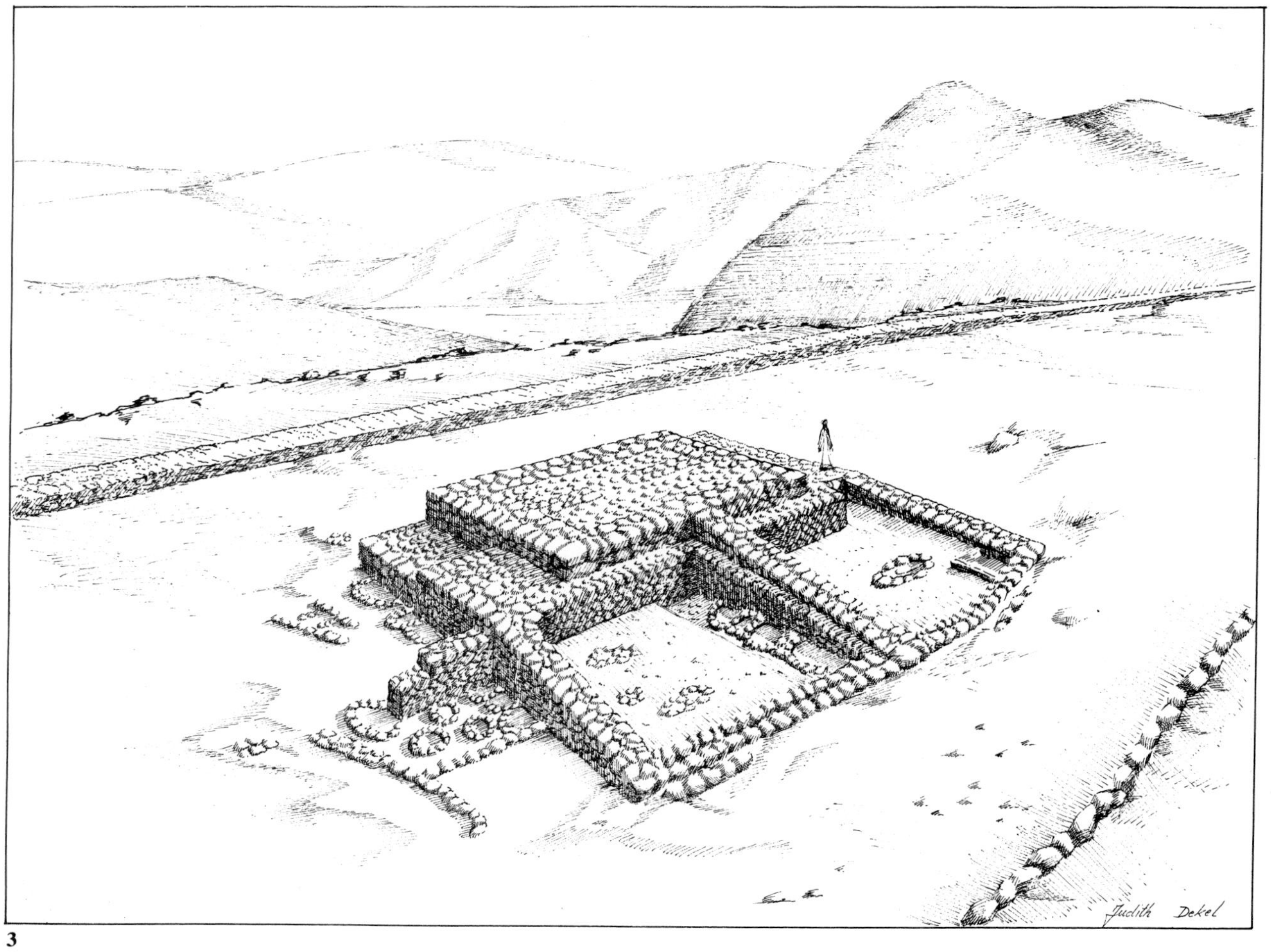

3

3 Reconstruction of the altar. Because the structure was so well preserved, this reconstruction only required minimal intervention by the artist. A ledge for the priests surrounds the central structure on three sides. A major ramp leads to the central structure of the altar, and to its left a secondary ramp ascends to the surround. The courtyards appear in the foreground and the temenos *wall in the background, at the foot of the mountains. Sketched by Judith Dekel.*

1

1 *A scarab, or Egyptian-style signet ring, found in the altar's fill. The use of scarabs – seals and charms prevalent in ancient Egypt – spread over the entire ancient East. This seal, carved in the shape of a beetle – an insect sacred to the ancient Egyptians – contains Egyptian religious symbols and scenes on its lower portion. Relatively crude in its workmanship, the scarab's ornamentation is geometric: a four-petal rosette with shoots between the petals, and a Uraeus (Egyptian cobra) emanating from each shoot. Discovering this scarab in the altar's fill enabled archaeologists to date the entire stratum, since the scarab can be ascribed with certainty to the great pharaoh Ramses II and to the latter part of his reign, 1245-1220 b.c.e. Similar scarabs, dating to the same era, have been found in Egypt and Cyprus.*

2 *Map of the allotment of the tribe of Manasseh in the central hill country. The location of the cultic site matches the biblical tradition about Mt. ‘Ebal.*

between Canaanites and Israelites, about movements of families, clans, and tribes, and about man struggling with rocks, forests and groves, and the local inhabitants. On the other hand, archaeological research has run into great difficulty studying this era, for which we have no external sources. Hence also the great interest which the isolated structure within the precinct on Mt. ‘Ebal had for us. Over two years elapsed, however, before we succeeded in raising the funds necessary to begin work. We excavated the site for seven seasons, each of which lasted approximately one month. There being no road to the site, we broke one through with our bare hands, so that we could reach the site by jeep and bring in tools, food and water.

Unlike other sites, where the archaeologist knows what he is excavating – a house, a room, a wall or other structure – the structure on Mt. ‘Ebal was enigmatic from the outset. To this day no architectural parallels to it have been found within Israel. Two years of work, comprising three seasons of laborious excavation, elapsed before we got the brainstorm which solved the riddle of the nature of the site by piecing together our scientific data with literary sources on Israelite cultic worship.

When we excavated the isolated structure in the center of the walled area which encompassed approximately one acre, it became clear that we were dealing with a far more elaborate complex than we had imagined at the outset. A large elevated structure, measuring 29.5 by 23 feet, rose in the center. It was built as a frame structure with walls about 5 feet thick, made of large, rough, unhewn stones. Inside the frame two thick walls were built facing each other and leaving an open space between them. The empty space itself was filled by the builders with four deliberately laid strata of fill. The lowest stratum contained a considerable quantity of ashes, above it was a stratum of dirt and stones, then another thick layer, approximately three feet deep, containing a large quantity of black ashes. In these ashes were hundreds of animal bones, some of which had been burned in a hearth. Many potsherds, belonging to the same period of early Israelite settlement, were found there as well. All this formed a filled platform which came to a height of about 10 feet above bed-rock. A sort of terrace, about a yard lower than the structure, was built adjacent to it, surrounding the high platform on three sides. Only the southeastern edge of the platform remained exposed. It is interesting that the corners of the platform point due north, south, east and west.*

A ramp of unhewn stones, 4 feet wide by 23 feet long, rises to the top of the platform from the southwest. The gentle incline, easily climbed, and the presence of the ramp itself accord with the explicit scriptural injunction: **"Neither shalt thou go up by steps unto Mine altar, that thy nakedness be not uncovered thereon"** (Exodus 2:23).

Adjacent to the northern side of the ramp is another small, narrow wall, somewhat lower than the one beside it. It turns out that this smaller ramp, which greatly intrigued us since we could find no constructional logic for it, was intended as a means of ascent for the priests to reach another part of the altar, the **surround** or **ledge.** This is none other than the above-mentioned terrace adjacent to the altar, which was reached by climbing the smaller ramp adjacent to the larger one. All this became clear to us only after reading the extremely precise mishnaic descriptions of the Second Temple in Jerusalem: **"The altar was thirty-two** [cubits] **by thirty-two** [cubits]. **It rose up one cubit and receded one cubit; this was the base.** [Thus] **we find left** [a square space of] **thirty by thirty.** [The next part built up on the base] **rose up five** [cubits] **and receded one cubit; this was the surround. Thus we are left with twenty-eight by twenty-eight... And there was a ramp at the south of the altar, thirty-two cubits by sixteen cubits in width..."** (*Middot* 3:1-3).

About the smaller ramp the Mishnah writes: **"How was this performed? The priest went up the ramp and passed around the ledge, and came to the southeast corner..."** (*Zevaḥim* 5:3).

The mishnaic description of the altar depicts a sort of graduated tower in which each successive level is somewhat smaller than the one below it. In the Second Temple period

* The practice of constructing sacred buildings so that their corners pointed in the directions of the compass was characteristic of Mesopotamia throughout its history. Temples, as well as altars, were always oriented in this way. The practice stems from the nature of the religion which developed in Babylonia and Assyria, based on four principal natural forces: earth, fire, air and water.

tribal allotment of manasseh

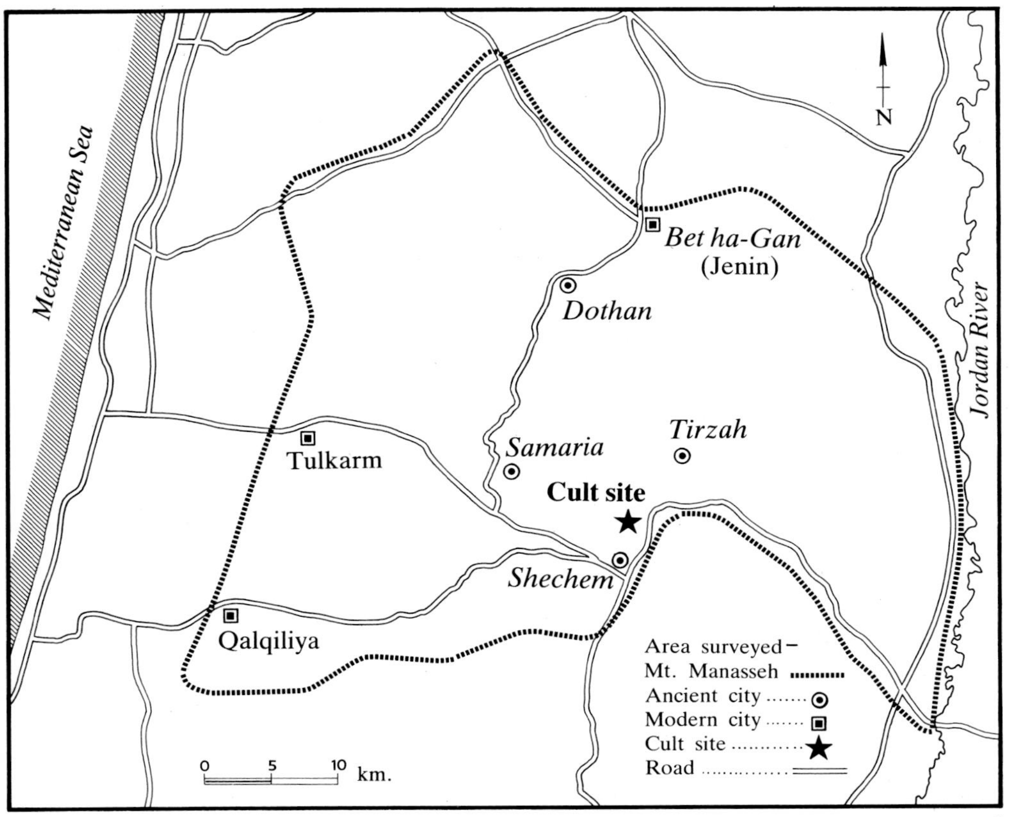

2

3 *The stone mound beneath which the burnt offering altar complex was discovered. As excavation began, thousands of potsherds, dating to the 13th century b.c.e., the beginning of the period of the Israelite settlement, were found among the stones. The excavators were surprised to find that the site had been deliberately buried under a layer of stones before it was abandoned, presumably to prevent its desecration. Perhaps abandoning Mt. 'Ebal was related to establishing a sacred site at Shiloh and the focus of the Israelite population shifting from the territory of Manasseh in the north to that of Ephraim in the central part of the country.*

4 *Strange installations in the northern court of the altar complex. Five box-like installations built of stone were discovered in a row near the ramp that ascends the altar. Some contained large quantities of ash and burned bones from animal sacrifices, others complete pottery vessels unearthed* in situ. *This discovery, like that of the altar, reveals the hitherto undisclosed world of religious ritual of the early Israelites.*

3

there were three levels, whereas the altar on Mt. 'Ebal has only two. These levels are formed by the surrounding ledge (see photographs and reconstruction). Interestingly enough, the future altar, described by Ezekiel, which most scholars believe reflects the altar in the First Temple, was also built in successive levels: **"And these are the measures of the altar by cubits – the cubit is a cubit and a handbreadth: the bottom shall be a cubit, and the breadth a cubit, and the border thereof by the edge thereof roundabout a span; and this shall be the base of the altar. And from the bottom upon the ground to the lower settle shall be two cubits, and the breadth one cubit; and from the lesser settle**

4

1

to the greater settle shall be four cubits, and the breadth a cubit. And the hearth shall be four cubits; and from the hearth and upward there shall be four horns'' (Ezekiel 43:13-15).

On the west, adjacent to the altar and the ramps, are two stone-paved courts. In these we found structures constructed and paved with crushed chalkstone. Some of them contained ashes and animal bones, others pottery vessels which had been deliberately placed in the spot, apparently for offerings. Similar structures containing pottery were found round about the altar.

bones provide the solution

Examining the bones in the laboratories of the Hebrew University's Department of Zoology took several months. These were tense months for us, the excavators. When Liora Kolska-Horwitz, who did the bone analysis, brought us the results, they were very surprising. Except for the bones of a wild rabbit and a hedgehog (that happened to die on this site at a later date), 942 bones were examined, representing 50-100 specimens. These were attributed to four kinds of animals: goats, sheep, cattle, and fallow deer. The latter is a light-spotted animal which inhabited the woodlands of our country in antiquity. Examination of the sex and age of the animals revealed that all those that could be diagnosed were young males, approximately one year old. This correlates remarkably with the laws of sacrifice in the book of Leviticus:* **And the Lord called unto Moses, and spoke unto him out of the tent of meeting, saying: Speak unto the children of Israel, and say unto them: When any man of you bringeth an offering unto the Lord, ye shall bring your offering of the cattle, even of the herd or of the flock. If his offering be a burnt-offering of the**

* The fallow deer does not fit the definition of sacrificial animals but is included in the list of animals fit for eating (Deuteronomy 14:5). It appears that in this ancient period fallow deer were sacrificed, as well.

1 *An aerial view of the inner* temenos *and altar complex, from the south. Extremely few sacred sites of the ancient Israelites have been uncovered in archaeology of the Land of Israel; for, in an effort to centralize religious ritual in Jerusalem, Kings Hezekiah and Josiah tore down the "high places" and altars scattered elsewhere across the land. Thus, an example such as this one, of a sacred precinct surrounding a burnt offering altar, is quite rare. The altar itself is comprised of a raised platform (excavated, in the center of the photo), two courts (on the left), and a ramp ascending between them to the top of the platform. As is characteristic in excavation of sacred precincts, no structures other than the altar complex were found within the* temenos. *Situated on one of the highest points in the land of Israel, the altar on Mt. 'Ebal accords closely with the ancient scriptural tradition of building sacred centers atop mountains: "They shall call peoples unto the mountain; there shall they offer sacrifices of righteousness" (Deuteronomy 33:19).*

2 *The sacred precinct on Mt. 'Ebal (viewed from the west). The situation of the inner* temenos *wall within the enclosure of the outer* temenos *wall is evident. The gateway to the inner precinct was by way of a broad entrance with three steps. On the inner side was a large courtyard with no other structures in it, save the altar complex. Twice the Bible uses the phrase "at Mt. 'Ebal," as distinguished from "on Mt. 'Ebal," by which it refers to the side of the mountain, not its summit. Indeed, the site lies on the northeastern side of the hill. Drawn by Judith Dekel.*

2

herd, he shall offer it a male without blemish" (Leviticus 1:1-3).

A great part of the bones, as we mentioned, had been burned over a fire and were cut near the joints. Being scorched in this way attests that the flesh was not intended for eating but was burned over an open fire (i.e. not in an oven). Thus the high correlation with the biblical laws of sacrifice, together with the great architectural resemblance to Israelite altars, confirmed the view that we were dealing with a cultic site and altar from the beginning of the Israelite settlement.

more surprises: a *temenos*, courtyards, and entrance

As the nature of the structure became increasingly clear, we began trying to solve the riddle of the enclosure. The thin enclosure wall was clearly not intended to provide a defense against enemies, but rather to delimit a sacred area, entry into which was permitted only to priests and levites, and perhaps other eminent persons.

Aside from the altar, no other structures were found inside the *temenos* (enclosure wall of a sanctified area). The entire area was laid out in the form of several courts. When we uncovered parts of them, it became clear that a considerable quantity of bones and potsherds lay scattered over the courts. However, unlike the bones found in the altar, they had not been burned and their flesh had been used for food. We called these courts the Maimuna* area, for here the big feasts were held, as we read explicitly in Scriptures: **"And thou shalt sacrifice peace-offerings, and shalt eat there; and thou shalt rejoice before the Lord thy God"** (Deuteronomy 27:7).

* The Maimuna is a celebration held by North African Jews on the last day of Passover and is noted for its great feasting.

The entrance to the enclosure was built in a broad depression in the natural rock, north of the site. Here three wide steps, paved with flat stones, were constructed between two parallel walls. This elaborate entrance is unparalleled in other sites of the settlement period. Both the width (approximately 26 feet) and the paving, at the entrance to such a small site, are indicative of what we call a processional gateway. Such gateways were generally built for cultic processions, carrying holy objects, to pass through.

an ancient cultic site beneath the altar

As we dug deeper into the strata of fill, it became clear that the cultic center, even the large altar itself, had been preceded by another cultic site. On the natural bed-rock, beneath the geometric center of the altar, we discovered a round structure, about 6.5 feet in diameter, built of unhewn stone. It was found full of yellowish material, above which was a thin layer of ashes and burned animal bones. At first we thought this was part of the altar. Shortly, however, levels of habitation preceding the large altar emerged in other parts of the site as well. Around the early, circular structure were signs of further cultic activity: an earthen floor paved with pottery, a large collar-rimmed jar, and other vessels. The pottery findings in both phases were very similar, so much so that we believe the same people, or the same generation, built both phases of the site. There is no difference in the pottery; but, in contrast, there is a fundamental difference in the perception of the site, which may be put briefly as follows: in the second half of the 13th century, as far as we can tell, a modest cultic site was established on Mt. ‘Ebal. A rough wall, constructed of large boulders, was built to enclose a sacred area. In the center was a round structure, possibly used for sacrifice, and around it other activities took place.

We do not know the origins of the great sanctity attributed to the mountain, but it appears that this sanctity only dates from the time of the Israelite settlement. For there is not the slightest sign of any Canaanite cultic tradition, nor any Canaanite finding which dates to the Late Bronze Age, anywhere on Mt. ‘Ebal. It stands to reason that founding a cultic center on Mt. ‘Ebal was intended as nothing other than a counter-weight to the presence of Canaanite Shechem and its cultic sites.

After several decades of the site’s existence, a revolutionary change occurred there. From a small place, sacred to one family or perhaps to the region, it suddenly became a central cultic site of supra-tribal or perhaps even national importance to the entire alliance of the tribes. A new *temenos* was built, as well as a broad, paved gateway. A large and complex burnt offering altar,* comprised of the platform itself, a surround, a small and a large ramp, and paved courts, was built on top of the earlier round structure. When this larger complex was constructed, so it seems to us today, the remains of bones and ashes from the earlier rites were gathered together and used to fill the new altar. Burying the earlier structure in the center of the newer one apparently symbolized the continuity of the tradition of sanctity attached to the site.

Many pottery vessels were discovered on the site, all belonging to the Early Iron Age (the time of the Israelite settlement, 1250 - 1000 b.c.e.). Prominent types include the *pithos* (large collar-rimmed storage jar), jars, cooking pots, kraters, jugs, and bowls. Yet what was most interesting was the discovery of two scarabs (Egyptian-style signet rings in the shape of a beetle, common in the Ancient Near East throughout the second millenium b.c.e.). One was found in the altar’s fill, the second inside an offering structure. One displays a geometric design consisting of a four-petal rosette in the center, with four shoots between the petals and a uraeus (an Egyptian cobra, believed in Egypt to have magical powers of protection and holiness) coming out of each shoot. The other displays a kneeling Egyptian archer and the cartouche of Thutmosis III, the great Egyptian conqueror. On the basis of similar findings in Egypt, Canaan and Cyprus, B. Brandl of the Hebrew University ascribes these scarabs to the second half of the 13th

* In the Bible a “burnt offering altar” is a structure to which animal sacrifices were brought and burned. The other biblical altar is a small incense altar, generally made of a single stone, on which incense was burned in the chambers of the Temple.

1

1 *A jar,* in situ, *as it was placed 3,200 years ago in the gift offering installation. It was a common practice among all cultures of the ancient world for pilgrims to bring priests offerings for the deity when arriving at a sacred place. Several scriptural quotations describe this custom and the types of offering that were brought: “... and there shall meet thee there three men going up to God to Beth-el, one carrying three kids, and another carrying three loaves of bread, and another carrying a bottle of wine” (I Samuel 10:3). In the altar complex on Mt. ‘Ebal archaeologists found dozens of stone installations containing vessels, like the one pictured here, in which offerings were brought.*

2 *A three-handled jar from the offering structure in the Mt. ‘Ebal altar, after restoration and treatment.*

2

century b.c.e. In other words, they date to the time of the great Egyptian pharaoh, Ramses II, who is considered the pharaoh of the exodus from Egypt. Finding these scarabs here does not mean they were brought directly from Egypt; that would be going too far. More important, however, is that they fix a date for the construction of the altar – approximately 1250 b.c.e.

shechem and mount ‘ebal in the bible: is this indeed joshua's altar?

In early Israelite sources Shechem is considered a central holy place for the tribes coming to settle the land. Moreover, Shechem's sanctity also finds expression in the stories of the patriarchs. When Abraham migrated from Mesopotamia to the land of Canaan, he came to Shechem first: **"And Abram passed through the land unto the place of Shechem, unto the terebinth of Moreh. And the Canaanite was then in the land. And the Lord appeared unto Abram, and said: 'Unto thy seed will I give this land'; and he builded there an altar unto the Lord, who appeared unto him"** (Genesis 12:6-7). This tradition was continued by Jacob: **"And Jacob came in peace to the city of Shechem, which is in the land of Canaan, when he came from Paddan-aram; and encamped before the city. And he bought the parcel of ground, where he had spread his tent, at the hand of the children of Hamor, Shechem's father, for a hundred pieces of money. And he erected there an altar, and called it God, the God of Israel"** (Genesis 33:18-20).

There appears to be a direct connection between this and the important tradition in Deuteronomy 27 and Joshua 8 concerning an altar erected on Mt. ‘Ebal and an important covenant made on the site: **"And Moses and the elders of Israel commanded the people, saying: 'Keep all the commandment which I command you this day. And it shall be on the day when ye shall pass over the Jordan unto the land which the Lord thy God giveth thee, that thou shalt set thee up great stones, and plaster them with plaster… And it shall be when ye are passed over the Jordan, that ye shall set up these stones, which I command you this day, in mount Ebal, and thou shalt plaster them with plaster. And there shalt thou build an altar unto the Lord thy God, an altar of stones; thou shalt lift up no iron tool upon them. Thou shalt build the altar of the Lord thy God of unhewn stones; and thou shalt offer burnt-offerings thereon unto the Lord thy God… And thou shalt write upon the stones all the words of this law very plainly.' And Moses and the priests the Levites spoke unto all Israel, saying: 'Keep silence, and hear, O Israel; this day thou art become a people unto the Lord thy God…' "** (Deuteronomy 27: 1-9).

The Book of Joshua describes the performance of this commandment: **"Then Joshua built an altar unto the Lord, the God of Israel, in mount Ebal, as Moses the servant of the Lord commanded the children of Israel, as it is written in the book of the law of Moses, an altar of unhewn stones, upon which no man had lifted up any iron; and they offered thereon burnt-offerings unto the Lord, and sacrificed peace-offerings. And he wrote there upon the stones a copy of the law of Moses, which he wrote before the children of Israel"** (Joshua 8:30-32).

No scholar challenges the fact that this is an extremely important and authentic tradition dealing with a central event in the life of the people. All agree that this event took place on Mt. ‘Ebal. As to the date of the event and the date it was recorded, however, views vary. Another tradition, in Joshua 24, accords special importance to Shechem. There Joshua made a covenant with the people, **"and set them a statute and an ordinance in Shechem"** (Joshua 24:25). According to the biblical redactor, Shechem and its environs were a major center for the emergent union of Israelite tribes. The central altar was erected on Mt. ‘Ebal, and there Israel became **"a people unto the Lord thy God"** (Deuteronomy 27:9); whereas the "statute and ordinance" (whatever this obscure expression means) were given to the people in Shechem.

Thus far, archaeological research has not been bountiful on the period of the Israelite settlement. In most of the major places mentioned in the stories of the conquest, such as Jericho, ‘Ai, ‘Arad, and others, no strata of destruction from the Late Bronze Age which would accord with the biblical account have been found. Reputable scholars have suggested that the entire

1

1 *The second Mt. 'Ebal scarab, found in an offering structure north of the altar. This finely-tooled scarab displays a kneeling Egyptian archer (left) holding a double bow. To his right is the* cartouche *(royal seal) of the great 15th century, b.c.e conquerer, Thutmosis III. Above the archer's head is a salamander and at his feet a boat. The drawing means "Pharaoh commands ten thousand archers." This rare memorial scarab, issued by Ramses II in honor of the great conquerer who lived two centuries earlier, has only four known parallels and can be dated with great precision to 1245-1220 b.c.e., thus strongly supporting the dating of the altar's construction to the latter half of the 13th century, b.c.e.*

2 *A view of the altar during excavation. Its central part is a stone structure, 24.5 feet by 29.5 feet. An open space was discovered inside, with specially constructed walls leading into it. The interior space was found filled with alternate layers of stone and ash. The man in the photo is kneeling on a layer of ash. To the archaeologists' great surprise, hundreds of animal bones, most of them burnt, were found in the layers of ash. Burnt bones are evidence of burnt offerings. The bones were attributed to four types of animal – cattle, sheep, goats, and fallow deer – and all were from young males, just as the Toraic laws on sacrifice prescribe. Fallow deer is the only animal not mentioned as one that may be sacrificed; thus discovery of its bones in the Mt. 'Ebal altar is rather perplexing. The varieties of animal bones discovered are evidence that the laws of sacrifice were followed from the very beginnings of the Israelite religion. Despite the presence of wild boars in the region, not a single bone of this animal, not fit for sacrifice, was found on Mt. 'Ebal.*

story of the conquest is nothing more than a later, etiological tradition which sets out to account for various manifestations in the light of mythological traditions and folklore. Recent extensive archaeological surveys of the central hill country, however, reveal clearly the process of Israelite settlement as a major settlement movement of the era (1250-1100 b.c.e.). Hundreds of newly-founded, small settlements were established within a short period throughout the hilly allotments of the tribes of Manasseh, Ephraim and Benjamin. The settlers used a characteristic type of pottery and their houses were generally built on a three- or four-room plan.* Although Israelite pottery and architecture were influenced by the Canaanites, they have certain prominent and unique characteristics. In our survey of the hill country of Manasseh we were able to study the ecology of the Israelite settlement and, using new research methods, we succeeded in reconstructing the process by which they penetrated the central hill country from the eastern Transjordan. Evidently the beginning of the penetration, sometime in the 13th century b.c.e., was made by semi-nomadic shepherd groups migrating from the edge of the desert, by way of the "ecological pipe" of Wadi el Far'a (Naḥal Tirẓah). Many sites with ancient pottery typical of the settlement period were discovered along the fertile and well-watered valley of this river, which is surrounded by broad pasture. In the next phase the Israelites established themselves along the edges of the internal valleys of the hill country of Manasseh: Tubas (biblical Thebez), Zebabdeh, Sanur, Dothan, and others. An economy based on olive and grape cultivation, which henceforth would characterize Israelite habitation of the hill country, did not emerge until the settlement process drew to a close at the end of the 12th century. As this complex and fascinating process was developing, the people's religious and ritual practice took shape. The cultic site on Mt. 'Ebal satisfies the three criteria necessary to identify a biblical site: chronological (beginning of the Israelite settlement), geographical, and the nature of the site (a cultic center with a burnt-offering altar). In view of this analysis, the identity of the biblical story and this site as the first inter-tribal center of the Israelite tribes can hardly be doubted.

This is the first time a complete Israelite cultic center, including an altar for burnt offerings, is available for study. Thanks to King Josiah's and King Hezekiah's activities in breaking up the "high places," only two small altars for burnt offerings have been discovered in Israel, one in 'Arad and the other (discovered no longer intact) in Beer-sheba, and both date relatively late. The altar on Mt. 'Ebal is not only the most ancient and complete altar, but also the prototype of the Israelite burnt offering altar of the First and Second Temple periods. The Mesopotamian architectural influence on the structure of the altar is also very interesting, both in its stepped construction and in the orientation of its corners to the north, south, east, and west.

2

* An architectural design for a residential structure, having three compartments running lengthwise and one crosswise. The living quarters were in the lateral room (sometimes of two storeys), while the livestock, kitchen, and storerooms were in the longitudinal compartments. The entrance to the structure was on the central longitudinal room. Its convenience and efficiency made this the prevalent and almost exclusive plan in the villages and habitations of the newly arrived Israelites, and in their later sites as well.

jericho and its winter palaces

Ehud Netzer

Historians of the Land of Israel have known of archaeological remains near the mouth of Wadi Qelet (biblical Naḥal Perath), in the western Jericho Valley, since the past century. Charles Warren, known for his excavation of Jerusalem, first dug here in 1868. Since then the site was thought to be Second Temple period Jericho – i.e. the site of Jericho in the Hellenistic and early Roman periods.

In the 1950's two American expeditions excavated this site far more extensively and discovered remains of various buildings, mostly Herodian. This led to the hypothesis that Herod's winter palace, described by Josephus, stood here. A large building discovered south of Wadi Qelet was thought by the American archaeologists who uncovered it to be a gymnasium, also from the time of Herod.

Two tels, locally known as Tulul Abu 'Ala'iq, stand out on the site in the western Jericho Valley. Charles Warren and one of the American expeditions excavated both tels, which they believed to have originally been the two fortresses, Threx and Taurus, which Pompey destroyed when he conquered the Land of Israel in 63 b.c.e.

Investigation of the site in an attempt to uncover its remains systematically was renewed in 1973. The expedition, directed by the author, was sponsored by the Institute of Archaeology of the Hebrew University with the participation of the Israel Exploration Society and the District Archaeologist of Judea and Samaria. While excavating it became clear that this was not the site of the city of Jericho in the Second Temple period, but rather an enormous complex of winter palaces built beside an extensive royal domain. The city itself apparently extended over the entire area of the Jericho Valley.

palaces and forts combined

The originators of the winter palaces as well as the royal estates were the Hasmonean kings, most likely Alexander Yannai (Jannaeus, 103-76 b.c.e.). The Hasmoneans were also the first to build the series of forts along the Jordan Valley and the Dead Sea, including Sartaba (Alexandrion), Hyrcania (Hureqanya), Masada and Machaerus. Remains of several of these forts stand above the Plain of Jericho: one, known as Dagon or Dok, on the summit of the Qarantal (Monastery of the Forty Days), and another, called Cypros (Kipros), south of Wadi Qelet. Threx and Taurus, the two forts destroyed by Pompey, were undoubtedly the same as two of these forts built by the Hasmoneans, overlooking the Jericho Valley. Cypros, like the other fortresses, was rebuilt by Herod, who named it after his Nabatean mother. Digging on the summit of this hill (with Emanuel Damati, in 1974), we revealed magnificent remains from Herod's time and ruins of the first Hasmonean fortress on the site. Dramatically situated in the Judean Desert, overlooking the Jordan Valley and facing the mountains of the Transjordan, these fortresses were not only places of refuge in

1

1 *Herod's third palace in Jericho, on the banks of Naḥal Perath (Wadi Qelet) – the northern wing. On the left is the magnificent hall, the heart of the palace. The marble floor tiles have been plundered, but their outlines remain clearly marked. The recesses for the plinths of the pillars can also be discerned in the floor.*

time of trouble but also excellent bases for palace-strongholds. In Cypros we uncovered some magnificent chambers, elegant artifacts, and even two Herodian bathhouses.

To build the royal domain – a large agricultural estate – a sophisticated watering system had to be devised. This system was fed by the plentiful springs near the valley and, like the irrigation system of Jericho to this day, operated by means of aqueducts. 'Ein Fara, 'Ein Fawwar and 'Ein Qelet, one group of springs watering the Hasmonean farmlands, issued from Wadi Qelet. 'Ein Nu'eima and 'Ein Duyuk, a second group of springs, issued from Na'aran (near the Jericho – 'Ofra – Bet El road). The aqueducts were built the length of the foothills, allowing irrigation of most of the land in the western part of the valley. Having been well constructed, sections of these aqueducts survive almost in their entirety to this day (see photo).

The royal estate covered an area of about 125 acres and was fenced in for protection against wild animals and thieves. The primary cultivated plants were date palms and balsam trees. The hot climate of the Jericho Valley is unusually well suited to these plants, whose products were marketed throughout the lands of the Mediterranean. Date palms were grown not only for the raw dates themselves but also for the date honey and wine which were produced from the fruit. Balsam trees supplied the raw materials for producing all sorts of spices and medicines, thus providing an inexhaustible source of revenue for the Hasmonean kings and for Herod after them.

a swimming pool and ritual baths

Jericho is scorching hot in the summer but pleasantly warm in the winter, thus offering a fine base for a winter resort. Next to the royal estates it appears that Alexander Yannai also built himself a winter palace, the first on the site near the mouth of Wadi Qelet. The central attraction of the Hasmonean palace was a large swimming pool measuring approximately 18 x 32 meters, almost as large as today's Olympic pools. The pool was surrounded by paved plazas and magnificent buildings. The palace itself is still largely covered by a man-made tel (the northern of the two tels of Abu 'Ala'iq), built later by Herod in order to erect buildings of his own on it. Remains of colored frescoes (see photo) were found in the few rooms which we uncovered in the Hasmonean structure buried under the tel.

The Hasmonean palace and its adjacent buildings are marked by a multiplicity of ritual baths (*mikvaot*). These are the most ancient *mikvaot* discovered to date. The Hasmonean kings

1

2

belonged to a priestly family and served as high priests in the Temple. Thus the need for frequent immersion to purify the body was an inseparable part of their way of life. Some of the *mikvaot* which have been unearthed were built as isolated units, while others were incorporated in the Hasmonean bathhouses.

The Hasmonean palace stood for several decades, during which it underwent various alterations and enlargements. Its last golden age appears to have been under Queen Salome (76-67 b.c.e.), Alexander Yannai's widow, who ruled after his death. When she died, bitter rivalry broke out between her sons, Hyrcanus and Aristobulus, rivalry which hastened the entrance of the Roman general Pompey into the land. He conquered the country in 63 b.c.e., bringing the era of independence won by the Hasmoneans to a close.

murder in the swimming pool

It appears that when Herod ascended the throne in 37 b.c.e. the Hasmonean family was still using its palace. Initially Herod tried to win over the hearts of the Hasmoneans, to which end he took Mariamne the Hasmonean for his wife. Somewhat later, under family pressure, he appointed her brother Aristobulus as High

1 *The cold room* (frigidarium) *of the bathhouse in the northern wing of Herod's third palace. The walls of the* frigidarium *are built of Roman concrete covered with small stones forming a diagonal mosaic design – a construction technique quite common in Italy but extremely rare in the eastern Mediterranean.*

2 *The area of ritual baths in the Hasmonean palace. These are the earliest ritual baths discovered to date. The Hasmonean kings were from a priestly family and officiated as High Priests in the Temple. The necessity of frequent ritual immersion for purification of the body was an inseparable part of their life style; hence the many ritual baths attached to the palace. Each* mikveh, *or ritual bath, consisted of two pools (right foreground); one pool held pure rainwater, whose sanctity was transferred via a connecting pipe to regular water, periodically filled into the second pool. The large swimming pool can be seen in the rear, and across it an elevated "bridge" for those wishing only ritual immersion. Mariamne's brother Aristobulus was drowned in this pool at the behest of her husband, King Herod.*

3 *Colored plaster designed to resemble marble, on the wall of a room in the Hasmonean palace.*

3

jericho and its winter palaces

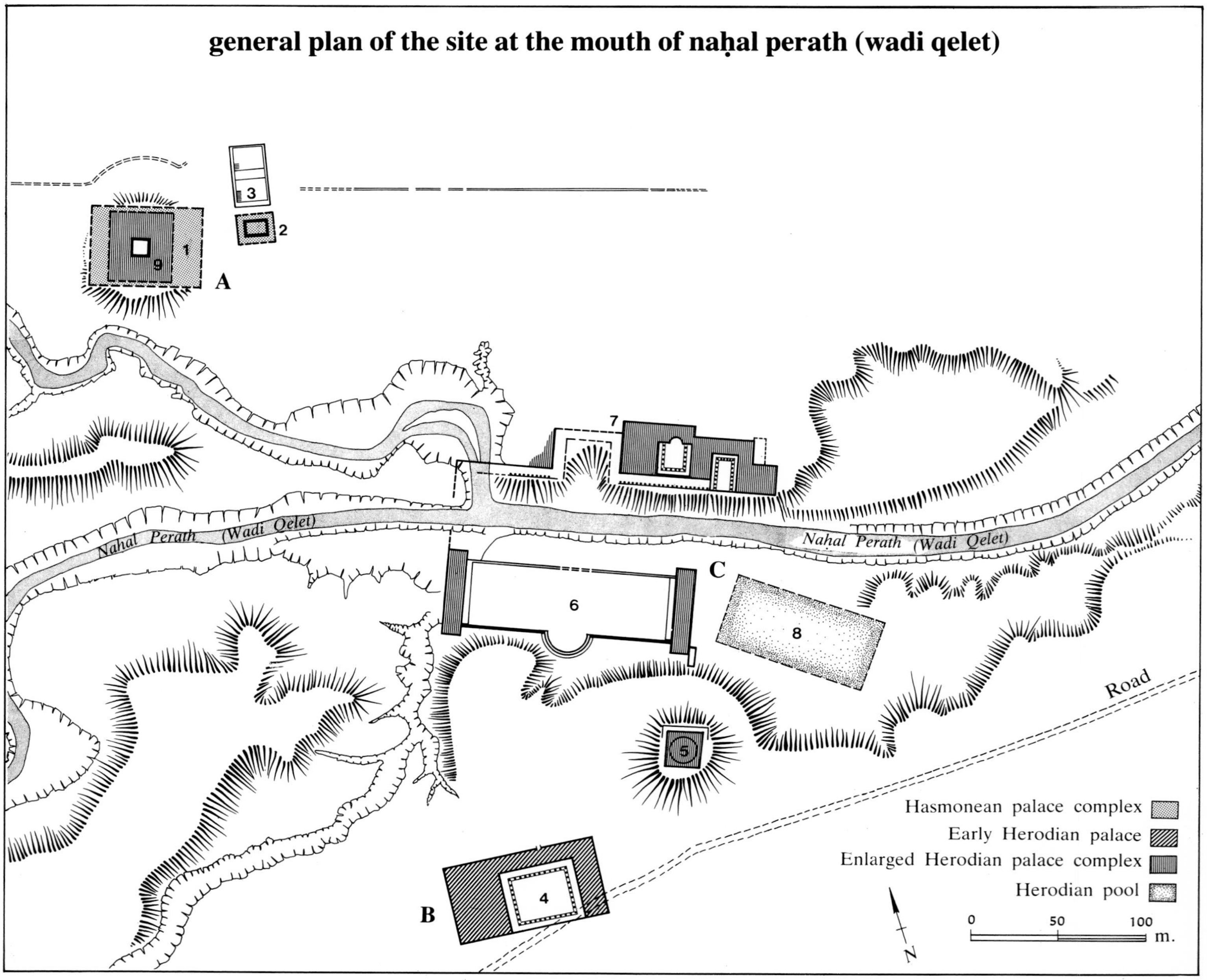

general plan of the site at the mouth of naḥal perath (wadi qelet)

1

Priest. However this appointment was not to Herod's liking, and shortly thereafter he resolved to get Aristobulus out of his way. The opportunity arose during festivities hosted by Alexandra, mother of Mariamne and Aristobulus, in the Hasmonean palace in Jericho. In the heat of the day the guests all went to the swimming pool, and as the day drew to a close Aristobulus was deliberately drowned at Herod's behest.

Shortly after this dramatic event, Mark Anthony, the Roman ruler, removed the Jericho Valley from Herod's hands and gave it to his beloved, Queen Cleopatra of Egypt. Herod, realizing the economic importance of the royal estates in the fertile valley, leased the plantations of Jericho from Cleopatra. It seems that during the same period Herod built himself a palace in Jericho, south of Wadi Qelet. This is the building which when first excavated was mistakenly thought to be a gymnasium. The building was reburied after the excavations and is no longer visible above ground.

After the dramatic suicides of Anthony and Cleopatra, Jericho returned to Herod, whose political stature was steadily growing. Herod then acquired possession of the Hasmonean palace and built himself an additional palace, this time on the remains of the Hasmonean building which in the interim had been damaged by a severe earthquake (31 b.c.e), recorded in the writings of Josephus.

italian construction

The two adjacent palaces in Jericho, it seems, were not yet enough for Herod. Over the years the king had come to know the nature of the place and realized that every few years after a rainy winter the dry streambed of Wadi Qelet would fill with large quantities of water which continued to flow for several weeks. In the best Roman tradition, therefore, Herod built yet

2

3

4

1 *General plan of the site on the mouth of Naḥal Perath (Wadi Qelet), according to its stages of construction:*

A. *Hasmonean period – winter palace complex:*
1. *main building;*
2. *pavilion?;*
3. *swimming pool.*

B. *Early Herodian building:*
4. *the winter palace.*

C. *Late Herodian buildings:*
5. *the southern tel;*
6. *the sunken garden;*
7. *the northern wing;*
8. *pool;*
9. *villa built on ruins of the Hasmonean structure.*

2 *The Hasmonean aqueduct which irrigated the royal domains near the palace.*

3 *Restoration work in Herod's palace.*

4 *A* mikveh, *a bath for ritual immersion. According to Jewish law the water in a* mikveh *may not have been drawn, i.e. it must be rainwater or water flowing from a spring. In the picture we see two pools; the one on the left, a course of steps descending to it, was filled with water channeled to it from nearby Naḥal Perath via a plastered conduit. Rainwater was collected in the pool on the right, a smaller pool called the* oẓar, *the "treasury." A pipe connected one pool to the other. Only when the water in the "treasury" came in contact with the water in the larger pool was the water in the* mikveh *considered fit for ritual immersion.*

1

reconstruction of the enlarged herodian palace complex

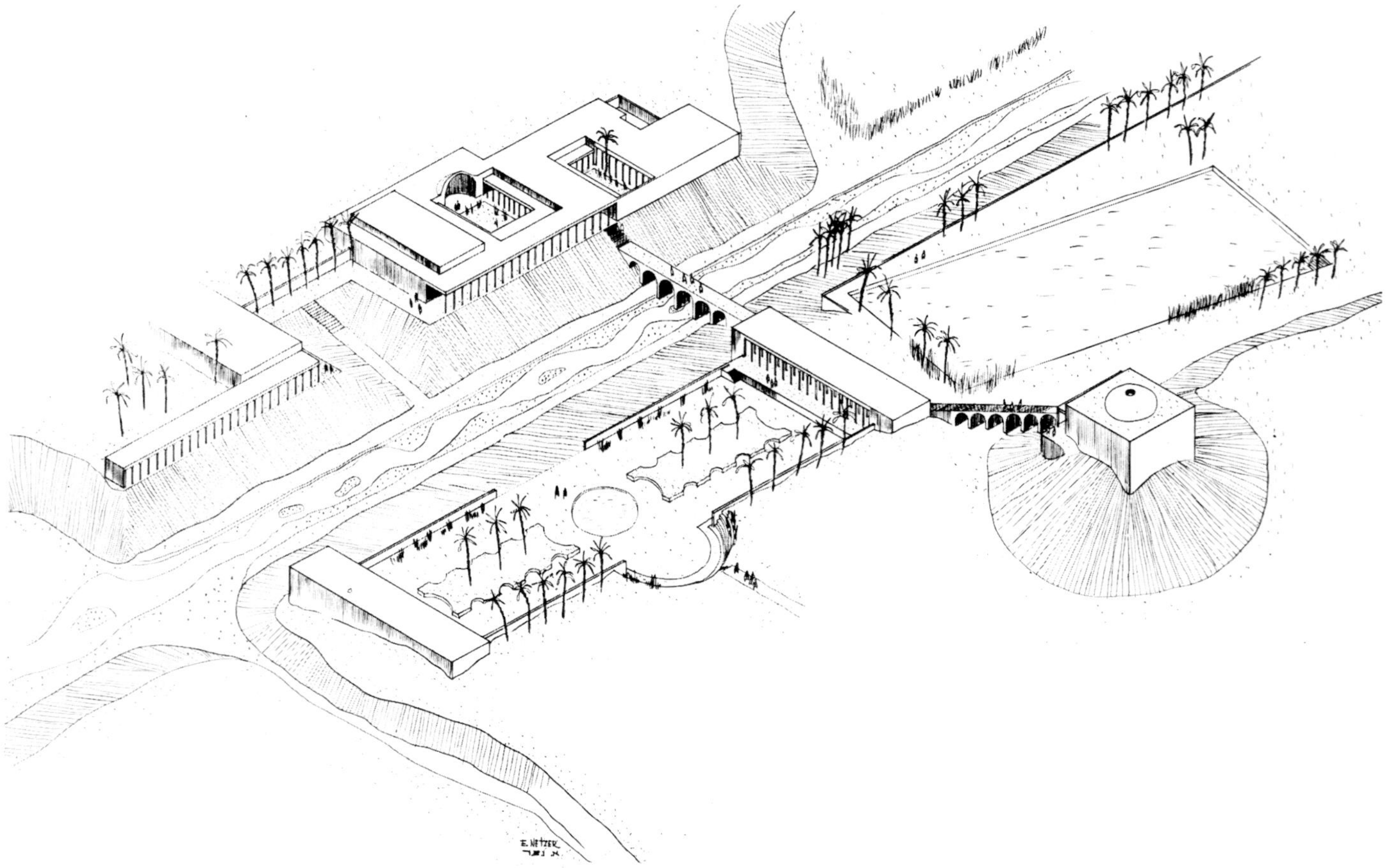

2

1 *Jericho, a garden city in an oasis. Three factors made Jericho a flourishing place during the Second Temple period: exploitation of the economic potential of the oasis, situation of the city on a main crossroads to Jerusalem, and its pleasant winter climate.*

2 *Reconstruction of the palace complexes on either side of Naḥal Perath (Wadi Qelet).*

3 *View of Jericho from Naḥal Perath.*

Panorama overleaf: Naḥal Perath, beneath which ran the southern border of the tribe of Benjamin.

3

another palace, his third in the vicinity of Jericho. This complex spread over both sides of Wadi Qelet and enjoyed the seasonal flow of water through the wadi.

In building the third palace Herod's builders worked side by side with guest masons from Rome, the supreme seat of the Roman government. The guest builders used a method of construction which was common in Italy but extremely rare in the eastern Mediterranean basin. This building technique (Roman concrete clad with small stones, forming a sort of diagonal mosaic) is only found in three sites in Israel, all of them Herodian: Jericho, the Banyas, and Jerusalem (near Damascus Gate). Although these stone-covered walls resembled a mosaic floor (albeit built of larger stones), unlike mosaics they had no ornamental objective, but were simply another technique of construction. All the stones of the completed wall were generally covered with colored plaster. Remains of this plaster can be discerned in the photograph of an elderly mason from Jericho reconstructing the corner of the wall built 2000 years earlier by guest masons from Rome. Archaeologists call this style wall, resembling a diagonal mosaic, "reticulated work."

Herod's third and magnificent palace has wings on either side of Wadi Qelet. The main wing is on the north bank, while an enormous pool (40 x 90 meters large), a garden with aqueducts and pools ("the sunken garden"), surrounded by ornamented walls and colonnaded balconies, and a building constructed entirely upon an artificial mound (the southern tel of Tulul Abu 'Ala'iq) are all on the south bank. By creating artificial mounds Herod could elevate himself above the date palms surrounding his palace on all sides, some of which may have been planted in the time of his predecessors, the Hasmoneans.

Various chambers have been discovered in the main wing, built north of the wadi: two garden courtyards surrounded by colonnaded porches, an elaborate bathhouse, and a huge ballroom or hall. The dimensions of this enormous hall reflect the broad scope of activity here when the king used to come with his family and friends to enjoy himself in his winter palace. Thirty meters long and 20 meters wide, this hall could hold hundreds of guests for splendid banquets and parties. Originally the entire hall was furnished with a floor of colored marble. The walls of the hall, like those of the other palace buildings and courtyards, were ornamented with frescoes similar to the frescoes in the northern palace on Masada. After the palace was abandoned all the flooring of the magnificent hall was stolen, leaving nothing today but the exact outlines of the marble tiles. Of the bathhouse chambers, the cold room or *frigidarium* deserves special mention. This is a round chamber with semicircular niches in each quadrant. It was undoubtedly covered by a domed ceiling, one of the technical innovations of Roman architecture (see photo).

Jericho's palaces were surrounded by gardens and orchards. Evidence of elaborate gardens, verdant and colorful, and providing ample shade, was discovered in the inner courtyards of Herod's third palace. The reconstructed diagram here gives the reader a feeling for the splendor of Jericho and its palaces in days of yore.

Herod was especially fond of Jericho, and it was here in his palace that he died. His funeral procession marched from here all the way to Herodion, where he is buried.

After the fall of the Second Temple the aqueducts in the western Jericho Valley were destroyed, and this part of the valley once more became dry and barren as it had been before the Hasmonean kings came to the area.

herodion – facing the desert

Ehud Netzer

When we stand on the southern side of Jerusalem, gazing towards the Judean Desert, Mt. Herod, sometimes called Herodion (or Herodium), catches our eye, not because of its particular height but because of its unusual shape. Herodion resembles a truncated cone, somewhat like a volcanic mountain. Although it is not an extinct volcano, there is a crater on its summit – a man-made crater which is part of a most unusual structure. King Herod, who immortalized his name in this unusual mountain, became known to no small extent for the many construction projects which he left after him. During the long years of his reign (37-4 b.c.e.), Herod's builders were busy at work. Among his most famous projects were the Temple in Jerusalem, the city and port of Caesarea, and Masada. Although Herod ruled by the grace of the Romans, who controlled all of the eastern Mediterranean at that time, he enjoyed a large degree of autonomy and managed his kingdom most skillfully, both in terms of foreign policy and in terms of economy and administration.

Herodion was built on the edge of the Judean Desert, facing the Dead Sea and the mountains of Edom, near the road connecting Jerusalem with Masada and Petra. The choice of this site for Herodion was not in the least incidental. In 40 b.c.e. Herod was compelled to flee from Jerusalem at the peak of an anti-Roman revolt led by Mattathias Antigonus the Hasmonean and supported by the Parthian army. The Parthians, then living in the region of modern Iran, were stubborn, harassing enemies of the Roman Empire. Herod, accompanied by his family and bodyguards, fled from Jerusalem in the dark of night towards the Nabatean kingdom, whose capital was Petra. When his escape became known, Mattathias Antigonus and his supporters went in hot pursuit, and here (east of Bethlehem) they fought a bloody battle in which Herod emerged the victor. Herod himself fled to Rome, where he was crowned king. Then, assisted by the Roman army, he returned to the Land of Israel and seized control of it.

Almost a generation passed before Herod returned to the site of the battle which had so decisively affected his life. This time he was accompanied by his engineers, who undertook a construction project here – one of the remarkable architectural monuments left by this great builder. The site became a memorial to the fateful battle which was fought here, a memorial to Herod's name and the place of the king's burial. There was, however, also a more practical side to building Herodion. The desert landscape on the one hand, and the site's proximity to Jerusalem on the other, inspired Herod to choose this location for a huge palace, an open palace where his guests could enjoy the breathtaking view and comfortable summer climate. They could also enjoy a measure of repose which they did not always have in the capital city of Jerusalem, a city which three times a year was a center of mass pilgrimage. Herodion was also the administrative capital of the district in which it was located. Herod's engineers succeeded in overcoming the aridity of the desert by building an aqueduct from the spring near Solomon's Pools, south of Bethlehem, all the way to Herodion.

1 *The mountain fortress palace of Herodion: "Having immortalized his family and friends he did not neglect to make his own memory secure. He built a fortress in the hills facing Arabia and called it Herodion after himself, and seven miles from Jerusalem he gave the same name to an artificial hill, the shape of a woman's breast, adorning it more elaborately than the other" (*The Jewish War, *Book I, 21:10).*

Few people realize that the peak rising at Herodion is only part of a larger area all of which was named after Herod. Herodion also extends over an area of 37 acres north of the mountain, which is called Lower Herodion. Remains of enormous edifices and an impressive pool in the area of Lower Herodion are easily discernible to this day. We must note that no other settlement preceded Herodion on this site. After Herod's death the site was maintained (although with interruptions) until the end of the Byzantine era, in the seventh century.

First we shall look at the volcanic-shaped mountain, and then we shall proceed to Lower Herodion. The original ascent up the mountain was not the same as the gently sloping path to its summit today. In Herod's time the mountain was ascended from the northeast in a straight line from bottom to top. Here there was once an impressive staircase, whose foundations alone can be discerned today. The mountain itself was originally a gently rounded hill resembling many other hills around it. First Herod's engineers built an impressive round structure some 55 meters in diameter and 30 meters in height (not including the towers, which soared even higher) on the summit. This structure has not survived in its entirety yet even the part which still stands today (to a height of some 15 meters or more) is most impressive. This circular structure did not stand on its own. As soon as it was completed a massive fill was intentionally poured around it. This fill, tens of thousands of cubic meters of earth, buried a large part of the structure and created the steep slopes around it, giving the hill its conical shape. Only the top of the structure and the towers on it showed through the fill.

a palace at the bottom of the crater

The round structure was multi-functional. A palace – a magnificent royal villa – lay concealed in the center (at the bottom of the "crater"). A large circular structure surrounded the palace like a wall surrounding a fort. Indeed the building was also intended to serve as a fortress in times of trouble. The steep slopes which the builders created around the building contributed further to its fortification. Visitors to the site today can see the

1

various details of the palace: the large colonnaded courtyard, the reception room, and the bathhouse which was part of the palace. The Roman bathhouse which has been restored on Masada is undoubtedly well known to many people. The bathhouse at Herodion was built in a similar style, except with one new element – a round room with a marvelously well preserved domed roof.

The round structure which surrounded the palace is easily discernible. But what lies inside this ring-like structure essentially has not yet been uncovered. In Herod's time a series of corridors, one above the other, encircled the palace. Aside from two basement levels, we can reconstruct five stories of corridors; the lower three have remains still standing, while the upper two can only be reconstructed today by the many stones which have fallen in the rubble. Four towers, facing north, south, east and west, rose above the walls. Three of them were semicircular and not particularly tall. The fourth, facing east, was an exception. What remains of it today (rising 16 meters high) is only a solidly filled foundation. Many more stories can be reconstructed above this foundation, in our estimation bringing the tower to a height of some 45 to 50 meters at the time of its construction. It is true that Herodion today offers no direct proof of this, but the writings of Josephus do provide some assistance. The foundation of the eastern tower at Herodion resembles the foundation in the courtyard of the Citadel in Jerusalem (Phasael's Tower), also built in the time of Herod. Josephus describes Jerusalem's three lofty towers (one of which was Phasael's Tower) in great detail, and according to his account two of these towers reached the impressive height of 45 to 50 meters.

an artificial hill, the shape of a woman's breast

The unusual shape of the structure which was erected on Mt. Herod, which should properly be called the "Mountain Fortress Palace," has turned the site into a monument. Indeed, recalling the functions of the site, intended to commemorate both a battle and the king's name, we realize that constructing an artificial mountain at Herodion accomplished this objective with great success. In Herod's day a number of large cisterns for water were hewn along the slopes of the mountain, thus assuring a reliable supply of water to the summit, both in time of peace and in time of crisis. The cisterns were hewn near the steps which ascended the mountain. The ascent itself was once very impressive, insofar as the upper part of the staircase essentially

1

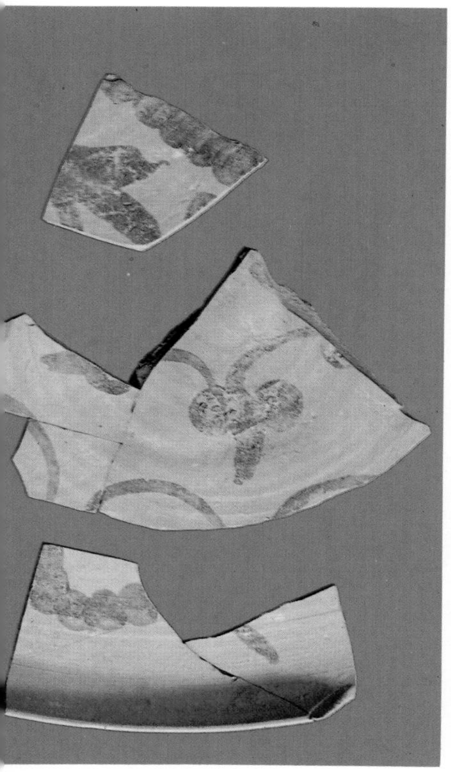

2

3

1 A Byzantine church uncovered in northern Lower Herodion. Dedications were set in the mosaic floor, as in the western vestibule, shown on the left. A Byzantine community settled in Herodion over the remains of the large palace complex.

2,3 Bowls decorated with floral designs, from the late Second Temple period, discovered at Herodion.

4 The central court (peristyle) of Herod's palace, recessed in the cone of the round mountain. In the background is the foundation of the eastern tower. The doorway on the left of the peristyle (with a man standing in it) leads to the palace vestibule, which was once reached by the corridor of steps built up the side of the mountain.

4

penetrated into the artificial fill surrounding the circular building. To defend these stairs buttresses with stone arches were built overhead. Several of these arches over the stairs have been uncovered and may be seen on the side of the mountain.

Reading the description which Josephus gives of Herodion, we are amazed at the correlation between what he describes and the remains which have been found here:

"Having immortalized his family and friends he did not neglect to make his own memory secure. He built a fortress in the hills facing Arabia and called it Herodion after himself, and seven miles from Jerusalem he gave the same name to an artificial hill, the shape of a woman's breast, adorning it more elaborately than the other. He encircled the top with round towers, filling the enclosed space with a palace so magnificent that in addition to the splendid appearance of the interior of the apartments the outer walls, copings, and roofs had wealth lavished on them without stint. At very heavy cost he brought in an unlimited supply of water from a distance, and furnished the ascent with 200 steps of the whitest marble; the mound was of considerable height, though entirely artificial. Round the base he built other royal apartments to accommodate his furniture and his friends, so that in its completeness the stronghold was a town, in its compactness a palace" (*The Jewish War*, Book I, 21:10; Penguin ed., p. 77).

As we see in the passage quoted, Josephus refers to the existence of a Lower Herodion. Today the best view of the remains of the site at the foot of the hill is from the summit. The ruins of a large pool built in the center of Lower Herodion and a broad area to its east, looking very much like a giant playing field, are most prominent. Looking closely one can discern that this broad area was completely man-made; an entire valley was filled in with earth to create it. The dam of earth, whose purpose was to support this gigantic field, can also be made out clearly from the summit.

1

2

The pool, 70 meters long by 45 meters wide and almost four meters deep, held a volume of water exceeding 10,000 cubic meters. The pool served as a reservoir for the water brought by the aqueduct (mentioned above) and as a swimming pool for hot summer days. One could row across this pool in small boats and thus reach the structure which stood in its center. Although only the foundations of this structure remain, a round building surrounded by pillars can easily be reconstructed here.

The areas encompassing the pool were intended as the foundation for an enormous garden laid out and planted in the best Roman tradition. The guests of this extended palace, aside from the king and his family, also including his friends and associates (we call them all guests insofar as this was essentially a summer palace and not a permanent palace used the year round), surely promenaded here for their pleasure. The garden was once surrounded by porticos, of which only a few ruins remain. The most magnificent portico of all stood on the eastern side of the garden, on the earthen dam mentioned above. The large pool was not only the center of the garden, but also the very heart of all Lower Herodion. Anyone who looked down from the mountain towards Lower Herodion in those days could

1 *View of Mt. Herod from the east. During the Great Revolt against the Romans Herodion was captured by the Zealots and was one of their last strongholds. Herodion, also a center of the Bar Kokhba rebellion, is mentioned several times in letters and documents of Bar Kokhba that were found in caves in the Judean Desert. Indeed, many remains testifying to its use in the Bar Kokhba revolt have been found here.*

2 *The large monumental edifice from Herod's day, discovered beside the pool complex, in the heart of Lower Herodion. The mystery of the building has not yet been solved; perhaps it is Herod's tomb.*

3 *Pieces of stucco decoration which embellished many buildings here in the time of Herod.*

enjoy the sight of the pool enclosed by gardens, all set against the surrounding desert background.

the enigma of the long track

The ruins of a long building, partially constructed of hewn stone, stand out to this day on the northern slope of Herodion, southeast of the pool complex. The edifice was 130 meters long and half as wide. Little remains of this monumental building: a few walls, some ruins of stone arches, and a single room which has survived intact, vault and all. The size and location of the building attest its importance. The most plausible hypothesis is that the central building of the palace stood here. This is where the main receptions at Herodion must have been held and where the honored guests must have stayed, except for the king's closest friends whom he invited to stay with him in his concealed and sheltered villa on the summit of the hill.

A long narrow area (resembling a racetrack) can be discerned at the foot of the long building. This area, over 300 meters long, straight and level, is clearly man-made. It is too narrow for horseraces (horse and chariot races were held in Herod's time in Jerusalem, Caesarea, and even Jericho), but perhaps was used for athletic contests. Or perhaps the ladies of the palace went on their daily walk here? Or perhaps this track has to do with the unique building which was discovered at its end? We shall return to this enigma later.

Lower Herodion also extends north of the pool complex on the northern side of the modern road leading from Bethlehem to Herodion (and continuing on to Tekoa and Hebron). This area was previously unknown to archaeologists and was only discovered in 1972 in excavations of the site by the author, sponsored by the Hebrew University and assisted by Emanuel Damati, District Archaeologist of Judea and Samaria. The mountain was first discovered by archaeologists from the Franciscan Order in Jerusalem in the 1960's, on the eve of the Six Day War. The dig was completed by the National Parks Authority with the assistance of the archaeologist Gideon Foerster.

Now let us return to the northern part of Lower Herodion. Although investigations here have been very limited, they reveal a series of palace wings spreading further north. Ornamented royal buildings stood here side by side with service buildings, an inseparable part of any palace deserving the name. Noteworthy among the palace buildings is another Roman bath in addition to the one on the summit, as well as other bathhouses which were surely once incorporated in various other palace buildings. Another building, uncovered here in its entirety, belongs to a much later period – the Byzantine era. A Byzantine community grew up in Herodion on the ruins of the extended palace. A small congregation of monks settled in the mountain fortress palace and even built themselves a small church, incorporated in one of the palace rooms. Mosaic floors, including several inscriptions which were worked into them, were discovered in the church in northern Lower Herodion.

On the fringe of the northern region, right by the turn-off of the road ascending the mountain today, we unearthed part of a large service building in which there was a long, narrow storeroom. The vaulted ceiling of this storeroom had collapsed, perhaps in an earthquake, and had buried dozens of large storage jars. Remains of a stable were also found on the site. Here the horses which carried the king and his entourage from the capital, Jerusalem, were stabled.

3

plan of the fortress palace in herod's day

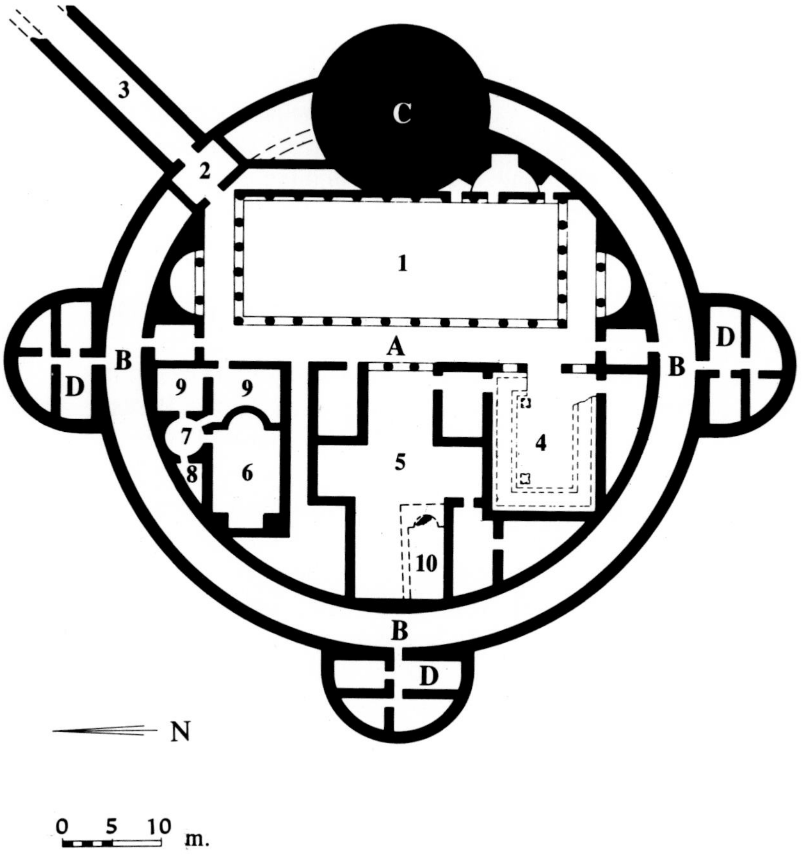

Legend:

A Interior structure
B Surrounding structure
C Eastern tower
D Three semi-circular towers
1. Peristyle court
2. Vestibule to the mountain fortress palace
3. Corridor of stairs ascending the mountain
4. Reception hall (over which the synagogue from the time of the Great Revolt against Rome was built. Remains of the synagogue's benches and pillars were found on the site)
5. Residential wing

Bathhouse:

6. Hot room *(caldarium)*
7. Tepid room *(tepidarium)*
8. Cold room *(frigidarium)*
9. Entrance and dressing rooms *(apoditerium)*
10. Byzantine church location

Let us return to the unusual building which we mentioned in connection with the long track. This building was the greatest surprise awaiting us in our work on Lower Herodion. The structure, which we called the "monumental building," is concealed slightly south of the pool complex at the beginning of the slope ascending the mountain. Even though this building has been completely unearthed, its riddle remains unsolved. It is built of large ashlars and has no external ornamentation. The interior, in contrast, reveals remains of a large and magnificent hall surrounded by half-pillars with niches between them. The hall was once covered by an impressive vaulted ceiling. What was the purpose of this building? We have no conclusive answer as of yet. The building is exceptional among the known Herodian remains in the country. Its thick walls lead us to believe it had additional storeys, or perhaps even some monument built over it. One theory which emerged as we were digging was that this had been intended as Herod's burial place.

a mountain tomb?

In Josephus we read about Herod being buried at Herodion. The funeral is described in the greatest detail (what we would call today a full military ceremony), but the exact grave site is not stated. This disappointment notwithstanding, it is still possible that the monumental building we discovered is associated with Herod's place of burial, which perhaps lies hidden somewhere nearby. Should this prove to be the case, it might imply that the long track which terminates near the monumental building was built especially for the pompous funeral ceremony held here.

Another possibility is that the tomb lies hidden within the mountain. Some scholars maintain that this accounts for the shape of the mountain, resembling the round tombs which several Roman rulers such as Augustus and Hadrian built for themselves. In our opinion a much closer source can be found to explain the shape of the mountain fortress palace, namely the Antonia fortress which Herod built in Jerusalem, next to the Temple Mount. The Antonia, like the palace of the mountain fortress, was a walled fortress with four towers (one of which was exceptionally tall) and steep glacis around the fort's walls. This is all based on the descriptions given by Josephus, since there are no extant remains of the Antonia fortress.

The history of Herodion after Herod's death merits a separate article. Let us mention simply that the fortified mountain attracted both the Zealots in the first revolt against Rome, which preceded the destruction of the Second Temple, and the followers of Bar Kokhba in his rebellion.

The first revolt left its mark on the site in the form of synagogue benches which were built in Herod's reception hall and ritual baths which were dug in the large colonnaded courtyard. The second, Bar Kokhba's rebellion, left a series of tunnels, veritable bunkers, hewn in the mountain.

Herodion has not said its last word. Future excavations will surely bring to light more information about the mountain and the buildings at its foot, and will enrich our knowledge of the history of Herodion, sitting on the fringe of the desert.

1 *The grandeur of Herodion, its palaces and gardens, attests its having been one of Herod's main summer palaces, a place offering a striking view of the desert and enjoying pleasant mountain air in the summer, yet situated quite close to Jerusalem.*
"He encircled the top with round towers, filling the enclosed space with a palace so magnificent that in addition to the splendid appearance of the interior of the apartments the outer walls, copings, and roofs had wealth lavished on them without stint. At very heavy cost he brought in an unlimited supply of water from a distance, and furnished the ascent with 200 steps of the whitest marble; the mound was of considerable height, though entirely artificial. Round the base he built other royal apartments to accomodate his furniture and his friends, so that in its completeness the stronghold was a town, in its compactness a palace" (The Jewish War, *Book I, 21:10*).
Herod was buried at Herodion, although his exact burial place has not been discovered to this day.
"After this was over, they prepared for the king's funeral, Archelaus taking care that his father should be buried in a very sumptuous manner. Accordingly, he brought out all his ornaments to add to the pomp of the funeral. The body was carried upon a golden bier, embroidered with very precious stones of great variety, and the bier was covered over with purple, as well as the body itself, which had a diadem upon its head, and above it a crown of gold, and a sceptre in its right hand. Round the bier were Herod's sons and numerous relations; next to these were the soldiers, disposed according to their several countries and names... And they went eight furlongs on the road to Herodion; for there by his own command Herod was to be buried. And thus did he end his life." (Antiquities of the Jews, *Book XVII, 196-199*).

1

secret hideouts

Yigal Tepper

Jewish and gentile sources, few and incidental, yield a paucity of detail about the intensity with which the Jews fought the Romans in 132-135 c.e., in what is known today as the Bar Kokhba rebellion. Because these sources are so scanty, great importance attaches to any archaeological finding which can shed further light on this historical event.

Jewish sources record very little about the course of the revolt itself, focusing primarily on its consequences and at that mostly on death, destruction, decrees and persecution:

"And they [the Romans] **massacred them** [the Jews] **until the horses waded in blood up to the nostrils..."** (Jerusalem Talmud, *Ta'anit* 21a).

"... and the [Jews'] **blood rolled along boulders... and flowed into the sea** [staining it for] **a distance of four miles..."** *(Ibid.)*.

"... and the blood flowed like water, filling two streams."

"... and the streams ran with two parts blood and one part water..."

"... the brains of three hundred infants were found dashed on a single stone..." *(Ibid.)*

"... The evil Hadrian had a large vineyard... and it was surrounded by a fence of those slain at Betar..." *(Ibid.)*.

These sources also mention that Jews were sold into slavery *en masse* after suppression of the revolt, flooding the market till the price of a Jewish slave dropped to the cost of one day's fodder for a horse.

Jewish sources record the punitive measures which ensued after the rebellion, but not its causes or battles. Other sources, however, indicate that protracted fighting between Jews and Romans lasted about three and a half years and resulted in the country being ravaged. The destruction was especially great in the land of Judea: many settlements were wiped out and others abandoned. After the revolt the Romans punished the Jews with the measures customary at that time by imposing heavy taxes on them, intended to reimburse the Romans' expenses in the war, and by seizing Jewish lands and apportioning them as prizes among the victors and their helpers. Other Jewish lands were abandoned, their owners having been killed, sent into exile, or sold into slavery.

These woes, which befell the Jews in their land after Roman suppression of the revolt, were similar to the troubles that beset other peoples throughout the empire who had revolted against the authority of Rome. However, unlike the fate of other peoples, the Jews suffered additional punitive acts, added to the retribution which the Romans were wont to inflict in similar instances. These were very serious punitive measures, different in their methods and purpose – punishment which in Jewish sources is referred to as **"decrees of persecution."** In addition to the physical desolation which the Romans wrought in the Land of Israel, through these decrees they aimed at bringing about spiritual and cultural ruin, with the objective of ending the existence of the Jewish people.

Among the decrees Jewish sources list prohibitions against circumcision, prayer, affixing a *mezuzah,* eating matzah, wearing *ẓiẓit* (fringes), lighting Hanukkah candles, ordaining rabbis, and assembling in synagogues or houses of study. Teaching or studying the Torah was proscribed. Jerusalem, which had been rebuilt by the Romans and named Aelia Capitolina, was barred to Jews. Anyone who violated these proscriptions was considered a rebel against Rome and was liable to a torturous end, as suffered by Rabbi Akiva, one of the Ten Martyrs put to death by the Romans.

Why did the Romans go to such excess, imposing on the few surviving Jews, who had paid the heavy price of the terrible war and its consequences, all these proscriptions, edicts, and decrees, far above and beyond their usual practice? Why did the Romans also attempt to quench the spirit of the Jewish people, after having struck such a severe blow at its body?

Perhaps the reason lies in the vehemence of the Jewish war against the Romans; perhaps in the Romans' desire to take vengeance on the people who had fought them over a relatively long period, causing their army heavy losses. Yet in this respect the Jewish rebellion was in no manner exceptional in comparison with revolts of other nationalities against Rome.

Perhaps the fury of the Romans was vented on the Jews because the latter had risen against them in massive, bitter revolt

three times over a relatively short period: once in 66-73 c.e., the revolt in whose wake Jerusalem and the Temple were laid waste; again in 115-117, when the Jews of the Diaspora revolted, stirring up the empire from Cyrene to Egypt and from Mesopotamia to the Land of Israel; and lastly, only a short while later, in 132-135, when a third Jewish revolt, much more bitter than the preceding ones, suddenly erupted. However this still is not enough to account for the vehemence of Rome's punitive measures, which were explicitly aimed at crushing the spirit of the Jewish people, its moral fiber, its religious world outlook, and perhaps even its capacity for national rehabilitation.

The Romans, it seems, discerned that the Jews were instilled with a certain spiritual strength which motivated them to rebel time and again, but could not perceive any just cause for such revolt. Perhaps the Romans concluded that it was this strength that gave the Jews the military capacity, despite their inferiority, to challenge Roman military might, a capacity which caught the Roman rulers of the land utterly by surprise.

This spiritual strength even amazes people today. We, however, are in a position to study the Jewish methods of warfare which surprised the Romans in the Bar Kokhba rebellion, causing them heavy losses. In this we are assisted by the recent archaeological discoveries of archaeologists surveying the foothills of Judea, which add a further dimension to our understanding, providing information hitherto unavailable to us. These findings are presented in the sketch which follows.

sources on the bar kokhba rebellion

The Great Revolt, the first revolt by the Jews against their Roman conquerors, is chronicled by the Jewish historian Flavius Josephus, who was a general in the revolt and the Galilean commander who turned himself over to the Romans after unsuccessfully defending Yodefat. Josephus described the history of the revolt for the people among whom he lived out the remainder of his life, having known the beginning of the revolt as an active participant and its end as an observer inside the victorious Roman camp. The Jewish calendar has a day commemorating this revolt, the day the Second Temple was destroyed: the ninth of Av. Jewish tradition also associates the destruction of the First Temple and the fall of Betar with this day of national mourning.

The Jews' revolt against the Greeks also has its written records – the First and Second Books of the Maccabees – as well as its commemorative days which have entered the heritage of the Jewish people for all time: the eight days of Hanukkah, celebrating the rededication of the Temple.

These literary testaments, as well as the commemorative days associated with the events chronicled, preserve important chapters in the annals of the Jewish people deep in the historical remembrance of the nation. Without these works our knowledge of these periods would be scant and haphazard, like what we know about the course of the Bar Kokhba rebellion, and far from sufficient to provide a full picture.

Unfortunately the Bar Kokhba rebellion had no chronicler. The reasons Jewish tradition bound the events of the revolt to the day of Lag ba-Omer are shrouded in mystery; and the customs associated with the day have become so deeply veiled in gentile folklore traditions, imposed during the Jews' exile from their land and their dispersal over Europe, that today we no longer know which of the customs surrounding the day are authentically our own and which belong to other peoples.

All we have to illumine the events of this great rebellion, its motives, and the course and termination of the fighting, comes from a patchwork of facts randomly scattered sparsely through Jewish and gentile sources, a patchwork in which the information missing far outweighs that which is present, even today. Even the first name of the Jewish general who by his personal leadership united all the ranks of the Jewish people in a revolt from which there was no retreating has only been recently identified: Simeon.

How then can we assess the intensity with which the Jews fought this revolt, when the sources available to us speak almost exclusively about the Roman punitive actions which followed in its wake? Archaeological findings from this obscure period, discovered recently in caves in the Judean Desert, Naḥal

Delayya in eastern Samaria, in the fortress of Herodion, and in Jerusalem, add some important details to the patchwork picture. Yet even these findings are not adequate to explain how the Jews, a small and humble people, managed to surprise the Romans, who were installed as overlords and rulers in the Jews' land; how they managed to deal the Romans a severe blow, driving them out of the land for a short period of time; how they managed to liberate Jerusalem and institute an independent administrative apparatus; how they held out against the military might of the Roman Empire for several years; how time and again they routed what was then the best army in the world, ultimately compelling Emperor Hadrian, in order to defeat the Jews, to raise what by ancient standards was a vast force numbering more than eight Roman legions and additional auxiliary troops – almost three times as large as the Roman force which Titus led when he destroyed Jerusalem. This army succeeded in overcoming the rebels only after suffering such heavy losses that Emperor Hadrian could not open his address to the Senate with the usual commander's greeting, "If you and your children are in health, it is well; I and the legions are in health," but had to omit it. Hadrian's forces returned to lick their wounds in camp and did not merit the customary victory march.

1

2

the vehemence of jewish fighting

The spiritual strength of the Jewish people, the magnitude of their hatred towards the Romans who conquered their land, and their determination to free themselves from "the yoke of this nation" account for the vehemence with which the Jews fought the Romans. However to strike at the Roman army, and at that with a considerable degree of success, requires tangible means capable of translating this hatred into terms of military strength. Uniting the Jewish people under the leadership of Bar Kokhba was one of these means. The physical strength of Bar Kokhba himself, as described in our sources, may be viewed as another means: **"He would catch the missiles** [from the Romans' catapults] **on one of his knees and hurl them back, killing many** [Romans]**";** and in gentile sources: **"For he spewed out flames from his mouth."** This did not suffice him, and therefore he also placed physical challenges before his fighters, trying the heroism of his warriors by cutting off their fingers. When the sages protested against his practice, he took their advice: **"Let anyone who cannot ride his horse and uproot a cedar of Lebanon be refused enrollment in your army."** So great was his faith in his own strength and in that of his army that he prayed of God in brazen self-confidence, **"Let Him neither aid us nor afflict us,"** in other words: He need not help us, for we shall manage on our own.

All this, however, was still not enough to defeat the Roman army. To do so required an army which was well trained, organized, and equipped; an army capable of successfully engaging the Roman forces without giving them an opportunity to train and prepare for the encounter. The Jewish army had to build itself and develop methods of warfare and self-defense that would enable it to call the tune in the battle engagements and to win decisive victories – all with the Romans and their henchmen keeping a close eye on the entire country.

On the nation's mobilization efforts, on preparing, organizing and training the army, on developing methods of warfare, on providing for the defense of settlements and organizing supply routes and stores – on all this we essentially have not a single reliable source. What little we do know rests on the testimony of the Roman historian Dio Cassius.

The works of Cassius disappeared into the fog of history. The few of them that survived were preserved in the books of a Byzantine monk who used quotes from the writings of Cassius to illustrate the evil which befell the Jews for refusing to accept the gospel of Jesus. Dio Cassius' record of the Jews' war against the Romans in the time of Hadrian is haphazard and fragmented, and is written in the idiom of an outsider, in Roman fashion viewing the Jews as a people following practices foreign to him and his culture, while in contrast beholding Hadrian as an enlightened emperor and noble member of Hellenistic civilization.

We cite Dio Cassius on the following subjects:

THE CAUSE OF THE REVOLT: **"At Jerusalem he** [Hadrian] **founded a city in place of the one which had been razed to the ground, naming it Aelia Capitolina... This brought on a war of no slight importance nor of brief duration..."**

PREPARATIONS FOR REVOLT: **"... they purposely made of poor quality such weapons as they were called upon to furnish, in order that the Romans might reject them and they themselves might thus have the use of them."**

OUTBREAK OF THE REVOLT: **"... but when he** [Hadrian] **went farther away, they openly revolted."**

FIRST STAGE OF THE REVOLT: **"They** [the Jews] **occupied the advantageous positions in the country and strengthened them with mines and walls, in order that they might have places of refuge whenever they should be hard pressed, and might meet together unobserved under ground; and they pierced these subterranean passages from above at intervals to let in air and light."**

SUCCESS OF THE JEWS: **"At first the Romans took no account of them. Soon, however, all Judea had been stirred up, and the Jews everywhere were showing signs of disturbance..."**

SECOND STAGE OF THE WAR: **"Then, indeed, Hadrian sent against them his best generals. First of these was Julius Severus..."**

ROMAN VICTORY: **"Severus did not venture to attack his opponents in the open at any one point... but by intercepting small groups, thanks to the number of his soldiers and his under-officers, and by depriving them of food and shutting them up, he was able, rather slowly, to be sure, but with comparatively little danger, to crush, exhaust and exterminate them."**

CONSEQUENCES OF THE REVOLT: **"Very few of them** [the Jews] **in fact survived. Fifty of their most important outposts and nine hundred and eighty-five of their most famous villages were razed to the ground. Five hundred and eighty thousand men were slain in the various raids and battles, and the number of those that perished by famine, disease and fire was past finding out. Thus nearly the whole of Judea was made desolate..."**

1 *The opening of a cistern at Ḥurbat Naqiq. Indentations made by ropes used for drawing water can be seen in the rock. Looking in from above, the entrance to the secret tunnel, located on the concave wall of the cistern, is hidden from view.*

2 *The central hall in the public shelter at Ḥurbat Naqiq, with doorways to smaller rooms opening off it. The photo was taken facing the entrance tunnel.*

3 *A large cistern in the center of an ancient settlement in the Judean foothills. It was transformed into a hideout by hewing a tunnel to it from a house above, the floor of the house concealing the entrance to the tunnel.*

3

CONSEQUENCES OF THE REVOLT FOR THE ROMANS:
"Many Romans, moreover, perished in this war."

This fragmentary account by Dio Cassius intimates that the Jews engaged in clandestine preparations for the revolt. They equipped themselves with Roman arms well in advance, and dug underground hideouts which served both as defense shelters and as bases for launching surprise raids on the Romans.

Not in keeping with the customary approach of contemporary historians, Dio Cassius gives no details about battle deployments. For this reason and because no other corroborative evidence had been found to date, doubt was cast on the reliability of Dio Cassius' testimony, which has even been considered a Roman apology written to explain the war's long duration and heavy toll.

Attempts to trace the footsteps of the Bar Kokhba rebels have also reached a dead end. On the one hand, an ostensibly historical source lay at their disposal; on the other hand, the archaeological discoveries possibly corroborating this source, or something close to it, have amounted to the findings of the Judean Desert caves, which actually attested to civilians hiding out in these caves. Archaeology has only recently begun to reveal facts perhaps capable of filling in the missing dimension, the dimension linking the testimony of Dio Cassius with the cause of the rebels' success. These findings are the subterranean chambers known as the "secret hideouts of the Bar Kokhba rebellion."

discovering the secret hideouts

The discovery of the "secret hideouts" attributed to the period of Bar Kokhba's rebellion is a fascinating story. While the description of these hideouts is very interesting, their main significance is their contribution to reconstructing Bar Kokhba's rebellion and understanding its main events, so obliquely alluded to by the Roman historian Dio Cassius.

The existence of secret hideouts was essentially discovered by Ehud Neẓer in his excavations at Herodion. Herod built his mountain palace as a fortress for the security of his own person and of his family, and as his destined burial place. The letters of Bar Kokhba, discovered in caves of the Judean Desert, plainly stated that the fortress of Herodion served as Bar Kokhba's headquarters during the first stage of the revolt, during which the Jews established their own administration in the country. Signs of this period have indeed been found among the ruins of Herodion.

Various tunnels and subterranean chambers were discovered inside the mountain. When archaeologists realized that these tunnels were obstructing the water system of the fortress and using its conduits as passageways to the tunnels, thus vitiating the usefulness of the water system, they surmised that the tunnels belonged to the period of Bar Kokhba.

Not far from Herodion, in Wadi 'Arub near Gush 'Eẓyon (the 'Eẓyon Bloc), another subterranean complex was discovered, also containing hollowed out chambers and tunnels. Yoram

1

Ẓafrir, who excavated this complex, attributes its date and use to the Bar Kokhba rebellion, in agreement with the testimony of Dio Cassius. These two finds were the first intimation that Dio Cassius' account may have been a true reflection of the situation during the Bar Kokhba rebellion. While this finding may have shed new light on the veracity of Dio Cassius, it did not yet explain how this historian attributed to such subterranean complexes as these the mightiness of the Jewish war effort or the reason for the Jewish successes and Roman losses.

Then in 1977 several subterranean complexes containing tunnels and chambers, as well as potsherds matching the period of the Bar Kokhba rebellion, were found in the Shefela (foothills) of Judea, south of Naḥal Adorayim, by the archaeologist David Alon. Local residents of the southern Hebron Mountain region revealed that coins and pottery had for many years been removed from these underground chambers and sold in antique markets in East Jerusalem. The coins that had been sold, when identified, proved to be from the Bar Kokhba rebellion.

Since then dozens of ancient ruins in the southern, central and northern Judean foothills have been surveyed by other archaeologists, including the author. These surveys revealed dozens of subterranean hideouts, some of which have been made public and have begun to attract hikers and sightseers.

The discovery that subterranean hideouts were common to most of the ancient ruins in the area defined by other criteria as a Jewish region in the time of Bar Kokhba's rebellion, corroborates Dio Cassius and in one fell swoop fills in an important dimension to our understanding of the revolt. Much work lies ahead, assembling all the findings and information about these secret hideouts in order to assess their full scope and understand their minute details. For the meanwhile we shall

1 *A columbarium (cave with niches resembling pigeon-holes) was transformed into a secret hideout by hewing a tunnel into its ceiling from the building above it and by camouflaging its original entrance.*

2 *An opening to a secret tunnel was hewn halfway up the vaulted wall of a cistern so that it would not be visible from above. A rope ladder, which could be rolled up in time of danger, was used to descend from the opening of the tunnel into the cistern.*

On the next page:

1 *A secret shelter for storing liquids. In the walls we can see the openings of containers hewn in the shape of jugs, used for storing water, oil, or wine. The opening on the upper right is the hidden shaft leading to the shelter.*

2

focus on two subterranean complexes, one at Ḥurbat Naqiq and another at Kh. Ḥazana. These sites, publicized in the press, have become an attraction for Israel's sightseers, offering them a new experience in seeing the land. Of the two sites, the complex at Ḥurbat Naqiq is the finer and more outstanding, in its details characterizing various aspects of the secret hideouts.

We wish to enhance the sightseer's visit to these hideouts by bringing certain important details to his attention, and at the same time request that he take care not to damage or deface the sites as certain visitors have done, ruining the findings in some of the hideouts and leaving their names behind on the walls of rooms and tunnels.

innovations in warfare and self-defense

Studies since 1977 have revealed as many as several dozen secret hideouts. Research on the subject, although still in full swing, has already yielded enough to assess the nature of these hideouts, the reason they were made, and how they were used. Beginning with their name, we may ask why they are called "secret hideouts"? Alternatively, were these complexes what Dio Cassius had in mind when he spoke of "places of refuge whenever they should be hard pressed," or did they also serve for attack?

Man has used subterranean hideouts for defense since time immemorial. The five Canaanite kings escaped from Joshua by fleeing to the caves of Makkedah (in the Judean foothills!); and David fled from King Saul, also to caves in the Judean foothills. The caves of the Judean Desert have served as hideouts for the persecuted since ancient times. This was so 5,500 years ago, when Chalcolithic man hid his great cache of bronze implements in them, and it was so in later periods as well. The caves of the Judean Desert were used by the Qumran sect for stowing their holy scriptures, and later by the refugees of the Bar Kokhba rebellion, who climbed up from 'En Gedi to hide in the Judean Desert caves.

In contrast to these and other examples, the man-made subterranean chambers which Bar Kokhba's men built as hideouts were an innovation. For the first time hideouts were prepared in advance, the form of the subterranean complexes being planned and built according to predetermined needs. A society which plans for the security of its members in advance, before the outbreak of hostilities, by setting up subterranean hideouts was something new in the history of human civilization. The continuation of this phenomenon may be seen in the subterranean hiding places which the early Christians built themselves in Rome and Turkey, and in our day in the underground hideouts which the Chinese made to defend themselves against their Japanese foe, a method which was later adopted by the Vietnamese in their war against the American army. Here we should also mention the Warsaw Ghetto insurgents, who built themselves bunkers and underground passageways for hiding and for launching a surprise attack.

What these hideouts and others not mentioned here have in common is a strategy employed since the time of Bar Kokhba by a weaker force preparing to take on a force which is normally stronger in open warfare. Dio Cassius' assertion that Bar

1

Kokhba's men developed the strategy of subterranean burrows as a means of warfare and self-defense, if true, essentially attests to an innovation in techniques of warfare and self-defense introduced by the revolt's leaders: rebels for the first time not only took into account immediate military advantages, but also considered the possible consequences of revolt for their civilian rear and hence also provided for its security. Although Dio Cassius attributes the Jews' strategy to their cowardice in not daring to come out in the open against the Roman army, the secret hideouts, which were planned and prepared in advance, long before the revolt – six years, as far as we can tell – actually show that the Jews planned their revolt very thoroughly. Aside from preparing weapons and building and supplying an army, the Jews developed a technique to prevent the Romans from enjoying their usual great advantage on the open battlefield. This strategy also provided the rebels a means of fortification, something they had been prevented from building for their towns in a conventional and open format because of Roman control of the country at the time.

All this implies that the Jewish revolt against the Romans was neither sudden nor uncalculated. On the contrary, it was planned and organized well in advance by a unified command, enlisting the entire Jewish community in a protracted military operation on the basis of a pre-charted plan of the stages of the revolt; and all this without the Romans knowing a thing about these preparations.

Only after being caught by surprise – after discovering how the revolt had been organized and planned, after paying the toll taken by the Jewish forces which sallied forth from underground at unexpected times and places, after finding themselves precluded from attacking the foe who would disappear into their secret burrows – only after all this did the Romans begin to consider the advantages of the technique which had been employed against them. Hence the tone of surprise which we detect in Dio Cassius' report on this technique of warfare. From his testimony it is clear that the Romans were caught utterly unawares and that much time elapsed before they developed their own method of warfare to meet the challenge of the Jews.

varieties of secret hideouts

The secret hideouts of the Bar Kokhba era have many features from which we may draw inferences about the intentions of the people who made them. Several varieties of hideouts have been found, each specifically adapted in its form and interior layout to

1 *A secret shelter for storing liquids.*

2 *"They [the Jews] occupied the advantageous positions in the country and strengthened them with mines and walls, in order that they might have places of refuge whenever they should be hard pressed, and might meet together unobserved under ground" (Dio Cassius, on the Bar Kokhba rebellion).*

On the next two pages:

1 *Narrow passageways (40 x 50 cm.) which could be blocked by stone doors openable only from within were built in the tunnels leading to the secret shelters.*

2 *A lead weight from the time of Bar Kokhba, found in a hideout in Ḥurbat Alim, north of Bet Guvrin. Its discovery in a typical burrow helps date the secret hideouts. Geometric designs and inscriptions appear on both sides of the weight. A rosette, the most common motif of the Second Temple period, is in the center of the side shown here and is surrounded by an inscription,* **"Ben Kosba Nasi Yisrael V-parnaso Shimeon Dasoi. Peras,"** *which translates:* **"Ben Kosba president** *(or head of state)* **of Israel and his economic chief Simeon Dasoi. Peras."** *The last word denotes a unit of weight.*

2

the intentions, requirements and attributes of the place.

Tunnel systems. In some settlements Bar Kokhba's fighters set up ramified complexes of tunnels, wending through existing subterranean hollows in the same area: bell-shaped caves, cisterns, caves used as oil presses, catacombs, columbaria, etc. Labyrinths of subterranean passageways with many entrances and exits hidden in existing caves thus came into being.

Public systems. These were generally larger. Some had halls for clandestine public gatherings; some served as headquarters or were used for any other public purpose.

Family systems. These were mostly small, generally in the form of a tunnel with an aperture in the floor of a residential building above ground, and with two or three rooms opening off the tunnel. These systems appear to have been built as secret shelters for the inhabitants of the residential buildings above them.

Supply depots. These were generally made for hiding and protecting provisions, supplies, war materiel, water, food, etc. – whatever the public needed to survive underground for any protracted time.

These types of systems appear time and again in most of the settlements where secret hideouts were found and essentially reflect a community decision to build itself an underground refuge. Some of the systems appear to have been built at the request of the settlement, pursuant to instructions issued by revolt headquarters to the entire Jewish community; others appear to have been privately constructed by one or another group of residents in a given town.

The Jews at that time were forbidden to fortify their cities, to build a wall around their towns, or make themselves a gate. The sites where secret hideouts have been discovered are characteristically unwalled settlements, farming villages without any signs of fortification. Their outward aspect must have been deceptive then, as now – a peaceful civilian scene. The idea of imparting such an innocuous appearance to Jewish settlements, while secretly preparing for revolt, was surely in the mind of the leaders when they invented their strategy of secret hideouts. It was the Romans' total unawareness of what was transpiring that gave the commanders of the revolt their sense of security. Thus they assured the welfare of the population by making an effective defense system immediately available to all citizens beneath their very houses and were spared having to gather the population into walled cities, as had been done in the first revolt.

shapes of the secret hideouts

The various types of hideouts have certain characteristic features by which we identify them today:

The tunnels were designed to make passage through them difficult and to provide convenient places for their defense. Meandering this way and that, they turn sharply left or right and frequently change level up or down. The tunnels are narrow and low, passable only by stooping. Tight doorways, which could be defended and locked with stone doors, were built into the tunnels.

1

The entrances to the tunnels were designed so that they could be blocked from within and defended. Most of the entrances were camouflaged in caves which served as columbaria or oil presses. Other entrances have been found in the floors of houses.

The rooms of the shelters were mostly narrow and low. It appears that the people who built these shelters did not provide more than the bare minimum for survival. Some rooms show signs of the people living in them trying to improve their quarters while in hiding.

Storage installations. Some shelters where containers for liquids and storerooms were found appear to have been designed exclusively for storage. Most shelters, however, had storage installations and supply rooms attached to them. Such installations, it seems, were built into family and public shelters to answer the day-to-day needs of survival of the people hiding in them.

Ventilation, of course, is one of the difficult problems in human survival underground. As Dio Cassius notes, those who built these secret hideouts were aware of the problem and saw to it that the caves had at least two openings, for air intake and exhaust.

Lighting was provided by small oil lamps most hours of the day. Such a lamp consumes about a liter of oil per day. Thus one problem of living in these shelters was to provide a steady supply of oil. To economize on oil, niches were built to house the lamps so that they would provide the most efficient lighting.

Sanitation becomes a serious problem when a large number of people live in crowded conditions beneath the ground. There are indications that the designers of the shelters noted this fact and set aside special places as bathrooms, mostly in remote, abandoned caves, reached by tunnels.

Blocking the tunnels and shelters. Several devices designed to block entrances to rooms, tunnels and passageways within tunnels have been found. Stone doors were the most common means of barring passage.

The great similarity between shelters discovered in different communities appears to confirm the hypothesis that they were built according to a single plan, prepared well in advance. Most appear to have been built inside settlements, solely for the purpose of concealment, thus fitting Dio Cassius' description of them as "places of refuge whenever they should be hard pressed."

Given living conditions in the shelters, it is hard to imagine that fighters could remain in hiding and at the same time maintain sufficient physical fitness to come out into the open and fight in an organized battle array. This leads us to suggest that the rebels had a different way of fighting, not tied to standard battle arrays; however, we have no proof of this.

2

tu b'av wears a new dress

Not the slightest remains of the people who defended these shelters have been found in them to date. While potsherds and other findings have been discovered, no human remains of people killed or otherwise having met their end in the hideouts have been found in a single shelter. This raises the question whether the hideouts were conquered and their defenders removed, or whether the defenders surrendered and fell into the hands of the Romans. Remember Flavius Josephus, who hid in a cave with the last defenders of Yodefat. There, too, the defenders faced a similar choice: to kill themselves or surrender to the Romans. Most chose to take their own lives, and only Josephus, the last to survive, surrendered to the Romans. Did the same thing happen in these secret hideouts?

There are indications that the Romans did not break into the secret hideouts. Most of the openings were found sealed, their closings in place. Today the shelters are entered by way of openings which were broken through the walls or ventilation ducts in a later period. There are also indications that the Romans filled stones and dirt into a number of caves which they thought opened on tunnels leading to the secret shelters.

Ostensibly it seems likely the Jews surrendered to the Romans and abandoned the shelters. This, however, is controverted by the testimony of Dio Cassius, who states that untold numbers of Jews perished in these shelters by "famine, disease and fire." The clue to resolving this contradiction lies in a Jewish source which mentions that after suppression of the Bar Kokhba rebellion the Jews petitioned the Roman government for permission to bury the fallen who had been abandoned upon their death. The same source states that on the 15th of Av (Tu b'Av, traditionally a day young maidens, bedecked in white, went out to dance in the vineyards, and young men selected prospective brides) the Jews were granted permission to bury their brethren who had fallen at Betar. This source reflects efforts by the Jews remaining in the land to observe the commandment of bringing those who had fallen in the revolt to a proper burial. This immediately reminds us of the State of Israel's concern to lay to rest its fallen soldiers whose bodies remained in enemy territory after Israel's wars.

Presuming this to be so, Tu b'Av takes on a new dimension as a sanctified day, which in the time of Bar Kokhba acquired renewed significance as a day of national remembrance.

The Jews who came to evacuate the bodies of those slain in the revolt knew secret shelters existed in the Jewish settlements, but due to circumstances at the time they did not succeed in locating the entrances to the shelters. Hence they had to enter the shelters by breaching their walls. In their wake, many years later, robbers broke into the shelters and removed most of the material findings which were there. Thus all that remains for us today are the shelters themselves, testimony to an unusual development in the history of the Jewish people.

the sanhedrin removed to bet she'arim

Menachem Zaharoni

On the Ninth of Av the First and Second Temples were destroyed, hence this day symbolizes the loss of national independence. When the State of Israel was established it was suggested that the day of mourning on the Ninth of Av be annulled. A similar suggestion, interestingly enough, had been advanced centuries earlier in Bet She'arim, the Jewish town in the Lower Galilee chosen as the seat of the Sanhedrin (the supreme Jewish council) after the Sanhedrin had been exiled from Jerusalem to Jabneh (near modern Yavne), and thence to Usha and later to Shefar'am.

One hundred years after the destruction of the Second Temple the Lower Galilee was actually a flourishing center of Jewish life, enjoying the sense of security of a people living on its own land and in its own country. This feeling was so strong that Rabbi Judah ha-Nasi, redactor of the Mishnah and leader of the Jewish community, wished to cancel the fast on the Ninth of Av altogether, which that year fell on the Sabbath and hence was observed a day later. The sages opposed him, and Judah ha-Nasi conceded to their wishes.

In the early ninth century b.c.e., during the divided monarchy, a new Hebrew settlement, most likely a small village, was founded on the hillock of Bet She'arim, northwest of the statue of Alexander Zeid. Like the statue of Zeid today, the houses of this settlement gazed upon the fertile expanses of the Jezreel Valley and the lofty hills of Mt. Carmel.

life on the margin of world events

The chalkstone hills north and northeast of Bet She'arim were once covered with forests of Tabor oaks. The prophecy of Hosea, **"And the earth shall respond to the corn, and the wine, and the oil; and they shall respond to Jezreel"** (Hosea 2:24), evokes a scene very much like the landscape of this area. In early summer golden fields of wheat and barley (corn) covered the expanse all the way to the foothills, even ascending the slopes of the hills, while vineyards (wine) and olive groves (oil) reached down toward the valley from the rocky slopes of the mountains and hillsides.

The farmers and wine-growers of Bet She'arim lived on the edge of political developments of the times, although their settlement surely felt all that transpired. In the years of prosperity and political glory enjoyed by the kingdom of the ten tribes, the settlement expanded and became more solidly based, while the years of decline affected it adversely, the storm of war and destruction seriously shaking it, possibly even wiping it out altogether. From the few extant remains, nothing definitive can be concluded regarding the fate of this settlement. Indeed Bet She'arim was of no political importance during the biblical period either demographically or militarily and hence is not mentioned in Scripture.

The major cities during this period were Megiddo and Jezreel, situated along the Via Maris, the international route which led from Egypt, along the Coastal Plain and the 'Iron Valley, to Syria and the lands of the Tigris and Euphrates. The swamps of the Qishon precluded a major route from developing along the line of the Carmel range and the foothills of Bet She'arim to the important Canaanite cities of Acre and Akhziv on the northern coastal plain of the Galilee.

After the fall of the Northern Kingdom a veil descends over the history of the Jezreel Valley, exposing very little to us of what happened there. What we do know for certain is that the conquering kings set aside the fertile lands of the "great valley" for themselves as their royal demesne. When Judah Aristobulus the Hasmonean conquered the Jezreel Valley from the Seleucids, ownership of these lands automatically passed to the Hasmonean kings and from them to Herod. Josephus mentions that **"a large quantity** [of corn] **belonging to Queen Berenice** [sister of King Agrippa II], **had been collected from the neighboring villages and stored in Besara** [Bet She'arim]" (Josephus, *Life,* Ch. 44). Bet She'arim is first mentioned in Jewish sources with respect to Josephus having seized this corn for the rebels revolting against Rome. Sometimes he refers to

1

1 The courtyard in front of the catacomb of Rabban Gamaliel and Rabban Simeon. The catacomb's façade has three arches, one of them without a doorway. Perhaps this is the cave where Rabbi Judah ha-Nasi is buried. The terraced benches above the catacomb were used by the people for public assemblies, perhaps even for memorial services for the illustrious Nasi.

*2 One of the three Hebrew inscriptions found in the catacomb pictured on the left. The inscription, painted in black, is bi-lingual, the first line in Hebrew and the second in Greek. It reads: "This is of Rabbi Gamaliel M." The other inscriptions mention Rabbi Simeon and Rabbi Ḥanina. Ever since the catacomb was discovered, scholars have wondered whether this might be the family vault of Rabbi Judah ha-Nasi. The Talmud (*Ketubbot *103b) recounts that, before his passing, Rabbi delegated various offices of the Sanhedrin, saying: "My son Simeon shall be a great scholar, my son Gamaliel shall be Nasi, and Ḥanina b. Ḥama shall preside [at the college]." Is it merely coincidental that three people by these names were found to have been buried in the same catacomb of Bet She'arim?*

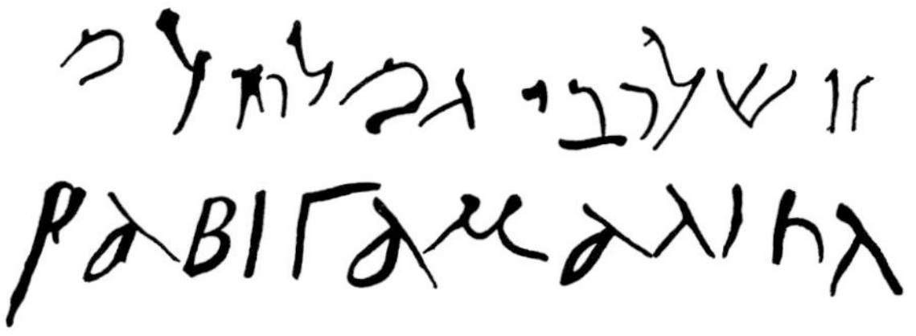

2

the place as a city, sometimes as a village. In his day it must have been a large village, inhabited by Jewish tenant farmers, and an administrative center for the estates of Berenice.

the seat of the patriarch and the sanhedrin

Bet She'arim gained historical significance only in the time of Rabbi Judah ha-Nasi, known in Jewish sources simply as Rabbi. The Jewish community in the land began to rally after the great devastation which it suffered with the failure of the Bar Kokhba revolt. But the Jewish community of Judea and the Judean foothills, which suffered more heavily from the horrors of war than the Galilean communities, was too impoverished for the center of autonomous Jewish rule to be re-established in any one of its towns. **"The Sanhedrin was exiled... from the Chamber of Hewn Stone to Ḥanuth** [buildings on the Temple Mount, outside the sanctified area]**, and then removed from Ḥanuth to Jerusalem and from Jerusalem to Jabneh, and from Jabneh to Usha and from Usha** [back] **to Jabneh and from Jabneh** [back] **to Usha, and from Usha to Shefar'am and from Shefar'am to Bet She'arim and from Bet She'arim to Ẓippori and from Ẓippori to Tiberias"** (*Rosh ha-Shanah* 31a). **"Justice, justice shalt thou follow: this means, Follow the scholars to their academies, e.g. Rabbi Eliezer to Lydda, Rabban Joḥanan b. Zakkai to Beror Ḥayil... Rabbi to Bet She'arim"** (*Sanhedrin* 32b). It was difficult for the nation's leaders to relinquish the idea of re-establishing the Sanhedrin in the vicinity of Jerusalem, yet the demographic reality determined that it be re-established in the Galilee. Nevertheless, from Usha in the western Lower Galilee another attempt appears to have been made to transfer the Sanhedrin back to Jabneh in the southern Coastal Plain. This attempt, however, failed ("... from Jabneh to Usha, from Usha to Jabneh, and from Jabneh to Usha").

Usha and Shefar'am were on the outskirts of the Jewish population center in the Galilee, too close to the eyes of the Roman authorities in Acre and on uneasy terms with the neighboring alien population living in the Zebulun Valley. In contrast, Bet She'arim, although not centrally located, lay in a purely Jewish area. Jewish settlements bordered it on all sides: Tiv'on on the north, 'Ardaskos on the northeast (on the site of the modern *kibbutz* Allonim), and on the south a village whose ancient name we do not know (Tel Yiẓḥakiya) but which, as synagogue remains on the site clearly attest, was certainly Jewish (its exact location is near the turn-off to Kefar Yehoshua' from the Tiv'on – Yoqne'am road). All the foothills to the east were densely covered with Jewish farming villages whose residents worked the land in the valley. The most famous of these was Simonia, the biblical Shimron.

1

1 *The large public building (basilica) was part of the city wall, which was formed by the outer walls of houses built contiguous to one another.*

2 *A large structure north of the synagogue. The arch indicates that at one time the building had a second storey.*

3 *Arcosolia style graves, hewn into the wall: each grave consisted of an arched niche above a trough-like hewn grave covered with a sarcophagus lid.*

Presumably Bet She'arim was chosen to succeed Shefar'am as the seat of the Nasi (Patriarch) and the Sanhedrin because it was the most important town in the region. Yet perhaps there was another reason for its selection.

Origen, a Church Father and approximate contemporary of Judah ha-Nasi, writes that the sovereignty of the Jewish Patriarch was no different from the sovereignty of any other king subject to the supreme hegemony of Rome. Talmudic sources, too, write of Rabbi Judah ha-Nasi's great wealth and exalted leadership. Surprisingly, however, they say nothing of the wealth of his father's house: **"Rabbi Simeon b. Menasya said in the name of Rabbi Simeon b. Yoḥai: beauty, power, wealth, honor, wisdom, longevity, and progeny are befitting the righteous and good for the world"... Rabbi Joḥanan says: "All seven qualities... which the rabbis attributed to the righteous were true of Rabbi** [Judah ha-Nasi]" (Jerusalem Talmud, *Sanhedrin* 11:4). Rabbi Judah ha-Nasi had estates in various parts of the country, from which he amassed a fortune in grain. **"Rabbi opened his storehouse** [of grain] **in a year of scarcity"** (*Bava Batra* 8a). Using the characteristic hyperbole of folklore, *Bava Meẓia* (85a) remarks: **"Rabbi's house-steward was wealthier than King Shapur** [of Persia]." **"Since Rabbi had not benefited from the community at all, and had not inherited property from his father"** (Genesis Rabbah 100:2), we may presume that the Roman authorities, who recognized him as the ruler of the Jews, viewed him as successor to Herod's dynasty and gave him

2

3

4 Stone doors like this one of Judah ha-Nasi's vault still swing on their hinges in the doorways to the catacombs. Nailheads and knockers are carved on the doors to imitate the appearance of wooden doors. They were locked from the outside by a bolt and iron key, since robbing graves was already commonplace when the catacombs were cut.

In the picture on the next two pages: The catacomb of the sarcophagi, apparently intended for Jewish scholars and their families. All the epitaphs are in Hebrew, and the title "Rabbi" occurs in most of them.

title to all the possessions of the extinct royal line, including the lands of the Jezreel Valley near Bet She'arim. If so, this gave Judah ha-Nasi further reason for establishing his residence at Bet She'arim.

As the Patriarch prospered so did Bet She'arim. The Jewish community gained the feeling of security, of a people dwelling on its own land, in its own country. Memory of the destruction grew dim, and the economic situation improved markedly, so much so that the community could afford to build splendid public buildings. The largest and finest of the buildings at Bet She'arim, discovered in excavations, are from the time of Rabbi Judah ha-Nasi. Perhaps it was this feeling of well-being that prompted the Patriarch to request that the fast of the Ninth of Av be cancelled.

the synagogue – the loftiest of houses

How did Bet She'arim look in the time of Rabbi Judah ha-Nasi? The town, covering an area of about 25 acres, extended 300 meters from the northeastern edge of the hill where the houses of the Zeid family stand today to the beginning of its southwestern slope. The large public building, or basilica, discovered in excavations northwest of the Zeid statue, was the boundary of the city and part of the city wall. A wall formed by houses built adjacent to one another enclosed the town. The northern gate of the city can still be discerned at the entrance to the ruins of the oil press.

The main entrance to the city lay on the east, since the gradient of the hill was less here in contrast to the north and west, where the hill was quite steep. It seems plausible that there were also paths leading south from the southern wall towards the well, which today is blocked up, at the foot of the hill. This was the primary source of water for Bet She'arim, in addition to the numerous water holes which were hewn into the impermeable chalkstone.

A section of road paved with stone slabs, leading westward from the eastern edge of the hill, was revealed in excavations. The road passed by the synagogue which once stood on a site west of the present-day Zeid house. The synagogue, unearthed in excavations, is from the first quarter of the third century.

4

This means it was built after the death Judah ha-Nasi or at the earliest during his last years, when he was living in Sepphoris. Insofar as the building belongs to the proto-type of early Galilean synagogues, built more or less according to the same plan, we may presume that the synagogue of Rabbi Judah ha-Nasi was quite similar. Perhaps it even stood in the immediate vicinity, for Jewish law requires that the synagogue be built in such a way that it rise above all the surrounding houses, and this was the only site on which a building could be constructed to conform with this principle.

Ancient synagogues characteristically were entered from the side facing Jerusalem and, unlike later synagogues, did not have a fixed place for the Holy Ark. Indeed the southern façade of the Bet She'arim synagogue, which faces Jerusalem, has three entrances. From its appearance we may judge that it was an unroofed façade, entered from the street.

The synagogue was a magnificent building, both inside and out. Decorated hewn stones and Corinthian capitals attest to its external splendor, while the colored plaster found on its floor in

the course of excavation provides evidence of its interior appearance. White panels of imported marble were incorporated in the plaster decoration, and on them were found commemorative inscriptions in Greek and Hebrew, honoring community leaders and generous men who contributed to building the synagogue. Two rows of columns divided the synagogue's interior into three spaces: a wide nave flanked on either side by narrow aisles. At the northern end of the hall, opposite the main entrance, there was an elevated platform which perhaps was used for reading the Torah. The side aisles along the eastern and western walls were lined with stone benches. The synagogue excavations have been covered over in order to preserve the antiquities. A pear-shaped well was hewn next to the synagogue to collect run-off water from the synagogue roof, probably used by worshippers to wash their hands.

a life of ease in the nasi's house

It is not hard to conjure up the figure of Judah ha-Nasi marching in all his splendor down the street on his way to the synagogue or his *Beit Midrash* (House of Study), surrounded by an entourage of disciples. Rabbi Judah must have spent most of his life in the *Beit Midrash,* where he worked for many years redacting the Mishnah, the second most important work for the Jewish people, after the Bible. In the Mishnah he summed up Jewish law, or *halakhah.* He found various collections of mishnahs by eminent rabbis before him, but often discovered that these works had contradictory rulings. Thus, the vast body of material which had been collected had to be arranged, and differences between versions had to be resolved. Scholars believe that what we know as the Mishnah today was based by Rabbi Judah on the mishnah of Rabbi Meir. Only a strong, authoritative personality could rule on the different versions, in most instances unifying the *halakhah,* and hand down to the people a book of Jewish law which would be accepted by the rabbis and serve as the basis of the people's spiritual development for generations.

Here, in Bet She'arim, this great work took shape in the minds of Rabbi Judah ha-Nasi and his colleagues and was committed to writing. Perhaps it was by virtue of his redaction of the Mishnah that Rabbi Judah ha-Nasi came to be called simply "Rabbi," the rabbi whose word is unchallenged.

The synagogue discovered at Bet She'arim may indeed postdate Rabbi's time there; however the finest building discovered in its vicinity was built in his time, perhaps even at his behest and on his own initiative. A grand edifice built of ashlars with wide, smoothly tooled bosses on their outer sides was discovered near the road north of the synagogue (for some reason a sign saying "Synagogue" was placed near the remains of this building). The building has many rooms in it, as well as a small pool which collected water from the roof. Remains of a structure containing an oven for manufacturing glass were discovered east of this building. Between the large edifice and the synagogue are foundations of several smaller buildings, perhaps associated with the synagogue.

1 *A sarcophagus, apparently locally made, decorated with rosettes and hanging garlands. It stands out from other locally produced sarcophagi in its high level of carving.*

2 *A marble carving of Leda and the swan, a Greek mythological theme* par excellence, *was discovered among the ruins of a mausoleum next to one of the catacombs – testimony to the influence of Greek culture on part of the population at Bet She'arim.*

1

2

3, 4 *Sarcophagi whose workmanship is crude and ornamentation simple were apparently carved by local Jewish artisans, since their decoration abounds in traditional Jewish motifs:* menorahs, shofars, etrogs *and* lulavs, *incense pans and even the Holy Ark. Aside from these motifs, motifs prevalent in the contemporaneous Greco-Roman world also appear in Bet She'arim: hanging garlands, rosettes, hunting scenes (a lion chasing a deer) and conch motifs, common themes in the art of Mediterranean peoples.*

3 *Several unfinished decorations demonstrate the primitive carving techniques used.*

4 *A primitive carving of spread-winged angels on a sarcophagus in the vault of the sarcophagi.*

3

4

The basilica (40 x 15 m.), the second monumental building discovered in the excavations, is also from the time of Rabbi. As mentioned above, it formed part of the city's western wall. It, too, is built of finely tooled ashlars with smooth, slightly projecting bosses. Its plan is that of a basilica: two rows of columns dividing a large hall into three – a nave in the center and two narrow aisles on either side. The building was entered through a vestibule (or narthex) on the northern side. Later the wall between them was taken down to lengthen the nave.

Water was apparently a serious problem at Bet She'arim, and hence any straight surface, even the roof of the building, was used for collecting rainwater. Large wells were dug in the rock beneath the flooring, and run-off water from the roof and the immediate area was channeled into these wells. On the eastern side of the building we can see a gutter used for this purpose.

Rabbi Judah ha-Nasi undoubtedly spent much of his time in this public building as well. Although an exedra is generally considered to be a roofed building with three walls, this may very well have been the building referred to in the Jerusalem Talmud, Tractate *Eruvin,* Ch. 1: **"Rabbi accepts the exedra of Beth Sharei** [the Aramaic name of Bet She'arim]."

The Nasi's household lived a life of ease, similar, according to legend, to the house of Emperor Antoninus: **"Antoninus and Rabbi never lacked lettuce, radish or courgette on their tables, neither in summer nor in winter"** (*Avodah Zarah* 11). In other words, even vegetables which were out of season and hence expensive were served at the Nasi's table. Rabbis and wealthy men frequented the house of Judah ha-Nasi, as we read: **"Rabbi honors the wealthy"** (*Eruvin,* Ch. 5). A considerable fraction of the population of Bet She'arim were common folk, not from the privileged class of sages. **"Rabbi once opened his storehouse in a year of scarcity, proclaiming: Let those enter who have studied the Scripture, or the Mishnah or the Gemara or the Halakhah, or the Aggada; there is no admission, however, for the ignorant"** (*Bava Batra* 8a). This makeup of the population is evident from the tomb inscriptions in the cemetery of Bet She'arim. Quite a few names include the title of rabbi, yet just as many appear without this title. Most illustrious of all was the Nasi: **"Between Moses and Rabbi we do not find one who was supreme both in Torah and in worldly affairs"** (*Gittin* 59a).

the city of the dead

Rabbi Judah ha-Nasi lived his last nineteen years in Ẓippori (Sepphoris), known for its clean, salubrious air (*Ketubbot* 103). The valley's swamps, which surely existed by then, brought the curse of malaria to Bet She'arim, driving the ailing leader out of the town. **"It was taught: Rabbi was lying** [on his sickbed] **at Sepphoris but a** [burial] **place was reserved for him at Bet She'arim"** (*Ketubbot* 103b). Rabbi Judah ha-Nasi was buried in Bet She'arim in a tomb which he prepared himself in advance, perhaps during his residence in the city. Bet She'arim may well have become a place where important people were brought for burial even before Rabbi's death. This is intimated by a story about Rabbi Ḥiyya: **"Our Rabbi was very modest, and**

would say: whatever a person tells me I do, except what the sons of Bathyra did to my elder, for they lost their greatness and exalted him. And if Rav Huna [the Exilarch] **were to come here, I would seat him above me... Once the great Rabbi Ḥiyya came in to him and said: Rav Huna awaits without... Rabbi's face turned yellow. Seeing that Rabbi's face had turned yellow, Rabbi Ḥiyya said to him: His coffin has come"** (Jerusalem Talmud, *Kilayim,* Ch. 9). This story implies that the coffin of the Exilarch was brought to Bet She'arim for burial while Rabbi was yet alive. The tomb of the prominent and illustrious Judah ha-Nasi, however, added an aura of holiness to the cemetery of Bet She'arim, which became the main cemetery not only for Jews of the Land of Israel but also for Jews of neighboring lands.

Bet She'arim has a large necropolis from which we may learn not only about burial practices of the times, but also about the way of life in Bet She'arim in the late second and the third and fourth centuries.

The earlier burial chambers of the city are located on the southwestern slope, west of the hillock of Bet She'arim. The catacombs here are spacious because this cemetery served only the local population, and there was as yet no shortage of burial place. The later catacombs lie on the northwestern slope of Bet She'arim. In contrast to the earlier catacombs, only one of the later ones is spacious and has few graves in it. Yet it was actually this catacomb that caused the central cemetery of Bet She'arim to come into being. This is the catacomb containing the tombs of Rabban Gamaliel and Rabban Simeon.

is this indeed rabbi's tomb?

Three impressive arches once decorated the façade of the tomb; the one on the right is original and the other two have been reconstructed after it. The right-hand arch was built as a decorative element from the outset, whereas the other two arches have doorways under them. The main entrance was under the central arch. Stone doors still swing on their hinges in the entranceways. Made to resemble wooden paneled doors,

1

2

they display prominent "nail heads" and knockers. They were shut by a stone bolt, using a special iron key.

Immediately upon entering the catacomb through the left door we find ourselves in a spacious chamber. In the corner of the wall on our left, above a tomb hewn into the wall, is an inscription: **"Rabbi Simeon."** Left of it, above a tomb hewn in the floor, one could make out the words **"Anina the younger"** when the catacomb was first discovered, but with exposure to light, this inscription has faded away. It is known that the Jews of the Galilee were declared unfit to lead prayers because they pronounced the Hebrew letter *ḥet* as an *aleph,* and the letter *aleph* as a *ḥet.* From this we may deduce that Anina is none other than Ḥanina.

From the large room we pass through a restored archway into the next room. In the side of the right-hand wall we come across another inscription: **"This is of Rabbi Gamaliel"** (with the name Gamaliel also appearing in Greek). In the right-hand corner of this room there are two parallel horizontal shaft-graves (cut deep into the rock) and surrounded by a man-made wall. No inscription was found here, but examination of the bones has shown that the grave on the right belonged to a man and the one on the left to a woman. Remains of a lead casket in which the woman was interred and a cylindrical mirror handle made of bone decorated with circular carving were found in the left pit. Three names associated with Rabbi Judah ha-Nasi were found in this catacomb: Rabbi Gamaliel and Rabbi Simeon, the sons of Judah ha-Nasi, and Rabbi Ḥanina, his disciple. Nahman Avigad, who excavated this catacomb, believes this to be far from incidental. One other detail contributes to the hypothesis that Rabbi Judah ha-Nasi himself is buried in this catacomb: in his will Rabbi requested that he be buried in the ground, not in a casket; and this fits in with the archaeological discovery of the two shaft-graves sunken in the floor of the inner chamber of Rabbi Simeon and Rabbi Gamaliel's catacomb.

These three names call to mind a story about Judah ha-Nasi's last day: **"When Rabbi was about to depart** [from this life] **he said, 'I require** [the presence] **of my sons.' When his sons entered into his presence he instructed them: 'Take care that you show due respect to your mother. The light shall continue to burn in its usual place, the table shall be laid in its usual place** [and my] **bed shall be spread in its usual place. Joseph of Haifa and Simeon of Efrath who attended on me in my lifetime shall attend on me when I am dead.' ... 'I require,' he said to them** [the presence] **of the Sages of Israel,' and the Sages of Israel entered into his presence. 'Do not lament for me,' he said to them, 'in the smaller towns** [to prevent quarrels from arising between the towns in which he would be eulogized and the towns to which his coffin would not be taken], **and reassemble the college after thirty days. My son Simeon is wise, my son Gamaliel Nasi, and Ḥanina b. Ḥama shall preside** [at the college]' " (*Ketubbot* 103a). Note that the distance from the graves of Gamaliel, Simeon, and Ḥanina to the sunken graves corresponds to their rank and their position in the Sanhedrin. It seems likely that the sunken graves in the inner chamber belong to Rabbi Judah ha-Nasi and his wife. That the names of the deceased were not inscribed on them is not surprising, for names were inscribed to help people locate the graves of their relations, and everyone knew where Rabbi was interred.

miracles on the day of the funeral

Let us close our eyes and imagine the events of the Friday on which Rabbi passed away in Ẓippori. The rabbis declared a fast day and prayed for mercy, while masses congregated in front of the house of the dying Nasi. **"They said: he who says that Rabbi is dead, will be stabbed. The Sages said to Bar Kappara: Go and investigate. He went and found that he had expired."** Nobody daring enough was found to carry the sad tidings to the assembled throng. **"He** [Bar Kappara] **went to the window and peered out, his head wrapped and his garments rent. He began to speak: My brothers, the sons of Jedayahu** [as the people of Ẓippori were known, after the Jedaiah priestly family which lived there] **harken to me! The angels above and the mortals have taken hold of the Holy Ark. The angels above overpowered the mortals, and the Holy Ark has been captured. 'Has he,' they asked, 'gone to his eternal rest?' 'You,' he replied, 'said it, not I.' They rent their garments, and the wailing of the mourners carried as far as Gufefaya, three miles away"** (*Ketubbot* 104a).

Vast numbers of Jews in the Galilee escorted the illustrious Nasi to his last resting place. He was eulogized in eighteen synagogues, i.e. in eighteen towns, apparently all the towns along the way from Ẓippori (Sepphoris) to Bet She'arim (thus preventing strife between the towns). Here, in front of this catacomb, throngs of people must have gathered, only the most eminent rabbis and members of the family being permitted into

1 *A special prominence has been given to one burial in the catacomb by its unique construction. This, the most important burial in the catacomb, is apparently the resting place of a head of family and his wife who were accorded especial honor. Since there is no inscription over the grave, one cannot say definitively who lies within. But, accepting the theory that the Rabbi Simeon and the Rabbi Gamaliel who lay here are from Judah ha-Nasi's family, it is quite possible that Rabbi himself and his wife are interred in the double grave in the far corner of the chamber, over which a hewn stone structure was built to make it stand out from the other graves. Why might the names of the sons have been written here, but not that of Rabbi Judah ha-Nasi? Why is there no inscription on what is apparently the most important grave in the catacomb? Perhaps the burial inscriptions in Bet She'arim were written to mark the resting place of the deceased, so that visitors could find their graves easily. Hence the brevity and carelessness of the inscriptions, which may have been the work of the unpracticed hand of relatives or grave guards, who wrote these inscriptions long after the interment, when there was a danger that pilgrims to graves of righteous men might not know where these rabbis were buried. However, we may hypothesize that the famous and important grave at the far end of the catacomb, unique in its large stone construction, needed no marking, for there was no danger it would be forgotten.*

2 *The end of a lead coffin, ornamented by Jewish ritual objects.*

3 *A stone paved street passing by the synagogue.*

3

the burial chamber itself. Here, in front of the shaft-graves, they parted from the body of the shepherd who had lifted up his flock and implanted in them a sense of confidence in their future on their own land. The people befittingly glorified the day of the funeral with stories of miracles: **"The day lingered on until every person reached his home and filled himself a jug of water and lit his lamp. As soon as the sun had set the cock began to crow. Becoming remorseful, they asked: Have we violated the Sabbath? A voice issued forth and said to them: whoever was not idle in eulogizing Rabbi, shall be assured a place in the world to come"** (Jerusalem Talmud, *Kilayim,* Ch. 9). The admiration accorded Rabbi Judah ha-Nasi after his death was even greater than that given him in his life. Before long he became known among the Jews of Israel and the Diaspora as "our holy Rabbi." In this light we are to understand the growth of the central cemetery at Bet She'arim. The wealthy, the respected and the leaders of communities all wished their eternal resting place to be in close proximity to the grave of "our holy Rabbi." Deceased from as far as Meshan in southern Mesopotamia, Ḥamiẓur in distant Arabia, and Palmyra on the edge of the desert, as well as from Beirut, Antioch, Tyre, Sidon, and of course the Jewish towns of the Land of Israel, were brought to the city of the dead at Bet She'arim. West of Rabbi's family catacomb is a cave known as the Syrian burial hall, where the bones of the head of Antioch's Council of Elders and his family were interred.

The site became a place for public gatherings. After Rabbi's death a terraced structure for these assemblies was built above his grave. Perhaps memorials for the illustrious Nasi were held here.

A burial "industry" soon developed in Bet She'arim. The catacomb chambers became smaller and were even hewn in several storeys; for example, the catacombs on the western slope of Bet She'arim, known as the Catacombs of the Steps. Burial caves consisting of many burial chambers branch off either

1

1 *Carving of a man with a* menorah *above his head. Many reliefs of* menorahs *were discovered here, even in catacombs of Jews from abroad. The symbol of the* menorah *was a prevalent national emblem and not without reason was chosen as the emblem of the State of Israel.*

2

2 *An engraved carving of a mounted horseman. Many of the reliefs and engravings are not the work of artists, but rather the handicraft of common folk.*

3 *A sarcophagus from the catacomb of the sarcophagi, decorated with a relief of an eagle with a garland, and a bull's head on the lid. Many sarcophagi at Bet She'arim are decorated with motifs from the plant and animal world, geometric designs, reliefs of human beings, and traditional Jewish symbols. Some portray the Holy Ark side by side with animal forms. Even a design of a human face, resembling portrayals of pagan gods, was found in the vault of the sarcophagi. How is it that the sages did not find fault with such things? The non-Jewish world by then had wearied of paganism; and worshipping the gods had become simply an empty civic ritual. No sanctity, only outward decorative value, attached to the figures of the gods.*

3

side of a hall. Above an opening in the left wall was a plaque inscribed in monumental Assyrian letters, with a Hebrew inscription, "This is the tomb of Rabbi Isaac, son of Moqim, Peace."

"I, the leonide, left the light"

Beth Sharei, a shortened form of Bet She'arim, was the Aramaic vernacular name of the site. Besara, its Greek name, discovered in an inscription on a marble plaque which was once affixed to a mausoleum, was derived from the Aramaic name. The mausoleum, which stood adjacent to a catacomb, was originally two storeys tall, although today only part of its lower storey can be seen. A reconstruction of the structure may be seen in the museum of Bet She'arim. It was a magnificent edifice, crowned by a triangular gable. A carved stone arch stood over the entrance, and reliefs of animals and floral motifs lined the façade. Some of the stones from the arch are now in the museum on the site. Among the ruins of the mausoleum was a white marble relief portraying Leda and the swan, a theme from Greek mythology *par excellence,* evidence of the impact Greek culture had on a segment of the population at Bet She'arim – perhaps the city's wealthy Greek-speaking class.

A Greek epitaph found on the site reads, in translation: **"Here I, Justus, the Leonide, son of Sappho, lie dead, who after having picked the fruits of all wisdom, left the light, the unhappy parents, who mourn unceasingly, and the brothers. Woe unto me, my Besara. And after descending to the netherworld, I, Justus, lie here with many of my relations, for such was the wish of mighty Moirai. Take comfort, Justus, for no man is immortal."**

The language of this inscription shows Homeric influence. The epitaph does not express Jewish concepts; instead there is a reference to *Moirai* (fate), a purely Hellenistic notion alien to Judaism. A Jew does not take comfort in the fact that "no man is immortal," but rather in the fact that he is summoned to the world to come. Thus we see that this catacomb belonged to assimilated Jews, detached from the culture of their people and imbued with Hellenistic culture. Several other inscriptions influenced by Greek ideas were discovered in the necropolis of Bet She'arim, but these inscriptions also displayed an admixture of Jewish ideas. While the epitaphs of a mixed Greco-Jewish nature can be ascribed, it seems, to Diaspora Jews, the purely Hellenistic epitaph of Justus incontrovertably belonged to a resident of Bet She'arim.

The epitaphs, most of which are Greek and a few Hebrew, Aramaic or Palmyrene, reveal, however, that only a minute fraction of the Jews of Bet She'arim were so assimilated. The Palmyrene inscriptions and some of the Greek inscriptions belong to Jews from abroad. Indeed, many Jewish inhabitants of the land used Greek, and apparently only the poor common folk used Aramaic. Still the majority of Greek speakers and people with Greek names were thoroughly Jewish in persuasion. This is attested by appellations containing such combinations as "Rabbi Prigorius."

Those with a Hellenistic education ("Greek wisdom"), like Justus, comprised a small and insignificant minority. The rabbis forbade teaching Greek and viewed those who learned it with disfavor, although the Nasi's sons actually learned Greek in order to be able to deal with the authorities. Rabbi Ishmael advised his nephew, "who had already learned the entire Torah": **"Go and find an hour which is neither night nor day, and in that hour study Greek wisdom"** (*Menaḥot* 29). The Sages distinguished studying Greek from studying Greek wisdom: **"It may be said that the Greek language is one thing and Greek wisdom is another"** (*Bava Kama* 83a). Knowledge of the Greek language was essential to the Nasi for negotiating with the government; Greek wisdom – philosophy and poetry – they viewed as posing a cultural threat.

This is the context for understanding Rabbi Judah ha-Nasi's remark: **"Why use the Syriac language in the Land of Israel,** [where] **either the Holy Tongue or Greek language** [could be employed]**?"** *(Bava Kama 83a,b)*. The bilingual inscription on the grave of his son, Rabban Gamaliel, was written in this spirit. In Rabbi Judah ha-Nasi's household, however, Hebrew exclusively was spoken. Indeed Rabbi's maidservant became so famous for her knowledge of Hebrew that disciples of the rabbis would come to her to clarify obscure expressions.

on agriculture and the burial industry

What were the occupations of the residents of Bet She'arim? Presumably they derived their main livelihood from agriculture. When a person's name appeared in an epitaph without mentioning his livelihood, he was a farmer. The oil press at the foot of the northern slope of Bet She'arim was used primarily during the Byzantine period, but undoubtedly was hewn and used much earlier. This relatively large press testifies to extensive olive cultivation.

The rocky hills of the Lower Galilee are well suited to growing olives. Only olives (and not grain) could be grown in areas where the soil was too shallow for cereal cultivation. Even in the Lower Galilee today olive groves abound in areas similar to this. At Ramat Yishay, not far from Bet She'arim, the hillsides of soft chalkstone and grey Rendzina soil (Mediterranean soil on limestone) are good for cultivating grapes, as well; hence the great number of wine presses hewn into the rocks around Bet She'arim. Crafts and commerce were of secondary importance to the livelihood of the residents.

We have already mentioned glass manufactory. A slab of raw glass, possibly brought from Jalama (Qishon Police Station), where there was a large glass factory, is on display in one of the caves of Bet She'arim which has been made into a museum. In Bet She'arim this raw glass was processed into vessels.

A goldsmith and a fabric merchant are mentioned in the epitaphs at Bet She'arim. Several carvings of ships were also discovered in the catacombs, perhaps evidence of maritime vocations and international commerce.

The occupation unique to Bet She'arim, however, was the "burial industry." Near the synagogue a memorial plaque for people who earned their living as undertakers was discovered: **"Of Rabbi Samuel, who shuts the eyes of the dead, and of Judah, who lays them to rest."** Hewing graves, as well, must surely have employed a large number of people. The catacombs had to be carefully planned and thoughtfully hewn, for the soft chalky rock tends to collapse easily. Indeed, here and there in the necropolis of Bet She'arim one encounters graves where digging was stopped for fear of collapse. On the other hand, developing such a city of the dead would have been impossible were the rock not soft and easily hewn. The stone was cut using a hammer and chisel. Traces of the hewing can be seen on the interior walls of the caves. Spacious courtyards were built in front of important catacombs. A narrow corridor led to the crowded catacombs on the western slope of the hill. The entrances to the catacombs all had stone doors similar to the door of Judah ha-Nasi's family vault, some of them ornamented with reliefs of geometric and floral designs. Every door was shut from the outside by a stone bolt and iron key, for in the time the catacombs were built pillage of tombs was commonplace. We have evidence of this in the tomb next to Judah ha-Nasi's catacomb, known as the "catacomb of the curses" because of its epitaphs cursing grave robbers: **"He who is buried here is Simeon, the son of Yoḥanan, and on oath, whoever shall open upon him shall die of an evil end."** Some of the epitaphs warned robbers that they would be punished by not receiving a place in the world to come.

An arched façade, whose stones were carved with geometric and abstract designs, ornaments important catacombs, such as that of Rabbi and a catacomb of sarcophagi. Reliefs and carvings have also been found in many caves, especially in the catacombs on the western slope, which apparently were for simpler folk.

greek funerary art – an outer facade

The reliefs and carvings are as crude as the drawings of children today. This is not the work of artists, but the product of popular craftsmanship. One of the more prominent carved motifs is the *menorah* or seven-branched candelabrum. Sometimes this motif was carved, inscribed, or cast on moveable objects such as marble or lead sarcophagi, and sometimes it was carved or inscribed on tomb walls. *Menorah* reliefs are also found in the tombs of Jews from outside Israel, such as the Syrian Jews' burial cave. The *menorah* was a national symbol and was deservedly chosen as the official emblem of the State of Israel.

Above a grave in one of the catacombs on the western slope an engraved drawing of a broad-shouldered Roman soldier dressed in armor was discovered on the wall. The epitaph next to the drawing informs us that the person buried there was named Germanicus and that he was brought from Palmyra; apparently he was a Jewish mercenary in the Roman army.

Most of the burials discovered at Bet She'arim are in catacombs; very few are isolated graves. Above the catacomb of the sarcophagi some graves were found cut into the rock and built of stone; these were apparently the graves of the poor. Inside the rock hewn graves, however, some lead coffins fortunately escaped the notice of grave robbers and were found still in place. Deeply cut shaft-graves, or pits, sunk in the floor of the catacombs are quite rare, although wealthy families did have family vaults. The fine cave on the slope of the hill facing the hillock of Bet She'arim, southwest of the town, appears to be one such catacomb. The burial cave of the Syrian Jews may also have been a family vault, since the family of Aidesios, the Head of the Council of Elders, has five tombs there marked with epitaphs.

Most of the catacombs are large, some even divided into several storeys – testimony to the great increase in demand for burial places once Bet She'arim had become the central cemetery for Jewish communities in the Land of Israel and abroad.

The catacomb of the sarcophagi appears to have been set aside for the sages and their families. All the epitaphs in this catacomb are in Hebrew, and many of the deceased buried here were given the title of "Rabbi"; and when a rabbi's family members were interred here, they were referred to as the children of rabbis. An example is provided by the epitaph on the sarcophagus near the entrance, inscribed in clearly legible Assyrian script: **"Here lie Atio, the daughter of Rabbi Gamaliel, son of Nehemiah, who died a virgin at the age of twenty-two, and Ation, the daughter of Rabbi Judah, son of Rabbi Gamaliel, who died at the age of nine years and six months; may they stand** [with the worthy]."

The chambers are generally connected to one another by arched doorways. The graves are hewn in the walls or floors of the chambers. Some are free-standing stone coffins beneath vaulted recesses; others are *arcosolia,* or arched niches cut into the wall, beneath which are hewn trough-like graves covered by stone slabs.

The niches near the graves were intended for ossuaries, in which the bones of the deceased were collected after the flesh had decayed: **"When the flesh had decayed away they collected the bones and buried them in their place"** (*Sanhedrin* 6:6). The burial chamber, and perhaps even the single grave, was the property of the family and was too dear to be used only once.

The duty of collecting the bones devolved upon the son. A person collecting bones and transporting them (for instance, from anywhere in the country to Bet She'arim) was even exempt from reciting the *Shema* and other prayers, and performing other commandments, since one actively engaged in fulfilling a commandment is exempt from performing others at the same time. The deceased were treated with the utmost respect. Bones were not placed in a wagon or a boat, or on the back of an animal, nor sat upon, but placed respectfully in an ossuary.

1 *A multi-storey catacomb. Due to the important cemetery in the city, Bet She'arim continued to flourish long after the Nasi and Sanhedrin had moved elsewhere, until it was burned down in the revolt against Gallus in 352 c.e. A hoard of coins found in a wealthy house north of the synagogue dates the city's destruction: the latest coins are from 351 c.e. Bet She'arim was not rebuilt, its cemetery passed into disuse, and in the Byzantine period the graves began to be plundered. The ruins of the abandoned settlement became covered over, the site grew desolate, and in time even its name was forgotten. In the Middle Ages, when Jewish pilgrims wished to prostrate themselves at the grave of Rabbi Judah ha-Nasi, the site of Bet She'arim was no longer known.*

1

the sanhedrin removed to bet she'arim

1 *The bronze statue erected in memory of the watchman Alexander Zeid, on the hills of Sheikh Abreik, the site of ancient Bet She'arim. Modern scholars tried unsuccessfully to locate the site of Bet She'arim, until Alexander Zeid settled on the hill where the tomb of Sheikh Abreik stands and ancient Bet She'arim was discovered. Identification of the site was confirmed when a Jewish inscription mentioning its name was discovered during excavations.*

A short distance from the sarcophagus of Atio and Ation, against the wall on the left, are two sarcophagi, adjacent to each other. On the outer sarcophagus is an epitaph which reads as follows: **"These coffins, the inner and outer, are of Rabbi Aniana** [Ḥanina] **and of... the holy, sons... this coffin... the daughter of Rabbi Joshua, righteous of blessed memory."** These, it seems, are the graves of martyrs. This hypothesis, if correct, makes this the earliest known burial of martyrs in Jewish history. What they were killed for, we do not know. They certainly did not sacrifice their lives in a struggle against pagan symbols and images of animals, fish and birds, as the people of Jerusalem had done before the Great Revolt. It seems that the sensitivity of these generations of Jews to animal forms had become dulled, for in Bet She'arim there are vast numbers of coffins ornamented with lions, or with a bull's head above and an eagle below. Even a figure of a human face, closely resembling drawings or carved representations of pagan deities, was discovered on the side of one sarcophagus.

How is it that the sages at Bet She'arim did not perceive any fault in ornamentation in which the Holy Ark appears with figures of animals? The non-Jewish world by then had wearied of paganism, and pagan worship had become merely a duty which people performed but no longer believed in. Hence images of the gods were no longer viewed as holy, but simply as decorative elements.

Rabban Gamaliel II used to bathe in the bathhouse of Aphrodite in Acre without the slightest reluctance. When Proclos, son of a philosopher, once asked him to explain how he could permit himself to do such a thing, Gamaliel answered: **"I did not come into her domain; she** [Aphrodite] **has come into mine. Nobody says: The bath was made as an adornment for Aphrodite** [i.e. the bathhouse is not for the purpose of pagan worship]**; but one does say: Aphrodite was made as an adornment for the bath. Another point: If you were given great wealth you would not go to worship the stars naked..."** We see that Rabban Gamaliel II viewed pagan symbols, not to speak of figures of animals and birds, simply as a decorative element to be treated offhandedly and even with contempt. This must surely have been how the people of Bet She'arim, including the sages, perceived the mythological images portrayed on the sarcophagi.

The sarcophagi whose workmanship is crude and ornamentation primitive were probably made by local artisans or by Jewish artisans from nearby places such as the Carmel, since traditional Jewish motifs are common: *menorahs, shofars, etrog* and *lulavs,* incense pans, and even a relief of the Holy Ark. Aside from these, motifs of contemporary Roman and Hellenistic art also appear in Bet She'arim: rosettes, garlands, hunting scenes (a lion chasing a deer), and conches, a motif prevalent in Mediterranean art. There is, for example, a sarcophagus decorated with a strange mixture of motifs from the animal world, geometric designs, and a Holy Ark with a large conch above it. Particularly interesting is the portrayal of spread-winged angels on a stone coffin in the sarcophagus catacomb. Another sarcophagus has a relief of a man with a dog, standing between elaborate columns, perhaps representing the façade of a palace.

From several unfinished decorations we learn about the technique used in carving the reliefs. For example, to carve a garland the artisan would first outline its geometric shape and then fill in the details, much as a child might do. There is little use of color, and rouge, apparently from a rust-colored chalk, is the only color which occurs.

The decorations in the city of the dead at Bet She'arim reveal the limited extent of Greek influence on the Jewish community of the Land of Israel. Only a minority became deeply involved in the Greco-Roman world; for the vast majority, Greco-Roman culture was nothing but an overlay, empty of the meaning of the Greek artistic tradition. The yearning for some sort of ornament was satisfied by extremely primitive decorations, which would have evoked a laugh from any man truly part of Hellenistic culture. Deep inside, the Jewish community of Israel was true to the tradition of its ancestors and to the Law of the Jewish people. The elite of the people were not philosophers and poets, but sages who knew and understood the Torah.

devastation and renewal

Bet She'arim flourished for about 175 years, from the time of Judah ha-Nasi until 352 c.e., when Gallus, upon orders from Emperor Constantius to suppress a revolt by the Jews of the Galilee, destroyed the city along with Ẓippori (Sepphoris) and other places. A hoard of 1200 coins found in the synagogue in a layer of ashes dates the destruction. The coins date to the time of Emperor Constantine the Great (308-337 c.e.) and Emperor Constantius; none are later than 352.

A poor town continued to exist on the ruins of Bet She'arim in the Byzantine and early Arab periods. Even in the Mameluke period a poor village stood here. The name Bet She'arim was forgotten, and the site became known as Sheikh Abreik.

When the Jewish National Fund redeemed the lands of Sheikh Abreik, a small poor village of tenant farmers stood on the site. Alexander Zeid, a watchman guarding JNF lands, was the first Jew to resettle here after a hiatus of over 1,500 years. It was he who rediscovered the catacombs (some were discovered and restored by Moshe Joffe, one of the first residents); and his discovery led to the archaeological excavations which brought to light the remains of the city of Judah ha-Nasi where the redaction of the Mishnah was planned and possibly even carried out.

1

alexander zeid

Born in Siberia in 1886, he was the son of a Vilna Jew who belonged to the Hebrew enlightenment and felt tied to Zion and, under the Czar, had been exiled to Siberia. His mother was a Subbotnik (Russian sect that sanctified the Sabbath and converted to Judaism). In 1904 Zeid immigrated to the Land of Israel. He worked as a hired hand on farms and in quarries in the early settlements in Judea and Jerusalem. One of the founders of the Bar Giora organization for guarding and defense, established in 1907, he also founded Ha-Shomer (The Watchmen) in 1909. Initially the aim of this organization was for Jews to take exclusive control of guarding and defense in the moshavot, early Jewish settlements. Later some members added the ideals of Jewish labor and settlement; thus in 1916 Ha-Shomer founded Kefar Gil'adi and Tel Hai in the Upper Galilee and Tel 'Adashim in the Jezreel Valley. The founding of Ha-Shomer marks the beginning of a Jewish fighting force in the renewed Jewish settlement of the Land of Israel.

In 1926 Zeid left Kefar Gil'adi over a difference of opinion regarding the future of the settlement and went to establish a new home in Sheikh Abreik as watchman over lands in the Jezreel Valley and surrounding area that had been purchased by the Jewish National Fund in the 1920's. There he, his wife Ẓippora and their sons lived alone in hostile surroundings. On July 10, 1938 Alexander Zeid was ambushed and killed by one of the Arabs living in the area. His family, however, still lives there today.

milk and honey at Ẓippori

Menachem Zaharoni

Edited: Ilan Zaharoni

Ẓippori (Sepphoris) is listed in the Mishnah as one of the **"walled cities in the time of Joshua the son of Nun"** (*Arakhin* 9:6). That its name, Ẓippori or Ẓipporin, was Hebrew attests that the city existed by the First Temple period* and only by chance was not mentioned in the Bible; however there is as yet no archaeological proof of this. The earliest mention of the city in an historical source is from the time of Alexander Yannai (Jannaeus), when Ptolemy Lathyrus, king of Cyprus and rebel son of Cleopatra, queen of Egypt, failed in his attempt to conquer the city during his war against Alexander Yannai. In time Ẓippori became the main city of the Galilee. When Gabinius, procurator under Pompey, tried to break up the conquered Hasmonean state by dividing it into five independent provinces, Ẓippori was made the capital of the province of Galilee. After Herod's death it revolted and was laid waste by Varus, the Roman procurator. Later Herod Antipas (4-39 c.e.) rebuilt it and settled it with hellenized Jews.

After the failure of the Great Revolt nationalist Jewish elements actually gained the upper hand in Ẓippori, and during and after the Bar Kokhba revolt it was the seat of sages and a vibrant center of Jewish life. Towards the end of the second century c.e. Rabbi Judah ha-Nasi moved the Sanhedrin (the supreme Jewish council) to the city, making Ẓippori for a while the capital of the autonomous Jewish community in the Land of Israel.

Historical sources speak of the ancient castra (fortress) of Ẓippori. The hillock of the ancient fortress, and the mid-18th century fortress of the bedouin ruler Dahir al-'Amr which is perched on it, may be seen from many points in the distance.

the fortress and the upper city

The present fortress undoubtedly stands on the same site as the Herodian one. Large ashlars dressed in Herodian style – smoothly tooled bosses framed by smoothed margins – were found in its lower courses, and sarcophagi were used to build the walls. The higher courses were built of smaller stones, apparently dressed in Crusader fashion, with a protruding face. The uppermost courses are Turkish, i.e. from the time of Dahir al-'Amr, an indication that he only repaired the fortress, whose upper courses had been ruined. The fortress is entered through a doorway in the southwestern wall of the building, decorated by a Moslem style arch characteristic of construction in the Turkish

period. Steps on the interior of the building lead to a second storey. The walls of the second storey are covered with many Arabic graffiti, a memento of Israel's War of Independence, during which time the fortress served as a central den for Arab gangs from which they used to sally forth on attacks against Jewish settlements. The fortress thus reveals traces of at least four eras:

1) The late- and post-Second Temple period (from the beginning of the Common Era), during which time the fortress appears to have been used as a Roman garrison. Jewish sources mention that once a fire started on the Sabbath in the yard of Joseph ben Simai of Shiḥin, an administrative official of the king, manager of the estates of Agrippa II, **"and the men from the Gastra** [castra or fortress] **of Sepphoris came to put it out, because he was a steward of the king"** (Babylonian Talmud, *Shabbat* 121a; Jerusalem Talmud, *Shabbat* 16: 7). The Roman soldiers living in the fortress came to the rescue to save the property of Agrippa II, who was trusted and accepted by the Romans.

2) The Crusader period (12th-13th centuries), during which Ẓippori was an important Crusader stronghold. The Crusader forces massed by the springs of Ẓippori before setting out for the Battle of Hattin (Qarne Ḥittim), where they suffered the crushing defeat which put an end to the First Crusader Kingdom.

3) The period of Dahir al-'Amr (18th century). The building

* Villages founded during the Persian and Hellenistic periods were given non-Hebrew names; to wit, 'Ardaskos, on the site of modern-day *kibbutz* Allonim. Only those villages which were founded by the First Temple period and whose population remained Jewish retained their ancient names.

Resh Lakish said: "With mine own eyes I have seen a land of milk and honey round Ẓippori, and it is sixteen miles by sixteen miles" Babylonian Talmud, Megillah 6a.

1 *"The castra of Ẓippori" (Lat.* castrum *– fort) was in use in Roman and Crusader times and in the 18th century. According to the sages the town's name was derived from the fact that it was "perched like a bird [Heb.* ẓippor] *atop the mountain" (*Megillah *6a). The fort provides a breathtaking view of most of the western Lower Galilee, known in the past as the "limits of Ẓippori."*

2 *Remains of two synagogues were discovered on the grounds of the 12th century Crusader church, next to the Franciscan monastery. The granite columns and capitals of the church were apparently taken from these synagogues.*

was constructed by Aḥmad, son of the bedouin ruler Dahir. The form of the building as it stands today actually dates from his time. The walls of the building are 15 meters long and about 4 meters thick on the bottom storey. All the arches are pointed, and the roof is vaulted.

4) The period of the War of Independence (1947-1948).

The area of the upper city (referred to in Jewish sources as the upper market), surrounding the fortress and the area south of it, is covered with wells, cellars, and ruins of buildings. The lower city (or lower market, in Jewish sources) spread over the sides of the hillock on the south and east. All these remains are from the Roman and Byzantine periods.

"and why was it called ẓippori?"

The Sages said: **"And why was it called Ẓippori? Because it is perched like a bird** [Heb. *ẓippor*] **atop the mountain"** (*Megillah* 6a). This explanation may seem strange, insofar as the hillock on which Ẓippori is situated is not particularly high. This difficulty, however, is resolved the moment we climb to the second storey of the building. The wide open windows reveal a panorama of the surrounding areas, near and far, as if through the eyes of a soaring bird.

To the east we see the hills of Nazareth flattening out into the

Tir'an Valley, and on the crest several houses of Upper Nazareth and part of the village of Mash-had (biblical Gath-hepher, birthplace of the prophet Jonah). The mountain northwest of Mash-had, about a kilometer east of ancient Ẓippori, is known as Mt. Jedaiah after the Jedaiah priestly division which lived in Ẓippori after the destruction of Jerusalem. At the foot of the Tir'an ridge we see the village of Tur'an. The Tir'an ridge, with a fire lookout at its eastern end, hides the eastern part of the Bet Netofa Valley from view. At the western end of the Tir'an ridge is a paved road leading to the religious *kibbutz* Bet Rimmon, and skirting the lower edge of the ridge are the scattered houses of the 'Arab el-Heib bedouin tribe. Near them to the north, over the ridge, is the Arab village of Rummana (not visible from Ẓippori), which was mishnaic Bet Rimmon. The Bet Rimmon Valley, the part of the Bet Netofa Valley near Bet Rimmon, is mentioned as a place where the Jews and their sages used to assemble in the early second century c.e.

Atop a small hill near the bedouin houses is Ḥurbat Ruma, site of a Jewish village from the time of the Great Revolt and home of Neiras and Philip, two of the heroic defenders of Yodefat in that uprising.

At this point the landscape opens out into the broad Bet Netofa Valley. At its northern end we see the ridge of Yodefat, rising sheer and high. A geological rift running the length of its base shifted the ridge upward. As is characteristic of all east-west valleys in the central Lower Galilee, the northern side of the Bet Netofa Valley rises rather steeply, while its southern gradient (towards the Tir'an ridge) is more gentle.

From Ẓippori (from right to left), the first summit we see is known as Har ha-Aḥim (Mt. of the Brothers), in memory of the two brothers, Neiras and Philip, heroes of Yodefat. Rising higher, further west, is the summit of Mt. Sha'avi, recalling another hero of the battle of Yodefat, Eleazar of Saba (Sha'av).

The sharp peak of Mt. 'Aẓmon (547 meters) stands out further along the ridge. Its Hebrew name bespeaks its mightiness (Heb. *'oẓmah*), while its Arab name, Dayedaba, means the watchman. Gazing at the mountain from Ẓippori or looking down from its summit on the surrounding area immediately affirms that its name is well merited. In the valley beneath Mt. 'Aẓmon lies the Arab village of Kafr Manda, which was the Jewish village of Mandi in the mishnaic and talmudic periods. Documents from the Cairo *genizah* indicate that there was also a Jewish village of Mandi here in the 11th century. Mt. 'Aẓmon was the refuge of the zealots and their families as they fled from the surrounding villages after Ẓippori opened its gates to the forces of Cestius Gallus. The Roman army encircled them and deprived them of water, then slaughtered them mercilessly (66 c.e.). The houses northeast of Mt. 'Aẓmon belong to the Arab village of Kaukab, talmudic Kokhava. To the west the Bet Netofa Valley borders on the hills of Allonim-Shefar'am, above which, at their western end, rise the hills of the Carmel and its continuation – Ramat Menasheh, the plateau of Manasseh. In the valley we can see an important section of the National Water Carrier – an open canal and control reservoir, Lake Eshkol, where a laboratory constantly checks the quality of our water and

prospect from the fort at ẓippori

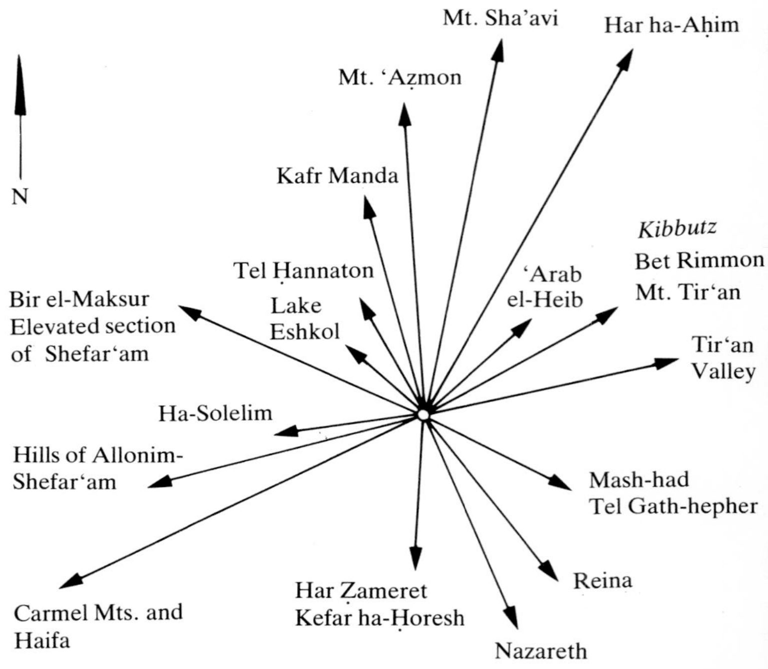

1

1 *Crusader construction is evident in the western wing of the fortress, where mishnaic and talmudic period sarcophagi from Ẓippori were used as quoins in the corners of the building. Most of the fort was renovated in the 18th century.*

2 *The springs of Ẓippori, which were channeled to water the "irrigated fields of Ẓippori" in the time of the Talmud, issue in the broad valley.*

2

chlorinates it. North of the lake we see Tel Shiḥin, the tel of the Canaanite and First Temple period city of Ḥannaton, situated on the main crossroads leading from the lands of Mesopotamia to Acre.

dipping their feet in cream...

As we proceed on our tour, the wealth and might of Ẓippori will become evident. Here, from atop this fortress, we can understand and actually feel the sources and reasons for this wealth and might.

The fertile fields of alluvial soil spread out in the valley before us are a source of wealth for their owners, even today. Although the eastern end of the valley has poor drainage and becomes flooded throughout the winter, in the past, as now, it was used for growing various melons and gourds, which grow well in the heavily soaked soil.

The plentiful springs of Ẓippori, which we passed on the road leading to the *moshav* and the site of the antiquities, lie along the wide and gently sloping banks of Naḥal Ẓippori. Such a combination of an ample water supply and smooth terrain, providing an abundance of easily cultivated agricultural land, is relatively rare and extremely important. Before the time of pumps, channels were used to divert water along a more gentle gradient than that of the stream, until the water was relatively high compared to the stream bed and could be channeled to the fields in the valley below.

The agricultural advantages of Ẓippori are tangible and have found expression in Jewish sources, as Resh Lakish said: **"With mine own eyes I have seen a land of milk and honey round Ẓippori, and it is sixteen miles by sixteen miles"** (*Megillah* 6); or as Rabbi Jose said **"to his son in Ẓippori: 'Go and bring us olives from the roof-top.' He went and found the roof-top flooded in oil"** (Jerusalem Talmud, *Pe'ah* 7:3).

The pride of Ẓippori was not only in agriculture, but also in commerce. The importance of Ẓippori as a commercial center is brought home by the existence of the Ẓippori pound, a unit of weight used throughout the Galilee.

from babylonia to egypt

The Bet Netofa and Tir'an Valleys, and their continuations in the Arbel and Yavne'el Valleys, cross almost the entire width of the country. Such a flat, gentle landscape provides an ideal route for crossing a hilly land such as the Galilee. Not far to the west lies the port of Acre, and to the southwest, the Jezreel Valley into which the ancient Via Maris branched near Megiddo.

Ẓippori, like Ḥannaton before it, lay on the crossroads of international trade routes linking the superpowers of the ancient world – Assyria, Babylonia and Egypt. It was approached from the south by a branch of the Via Maris cutting across the Jezreel Valley from Megiddo to Shimron (near Nahalal) and from there turning into the low hills towards Naḥal Yiftaḥ'el and the western part of the Bet Netofa Valley. The road from Acre, which is to the west, passed through the valley of Naḥal Evlayim, then mounted the low hills southwest of Mt. 'Aẓmon and crossed into the valley near Tel Ḥannaton (Shiḥin). Here the roads joined and shortly thereafter left the Bet Netofa Valley, crossed the Tir'an Valley, and turned down to the Yavne'el Valley and the Jordan River crossings south of the Sea of Galilee.

sites of interest in ẓippori

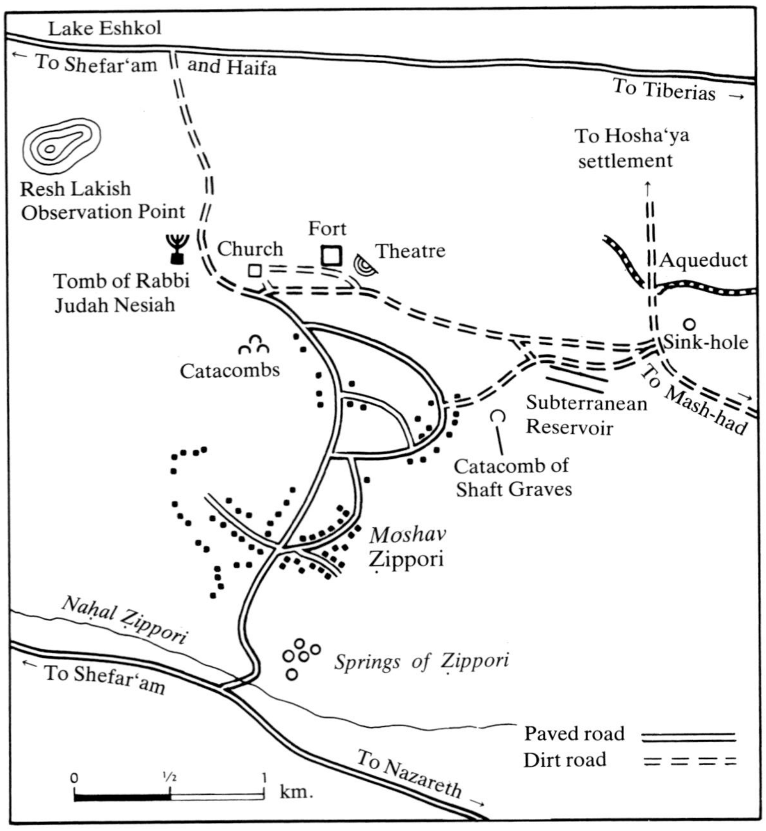

1 The tomb attributed to Judah Nesiah, grandson of Rabbi Judah ha-Nasi. The building is from talmudic times, although repairs were done on its upper portion at a later date. In the Middle Ages and even in modern times it was erroneously thought to be the tomb of Judah ha-Nasi, whose burial place in Bet She'arim had been forgotten. Judah Nesiah presided over the Sanhedrin in Tiberias, but before his death requested to be buried in Ẓippori, his birthplace.

A piquant story illustrates the importance and antiquity of these crossroads. The story originates in the letters of Tel el-'Amarna, Egypt, a royal archive from the time of Amenhotep III and his son Amenhotep IV (14th century b.c.e.). Several of these letters mention a certain King Lab'ayu of Shechem, who was downright roguish. His roguery – robbing people throughout the land – did not find favor with the kings of the cities attacked, who repeatedly complained to the king of Egypt about his carryings on. When the complaints had become so numerous that the Egyptian king (in whose realm the Land of Israel lay) could no longer remain silent, he sent an army to capture Lab'ayu and bring him to trial in Egypt. The Egyptian army led him from Megiddo to Ḥannaton, intending to proceed to Acre in order to sail from there to Egypt. Lab'ayu escaped from his captors and fled to Megiddo, and from there to Gina (Jenin), en route to Shechem. In Gina he was killed by townfolk loyal to the king of Egypt. Of particular interest to us in this episode is the complaint lodged by the king of Babylonia who protested that a Babylonian merchant by the name of Aḥitav had been robbed by the king of Shimron and the king of Acre at Ḥannaton. This complaint is evidence of the international traffic passing along the route outlined above.

What benefit is it to a city to be situated on the crossroads of an international trade route? The military importance is incontrovertible, but it is not always an asset. The residents of Arbel and Ḥannaton learned this lesson the hard way, when their cities were destroyed by the kings of Assyria passing by them on their campaigns (eighth century b.c.e.).

The great advantage enjoyed by the residents of a city situated on a crossroads is the economic benefit its location brings. The good living earned by people offering services on main thoroughfares is evident to this day. Moreover the contacts afforded by international commerce supplied a wealth of information and opportunities to those dwelling mid-way between the superpowers of the time.

Imagine a trader carrying goods from Babylonia to Egypt. Let alone the difficulties of the long journey, he also faces the fear of meeting bandits along the way, and perhaps has escaped from them by the skin of his teeth. Various illnesses befall his men, and wild animals surely take their toll as well. Half way along the road he meets a resident of Ẓippori who offers to buy his goods at

1

a lower price than they would command in Egypt. At first he refuses, but the man of Ẓippori, who from his contact with traders is well aware of the market in both countries and no less aware of the hazards of the journey, holds his own. The Babylonian trader then begins to waver. The price is low, but Egypt is still far off and the way there fraught with danger. The Ẓippori merchant sets him worrying about the market in Egypt and magnifies his fears of the dangers along the way. It is only natural for the trader to give in to temptation and sell at a low price. Thus we have an economic advantage of the first magnitude.

These agricultural and commercial advantages convinced rulers in various periods to make the city a regional capital, thus adding to the importance, development and wealth of Ẓippori – all the more tangible when we see its ruins. Wealth, however, was not what won the city its venerated place in our history.

the synagogues of ẓippori

Ẓippori reached its zenith in the time of Judah ha-Nasi (late second century c.e.), who moved the Sanhedrin to the city, making it the capital of Jewish "autonomy." Some meagre signs of this Jewish golden age, which culminated in the redaction of the Mishnah, can be seen in the few remains of synagogues here.

Ẓippori once had many synagogues, including special synagogues for the members of various vocations such as weavers, or synagogues for congregations from a given place such as the Jerusalemite synagogue, or the Babylonian synagogue.

Remains of two synagogues were discovered in the vicinity of the ancient Crusader church, down the western side of the hill (the key to the church is kept in the monastery next to the fortress). North of the church, near the stone wall enclosing its courtyard, the mosaic floor of a synagogue was uncovered, bearing an Aramaic inscription whose approximate sense was: **"In appreciation of Rabbi Judan ben Tanḥum ben... who donated one** [dinar]**..."** This is a commemorative inscription of a sort customary in the Galilee in that era, honoring one of the donors who helped build the synagogue, which in those days were built by contributions from a number of individuals. The inscription is now preserved in a room to the left of the apse of the Crusader church.

In the courtyard of the church, leaning against the wall to the left of the gate, is a stone lintel bearing a Greek inscription from the fifth century, which translates as follows: **"By the illustrious, learned Gelsius** [Isaac] **son of Aatius the minister; by Judah, the head of the synagogue; and by Sidonius, the head of the synagogue, these walls** [were built] **in honor of Jans** [Johanan] **Aphro** [dysius], **the illustrious head of the synagogue of the men of Tyre."**

The ornate capitals and finely polished granite columns belong to buildings from Roman times. Perhaps they are none other than the remains of synagogues and other buildings in Ẓippori from the era of Judah ha-Nasi. Jewish sources mention the largest of the synagogues, "The Great Synagogue of Ẓippori,"

1

and "The Great House of Study" where the Nasi taught. Maybe Judah ha-Nasi actually leaned against one of these columns during his prayers.

christianity – a foe on the threshhold

When Christianity became the official religion, the apostate Joseph, "Friend of the Emperor" (an honorific title), who according to Christian sources was close to the house of the Nasi, tried, with the aid of the Byzantine government, to build churches in the Jewish towns of the Galilee, including Ẓippori. The Jews vehemently objected and the authorities stepped up their persecution of the Jewish community. This led to the outbreak of another revolt in 352 c.e., suppressed by Gallus; hence its name, the "War of Gallus." Ẓippori was destroyed in this revolt, and apparently also Bet She'arim. Ẓippori, however, was soon rebuilt, and a Jewish majority was restored to the city until the close of the fifth century, as the synagogue and its Greek inscription testify. During this period the city already was the seat of a Christian archbishop. Little by little Christians penetrated into Ẓippori, displacing the Jews. Christian tradition claims Ẓippori as the home of Hannah and Jehoiachin, the parents of Mary; the monastery built here is named after them. However, there is evidence of a Jewish community existing in Ẓippori into the early Arab period and possibly surviving until Crusader times.

The ancient church, whose eastern wall still stands intact, is from the Crusader period. Ẓippori was of far greater military importance to the Crusaders than Nazareth, insofar as it was located on the road to Tiberias, the capital of Galilee under the Crusaders, and was an important source of water for their horses. (Remember that the Crusaders' main source of strength was their cavalry, and that supplying water for their horses was very important.) Little wonder, therefore, that the Crusaders built a large, magnificent church in Ẓippori in the 12th century. The huge apse and large vaulted recesses on either side of it remain in the eastern wall and attest the former splendor of this building. The surviving columns are typical of Crusader construction, with a cross-section roughly in the shape of a cross formed by the adjacent placement of four cylinders. In the Crusader period Ẓippori was a fortified city. Near the springs of Ẓippori the Crusader army massed before the Battle of Hattin (1187), and from that city it set out to its crushing defeat.

the grandson who remembered the town of his birth

A dirt road, branching west off the road to the monastery, leads down the hill to the cemetery of the *moshav* of Ẓippori and to an ancient structure standing next to it – a tomb attributed to Rabbi Judah ha-Nasi's grandson, Judah Nesiah, which still attracts pilgrims today. Niches to house caskets, which have been plundered over the years, were built in the inside walls. The building is from the talmudic period although its upper portion was rebuilt at a later date. Throughout the Middle Ages and even in modern times the tomb was erroneously attributed to Judah ha-Nasi, whose tomb in Bet She'arim had been forgotten. For generations, as we read in various travelogs, Jews have come to pray at this grave.

Ẓippori, as we have said, was a mostly Jewish city with a very lively community and center of Torah study. It was the birthplace of many of the authors of the Talmud, among them the great *amora* of the Land of Israel – Rabbi Joḥanan. Ẓippori's rival city was Tiberias, also built by Herod Antipas. Sages and devout Jews, however, refrained from settling in Tiberias for fear of ritual impurity, because the city was built over ancient graves.

Rabbi Simeon bar Yoḥai, wanted by the Roman authorities, lay in hiding, according to tradition, in Peqi'in in the Galilee. After the Romans had given up their pursuit of him, he came out of hiding and bathed in the hot springs of Tiberias. Understanding the national importance of Tiberias, he cleansed it of ritual impurity, thus ushering in massive Jewish settlement of the city, so much so that it became the largest city in the north of the land. In recognition of this, Rabbi Judah Nesiah (230-270 c.e., known as Judan Nesiah in Aramaic, the vernacular of Galilean Jewry) transferred his domicile and the seat of the Sanhedrin to Tiberias. Before his death, however, according to Jewish sources, he requested to be buried in Ẓippori.

up hill again – to the theatre

After the failure of the Bar Kokhba revolt (135 c.e.) the Roman authorities tried to wipe out the Jewish character of Ẓippori, changing its name to Diocaesarea, the city of the god (Deus) Zeus and the Caesar. Administration of the city was handed over to gentiles. The new name, however, was rapidly

2

1 *The entrance to the underground cistern, about a kilometer and a half east of the fort, along the road to the village of Mash-had.*

2 *"Drop by drop the measure is filled" (*Ta'anit 9*). A subterranean water reservoir from the Roman period. Signs of the plaster which sealed the fissured stone walls are still visible. An aqueduct ran from the springs of Mash-had and Reina to the reservoir, which consisted of two pools. After the upper pool filled, the water flowed over into the lower one.*
Long and narrow, the reservoir is 189 meters long by 2.0 - 6.5 meters wide and at most 7.9 meters deep. Hewn into chalky rock, harder at the northern end, excellent use was made of a natural geological break to cut the reservoir.

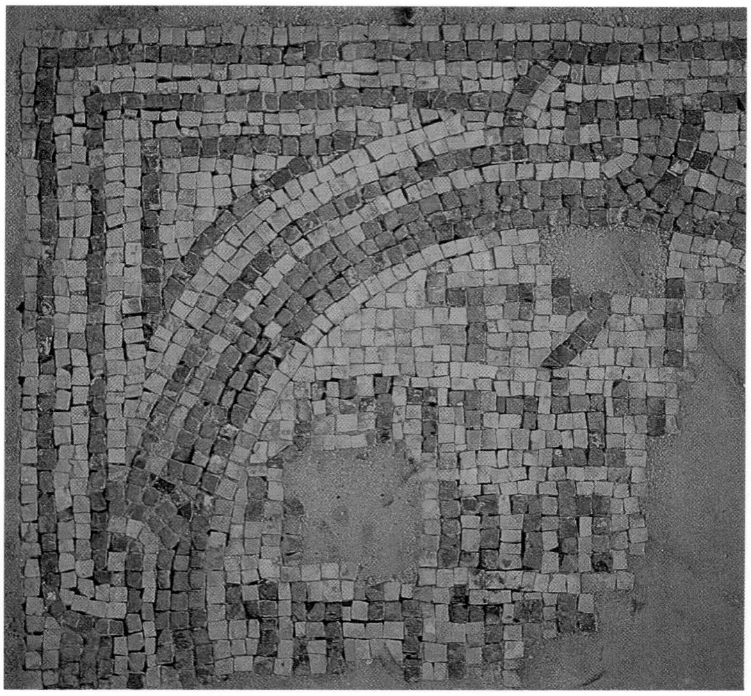

1

forgotten, and the city administration returned to Jewish hands.

In the time of Rabbi Judah ha-Nasi (circa 200) Ẓippori was the seat of the Nasi and the Sanhedrin and an exuberant center of Jewish life. Still the city always had a Roman garrison stationed in it and Roman officials living there with their families. Under Hadrian a road cutting across the Jezreel valley was paved from Kefar Otnay (near Megiddo) to Ẓippori, undoubtedly increasing Roman traffic to the city. Behind the fortress which we see today, northeast of it, the Romans also built themselves a theatre. Like other Roman theatres in the country, it was built on the side of the hill, facing a beautiful landscape. The theatre had three tiers of seats, accomodating 4,000 people. The orchestra, where the chorus stood, was cut into the rock and paved with stone panels. Behind it was the stage, at the foot of the hill.

West of the theatre a Roman villa with several interesting architectural elements, including Ionic columns and capitals and a mosaic floor, was unearthed in excavations. Descending southwest from the fortress one comes across many remains of ancient buildings and even the ruins of a wall which apparently enclosed the ancient castra (the upper city).

The theatre to no small extent symbolizes the perennial striving to preserve Jewish identity. Throughout its existence Judaism has had to fight against cultures which in their outward aspects, their simplicity and colorfulness, have beckoned to and attracted the people. Hellenistic culture, especially its surface manifestations and the style of life which it advocated, posed a threat to the cultural and national distinctiveness of the Jews. It was this threat which led to the outbreak of the Hasmonean revolt and which sowed fear in the hearts of the sages as they saw the royalty and the nobility becoming hellenized. Even at the end of the Roman period, when Hellenism had begun to decline, the sages feared lest Jews be enticed by this style of life. In mixed cities, such as Ẓippori and Bet She'an, this life style, focusing around entertainment and pleasures of the body, had a deeply threatening impact, as is reflected in Jewish sources: **"Rabbi Simeon ben Pazi expounded: What is meant by: 'Happy is the man that hath not walked in the counsel of the wicked... nor sat in the seat of the scornful'** [Psalms 1:1]**? Happy is the man who has not gone to the theatres and circuses of idolaters"** (*Avodah Zarah* 18b).

along the road to tiberias

There was always lively traffic between Tiberias and Ẓippori. The region was almost entirely Jewish. The road from Ẓippori to Mash-had (now an Arab village in the hills of Nazareth) was apparently part of the ancient route to Tiberias. From Mash-had, ancient Gath-hepher, the road continued on to Tiberias roughly along the route of the modern road. Traffic along this road was so overwhelmingly Jewish that **"Rabbi Ḥanina once found a slaughtered kid between Tiberias and Ẓippori... and as regards the method of slaughter** [it was deemed proper]**... and seeing that they were permitted in regard to the method of slaughter, the majority** [of the people along this road] **must have consisted of Israelites"** (*Bava Meẓia* 24b).

The road which winds eastward down the hill from the fortress is the ancient road to Tiberias. Near the bedouin tent along the side of the road is a row of bramble bushes, whose appearance gives added spike to Jotham's fable (Judges 9:3-15). What actually captivates our attention, however, are the ancient olive trees with their hollow, scarred trunks. Did these olive trees behold the glory of Ẓippori, or perhaps listen to the conversation between Rabbi Joḥanan and his disciple, Rabbi Ḥiyya b. Abba, as they walked along this road from Tiberias to Ẓippori: **"They came to a certain plot of land and Rabbi Joḥanan said: 'This land was mine and I sold it in order to acquire the Torah.' They came to a certain vineyard and he said: 'This vineyard was mine and I sold it in order to acquire the Torah.' They came to a certain olive-grove and he said: 'This olive-grove was mine and I sold it in order to acquire the Torah.' Rabbi Ḥiyya began weeping. 'Why are you weeping?' asked Rabbi Joḥanan. He answered him: 'Because you have left nothing for your old age.' He said to him: 'Ḥiyya, my son, is it a light thing in your eyes what I have done? That I have sold a thing which was created in six days and acquired a thing that was given after 40 days? For whereas the entire world and the fulness thereof were created in six days, the Torah was given at the end of forty days.' "** (Exodus Rabbah 47; Leviticus Rabbah 30:1).

... yet wherein lies its greatness?

As we walk along, visualizing scenes from the past, we begin to consider why Ẓippori was so special. The explanation is neither in the stone ruins nor the glory of the past but in an analysis of the period beginning with the suppression of the Bar Kokhba revolt (135 c.e.) and continuing until the redaction of the Mishnah in approximately 200 c.e. The Bar Kokhba revolt had dire consequences – almost complete annihilation of the Jewish community in Judea and apparently serious damage to the Jews of the Galilee. Hadrian's decrees made it impossible to lead a Jewish life according to the laws of the Torah. Hadrian, motivated not only by political pragmatism but also by wrath and injured pride, took action against a small nation which had revolted and drawn the blood of the gigantic superpower. Prohibitions against circumcision, rabbinical ordination, and studying the Torah, along with economic and physical persecution, were intended to put an end to this unique people.

The following episode, left us from that period, speaks for itself: **"Hadrian the accursed** [lit. "his bones be pulverized"] **set up three garrisons... saying, 'Whoever tries to flee from one will be captured at another and vice versa.' The Romans announced, 'Wherever a Jew is hiding, let him come forth, for the king will treat him well.' Those who were shrewd did not come out, but those who were naive came out into the open and were trapped. They all assembled in the valley of Bet Rimmon, and Hadrian said: 'By the time I eat this slice of cake and this leg of fowl, there had better not be a single one of them alive here.' His legions immediately surrounded them and slaughtered them, so that their blood flowed as far as the River Kipros. Those Jews who remained in hiding** [in the caves] **used to venture forth at night, following the scent of their slain brethren, and bring back the corpses and eat them... Once a young man among them found the slain body of his father; he took the corpse, buried it, and marked the spot; then he returned and said, 'I found nothing.' Somebody else went out and followed the same scent, discovered the body, and brought it back. After they had eaten it, they asked him, 'From where did you bring this corpse?' 'From such and such a place.' The young man then asked, 'What distinguishing mark was over it?' 'Such and such a sign,' he replied. 'Woe is me,' wailed the young man, 'for I have eaten the flesh of my father!' "** (Lamentations Rabbah 1:16).

And so the people fought for their survival, struggling against economic hardship and decrees threatening their existence and identity. Rabbi Ḥanina ben Teradyon, caught bringing together groups and teaching them Torah, was sentenced to be burned at the stake; his wife was sentenced to death, and his daughter condemned to serve as a prostitute. Rabbi Judah ben Bava was killed by the Romans, but not before he had ordained five rabbis from Usha to Shefar'am. In addition to these men, the other of the Ten Martyrs, including Rabbi Akiva, were killed; and many others, whose names remain unknown, perished in this struggle.

It was this steadfastness, this struggle fraught with danger, that kept the embers burning. A spirit of brotherhood reigned among those keeping the fire alive; and in one of their gatherings they ripped their prayer shawls to provide enough to share all around. When the persecution abated somewhat, the

2

1 *A mosaic inscription from one of the synagogues at Ẓippori, now preserved in the Crusader church in the room to the left of the apse. Honoring one of the donors who contributed to construction of the synagogue, as was customary in the Galilee at that time, the Aramaic inscription reads: "In appreciation of Rabbi Judan ben Tanḥum ben ... who donated one [dinar] ... ."*

2 *The upper city was inhabited by Roman officials and their families and by wealthy Jewish families. Northeast of the fortress a theatre was built for their benefit. It had seats of stone and, as in other theatres of the same period, was built on the hillside, facing a striking landscape.*

1

sages assembled in Usha (east of present-day Ramat Yoḥanan) and proclaimed: **"Whoever has learnt, let him come and teach, and whoever has not learnt, let him come and learn"** (Song of Songs Rabbah 2). Later a Nasi was elected and the Sanhedrin reinstated.

The Nasi and the Sanhedrin moved to Shefar'am and later, in the time of Judah ha-Nasi, to Bet She'arim, and from there to Ẓippori. Rabbi Judah ha-Nasi was venerated and beloved of his people, and followed an astute political policy, which even led to cordial relations with Roman Emperor Antoninus and won the Jews a degree of autonomy in managing their life, permitting the survival of their distinctive national ways according to the laws of the Torah. Here in Ẓippori the halcyon days of Jewish cultural-religious life reached their zenith with the conclusion of a vast undertaking – the collation of the Mishnah, an enterprise which assured the continuation of Jewish thought, deliberation and rulings affecting all walks of life, even in times of hardship and oppression, and thus protected the people from assimilation in its lands of exile.

Thus Ẓippori symbolizes resurrection out of dreadful persecution. From the time when Jews here in the Rimmon Valley were mercilessly oppressed, from the day Judah ben Bava died a martyr somewhere between Shefar'am and Usha, only 65 years had elapsed until the day the Mishnah was completed in Ẓippori, the day Jewish life was restored to full vigor in the Galilee, and its future was assured.

a large tunnel and a small adventure...

The springs of Ẓippori are located near the turn-off of the access road to the *moshav of* Ẓippori from the main Shefar'am – Nazareth road, and near the stream bed of Naḥal Ẓippori. A pump house now stands over the main spring. Here, in the time of the Talmud, lay the irrigated fields of Ẓippori, mentioned in talmudic literature. In those days the water could not be brought up to the town itself or to the higher fields on the eastern side. For drinking, and possibly also for irrigating the eastern fields, an aqueduct was built to carry water from the smaller springs, 'En Avel and 'Enot Amitai, in the vicinity of Mash-had. Parts of the aqueduct are hewn into the rock, parts built of stone. Along the way is a large and interesting subterranean cistern, about a kilometer and a half east of the fortress of Ẓippori. The cistern is 200 meters long by four meters wide and six meters high. It may be reached by any path leading from Ẓippori towards Mash-had, but is best approached by the dirt road to Mash-had which leaves from the northeastern spur of the *moshav*. Slightly northeast of the cistern there is a pine grove.

1,2 *Ẓippori's water works are comprised of two aqueducts, one beginning at the springs 'Enot Amitai and 'En Avel, on the northern slope of Mt. Yona, the other at the Reina springs. Five kilometers from their respective sources the two aqueducts join, then, before entering the city, they split again, the northern one carrying water to a pool and the southern one to the subterranean reservoir and from there to the city. Parts of the aqueducts are hewn into the rock, parts built of stone, according to the terrain.*
The joint portion of the aqueduct, shown in the pictures, is cut into the ground at its eastern end and constructed on a man-made foundation, preserved to a height of 1.5 meters and a width of 1.4 meters, at its western end. The wall is of dry construction, consisting of boulders with smaller stones filling the interstices. The joint segment of the aqueduct is approximately 5.2 km. long and has an average gradient of only 10.6 per thousand.

These being the only closely planted trees in the area, save for some ancient olive groves, we can use them to help locate the cistern. The cistern is quite high and in many places retains its original plaster. Plant ashes were added to the plaster to prevent the water from seeping through the fissured stone. The cistern is relatively well preserved, although part of the ceiling has collapsed in the middle. One branch of the aqueduct from the vicinity of Mash-had reaches the cistern. Another branch turns north and makes a circuit around Mt. Jedaiah. Where it continues we do not yet know, for it is not visible above ground; but about 500 meters from where it breaks off there is a pool cut into the rock. Perhaps the aqueduct channeled the water here. So far we do not know where the water system continued from the pool, but there may have been an aqueduct which carried water to the city of Ẓippori, perhaps even to the castra, the upper city. The existence of an aqueduct passing through the city and even into the yards of the houses there is intimated by a question of Jewish law concerning the Sabbath, recorded in Tractate *Shabbat* of the Mishnah. Indeed it is quite possible that a water system on such a grand scale did exist, for it is integrally tied to the Hellenistic style of life which required vast quantities of water, far beyond the amount stored in the city's many wells, to maintain the baths and fountains.

Walking the length of the tunnel, from west to east, is not particularly difficult but involves a small adventure of descending the walls which separate the pools. Whoever has not had his appetite sated by this little adventure has a much larger one in store. In the pine grove not far from the ruins of the ancient aqueduct a huge crack gapes in the hard rock. This is a sink-hole, a geological formation resulting from dissolution of the rock. If you wish to descend into it, you must be agile and have ... candles or a flashlight. First you descend into a spacious room, then through a narrow passageway at its edge, and on into the depths of the rock – a real adventure.

far from the last word

During the War of Independence, and in all the massacres which preceded it, Arab murder gangs used Ẓippori as a base. After the gangs were quashed, the residents fled and the village was abandoned, when, in "Operation Dekel," a column of the IDF progressed from Shefar'am towards the Nazareth road.

In 1949 the *moshav* movement founded a settlement on the site. According to the testimony of one of the residents of *moshav* Ẓippori, there are two Arab families from Nazareth, former Ṣaffuriyya residents, who maintain they are of Jewish origin and, in the best tradition of apostates, hold extremist anti-Israel views.

The hill above the tunnel provides a view of the houses of the *moshav* and the fortress atop the hill. The Jews renewed their tenure in Ẓippori by establishing a *moshav* on the site of the city which was such an important symbol and landmark in its history.

Traces of remains from various periods extend over a vast area. Ẓippori, which has long waited for someone to deliver it from shameful neglect and bring to light secrets still concealed beneath the ground, is finally being excavated by a joint expedition from Duke University in North Carolina and the Hebrew University of Jerusalem, under the direction of Eric Meyers, Ehud Netzer and Carol Meyers, and a second expedition from the University of Florida, directed by James Strange.

2

the synagogue at capernaum

Irit Zaharoni

Set among the black basalt stones on the shore of the Sea of Galilee, the splendid remains of the synagogue at Capernaum (Kefar Naḥum in Hebrew) stand glistening white. This is a prime example of the "earlier type" of synagogue, one among many discovered throughout the Galilee, the Bashan and the Golan.

Ancient synagogues are generally classified by scholars into two principal types. The "later type" comprises synagogues which have a fixed place for the Ark and are characterized by strikingly beautiful mosaic floors and meager external architectural ornamentation. The most famous of these synagogues is the one at Bet Alfa. The main era of construction of these synagogues was from the fifth to the seventh century c.e.

Other synagogues, most likely constructed in the third-fourth century, are considered to belong to the "earlier type." These were discovered mostly in the Galilee and hence are also known as the Galilean type. These monumental edifices were built of dressed stone and decorated in the best Roman style of the third-fourth century. The plan and interior layout of these buildings is extremely uniform despite variations evident in the form of buildings constructed in different places, according to the economic status of the various communities and the generosity of the donors.

Every Jewish community, be it a town or a village, undoubtedly invested its greatest effort in building a synagogue. The synagogue was the spiritual and social center of the Jewish community. The site for the synagogue was selected in accordance with the prinicples of Jewish law (Tosefta, *Megillah* 4), which stipulated that the synagogue was to be built on the highest spot in the city. The logic behind this rule was to enhance the glory of the house of worship. From the porch of the synagogue, built on the crest of a hill or overlooking a hillside, worshippers could gaze at the marvelous views of the hilly Galilee. Building a synagogue on the shore of a lake (as in Capernaum) or by a stream or spring (like the synagogue near the stream of Gush Ḥalav) was also allowed, although this is not explicitly stated in Jewish texts. Selection of such sites appears to have been based on an ancient tradition.

plan of the synagogue at capernaum

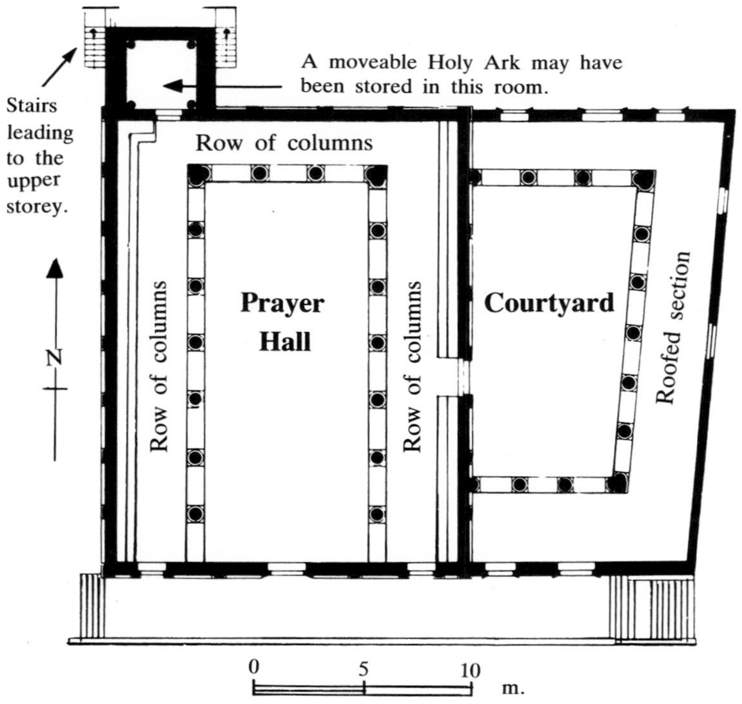

1 A vase with grape clusters and acanthus leaf motifs carved in relief on one of the capitals of the synagogue.

2 A segment of a frieze with a relief of a chariot in the shape of a shrine. It is thought to represent the Holy Ark, which was customarily transportable and was brought into the prayer hall on a hand-pushed cart when the Torah was to be read. In Capernaum the Ark was stored in a side room, and only in later synagogues was a special niche built to provide a permanent place for housing the Holy Ark.

Quite a few scholars believe the origins of the synagogue date back to the Babylonian exile. Being far from their traditional center of prayer, the ravaged Temple in Jerusalem, and refusing to recognize the superiority of the Babylonian deities, ostensibly the victors, the leaders of the Jews held gatherings for prayer and thanksgiving "by the rivers of Babylon," directing their eyes towards Jerusalem, whose memory they cherished.

Once the Jews became accustomed to gathering for prayer in the synagogue, the practice never ceased, even after the return to Zion and reconstruction of the Temple. In Jerusalem itself an inscription was discovered attesting the existence of a synagogue not far from the Temple.

That synagogues existed by the Second Temple period, both in Israel and the Diaspora, is attested by various written sources. Actual remains of synagogues coeval with the Temple (and thus predating the "earlier type") were discovered at Masada, Herodion, and Gamla.

Establishing the synagogue introduced a great innovation in holy worship, both with respect to the Temple in Jerusalem and with respect to all the shrines of other religions. A temple or shrine was a place for offering sacrifices, hence the public would throng in the courtyard, while only a small handful of priests would be allowed entry into the building. The synagogue, however, was for reading the Torah and for prayer, and hence it was meant for all the congregation to assemble within its walls.

Years later Christian churches and Moslem mosques followed in the wake of synagogues, themselves adopting this principle.

The largest, most magnificent and famous of the earlier type of synagogues is the one at Capernaum, with an area of 360 sq. meters, easily accomodating several dozen worshippers. The wealth of the community at Capernaum, a commercially flourishing fishing town situated on the highroad, and the great effort invested by this community in its synagogue are evident in

1

2

the synagogue at capernaum

the building's elaborate façade. To begin with, the synagogue stood out in its color. Only this building was constructed of white chalkstone, which had to be brought from afar, while all the houses in the area were built of local black basalt.

In general appearance the synagogue at Capernaum, like other Galilean synagogues, resembled magnificent Roman buildings of the same era. Many Roman buildings with comparable architectural details and artistic stone carvings have been discovered in Syria, the Golan, and the Hauran, although few remains of buildings of this type have been found in the Land of Israel itself. The stone carvers here combined designs of ornamentation prevalent in the East at the time with traditional Jewish motifs common in the Land of Israel.

The walls of the synagogue were ornamented on the interior and exterior with stone carvings. The broad scope of ornamentation included motifs from the plant and animal world, as well as geometric shapes. Few human shapes are found here.

Carvings of a horse and of eagles carrying garlands have survived from Capernaum. At other synagogues even human figures from Greek mythology have survived. During the time of the Mishnah and the Talmud observant Jews carved mostly floral and animal forms, although sometimes they carved human forms as well. They understood the Torah's prohibition, **"Thou shalt not make unto thee a graven image,"** as applying to carving which was done with the intent of idolatry, whereas decoration of the synagogue they viewed as nothing more than ornament, solely for the purpose of adornment and not in the least alluding to pagan rites.

Although, as we have said, the decorations were purely ornamental, some had symbolic value. The *menorah, shofar* and incense pan which are carved on a Corinthian capital, and the chariot in the shape of a shrine (representing a Holy Ark like the one painted at Dura Europos) which is carved on one of the lintels are religious symbols common in synagogue art. Grape vines, pomegranates, and date palms apparently represent three of the seven varieties of fruit with which the Land of Israel was blessed. What we call the Star of David today was not a Jewish symbol at the time. All the animal representations, save for one, were intentionally defaced in a mounting wave of opposition to carving such forms which, as far as we can tell, set in at the beginning of the Arab period.

1

2

3

The synagogue plan is square. The main part of the building is the assembly and prayer hall. The highly ornate façade of the synagogue faces south, towards Jerusalem. The façade, the most adorned part of the building, had three entrances. Thus the worshippers must have first entered the building and then,

4

during the prayers, turned around to face Jerusalem.

In contrast to the practice which took hold later and is followed to this day, the Holy Ark, or Torah shrine, did not have a fixed place in the wall facing Jerusalem. According to many scholars the Ark was portable and was kept in one of the side rooms of the synagogue, whence it was carried into the hall during the service. The synagogue at Capernaum has such a side room near the northern wall.

1 *A cornice showing figures of mythological sea-horses and two eagles holding a garland.*

2 *A cornice showing medallions decorated with floral motifs and geometric designs such as a Star of David (on the left).*

3 *A medallion containing a five-pointed star, part of a frieze from the synagogue at Capernaum. Other medallions on the frieze contain rosettes, clusters of grapes, pomegranates, and other designs.*

4 *A capital from the synagogue, showing a seven-branched candelabrum, with a* shofar *on its right and an incense pan on its left.*

Rows of columns apparently supporting an upper gallery were built opposite the side and back walls. (The presence of a third row of columns parallel to the façade, in addition to the two rows along the sides, and the absence of an apse are characterisitic features of ancient synagogues.) The remains of steps discovered at Capernaum further attest the existence of a gallery. Perhaps this gallery, or part of it, was set aside as a women's section.

Two rows of stone benches were built along the walls of the prayer hall for use by the worshippers. The floor of the hall was paved with large stone tiles.

On the eastern side of the synagogue was a large enclosed courtyard.

Two inscriptions, one Greek and the other Aramaic, both naming donors to the synagogue, were discovered on the pillars. The Greek inscription translates as follows: **"Herodes son of Mo[qi]mus, and his son Justus, together with their children, erected this column."** The Aramaic inscription states: **"Ḥalfo son of Zeveida son of Joḥanan made this column; may he be blessed."**

The inscriptions in Galilean synagogues are not themselves part of the decoration or architectural ornamentation of the synagogues, yet they deserve mention due to the light which they shed on the atmosphere which enveloped these synagogues. Save for one inscription in Greek – the one at Capernaum – all the dedicatory inscriptions were written in Aramaic.

These inscriptions reveal that donating all the funds necessary to build a synagogue was beyond the means of a single individual, and that many individuals worked together to build the edifice, insofar as each person contributed a particular part, columns or stairs or other items. Nevertheless, despite the many donors, the plan of the building did not suffer, but remained an integrated and harmonious composition.

Capernaum became holy to Christianity as one of the places where Jesus was active in the early 1st century c.e. Christian scholars who came to the site hoped to discover that this synagogue was the very building in which Jesus had prayed. However there are no remains on the site which can be dated to that period. It has recently been suggested that the synagogue at Capernaum was actually built later, in the 5th century. This theory was based primarily on coins found on the site. Nevertheless the more widely accepted view remains that the

1 *The protruding end of a stone beam with a remarkable palm-tree relief.*

2 *Lake Kinneret, the Sea of Galilee, mentioned in historical sources also as the Sea of Tiberias, the Sea of Gennesareth (Ginnesar), and other names.*

1

building was founded in the 3rd or 4th century and continued to serve as a Jewish center of prayer for many years.

In their appearance and craftsmanship the synagogue at Capernaum and other Galilean synagogues represent the golden age of Jewish creative life in the Land of Israel – the time of the *tannaim* and *amoraim* – and within their walls many of the rabbis who gave us our heritage of the Mishnah, the Talmud, and Jewish homiletical literature must have prayed.

For further reference see:
1. Gideon Foerster, "Notes on Recent Excavations at Capernaum," *Israel Exploration Journal,* XXI (1971), 207-216.
2. Articles by Gideon Foerster in L. Levine (ed.), *Ancient Synagogues Revealed,* (Jerusalem, 1981), 45-49.

2

the zodiac ever and anon

Magen Broshi

Towards the end of the First World War, in September 1918, the explosion of shell which was fired at British positions in Na'aran, north of Jericho, revealed the mosaic floor of a synagogue. This was a surprising discovery, for it was the first Jewish mosaic floor to be found in the Land of Israel. Of this once magnificent mosaic floor only segments, albeit quite large ones, remained, depicting a biblical scene – Daniel in the lion's den – and the signs of the zodiac.

Ten years later, while an irrigation ditch was being dug, the mosaic floor of the Bet Alfa synagogue (on the grounds of *kibbutz* Ḥefẓi Bah in the Ḥarod Valley), also depicting a biblical scene – the binding of Isaac – and the zodiac, was discovered. This time the floor was well preserved and, understandably, aroused considerable excitement. There were people who recollected hearing a scholar once say it was impossible that mosaic floors should be found in ancient Jewish synagogues, and certainly not mosaics depicting human and animal figures or such pagan themes as the signs of the zodiac.

Thus far around twenty mosaic synagogue floors have been found in Israel, four of them depicting the zodiac: besides Na'aran and Bet Alfa, fragments of a zodiac mosaic have also been found at Ḥusseifa (a Jewish town from the Roman and Byzantine era, now the Druze village of 'Isfiya) on the Carmel and in the magnificent floor at Ḥammat Tiberias. A fifth synagogue, at 'En Gedi, lists the zodiac signs but does not depict them.

Earliest of all is the synagogue at Ḥammat Tiberias, dating to the fourth century c.e. The synagogues at Ḥusseifa and 'En Gedi are from the fifth century, and the ones at Bet Alfa and Na'aran from the sixth These centuries are known in the history of the area as the Byzantine period.

The zodiac design in these synagogues has a fixed form. It is situated in the center of the floor and consists of two concentric circles inscribed in a square. The figure of the sun god appears inside the inner circle, the twelve zodiac signs in the outer circle, and the four seasons in the corners.

The sun god (Gk. *Helios,* L. *sol*) rides a chariot hitched to

1 *Against a sky covered with moon and stars, Helios the sun god rides on his chariot, drawn by four horses. This drawing appears in the center of the zodiac design in the mosaic floor of the Bet Alfa synagogoue. The primitive, naive style has the charm of rural folk art.*

1

1 *The mosaic floor in the synagogue at Ḥammat Tiberias. The corners of the "carpet" with the zodiac in its center display four female figures representing the four seasons. In that era they were named according to the Hebrew months: "The Period of Tishri" (fall), "The Period of Tevet" (winter), "The Period of Nisan" (spring), and "The Period of Tamuz" (summer). Each figure is adorned with the harvest of the season; for instance, a ripe cluster of grapes in the hand of "The Period of Tishri."*

2 *"Balance" (Tishri) and "Virgin" (Elul), the beginning and end of the Jewish year. The mosaic in the synagogue at Ḥammat Tiberias appears to have been executed by a gentile artisan. He naively portrayed the figure holding the balance as uncircumcised, even though this was a synagogue. And, not knowing Hebrew, he mistakenly copied the letters given him for "Water-bearer" in mirror writing (see the upper right of the zodiac picture on the previous page).*

2

two thousand years later, indeed?

Meir Ben-Dov

"For the first time in two thousand years" became a common expression often heard in connection with the renewal of Jewish settlement in the Land of Israel at the end of the previous century, and asserted even more often in our own day: "the first settlement in the 'Arava in two thousand years"; "the first wedding on the summit of Mt. Meron in two thousand years"; and even "the first Yemenite pilot in two thousand years."

What lies behind such expressions? Taken most simply, two thousand years ago we, the Jews, were exiled from our land. Actually it was in 70 c.e., 1900 years ago, when the Second Temple and Jerusalem were destroyed, at the end of the Great Revolt of the Jews against the Romans. "For the first time in two thousand years" implies that the Land of Israel was quit by its Jewish inhabitants, who went into exile with the destruction of the Temple, essentially putting an end to the Jewish community in the land, save for a handful of small villages or isolated Jews residing here or there as an insignificant minority in a country most of whose inhabitants were gentiles.

Was this indeed the case?

Anyone the least bit versed in Jewish sources knows that this view of the situation has no roots in reality. The Mishnah and the Jerusalem Talmud, legends and homiletical literature, all tell of large, influential Jewish communities inhabiting considerable parts of the Land of Israel in the centuries after the destruction of the Temple. Contemporaneous historical sources also tell of significant Jewish populations living in the country and taking part in the various historical events which transpired in the region. Besides all this, we have the tangible evidence encountered by anyone traveling around Israel: ruins of ancient synagogues. Many have been discovered in various parts of the country, some concentrated in especially great numbers in specific regions. Go to the Golan Heights and you find synagogues in Qaṣrin, 'En Nashut, Dikke, Dabura, and many other places. Go down to the area around the Kinneret (Sea of Galilee) and you find them in Kefar Naḥum (Capernaum), Tiberias, Ḥammat Gader, Korazim (Khorazin), and the Arbel. Continue to the Bet She'an Valley and there you find the synagogues of Bet She'an, Reḥov, Kokhav ha-Yarden (Belvoir), Ma'oz Ḥayyim, Kefar Dana, and the like. In the Upper Galilee you will find their remains at Bar'am, Gush Ḥalav (Gischala), Meron, Ḥurbat Shema', and as far as Yafa (Japhia), near Nazareth, in the Lower Galilee. You find them also further south: at Jericho, Na'aran, and 'En Gedi in the Jordan Valley, and at Suseya, Eshtemoa' and Ḥurbat Kishor in the Hebron Hills. You find remains of synagogues in Ashdod, Ashqelon, and 'Aza (Gaza) along the coastal plain, as well as Ma'on in the Negev. Only the major synagogue ruins are listed here, for an exhaustive list of the 120 and more sites where such ruins have been found would be too long.

Archaeologists have classified ancient synagogues according to various periods, identifying some as earlier ones, i.e. from the second and third centuries c.e., and others as later ones, dating up to the 10th century. Between the early and late periods,

1

naturally, there is also a middle period. Recent studies have actually tended to ascribe later dates to synagogues than previously believed. Once it was thought the impressive buildings in the Galilee, such as the synagogues at Kefar Naḥum and Bar'am, belonged to the early period, whereas those with mosaic floors, like the one at Bet Alfa and others, were later. Recent studies, however, have revealed that almost all the synagogues whose remains have been discovered belong to the later period, i.e. the late six and seventh century c.e. Some may have been founded earlier, but their main period of use before being abandoned or destroyed was primarily during the centuries stated. Some synagogues even continued to exist as active houses of worship into the eighth century.

A map of ancient synagogues thus shows centers of dense Jewish habitation in various parts of the country, a picture which fits in well with other data and sources on the history of the Land of Israel during these centuries. We must bear in mind that every such synagogue discovered in digging, often quite by accident, was a community center serving a large number of Jews. Every synagogue always had a large Jewish population behind it, a population which needed such a center and had the economic means to build and maintain it.

the jewish peasant was different

Thus we may infer that in the sixth and seventh centuries – five and six hundred years after the destruction of the Second Temple – the Land of Israel was still inhabited by a large, concentrated Jewish population, which constituted a weighty part of the general population of the land. This Jewish community had a strong leadership, which was capable of supporting its works and which also produced from its ranks eminent creative men, primarily poets. And, as had been the case in the generations preceding the destruction of the Temple, this was still a community consisting mostly of farmers living on their land in villages and small towns. Only a small fraction of the Jews of the Land of Israel at that time were urbanites employed in commerce or petty crafts. However, among the cities of the land, there were some, such as Tiberias, whose residents were mostly Jews.

The Jewish farmer of those days was different from his fellows the world over. A typical farmer then, like most farmers today, spent most of his time toiling hard at agriculture, remote from the world of study and education, while the Jewish farmer, on the other hand, aspired for at least one of his sons to study Torah. Thus a foundation of an educated, broad-minded peasantry came into being and left its mark on the level of agriculture as well. The farmers of the Land of Israel grew a wide variety of crops. The country's farms were mixed and exported agricultural produce such as wheat, olive oil and date honey. These were the basis of industry in the ancient world: oil was used for lighting, preserves, cosmetics, and manufacturing soaps and medicines, and date honey was the principal sweetener used by a world which did not yet know the use of sugar.

Can we estimate the number of Jewish residents in the Land of

1 *Stone relief of a palm tree, among the decorations of the synagogue at Kefar Naḥum on the shore of the Sea of Galilee. A wealthy Jewish community still existed here in the sixth century, as attested by the Aramic inscription in the mosaic floor of the synagogue at Ḥammat Gader.*

2 *The synagogue at Eshtemoa' (Sammu') in the southeastern Hebron Hills, like the synagogue at Ḥurbat Suseya a bit further east, was still used for prayer at the close of the first millenium c.e.*

3 *A mosaic synagogue floor, destroyed in the mid-seventh century, was also discovered at Maiumas, a suburb of the port of Gaza. The picture shows a lioness suckling a lion cub, and grape vine arabesques.*

2

3

1

1 *A carved basalt capital from the synagogue at Qaṣrin in the Golan. The Jewish farming community of the Golan appears to have survived until the Moslem conquest.*

2 *At Jish, a mostly Christian Arab village in the Galilee, the site of ancient Gush Ḥalav or Gischala, the remains of two synagogues have been unearthed. One was on the hill, where the village's church now stands over its ruins. The other, shown in the picture, was discovered in an olive grove at the eastern foot of the village.*

Israel in that period and calculate what fraction they comprised of the land's total population at the time?

Michael Avi-Yonah assessed the Jewish population in the Land of Israel in the early seventh century at two hundred and fifty thousand. His estimate was based on the report of a Christian monk that in the Persians' war against the Byzantine Christians, in 614 c.e., twenty-five thousand Galilean Jews joined the Persian army in their siege of Tyre. In Avi-Yonah's opinion, a population is capable of raising an army about a tenth its size; hence he assumed that the Jews of the Galilee numbered approximately a quarter of a million. However this estimate, which was made some 50 years ago, assumed that in the sixth and seventh centuries Jews lived only in the Galilee and that the south was inhabited primarily by gentiles. Subsequent studies, however, both in the field and in historical sources, have indicated that many Jews still lived in other parts of the country. Moreover, even if twenty-five thousand Jewish soldiers from the Galilee came to the aid of the Persians, how do we know that this exhausted the draft potential of the Galilean Jews? It is fully possible that not every able-bodied man enlisted to aid the Persians; in which case we must estimate the Jewish population of the Galilee at more than a quarter of a million, to which we must add the large number of Jews living in other regions of the country, as well.

There is, we believe, another way of obtaining a feel for, if not calculating exactly, the size of the Jewish community in the Land of Israel during that period. Firstly, we must assess the relative weight of the Jewish population among the rest of the major groups in the population, especially their relative weight as compared to the Christians. The Christians living in the Land of Israel at the time comprised the gentile population of the country which over the years had adopted Christianity. Among them were the descendants of the Canaanites, the Philistines, and the Phoenicians, who were joined by the offspring of the foreign legions which had come to the country in the various waves of conquest and had sunk roots here or been settled here as part of a deliberate policy of the conquering powers, especially the vestiges of the Greek and Roman forces. Besides all these, the Christian population also included descendants of Jews, converts to Christianity, of their own free will or by coercion. The Byzantine government pursued a policy, like that of its official religion, of bringing as many of its residents as possible under the wing of the Christian faith. This suited Christian ideology as well as the political aims of the secular government.

The Christian population had its churches, whose remains have been uncovered in archaeological excavations along with the remains of synagogues. Thus we may draw some demographic conclusions by comparing the number and distribution of synagogues as against churches for the same period. The number of churches coeval with ancient synagogues turns out to be over two hundred and thirty. In other words, we have twice as many churches as synagogues. Does this mean that the Christian population was twice as large as the Jewish? Not necessarily, for several reasons. To begin with, not every church was affiliated with a Christian settlement. Some were commemorative churches, or in other words edifices built in places associated with events in the life of Jesus and the Apostles

3 *The Holy Ark, seven-branched candelabra, and representations of the* shofar *and incense pans have been worked into the mosaic floor of the synagogue at Bet She'an, dating from the talmudic period. Other mosaic floors from the same period have been discovered in the Bet She'an Valley, notably at Ma'oz Ḥayyim and Ḥurbat Reḥov, where instead of pictures the mosaic floors display a detailed verbal description of the borders of the Land of Israel according to talmudic law.*

4 *"Shalom 'al Yisrael [Peace be over Israel]" – an inscription in the mosaic floor of the synagogue at Jericho. A mosaic synagogue floor was also discovered at Na'aran, somewhat further west.*

or with the lives of the Prophets, and were erected only by virtue of the wealth and power of the government. For instance, the church on Mt. Gerizim was built to mark the victory of Christianity and the Byzantine Empire over the Samaritans and their faith, after their revolt against the central government had been quashed. The purpose of the church built on Mt. Tabor was to extol an episode in the life of Jesus, as were the churches in Jerusalem and Bethlehem. Secondly, some churches belonged to monasteries. Such churches were the focal point of a community of men and not of an urban or rural population center. Other churches represent another component of the country's population, Christian in faith, yet ethnically belonging to another group. These were the descendants of the Nabatean tribes in the Negev, who remained Arab despite their conversion to Christianity. Some of their settlements in the

2

3

4

Negev have several churches each. This is less an indication of large population than of economic prosperity, which a settlement expressed by building churches beyond those necessary for its ritual and congregational needs. It should be noted that the Arab Nabatean tribes, who adopted Christianity out of convenience, were also the first to leave this religion and go over to Islam with the Arab conquest. Throughout the course of their history the Nabateans remained a separate ethnic group from the rest of the country's population.

For the above reasons, we conclude that even if twice as many churches as synagogues were discovered with respect to the same period, this does not means that there were twice as many Christians as Jews in the country. Aside from Jews, Christians, vestiges of the land's ancient pagan ethnic groups, and Arab elements, the population of the Land of Israel included another significant component – the Samaritans. While admittedly not Jews, they unquestionably rejected Christianity. In the regions where they lived, the highlands of Samaria and the surrounding area, they comprised almost the exclusive ethnic group in the population.

1200 rather than 2000 years

What was the total populaton of the Land of Israel in the sixth and seventh centuries, and what fraction of it was Jewish? Datable archaeological remains, such as destroyed villages, ruins and the like, as well as potsherds and pottery findings belonging to the same centuries, yield an estimated population of three million people during that period. Thus this was one of the more heavily populated periods for the Land of Israel, and, significantly, most of the population lived in villages. Aside from several large cities such as Jerusalem, Caesarea, Tiberias, Banyas (Panyas), and Ashqelon, there were no large population centers in the country. Bearing in mind that roughly the same number of people inhabit the country today, and that the large urban centers of today did not exist then, nor could they possibly have existed, we realize that most of the agricultural regions of the land were populated more densely than today.

1

Among the three million inhabitants, Christians numbered one million, seven hundred and fifty thousand and constituted the majority. Jews numbered roughly seven hundred and fifty thousand, Samaritans about two hundred and fifty thousand, and Arabs who embraced Christianity and were essentially the successors of the Nabateans and other tribes in the southern part of the country numbered another two hundred and fifty thousand.

The Jews, numbering about three quarters of a million, were certainly a significant part of the population. Moreover, being mostly agricultural, they dwelled in the villages and small towns and even constituted the majority in some localities.

Thus we can sense the existence of a very powerful Jewish community in the Land of Israel five hundred and even six hundred years after the destruction of the Second Temple. Therefore we must really change the expression "after two thousand years" to "after one thousand two hundred years." True, indeed, "the first wedding on Mt. Meron," but after 1200 years, since the region had a dense Jewish population up to then, with the Jews perhaps constituting the bulk of the inhabitants in their area at the time.

This leaves us with the question of how this extensive Jewish community disappeared. What became of those seven hundred and fifty thousand Jews? The question becomes even more poignant when we encounter the Jewish community of the Land of Israel in the ninth century, and even more so in the tenth century. Sources from this period reveal a small although quite significant community dwelling primarily in towns and cities, and no longer a rural agricultural population. What brought about this radical change?

The Jewish community began to suffer toward the close of the sixth and the beginning of the seventh centuries. The heavy fighting between the two superpowers of the time, Persia and Byzantium, which went on in this region, sorely afflicted the inhabitants of the land. The armies which swept through the lands of the region, fighting on their soil, ravaged and ruined the land. The Jews suffered along with other groups in the population. In addition a serious spiritual crisis descended on the Jewish community in the wake of the Byzantine victory over the Persians in 628 c.e. The victory of Byzantine Emperor Heraclius had been preceded by a Persian victory in which the Byzantines had been overcome and all the Land of Israel, including Jerusalem, had been taken out of their hands. The Jews had assisted the Persians, who had agreed to pay them considerable recompense for their assistance. The Jews thought of Chosroes II, then king of Persia, as Cyrus, and perceived signs of the Messiah's imminent arrival. The Jewish people sensed, and almost tangibly felt, the renewal of its religious and national independence, whose crowning glory would be the rebuilding of the Temple. Those were days of general spiritual elation and of strengthened faith in the Rock of Israel, its

2

1 *A basket of pomegranates, from the mosaic floor of the synagogue at Ḥurbat Ma'on in the western Negev, near* kibbutz *Nirim. The mosaic was made by the artisans who executed the mosaic floor in the synagogue on the Gaza coast.*

2 *The elaborate entryway to the nave of the great synagogue at Bar'am, a typical Galilean synagogue. The ancient Hebrew names of the villages have been retained by the Arabs in slightly distorted form to this day, thus providing further testimony to the continuity of Jewish habitation in the Galilee.*

two thousand years later, indeed?

1 *A detail from the mosaic floor of the synagogue at Hurbat Ma'on, showing a deer now extinct in this area. A prime example of the "later" type of synagogue (6th-7th centuries), in which the Holy Ark has a fixed place in an apse facing Jerusalem, it is the first of its kind discovered in the Negev.*
The mosaic is divided into 55 circles, arranged in rows and formed by a design of grape vines with occasional clusters of grapes, leaves, and tendrils. Specifically Jewish symbols are concentrated around the apse: a seven-branched candelabra, standing on three legs resembling lion's paws, with seven oil lamps burning in the candelabra and two lions, etrogs, *a* shofar *and a* lulav *flanking it. The circles in the next few lines frame pictures of various objects, such as baskets, bowls, etc., while the remaining circles frame pictures of animals and birds.*

2 *A section of the mosaic floor of the Meroth (Merot) synagogue in the eastern Upper Galilee. The part which has survived shows a young Jewish warrior with a sword, bronze helmet and shield beside him, perhaps representing David with the arms which he took from Goliath (I Samuel, Ch. 17). An Aramaic inscription, "Judan bar Simeon Mani," is worked into the mosaic beside the figure of the warrior, perhaps naming the donor or artist who made the mosaic.*
Until the discovery of this mosaic floor, the first one discovered in a synagogue in the Upper Galilee, stone paving was considered a characteristic feature of Galilean synagogues. Built in the late 4th-early 5th century c.e., the Meroth synagogue survived until the town's destruction in the late 12th century, during the Crusader period.
Ancient Meroth was founded in the 2nd century, b.c.e., probably in the Hasmonean period. Its economy was based primarily on olive cultivation for oil and on vineyards, grain and vegetable cultivation, and herding.
A treasure of 485 coins, from the time of Alexander Yannai (Jannaeus) through the Crusaders, was found in the synagogue's coffer, discovered in a recess hewn in the rock, beneath the floor. Of the coins, 245 are gold – evidence of a prosperous town with an active community that donated liberally to the public weal.
Next to the synagogue a classroom for young children was discovered, as well as a Bet Midrash, *apparently the earliest "house of study" discovered thus far in an ancient Jewish settlement. The lintel bears an inscription from the Bible: "Blessed shalt thou be when thou comest in, and blessed shalt thou be when thou goest out" (Deuteronomy 28:6).*

1

Redeemer. But before long the Byzantines returned and defeated the Persians. Emperor Heraclius, reestablishing control over the country, behaved judiciously. He did not massacre the Jews, nor launch a campaign to convince the Jews that the key to their national spiritual existence lay in abandoning Judaism and embracing Christianity. The great crisis of faith, however, suffered by the Jews of the Land of Israel, played into his hand in Christianizing the population. Rabbi Benjamin, for instance, leader of the Jews of Tiberias and perhaps one of the main public figures among the Jews of the time, was among the first to voluntarily embrace Christianity. If that was what the leader of a Jewish community did, we can well imagine what path tens of thousands of other Jews followed.

Nevertheless many Jews remained in their villages, despite the hard blows which descended on them. Where, then, did these Jews disappear? What led to the synagogues being abandoned? Where did all the Jews of the villages go?

islam or death

The Byzantines had barely enjoyed a respite from their wars before a new and energetic group was at the gates of the land. Arab tribes burst violently into the heart of the Land of Israel and Syria, waving the banner of their new faith: Islam. The two superpowers, Persia and Byzantium, weakened by their mutual wars and decayed from within, fell into the hands of the Moslem Arabs like ripe fruit. It was only a few years before the entire area which they had controlled came under the domination of the new conquerors. The latter wished to increase the number of adherents to their faith and had no desire to rule over depopulated lands. Therefore they began pressing the conquered populations to accept Islam.

2

Initially the conquerors adopted a policy of "convert to Islam or die." Later, when it became evident that although many had converted, many others, especially Jews and Christians, refused to adopt the new religion, the Moslems looked for a compromise which would not depopulate the land of its farmers or destroy the infrastructure of commercial or administrative life, two spheres in which the Christian component was quite significant. Therefore the Moslem authorities enacted a law granting special status to "People of the Book" – members of religions acknowledging scriptures which were also accepted by Islam and had preceded the Koran, namely the Old and New Testaments. Thus the Jews and Christians could continue adhering to their faith in exchange for paying a poll-tax.

The poll-tax payments were quite substantial and were an especially heavy burden on the agricultural inhabitants of the land. Many could not withstand the pressures and converted to Islam. Thus many Jewish peasants became Moslems. Indeed to this day many agricultural terms in the language of Israeli Arabs originate from Hebrew or Aramaic, the two languages spoken by the Jews of the Land of Israel in that period. Also, many Hebrew place names can be distinguished, although years of Islamification and Arabization have given them an Arab sonance.

There were also tens of thousands of Jews who remained true to their faith. For them a new door opened, but it led to abandoning the Land of Israel and quitting the soil. Although the relations between Christian Europe and the Islamic world were hostile, both sides were interested in trading the goods which they produced, but the hostility between them, which even led to outright war, prevented direct commercial relations from developing. In such a situation the Jews were able to be the middlemen; they were not particularly well liked by either side, but were hated less than the two hated each other. As merchants the Jews also could use the Hebrew language for inter-bloc communications, a necessary foundation for commerce. Every Jew knew Hebrew, for it was the language of prayer and Torah study. Equally important to commerce was a system of legal protection. In the absence of international law, any mercnant in a foreign land was without legal protection. The Jewish merchant, on the other hand, could hold his fellow Jew in a foreign land accountable under Jewish law. Thus the *halakhah* and Jewish law became a tool of international commerce.

These advantages, plus the elementary education enjoyed by the Jewish peasant in the Land of Israel, provided the foundation for his becoming a merchant. Thus he could keep his religion, escape the oppressive taxes which weighed down the peasants, and enjoy the promise of a livelihood in the burgeoning field of international trade.

In the course of several decades the Land of Israel became depopulated of its Jews, particulary its Jewish farmers. Some adopted Islam and remained on the soil, while others left their villages and headed for Europe. Among the latter, some did not switch to commerce, but continued tilling the soil, now in Spain, which lay on the border of the Moslem empire and Christian Europe. This wave of Jewish emigration, incidentally, contributed greatly to the development of Spanish agriculture, as is evidenced by Spanish traditions to this day. The shift of Jews from the Land of Israel to Spain, in large numbers and high quality of human material, established one of the marvelous Jewish communities in the history of our people: "The Golden Age of the Jews in Spain." This explains the background and the reason for the emergence of the great works of Hebrew poetry and prose, created in Spain but rooted in the Land of Israel. The yearning for the Land of Israel, which speaks through this wealth of literature, bears testimony to the close ties of the Spanish Jewish community, only recently arrived in its land of exile, with its home.

Indeed we became exiled from our land only one thousand two hundred years ago by force of historical developments in the Land of Israel in the seventh and eighth centuries, and not "two thousand years ago."

1

The earliest synagogues, the Jewish community's places of gathering for prayer and reading the Torah, apparently originated in the Babylonian exile following the destruction of the First Temple (586 b.c.e.). The oldest synagogues whose remains have been discovered in the Land of Israel, at Masada, Herodion, and Jerusalem, were in use before the destruction of the Second Temple (70 c.e.). Aside from serving as a place of Torah study and prayer, the synagogue also served as a center of public community life.

The synagogues that came into being in the Land of Israel after the expulsion of the Jews from Spain (1492) were as varied as the background of the communities that began returning to the country at the time. In the four holy cities – Jerusalem, Hebron, Tiberias and Safed – Jews from the Diaspora founded synagogues similar to those they had had in their lands of exile.

1 *Remains of the Bet Ya'akov Synagogue, also called Ḥurbat Rabbi Judah he-Ḥasid, the most magnificent synagogue in the old city of Jerusalem. Built in 1856-1862, it was the center of the Ashkenazi pharisee community in Jerusalem. After the fall of the Jewish Quarter, on May 27, 1948, the synagogue was pillaged and blown up by the Arabs.*

2 *The Western Wall – what remains of the Second Temple, destroyed by the Romans.*

2

safed, city of the kabbalists

Yeshayahu Ashni

There seems to be an unwritten law that one place being destroyed gives rise to another place being built. This was the case with the expulsion of the Jews from Spain in 1492. The inquisitor general Torquemada, a cruel and fanatic monk, confessor to Queen Isabella of Spain, sought to convert the Jews through the use of force and torture. Those who were strong in character and faith remained undaunted in their refusal, preferring to be burned at the stake of the Inquisition; whereas the weaker in character accepted the Christian religion for appearances sake, while clandestinely remaining true to the faith of their forefathers. The elite leadership immigrated to Safed. But why Safed?

Safed had two attractions: one spiritual – the grave of Rabbi Simeon bar Yoḥai on nearby Mt. Meron; the other – the economic prosperity of the city, especially its wool and textile industry, which had won a reputation throughout the world. Safed textiles, a famous export product, reached as far as Venice, Italy, and were eagerly bought up by connoisseurs. During this period the vast majority of Safed's inhabitants were Jews, comprising eighteen thousand of the city's total population of twenty-five thousand.

safed's golden age

The immigration of the Jewish exiles from Spain in the 16th century ushered in the golden age of Safed. The city became the center of the kabbalists and a main focus of Jewish mysticism.

The kabbalah is a philosophical system and a religio-moral ethos, teaching that as morality in the life of the individual, abstinence, purification and spiritual refinement prevail, the coming of the Redeemer is hastened.

Man's behavior in the lower world affects the higher spheres, just as the upper spheres influence the behavior of man below.

According to S. A. Horodezky's book, *Ha-Mistorin be-Yisrael – Ha-Ari ha-Kadosh* ("Jewish Mysticism – The Holy Ari"), **"The teaching of the Ari instructs the Jew to seek the mysteries of everything only through spirituality, for there is an occult, and an occult concealed behind the occult"** *Sefer Limudei Aẓilut* ("Doctrines on Emanation"), 34; **"The principal thing is not the Torah in its simple level, for in this level it belongs only to matter. The principal thing in it is the occult, and then the Torah becomes the Holy of Holies."**

The rabbis of the kabbalah drew their inspiration from the *Zohar* ("Book of Splendor"), attributed to Rabbi Simeon bar Yoḥai, a book which appeared at the close of the 13th century. Although some scholars attribute the *Zohar* to Rabbi Moses de Leon, the people gave the work sanctity by associating its composition with the name of Rabbi Simeon bar Yoḥai.

This was the era of Rabbi Moses Cordovero, erstwhile teacher of Rabbi Isaac Luria Ashkenazi (the Ari) and author of *Pardes Rimmonim,* a book on theoretical kabbalah. Two systems of kabbalah, the theoretical kabbalah of Moses Cordovero and the system of practical kabbalah of Isaac Luria, in the final analysis were united into one system. The rift in the name of religion ended in a single teaching accepted by both men. Cordovero called for tolerance, respect, and consideration of the views of one's fellow man, showing kindness and understanding – something which we would do well to follow today. Cordovero wrote to his friends, in "General Rules of Moral Behavior": **"... to make their hearts always a dwelling place for the Divine Presence; not to be angry at all; not to speak ill of any man; not to curse any man, but to bless him; not to swear, even the truth; not to utter a lie ... to be congenial with one's fellow man ... and to be gentle even to those who violate the Torah..."**

Indeed the patience and tolerance, the restraint and forbearance of a philosopher, and not of a raving extremist, mark the general principles of Cordovero. Soft-spoken admonishment is the root of his strength and power of persuasion.

Legend has it that when Cordovero's disciples saw their teacher was about to die and return his soul to his Maker they stood around his bed and saddened him by wailing, "Whom do you leave for us, Rabbi? Who will instruct us in your teachings, in the Torah of Moses, and who will take your place?" Cordovero replied, "Whoever shall see two pillars of fire, going before my bier on my way to my eternal rest, he shall take my place." Cordovero departed this world, and his disciples carried him to the cemetery in Safed; but not one of them saw a pillar of fire, and they went in the wrong direction. Isaac Luria, who happened to have been away from the city, returned at the last moment, after the funeral procession had started, and hurried to catch up with the mourners. As he approached them, he suddenly cried out: "Where are you going? Turn right, for I see two pillars of fire over there." The mourners halted with Cordovero's coffin and said, "Our rabbi is dead, long live Rabbi Isaac Luria, for you are our rabbi."

This story echoes the lessons from Safed's glorious age, for Cordovero appointed the man who had been his rival to succeed him, showing the nobility of the men of stature of the 16th century.

the ari – rabbi isaac luria ashkenazi

The lion of his society, Rabbi Isaac Luria Ashkenazi, head of the kabbalists, known as "the Ari" ("the sacred lion"; acronym from the Hebrew, *ha-Elohi Rabbi Yiẓḥak* – "the divine Rabbi Isaac"), left his mark on his own generation and generations to follow. Many stories and legends grew up around this personage, whose spirit can be felt living on and guarding the alleys of Lurianic Safed, the very heart of ancient Safed, which stands in ruins to this day, crying for someone to restore and renovate it.

Safed has been known by many names, but only one has lasted, on the merits of a single man: Safed, the city of the Ari. His morality and humility, his wisdom and learnedness, the simplicity of his ways and his abiding aspiration to improve the individual, society and the entire world – all these left their

1 The Synagogue of Rabbi Isaac Aboab, author of Menorat ha-Ma'or. *An elevated almemar stood in the center, under a painted dome from which a chandelier was suspended.*

2 The house of Rabbi Isaac Luria (the Ari) and the ruins of the Beit Midrash *and* mikveh *(ritual bath) adjacent to it in the old Sephardic quarter of Safed.*

3 The Ari Synagogue in the Ashkenazi Quarter of Safed. The Heikhal *– the Torah shrine and its ornamentation – was a present from a Galician Jewish artist.*

1

2

3

safed, city of the kabbalists

mark on his contemporaries in the Land of Israel and the Diaspora; and his ways continue to radiate on hundreds of thousands of people in the Jewish world to this day. Miraculous events were ascribed to him even before his birth. *Sefer ha-Kavvanot u-Ma'aseh Nisim* ("Book of Intentions and Miraculous Deeds") relates the following tale:

"There was once a simple man in the Land of Israel, named Rabbi Solomon Luria. This man was simple and straight, a god-fearing man who shunned evil. One day he remained in the synagogue by himself, studying, when Elijah the Prophet appeared to him and said: I have been sent to you by the Almighty to bring you tidings that your wife shall conceive and bear a child, and you shall call him Isaac; and he shall begin delivering Israel from the *kelippot* ["shells" or "husks" of evil], and through him several incarnated souls shall be perfected, and he shall reveal the hidden mysteries of the Torah and expound the "Book of Splendor," and his name shall spread throughout the world. Therefore take care that you not circumcise him until I come and be the *sandak* [one who sits in the Chair of Elijah and holds the child during the circumcision ceremony] of the child. Upon finishing his words, he disappeared, and the man went home in the night and did not reveal the secret even to his wife. When the son was born the entire house filled with light, and on the eighth day they brought him to the synagogue to circumcise him. His father searched in all corners of the synagogue to see if Elijah had come as he had said, but he did not see him.

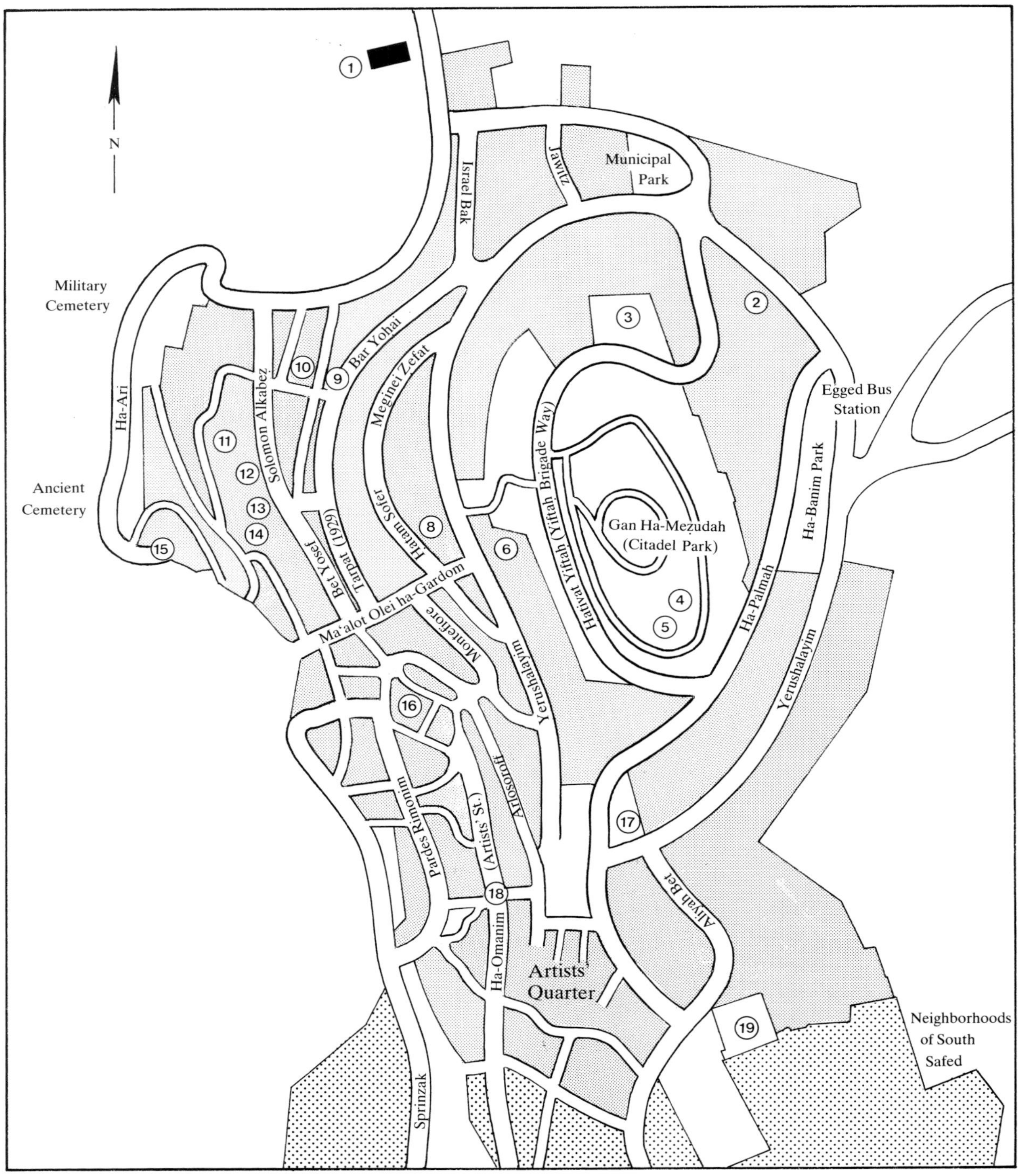

sites of safed

Legend:

1 Safed Yeshiva
2 Municipality
3 Municipal Museum
4 Memorial statue to the fallen soldiers in the War of Independence
5 Citadel – archaeological excavations
6 Government offices (Safed police station, 1948)
8 "Davidka" – One of the mortars used in breaking the Arab siege of the Jewish quarter of Safed, on May 10, 1948.
9 Kikar ha-Meginim (Defenders' Square)
10 Ashkenazi Synagogue of the Ari
11 Yose Benea Synagogue
12 Aboab Synagogue
13 Joseph Caro Synagogue
14 Alshekh Synagogue
15 Sephardic Synagogue of the Ari
16 Artists' House (Mosque)
17 Cave of Shem and Eber
18 Museum of Printing Art
19 Government House (Turkish governor's headquarters)

1 *The Ari Synagogue marks the spot, formerly outside the city, where the Ari customarily greeted the Sabbath. His kabbalist disciples called the spot "Ḥaqal Tapuḥin Kadishin" (lit. "field of holy apples," a mystic concept associated with the festive Sabbath meal).*

1

Everyone was urging him to proceed, but he replied that not all the guests had arrived. Thus half an hour went by, but Elijah did not come. Then he thought bitterly to himself: since Elijah has not come, my sins must have caused his tidings not to be fulfilled; and as he was crying, Elijah appeared to him and said: Do not cry, servant of the Lord. Draw nigh unto the altar and make your offering, which is entirely given to heaven, and sit on my chair and I shall circumcise. Those assembled, however, saw nothing."

Rabbi Isaac Luria was born in Jerusalem in 1534 to a father from Ashkenaz (Franco-Germany) and a mother from Spain. He lost his father at the age of eight. His father, from the family of Rashi, traced his ancestry back to Rabbi Joḥanan the Shoemaker. After his father's death he went to Egypt with his mother, Rebecca, to live with his uncle, R. Mordechai Frances, in Cairo. He studied Torah under Rabbi Bezalel Ashkenazi and Rabbi David Ben Zimra (Radbaz). At the age of fifteen he wed his cousin. From an early age he grew accustomed to seclusion, and would spend hours studying and listening to the song of the universe and the birds, in a hut on the banks of the Nile. The Ari led a life of fasting and abstinence; all week long he spent away from his wife, only coming home on the Sabbath eve and returning to his secluded hut by the close of the Sabbath.

At the age of sixteen he began delving into the mysteries of kabbalism, trying to fathom the depths of the miraculous and the occult in the "Book of Splendor."

"He was privileged every night to have his soul be raised and asked to which celestial court he wished to be elevated – the court of Rabbi Eliezer the Great, or the court of Rabbi Simeon bar Yoḥai. Wherever his soul wished, there it would be brought, and would receive awesome secrets. In the morning he would have forgotten nothing, and would reveal all to his disciples" *Sepher Shivḥei ha-Ari* ("The Tributes of the Ari").

In 1570 Isaac Luria moved to the Land of Israel and, after hearing heavenly "heralds" tell him "Go to Safed," settled in Safed. The Ari lived in Safed less than two years, keeping in the background, at first studying in the Beit Midrash of Rabbi Moses Cordovero, author of the kabbalistic work, *Pardes Rimmonim.* His fountainhead of wisdom soon came to the fore. The disciple became a fellow teacher, and upon Cordovero's death became the head rabbi. The Ari won the hearts of all and became leader of the kabbalists, unparalleled since the days of Rabbi Simeon bar Yoḥai. His figure became enveloped in countless legends and stories.

The Ari instructed the people:

"Minimize all that you consume in the pleasures of this world, taking only that which is essential for the survival of the body." "For man to keep the holy precepts alone does not suffice; he must also be a person of good attributes. The two together, commandments and attributes, can bring man to perfection" (*Sha'arei Kedushah,* Part 1, Ch. 3: The Fruit of the Tree of Life).

"The principal categories of evil attributes which man should shun are: pride, anger, idle talk, lust for pleasure, and melancholy; their opposites are the principal categories of good attributes. Humility man must acquire to such an extent that he neither feel joy from honor, nor disgrace from reproof, and that both be equal in his eyes." "Man should love his fellow, and receive every man with joy, even if he be his adversary, and not cause sorrow to any creature in the world," for **"no creature was created for nought, and man must not kill any creature**

needlessly. Even lice should not be killed, nor should they so much as arouse disgust." "Man should be chary of his words – one of the conditions for attaining wisdom – and should speak softly, in a low voice."

"Melancholy is a bad attribute. It prevents man from working and observing the commandments, deflects one from studying the Torah and praying with devotion, and abrogates good thoughts" (S. A. Horodezky, *Ha-Mistorin be-Yisrael – ha-Ari ha-Kadosh*).

To this day people still recount his miraculous deeds and praise his greatness and insight. According to Rabbi Meshullam Zusha Luria, a descendant of the Ari, in the time of the Ari the Jews of Safed used to pull their caps down to their noses in order to cover their foreheads, since, by looking at a man's forehead, the Ari could decipher the origins of a man's soul, the secrets of his incarnations, and the way to perfect his soul. "To be safe they would cover their foreheads, for everyone feared lest the Ari read on his forehead his innermost thoughts" – and everyone had something to hide.

1

The Ari's twelve disciples, who venerated him greatly, used to travel over the Galilee and wander in the gardens of Safed. On these trips, called in kabbalistic language "divorces" (since they divorced themselves from everything physical, and dealt exclusively with the spiritual), they would receive his teaching. The Ari used to reveal the holy tombs of *tannaim* and *amoraim,* ancient military commanders and mystics.

Rabbi Isaac Luria himself did not write any books, essays, or commentaries. His disciples wrote from what he taught them. When he was living in a small crypt in Safed, above which the synagogue named after the Ari was later built in the ancient Sephardic quarter, the Ari was entreated by his disciples: **"Rabbi, why does not His Excellency write but one fine essay, so that his teaching not be forgotten in Israel?"** He replied as follows: **"If all the seas were ink, and all the heavens scrolls of parchment, and all the nests in the world quills, they would not suffice to write down all my wisdom"** *Shivḥei ha-Ari* ("The Tributes of the Ari").

The Ari lived in Safed less than two years. Yet by his brilliant spiritual leadership he wrought a revolution in the way of

2

3

1 *The secret of Safed's blue: "Safed is the gate to heaven." Simtat Beit ha-Din ("Rabbinical Court Alley") of Rabbi Joseph Caro, author of the* Shulḥan Arukh.

2 *The Ari Synagogue in the Sephardic Quarter. The Torah shrines or the* Heikhal, *whose doors were carved in Damascus, house ancient Torah scrolls.*

3 *A 16th century fulling mill in Naḥal 'Ammud, below Safed. The mill, operated by water power, was used to beat raw wool with wooden hammers.*

thinking and the economic, social and ethical life of the inhabitants of Safed.

rabbi joseph caro – author of the shulḥan arukh

Safed was the home of the eminent Rabbi Joseph Caro, author of the *Shulḥan Arukh,* which was written in Safed and Biriyya and became the standard code of Jewish law and practice. Rabbi Joseph Caro spent twenty years writing his opus, and another twelve redacting it and adding marginal notes. The *Shulḥan Arukh* first appeared in Venice (1565-1566). Esteemed by his disciples, Joseph Caro was given the honorific title of *Maran* (meaning ordained by two hundred rabbis) and was addressed as "The Holy King" and "The Prince of God." Nevertheless he remained modest and humble, in life as in death. On his tombstone in the cemetery of Safed we can read the simple modest epitaph: "Here lies R. J. Caro, author of the *Shulḥan Arukh."* Stories about his personality and his way of life are heard in the streets of Safed to this day.

an attempt to renew the sanhedrin

In the 16th century Rabbi Jacob Berab settled in Safed and served as the rabbi of the city for 24 years. Believing the messianic age to be at hand, he sought to reinstate rabbinic ordination and set up the Sanhedrin (the supreme Jewish council of mishnaic and talmudic times) anew in order to restore legal power to Jewish institutions and thus establish the beginnings of Jewish sovereignty. He was strenuously opposed by Rabbi Levi ben Ḥabib in Jerusalem, who objected to having the center of ordination in Safed and not Jerusalem. A sharp controversy erupted, defamatory stories reached the authorities, and Rabbi Jacob Berab had to leave Safed. Thus the historic attempt to establish a political-administrative apparatus which might have united the nation under the authority of a new Sanhedrin came to nought.

1

The famous liturgical poet Rabbi Solomon Alkabeẓ, author of the Sabbath hymn "*Lekha Dodi,*" which was considered the Jewish anthem until Imber wrote "*Ha-Tikvah,*" also lived in Safed during this period. A wealthy Arab efendi is said to have become enraptured by the beauty and wisdom of Rabbi Solomon Alkabeẓ, to have murdered him, and buried the body in his garden as a charm to bring him blessings and good crops. The burial place of Rabbi Solomon Alkabeẓ is unkown to this day. A monument in his memory has been erected in the ancient cemetery of Safed, a distance from the tomb of the Ari and beside the grave of the Ari's son, Moses.

yom zeh l'yisrael

A Sabbath table hymn by the Ari, with his name worked into the verses as an acrostic. Early prayer books have the five stanzas freely translated here, more recent prayer books have more stanzas, apparently added by a later author.

This day is for Israel light and rejoicing, a Sabbath of rest.
Thou badest us standing assembled at Sinai That all the years through we should keep thy behest – To set out a table full-laden, to honor
The Sabbath of rest.
This day is for Israel light and rejoicing, a Sabbath of rest.

Treasure of heart for the broken people, Gift of new soul for the souls distrest, Soother of sighs for the prisoned spirit –
A Sabbath of rest.
This day is for Israel light and rejoicing, a Sabbath of rest.

When the work of the worlds in their wonder was finished, Thou madest this day to be holy and blest, And those heavy-laden found safety and stillness,
A Sabbath of rest.
This day is for Israel light and rejoicing, a Sabbath of rest.

From the Authorized Daily Prayer Book by Dr. Joseph H. Hertz

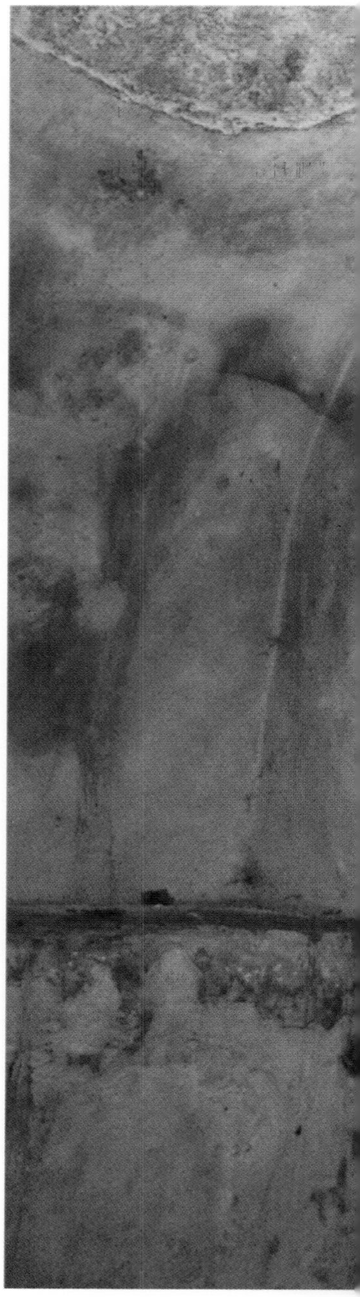

Another resident of Safed from that era was Rabbi Israel Najara, a spicy, unconventional poet, author of *Zemirot Yisrael* ("Hymns of Israel"). *Yah Ribbon Olam ve-Almayya,* one of his compositions, is sung at the table on the Sabbath eve. Many other rabbis lived and wrote in Safed in those days.

safed – a legend in blue

Blue has been a color of Safed for four hundred years. Almost every ancient ruin has a touch of blue somewhere. I asked the last kabbalist, Rabbi Asher Saltz, why blue, of all colors?

The elderly man answered with a thin smile on his lips: "How is it you do not know? It is completely self-evident: Safed is the gate to heaven, the bridge to heaven; the reception-room of the Holy One, Blessed be He, is blue, and the seven heavens are

1 "Me'onot ha-Arayot" – *the graves of the great Kabbalists, the mystic philosophers of the Lurianic age.*

2 *The crypt where the Ari used to seek seclusion. The Sephardic Synagogue of the Ari was built over it in later years.*

2

blue; therefore the gate and the bridge which lead to the vestibule and the reception-room of the Almighty must also be blue."

There are many other explanations. Dr. Leon Galatner, former director of Asaf Ha-Rofeh Hospital, who studied with me in *Ḥeder* (Jewish school) in Botschatz, explained that the color blue has special medicinal and hygienic properties: flies cannot tolerate blue, and hence the color keeps them away.

To this day the elderly women in the ancient Sephardic quarter of Safed paint the walls of their houses blue. For Sabbath and Festival eves they also paint the cracks between the tiles in the yard blue, as if they were spreading out a blue carpet to welcome the Sabbath Queen. They even used to come to where the Ari once lived, paint the ruins of his house blue on the inside and light oil lamps in his memory. In the early years of the state they painstakingly maintained this pleasing practice in the house of the Ari, which was ruined several years ago in the course of construction work on a Ḥassidic neighborhood. Also painted blue are *Me'onot ha-Arayot* ("The Lions' Dens") – the tombs of the great leaders of Safed from the 16th century: the Ari, Rabbi Joseph Caro, Rabbi Moses Cordovero and others.

The blue of Safed is also associated with a romantic historical story. Diego Pires, also called Solomon Molcho, the right-hand man of David ha-Reuveni, who wanted to re-establish the kingship in Israel, came to Safed and fell in love with Rabbi Jacob Berab's beautiful daughter. The Portuguese aristocrat became engaged to the good-looking Safed damsel. Having had to leave Safed on political business, he wrote her love letters. In his first letter he wrote: "Three things captured my heart in Safed: the blue sky, the blue walls, and your blue eyes."

Safed is indeed a fantasy in blue of legends interlaced with an endless shimmering golden landscape.

hebron – jewish life of yesteryear

Irit Zaharoni

Hebron, before the outbreak of the Arab riots, had the smallest Jewish community of the cities sacred to the Jews (Jerusalem, Safed, Tiberias and Hebron). Nearly 600 Jews, Sephardic and Ashkenazi, resided in Hebron. The Sephardic Jews were craftsmen and merchants, while the Ashkenazi Jews were for the most part supported by *Ḥalukkah* funds (contributions from Diaspora Jewry to those resettling the Land of Israel).

"Most of the Sephardic Jews live in one large court, with several lanes and alleys, called Ḥart al-Yahud (Arabic: "Court of the Jews"; known in Spaniolish as "El Cortijo"); the Ashkenazi Jews live in individual houses on the neighboring streets" *(Moreh Derekh be-Ereẓ Yisrael* [Guide to the Land of Israel], A. M. Luncz, 1891).

The Hebron ghetto was surrounded by a Moslem settlement in which the houses were built so close to one another that it was easy to jump from roof to roof and reach the street of the Jews, a situation which bred numerous troubles. The ghetto had three gates. The Market Gate had a hole large enough to put a fist through and deep recesses in the doorposts. The hole was apparently intended for peeking through in time of emergency, to watch what was happening beyond the gate, and the recesses for bolting the door.

Legend has it that "the door of the gate to the court has a hole below, and today it is said to commemorate a miracle. Once a certain ruler decreed that the Jews must pay a vast sum in specific coins which he knew they could never obtain. But our brethren, the Jews, prayed to the Lord and He was merciful unto them. And lo, when morning came the rabbi found a hole in the door, with the entire sum of money, in the requisite coins, stashed in it. When they gave it to the official, he was greatly astonished, and they told him the entire story" (*Ḥibbat Yerushalayim* ["Love of Jerusalem"], A. M. Luncz).

The two other gates were the New Gate, which led through dim vaulted passageways to the institutions of the community, and the Bathhouse Gate, through which the joyous processions of brides would pass as they came out of the bathhouse.

a miracle on the holy day

In the center of the ghetto was a plaza used by the community for meetings on joyous or sad occasions. Here the procession accompanying the bride and her bridesmaids would halt and all would sing and dance around her. Here the dead were eulogized; here the Arab water-bearers who served the residents of the ghetto would rest, and here the descendants of Ishmael would hold their market on the eve of Sabbaths and Festivals.

The Jewish community in the city of the Patriarchs was served by many and important institutions. There were nine synagogues and houses of worship, two religious schools for children, and three yeshivas: the Yeshiva of Eliyyah Mani, the Yeshiva of the Gaon "Sedei Ḥemed," and the Hebron Yeshiva. Each yeshiva had a rich library of old books. There were religious courts, a clinic and a hospital, a ritual bath, two guest houses, two bakeries, inns and other public institutions.

Within the ghetto were four synagogues, two ancient and two recent. The Great Synagogue of the Patriarch Abraham stood in the center of Jews' Street. The earlier dating ascribes it to the time of the *geonim;* the later dating to the era of immigration of the Spanish exiles. This synagogue, which served the Sephardic community, is supported on four mighty pillars, above them a dome surrounded by twelve windows. The synagogue, having been destroyed by the Arabs, has recently been reconstructed. Near it is a small, dimly lit synagogue, called "The Small Synagogue," where the first Ashkenazi Jews of the city prayed.

Legend tells of a miracle which occurred in Hebron on the Day of Atonement. "Once, on the eve of the Day of Atonement, there were only nine men in Hebron, and they waited for the villagers to arrive [to constitute a *minyan,* a quorum of ten necessary for public worship]. But no one came, for they had all gone to Jerusalem, to the Holy City. The nine men were deeply grieved at having to pray privately and cried long. As the sun was beginning to set and the day draw to a close, they lifted up their eyes, and behold, an old man was approaching. Extremely happy to see him, they set before him a meal before the fast. He greeted them with blessings and said he had already eaten along the way. Thus they prayed with a *minyan* on the Holy Day and rendered great honor to the man. On the eve after the Day of Atonement they began debating who should have the

1 *The Cave of Machpelah. The monument Herod built to mark the site of the cave stands out in its vast proportions and typical Herodian construction, resembling a scaled down model of the Temple Mount. The Crusader church which was erected in its center was later converted into a mosque.*

2 *"And Abram moved his tent, and came and dwelt by the terebinths of Mamre, which are in Hebron" (Genesis 13:18).*

honor of welcoming the guest in his home. They resolved to settle the question by casting lots, and the lot fell on the cantor, a holy man who saw dreams and visions. The cantor went to his home, followed by the guest. As he approached his home, the cantor turned around to give his guest the honor of entering first; but lo, the guest was gone. They looked for him, but he was nowhere to be found in all the court. Everyone was greatly dismayed, for they thought he had gone on his way the same night, eschewing their hospitality. That very night the old man appeared to the cantor in a dream and said that he was the Patriarch Abraham, who had come to complete the *minyan,* because he had seen them so distressed at having to pray privately. They rejoiced greatly and blessed the Lord" (*Sefer Emek ha-Melekh* ["Valley of the King"], R. Naphtali b. R. Jacob Katz).

Medical services were rendered free of charge to the Jews of Hebron, both Sephardic and Ashkenazi, and both communities shouldered the financial burden. The doctors, pharmacists, and medicines were paid for by the *kolelim* (groups of Ashkenazi Jews who settled in the holy cities and devoted their lives to studying the Torah) by agreement between the communities. Among the Jewish doctors who faithfully served the Jewish community and even the Arabs, who used the clinic opened by Hadassah, were Dr. Ḥassin and Dr. Mani, Hebron-born Jews who received their medical training abroad and returned to practice in their community. Also serving the community was

1

1 *A decorative structure marks the opening in the floor of the mosque which leads into the depths of the Cave of Machpelah, beneath the mosque.*

2 *The Guest House of the Ḥabad, near the entrance to the Casbah.*

3 *A depression for a* mezuzah *on the right-hand doorpost is the identifying mark of a Jewish home. Jewish homes in the Casbah (old city) of Hebron can be identified by this sign to this day.*

the pharmacist Ben-zion Gershon, who, with his wife, was murdered in the 1929 riots. Ironically, he was killed by those very descendants of Ishmael to whom he had dispensed medicines, free of charge, and many of whose lives he had saved.

sephardic and ashkenazi jews

"The residents were known for their hospitality to strangers, and aside from the special house for guests, each family welcomed guests in its home, honoring them with a festive meal which they called the 'Feast of the Patriarch Abraham,'" we read in Luncz's *Moreh Derekh be-Ereẓ Yisrael.*

At the turn of the 20th century tourism to Hebron was organized by the long-established travel company, Cooke's Tours, which brought wealthy tourists to Hebron in coaches, while simpler folk came from Jerusalem to Hebron on foot or on donkeys or asses.

Since such pilgrims could not afford a room in a hotel they were lodged in the Guest House of the *kolel* in the Jews' Court. This was a public building with several spacious rooms with mats spread over the floors. The guests would lay down mattresses and sleep, about twenty people to a room, men in one room and women in another. A large room served as a dining hall where the guests received hot meals prepared by the Sephardic Kolel, at its expense. Any guest was entitled to this hospitality for three days, free of charge.

Honored guests were lodged in the home of the "Ḥakham Bashi," and wealthy visitors stayed in the Jewish hotels.

"The Sephardic and Ashkenazi Jews were on good terms with each other and maintained close ties. They visited in each other's homes and socialized together, but did not inter-marry. For the Sephardic Jews said: the Ashkenazi women do not speak Spaniolish, do not know how to cook eastern delicacies, and are not thrifty; and the Ashkenazi Jews said: we are willing to take your daughters for our sons because they are excellent housewives, know how to be thrifty, and are remarkably obedient; but not the young men – for they do not make the Torah their livelihood, are not punctilious about performing the commandments, and they institute excessive regimen in the home. And thus they remained always" (*Sefer Ḥevron* – "Book of Hebron").

in the shadow of religious fanaticism

The Arabs of Hebron, zealous Moslems, tolerated the presence of a small handful of Jews, but the Jews had to be extremely careful of the religious sensibilities of their fanatic neighbors. The latter forbade them to enter the Cave of the Machpelah, burial place of Jewish patriarchs and matriarchs.

The leader of the Hebron Jewish community, A. D. Slonim, born in Hebron, branch manager of the Anglo-Palestine Bank (now Bank Leumi), and a member of the City Council, maintained ties of commerce and friendship with many Arabs and was well liked and accepted by them.

In early 1929, the pro-Arab officials of the British Mandate, under the leadership of Chief Secretary and acting High

2

3

Commissioner Luke (his father converted from Judaism, and he himself changed his surname and kept his Jewish origins a closely guarded secret), banded together with the Supreme Muslim Council, led by Mufti Haj Amin al-Husseini. It was not long before this alliance spoiled the atmosphere of relative political calm which had reigned in the country for close to seven years, and brought on the 1929 riots.

The Mufti used religion to stir up the Arab masses. They had a time-honored heritage of religious zeal, and when the pronouncement that "the religion of Mohammed came with the sword" was combined with nationalism and with lust for pillage and murder, vast numbers of people could be roused to any crime.

A pretext for religious propaganda was soon found. On the eve of the Day of Atonement (September 23, 1928) hundreds of Jews gathered to pray at the Western Wall. The beadle set up a partition in the middle to separate the men from the women. The Deputy District Commissioner of Jerusalem, Keith-Roach, passing the plaza at the Western Wall with Police Inspector Douglas Duff on their patrol of the area, saw the partition and was appalled. He viewed this as a violation of the status quo which had been established regarding Jews praying at the Western Wall. He immediately asked the sheikhs guarding the Waqf whether they had seen what the Jews had done. "Those sly elders," said Duff, "immediately put on a show of offended righteousness and began interpreting the affair as a bald attempt to turn this spot holy to the Moslems into a Jewish house of worship." Keith-Roach ordered Duff to remove the partition.

On the morrow a delegation of worshippers came to Keith-Roach and petitioned him to postpone carrying out his decree until the end of the Day of Atonement. The Deputy District Comissioner immediately sent Duff to take down the partition by force. This desecratory act, crudely performed on the Day of Atonement, next to the Western Wall, aroused anger throughout the Jewish community of the Land of Israel and the Diaspora. The institutions of the *yishuv* (the Jewish settlement in pre-State Israel) lodged a complaint about the incident before the British Government and the Mandate Committee. On the opposing side, the Arab press, and the agitators who worked hand and glove with it, rushed to raise a hew and cry that the Jews were plotting to desecrate sites holy to Islam. The Mufti himself moved from his apartment on the Mt. of Olives Road to the building of the Moslem Council, next to the Wailing Wall, in order to instigate trouble from there. "Every few weeks a new pinprick was given in order to undermine relations between Jews and Arabs" (Kisch). The agitators suddenly learned that the Western Wall, whose sanctity had been desecrated more than once by troublemaking Arab youngsters throwing stones and animal dung, was a site sacred to the Moslems. Studying the matter, they discovered that el-Burak, the prophet Mohammad's winged steed, had been stabled close to the Western Wall when the prophet ascended to Heaven. This vapid story, which at first was derided by many Moslems themselves, became the point of departure for a libel accusing the Jews of plotting to conquer the sacred mosques on the Temple Mount. The Arab press published inciting articles that called for a holy war against the Jews. The government paid no heed to any of the Arab provocations, leaving their leaders feeling free to do as they pleased.

The Arabs of Hebron, known opponents of the Mufti, became engaged in a bitter quarrel with the Mufti over funds of the local Waqf. The Mufti did not succeed in embroiling them in

1

his murder schemes so quickly, yet nothing could win over the hearts of the Hebron Arabs as easily as religious incitement. Religious fanatics, with Sheikh Taleb Morke, head of the Moslem-Christian Association in the city, at their lead, joined the Mufti in the incitement against Jews and Zionism.

Nevertheless the Jews of Hebron trusted in their fellow townsmen. Thus on August 20, 1929, when Sa'adia Kirshenbaum and A. H. Cohen, two emissaries from the *Haganah,* arrived from Jerusalem with an offer to Slonim either to send him a unit of defenders (ten men with arms) to protect the Jews in the event of an attack or to bring all the Jews of Hebron to Jerusalem until the crisis passed, Slonim responded, after conferring with several of the city's dignitaries, both Jews and Arabs, that the Jews of Hebron did not fear for their safety insofar as they trusted the Arabs' good relations towards them and relied on their ties with the Arab dignitaries. He requested that no defenders be sent to the city, feeling that if such an action became known it would rouse the Arabs' wrath.

On Friday morning an Arab apprentice, reared in the home of Jewish carpenters, reported as follows: "Despite the fact that by revealing this secret to you I am placing my life in jeopardy, because I love you I wish to tell you that the Arabs are preparing to attack you and that a letter has come from the Mufti calling upon the Arabs to come to Jerusalem and beat the Jews, and that the mobs in Hebron are preparing a pogrom against the Yeshiva" (from the testimony of Rabbi Slonim).

The city's two rabbis, Ashkenazi and Sephardic, turned to the city's governor, Abdallah Kardus, who assured them that their fears were unfounded, that the government had sufficient military force at its disposal to handle the situation, and that many plain-clothes policemen were on guard. At two-thirty in the afternoon some cars arrived from Jerusalem, and Arabs climbed on the roof of one of the cars and broadcast that the Jews were allegedly massacring Arabs in Jerusalem. Sheikh Taleb Morke stood among the mob and delivered a rabble-rousing address, shouting: "Allah and Mohammad call on you to kill the Jews." The mob shattered the windows of the Jews' houses and burst into the building of the yeshiva, which, being Friday afternoon, was empty. Only one young man, a diligent scholar, was there, studying Torah. He was slain and his body was left lying in the empty yeshiva until Sunday.

The Jews of Hebron, seized by fear of the mob, shut themselves up in their houses at orders from Police Commander Cafferata.

heroism in the wake of despair

In the evening the *mukhtars* of the village of Dura came to the commander of the police force and told him that a messenger had come and called them to go to Jerusalem and fight the Jews, otherwise they would be fined by the Mufti. Cafferata ordered them back to their village and at dawn phoned Jerusalem, Jaffa, and Gaza to request reinforcements. He was the only British government official in the city and had a police force comprised entirely of Arabs, save for one Jew.

Early on Saturday morning, August 24, 1929, Slonim and several of his colleagues set out to see the commander. On their way they met one of the Hebron dignitaries, who offered them a typical Arab "compromise": turn over the "aliens," i.e. anyone not born in Hebron, to the Arabs. Slonim rejected this "noble" offer with equanimity and continued on his way to the police. Cafferata received the delegation with insults and abuse and ordered them to go back and lock themselves in their homes, for only in such a way could he guarantee their safety.

At about nine a.m. the Arabs of Hebron and the neighboring villages ganged up in the streets and called for a massacre of the Jews. Sheikh Taleb Morke and other notables took the lead, proclaiming in the name of the Mufti "that the day had come to kill and annihilate all the Jews, from young to old, and that the religious leaders had said they could take the Jews' women and property." The rioters went from house to house unhindered, indiscriminately killing and slaughtering young and old, men and women. Cafferata attempted to control the mob, shot into the crowds, and even killed two of the rioters, but the mob pelted him with stones until he fell from his horse. Then he brought armed police opposite the building of Hadassah and ordered them to shoot the rioters, but the police, Arabs, shot into the air and refrained from hurting their brethren. The rioters set fire to the synagogue, Hadassah hospital, and other buildings. Then from the quarter in the new city they turned toward the old ghetto, easily overcame the small police force standing guard at its entrance, and continued their massacre. Cafferata himself and the Jewish policeman, Ḥanokh Brozhinsky, killed about eight of the rioters.

The Jews of Hebron also displayed the heroism which comes in the wake of despair. "I saw a youngster on a roof top," one of the survivors of the Hebron massacre reported, "heroically fighting off eight Arabs. Even as he was about to fall, from time to time he would strike out with his hand in which he held an iron rod, until the eight overcame him and all started knifing him at once, and he fell dead. Moses Keizlstein grabbed hold of a meat

1 *A rabbi being beaten by Arab rioters – by Ze'ev Tishbi (1916-1958), painted after the 1929 riots in Hebron (Gabriel Davrah collection).*

2 *A boy who was bereft of his entire family and himself was wounded in the Arab riots. "... I saw Eliezer Dan, his wife Hannah, and their son Aaron lying in a pool of blood. His father-in-law Rabbi Orlinsky and his wife also lay dead... and many more were killed or wounded. Almost all had bullets shot through their heads and their stomachs ripped open... Among the victims I recognized my brother, wounded in the head by an ax and a knife..." Testimony of one of the survivors of the Hebron riots which, nine days after the Ninth of Av (date of the destruction of the Temple), 1929, turned the City of the Patriarchs into the City of Slaughter.*

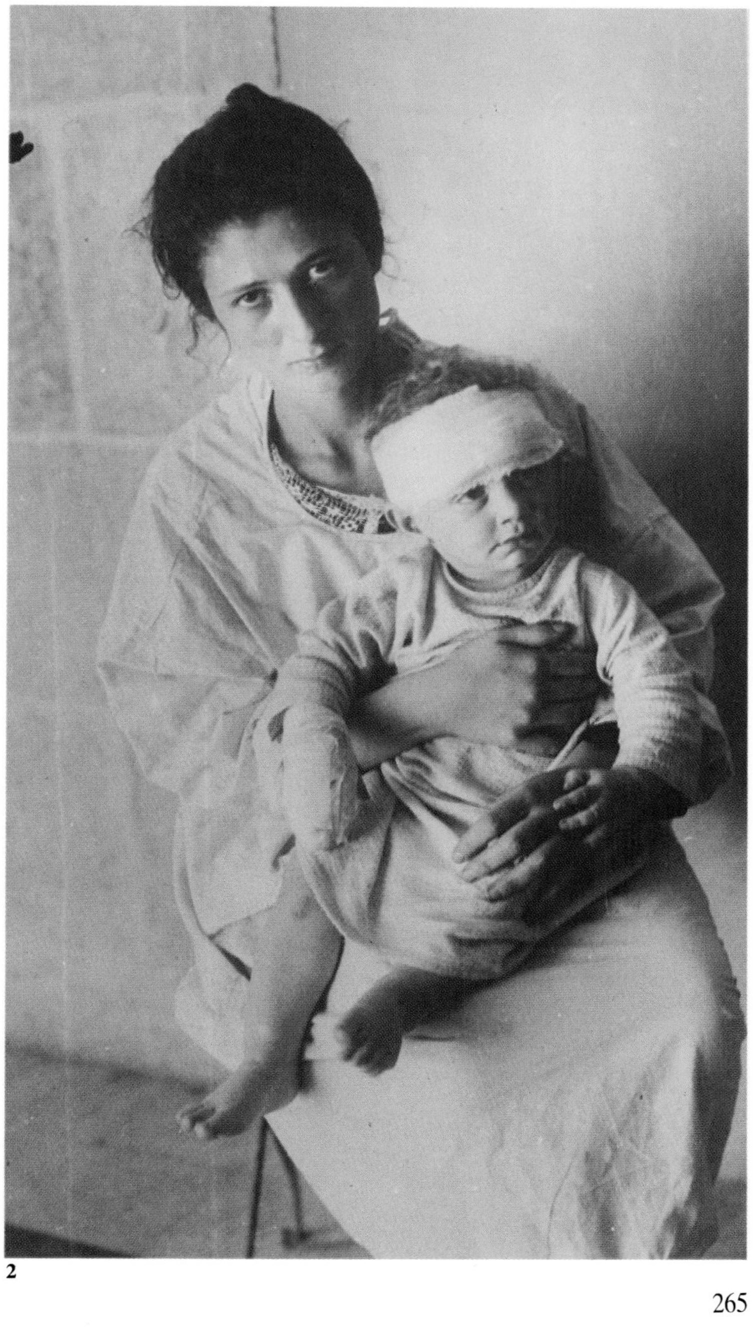

2

1

1 *The lintel over the door of David Rozman's and Shelomo Slonim's house, in an alley of the Casbah, outside the Jewish quarter, was taken from an ancient synagogue. Three* menorahs *are carved on the lintel, the middle one upside down to commemorate the destruction of the Temple.*

2 *A view of Hebron, a city of great importance in the early history of the Jewish people and the Land of Israel. According to Scripture, Abraham pitched his tent here (Genesis 13:18) and purchased the field of Machpelah, acquiring the property for our ancestors in the Land of Israel (Genesis, Ch. 23); he received annunciation of Isaac's birth here (Genesis, Ch. 15); and his son Isaac lived and died here (Genesis 35:27). The three patriarchs and three of the matriarchs were buried here, in the cave of Machpelah (Genesis 49:31 and 50:13). King David reigned here for seven years (II Samuel 2:11) and later was anointed king of all Israel here in Hebron...*

grinder and used it to defend himself. He was seriously wounded and, having passed out, was taken for dead and left alone. Ze'ev Greenberg, a 17 year old from the yeshiva, who was defending himself with a stick, was taken out to the street and killed. Eliyahu Abu-Shedid defended himself with all his might and chopped off the fingers of one of the rioters. His two sons did likewise. He called out to the Arabs that if any Jews should survive they would know from whom to avenge his blood. Abraham Dov Shapira, from the yeshiva, faced the wild murderers, fighting them heroically, knife in hand, until he perished."

When the murderers reached Slonim's house, where some 70 people had taken refuge, several yeshiva students stood guard at the entrance to the house and protected the door until the rioters broke in through the roof and killed the defenders on the threshhold. Only at the last moment did Slonim shoot his gun at the killers, who jumped on him gleefully and condemned him to death, along with whomever else fell into their hands there.

People hid in every corner, behind wardrobes, in bathrooms and lavatories, "twenty people in a single hole, and thirty in one corner." Many were saved by the grace of their Arab friends.

About twenty people hid in the house of Rabbi Slonim, who lived across from his son. The Arab landlord and his son stood in the doorway and defended the Jews for six hours, until the British police finally arrived on the scene. The Arab, Abu 'Iyd Zeitun, with his brothers and son, gathered many Jews in the basement of his house and protected them there, until the police came to conduct them to the police station.

Were it not for several Arab families who protected the Jews, said a memorandum from the Jews of Hebron to the High Commissioner, not a Jew would have survived in Hebron.

The mobs did not begin to disperse until 10:30. The Jews were all gathered in the police station. Some 500 people sat on the blood-stained floor of the barracks, including widows and orphans who, at one stroke, had lost all that was near and dear to them. Fifty-nine dead were collected (another seven died of their wounds after being transferred to Jerusalem). Arab prisoners from among the rioters were taken to dig five mass graves in the Jewish cemetery. Only five people were allowed to take part in the funeral and they were accompanied by a British police guard. When the Jews appeared with the bodies of their martyrs, the Arab grave-diggers burst into song. One yeshiva student approached the English and demanded that they silence the villains. Their request was granted.

The women and children were moved to Jerusalem on Monday, and on Tuesday cars came for the rest.

"Two files of policemen closely lined the path from the door of the police station to the road. One by one the Jews came out, exhausted and depressed, and, filing between the rows of police, entered the cars. Arabs crowded the surrounding rooftops and barricades by the hundreds, looking on with curiosity as the last Jews left the city of slaughter."

The cars set off, and Hebron became "Judenrein"...

Had Jewish settlements been established around Hebron in time, perhaps the fate of the city would have been like that of Safed, which in the fullness of time, after all that transpired, remained within the State of Israel. However the attempts made in this regard, such as settling discharged soldiers in Tel Arad, failed, leaving the Jewish town of Hebron isolated.

The Hebron massacre in 1929 put an end to a long period of peaceful coexistence between Jews and Arabs and extinguished a vibrant Jewish community. A subsequent attempt to reestablish the Jewish community was quashed by the 1936 Arab riots. Jewish settlement was not renewed in Hebron until 1968.

Information for this article was gleaned from a number of books, especially Oded Avisar (ed.), *Sefer Ḥevron* (Jerusalem: Keter Publishers, 1970).

2

The New Gate

Jeremiah 26:10

The Land of Israel Reborn

a dream come true in "mikveh"

Zvi Ilan

Mikveh Israel, in existence for 110 years, is an important landmark in the history of the *yishuv* (pre-State Jewish community). Ben-Gurion said: "The State was made possible due to the founding of Mikveh Israel. Were it not for Mikveh Israel the State of Israel might not have been born. Everything dates back to then, and we today have only brought things to their national-political completion."

"Mikveh" is also special in that it has remained a nature reserve adjacent to a bustling town. One of the oldest institutions in the country, its buildings and grounds provide excellent places for hiking, immediately enveloping you in its charm and making you forget you are so close to a city and just off a busy highway.

The most comprehensive of all the books written about Mikveh is Joseph Shapira's *100 Shanah le-Mikveh Yisrael* (100 Years of Mikveh Israel), but we will give a brief account of the founding of the school, then skip over its hundred and ten years of existence, and learn how this venerable institution functions now.

The founding of Mikveh Israel is bound up with the situation of the *yishuv* in the Land of Israel in the second half of the previous century and with the operations of the Paris-based, Jewish philanthropic and educational organization, the *Alliance Israélite Universelle.*

In 1868 the *Alliance* sent its secretary, Charles Ya'akov Netter, on a tour of the Near East to survey the condition of the Jews there and report back with proposals for ways to help them. Among the places he visited was the Land of Israel, then with only thirteen thousand Jewish inhabitants, ninety percent of them living in Jerusalem, Hebron, Safed, and Tiberias, the four holy cities. Small communities existed in Jaffa, Sidon, Haifa, Acre, and Shechem. Of the 2500 males in this population only a sixth engaged in some sort of productive labor or in commerce. Many others studied Torah and lived off contributions from abroad, the *ḥalukkah* ("distribution" or "dole") funds sent to the Land of Israel by the Jews of Eastern Europe. Only an isolated few engaged in agriculture – one Jew who owned land in Moẓa, outside of Jerusalem, and the Zeynati family in Peqi'in in the Galilee.

hard-earned bread replaces hand-outs

In Jerusalem construction of a school to promote education and crafts was under way, funded by philanthropists from the Diaspora. Netter's visit to the country was actually due to this school. After Sir Moses Montefiore's second visit to the Land of Israel in 1839, more and more people in the holy cities began speaking of breaking out of the vicious circle of *ḥalukkah* funds and launching a productive life in agriculture, albeit for some this only meant leasing land to others. Towards the end of 1867, 37 people, most of them young men from Jerusalem, some Jews who had come from Georgia (Russia), sent a letter to Joseph Krieger, the representative of the *Alliance* in Jerusalem, asking him: **"Provide us land, give us tools, and send us people who will teach us to till the soil."** This letter, forwarded to Netter who was then in Egypt, led him to extend his visit in the Near East and examine the condition of the Jews here.

During Netter's stay in Jerusalem a great number of people flocked to his door, clamoring for work. Lacking a state and institutions for dealing with employment, people were forced to rely completely on help from abroad. To explain the purpose of his mission to the Jews of Jerusalem, Netter called a meeting in the courtyard of the *Battei Maḥasseh* (a neighborhood in the Jewish Quarter of the Old City), where he received an enthusiastic response to his question whether they were prepared to give up living off the dole from abroad, and live instead by the sweat of their brow.

Netter relied on the experience of travelers and researchers, who had concluded that only tilling the soil could save the Jews and that an effort must be made to introduce farming into their lives. He proposed that the *Alliance Israélite Universelle* establish an institution to train the young generation to work the soil, and believed that in this way the entire situation would gradually change for the better.

On January 11, 1869, the *Alliance Israélite Universelle* decided to establish the school. President of the organization,

1 *"Provide us land, give us tools, and send us people who will teach us to till the soil" (1867). The objective of Mikveh Israel was to train the younger generation to till the soil and to raise a new generation of Jewish farmers. Mikveh Israel of today is a green island in the sea of concrete of the Tel Aviv metropolitan area.*

Adolphe Crémieux (after whom a *kibbutz* on the southern coastal plain is named), delivered a speech supporting the idea of establishing an agricultural school; by-laws for the school were drafted: ten students would be accepted annually; the course of studies would last three years; students would live in a dormitory, and all would be fully supported by the management. Additional students spending time in the school would be supported by various communities.

Beginning with the second year, it was decided, a sufficiently large plot of land to support ten families would be purchased every year. This land was to be sold to Jews who took in graduates of the school to work on their farm. Should there be no Jews wishing to purchase the land, the management would work the land with the help of the students, who would receive a fraction of the revenue. The management would give preference to Jewish labor and would try to find work for the unemployed.

The by-laws show how the *Alliance* hoped to gradually increase the number of farmers, building around the nucleus of the school and its graduates, and to supply work for new immigrants. There were at the time many plans drafted to provide members of the *yishuv* employment, but they all came to nothing. Netter illustrates the force of the individual personality in shaping history. Far from resting on his laurels once his plan was adopted, Netter proceeded to publish a manifesto to the Jews of the world to lend a helping hand. The Jews greeted his plan with applause, but proffered little assistance. Netter, previously a merchant, set out for the Near East himself. With hard work, demanding all his talent and energy, he convinced the Turkish government to give him land for his school near Jaffa, and obtained funding and support for his enterprise.

the hills of abraham and sarah

Netter, consulting an agronomist, built the school with his own hands. He invested enormous effort in the planning of every detail and thus determined the future shape of the institution, its houses and fields, its livestock sectors and workshops. Although not especially wealthy, he contributed a large sum of his own money to the establishment.

Despite schemes by the Arabs from the neighboring village of Yazur to thwart him, Netter went into the fields and got under way, beginning with a well for drinking water and irrigation. He lived in an old cave which he had discovered on the lands of the school, until the first hut was built.

He imparted a biblical atmosphere to the area, naming hills after Abraham, Sarah, Isaac, Jacob and Benjamin, plains after Moses and Samuel, and valleys after Rebekah and Rachel. The name of the institution was proposed by the tailor, Elḥanan, whom Netter brought from Jerusalem to clothe the children and take charge of religious life. The name was taken from Jeremiah 17:13: **"Thou hope of Israel** [Heb. *mikveh yisrael*], **the Lord! All that forsake Thee shall be ashamed."**

Buildings were erected, and plowing began. Netter, who of course was not a farmer, wanted the school to be modern and to grow crops which were as yet unknown in the country.

The *Alliance Israélite Universelle* was not motivated by nationalist ideology, as was *Ḥibbat Zion* (Love of Zion – a Jewish nationalist movement centered in Eastern Europe and forerunner of the Zionist Organization). Rather, the *Alliance* primarily desired to help Jews all over the world, as human beings, and to work for their civil equality. Yet Mikveh Israel was invaluable in laying the foundation for Jewish settlement of

1 *The former barn, now used as a student residence hall.*

2 *The synagogue at Mikveh Israel, inaugurated in 1895. The institution itself was inaugurated on the Sabbath whose weekly* haftarah *portion included the verse: "Thou hope of Israel [Heb.* mikveh yisrael*], the Lord! All that forsake Thee shall be ashamed" (Jeremiah 17:13); hence the name of the school.*

1

the Land of Israel. Mikveh provided employment and training (albeit often under criticism) for the pioneers of the first *moshavot* (lit. "colonies," early agricultural settlements), the settlers of Rishon le-Ẓiyyon, and the *Bilu* pioneers (early Russian Zionists) who founded Gedera. Jews from the Diaspora who wished to settle in the Land of Israel and needed advice generally turned to the director of this institution.

Three years after the foundation of the school (1870), Netter, disabled after falling off a horse, passed his mantle as director to his assistant, Isaac Shamash. Subsequent directors included the learned Dr. V. Herzberg, and Samuel Hirsch, Joseph Niego, Eliyahu Krause, and Asher Malkhin. Since 1965 the school has been directed by Dr. Gideon Katz. Through the years Mikveh Israel has trained thousands of graduates who have established agricultural settlements, applying themselves to all branches of agriculture. In its early years Mikveh was criticized for its French atmosphere, for not being religiously observant, and for being detached from the concerns of the *yishuv*. In time, however, Mikveh found its place alongside other institutions in encouraging agriculture and building the land.

Groups and individuals wishing to visit Mikveh not on weekdays must obtain advance permission. Cars may enter only through the Krause gate, bordering on Ḥolon, and pedestrians may use the gate facing the Jaffa-Jerusalem road. Now we shall take a look at some interesting sites at Mikveh.

along the paths of mikveh israel

Netter's Cave, his home for six entire months, is located in the center of the park in front of the administration building. Potsherds from the Hellenistic and Crusader periods have been discovered here. Remains of a Bronze Age and Hellenistic settlement were found on the hill of Mikveh's water tower. Hellenistic tombs were discovered west of the school. Even without excavating we may surmise that Mikveh was built over an earlier settlement also based on agriculture.

On **Netter's grave,** in the grove on the southern side of the school's property, the epitaph reads: **"Here lies Ya'akov Netter of everlasting memory. Born on 12 Elul, 5586 (1826). Died on 19 Tishri 5643 (1883). For his brethren he wrought well. His goodness more than words can tell. The work of his hands: Mikveh Israel."**

A tomb decorated with stone carving, at the side of the quadrangle, is the grave of Samuel Hirsch's two young children, his son Ya'akov and daughter Jana, who died of diphtheria within a week and a half of one another, in 1885.

Netter's house, one of the school's first buildings. Netter's room was on the northern side. The building, recently renovated, contains a room commemorating the men who contributed to Mikveh, and beside it a museum. Near the building, on the north, is the central pool of Mikveh, now partially in ruins.

The **old gate** faces the road to Jerusalem. Nearby are the remains of a pool, a well, and the guard's house. This is apparently the house where the *Bilu* pioneers lived. Beside the

1 *A photograph of the tobacco harvest in 1922, showing the pickers against the background of the tobacco field. Their varied garb reflects the various cultures characteristic of the early waves of* aliyah *(immigration): the Russian* rubashka *(shirt) from Eastern Europe, with the Arab* kafiya *(headdress) which people liked to view as a return to the dress of our forefathers.*

2 *The smithy at Mikveh Israel. The school was based on self-sufficiency.*

3 *Mikveh Israel has a botanical garden with native and imported species. It was planted in 1929 and today has 1200 varieties of plants. The garden is designed in French style, another instance of the French mark which the* Alliance *has left not only on the garden but on the institution as a whole.*

house is a plow mounted on a concrete platform, indicating the nature of the school. On 27 October, 1898. Theodor Herzl met with the German Kaiser, Wilhelm II, on his way to Jerusalem, beside this gate.

An avenue of palm trees leads to the center of the school. On our right we see the pump house, whose mechanism, unfortunately, has not survived, and beyond it, one of the **concrete bunkers** of Mikveh, which was on the front line during the War of Independence. Close by is a **gigantic tree** – a Bengal Ficus, planted in 1888, whose air roots form a veritable little grove around it.

The **synagogue** is a handsome building with a fine interior and an elaborate sign over the entrance. This sign, a work of art, is a carved marble plaque with colorful reliefs showing a plow and a cluster of grapes, and an inscription in Hebrew, Arabic and French, mentioning that the synagogue was dedicated in 1895.

The **winery** is a broad building with several wings. Several years ago it was renovated and reopened under the name of Carmiya, but has since been shut down again. There are, however, two things worth seeing here. One is the arms cache of Mikveh, in the winery's western wing. A covered rectangular entrance opened on a short, round tunnel with steps leading to a small room. This room, which was intended for storing arms, was not discovered by the British. The cellar beneath the eastern wing was used by the *Haganah* in the Tel Aviv area for training fighters clandestinely. The site is now used by the Civil Defense for inauguration ceremonies. The building is in a terrible state, its basement and roof falling apart. It is imperative, while several of the winery's machines still survive, to save at least some parts of the building and preserve them in memory of the heritage of wine making in Israel.

The first buildings erected at Mikveh have been declared national monuments, and some are now being renovated and restored. In 1976 the *Knesset* enacted the Mikveh Israel Bill, legislating that the school's 800 acres and its buildings are not to be touched, thus saving the school from repeated proposals to build more high-rise housing projects on its land. The people living in the neighboring city were also thereby assured greenery and clean air.

The **botanical garden,** founded in 1929, grows 1200 different species of plants. Topiary pruning, reminiscent of the

1

2

3

1 *A group of Jewish students from Bulgaria, at Mikveh Israel (1899). Shmuel Anavi is in the bottom row, first from the right. Mikveh Israel had 102 students that year, some of them sons of Jewish farmers from the* moshavot, *others children from the Diaspora, mostly from Russia.*

2 *Eliyahu Krause, director of Mikveh Israel, speaking at convocation at the end of the school year. Seated beside him is David Ben-Gurion, then Israel's prime minister. Krause, born in the Crimea, Russia, immigrated to the Land of Israel in 1892. He attended Mikveh and upon completion of his studies was sent to study agriculture in France. In 1901, after holding various positions, he was appointed director of Mikveh. He transformed the institution with its French heritage and atmosphere into an important Zionist and national educational center.*

1

magnificent gardens of France, is practiced here. There is a long pavilion in the garden, in memory of Eliyahu Shamir, brother of the novelist Moshe Shamir and hero of the latter's book, *Pirkei Elik* (Stories of Elik), who fell, along with six other fighters, as they were passing through the hostile village of Yazur (today Azor) in an open truck. Mishmar ha-Shiv'ah (Watch of the Seven), a *moshav* east of Azor, is named after them.

Near the gardens is a **memorial to the fallen soldiers,** killed at Shilta in the Modi'in region, at Malkiyya, Ḥuleiqat and Beit 'Afa. Those killed were Mikveh graduates training at *kibbutz* Geva'. Seeing this memorial to youngsters from 17 to 19 years old brings to mind the youths who sacrificed their lives to give us a State of Israel. The name 'Oved Ladizhinski, their colleague in agricultural training, who was killed in the Mitleh Pass in 1956, has been added to the names on the memorial. Mikveh has in addition a *Yad la-Bannim,* a memorial center honoring all the fallen connected with Mikveh Israel. This building houses a large model of the campus.

But the weighty heritage of the past is not too heavy a burden for Mikveh Israel today, as talking with students, and with the school's director, Gideon Katz, indicates. The institution has charted its course successfully and adapted innovations and modern developments. It has an annual enrollment of 800 students and 200 graduates every year. Its student body is divided into a general group and a religious group, living in harmony. There is also a school for agricultural technicians on the premises. Its students include young men and women who have completed their army service, and high school graduates with draft deferrals from the IDF. The school is ideally situated for a national agricultural institution; its climate, soil and growing conditions are suitable to the entire spectrum of Israeli agriculture, and its proximity to Tel Aviv makes it convenient for students coming from all parts of the country. Thus Mikveh holds the unrivaled title of the largest agricultural boarding school in the country.

Mikveh remains a credit to its earlier days. Alongside a hundred year old orchard which still bears fruit, the school fosters the development of new branches of agriculture. Graduates of Mikveh, who live all over the country, come to visit their *alma mater* at every opportunity and are proud of being products of Mikveh Israel. Netter's dream has in large measure come true. Much of what has been done in the country began at Mikveh. As you wander along the paths of Mikveh we hope that you, too, will sense its atmosphere of modest beginnings, and the developments which come from men of vision who are willing to work hard to realize their dreams.

2

reminiscences of a young man of 95

"Herzl spoke with our headmaster about preparing a reception for the German Kaiser, who was scheduled to pass by our school on his way to Jerusalem. We set up a plaza by the gate and decorated it with flowers and tools. Herzl came a day in advance to check that all was in order. As the Kaiser approached, Herzl gave a sign and we, the students, sang the German national anthem. I saw the Kaiser signal to Herzl to approach him. They shook hands and talked for several minutes. I stood beside Herzl just as I am sitting beside you right now."

This is not a quote from a book or a newspaper yellowed with age; it is from a conversation which I had with the very man who witnessed this event. The man, Shmuel Anavi, was a student at Mikveh Israel in the 19th century, and at the time of this interview (February 1980) was 95 years old. Herzl's meeting with German Kaiser Wilhelm II, which took place in 1898, he witnessed with his own eyes.

Coming to visit him one dreary morning, I was not sure I had heard correctly when I was told that he had gone out to the bank and to do some other errands... When he returned, I saw a short but erect man, his large moustache and hair silvery white, and his eyes still without glasses.

Shmuel had been a student at the Alliance *school in Plovdiv, Bulgaria. When the students were asked to write what they would do if they had a lot of money, Shmuel wrote that he would use the money to buy a farm where he would grow fruits and vegetables, raise chickens and have a cow. This, Shmuel thought, was because he used to accompany his father Ben-Ẓion, a greengrocer, and therefore dreamed of he himself owning a farm of the sort he saw when traveling with his father. His teachers, seeing that this was his dream, sent him to study at Mikveh Israel along with one other lad. His parents remained in Bulgaria.*

Among the 102 students in the school at the time were several other young men from Bulgaria. The rest of the students were the sons of farmers from the moshavot *and children from all over the world, especially Russia. Shmuel came to the Land of Israel in 1898, at the age of 14. The school then had six teachers, aside from the headmaster and agronomist from Turkey, Joseph Niego. Anavi had endless praise for Niego, both as a headmaster and as a human being.*

In those days, so Anavi tells, Mikveh taught everything a farmer needed to know: cultivating field crops, plowing with horses and oxen, raising chickens and livestock, growing seedlings and hothouse plants. "We used to do deep plowing, with four pairs of oxen, as far as half a meter down, in order to remove the weeds. We generally worked at night. Once I was plowing together with an older student when Arabs suddenly descended upon us and tried to steal the oxen. I rushed back to Mikveh and rang the bell. Everyone, including the Arab watchman, rushed to the rescue and the thieves fled. Two thirds of Mikveh's land was planted with vineyards. The distillery functioned then, and the wine which we produced was exported. Merchants used to come from Russia and buy many casks of wine."

This 95 year old youngster (his family claims he is even older) now speaks somewhat falteringly, and his Hebrew is not the best. He is quite regretful about this. His advice to every newcomer is: "First thing, learn Hebrew!" He himself did not have the opportunity, since all his studies at Mikveh were conducted in French, and only one hour a week was devoted to studying Hebrew.

After four years at Mikveh he fell ill from longing for his family, and returned to Bulgaria. The studies at Mikveh, so he says, were so thorough that they prepared the graduates for any craft or occupation they might be called to do. Many students left the Land of Israel for Egypt. One went to Australia. He himself went into trade in paprika and nuts. Because he held a diploma from Mikveh, he was sent to officer training school, and before the First World War fought in the Balkan Wars.

Back in Plovdiv Anavi did not forget his training. He became the chairman of the Palestine Council, which sent children and adults to the Land of Israel. When Ben-Gurion came to visit Bulgaria, several of the Zionist leaders of his city, including Anavi, traveled in a special train car to Sofia, where they heard Ben-Gurion address a public gathering. When the gates opened, and anyone who so desired could go to Israel, Anavi came with his family in 1949. His wife has since passed away, but he has two sons and a daughter, and from them has had the joy of seven grandchildren and six great-grandchildren.

The present director of Mikveh, Dr. Katz ("a very good man"), invited Anavi to visit Mikveh and arranged a large reception for him. "The difference in the place since those days is enormous, without comparison. To begin with there are many more students, many new buildings. Now everything is mechanized; back then everything was done by hand. We had only two machines, for harvesting and for threshing. In our day there was no electricity. Everything ran on oil."

One other man from Anavi's class is still alive, his name – Shelomo Cordova. But he is a young man – only 94 years old, and ailing.

Before leaving for the tempestuous twentieth century beyond the walls of this institution, I gave my blessings to the vigorous spry old man, who may yet live to see the twenty-first century and reminisce to future generations about days of yore...

rosh pinna
renewing jewish settlement in the galilee

Yair Nafshi

Edited: Tamar Dror

The hundredth anniversary of the First Aliyah was celebrated in 1982. (The First Aliyah was a wave of immigration to the Land of Israel of Jews influenced by the ideas of *Ḥibbat Zion* [Love of Zion], a movement whose motto was to till the soil. Successive waves of immigration, until the establishment of the State, have been identified according to the primary composition of each wave of immigration and have been named the First Aliyah, the Second Aliyah, etc.) Nineteen eighty-two, proclaimed "Settlement Year," saw the centenaries of Rishon le-Ẓiyyon, Rosh Pinna, and Zikhron Ya'akov. Actually Rosh Pinna has three "birthdays." The first commemorates a group of young men and women from the "old *yishuv*" (pre-Zionist Jewish community in the Land of Israel) in Safed, who in 1878, several weeks before the founding of Petaḥ Tikva, "Mother of the *Moshavot,*" settled in the village of Ja'uni, at the foothills of Mt. Canaan, and called their settlement Gai Oni (Valley of My Strength). This settlement attempt failed. It was succeeded by a group of immigrants from Moinesti, Rumania, who in August 1882 established a new settlement there and in remembrance of the travails of their predecessors named it Rosh Pinna, from the biblical verse, **"The stone which the builders rejected is become the chief corner-stone (*rosh pinna*)"** (Psalms 118:22).

The founders of Rosh Pinna, however, reckoned the age of their settlement from the day they plowed the first furrow in their land, December 12, 1882. This day they proclaimed the anniversary of their *moshavah.*

reb eleazar rokach fights *ḥalukkah*

R. Eleazar Rokach*, born in Jerusalem in 1854, moved to Safed in his youth. Impassioned by the idea of sinking roots in the soil of the Jewish homeland, he drew his chief inspiration from the vision of his grandfather, Israel Bak, the printer and doctor from Berdichev. Israel Bak and his son Nisan established a Jewish village on Mt. Jarmaq, now known as Mt. Meron, and had visions of establishing 200 Jewish settlements in the Galilee. Their philosophy was, **"Without soil one is not a man, as it is written, 'The heavens are the heavens of the Lord, but the earth hath He given to the children of men'** (Psalms 115:16)."

With respect to the problem of Jewish existence, Israel Bak said: **"If you do not want to live in castles in the air, you must acquire some land under your feet."** The village of Jarmaq was destroyed in 1840 as a result of a change of rule in the land, and Israel Bak was forced to move his residence to Jerusalem. His life's work was continued by his grandson, who fought to realize the dream of settling on the land in Zion.

Repelled by the idea of *ḥalukkah* (living off charity from Jews of the Diaspora), he led a crusade against that institution, even at the risk of his life, fighting the beadles of Safed and the city fathers as well as the Jews of the Diaspora to whom he was sent as an emissary to spread his teachings.

Ḥalukkah was a *weltanschauung* and way of life which had been supporting most of the Jews living in the Land of Israel, in its four holy cities, for generations. The prevailing view among the Jews of Zion and of the Diaspora was that holy study in the Land of Israel would hasten the coming of the Messiah. The Jews living off donations from the Diaspora organized themselves in communities known as *kolelim* (sing. *kolel*), according to their country of origin. Each *kolel* thus received philanthropic support according with the standard of living and the religio-messianic consciousness of the Jews in their country of origin. The fund raisers, called "emissaries of the rabbis," were highly respected persons. The Sephardic Jews were an exception; refusing *ḥalukkah,* most of them worked for a

* Note: In this article R. is an abbreviation for Reb, a title equivalent to Mr. The title of respect, Reb, was common in the shtetl.

1 Reḥov ha-Rishonim *(Street of the First Settlers) in Rosh Pinna.*

"a society devoted to tilling the soil"

In 1878, several Jewish families from Safed, on the initiative of R. Eleazar Rokach, purchased part of the land of the Arab village of Ja'uni and settled there, calling their settlement Gai Oni (Valley of My Strength). The July 22, 1878, edition of the newspaper, *ha-Ẓefirah,* recounts the story of **"thirty people who grew disgusted with the bread of adversity and with charity, and therefore set out and purchased land in the village of Jana', in order to farm the Land of Israel. The signatures of the thirty reached the editorial board of the Hebrew newspaper after they had been endorsed by the court of the holy city of Ṣarfat [Safed]."** The Galilean settlers had requested a loan to purchase the land, build their houses, etc., and stressed that they would pay back the money.

It appears that several Jews had fled from Syria in the wake of the Damascus Affair* and the ensuing anti-Jewish riots there and had relocated in the Arab village of Ja'uni from 1840 to 1850. The Jews of Damascus rose in organized self-defense and emerged victorious in the battle against their persecutors. Among the Jewish insurrectionists was a man named Musa Silas, who beat one of the rioters to death. Fearing revenge, he fled his city and took refuge in the village of Ja'uni, where he settled and lived off the soil. In time several more refugees from the blood libel migrated to the village. However they lived there only until 1850. Thus, when the settlers of Gai Oni arrived in Ja'uni, they found nothing but a poor Arab village consisting of two clans – Tamyami and Jalvut – and numbering 150 people in all.

Although a number of Galilean villages – such as Peqi'in, Bar'am and 'En Zetim – were more or less continuously inhabited by Jews from the Second Temple period to the modern era, and there had been a settlement on the Jarmaq (which apparently lasted five or six years and numbered several families), the idea of a Jewish village in the Galilee was still relatively new. The settlement effort in Gai Oni received wide coverage in the contemporary press, thanks to the activities of Eleazar Rokach. These articles indicate that the intention of the settlers from Safed was to establish a Jewish colony (Heb.: *moshavah*) and live as farmers on the soil of the Jewish homeland.

The decision to settle in the village alongside the Arabs was based on security considerations; Jews and Arabs could join to defend themselves against bedouin attacks. Somewhat later several of the Arabs of Ja'uni moved to Ḥoran, where the Turkish government made a present of good land to them; while

living. Eleazar Rokach and his young group from Safed, like the young men and women who left Jerusalem to found the agricultural settlement of Petaḥ Tikva, considered supporting oneself on these welfare funds like leaning on a broken reed, and set out to fight *ḥalukkah* to the end.

A memorandum from Rokach to Montefiore, in 1875, published in the newspaper, *Ha-Ḥavaẓelet,* gives us an idea of his battle against *ḥalukkah.* Rokach stated in his memorandum, later reproduced in the anthology, *Maẓav ha-'Ir ha-Kedoshah Ẓefat ve-Toshaveha ha-Ashkenazim* (The Condition of the Holy City of Safed and its Ashkenazi Inhabitants) as follows: **(a) the Jews of Safed must support themselves by their own labor; (b) there must be workshops to employ Safed's younger generation to enable them to earn a living; (c) tilling the soil must be paramount, for therein lies the salvation of the people and the homeland.** The memorandum is signed Eleazar Rokach, "Head and Delegate of the Society of the Holy Land in Gai Oni in the Upper Galilee."

* A blood libel in Damascus in 1840, in which Franciscan monks accused Jewish notables in the city of murdering the monk Thomas, in order to use his blood in the preparation of their *matzah* for Passover.

they sold their land in Ja'uni to the Jews for a handsome sum.

A severe drought in the winter of 1878-79 plunged the settlers into grave difficulties. In 1880 they issued repeated appeals for aid, published in the press in the Land of Israel and abroad. They also turned to Eleazar Rokach, requesting him to intercede on their behalf and raise funds for them. He went abroad and established a base of operations in Bucharest. From his speeches it is clear that he viewed the settlement in Gai Oni as the beginning of organized re-acquisition of land in the country for the sake of Jewish settlement, ultimately to spread over the entire area of the land of our forefathers. The *Alliance Israélite Universelle* (an international Jewish organization founded in France in 1860, in the wake of anti-Semitic events of the times; its goal – to promote world Jewish unity and render political and cultural assistance to Jews wherever they may live) responded to his appeals, and with their aid he tried to save the farmers of Gai Oni. The *Alliance* had no objection to the fund-raising campaign for settlement of the land and agreed to lend its name and full support to the undertaking. Eleazar Rokach, a gifted orator, inspired many people to view pioneer settlement as the beginning of Jewish national redemption. R. Eleazar charity boxes, the first charity box for land acquisition, were introduced into many Jewish homes. This charity box came to overshadow the R. Meir Ba'al ha-Ness box, whose beneficiaries were supported by the *ḥalukkah,* Rokach's sworn enemy, and paved the way for the blue box of the Jewish National Fund.

Rokach's endeavors did not save the settlers of Gai Oni. They were beset with one crisis after another, until their strength failed them. In dire straits, they abandoned their settlement (1880-1881) and returned to Safed. A very few remained, sorely destitute, combing through the Arabs' fields after harvest, gathering lone stalks of grain, like Ruth the Moabite.

Nevertheless Rokach's work was not altogether in vain. The May 26, 1880, issue of *ha-Magid* publicly proclaimed: **"The learned R. Eleazar has come hither from the Holy Land and has enlightened our fellow Jews to found a society devoted to tilling the soil."** In another issue of *ha-Magid* Eleazar Rokach explained: **"The Jews suffer the wrathful attacks of anti-Semites because they do not work like all other peoples, but rely only on commerce for their livelihood."**

The seeds of propaganda which he sowed in the Jewish communities of Rumania began bearing fruit. Here and there Jews decided to liquidate all they had and set out for the Land of Israel. The meeting in the home of R. Falk in Moinesti, at which the Society for Settling the Land of Israel by Tilling the Soil was founded, is mentioned in the memoirs of R. Joseph Ẓevi Falk's son: **"That very evening almost eighty families signed**

1

up, pledging large sums of money, each according to his means. The same evening two people were chosen and delegated to go to the Land of Israel and purchase land. One was R. David Schub and the other R. David Bukshester. Everyone agreed that since, God willing, they would go to the Holy Land, which is under the Lord's eye from the beginning of the year to the year's end, they all must therefore abide by the precepts of the religion to the last detail, including observance of all the commandments pertaining to the land, such as heave offerings and tithes, etc. Then there was great rejoicing." Ẓevi Falk then adds, **"Jews began awakening and founding societies for immigration to the Land of Israel."** It should be noted that these were all God-fearing, learned and devoutly observant Jews. Free-thinking Jews did not support *aliyah* and became assimilated.

rosh pinna is founded

While still in his home town, David Schub heard from a Safed resident passing through Moinesti that "several Jews from Safed bought land in the village of Ja'uni, near Safed; and, lacking the means to till the land, they wish to sell it." David Schub set out from Safed with his escort, who owned land in Gai Oni, to survey the possibilities. Schub writes in his memoirs, *Zikhronot le-Veit David,* "After seeing the land of the village ... and inquiring as to the price of the land, I decided it was a good place and reported back on it to my society."

Before any reply reached him, David Schub traveled throughout the country along with David Bukshester. Contrary to the recommendation of the latter, who preferred land on the plain, it was decided to purchase land in Gai Oni. David Schub notes that two Jews, the brothers David and Ẓevi, lived in the village and supported themselves by gleaning. David Schub's arguments for purchasing the land were as follows: "... three springs originate in the valley between the mountain on which the village is situated and Mt. Canaan. They issue forth three

1 *The Kalischer house. When its foundations were being dug, a cave containing an olive press from the Second Temple period was discovered. The olive press was renovated by the early settlers and used to extract oil until 1952.*

2 *The old cemetery overlooks the Gai Oni valley and the first houses of the* moshavah.

1 *The Friedman house. The father of the family, known by the nickname of Yusuf Effendi, was one of the early settlers of Gai Oni. He bought the first plot of land from the Arab villagers and planted a garden of citron trees on it.*

2 *The first hotel in the Galilee, owned by R. Alter Schwarz, grandfather of Yigal Allon.*

3 *The synagogue, built by the settlers in 1885, was funded by Baron Rothschild. Beneath it is a* mikveh *(ritual bath) and bathhouse, run on the eves of Sabbaths and Jewish festivals.*

4 *The first group of* Ḥovevei Zion *(Lovers of Zion) from Rumania, at Galatz port, before boarding the* Thetis *in 1882. The pioneers allegorically dubbed the ship the* Titus, *saying: "Titus exiled the Jewish people; and so they shall return to their land aboard the* Titus."

hundred meters above the village and water the gardens and orchards in the valley. Therefore I decided the place would be good for our society. The land of the village is mixed, some hilly and some plain, with hills encompassing a large, expansive plain called El-Ḥat after the large amount of wheat (Heb.: *ḥittim*) that grows there... and above it, rising before our eyes, is Mount Hermon, with a northerly wind blowing from it, cooling and cleansing the air from the heat of the summer" (from which we learn how little geography he knew, for the afternoon breeze at Rosh Pinna blows from the west). David Schub saw two principal drawbacks: the lack of roads providing access to the coastal cities and the center of the country, and the stoney soil. These, however, are shortcomings which it is within man's hands to change, whereas sources of water and fresh, cool air are advantages given by the mountainous nature of the region.

Thus it was decided to buy Ja'uni. On July 24, 1882, David Schub purchased two thirds of the village's land. The remaining third was purchased by families who came from Russia, with the encouragement of R. Mordechai Segal. The end of that month thirty families (130 people) set out from Moinesti. They sailed in a ship called the *Thetis,* but allegorically dubbed the *Titus* by the immigrants, saying that the Jewish people had been exiled by Titus and now were returning to their land in the *Titus.* The ship docked in Beirut, whence, after an arduous trek, the group reached Safed.

David Schub describes the founding of the *moshavah* in his book: "At the close of *Shabbat Shuvah* (the Sabbath between the Jewish New Year and the Day of Atonement; September 16, 1882), I convened a meeting of all those who had come, to found the *moshavah,* to discuss the first steps necessary to begin work and set up a leadership body, to elect a council and to establish the by-laws which would govern all affairs of the *moshavah.*" In the course of the meeting it became clear that **"a large number of those who came did not have enough money, and others were utterly destitute. I realized that if we let every man be for himself, each tilling his own plot of land, and split into wealthy, middle-class and poor, it would have the gravest consequences... I proposed that at least for the first year we should all work the land jointly... We must have unanimous consent to this point; and any man who is fearful and faint of heart may leave our society and retrace his steps to Rumania."**

Thus the settlers agreed to his proposal, save for six families who returned to their land of birth. In accordance with Schub's proposal, the settlers drew up by-laws (which appear in his book) including the following regulations, adopted at their first meeting:

"The general objective of the society is to promote the material and moral weal of the *moshavah,* and to set an example to our fellow Jews, wherever they be; to encourage Jews to settle the Land of Israel and rebuild the ruins of our nation, and to help with all our ability those who love the Holy Land.

"The members of the society are obliged to work wholeheartedly and to the best of their ability for the welfare of the generality and to promote the ideal of settling the Land of Israel; to follow the spirit of our sacred Torah and the Jewish nation. In general it shall be the duty of the council to supervise all commerce and workshops, seeing to it that they be founded on a basis of fellowship, so that all the members of the *moshavah* shall benefit from them and no man shall eat at the expense of his neighbor.

"In the event, Heaven forbid, that a member of the *moshavah* pass away, the society shall care for his widow and children and support them to the best of its ability. If the deceased was a member who worked the land himself, all the members of the community shall continue to work his land and protect it. If his land was worked by hired hands, it shall continue to be worked by hired hands at the expense of the

1

widow, and a supervisor on the part of the community shall oversee them as long as the council deems necessary.

"If there be a quarrelsome troublemaker among the members of the *moshavah,* whose ways are against the spirit of the community, the council shall admonish him three times; after that a general meeting may by majority vote force him off his holding and pay him for his land such sum of money as they justly assess, or may even take over his land without paying.

"Each and every morning, from six o'clock (European time) or twelve o'clock Turkish time, everyone is obliged to go out to work, until the same hour of the evening.

"Daily, at midday, everyone shall have two hours rest from his work.

"No one shall despise his neighbor or call him by a deprecatory name. There shall reign only peace, brotherhood, and unity among us, so that we may be of honor and good repute throughout the land. Anyone who despises his neighbor or calls him by a deprecatory name shall be punished by the council.

"The members of the *moshavah* shall not begin working the fields until the majority have decided what work they shall do and what crop shall be sown. At plowing time all shall plow together, and at sowing time all sow together, and likewise at harvest time. In all work they shall apply themselves to one endeavor acceptable to the whole, and not have one man tending his olives and another his vineyard.

"Each and every man shall be obliged to do guard duty, to go

2

3

4

out into the *moshavah* and stand on the look-out and guard at night, as arranged by the council. No one may cancel his guard duty, but only trade days with his neighbor or some other person. Every man must do his guard duty himself, or trade with someone in the colony, and no man may be hired to guard in his stead for pay."

building the *moshavah*

David Schub describes how the *moshavah*'s houses were built. A Safed Jew served as architect and building contractor, while the members of the *moshavah* were the laborers. They applied themselves to all sorts of heavy labor. The fine ladies put aside their past and, along with the men, plunged their hands into the plaster and whitewash used in construction work. When a house was completed, lots were cast to determine who would move in, and all continued building the remaining houses. Thus twenty houses were built.

The first houses of the *moshavah* were built very close together. Schub explains: "Noting conditions in the country, and that our property be more secure, it was decided to build the remaining houses in proximity to the two above-mentioned houses (remaining from Gai Oni), despite the crowding, which allowed no further construction." Further reasons listed for close construction were: lack of financial means, proximity to springs, and the Turkish law forbidding construction on land owned by the Ottoman Empire but with rights of use and possession in the hands of those working them, on land previously not built up, etc. Thus he concludes, "For all these reasons we were constrained to build close to the village of Gai Oni, in a narrow area, in two crowded rows, one house backing up on the next, without any space between them. Each house consisted of two rooms, a barn and a small yard."

Here we must note that Rosh Pinna at the time had two separate societies of settlers in it: the Jews from Moinesti, headed by David Schub – the group with the "by-laws" – and another group of six families lead by Joseph Friedman, one of the founders of Gai Oni. The latter called themselves the "Russians in the colony of Rosh Pinna." Later, when Baron Rothschild's steward, Elie Scheid, came to Rosh Pinna, he extended his patronage only over the Rumanian group.

the first day of plowing – joy and woe

That year severe drought struck the land. The earth, "hard and barren as a rock," could not be plowed. All eyes were cast towards the heavens, anxiously awaiting rain. It was not until December that Rosh Pinna had the first rain of the season. The farmers rejoiced and started preparing to plow. On December 12, 1882, the settlers went out to plow their soil for the first time. David Schub describes the events of that day: **"With tears of joy in our eyes we walked behind the plow, seeing our great dream – to dwell in the land of our forefathers and to work its soil with our own hands – come true...** After finishing our work we gathered in the field; and of course there was no lack of enthusiastic speeches and song. I myself chose Psalm 126 ('A Song of Ascents. When the Lord brought back those that returned to Zion...') as the theme of my address. The rejoicing was great indeed. We decided to declare this day, the 2nd of Tevet (Dec. 12, 1882), a holiday celebrating the founding of the *moshavah*. With song and rejoicing we returned from the fields to the *moshavah*, to where the houses stood. There in the middle of the street we set a dinner table. Each of us brought his meal, and we sat down together to eat and rejoice, and to give thanks for the kindness bestowed upon us by God."

That day the *moshavah* also celebrated the marriage of two of its younger members, Malkah Blum and Fischel Rubenstein, who had become engaged on the ship on their way to the Land of Israel. "All the *moshavah* took part in the wedding. We made plenty of raisin juice, as well as various cooked dishes of mushrooms and of *ḥubeiza* (a plant colloquially known as "Arab bread," which grows wild in the fields. It was used for food by the besieged Jews of Jerusalem during the War of Independence), borscht and herring brought from Safed on credit, and loaves of bread – half bran and heavy as rocks – baked the previous day. A most unusual musical ensemble was put together to escort the couple to the bridal canopy. First came R. Samuel Katz with his instrument – a tin funnel. Next came the bride's brother, R. Benjamin Blum, making music upon two brass candlesticks which he struck one against the other, and third R. Reuben Rottenberg, a dark-haired bachelor already tawny-skinned from the sun of the Land of Israel and talented at drumming on a tin can with two sticks. The young ladies, even the more modest among them, cast their eyes upon him, intently watching his animated performance.

"...Abruptly our rejoicing ceased. The cry of a dying man pierced the air: an Arab had been killed! Stunned, we rushed to the scene and discovered that one of our number had been digging foundations for a building. With him was a young Arab, sitting and playing with a pistol which he got his hands on but did not know how to use. Suddenly a bullet shot out and hit him,

1

Mulberry trees and silkworms were grown in Rosh Pinna, and a factory there processed the cocoons to make thread, wove silk fabric and sewed it into various items.

1,4 *A dark mulberry – various stages in ripening of the fruit. It originates from western Asia and was known in the Land of Israel in the Second Temple period (confare:* Tosafot Terumot *4:5).*

2 *A silk* tallit *(prayer shawl) made in the Rosh Pinna factory, woven in shades of light blue and white with unusual geometric designs.*

3 *A silk bag woven and sewn in the Rosh Pinna factory between 1901 and 1905. The bag and* tallit *belong to Professor Romanov of Jerusalem.*

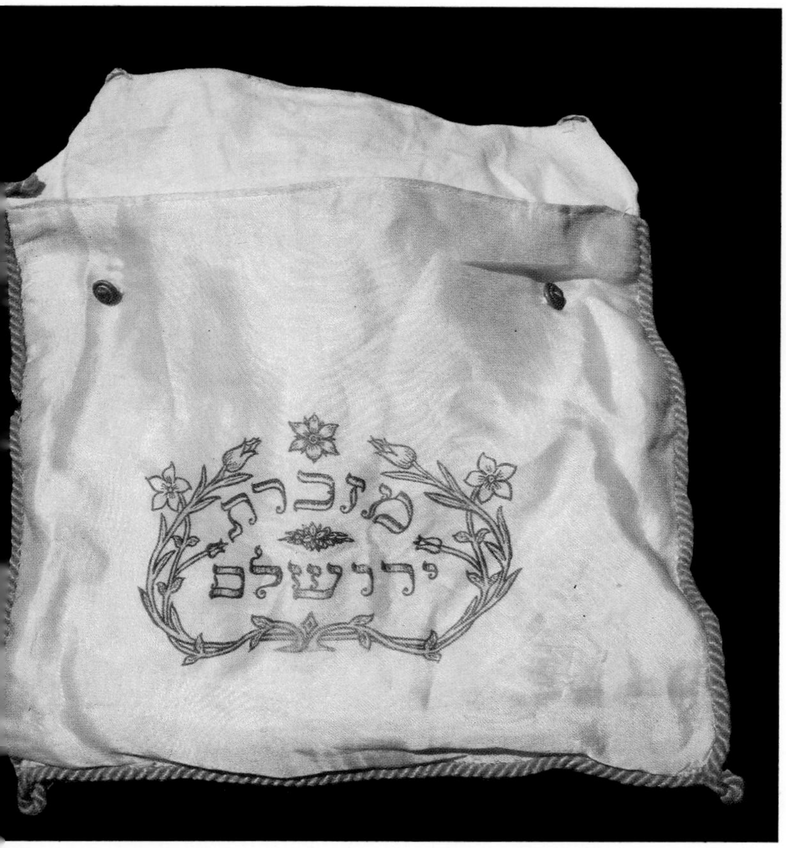

3

4

2

and he tumbled over, dead, into the excavated foundations." The young man who was killed belonged to the Ḥusseini family, a large Safed family descended from Mohammed. When word of the event reached Safed, a horde of Arabs descended on Rosh Pinna to finish off the "murderers." The sheikh of Ja'uni hurriedly gathered the Jews into his house and saved them from the Arabs' revenge until the Turkish police arrived and took the owner of the pistol to prison. A blood feud was averted by the intervention of the French Consul in Safed, Ya'akov Ḥai Abu, and the Arab dignitaries – and the wedding went on. December 12 was declared the anniversary of the *moshavah,* in the wake of the "miracle" of the Jews being saved from Arabs avenging the blood of their brother.

Relations between the farmers of the *moshavah* and the family of the victim remained strained for eight months. When the trial was over and the young Jew had been acquitted, the *moshavah* paid 8,000 francs blood-money. The appropriate ceremonies were held and peaceful relations were restored; but the coffers of the *moshavah* were emptied.

trials and tribulations

Preparing the soil for cultivation was back-breaking labor and took its toll. Clearing stones and deep plowing required everyone's help. All the settlers, men, women and children, pitched in and cleared stones from dawn to dusk.

"...In those days we did not drink a glass of water without giving thanks to God, for we had to bring our water from two or three kilometers away." Supplying the house with water was the job of the youngsters: "At dawn, Mother, full of pity at having to rouse her son, used to wake him from his pleasant dreams. 'To the water-hole, my child,' she would say tenderly.

Recognizing the value of performing this important task banished the sleep from your eyes. The oldest child in the family, having risen before you, fastened the pack-saddle on the donkey and loaded it with two special crates, each containing two large tin cans. You rode on the animal, perched between the crates, plodding towards the well. Since it was too dangerous to go anywhere alone, we used to go in a troop and set out singing noisily to dispel our fears."

"Providing water for our meager herd was a difficult undertaking. Water had to be channeled to a pool built near the *moshavah.* The pool used to fill overnight, and in the morning we used to draw the water with buckets and fill the trough by the side of the pool; thus we quenched the thirst of our animals. Channeling the water to the pool was far from easy, and when, after much labor and travail, we at long last succeeded in bringing water to the pool, our neighbors, the villagers of Ja'uni, became wily and diverted the flow to their gardens. Thus we were forced to set up a roster of two or three men to guard the water conduit every night."

The bedouins, as well, tried to steal the water of the *moshavah.* Once they attacked the guards at the pool, but the guards succeeded in driving back the intruders. Seeing that their sheikh had been injured, the bedouins turned tail and fled. The flight of the bedouins led to strained relations once more. After the sultan's judges found for the defenders, a *sulḥa,* or reconciliation ceremony, was held. This, too, cost Rosh Pinna a considerable sum, and once more the coffers were left empty.

The farmers were in dire straits. Court cases and peace settlements had cost them a fortune, while contributions came only in dribs and drabs. The Council's activities reached a standstill for lack of funds. Things reached such a pass that land was not plowed because not a grain of wheat or barley remained for sowing.

In 1883, a year after the founding of Rosh Pinna, the moshavot *were taken under the patronage of Baron Edmond de Rothschild, "the well-known philanthropist." The settlers spent years of hardship eking out a meager living cultivating field crops, fruit trees and vegetables and raising sheep and cattle until the baron decided to establish industries based on processing agricultural produce in the* moshavot. *Wineries were built in Rishon le-Ẓiyyon, Zikhron Ya'akov, and Rosh Pinna, and special plants were cultivated for a perfume industry set up in Yesud ha-Ma'alah, etc. In 1890 a decision was also taken to develop a silk industry, and for this purpose mulberry trees, whose leaves are used to feed silk-worms, were planted in the* moshavot *of the Land of Israel.*

rothschild comes to the rescue

The *moshavah* was in a crisis. With no prospects of improvement at home, David Schub set out once more to find help from abroad. However he got no further than Egypt and raised not a cent. In the meanwhile the *moshavah* received a visit from Elie Scheid, an emissary of the Baron de Rothschild, whom the council had invited after his earlier visit to Zikhron Ya'akov.

Scheid came as the "savior" of the *moshavah* on November 3, 1883. R. Zalman Bendel, who chronicled the events of the times in his book, *Sefer Mazkeret Ya'akov* (Ya'akov Commemorative Book), describes Scheid's activities and the significance of the change which the *moshavah* underwent once it came under the patronage of the baron: Rothschild's steward "doled out a monthly sum for each person" (20 francs) and paid off the *moshavah*'s debts. He even "gave orders to purchase oxen and equipment for plowing and sowing." Nor did he forget that a farmer needs "a cow for milking, a donkey, a horse to ride, barley, straw and fodder, etc." Even working hands and

rosh pinna's school

The school of Rosh Pinna holds an important place in the history of Jewish education in the country. In 1899 Isaac Epstein, who had come to the Land of Israel ten years earlier, was made principal of Rosh Pinna's school. Epstein worked in agriculture in Zikhron Ya'akov for four years and, beginning in 1891, he worked as a teacher, initially in the school for girls in Safed, and afterwards in Metulla, whence he came to Rosh Pinna. Despite the lack of professional training and the absence of basic text books, he succeeded in advancing education in the moshavot *of the Galilee, introducing the study of Hebrew in Hebrew, nurturing his pupils' nationalist feelings, and educating them to work the soil.*

Epstein taught at Rosh Pinna for three years, after which he was succeeded by Simḥah Ḥayyim Vilkomitz. He shaped the character of the school, which combined studies in science and agriculture and laid emphasis on the principles of labor and agriculture. During his tenure Hebrew was introduced as the language of instruction for all subjects taught at school. Vilkomitz served as principal of the school in Rosh Pinna until 1918.

Dr. Joseph Klausner, editor of Ha-Shiloaḥ, *who visited Rosh Pinna in 1912, was full of admiration for what he saw in the school of the* moshavah. *He notes that this school gained fame throughout the entire country as one of the modern and thoroughly Hebraized schools. Many Hebrew words necessary for education and tilling the soil were revived in the school. Even the Sephardic Hebrew accent, which became the norm in the country, received a special touch in the Galilee: there only a strong* bet *or "b" was used, and not a "v".*

Epstein introduced this pronunciation, and Vilkomitz after him fought to preserve this special Galilean way of speech, since they found in ancient sources that the former Jews of the Galilee had spoken this way.

1 *The silk spinning factory built in Rosh Pinna in 1894 and funded by Baron de Rothschild. Part of the silk cocoons were gathered in the* moshavot *and then brought on donkey-back to the factory. Most of the cocoons required were purchased in Lebanese villages. Adults and children from Safed and Rosh Pinna worked in the factory. Its spinning wheels continued to turn for ten years, producing fine silks that were sold to the wealthy of Europe. The enterprise was shut down in 1905 due to economic unprofitability.*

2

builders were rushed to Rosh Pinna with instructions to complete "the houses, barns and farmyards" at the great philanthropist's expense. The conduits channeling the water of the spring to the settlement were installed properly, as well.

The terms of the agreement between the farmers and Scheid are spelled out in issue no. 50 of *Ha-Magid* (1883). The farmers agreed to transfer 1,240 dunams of land, the 19 houses already built, and their livestock to new ownership, to be managed by Erlanger, and Scheid undertook to complete construction of the houses, as well as to give each settler "an ox, a cow, a horse and donkey, and twenty plows." Likewise he undertook to build a synagogue and a school. The agreement was signed by the parties on September 4, 1883.

According to R. Zalman Bendel's book and *Ereẓ Ḥemdah* (Lovely Land) by Sokolow, the severe crisis was brought to an end. The farmers took heart, continued their work, and even saw the fruits of their labors. But the baron's patronage was a mixed blessing: the quiet *moshavah* became an administrative center. An apparatus of officials grew up in Rosh Pinna, and these soon forgot the task delegated them. They dominated the farmers and ruled them with an iron hand. The first chapter in the history of Rosh Pinna drew to a close, and a new era began.

Today, one hundred years later, Rosh Pinna is a blossoming *moshavah* with pleasant houses surrounded by greenery. Although it has taken in many immigrants and has grown and expanded, as a matter of principle Rosh Pinna has preserved its rural character and agricultural coloration. Many of its present inhabitants are fourth and fifth generation descendants of those who settled in Gai Oni and Rosh Pinna one hundred years ago.

Builders are at work once more on the hillside where the founders of Rosh Pinna built their homes. Here the Association for Restoration of the Early *Moshavot* is restoring the original nucleus of the *moshavah* to the way it looked one hundred years ago. Thus far the synagogue, offices of the baron's clerks, and the Park of the Baron have been restored. Pika House, the first house to be restored, has become the Rosh Pinna Academy for studying the history of Jewish settlement in the Galilee.

ḥadera

a city rises out of swamps

Yehudah Ziv

To this day five Jewish localities have clearly Arabic names, names not ostensibly connected to an ancient name and not Hebraized: Metulla, ʻAfula, ʻAtlit, Karkur, and last but not least, Ḥadera, now nearing its hundredth anniversary. Its Arabic name, el-Khudeira, means "The Green."

Before it was founded and in its early years "greenness" was no sign of blessing; rather, it was the green of festering swamps which existed in the area for hundreds of years. The Crusaders, in fact, called the place Lictera – a corruption of the Arabic name, el-Khudeira.

From the outset, interestingly enough, attempts were made to give the new *moshavah* (colony) a Hebrew name. About a year after it was founded, Jawitz suggested that "the *moshav* of Ḥidere is really Ḥaẓor" (*Mi-Yerushalayim* [From Jerusalem], 1892, p. 13). Goldhahr, Baron Rothschild's surveyor, who was closely acquainted with Ḥadera and its environs, wrote a while later: "It was called Ḥideira, but Gedera was originally its name – for this *moshavah* was built on the same place where Gedera by Caesarea formerly stood" (*Admat ha-Qodesh* [The Holy Land], 1913, p. 42). Indeed this identification is confirmed by Benjamin Mazar, the noted historical geographer of Israel, who locates ancient Gador (formerly known as Gedera by Caesarea to distinguish it from other localities with the same name) on the tel on the shore of Ḥadera, south of Givʻat Olga – i.e., Tel el-Akhṣar (pronounced Aḥdar, meaning green), now known by its original Hebrew name, Tel Gador. This is also the name of the seasonal lake – the Pool of Gador – which lies to the east of the foot of the tel. Thus ancient Gedera has come back into its own.

1

For some reason the settlers of Ḥadera did not listen to Jawitz's proposal of the name Ḥaẓor, or even Goldhahr's suggestion to return to the name of Gedera, perhaps because the Bilu pioneers had pre-empted them nine years earlier, naming their settlement Gedera. The settlers of Ḥadera may have been apprehensive of having two "John Smiths." Yet this seemed to be a golden opportunity for using the original historical name in its full form, with the added qualification: Gedera by Caesarea. The opportunity was missed, however, and Ḥadera, a garbled version of the Arabic name, came into common use, without having any significance in Hebrew.

what's in a name?

When the Land of Israel was conquered by the Moslems in the seventh century, the Arabs generally distorted the names of Jewish settlements which fell into their hands. In many instances they changed the spelling, substituted or reversed letters, and at times even broke up a name into a phrase – all so that the name would be easy to pronounce, pleasing to the Arabic ear and comprehensible to the Arabic speaker. Here, too, as far as we can tell, the former name of Gedera by Caesarea was changed and became Khudeira-Ḥadera, the "green."

Rabbinic texts of the talmudic period indicate that Gador was a Samaritan city, whose wine is forbidden to Jews because of its proximity to a place of pagan worship. On the other hand, Gador was known for its fruits, including some which ripened late: **"Rabbi Simeon said: the term three lands** [with respect to the sabbatical year, during which the land is supposed to be left fallow] **refers only to Judea. From the rest of the lands one may eat until the last of the produce edible even by wild animals is gone from Beth-el and from Gedera by Caesarea"** (Tosefta, *Shevi'it* 7:10). Be that as it may, these religious rulings reflect the fertility and abundance of the fruit of Gador, all of whose environs were surely planted and farmed, then just as now, before the coastal plain became desolate. The western Sharon became an area plagued by swamps and remained thus until the founding of Ḥadera, the trail blazer of settlement in the Sharon region. In the wake of Ḥadera, founded in 1890, came numerous other villages and cities, from Ḥadera to Gedera – or perhaps from "Gedera... to Gedera" – forming the continuous strip of Jewish settlement which today comprises most of Israel's population.

Nevertheless, could the name of this veteran *moshavah* (which in the meantime has become a full-fledged city) still be changed back to its original appellation – Gador? There seems not the slightest chance, nor is there any need. The heroic battle of Ḥadera's pioneers has won renown. They doggedly fought the swamps and plagues such as locusts, malaria, and drought, while coping with occasional Arab attacks and the plots of the Turkish authorities. Ḥadera has become a symbol in the history of modern Jewish settlement of the Land of Israel, and its name is inscribed on the banner of this endeavor.

Furthermore, who are we to come and change its name – a name set by history – even if it is an Arabic one, and even if we

1 *Naḥal Ḥadera, in the early days of the settlement. Its Arabic name is el-Mafjar, meaning "the one which breaks through." Only when it rains does the stream rise and succeed in breaking through an egress to the sea. The residents of Ḥadera had their own interpretation of the name given the blocked stream and the swamps which lay beyond it, and dubbed it ha-Mefager ("the retardate").*

2 *Ḥadera Swamp – the formerly desolate landscape is now a nature reserve.*

2

1

do know the original name of the place from ancient times?

The land of the area of Ḥadera was purchased by Yehoshua' Ḥankin in 1890. It was the largest unbroken plot of land acquired in a single transaction that year; small wonder that there was great excitement at the news that **"at the entrance to the Shomron, on the seashore, a large property – thirty thousand dunams – has been purchased. Hearts pounded with joy and hope: thirty thousand dunams! Such an acquisition had never been heard of before in the country... Land, unparalleled in all our colonies: choice land for sowing, valleys enveloped in grass and grain, and choice land for fruit trees – all in one spot... On the seashore, with its natural harbors which could provide a port; the first *moshavah* on the shore, bringing the hope of a Jewish port city!"** (Smilansky, *Ḥadera,* 1930).

the khan – the beginnings of ḥadera

In a short while Ḥankin managed to sell Ḥadera's entire area to the deputies of Zionist associations in the Diaspora – Vilna, Kovna, Riga – and even to individual settlers. Before the winter of 1891 was out, the first pioneers had already settled here, **"for since time immemorial it has been customary in the country that land is not acquired by money alone, but also by right of possession. Thus the first stake was laid in the soil of Ḥadera..."**

The beginning of settlement in Ḥadera was in the one and only building there, the khan (inn for travelers), which stood on top of a hill surrounded by swamps. This was "a strange, black stone building, abandoned and partially ruined, with its gate open towards us like the jaws of some gigantic beast, ... large and square, perhaps with several dozen rooms and storerooms, a dreary vestige of the former owners of Ḥadera.... The large courtyard inside the khan was filled with heaps of trash, garbage and filth." The courtyard of the khan is preserved to this day. Ḥadera's synagogue now stands in its center, along Giborim Street; whereas the rooms, formerly used by Ḥadera's first settlers, have been turned into a museum of the history of the city.

"We could not wait for the Turkish government to give us permits to build.... On Tuesday of the week when the Torah portion of *Matot* was read (early July 1891) the first cornerstone was laid.... Then along came armed military men through the *moshavah* and began destroying the foundations which we had started to build. The order had been issued by the *mudhir* in Caesarea on the pretext that our buildings did not yet have roofs." Thus, for several years the founders of the *moshavah* lived crowded and congested in the dilapidated khan and in a number of shacks which they built nearby; until on June 7, 1896, news came that "a permit has been received from Constantinople to build forty stone houses in Ḥadera." Dr. Hillel Joffe, "doctor of the *moshavot* of the Shomron" and one of the first to study malaria in the Land of Israel (for whom the regional hospital in Ḥadera is named) laid the cornerstone of the first permanent building, saying: "Raising a heavy stone to build one house requires great exertion; raising stones to build a *moshavah* requires a seven-fold effort.... You have shown that you can exert yourselves. May your strength stand the difficult trial to the end. Face the hard battle with courage and confidence, for in the end victory shall be yours!"

a rosy dream – a bleak reality

Ḥadera's first settlers lived in the khan and dreamed of a rosy future: "One envisions Ḥadera fully built; and behold, it is one of the centers of our new state, one of the loveliest cities on the coast. The Ḥadera of dreams extends from its eastern side to the seashore.... On the shore is a large port, bustling with activity and life. With open arms it harbors merchant ships from all over the world. There, on the sand dune – the "mountain of gold" – stands the municipal theater, the university, the public library and museum... and further down, now the great swamp – gardens and parks, walks for grownups and playgrounds for children ... encompassing the town, hundreds of Jewish villages, just like it ... and from here shall come wheat, and milk and honey for all the cities of the land ... and from here shall come fruits for the entire world...."

It is interesting and thrilling how this dream has come true, almost to the last detail.

But the reality in those days was quite different – a bleak, bitter reality. The hill on which Ḥadera was settled was surrounded by extensive swamps. To the west were Birkat Rushrashi, Birkat Ẓafra, and Birkat Ibereikhtas (today the eucalyptus grove known as Ḥadera Forest, planted between Ḥadera and Giv'at Olga), and Birkat 'Ata, or the Forest Pool, to the southwest, which in a rainy winter fills again with water, a reminder of bygone days, but is no longer the malignant swamp which it once was; to the north – Birkat el-Batiḥ and the Cherkess swamp; to the east – the swamps of Ẓeita (the only swamp nature reserve with all its flora and fauna, which remains from the once uninhabited landscape – alongside the eastern train station of Ḥadera) and Gazaza, today the Bet Eliezer neighborhood.

A malaria epidemic erupted unexpectedly at the end of the

1 *Ḥadera's first street was called Giborim Street, Street of the Brave, for good reason. Some of the first houses of the* moshavah *can still be seen along this street.*

2 *Eucalyptus trees in Ḥadera Forest. Whether the eucalyptus trees dried the swamp is unclear; but the work in the forest was undoubtedly what saved the residents of Ḥadera. Baron Rothschild funded planting the forest; and years later cutting down the trees saved the settlers of Ḥadera from forced labor and from being drafted into the Turkish army.*

3 *Yad Avshalom at Ḥadera – a memorial to Avshalom Feinberg, a member of the* moshavah *and one of the* Nili *spy ring, who fell on the outskirts of Sinai and was buried in the sands of Rafiaḥ. Where he lay was not discovered until after the Six Day War.*

4 *Ḥadera's main street in 1912. Today it is called Reḥov ha-Giborim (Street of the Brave).*

Pictures on pages 294 and 295:

1 *Naḥal Ḥadera was also a place for recreation (photo: Sonya).*

2 *Picking oranges: the workers are new immigrants, just arrived and still dressed in European clothes (photo: Crystal).*

2

4

3

first summer. Moshe Smilansky writes in his memoirs: "I woke up in the night with my head spinning and all my limbs filled with heaviness. Chills ran through my entire body, my teeth chattered and I shivered all over... Fever followed the chills, sweeping over me from the tips of my toes, through all my insides, to the top of my head.... Then chills seized me again, worse than the first time, and threw my body into convulsions. Still shivering from chills, a wave of fever swept over me and engulfed me. And my head pounded like a hammer, pounded and pounded away incessantly. I felt as if my face were on fire, as if my eyes were growing out of their sockets; my tongue clung to my palate and was so dry, so parched.... For a moment it seemed to me as if I were in a boat, being cruelly tossed to and fro.... Fever and chills attacked me alternately, and sometimes together; and I did not know which was the harder to bear."

The malaria epidemic began claiming lives. There was hardly a house where someone had not died; and sometimes the disease wiped out entire families....

"We were forlorn. Pale, with knees shaking, we walked around, the sign of death on our foreheads, and fear and trembling in our hearts. Friends, relatives, and acquaintances came from all the colonies, bringing us their counsel and prayer: leave the place, save your lives, save the reputation of the *yishuv*... lest word get out to the Diaspora, and wrath descend on the entire country – a land which kills off its inhabitants! But not a soul left the place. Are we to flee from the battlefield? Shall we leave Ḥadera, this Ḥadera of ours, to be desolate and uninhabited as it was before? Some people even said: Better we should die in Ḥadera than live outside it!"

ḥadera forest

To the settlers of Ḥadera the eucalyptus tree seemed a marvelous salvation: "This tree has the splendid characteristic of drying up swamps, thus it brings health to those places where malaria reigns. This property is a factor of the tree's rapid growth: a tree only six years old may be as much as twenty meters high and one meter in circumference. Hence it draws up the moisture from the soil and dries it out. Moreover, since the tree is noted for its straight and tall trunk, it can provide the country with the timber for construction and wood for making tools, so lacking in the land" (Israel Belkind, *Ereẓ Yisrael Shel Zemanenu* [The Contemporary Land of Israel], 1899; Hebrew, 1928).

Upon Dr. Joffe's suggestion, in the summer of 1895 the general assembly of Ḥadera's settlers decided to write to Baron Rothschild as follows: "Our entreaty is laid before his right honorable lordship, the most generous baron, requesting that he have pity on us and our children and that he take our swampland; and that he order to have it cleaned, to remove from us the flaming sword which turns every way, the sword of death always hovering before our eyes. The swampland we hereby give to his honor, in full and absolute possession, for all time, to him and his descendants..." (Ever-Hadani, *Ḥadera*).

As soon as the "well-known philanthropist" gave his consent, and the bill of sale was duly signed by all the landowners (including some *Ḥovevei Zion* from Russia, for whom land had been purchased prior to their departure from Russia), the work of drying the swamps began. In the summer of 1896 imported Egyptian laborers dug the first canal – 700 meters long – and gradually the land began to dry out. The hardest work of all was planting the eucalyptus trees: "Bare to the waist, we stood in the swamp, took a seedling out of its pot, placed it between the second and third toe of the right foot, shoved the seedling into the loose soil, about half a meter or more into the water, and there we fastened it tight with our feet.... Naked and barefoot, we were covered with mud all day long, in a thicket of bushes and reeds. The sun warmed the swamp, raising a malodorous vapor, making the head spin till you felt like fainting; and swarms of various genera of mosquitoes, malaria-carrying mosquitoes, always with us, following us step by step, with no escaping them. Sometimes you raised a leg out of the swamp to take a seedling from the hand of a friend walking behind you with a basket of seedlings, and you lost your balance on the slippery soil or were tripped up by one of the roots, and you fell headlong

1

1 Yehoshua' Ḥankin with Arab notables on the land of Yoqne'am. Through his agricultural work Ḥankin forged friendships with Arab peasants and landowners and learned their language, etiquette, customs, and manner of speech. Later the knowledge he acquired served him in his negotiations to purchase land from them throughout the Land of Israel.

2 Yehoshua' Ḥankin on top of Mount Gilboa', the land he purchased in the Jezreel valley in 1920 spreading out behind him. He was buried in the foothills of this mountain, near the Ḥarod Spring.

ḥankin – redeemer of the land

Several figures stand out in the history of Jewish settlement of the Land of Israel in the modern era, having become legends in their own lifetime. One of these figures is Yehoshua' Ḥankin, a man of vision with a great dream and iron determination guiding his endeavors.

Yehoshua' Ḥankin was born in 1864 in the town of Kremenchug, in the Ukraine. His father, Yehudah Leib, and his mother, Sara, owned a farm there and worked in agriculture. In the wake of the pogroms in southern Russia in 1881-1882 they immigrated to the Land of Israel. Yehudah Leib was among the ten founders of Rishon le-Ẓiyyon. His son, Yehoshua', worked devotedly on the farm, helping defend the moshavah *against attack. Due to the uprising against Baron Rothschild's administrative staff, however, the Ḥankin family was forced to sell their land, home and farm and in 1887 moved to the* Bilu *colony of Gedera. Here Yehoshua' wed Olga Belkind, from one of the first families of* Bilu *pioneers. Her strong personality played a major role in her husband's undertaking of land redemption and national rebirth.*

In those days arbitrariness and chance ruled the land, and life was to a large extent dependent on the will of the rulers, whose primary criteria guiding their actions was the benefit that they themselves and those near them would receive. The central government took no interest in the good of the country or its inhabitants and was not willing to work to develop it or rebuild it from ruin. The land, ravaged by wars and plundered and destroyed by nomadic tribes, remained desolate. Foreign nationals were forbidden to purchase land in the country. Forming a company whose aim was to purchase land was also forbidden, and all transactions were made clandestinely. Thus over the years real estate holdings became concentrated in the hands of a small group of wealthy people, while most of the country's inhabitants suffered from abject poverty and poor health. Under such conditions only individuals with vision, with undaunted spirit and with steadfast determination could accomplish something.

Through his work in agriculture Yehoshua' Ḥankin established friendly relations with Arab peasants and landowners and learned their language, etiquette, customs, and manner of speech. In addition, he had personal charm which swayed these acquaintances of his and was unusually well-versed in all that concerned real estate laws and arrangements enabling land purchase. He began putting these talents to use in purchasing land.

Ḥankin, a remarkable negotiator, was not a profit-mongering merchant but a man of vision. For him redeeming the Land of Israel meant working for the general interest of the Jewish people, buying land to broaden the scope of Zionist settlement and thus making it possible for greater numbers of Jews, fleeing anti-Semitism and persecution in Europe, to immigrate and find a home in the Land of Israel.

"Along the road, between the moshavot *Nes Ẓiyyona and 'Ekron, is a tract of close to two and a half thousand acres of land lying desolate and abandoned. The land once belonged to one of the effendis in Jaffa and was called Tel Kh. Doran. In ancient times there was a settlement here by the name of Doran, destroyed when most of the country fell into ruin. It has no water, no trees, no houses on it. The land lay desolate for very many years, no one knew who owned it, no one tilled it or sowed it, and no one paid property taxes on it to the Turkish government. In 1873 the land was put up for auction to collect the taxes owed on it, and a Christian Arab effendi from Jaffa, one Butrus Roq, bought it for a song.... He paid up the taxes on the land and waited for an opportune moment to sell the land to the Jews, who were beginning to purchase land in the country at the time..." (Yehoshua' Ḥankin; Moshe Smilansky, Jerusalem 1946).*

2

Audaciously Ḥankin purchased the area of Doran even though he did not yet have the purchase price in his hands: "His friends discouraged him, saying he would not find a buyer for the land and would lose the down payment he had invested in it; but he had faith in the Jewish people... and indeed a company called Menuḥah ve-Naḥalah *(Resting Place and Inheritance) bought the land and founded the* moshavah *of Reḥovot" (Smilansky).*

In his lifetime Ḥankin bought back into Jewish hands over 150,000 acres of land. His most important purchases were the land that later became Reḥovot (1890), Ḥadera (1891), and most of the Jezreel Valley. In 1910 he purchased 2.5 thousand acres in the heart of the valley – now Merḥavya, and in 1920 he realized his dream of acquiring a large and continuous tract of land by purchasing 17.5 thousand acres in the eastern part of the valley (Gush Nuris – 'En Ḥarod) and the western part (land of Nahalal and Ginnegar). These purchases won him the name "Redeemer of the Jezreel Valley."

Ḥankin acted on behalf of Zionist organizations and private investors. Often his vision, enthusiasm and enterprise exceeded the financial capabilities of the Zionist community, but his personality, expertise, and ardent faith stood by him, keeping him from surrendering, from becoming a slave to harsh realities.

The farm of Ḥefẓi-Bah was established in 1905 on the sandy land northwest of Ḥadera and became a success story of making desolate land blossom. Neta'im Association, a shareholder company whose core consisted of settlers from the new yishuv, *joined by hundreds of shareholders who were Diaspora Jews, bought the land from Yehoshua' Ḥankin to develop it into a plantation center that would provide agricultural work for Jewish farm-hands. The members of the association who lived in the Diaspora were to immigrate later to the Land of Israel and earn their living from the fruit plantations prepared for them by workers of the Association through the efforts of pioneers from the Second Aliyah.*
Olga Ḥankin, who loved the Land of Israel and was well-versed in the Bible, proposed the name of the settlement, drawing on chapter 62, verse 4 of Isaiah: "Thou shalt no more be termed Forsaken, neither shall thy land any more be termed Desolate; but thou shalt be called, My delight is in her [Ḥefẓi-Bah]. *" This name for Olga symbolized the redemption of the desolate and forsaken land by modern Returners to Zion.*

into the water of the swamp.... By evening you returned home, weary and exhausted, and suddenly a bitter chill passed over your body, shaking and tossing it, and then a hot wave passed over every limb and organ of your body. A frightful slumber descended over you, nightmares plaguing you all night, then in the morning – out to work again!" (Joseph Weitz, *Ha-Ya'ar be-Ereẓ Yisrael* [The Forest in the Land of Israel], 1929).

"tower and stockade" in ḥadera

The plague of malaria was not quickly vanquished and continued to claim many victims; and, there being no alternative, Ḥadera was abandoned temporarily every summer. Towards summer's end, 1898, Dr. Hillel Joffe advised that all the residents of Ḥadera move to the seashore "where the foulness of the swamps will not reach."

The "exiles" of the *moshavah* assembled in Jaffa, "in the dark room of a poor Jewish inn. The room was bleak, and so were

1

the residents of Ḥadera, gathered for the first time on strangers' land, far from their cherished *moshavah* – a community of men going to the gallows, the mark of death on their foreheads and in their hearts. This meeting of mourners decided unanimously: the people of Ḥadera will not leave their *moshavah* and will not settle on someone else's land. And if it be decreed on them from on high that they must depart from their *moshavah* until the work of drying the swamps is completed, they shall pitch their tents on the borders of their land, on the hills along the seashore, where the malaria will not reach them."

Using the argument that they had to "watch over distant fields," the settlers obtained a temporary permit from the Turks to build thirty small wooden huts near the sea. Fearing lest evil befall them – primarily on account of the opposition of the bedouins who lived in the area – this project was executed using a technique similar to that which many years later became known as "tower and stockade." The walls of the huts were built clandestinely in Jaffa and, when German Kaiser Wilhelm II was visiting the country and all eyes were focused on this festive event, were brought by boat to the Ḥadera coast, in the dark of night. Within another day and night all the huts were standing, covered with tile roofs.

The new quarter, Qadima ("onwards," also known as Ḥadera *Bet*), proved a disappointment as well. The malarial mosquitoes came here in droves, and the disease continued claiming lives. The people of Ḥadera remained in Qadima an entire year, and when they returned to their *moshavah,* the huts continued to stand on the shore until they were destroyed by the bedouins. The former site of Qadima is now Giv'at Olga, the largest of Ḥadera's suburbs, named after the wife of Yehoshua' Ḥankin, "redeemer of the lands."

everlasting fire on the altar of ḥadera

"On November 12, 1899, another general meeting was convened, at which it was decided to leave the *moshavah* until the drying of the swamps was completed and to lease land elsewhere in the country, where all the families would be transferred and would continue farming on a temporary basis.... The resolutions were adopted, but the carts stayed put. Getting up and leaving the *moshavah* in public was beyond them, for no one in Ḥadera could find the courage in his heart to do so.... The everlasting fire on the altar of Ḥadera did not die out, and lives continued to be sacrificed."

In Ḥadera's first twenty years 214 of the settlement's 540 residents died of malaria. In 1911, twenty years after the founding of the *moshavah,* malaria still took a high toll. In Zikhron Ya'akov, too, where Dr. Joffe's hospital was located, new graves were dug for malaria victims. A special plot had to be added to the old cemetery of Jaffa – "which, during the war, was leveled by the Turks and made into a road for travelers and carts to pass."

Among those who died of malaria that year were Mendel Wasilinsky, one of the first three people to stake a claim in the soil of Ḥadera; Esther, granddaughter of R. Joel Lubin (who suffered the same fate); and Israel Feinberg, known as "Lolik."

From the beginning of his career in the Land of Israel, in Rishon le-Ẓiyyon, Lolik defended the tender young *moshavah* against the bedouins bravely and heroically.... When Rothschild's stewards banished him from Rishon, he went to Gedera with its first settlers. There he was often set upon by the local population, but he gave as good as he got and became known as a formidable adversary.... He, too, settled in Ḥadera among its founders.... There he was feared but highly respected by the neighboring population: "Whatever Abu-Salim ("father of Avshalom") says, so it shall be!" He was one of the first to plant orchards far from the *moshavah,* near Birkat 'Ata (the Forest Pool). For many years Feinberg headed the *moshavah* council, worked, fought, defended, and won; but in the end he succumbed.... At the age of forty-eight he surrendered his life, still full of youth and fervor...."

When the First World War broke out, the finest sons of the farmers in the *moshavah* belonged to the *Nili* underground ring, assisting the British by transmitting information and engaging in espionage against the Turks and their German allies, then in the country. As the British forces began advancing through northern Sinai towards the Land of Israel, Avshalom Feinberg and Yosef Lishansky set out southwards, dressed as bedouins, and headed for the British lines. Avshalom was murdered by bedouins near Rafiaḥ, and for many years his resting place remained unknown; his comrade escaped, wounded. On the main road of the southern outskirts of the *moshavah,* at the edge of the Feinberg orchard, opposite the Forest Pool, his sister erected a monument in his memory: Yad Avshalom of Ḥadera.

Avshalom's burial place was discovered only after the Six Day War; a palm tree was found growing out of his grave. His bones were transferred in a state ceremony to the military cemetery on Mt. Herzl in Jerusalem. The crossroads near where he fell, which the IDF fought over in three wars (the War of Independence, the Sinai Campaign, and the Six Day War), was named Avshalom Junction in his memory.

the eucalyptus trees saved ḥadera

In 1917, when the front line reached the southern Sharon region, the eucalyptus groves, planted in Ḥadera with great effort and sacrifice by its settlers, faced total devastation at the hands of the Turkish army which needed large quantities of wood to fuel its steam engines, to lay railroad tracks, and to put up telegraph poles. Ḥadera Forest was very fortunate; for Shimon Rokach, manager of the citrus growers association, received the concession for supplying the Turks with wood and coal. The Turks permitted him to hire laborers and carts and to issue his workers certificates exempting them from other military service. In 1918, when the Germans demanded that the quantity of wood be increased, soldiers were sent to work in the forest, as well. In spite of all this, Rokach succeeded in saving the trees by insisting that the trunks be cut down with saws and not felled with axes; thus the trees could renew their growth, and the forest once more rose to its former height.

To this day it is debated whether or not the swamps of Ḥadera would have dried out were it not for the eucalyptus trees which were planted there. Be that as it may, Ḥadera's forest saved the town in another way: the laborers who worked cutting down the trees were exempt from the Turkish draft and were not taken for forced labor. Thus they were spared the terrible conditions of service and perhaps even danger of death in the war. Moreover, in after-work hours the residents of Ḥadera could continue working their farms and thus protect their property. These very years were actually years of economic flourishing for the *moshavah,* and Pardess, the citrus growers association, earned a considerable profit for its members.

2

herzl's visit to the land of israel

Benjamin Gevirtzman

A festive atmosphere prevailed in the Land of Israel in the second half of 1898: Kaiser Wilhelm II, ruler of Germany and ally of the Turkish sultan, announced his intention to pay a visit to the Holy Land.

Since it is not every day that guests of such rank come to Turkish provinces – even the Land of Israel – preparations for receiving Wilhelm II began immediately. In Jerusalem the activity was particularly noticeable: piles of trash which had accumulated along the streets for years were now cleared; the walls of the houses lining the narrow roads were painted; thousands of lanterns were installed to light the streets at night; the approaches to the city gates were plastered white, and a new gate was cut into the wall to enable the Kaiser to enter the city in his carriage.

The festive atmosphere was doubled in Jerusalem's Jewish community as they anticipated the arrival of the new national leader: Theodor Herzl, of whom it was said that the majesty of King Solomon lay on his face and who was to meet with the Kaiser here.

Both the Kaiser and Herzl came to the Land of Israel as pilgrims to the holy places. For the Kaiser this was the high point of his long-range political activity, aimed at expanding German influence in the Near East. Herzl, who sought to integrate the Zionist movement into this German policy, found it a fitting opportunity for presenting himself to the Kaiser and persuading him to spread his wings over the movement.

In the middle of the latter half of the previous century Germany did not yet have any interests in the Near East. Bismarck, the Iron Chancellor who united Germany, was anxious to improve relations with Russia – at the time Turkey's enemy – and therefore did all he could to preserve neutrality with Turkey. For a while he even weighed the possibility of Germany supporting a Russian conquest of Turkey in exchange for cooperation between Moscow and Berlin.

But in 1888, with Wilhelm II's accession to the throne, all this changed. Wilhelm II was an ambitious ruler who sought German colonial expansion and wished to extend German political and economic influence throughout the world, including the Near East. He saw Turkey as a good economic outlet and a promising market for Germany's expanding industry, imprisoned, as it were, in central Europe. Thus the new German policy called for doing everything to strengthen Turkey and to assure that her independence not be threatened. The Kaiser took the first step by the second year of his rule: in November 1889 he paid a state visit to Constantinople, where he laid the foundations for enlarging the scope of Germany's economic and military activity in the Ottoman Empire.

money in exchange for a charter

In the wake of this visit the German rallying cry, *"Drang nach Osten"* (drive to the East), was coined. German assistance to the Turkish army, begun earlier, was now greatly expanded. German merchants began to appear in Turkey, and the German embassy in Constantinople, along with the consulates which had been opened in various cities of the Near East, launched a campaign of unprecedented commercial activity.

Even when world public opinion was incensed by the Turkish slaughter of the Armenians in 1894-1896, the German Kaiser did not hesitate to give the sultan political backing in order to further strengthen relations between the two states and to expand German influence in the Near East. When it appeared that his program was indeed coming to fruition, Wilhelm II set out on a round of visits to Constantinople, Jerusalem and Damascus.

Among the subjects dealt with by Kaiser Wilhelm was his attitude towards the Jews. Far from being a Judophile, he

1

1 *The boulevard of palm trees lining the entrance to Mikveh Israel. Here Herzl awaited the retinue of Kaiser Wilhelm II and his entourage, on their way from Jaffa to Jerusalem, in 1898.*

2 *The place where Herzl met with Kaiser Wilhelm II, today the courtyard of the ORT School on Ha-Nevi'im Street in Jerusalem. Here the Kaiser's magnificent royal tent was pitched.*

3 *The Jerusalem train station looks the same today as it did in Herzl's time, the main building remaining as it was under the Turks.*

2

3

wished, in fact, to see the Jews leave his country. When the First Zionist Congress was held in Basel in 1897, the Kaiser instructed the German ambassador to Switzerland to be present and to give a detailed report on the meetings. The Kaiser read the report closely and wrote in the margin: "I am in favor of the Jews going to the Land of Israel, and the faster they go there, the better. I shall not put any obstacles in their way."

Herzl was then working on the first stage of his program to obtain permission from the Turkish sultan for Jewish settlement of the Land of Israel. This program called for the Jewish people to return to its land, not through small scale, unplanned settlement – as the early *moshavot* or "colonies" had done – but according to a properly drafted program which would bring about the absorption of mass immigration in an orderly, structured manner. This, however, necessitated first receiving a charter from the Turkish government. Therefore, from the outset Zionist activity had to be aimed at obtaining this charter.

Herzl planned to propose that the Turks give the charter; but, knowing that they would not agree without receiving some *quid pro quo,* he was prepared to promise the Turks that in exchange the Jewish people would take upon itself to pay up Turkey's enormous debt.

In June 1896 Herzl went to Constantinople himself, hoping to have an audience with the sultan and to present his program to him. The meeting never came to pass, and the Turkish government officials with whom he did meet recoiled at his suggestion. They were well aware that massive immigration of Jews to the Land of Israel would in the end lead to the establishment of a Jewish state and the loss of the territory to the Ottoman Empire.

Herzl left Constantinople empty handed, but he did not abandon hope and, being a superb diplomat, began looking for a circuitous route to the sultan's heart. In view of the improved relations between Germany and Turkey, Herzl decided to work through the Kaiser. He was even prepared to suggest to the Kaiser that Germany spread its wings over the Zionist endeavor by granting it a protectorate, and that in return the German- (or Yiddish) speaking Jews would increase German cultural influence in the Near East.

According to various evidence, Herzl had some initial success in gaining the Kaiser's enthusiasm for his plans. Wilhelm's minister of foreign affairs, von Bülow, writes in his memoirs that the Kaiser was glad to have the opportunity "of getting rid of undesirable elements" in his country. Also, Wilhelm sent a letter to the Duke of Baden in which he expressed his opinion that Jewish settlement of the Land of Israel was likely to strengthen Turkey economically, and since that was in Germany's interest, the idea should be supported. The Kaiser did, however, add the anti-Semitic remark that Jewish settlement in the Land of Israel would create a base to bolster Jewish international capital, but that if this was the price that had to be paid for the Jews to cast their eyes towards Germany, it was well worthwhile.

In the wake of these events the Kaiser agreed to meet with Herzl in Constantinople during Wilhelm's visit there. The meeting took place on October 18, 1898, and was held in a very

1

cordial atmosphere. Herzl sketched the basic outline of his program, and the conversation turned to the Jewish question in general, to the Dreyfus trial, and to German influence once the question of the Jews was solved and Europe was freed from anti-Semitism.

There can be no doubt that Herzl's words, his polished appearance, and his Viennese-German manners made a deep impression on Wilhelm. Be that as it may, at the end of the conversation he asked Herzl: "Tell me one more thing: what must I ask of the sultan?" "A chartered company under German auspices," Herzl responded.

Everything seemed to be going fine. Behind the scenes, however, other powerful forces were coming into play against German support of Herzl's program. Leading the opposition was the German foreign office. Among the grounds for their opposition was the report of the German consulate in Jerusalem, which asserted that the Zionist aspiration of gathering all the Jews together in the Land of Israel was a utopia which had no chance of realization since most of the Jews in the country were themselves opposed to Zionism. It pointed out that Turkey perceived Zionism as a political threat and hence was opposed to immigration and purchase of land by Zionists. The report recommended that Zionism not be supported.

The German foreign office, influenced by this report, feared political complications in Constantinople on account of the Jews. Therefore they did all in their power not to provoke the Turks and tried to persuade the Kaiser not to support Herzl's

1 *The bell of the Jerusalem train station, which announced the trains' departure.*

2 *The Zionist delegation to Kaiser Wilhelm II, with the Stern family, in whose house (on the left), Herzl stayed during his visit to Jerusalem in 1898.*

3 *The Stern house on Mamilla Street.*

4 *The Zionist delegation to the German Kaiser upon its return from the Land of Israel. From right to left: David Wolffsohn, Theodor Herzl, Moritz Schnirer, and Max Bodenheimer.*

2

4

3

program. Foreign Minister von Bülow himself used his enormous influence on the Kaiser to dissuade him from supporting Zionism. Nevertheless the Kaiser brought up the subject in his meeting with the sultan, but 'Abd el-Ḥamid's reaction was so negative that the Kaiser was taken aback and never again brought up the matter with the Turks.

Herzl, of course, knew nothing of all this. Full of hope, he set out for the Land of Israel, where he was to have another audience with the Kaiser in order to receive his final response, as had been agreed at their meeting in Constantinople.

herzl the "king" and "messiah"

Herzl arrived in Jaffa by boat. He and his entourage took advantage of the time until the Kaiser's scheduled arrival to visit the Jewish colonies around Jaffa. They were received with great honor in Mikveh Israel and in Rishon le-Ẓiyyon, where they spent the night. The next day they continued to Nes Ẓiyyona, where the entire colony came out to greet him with cheers and the symbolic offering of bread, salt and wine.

Herzl and his party continued on to Reḥovot, where sixteen members of the colony greeted him on horseback, crying: "Hurray, long live Herzl!"

Legend has it that, of the small Jewish community living in Ramla at the time, two men came to Reḥovot to greet the "King of Jews." They approached Herzl, bowed down before him, and kissed his footsteps in the sand. The European Herzl drew back in alarm, at which one of them explained to him that "Thus shall be done to the Messiah son of Joseph ... as a magic charm to assure that the coming of the Messiah son of David not be delayed..."

Herzl spent an entire day in Reḥovot, visiting the homes of the residents and looking at their farms, before returning to Jaffa.

Knowing that the next day the Kaiser was to pass Mikveh Israel en route to Jerusalem, Herzl and his company awaited him on the road. Turkish horsemen led the Kaiser's retinue. As he rode behind them, the Kaiser recognized Herzl in the distance and drew up beside him, holding up the entire procession. He extended his hand to Herzl, and the following exchange took place between them:

Kaiser: "How do you fare?"
Herzl: "Very well, thank you, Your Majesty. I have been touring around the country. And how has Your Highness's trip been thus far?" Kaiser: "Very warm. Perhaps there is a future for this land; but for the moment it is still very ill. It needs water, very much water."
Herzl: "Yes, Your Majesty. Large scale irrigation is needed."
Kaiser: "This is a land with a future."

1 *German Kaiser Wilhelm II informed Herzl he was willing to give him an audience in Jerusalem during his upcoming visit to the Land of Israel and that he was prepared to recommend the Zionist movement to the sultan and take the Settlement Association for Syria and the Land of Israel, to be founded by Herzl, under his patronage. Herzl made a journey to the Land of Israel in order to meet the Kaiser. He was received enthusiastically by the residents of the Jewish* moshavot *(colonies), Rishon le-Ẓiyyon, Nes Ẓiyyona, 'Ekron, Reḥovot, and Moẓa (Judean* moshavot*).*

2 *During his visit he wore the characteristic garb in fashion among travelers in the Near East at the time.*

1

binyamin ze'ev herzl

Herzl, the father of political Zionism, raised the Jewish question to the level of an international political issue.

Herzl, born in Budapest in 1860, grew up in an assimilated family and was not deeply attached to the Jewish people or its culture. The Dreyfus Affair and anti-Semitism in France awakened Jewish nationalist sentiments in Herzl and brought him to the conclusion that the solution to the Jewish question lay in the mass exodus of the Jews from areas affected by anti-Semitism and their resettlement in a territory of their own.

Herzl convened the first Zionist congress as a national assembly of the Jewish people wishing rebirth. He founded the World Zionist Organization as the political body of the "Jewish people in the making." From 1897 to 1902 Herzl convened six congresses, in which the apparatus for Zionist activity was set up: a national bank, movement newspaper, the Jewish National Fund (land purchasing and development fund of the Zionist Organization), and other bodies.

The aim of Zionism was to establish a homeland for the Jewish people in the Land of Israel.

2

The Kaiser shook hands with Herzl once more, and the procession continued along its way.

These remarks of the Kaiser's do not give the slightest inkling of what had gone on behind the scenes after his meeting with Herzl in Constantinople. Herzl, at least, was certain that they actually hinted at a favorable stand on the question of a charter. He therefore hurried to the train to Jerusalem for his promised interview with the Kaiser, where he hoped to receive the final response to his proposal.

It was a Friday, and the train arrived late in the day. Herzl won the hearts of the Jews by continuing on foot from the train station to the Stern house, where he stayed, in order not to desecrate the Sabbath.

Herzl traveled in and around Jerusalem while awaiting his invitation for an interview with the Kaiser. He was shocked at the filth and refuse filling the streets of the Old City. His thoughts about building a new, clean city on the surrounding hills later found expression in his book, *Altneuland.*

Throughout his visit the authorities had Herzl followed by a Jewish-Turkish detective, for fear that he might try to undermine the government....

At long last Herzl received the invitation to the promised interview. It was held on November 2, 1898, in the Kaiser's magnificent pavilion, set up on the site of the present ORT School on Ha-Nevi'im Street.

Contrary to all Herzl's expectations, the meeting with the Kaiser was extremely cold. Herzl had but to hear that "the matter requires examination," when he suddenly realized that all his efforts with the Kaiser had come to nought.

Despite his disappointment, Herzl went to visit Moẓa, a settlement close to Jerusalem. There, on the land of a farmer called Broza, he planted a tree commemorating his visit to Jerusalem. Perhaps this has a symbolic significance and is in keeping with what became of his expectations of his meeting with the Kaiser in the Holy City; for, several years later, the tree he planted was chopped down by the Arabs....

The next day Herzl and his entourage left the country, deeply disappointed.

deganya – a new endeavor
pioneers in the jordan valley

Muki Tzur

There is something deceptively magical about the colorful idyll of the Jordan Valley. A picture of the valley taken at the turn of the century reveals how misleading the idyllic image is; for this lush valley was then a desert with a lake at its heart. The Jordan River, now winding unseen beneath heavy vegetation, then meandered in full view; in place of today's valley of palm and eucalyptus, of homes, fish-ponds, and banana plantations, was desert, a few adobe huts and bedouin tents, a khan atop the hill, and a small train station across the Jordan River. A small German motorboat ferried passengers from Tiberias to the train station at Ẓemaḥ, and now and then a caravan of camels crossed the Jordan. There was no bridge, and the river was forded on foot or donkey.

The colorful, idyllic landscape of the Sea of Galilee today embodies not an idyll but a drama. Gazing down on the valley from above, one sees well-established settlements, full of greenery and shade; white concrete houses, sometimes with red tile roofs; grand avenues of trees – security, stability. But behind this lies a saga of human endeavor, of man struggling with himself and with his society. This is the birthplace of the *kibbutz,* today a movement of close to 240 settlements, approximately 130,000 people (slightly more than 3% of Israel's total population) spread throughout the State of Israel.

In 1908, however, when a small group of workers came to the shores of the Kinneret (Sea of Galilee), a vigorous debate took place about whether it was at all possible for Jews to return to the soil, to be laborers. The attempt was made with the establishment of Ḥavat Kinneret, a workers' farm, whose role was to teach men and women to work the soil. These Jews who wished to become workers came to the Land of Israel from 1904 to 1914 as part of the Second Aliyah, a wave of immigration which came in the wake of the Kishinev pogroms*, during the First Russian Revolution and following subsequent pogroms. This was a time of great awakening, of youths determined to attempt a new way of life. Most of the Jews who sensed the change, the spiritual awakening of Russian society, and, at the same time, its anti-Semitism, either turned towards revolutionary activity in Russia or emigrated to the United States. But a handful turned to Zionism in search of a solution, endeavoring to build a society with new values in the Land of Israel.

These young laborers in the Land of Israel dreamed of cooperation stemming from freedom, of a life of working and creating which would reflect their belief in the equality of man. Reality, however, was quite different. Lack of work forced them to wander from place to place, or to return to their homes in Europe. Their relatives worked and dreamed in New York's East Side; in the Land of Israel they wondered if they could succeed at all. One of them described their condition thus: "We had the heart of a dove, and the wings of an eagle."

Deganya, the first *kibbutz,* was not the first experiment in collective living. There had been cooperative dining halls, and other groups, some of which undertook to work together in the orchards for a season. Here and there groups of six or seven workers lived together in communes. A neighborhood for laborers was built near Petaḥ Tikva and was called by its founders the "First Socialist Republic." An order of guards who lived collectively was founded on a country-wide scale. But these cooperative endeavors did not constitute a *kibbutz* or *kevutzah.*

How was Deganya, the first *kevutzah,* different from all the earlier cooperative endeavors? The first workers who had tried to band together assumed that their organizations were essentially temporary, since a hired hand must move on from place to place. A permanent home, a field, an orchard, a plow, would change a proletarian laborer into a farmer, a home-owner. It was the combination of the idea of a commune with that of settlement, Zionist settlement of the land, that made Deganya into a *kevutzah.*

This was not the first time Jews settled in the Land of Israel. Generation upon generation of Jews had come to the Land of Israel and settled there, but all the colonization efforts which preceded Zionism had one or another religious tone and were clearly marked by a philanthropic tenor. During the Second Aliyah, with the beginning of the Zionist Organization's

* Massacres of Jews, which took place in Kishinev, in southern Russia, in 1903 and 1905. Ḥayyim Naḥman Bialik's "City of Slaughter" was written in reaction to these pogroms.

1 *The "courtyard of Deganya" in the twenties, with a dovecote in the center and a stable on the left. Hay for the cows was stored in the loft above the barn (right).*

attempts to populate the land, settlement was examined in socio-political terms, in terms of explicitly desiring to improve the life of the Jewish people, in terms of seeking responsibility for solving the problem of the entire Jewish nation.

The Zionist Organization began purchasing land in 1905. In 1908 it established two farms for training workers, one at Ben Shemen, near the present-day Ben-Gurion Airport, and the second at Kinneret. Both reflected the necessity of training people for work. A fateful change, however, took place beginning in 1911, with the founding of Deganya. A commune already existed on the land of Deganya, but in 1911 a new commune came to settle there and construction of permanent homes began. At the time Deganya's members lived in Umm Juna, south of present-day Deganya, in several adobe huts and a shack which had been brought from Haifa. In contrast to the transient character of the structures in Umm Juna, the houses which were built on the banks of the Jordan River were solid basalt buildings. The members of the *kevutzah,* especially the younger ones, were afraid the revolutionary spirit would wither away if they moved into the houses. A stormy debate developed among the members. The romantic younger group, which wanted to continue working wherever they were needed, was headed by Shmuel Dayan (father of Moshe Dayan), and the group that wanted to settle down was led by the older members, Yosef Busel and Tanḥum Tanpilov. Busel maintained that true heroism does not lie in making radical changes but in being able to sustain them. Tanḥum Tanpilov added that young Jews knew how to begin revolutions; now they must learn what to do with them. It was decided to remain and move into the houses which were being built.

from commune to home

It was not easy to make the fateful decision to be steadfast to the commune and to transform it into a permanent home. Deganya had already experienced the failure of cooperative societies. Its members were wary of rigid ideologies. They wanted to act intuitively and ascribed great moment to the immediate apprehension of reality. Idealistic but not doctrinaire, they often said that their *kevutzah* must grow "out of the experiences of life."

All of Deganya's workers were young, unmarried men, except for one family which joined them only in order to assist the group in its first steps. The founders of Deganya had a long road to travel, working through ideological changes and various ways of expressing the spirit of community, freedom, and equality, and finally becoming, 80 years later, the *kibbutz* which it is today.

From the outset Deganya was influenced by A. D. Gordon, thinker, faithful leader, and laborer. Fearing he would be a burden as an elder among young comrades, Gordon refused to join the society. In his later years, however, when he fell ill, he did consent to become a member of Deganya. Until then he preferred moving from group to group, working for a short while with each, keeping in touch with all, and at night writing his philosophy. He believed in the simple life, in working the soil, in the self-taught individual, in the need to build a new way of life for the Jewish community, but one which would still be rooted in respect for the Jewish tradition.

Despite the fact that he himself was a wanderer and that his own family life was in many ways tragic (his son severed relations with him and his wife passed away a year after coming to the Land of Israel), he considered it his responsibility to see to it that the young workers formed families. He conversed with many of them and, according to the testimony of one of his friends, wrote at least fifty letters trying to dissuade them from voluntary abstinence, so likely in their circumstances. The workers, who had rebelled against their families and were influenced by revolutionary thought, grappled hard with this question. At Deganya, Shmuel Dayan proposed that no one marry for five years. His suggestion was accepted – but he was the first to break the resolution.

deganya – a new endeavor

1 *Deganya was built across the Jordan River before a bridge connected its banks. The river could only be forded in summer, when the water was shallow. In the background are Deganya's buildings at the end of its first decade.*

2 *"Here is my home, facing the Golan, regally encompassed by plantations and vineyards" – Yosef Netzer. The dream of Deganya's founders came true: a blossoming valley, dotted with* kevutzot *and* kibbutzim.

Gordon called on the *kevutzot* not to be seclusive, but to assume responsibility towards the public and other workers outside the *kevutzah*. He fought against idolizing one or another way of living. He called for an organic structure, from the individual through the family and on to the community and the entire nation.

These two demands of Gordon's, accepted by Deganya – assuming public responsibility and building a multi-generational society – embody two of Deganya's characteristics. The changes which took place in Deganya over the years are the result of its economic and demographic development and the product of its fundamental principles. From a commune of young bachelors it has evolved into a society where people have been living together, from infancy to old age, for four generations. Over the years it has taken in people from a variety of cultures. Tanḥum Tanpilov, one of Deganya's early leaders, stressed preparing for the future. As he planted trees for generations to come, he urged new members to adapt themselves to the pace of the life of the soil and the growing seasons. When a new worker arrived, full of enthusiasm on his first day of work, Tanḥum used to rest his hand on the young man's shoulder and say: "Work at such a pace that you will be able to keep on working for another forty years."

Yosef Busel was Deganya's leader. From its earliest days he knew that establishing a cooperative society entailed thinking about its values, the equal worth of man, each member's responsibility to the *kibbutz,* and the need to accept responsibility for all the workers. He received support but also encountered misunderstanding. The tension between reality and what he was demanding soon became apparent. He believed this tension was temporary, stemming from people educated in one society having to function in another society whose principles were not familiar to them. He thought that if the *kevutzah* were to raise a second and third generation, the tension would dissolve, as these generations lived the principles more as a matter of course. He believed that finally the *kevutzah* would emerge victorious, and the entire land would be filled with copies of Deganya. A rebel against traditional education, a man who adopted a life of labor, pioneering settlement and the collective, he was indeed a man of messianic fervor.

Communal life in Deganya's first years was constantly put to the test: clashes between men and women over the women's demand for greater involvement in the work and life of the community; difficulties in adjusting to physical labor; the need to build families within a communal setting. The hardships of the community's routine life, separated from the rest of society,

1

Malaria and an extremely hot climate made life in the Jordan Valley difficult. In addition, the first ten years were marked by developing a new society and finding a suitable economic base. After World War I Deganya was beset by economic and social crises: a large debt hung over the head of every settler; their leader, Busel, had drowned in the Sea of Galilee; some of Deganya's settlers had given up the collective life-style on kibbutz *and had left to found the first* moshav, *Nahalal. But the influx of newcomers in the Third Aliyah and the policy of the Zionist Organization saved Deganya as a* kibbutz *settlement. Deganya championed the idea of a small, intimate collective settlement – a* kevutzah *– whose members are tied together by economic relations and personal bonds.*

living for months at a time out in the fields in the scorching heat of the Jordan Valley which in the summer exceeds 108°F, meant that quite a few members left. However new people also came.

During the First World War Deganya faced many trials: exports ceased, there was a plague of locusts, the members feared being drafted into the Turkish army, and disease was prevalent. The economic infrastructure of the country was destroyed. Many people left the country or, as nationals of enemy states, were exiled from it. Toward the end of the war most of the Jewish residents of Jaffa and of Jewish settlements such as Tel Aviv and Petaḥ Tikva were banished from their homes and went north, some of them reaching the shores of the Sea of Galilee. The young *kevutzah* of Deganya, fighting for its survival, also had to extend a helping hand to the victims of hunger, disease, and unemployment. As thousands of Jews in the country were dying of hunger and disease, Busel and his comrades worked night and day to alleviate the terrible situation. After the war Busel himself was in such bad health that when his boat capsized in the Sea of Galilee, as he was sailing back to Deganya from a meeting in Tiberias, he had not the strength to save himself, and drowned.

1

1 *Geese, sheep, and a cow – the first livestock farm of the settlement at Umm Juna (1910). The first buildings of the* kevutzah *are in the background.*

2 *Deganya's pioneers in the courtyard of Umm Juna (1910). On the left is the first adobe hut, on the right, the shack where they lived.*

the split

When the war ended, Deganya faced another crisis. Several of its members came to the conclusion that it was not possible to raise a family within the communal setting, and that one must create a pattern of settlement based on independent family units. Several of Deganya's founders were among the first to establish the *moshav,* a form of settlement based on mutual aid and cooperative marketing, but in which each family in the settlement has a farm of its own, and as a result there are differences from one family to the next.

Retrospectively, Deganya's members thought that the split in their ranks occurred because the *kevutzah* had grown too large, that a small core group could have preserved the fundamental principles better. Irrigation of the Jordan Valley meant that the soil of Deganya was capable of supporting a larger number of settlers, but Deganya's members did not wish to enlarge their *kevutzah,* preferring to give up some of their land for another *kevutzah* to be formed. Thus Deganya *Bet* came into being, with the hope that a chain of Deganyas would one day encompass the entire country. A Deganya *Gimel* was also established in the Jordan Valley, but later moved to the Jezreel Valley and founded *kibbutz* Ginnegar.

The waves of immigrants who came to the country in the twenties formed new settings for cooperative living. Deganya served as an important model for them all and as a point of departure for their searchings. Some groups were more extreme than Deganya in the degree of communal life which they demanded. Communal education began to take shape, children's houses were built, members' private accounts were closed, and extreme communal practices regarding clothing were adopted, a member taking whatever clothing he required from the communal supply room. Deganya adopted some of these changes. While in most *kibbutzim* children slept in children's houses, Deganya's children slept in their parents' houses.

The *kibbutz* reached its fullest development in the thirties. Many groups of Jewish youth hoped to come to the Land of

2

Israel; Europe had become a dangerous trap for them. In *kibbutz* training centers in Europe they prepared themselves for building *kibbutzim* when they would be brought to the Land of Israel. However, even after arriving in the country they had to wait many years until they could be given land – but finally they established many settlements. Deganya's members assisted the immigrant members of the young *kibbutzim* and shared their special experience with them.

The Holocaust brought to an end the immigration of young people who dreamed of founding *kibbutzim.* The vast majority of them, some of whom were organizers of Jewish resistance, perished. After the Holocaust the *kibbutz* movement found itself without a pool of manpower in Europe and could draw only on Jewish youth living in the Land of Israel and those from western countries who shared the dream of the *kibbutz*.

With the establishment of the state, many new *kibbutzim* were founded, but they faced difficult problems. Deganya went through waves of crisis and growth. The family, which slowly became the extended family, actually proved to be an important factor in the growth of the *kevutzah.* Busel's prediction that the children of the *kibbutz* would accept its principles as a matter of course proved false. Every child raised on the *kibbutz* must decide whether or not he wants to continue living on the *kibbutz*.

Visitors to Deganya today will discover a large community, some 650 people. Industry has become the center of its economic activity. The community lives well, but the search for social configurations continues. The classic problem of a commune was put by a writer who visited Deganya and wrote an enthusiastic monograph on it. It is how to reach the balance, attained by Deganya, of "emotional closeness and a measure of personal distance." Deganya and every other *kibbutz* continues to face this problem, as well as the problem of maintaining a proper balance between the internal life of the community and involvement with the outside world.

Although the *kibbutz* is deeply rooted in the Israeli experience and is a "tourist and pilgrimage attraction," the dilemma of Deganya remains: is it possible to build a society which believes in the equality of man, and maintains mutual responsibility as an expression of this equality in everyday life? Is it possible to maintain a society in which work, art, and science are not the means for man to attain domination over his fellow, but rather are avenues of creative activity? Is it possible to maintain the delicate balance of human freedom, through the relations of one man to another, not as a political regime but as a mode of civilization? Can all these things exist through a bond with the roots of Jewish civilization and through universal horizons?

For the *kibbutz* of today these are not philosophical issues; they are the issues of life itself.

one's own labor and own responsibility

The principal factor deciding the group in favor of going to Umm Juna was the aspiration for one's own labor under self-imposed responsibility, without the authority or supervision of an outside body.

"Conquering work" in the existing moshavot *(early agricultural settlements) did not satisfy us. The structure of the farms in Judea, plantation farms totally dependent on foreign markets, we also found unsatisfactory. To have Jewish farm-hands instead of Arab farm-hands, to have Petaḥ Tikva and Rishon le-Ẓiyyon filled with Jewish hired labor instead of Arab hired labor, would be considered a great accomplishment; but no national revival or change in values would be achieved thereby. Even if the ignominy of our people could be reduced by work being done by Jews, this type of farm, entirely dependent on domestic or foreign market prices and existing only on hired labor, was incapable of bringing about individual redemption or national renaissance. Therefore we sought other forms of settlement – settlement founded on one's own labor and on an economic structure which could, first of all, answer the needs of the place itself.*

Yet how were we to realize this aspiration, and how could we assure our survival? We had but one answer to all these qualms: united force, the collective – that would succeed. The single individual was likely to succumb under the burden of the difficult life, especially in the conditions of the Land of Israel, but living together and working together would give us the strength to withstand the downhill slide. Mutual aid was the first and primary assumption, the root and foundation of work and success. In collective life we saw the way to create a just and congenial social order. We wished to see the kevutzot *as our family.*

Yosef Baratz, a founder of Deganya; from his book, *Village on the Banks of the Jordan* (Hebrew).

by the light of the blue glass lamp

When I first came to Deganya, I was amazed to see that Gordon, the elderly man and philosopher, who worked together with the younger settlers (which was not surprising), lived just like the other bachelors, together with another three comrades in a single room. Just like them, he kept all his personal belongings in a wicker basket under his cast-iron bed. He never requested any special privileges, and protested vehemently against any discrimination in his favor.

We, the young women, lived four in a room, directly across from the room Gordon shared with another three men. Sometimes, as we were going to bed, loud laughter would reach us from the men's room. On such evenings we knew that Gordon was relating one of the vast store of excellent folk tales which he told so skillfully at any opportunity.

Often, especially on cold winter nights, as the palm trees rustled outside the windows and large drops of rain hit the panes while we huddled in our warm blankets, at three o'clock in the morning in the hall separating the girls' room from the men's room, the kerosene lamp would be lit, and the sound of heavy boots would be heard plodding down the hall. At this cold, early hour Gordon used to rise and sit down to write. Once, at three a.m., while everyone was fast asleep, I stealthily opened the door a crack and peeked into the hall. I shall never forget the picture which met my eyes: a small, blue-glass kerosene lamp, covered with a green paper lantern, lit a table covered with green blotting paper. Gordon, leaning over a writing pad with sheet after sheet of closely written paper, sat deep in thought, his head propped on his right hand, which rested on the large table.... This is how he wrote all his essays. This elderly man used to rise early, with unbelievable energy, on cold nights as on hot nights. Then he could be alone, no other person with him, for they were all in the world of sleep. In this isolation, attained with difficulty, he created his spiritual work.

At dawn, dressed in workshirt and high boots, he used to go out to work with everyone else, his expression always easygoing and warm. There were jobs which he grew to like very much. He preferred working alone in the field and liked work which requires patience and perseverance, such as weeding. With hoe in hand he used to stand in the trench the whole day and carefully weed out couch-grass roots often a meter long, and gather them into an Arab basket. I also remember a small plot of land, not far from the farm buildings, which he himself made into a threshing floor. Like an ant, he carried sheaf after sheaf and piled them in a stack. Sometimes, however, there were jobs for which all the comrades were enlisted, such as clearing a neglected field, and then Gordon, of course, was no exception. He stepped in line with all the rest and again was the most lively, the most jovial of the gang, amusing the others with his stories. Frequently he used to express deep thoughts, talk about art and artists, about life....

Miriam Singer, from *Ha-Po'el ha-Ẓa'ir*

human beings are not herrings

One way or another, the main thing is people, not form. And the more one relies on form, the less one pays attention to the human aspect. Not only do I not require specially talented individuals for the kevutzah; *quite the contrary, I would like to see all sorts of common men off the street come into the* kevutzah *and there grow into decent, important individuals, and this is feasible.*

The general rule: if you wish a specific mold in the kevutzah, *do not view the mold as some sort of barrel in which you are pickled, in which each person rests on the next like herrings,*

1 *The hut which was the beginning of Deganya, the* kevutzah *founded on the land of Umm Juna, purchased by the Jewish National Fund in 1907.*

1

neatly arranged. Human beings are not herrings, and they are not to be arranged in a barrel in a fixed pattern. Human beings have motion, life, an entire world in them. Put life and the world into the form, or more correctly, make the form pervade all spheres of life, all worlds, and then the form shall exist as life and the world exist.

From a letter by A. D. Gordon to the members of Deganya, 1921.

the leader of deganya's founders

"The death of Yosef Busel, who drowned in the Sea of Galilee in 1918, was a severe blow to the kevutzah *[Deganya]. In the last five or six years of his life he not only devoted himself heart and soul to the business of the farm, but also was the spiritual leader of the* kevutzah. *He was blessed with outstanding qualities of leadership and a crystalline pure soul. It was he who laid the foundation for developing the extensive farm economy into an intensive farm economy. And by virtue of his purposefulness and his knowledgeability in the ways of agriculture, Deganya gained prestige and repute even in those circles which previously were disparaging of the value of the* kevutzah's *work."*

This paragraph, translated from Arthur Ruppin's autobiography, summarizes Busel's personality and his personal contribution to the pioneering endeavors of the Second Aliyah.

Yosef Busel was born in the town of Lakhovitza, Russia. He immigrated to the Land of Israel after receiving agricultural training on the PICA [Palestine Jewish Colonization Association] farm in the Ukraine, and joined the group of laborers who took upon themselves to farm Ḥavat Kinneret (1908).

Busel became the ideologue and leader of the kibbutz. *He formulated its principles of life: work and full sharing, full participation of women in the work, cooperative education of the children.*

His wife, Ḥayuta Busel, recounts how during the First World War Busel devoted himself to helping the Jews evicted from Tel Aviv-Jaffa. "He organized the farmers of the Galilee, and carts were sent to Tel Aviv and Jaffa to help the weak and poor move to Petaḥ Tikva."

Yosef Busel, debilitated by many years of malaria, drowned in the Sea of Galilee when the boat in which he was sailing from Tiberias to Deganya capsized in a storm.

Dan Giladi, from *Eretz Nosha'at be-'Amal Kapayim* (A Land Redeemed through Toil), Revivim Publishing House.

stand and defend – or abandon?

Mordechai Naor

The winter of 1919-1920 was hard and rainy throughout the country, especially in the Upper Galilee, then a remote and desolate region, not well served by roads, and lacking sufficient shelter in its few settlements. There was even heavy snow in the Galilee that year. However Monday morning, March 1, 1920, dawned bright and sunny, promising to be a pleasant winter day.

The expectations the clear dawn had aroused were not fulfilled, and the day belied the hope of its first few hours. A fierce battle raged in Tel Ḥai that day, known thereafter as Tel Ḥai Day. In the twenty-four hours of that day six of the defenders of Tel Ḥai, among them their commander Joseph Trumpeldor, fell.

What actually occurred in Tel Ḥai that fateful day, March 1, 1920?

the bone of contention

To answer this question we must explain, if only briefly, the background to the events which reached a head on that day. The beginning, September-October 1919, takes us back to the confrontation between England and France over who would control the northern part of the country in the period following World War I. These two powers wished to divide the countries of the region, which until the end of the war had been in Turkish hands, among themselves. They attempted to settle their quarrels through various agreements, such as the settlement, in September 1919, which set the border between the British mandate over Palestine and the French mandate over Syria (in those days including Lebanon, as well) along a line running from Rosh ha-Niqra eastward, passing north of Lake Huleh. As a result of this agreement the British withdrew their forces south and were replaced by the French in the area known today as the panhandle of the Galilee.

Actually the French did not succeed in establishing control over the area, whose Arab inhabitants were vehemently opposed to the change in authorities and to the French in general. French military forces sent to this region were only occasionally successful in their attempts to impose their authority. When, after each action in the area, they retreated to their main bases, these retreats were interpreted by the insurrectionist Arabs as great victories of their own.

What accounts for the French failure in this battle? It seems they should have won by virture of their military might. Was this struggle with the Arabs of the area connected with the story of Tel Ḥai? *Sefer Toledot ha-Haganah* (The History of the *Haganah*) offers the following answers:

"A. For many months the French command did not have sufficient infantry forces to take control of this unbridled area. At least such was the assessment of the command; and it is a fact that General Gouraud, French High Commissioner of Syria and Lebanon, threatened to resign if thirty thousand soldiers were not put at his disposal.

"B. Some of the soldiers were Moslems from Africa and felt a measure of attachment for their fellow Arabic-speaking Moslems who were revolting against French rule. The French officers were not overly trusting of the loyalty of the forces at their command and did not wish to put them to the test.

"C. It is not beyond the realm of possibility that, at times, this was an intentional tactic of the French authorities, designed to increase the lawlessness and anarchy in the area, so that when the time came they could use this as a convenient pretext for clamping down with an iron hand."

Caught up in this mess were four small Jewish settlements, each numbering no more than 20-30 people: Metulla, Kefar Gil'adi, Ḥamara and Tel Ḥai. These settlements were not in the least involved in the controversy between the French and the Arabs of the region (the Moslems, that is, for the Christian Arabs were considered allies of the French).

Nevertheless, through the winter, as the tension between the French and the Arabs and bedouins of the north mounted, the pioneers in these settlements often found themselves caught in the middle of the turmoil, with the Arabs more than once accusing them of being in league with the French. At the same

"Never mind. It is good to die for the sake of our country." These were Joseph Trumpeldor's last words. He continued commanding his men even after he was seriously wounded in battle. The decision to retreat to Kefar Gil'adi was not taken until nightfall, when munitions had run out. Trumpeldor expired on a stretcher, along the way....

1 *The courtyard of Tel Ḥai, facing the green and settled Ḥula Valley and snow-capped Mount Ḥermon.*

time there was a rise in the number of attacks on Jewish travelers and on the settlements themselves.

"make haste, else it will be too late"

The first alarms sounded in the beginning of the winter. On November 22, 1919, work-animals were stolen from Kefar Gil'adi, and three weeks later (December 12) Tel Ḥai was fired on, and one of the settlers – Shneur Shaposhnik – was killed.

The tragedy aroused the inhabitants of the area as well as outside forces. Supplies, arms and munitions were sent from the south, from the English area. People were sent to help, as well. However both the supplies and the number of people sent were insufficient, and only partially answered the demands of the northern settlements.

At the end of December 1919 the defenders of the Galilee were joined by a man of action, whose reputation had preceded him: Joseph Trumpeldor*, former officer in the Russian army, a war hero who had lost his left arm in the Russo-Japanese War, a pioneer at Migdal and Deganya, one of the founders of the Zion Mule Corps, which participated in the battle of Gallipoli in the First World War, and a commanding officer in this corps. His military experience, unusual personality, and reputation as a commander and human being made him the most outstanding figure in the defense of the region. In actual fact Trumpeldor was the commander of Tel Ḥai.

Over the next two months (January-February 1920) the situation deteriorated further. Because of attacks by local Arabs, Ḥamara was abandoned, thus reducing the number of Jewish settlements in the area from four to three. Four days later Trumpeldor wrote to the defense council in Tel Aviv, demanding aid, especially arms and food: **"We do not have enough armed men. We need one thousand bullets, at least five hundred for each rifle, yet we have only a hundred per rifle. We have no hand grenades at all, and no machine guns. Our food supplies are running out. Even our flour supply is low, and in a week we shall literally be starving."**

Reinforcements and supplies made their way north, but all too slowly. Meanwhile the French position in the region was weakening, and towards the end of January they pulled out their forces which had been encamped at Metulla. Several days later Metulla's handful of residents were evacuated to Tel Ḥai. On February 6 the members of Tel Ḥai were attacked while sowing the fields, and Aharon Sher, one of the men recently sent with the reinforcements to the Galilee, was killed in the fighting.

The situation worsened from day to day. Trumpeldor trained the men he had and at the same time continued demanding arms, supplies, and men from the south. The next few days brought extremely bad news: shooting on Jews, ambushes of carts and riders, and worst of all, a resolution adopted by the council of the Arab rebels to destroy the Jewish settlements in the Upper Galilee at the earliest opportunity. On February 8 Trumpeldor wrote in his diary: **"We can wait no longer for help. Make haste, else it will be too late."**

to stand fast – or to evacuate?

In the southern settlements, in Tel Aviv and Jerusalem, various committees and bodies were established to aid the Galilee,

* Trumpeldor came to the country in 1919 in order to prepare for the immigration of a large number of members of *He-ḥalutz*, a pioneer organization from Russia, some of whom were already assembled in Constantinople. Due to the tense situation in the north of the land he had come to the aid of the settlements there, all the while hoping that he would be able to free himself from his duties in the Galilee shortly and return to Constantinople in order to bring the members of *He-ḥalutz* to the Land of Israel.

1 *The courtyard of Tel Ḥai. It was customary to plan Jewish settlements in such a way as to have the residential and farm buildings flanking three sides of a yard, and a wall with a single gate in it closing in the fourth side (as in the courtyards of Kinneret and Ḥulda). To preserve the spirit of the era, the argricultural implements used then are displayed in the yard today.*

2 *Joseph Trumpeldor – a rare photograph from an old album* (Haganah *Archives).*

including even offices to enlist volunteers to go north. Yet action was slow, and the organs of the *yishuv* (pre-State Jewish community in the Land of Israel), who were called to discuss the matter, were divided over the question of whether a small number of remote points should be defended at any price, or whether they should be evacuated. As usual, they were also hampered by budgetary difficulties.

On February 23 the Temporary Council, the elected representatives of the Jews in the Land of Israel, convened to discuss the steps which should be taken to solve the problem of the northern settlements. The labor parties were in favor of sending reinforcements, allocating financial resources and, above all, standing fast to the principle that settlements must not be abandoned. **"It is clear to us that we must defend every place where there is a Jewish laborer… If we run away from robbers, we shall have to abandon not only the Upper Galilee, but also all of the Land of Israel,"** David Ben-Gurion proclaimed. And Tabenkin declared: **"If we fall there, we shall fall even as far as the desert."**

Opposing them, Jabotinsky and others maintained that in the current situation there was no chance of defending the Jewish outposts in the Upper Galilee. Serious defense required hundreds of fighters, and these were not to be had for lack of funds. There was also a political side. The Jews were demanding that the British take all of the Land of Israel under their protection, maintaining that it was out of the question for Britain to accept responsibility over only part of the land (especially when some areas were under the control of another great power). **"I ask you, as comrades in thought, to tell the youth who understand the bitter truth, and perhaps we can thereby save the situation… You must tell the comrades: Come back from there, and build up what exists here,"** Jabotinsky summarized.

1

The deliberations ended with the adoption of a resolution stating that the settlements of the Galilee must be defended and must be assisted with manpower and supplies. Further, a committee was elected to go north as soon as possible to examine the problems at close hand and suggest solutions.

The deliberations of the Temporary Council were held from Monday to Wednesday (February 23-25, 1920). The very day they closed, Trumpeldor set out at the head of a group of fighters and recaptured the abandoned outpost of Metulla, beating back the Arabs who had taken over there. Three days later, on February 28, it appeared that the situation had taken a turn for the better. A group of 35 young men and women, most of them discharged soldiers from the Jewish battalions, Dr. Geri among them, arrived from the south to join the defenders. By the end of February each of the three outposts (Tel Ḥai, Kefar Gil'adi, and Metulla) had some 30 to 35 men to defend it – more than they had had several weeks earlier, yet too few and too insufficiently equipped to be a match for the hundreds and thousands of Arabs who were gathered in the region. The latter, it is true, were not well trained, but their vast numbers, and especially their arms and supplies, constituted a very tangible threat to the small settlements.

As February drew to a close, the situation in the Galilee appeared on the point of exploding. The question was only when the explosion would occur. Indeed, it came on the first of March, 1920, which by the Jewish calendar was the eleventh of Adar, 5680.

the battle

Monday morning, March 1, dawned bright and clear, after a number of days of cold and rain. Life in Tel Ḥai went on as usual – tending the animals, doing guard duty, and working in the yard. Trumpeldor, the commander, went off to Kefar Gil'adi to take care of some business with the neighboring outpost. That morning one of the settlers from Kefar Gil'adi, Pinḥas Schneersohn, a member of *Ha-Shomer,* took the flock out to pasture not far from Tel Ḥai. He tells of running into Trumpeldor, who was on his way to Kefar Gil'adi:

"When he saw me coming with the flock, he stopped, sat down next to me and began to talk. He outlined his upcoming plans to me and disclosed that he had resolved not to postpone going to Constantinople any longer. His plan was to hasten the immigration of 200-300 pioneers from Russia to serve as a decisive force in solidifying the defense of the Upper Galilee.

'With hundreds of pioneers it will be possible to overcome the anarchy which reigns in the region and to assure all our settlements in the Galilee the security they need to live and create,' he said."

The two talked for a while, then Trumpeldor continued to Kefar Gil'adi. There, during breakfast, shots were heard from the south. One of the women burst into the dining hall and said the Arabs were shooting at Tel Ḥai. Trumpeldor gathered a number of young men and set off with them for Tel Ḥai. The picture which unfolded before his eyes was far from encouraging: many hundreds of armed Arabs and bedouins had gathered not far from the settlement. Pinḥas Schneersohn who, upon hearing the first shots, gathered his flock and rushed over to Tel Ḥai, tells about the moments before Trumpeldor's arrival:

"We saw a large band of Arabs approaching Tel Ḥai. They stopped several tens of meters away from the entrance to the farm. An Arab horseman rode up to the man on the lookout tower and asked him for his field glasses, ostensibly to follow the movements of the French army which, he claimed, was massing on the mountains. The Arab got them and refused to give them back. I went up to the horseman, with Moshe Eliowitz, and demanded forcefully that he return the field glasses to their owner. The Arab jumped off his horse, drew a dagger, and began brandishing it in the air as if to challenge us. 'You are spying for the French; soon we will wipe you out,' he yelled at us, and in so doing summoned the band to the gates of the farm. I ordered Moshe to go into the yard and warn the watchmen. As for myself, I retreated, all the while facing towards the rider, keeping my eyes on him. When I reached the yard, I gave the order to load the rifles. The noise of the triggers put the Arabs off, and they began to retreat. Suddenly a group of our comrades, under Trumpeldor's command, appeared on the horizon, approaching in a scattered chain."

Shortly after Trumpeldor's return, Kamal, the Effendi of

2

1

1 The only remains of the Jewish colony of Ḥamara (near kibbutz *Ma'yan Barukh), which was abandoned in January, 1920. Ḥamara means red, the color of the soil in the area.*

2 The first stone building in Kefar Gil'adi was not built until after the battle of Tel Ḥai. It comprises a stable, barn and residence.

3 The Arabs called Kefar Gil'adi "taḥshiba," *meaning hut, after the first and only hut which stood there in 1917.*

The Balfour Declaration, expressing Britain's support of "the establishment ... of a national home for the Jewish people" in the Land of Israel, was published in London on November 2, 1917. The declaration did not specify geographical boundaries. When the peace treaty was signed in Paris and the British and French were negotiating how the northern border would be drawn, the Zionist delegation to the convention began outlining the ideal preferred borders of the "national home," borders that would assure its future as an economic unit capable of supporting itself and providing for general comprehensive development. Especially, they requested that the headwaters of the Litani and Jordan rivers be included.

2

Khaliṣa (an Arab village situated on the site of present-day Qiryat Shemona), arrived at the yard of Tel Ḥai, accompanied by several companions armed with rifles, pistols and hand grenades. They demanded to be let in to see if any French were hiding in the outpost. Trumpeldor permitted them to enter. In retrospect granting them entry is thought to have been the fatal mistake, since from then on the situation rapidly deteriorated. *Sefer Toledot ha-Haganah* (The History of the *Haganah*) notes that the adversary used a ruse to penetrate the compound, and "Trumpeldor, true to his line, allowed Kamal, along with several officers, to look through the rooms. **This time** (emphasis in the original) it proved a fatal mistake." Even Pinḥas Schneersohn believes Trumpeldor's act "had a fatal impact on the entire course of battle in the Upper Galilee." Shulamit Laskov, on the other hand, writes in her book, *Trumpeldor,* that granting Kamal entry should come as no surprise, since similar incidents occurred on the preceding days, not only in Tel Ḥai but even in Kefar Gil'adi, a settlement of *Ha-Shomer.* "Even people in *Ha-Shomer,* who were considered experts in everything concerning behavior of the Arabs, followed the same rule," she says with respect to the practice of allowing Arabs into the settlements to check that no French were there.

Be that as it may, Kamal and his armed companions entered the fortified court of Tel Ḥai, whose buildings were surrounded by a stone wall, and headed for the attic to make sure no French were hiding there. What their true intentions were it is hard to say. The most extreme view claims in all certainty that the Arabs entered with the intent of attacking the defenders from within, coordinating their action with the many attackers from without. Others, however, hold that Kamal and his men entered in all innocence to search for Frenchmen.

What we know for certain is that within a short while a gun battle broke out in the yard and the attic. As far as we know, one of the Arabs tried to disarm Devorah Drachler on the second storey, and she shouted to Trumpeldor: "He is trying to take my gun away!" Trumpeldor told her to resist with force. Next a shot was heard. Who fired the first shot that set off the entire battle? Again, it is hard to say. Schneersohn believes that it was Kamal or one of his men. Trumpeldor, realizing that the battle had begun, instructed the defenders to open fire on the masses of Arabs besieging the fort and trying to break through the gate. As we recall, in the yard at that moment was a group of armed Arabs, headed by Kamal, who opened fire on the defending forces on the first storey and in the yard, with tragic consequences: Ya'akov Toker, an American Jewish volunteer in the Jewish Legion, who was standing by the gate, was seriously wounded. Similarly Trumpeldor, hit by a bullet shot from the attic, and then by a second, lay in a pool of blood with a serious wound in his stomach and another in his hand.

Salvos of gunfire masked the explosion of the hand grenade the Arabs threw into the room in the attic, where there were five members of Tel Ḥai – three men and two women. At that moment all attention was fastened on the Arabs in the attic and on repulsing those trying to break into the yard. Pinḥas Schneersohn noticed an Arab who had entered with Kamal and was hiding on the first floor, a machine gun in his hand. Without a moment's hesitation he shot him. Then he was summoned by the wounded Trumpeldor, who told him: "Schneersohn, take over the command."

atrocities on the second storey

The gunfire exchange continued. While some of the defenders provided cover, the wounded Trumpeldor and Nathan Zolti, who had been wounded while trying to help Trumpeldor, were

3

1 *Abraham Melnikov's Roaring Lion commemorates the eight who fell defending Tel Ḥai. The town of Qiryat Shemona ("City of the Eight") was later named after them. The stone for the sculpture was hewn out of the nearby mountain by Yiẓḥak Sadeh, friend and disciple of Trumpeldor.*

2 *The northern border of the Land of Israel under the British Mandate was a compromise between Zionist demands, supported by Britain, and French demands. This compromise was reached in the context of political developments in the region, foremost of which was King Faisal's coronation in Damascus, which was accompanied by Arab attacks on the French forces that had conquered Syria and Lebanon. In the course of these attacks the Arabs also attacked the four Jewish settlements in the panhandle of the Galilee: Tel Ḥai, Ḥamara, Kefar Gil'adi and Metulla.*

1

dragged to a more secure place. The situation was grave. The attackers on the outside fired without respite, while inside, on the second storey, Kamal and his men took up position. For the moment no one knew what had happened to the defenders.

Trumpeldor, despite his serious wound, retained his composure and instructed the people tending him how to bandage his wounds. Every now and then he asked Schneersohn for a progress report on the battle. He had few illusions about his own condition. When one of his comrades tried to cheer him, he said: **"These are my last moments. Tell the defenders to stand to the bitter end, for the sake of the people's honor."**

Later Schneersohn wrote about the defense array of Tel Ḥai on that day: "The plan of the building provided a central defense position. Its northern wing contained five rooms, connected only by inside entrances. Above the central room was a window looking down on the yard from the upper room. The Arabs who succeeded in seizing the upper storey blasted off the roof, which flew into pieces (for the building was covered with tiles and had no ceiling). This essentially gave them control over all the passages through the building. Comrades were shot while trying to run from one room to the next.

"In the stable in the western end of the yard was a fortified position manned by four comrades. Three men and two women stood on guard in the loft.... Kamal began shouting at me, trying to coax me into believing that his intentions were peaceful and that the first to open fire had not been his men, but ours. He begged me to halt the attack and to allow him and his men to leave the building. At that time we did not yet know what had happened to our comrades on the upper storey. Figuring that as long as Kamal and his men were abroad in the upper room, they would have control over all the rooms, I informed Kamal that he could leave. The comrades in the western position, however, continued shooting incessantly on Kamal and his men, and the latter did not succeed in coming out into the yard. Several times I ordered the western guard to cease firing, but my voice did not carry to them."

Suddenly the shooting stopped. The Arabs inside the building, led by Kamal, took advantage of the brief respite to slide down from the second storey to the yard. At the very same moment Ben-Yosef himself, one of the four defenders of the position in the stable, appeared. Schneersohn and the rest of the defenders aimed their guns at the Arabs. But upon seeing Ben-Yosef they held fire, and in this brief lull the Arabs slipped out of the yard. It is clear from Ben-Yosef's words that the four people manning the position had not heard Schneersohn's calls at all, and that every time they saw the Arabs trying to escape from the upper storey they shot at them. The entire situation seemed to them beyond hope. They assumed that all the defenders, save for themselves, had been killed in the battle. They decided that when they each had only one bullet left they would commit suicide, but beforehand they decided to check out the other rooms and sent Ben-Yosef to do so.

During the lull in the battle, after several hours of exchanging fire, an interim assessment of the situation could be made: Trumpeldor, the commander, was seriously wounded; Zolti, who rushed over to help him, was also badly wounded; Ya'akov

Toker had died. Several defenders had been hit and scathed by ricochets. The fate of the five in the loft was at the time as yet unknown. It was not until later that one of the comrades went up and discovered the grievous sight: the five – Devorah Drachler, Sarah Chizhik, Benjamin Munter, Ya'akov Scharf and Yiẓḥak Kaniewski – had been killed. (Later it turned out that Kaniewski, who was taken for dead, had only been badly wounded). On his return he told Schneersohn, who decided to keep the ghastly secret from the rest of the comrades so as not to break their morale.

During the lull the Arabs were allowed to evacuate their wounded who lay around the yard. Schneersohn estimates that at that point they had about 14 dead and numerous wounded. The defenders reorganized and broke a hole in the wall between the dining hall and the munitions storeroom, which they could not reach any other way. While in the storeroom they heard groaning from above. It was Kaniewski, and it was that which saved his life.

The arms and munitions taken from the storeroom helped the defenders in the coming hours. As the day drew to a close the attacks intensified, as masses of Arabs pressed against the southeastern wall of the yard. A few hand grenades dispelled their attack, causing them heavy losses.

The Arabs did not let up. They continued showering fire on Tel Ḥai and towards nightfall tried to set fire to the stable and adjoining hayloft by throwing burning kerosene-soaked mats at it. The defenders prevented the fire from spreading and repulsed the attackers once more.

"yet they were not vanquished"

As dark fell, the shooting died down. Schneersohn went once more to see the wounded Trumpeldor. "He lay motionless, silent, his face deadly white. His robust, sturdy body had somehow shriveled, yet his strong, bony face, expressive of inner strength, endurance and balance, had not changed.... I told him how things were. His mind remained clear. He asked me to encourage the comrades to hold their guard and defend themselves honorably, to the last bullet. When nightfall came Trumpeldor sensed that his condition was worsening and asked to have the doctor brought to him from Kefar Gil'adi.

Three of Tel Ḥai's defenders set off for Kefar Gil'adi, literally crawling there so as not to draw the attention of the Arabs still surrounding the spot. Shortly thereafter reinforcements arrived from Kefar Gil'adi, and with them Dr. Geri. Then it became known that, while it was still day, the settlers of Kefar Gil'adi had attempted to come to the aid of their beleaguered neighbors but had been unable to break through the siege of Tel Ḥai.

The newcomers replaced the defenders, worn out from the long day's battle, while the doctor tended to the three seriously wounded men. Trumpeldor's condition was critical. Dr. Geri

the battle of tel ḥai, march 1, 1920

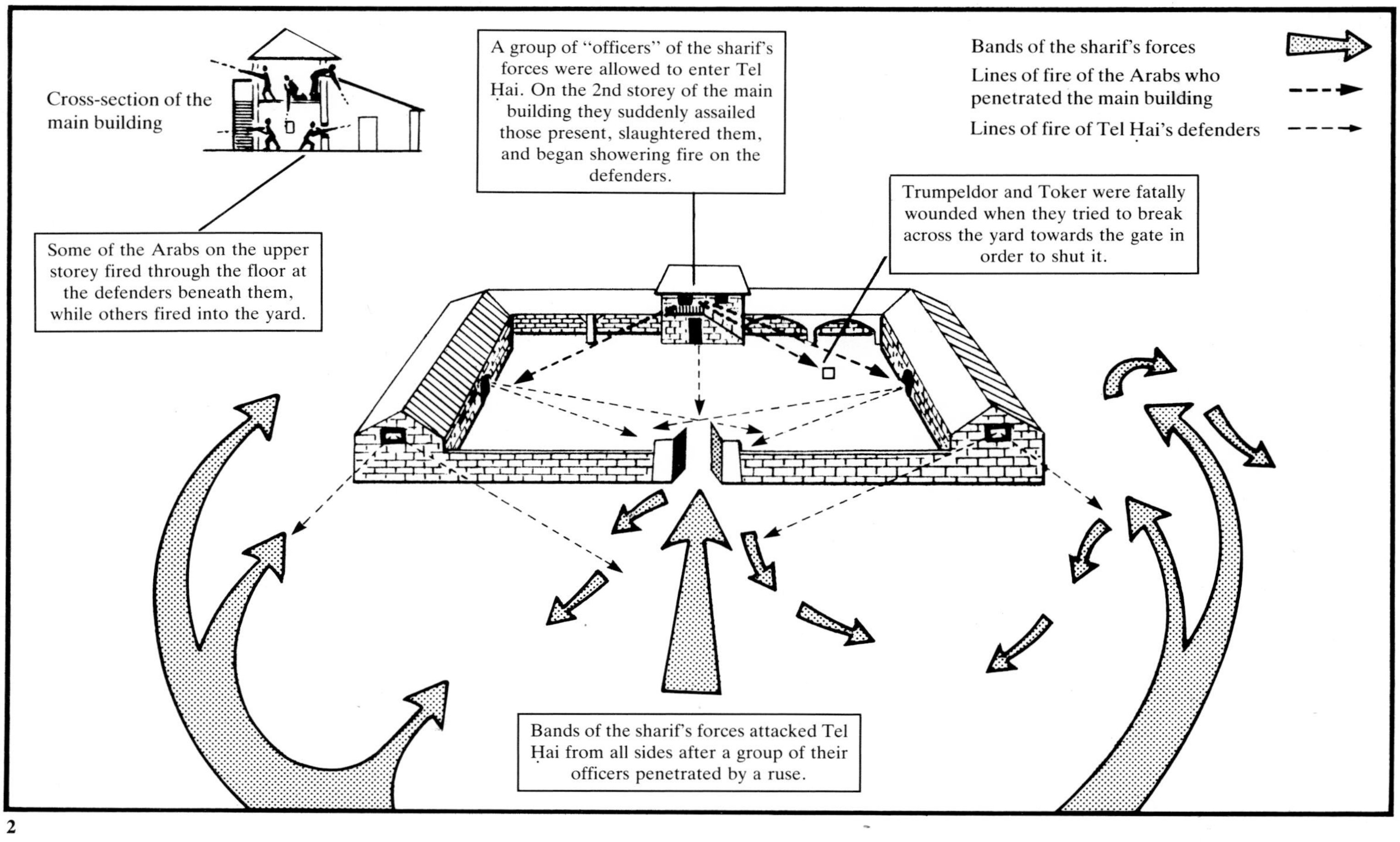

Cross-section of the main building
A group of "officers" of the sharif's forces were allowed to enter Tel Ḥai. On the 2nd storey of the main building they suddenly assailed those present, slaughtered them, and began showering fire on the defenders.
Bands of the sharif's forces
Lines of fire of the Arabs who penetrated the main building
Lines of fire of Tel Ḥai's defenders
Trumpeldor and Toker were fatally wounded when they tried to break across the yard towards the gate in order to shut it.
Some of the Arabs on the upper storey fired through the floor at the defenders beneath them, while others fired into the yard.
Bands of the sharif's forces attacked Tel Ḥai from all sides after a group of their officers penetrated by a ruse.

2

1 *Metulla was founded by Russian immigrants in 1896, on land purchased by Baron Rothschild. After the battle of Tel Ḥai the colony was evacuated, but its residents returned before long.*

2 *The beginnings of Tel Ḥai date back to 1918, to Turkish rule. A small group of Jewish shepherds, belonging to the organization of* Ha-Shomer, *settled in the courtyard and grazed sheep in the area.*

In the picture: Abramson and Koszcuk, grazing sheep.

gave orders to transfer the wounded on makeshift stretchers to Kefar Gil'adi, where he intended to operate on them.

On his arrival at Tel Ḥai, Dr. Geri asked Trumpeldor how he felt, and Trumpeldor responded, "Never mind, it is good to die for the sake of our country." From that day on this utterance has symbolized the legend of Joseph Trumpeldor's life and the story of Tel Ḥai.

Occasionally one hears rumors that what Joseph Trumpeldor uttered was not the saying attributed to him – "It is good to die for the sake of our country" – but in fact a ribald Russian curse. We are sorry to disappoint these cynics and men of little faith: Trumpeldor said precisely what is attributed to him. All the sources confirm this: Dr. Geri, who heard it directly from his lips; Abraham Harzfeld, who arrived at Tel Ḥai from Kefar Gil'adi in the evening hours of the day of the battle; and articles in the contemporary press, only a few days after it was uttered.

Trumpeldor survived only a short while longer. On the way up the hill to Kefar Gil'adi his body was seized with convulsions, and he passed away. At about the same time a cart arrived from Kefar Gil'adi to transport the wounded and to take several essential things which had to be evacuated from Tel Ḥai. That night the settlers of the outpost, exhausted and stunned by the death of their commander and five of their comrades, decided to move to Kefar Gil'adi to continue defending the region from the two remaining outposts – Kefar Gil'adi and Metulla.

Thus Tel Ḥai was evacuated and, after the animals were taken out of the yard, was set afire so that what remained would not fall into the Arabs' hands. That same night the six dead were buried, the four men in a communal grave, and the two women in a second grave.

During the next two days, for fear of further Arab attacks, Kefar Gil'adi and Metulla were evacuated as well, but not for long. Seven months later, in October, 1920, Kefar Gil'adi was re-established, and in its wake Metulla and Tel Ḥai were also rebuilt. Before many years elapsed, a tradition arose of pilgrimage to Tel Ḥai on the 11th of Adar every year, to commemorate the heroic battle and the fall of eight of Tel Ḥai's defenders, the six who fell on the 11th of Adar and Shneur Shaposhnik and Aharon Sher, who fell earlier. A monument to the heroic fight was commissioned from the sculptor Abraham Melnikov. His statue, The Roaring Lion, which stands between Tel Ḥai and Kefar Gil'adi, commands a wide prospect and is visited by tens of thousands every year.

Over the years, especially before the establishment of the state, the battle of Tel Ḥai and the statue of The Roaring Lion became symbols of heroism, of standing fast, and of recovering in the face of tragedy.

This indeed is the value and importance of these symbols to the generations which preceded us and to our generation as well.

by their merit the upper galilee is ours

the lessons of tel ḥai*

"From a military-tactical point of view, Tel Ḥai's stand was far from exemplary. Quite the contrary, even some of the defenders criticized Trumpeldor, who believed the words of the commanding Arab officer. Kefar Gil'adi and Metulla were abandoned before giving fight, as soon as attackers were detected massing at Khaliṣa in the Huleh Valley (today Qiryat Shemona, City of the Eight, so named after the eight who fell at

1

Tel Ḥai), and the defenders retreated to the villages of the Methualites in the hills of Naphtali, and from there southwards. Thus practical combat lessons could not be drawn from what happened. From a purely tactical standpoint the entire defense failed, confirming the professional military vision of Jabotinsky.... The special distinction of Tel Ḥai was not in the military outcome of its courageous stand, but in the readiness to fight, as Berl Katznelson put it:

"They stood up and fought like lions, but they were inadequate to the fight, and they fell. Nevertheless they were not vanquished, for they turned their defeat into a message... And from that time on, this heritage of Tel Ḥai became a movement, a supreme virtue: to meet the foe, standing brave and upright, to encounter enormous obstacles and not be deterred, to defend even if there is no guarantee of success, and if fate decree that the stand be lost, to overcome and turn the loss into a renewed thrust of reinforcement and victory.

"Indeed Tel Ḥai's stand was not in vain, even in terms of territorial achievements. The wave of attacks in the spring of 1920 hit the entire country, reaching its climax in the riots on Passover, in Jerusalem itself, before the very eyes of the British military government, which did not manage to defend the Jewish quarter in the Old City; whereas Jewish self-defense, led by Jabotinsky, successfully prevented incursions into the Jewish neighborhoods of the new city. In April, France and England met at the San Remo Conference, where they set the political boundaries between the British and French Mandates. The line which was drawn then – its principles and details finalized later in stubborn negotiations – projected north of the Rosh ha-Niqra – Huleh line in the eastern Galilee in order to extend the territory of the British Mandate over the destroyed Jewish settlements and the headwaters of the Dan River, the main tributary of the Jordan River. Incidentally, the border which was set then, and lasted until 1923, included the ascent of the Golan Heights as far as the tels of Quneitra.

"This political act, however, would have remained nothing more than another transient resolution had the pioneers of the Third Aliyah not decided to return and resettle Kefar Gil'adi and Tel Ḥai. In the summer of 1920 the Joseph Trumpeldor Labor Brigade was founded. (This is the full name of the Labor Brigade; the *Haganah* was not mentioned publicly for underground reasons.) Only half a year after the outposts were abandoned, the Brigade set out to renew the settlement, and a number of days later several of the farmers returned to Metulla. The Anglo-French resolution turned into a reality of Jewish life and renewed settlement in the panhandle of the Galilee....

"Tel Ḥai Day became *Haganah* Day, and generations of youth were reared on the example set by Trumpeldor and his comrades. In the movement and its educational undertakings the emphasis was laid on the heroism of those who fell, and the phrase Trumpeldor uttered as he was dying, 'It is good to die for the sake of our country,' was changed to the positive statement: 'It is good to live for the sake of our country.' "

2

* The Lessons of Tel Ḥai, excerpts from Elḥanan Oren's article, "*Moreshet Tel-Ḥai be-Mivḥan ha-Ma'aseh*" ("The Heritage of Tel Hai in the Test of Deeds"), Shorashim, I, 1979.

swamps and malaria in the jezreel valley

1

Ilan Zaharoni

The picture of Ereẓ Israel (the Land of Israel) before Zionist settlement of the land is so different from the picture of the land today, although so close in time. Only seventy years ago the swamps of Nahalal and the Ḥarod Valley were dried and the foundations for cooperative settlement of the Jezreel Valley* laid.

Today the valley is covered with dozens of thriving *kibbutzim* and *moshavim*, and not a strip of land remains that is not either plowed or planted or built up.

Ze'ev Carmi, passing through the valley in the summer of 1910, describes the Jezreel Valley before modern Jewish settlement:

"Pathetically the half-empty train crossed the Jezreel Valley, dull and deserted. Save for two hills, Mount Tabor and Giv'at ha-Moreh, we found nothing interesting – only the sorry sight of a plain without tree or brook ... everything in ruins. Only an occasional poor hut of some *felaḥ* (peasant) or tenant farmer." (From an account of a summer journey from Jaffa to the Lower Galilee.)

But when our pioneers set eyes on the landscape of dramatic events from the Bible they were deeply moved. The power of these feelings, of the sense of history, can be seen in Yehudah Almog's description of coming to 'En-Ḥarod to found a settlement there: "... Amidst lakes and swampy ponds we traveled on until we reached the slopes of Mount Gilboa' and arrived at the opening of the cave from which the spring, 'En-Ḥarod, gushes forth.... Like our forefathers, who "lapped" the water and followed Gideon for the deliverance of Israel, we knelt down by the spring and lapped the water joyfully" (*The Book of the Third Aliyah*, "Staking a Claim in the Valley").

a rich valley with a small drawback

The Jezreel Valley is the largest of the valleys in the land, and its deep rich soil provides vast economic agricultural potential. In those days, however, it was only inhabited by some 4,000 peasants, poor tenant farmers; for swamps and malaria stood in the way of realization and exploitation of the valley's rich potential.

Yehoshua' Ḥankin, redeemer of the land of the Jezreel Valley, was cognizant of this shortcoming in the valley but was inspired by the possibility of purchasing a large and continuous tract of land (approximately 50,000 acres) and beginning large-scale Jewish settlement,* something which could not be done in other areas where title to the land was in several different hands.

The land of the Jezreel Valley was owned by the Sursuk family (Beirut bankers), who had bought the land in 1872 for the sum of 0.36 pounds sterling per acre and in 1920 sold part of their estate (17,500 acres) to Yehoshua' Ḥankin, representing the Zionist Organization, for an average price of 17.2 pounds sterling per acre, in other words more than 50 times what he had paid. The tenant farmers who tilled the soil before the Jews bought the land and who abandoned it after its purchase were paid compensation even though the land had not actually belonged to them.

In 1920 Ḥankin managed to realize his great dream, purchasing 17,500 acres in the eastern part of the valley (Gush Nuris and 'En Ḥarod) and its western part (Nahalal and Ginnegar).

---

* The valley is named after the city of Jezreel, founded by the Israelites and included in the tribal allotment of Issachar (Joshua 19:18). Under King Ahab, Jezreel was the second capital of the Israelite kingdom, most likely its winter capital (I Kings, 18:45-46). Today the eastern part of the valley, draining into Naḥal Ḥarod, is known as the Ḥarod Valley.

* In 1881 Jews began leaving Russia en masse to escape cruel persecution and pogroms, and some of them wished to come to Ereẓ Israel.

2

swamps and malaria in the jezreel valley

Pictures on the previous pages:

1 *'Ein Sheikh – the swamps of Nahalal before they were drained. The swamps that formed around the springs were a breeding ground for mosquitoes that carried the malaria parasite. These were the permanent swamps that covered relatively small areas but existing the year round and not drying up in summer.*

2 *Nahalal, as seen from the air today.*

On these pages:

1,2 *Drying the land of Nahalal (1922-1924) was accomplished by draining the swamps into open channels and into ceramic pipelines laid deep underground. All the work, including digging the channels, laying the pipelines and covering them, was done manually. 25,000 man-days were invested drying the swamps of Nahalal at a time when the adult Zionist population in the Land of Israel was not much more than 30,000. Moreover, this project was accomplished when the workers had little to eat, lived in tents, and were exposed to anopheles mosquito bites and malaria.*

3 *Swamps in the Ḥarod Valley, the eastern part of the Jezreel Valley, before being drained (1921). The same year 'En Ḥarod, the first large* kibbutz, *was founded at the foot of Mount Gilboa' by members of the Joseph Trumpeldor Labor and Defense Brigade. The aims of the Brigade were to promote Jewish labor and defense and cooperative settlement, building the land by means of a general commune of laborers in the Land of Israel. Brigade members worked drying swamps, paving roads, doing other public works for the British army and the Zionist Organization, etc.*

1

2

swamps and the plague of malaria

The swamps of the Jezreel Valley fell into two categories:
1. Seasonal swamps that covered extensive tracts of land in winter but dried up completely when the rainy season was over.
2. Permanent swamps that covered relative small areas but lasted the year round.

The damage caused by the seasonal swamps was purely economic and could be dealt with by a relatively simple measure: digging drainage channels and planning crops according to the drainage conditions on each plot of land. It was the permanent swamps, however, that presented a serious problem even though they covered only a relatively small area. These swamps were formed by the unregulated flow of springs and brooks over level terrain with heavy soil that did not absorb the water. The economic damage of these swamps was minimal, but the bodies of water that did not dry up in summer were a breeding ground for anopheles mosquitoes, carriers of malaria, and drying these areas presented a complex technological problem, very costly to solve.

Malaria, or swamp fever, is a disease characterized by fever suddenly rising to 104° F or more, aches, chills, accelerated pulse, and injury to various organs, often leading to death. The symptoms occur cyclically.

"Our comrades used to say that he who has not experienced a raging fever does not know the taste of life in Ereẓ Israel (the Land of Israel). Some of our members came down with "tertian," a type of malaria where the patient's fever rises and falls intermittently ... for a week or two, sometimes even longer. The fever was not especially high, and during the day, when it fell, most of the sick went out to work even though they were weak, otherwise there would have been no one to work at all. But some came down with "tropical" fever, and those who did ... would be hit by a high fever that lasted weeks on end" (Ze'ev Dorsinai, *From the Banks of the Dnieper to En-Harod*).

The early settlers of Nahalal and 'En-Ḥarod were acquainted with this deadly disease, either from personal experience or from stories of the not so distant past. In settlements such as Ḥadera and Yesud ha-Ma'alah malaria claimed many lives and caused the settlers great suffering. Quite a few settlement attempts failed when the disease struck down a large number of the settlers. The founders of Nahalal and 'En-Ḥarod were well aware of what they were undertaking when they decided to settle where they did. The risk was there for all to see, but the promise lay hidden in their hearts and in their faith.

how is a swamp drained?

By 1921 considerable experience had been acquired dealing with malaria and swamps in Ereẓ Israel. Living with malaria meant suffering and death and impeded faster development of Jewish settlement. The conclusion was clear: to wipe out malaria the swamps had to be drained. The Zionist bodies gave priority to this undertaking, allocating it a large fraction of their meager budget.

The settlers of Nahalal were joined by another 300 pioneer workers who had come to help drain the swamps, and together they worked for two years, from 1922 to 1924. To bring home the extensiveness of the undertaking of draining Nahalal's swamps we must present several facts and figures, placing them in the context of the times: 14,500 meters of baked ceramic pipeline and 2,500 meters of iron pipeline were laid for drainage; 1,500 meters of riverbeds were adjusted; 9,000 cubic meters of earth were dug; approximately 7,000 meters of main pipelines were laid for water supply; the six springs in the area were enclosed in special concrete structures; most of the water from the springs was concentrated to a single place so that it could be utilized; 25,000 man-days were invested in the project; an area of 4,000 acres was drained; and the total cost came to 13,900 Ereẓ Israeli pounds (whose value was equal to that of the pound sterling).

Such an undertaking would be considered a vast project even in current terms, when digging a trench a meter long by a meter deep can be done by a steam shovel in a matter of minutes and when a cubic meter of dirt can be carried off by a bulldozer in a single shovelful. Yet all these jobs, including digging the trenches, laying the pipes, and covering them over were done *by hand*, and the investment of 25,000 days of labor was made when the adult Zionist population of Ereẓ Israel numbered little more than 30,000 people. And all this was done at a time when the workers had little more than bread to eat, lived in tents, and were exposed to anopheles mosquito bites and the danger of malaria.

The undertaking of drying the swamps of the Jezreel Valley is an outstanding example of man fighting the ravages of nature, of firm resolve and courage, but above all of vision that enabled man to accomplish the impossible.

Coping with the tremendous difficulties of life in Ereẓ Israel, striving to realize the dream of establishing a Jewish state – the ultimate goal – required unique and exceptional tools. Since the days of Deganya and Ḥavat Kinneret the Zionist Organization began to view settlement as a national undertaking and principal tool for realizing the Zionist idea, hence it also felt a need and obligation to take the settlement effort into its hands, providing it with a budget and guiding it. The immigrants of the Second Aliyah did not make do with the revolutionary act of leaving the Diaspora and returning to manual labor in Ereẓ Israel, but added the dimension of social revolution, striving to found a just and equal society. This combination gave birth to cooperative settlement, unique to the Jewish community in Ereẓ Israel, starting with the *kevutzah* (cooperative) at Umm Juna which became Deganya, and continuing with the *kibbutz* of 'En-Ḥarod and the *moshav* of Nahalal.

3

a village in the jezreel valley

Ilan Zaharoni

One cold and rainy winter eve in January, 1940, a sledge hitched to two mules slowly made its way to the main road.

On the sledge, its runners slicing through the boggy mud, sat a woman seized by pains of childbirth. Shrinking from the bitter cold and the steadily pelting rain, the passengers on the sledge huddled in their coats and rode in silence.

In the dark of night the beating rain and the howling wind mingled with the mules' heavy breathing, the patter of their hooves, and the smacking of the driver's lips as he goaded them on their way.

At the road a car was waiting to take the woman to the hospital ... I returned to the village, a babe of three weeks, cooing in its swaddling; the village, green but muddy, was then 13 years old.

The entry on Kefar Yehoshua' in E. and M. Talmi's lexicon, *Mi-Ḥermon 'ad Sharm esh-Sheikh* (From Ḥermon to Sharm esh-Sheikh) reads: "Kefar Yehoshua'. A *moshav* (affiliated with the *Moshav* Movement). Founded in 1927 in the Jezreel Valley. Named after Yehoshua' Ḥankin, redeemer of land in the Jezreel Valley and in many other parts of the country. The village has a regional museum called Ḥankin House."

Who could imagine that 60 years of struggle, toil, and creativity lay hidden in this village? Who would think that these few sentences encompass a great revolution in the life of the Jewish nation – freeing itself from the baggage of its existence in exile and paving the way for renewed independence and sovereignty?

a rebel dreamer

The picture of the bearded man with the long hair and soft, caressing eyes gazed down on us from the wall of the classroom, at once close and distant. To us Yehoshua' Ḥankin was a tangibly real yet legendary figure – the farmer's son who rebelled against the clerks of Baron Rothschild in Rishon le-Ẓiyyon and who dreamt of redeeming and settling the land, feverishly pursuing and realizing his dream through his indefatigable devotion in the face of hard work and danger.

The broad valley – which until thirteen hundred years ago was a fertile blossoming valley but subsequently became a poor, sparsely inhabited place of disease-ridden swamps – stirred a passion in him, which burned ardently his entire life.

His first attempt at purchasing land in the valley from the Sursuk family living in Lebanon, dates back to 1891.

Spurred on by his vision, his love of the valley, and the prospect of acquiring some 250 million dunams of land held by a single family, Ḥankin opened negotiations. He succeeded in getting the better of land speculators, who tried to foil the deal by offering the owners a high price, and the contract was signed. Its terms promised the sale of 160 thousand dunams in the Jezreel Valley and along the Acre coastal plain, at a price of fifteen francs per dunam.

1

1 *"The Zionist movement to settle the land brought running water into the home of the settler" (Arthur Ruppin). The water tower, built in 1929, in the center of Kefar Yehoshua'.*

2 *The Turkish railway station of Tel Shamam, near Kefar Yehoshua'. A branch of the Hijaz Railway once ran from the Bashan (Transjordan) to Haifa, passing through northern valleys. This was the legendary Jezreel Valley Railroad.*

3 *Harvesting forage for the dairy farm.*

4 *"Families living on the* moshav *shall support themselves by their own labor and shall not prosper from the labor of others" (Eliezer Joffe, idealogue of the* moshav ovedim, *or Workers' Cooperative).*

3

2

4

As the transaction was about to be closed, the Turkish government dealt it the death blow. Jewish immigration was prohibited. The money which had been raised for the purpose in Russia did not reach its destination, and the deal fell through.

The dream of redeeming the Jezreel Valley continued to inspire Ḥankin. On a rainy, stormy day in the winter of 1910, Ḥankin and Ruppin traveled to Beirut to persuade the *wali* (the General Commissioner) to direct the ruler of Nazareth, a fanatic and an opponent of Zionism, to approve the purchase of land in Fuleh (present-day Merḥavya).

These endeavors were to no avail. Only Ḥankin's connections in Constantinople, the capital of the Ottoman Empire, finally led to the contract's acceptance. Thus the first ten thousand dunams passed into Jewish hands, laying the corner-stone for redeeming and settling the land of the Jezreel Valley.

Redeeming the land was no easy task, requiring a life of wayfaring under difficult conditions, and it was fraught with great personal danger. Ḥankin's courage, perseverance, and personal integrity stood him in good stead on his difficult road. These qualities caused all who came in contact with him, especially Arabs, to respect and even admire him.

Despite great efforts, ten more years elapsed before he succeeded in buying more land in the Jezreel Valley. In 1920 Gush Nuris (today the Ḥarod Valley) and Ma'lul (now Nahalal) were purchased. By 1925 most of the Jezreel Valley, including Tel Shamam (Kefar Yehoshua'), had been bought back into Jewish hands. Jewish settlements were established one after another, hand in hand with the redemption of the land.

This is the man after whom the village is named, and this is part of the land he redeemed.

One day I happened by the home of the son of the former overseer of the Sursuk family's tenant farmers in Sulam (an Arab village near Merḥavya, site of biblical Shunem). The father, who was generously recompensed by the Jewish National Fund when the land was purchased, used the money to buy 600 dunams of land in the fertile Dothan Valley, and there he settled.

As we sat in his home, relaxing over coffee and delicacies, I asked the master of the house if he remembered Ḥankin.

The man, who at the time had been a young lad but now was well on in years, gave a smile. Yes, he remembered Ḥankin well. Many a time he had slept in their house. I wondered what they thought of Ḥankin's life's work; so I asked. Although he had been only a youngster and many years had since elapsed, the following incident was engraved in his memory: on one of his visits, when Ḥankin was in his riper years, he stayed in their house. They sat and talked. The father asked him, "Mr. Ḥankin, you are old and weary. Why do you continue running about and wearing yourself out buying land for others?" Ḥankin raised his eyes and said, "Future generations will appreciate my deeds.... They will go down in history in golden letters."

the hut on the hilltop

Tel Shamam is a small ancient tel (the site of Dabbesheth, mentioned in the delineation of the inheritance of the tribe of Zebulun, in Joshua 19:11) with several rusty tin shanties of Sursuk's tenant farmers and a picturesque railway station. Slightly south of the tel flows the Kishon, in summer, a small, unassuming brook, but in winter, with the onset of the rains, a broad, gushing river. North of the train station, on the hilltop, stood the first hut, left by the last tenant farmers to be compensated and leave the place.

I have never set eyes on this hut, yet I feel as if I had. Initially it was used by the earliest settlers, then it served various other purposes, until one day it caught fire and burned down. Later my father told me the story of the hut and the fire which demolished it. It was being used as a meeting house and library when the fire broke out. The people of the village all rushed to extinguish it, but to no avail. The hut collapsed under the flames, and only a fraction of what it had housed was rescued.

Among the items salvaged from the fire was a bookcase laden with books. When the fire broke out, one of the teachers charged into the hut, lifted the heavy bookcase on his back, and carried it out. When he tried to lift it again, after the fire died down, he could not budge it even a hair's breadth....

Huts are by their very nature transient; and the life of man, fleeting. Just as we feel sorrow and pain at the passing of a human being, so too the disappearance of this hut, used by our earliest settlers, sorrowed us all.

Eliyahu 'Amiẓur, one of the founders of the village, writes:

1

"The founders of this Jewish village, city folk with no agricultural background, unaccustomed to heavy physical labor, said to themselves: Let us be farmers"...

"The entire history of the Jewish people," Eliyahu continues, "is an anomaly: the people of Israel returning to its land, settling there before becoming a state, establishing the State of Israel, founding hundreds of settlements after the rise of the state, resurrecting the Hebrew language, establishing the IDF – and this by the sons of a people who throughout the world had a reputation as cowards, draft evaders, and deserters from all armies, who were considered to lack the least approach to the military in general and to war in particular – all these so unlike the history of all other nations. Therefore it seems a miracle, an unbelievable feat."

in praise of tools

Indeed, it was a miracle – the first plowing of the village fields, the first sowing.... When I was a child most of the tools, as well as the methods of cultivation, sowing, and harvesting, remained from the early days of the village and were still doing active yeoman's service. Those which had been replaced by newer ones still rested with honor in the lot adjacent to the tractor shed and were a source of interest and investigation.

Something of the sense of an intimate bond with the earth and nature was lost when the tools which had been pulled and operated by animals and man were replaced by heavy farm equipment, powered by tractors and engines.

Then the villager used to rise at dawn, hitch a pair of mules to a wooden cart rolling on large, iron-rimmed, wooden wheels, tie the two-bottom plow on behind, and set out for the day's plowing. Marching behind the plow the entire day, watching, as its blades cut into the black soil, was not easy, but it gave a sense of satisfaction and closeness to mother earth, to the source of life, to the foundations.

I myself can recall the two-bottom plow, the single plow, the Arab plow, and the one numbered four, the sowing machine, the combine, the threshing machine, the baling machine, and others... (all the tools and machines mentioned here, and many others, are in the museum of agricultural tools in Yif'at).

For the children of the village, threshing season was the best time of year. In early summer the wheat was threshed, and at the season's end, the corn.

The threshing floor was full of action. The threshing machine quivered as it swallowed the sheaves of wheat thrown with sharp-pronged pitchforks into its gaping mouth. The iron-wheeled tractor roared as a small wheel attached to its side moved a wide belt which, turning noisily, rotated the wheels of the thresher. Sacks were filled with kernels of grain, while straw was spewed out a wide shute and formed steadily swelling heaps. Even the scolding of the grownups could not dampen the children's enthusiasm as they romped amongst the enormous piles of straw.

Threshing required team work. One group loaded the machine, another replaced the filled sacks with empty ones, and

1 *Israel has approximately 100,000 cows of an Israeli breed, resulting from cross-breeding and developing local, Dutch and American breeds. They give on the average about 8,000 liters of milk per year, the highest yield in the world.*

2 *The first tractor, the cornerstone of the village's cooperatively owned heavy farm machinery.*

3 *Yehoshua' Ḥankin's study. The original furniture is on display in Ḥankin House, a regional center for nature and Land of Israel studies in Kefar Yehoshua'.*

4 *The family working in the hothouse.*

2

4

yet a third drove carts laden with bales from the field to the barn.

Harvesting the corn, picked by hand with the entire family helping, was arduous work and made all who did it itchy and scratchy.

Threshing it, however, made up for everything. The corn thresher was smaller than its counterpart, but more interesting and picturesque. Here, in addition to the kernels and the white husks, the machine spewed out scraped cobs, one after another, from the top of the narrow lift. These cobs were almost our only fuel for heating water and kitchen ovens.

When the activity on the threshing floor was over, baling the straw began. Mules with blinders walked round and round, rotating the knob of the baling machine. The straw was tossed with pitchforks to the top of the shute, and, at the ring of the

3

1 *"Thy children like olive plants, round about thy table" (Psalms 128:3). The children of the* moshav, *the next generation, from an early age a part of life in the* moshav *and work on the farm. The farmers' houses are laid out in a circle, facing the center of the village, where the public buildings are located. Behind each house are various farm buildings – chicken coops, cow sheds, straw storage structures, etc. – and beyond them the village's farmland.*

bell, an iron wire was threaded in to bind the bale.

We rejoiced when we received our first combine, but a touch of sadness was mixed with our happiness. Henceforth we were spared hard manual labor, but along with it the excitement of threshing, the stacks of sheaves, and the straw ... were lost. The amusements of threshing season had become a thing of the past; a new era had dawned.

a just and equal society

The idea of the *moshav* (cooperative smallholders' village) – as presented in Eliezer Joffe's pamphlet, "Founding Workers' Cooperatives" (1919), which guided the founders of the village – was not based on materialist aspirations. The poor training of the settlers, the primitive level of agriculture, and many other difficulties presented no prospects of growing rich from tilling the soil. Indeed at times one even began to wonder whether one could earn a decent living from farming. Much hope and faith were necessary in order to believe in one's own ability and the ability of the land to provide a livelihood. The wish to provide an outlet for individual ability and enterprise, coupled with the desire to shake off the intimate, and sometimes oppressive, setting of the *kevutzah* (collective settlement designed along the lines of an enlarged family) is what brought the idea of the *moshav* to fruition.

Private agriculture in the style of the early *moshavot* (colonies), in which the farmers often became colonists supported by Arab labor, contradicted the ideals of the founders of the first *moshavim.* The latter aspired to more than settling the land and reestablishing a Jewish state; they ardently held the ideal of building a new society which would be equal and just. Thus they saw themselves as blazing the way for others and as enacting their views and ideals with their own lives.

The principles of the *moshav* include the following: equality in means of production and opportunity; living by one's own labor, and maintaining a socio-economic system for mutual aid; supporting and promoting development of the individual and of the entire group alike.

A. Nationally owned land. The land does not belong to the villager, but is made available to him for him to farm and earn a living from it. He may not lease it or sell it. An equal quota of land is given to every person.

B. One's own labor. Families on the *moshav* live by their own labor, not the labor of others. Labor has a cleansing value and is the answer to the anomaly in the life of the Jewish people.

C. Mutual aid and responsibility. The entire society must extend help to the sick or disabled. When help does not depend on personal relationships or the kind-heartedness of one or another individual, but rather is the responsibility of the society as a whole, the weak and injured are not left to suffer alone.

D. Cooperative marketing. All the farm produce is marketed jointly, and the proceeds credited to the producing member. Cooperative marketing makes the socio-economic system feasible and assures its existence, and thus in turn guarantees maintaining other principles. Cooperative capital and pooled revenues make it possible to extend mutual aid in the form of credit, and to establish and maintain public institutions and enterprises.

E. Family labor. Running a farm with one's own labor requires the cooperation of the entire family in sharing responsibility and in execution. Husband and wife are equal partners in ownership of the farm and in signatory rights.

F. Prohibition against owning property outside of the *moshav*. This principle, in addition to its economic importance in assuring a concentration of resources for a strong, cooperative economic system and in avoiding conflict of interests, also expresses the world outlook of working people who view profits derived from speculation as pernicious.

The reader may wonder whether anyone still holds and lives by these principles. Indeed many people have abandoned the philosophy of the founding fathers and, worshipping Mammon, have been enticed to follow other paths. Yet there are still many, including the members of Kefar Yehoshua', who religiously adhere to the principles of these first settlers. There have always been dissatisfied people; there are always those who try to cast off the yoke and those who grumble about the difficulty of maintaining these principles. Yet the society as a whole, by using persuasion and precaution, closes up loopholes and preserves its existence as a unique society with its own values. The setting is more than the sum total of the restrictions and proscriptions which the members assume, and herein lies the strength of the village to develop and grow, for a strong socio-economic framework is a tremendously powerful tool which supports and advances the welfare of the individual as well as the group.

the legend of the jezreel valley train

On the broad hillock in the heart of the Jezreel Valley the village gradually grew. It had no roads and was far from the main thoroughfare (the famous Haifa-Jeda road – from Haifa to Nazareth to 'Afula). The first means of transportation serving the village was the train. The Tel Shamam station pre-dated the founding of the village, and the train – The Jezreel Valley Train – was even more famous. Much has been said in its praise, and the jokes about it could be told all the way from Haifa to Tel Aviv....

Although as a means of transportation and haulage this train was not the most comfortable or reliable, as a source of fun and adventure for the children of the village it was unbeatable.

1 *Wash day on the* moshav. *For many years, until the establishment of the State, the women of the village did their laundry in a large boiler which they heated with twigs in the back yard of their house, under the open sky.*

2 *A new page is hewn in the history of the village: the memorial to the sons who fell in Israel's wars, sculpted by Batia Lichansky. The two figures in the foreground represent the readiness to come to the defense of one's people and country, while the figure in the background, holding onto a plow, symbolizes the bond to the soil and the village.*

1

A paved road, full of potholes, led to the station; and at the end of the road were the station's stone buildings, crowned with red-tiled roofs, and the various installations of the railway. Once you arrived at the station and purchased your green tickets at the booth of the Turkish cashier with the grand moustache, you were free to tread along the gravel strewn platform. When the train would arrive was purely a matter of speculation; meanwhile, being bored was farthest from your mind.

First you went to Abu-Yusuf in the water tower next to the coal-house. This stout little Arab in his tarboosh liked the village children, and they him. He greeted you with a smile and invited you to come watch him work. He used to climb up the ladder to the tower, close and open faucets, pile up coal, open and close doors – all for the steam-engine which was dilatory in coming. Then came the turn of the switches, the wagonettes, the semaphores and the passengers.... The train passengers, especially the Arabs among them, their bundles, their dress, the animals traveling with them, were always very interesting.

A distant whistle announced the approach of the train, puffing and chugging along, till it screeched to a halt in a burst of steam. Then Abu-Yusuf used to rush to adjust the large fabric hose on the opening of the water tank, while the coal-stained faces of the engineers, the heroes of the train, peered out of the locomotive's window. The train cars bustled with strange and different people, with hens, pigeons, and even goats.

The slow moving train merited the gamut of jokes told about it: once a man who had tired of life tied himself to the train tracks; some time later he was found in agonizing pain – from starvation. It is said that passengers used to jump off the train as it was traveling, pick flowers, and catch it up again.

Jokes by their nature exaggerate, yet every joke has a kernel of truth. The train was not, to put it mildly, one of the faster ones. But for us, the children, who liked to draw out our adventures, this of course was an asset.

In time a stone road was paved to the main road and the importance of the train declined, until, with the outbreak of the War of Independence, it ceased running altogether. One can not even begin to imagine our disappointment when we realized, after the war, that the train would no longer pass by here. Only the silent station buildings and the rustle of the giant eucalyptus trees remain as a token of its past glory.

mud and narcissus

Life in the village was not all fun and games; the latter floated over the surface of the gray, arduous, daily life like foam on the face of the sea. Work was done with a will, out of a sense of renewal and creation, yet it was difficult, back-breaking toil. The workday was from dawn until dusk. During the Arab riots the burden of guard duty and other security-related tasks, which filled the days and nights, grew heavier.

Fields were set on fire and members of the village were called urgently from their work to put out the fires which were devouring the fruits of their labors.

Henya Shulami, as she went out to the barn in her farmyard, was killed in cold blood one night.

The children participated in the work, the responsibilities, the sorrows, and the joys of the community. On the farm, where hired hands never set foot, the children shared in the burden of work as a matter of course. Morning hours were devoted to studies, and afternoons to working on the various parts of the farm.

School itself was also something special. The society

2

the artist batia lichansky

In her work the sculptress Batia Lichansky produced everlasting testimony to the heroic fate and long suffering of the Jewish people in the Diaspora and the Land of Israel.

Through arduous labor she fashioned stone monuments in memory of sons who fell defending their homeland, in memory of the Holocaust and pogroms suffered by the Jews of the Diaspora, and other memorials expressing Jewish youths' vision of the future.

Aside from her large monuments, Batia Lichansky also sculpted busts of leaders of the renewed Jewish settlement in the Land of Israel, of novelists and poets from the period of the rebirth of the Hebrew language, and of her parents and sisters.

In her works one sees a visionary spirit and faith on the faces of thinkers and fighters alike, one sees faces looking to the future and bearing the very strength of purpose that made it possible to advance the Zionist idea.

Batia Lichansky was born in 1900 in a village in the Ukraine. She immigrated to the Land of Israel at the age of 10 and studied in the Hebrew Gymnasium in Jerusalem and in the Herẓlia Gymnasium in Tel Aviv. In 1919 she began to study painting in the Bezalel School of Art in Jerusalem and continued her studies in the Royal Academy in Rome. When the 1921 riots broke out she returned to the Land of Israel, enlisted in the Labor Brigade, and joined the settlers founding kibbutz 'En-Ḥarod (1922). Later she continued her studies in Berlin and at the Ecole des Beaux-Arts in Paris and returned to the Land of Israel at the end of 1929.

In 1986 she was awarded the Israel Prize for her life's work of artistic creativity extending over a period of more than sixty years.

understood that its continued existence and the preservation of its values depended to no small extent on educating the younger generation. This understanding was not simply theoretical; forty percent of the total public budget of the village was allocated to education.

The school had no janitors, gardeners, maintenance workers or secretarial staff; everything was done by the pupils and their teachers.

The teachers were full and equal members of the village, involved in its everyday life, close to their pupils, even forming lasting bonds of friendship with them.

Here too, life was not without friction and difficulties, between teachers and parents, and between these and their children or pupils. Yet this friction always stemmed from caring and from a sense of the importance of education. Teachers left their mark upon their pupils through personal example and by molding new and original ways of educating.

School, with its restrictions, studies, hardships, responsibilities, and sometimes boredom, also provided us enriching experiences, laid the foundation for our social cohesiveness, and gave us a sense of direction. The crowning glory of the education we were given lay in nurturing our bond to our country, its history and nature. The program of annual class trips covered all areas of the country. Every year we went on long hikes, even when there were Arab riots.

These trips, organized and led by David Barash, agronomist and part-time teacher, by Menachem Zaharoni, and by other teachers, inspired the youngsters and teenagers to hike on their own initiative, spontaneously and independently.

The eucalyptus grove full of wildflowers, the Sheikh Abreik woods, and the excavations at Bet She'arim, in which the children of Kefar Yehoshua' took part, all beckoned to us.

In winter the Kishon River fills with water, overflowing its banks and inundating plowed fields sown with wheat and ... narcissus.

Mire and mud did not deter the children from going out to the fields to inhale the fragrance of the narcissus and to gaze on the small, innocuous-looking brook which overnight had become a mighty river.

dancing in pajamas in the village square

In general, farmers are thought to be conservative, provincial people, for the most part uneducated. Among us, in the re-emergent Jewish village, different in its motivation and its way of life, a new kind of farmer emerged: an educated, cultured person, close to books and the world of ideas.

Even after a long and wearying day of work we set aside time in the evening for books, lectures, and theatrical productions. Every home had its books. There were also lecture series and public libraries which lent books to children and adults. Holidays were celebrated in a manner especially adapted to our rebirth in our own land. Plays were performed under the starry sky, on a stage built earlier that day, before an audience seated on bales of hay. Movies were also shown in the open air. The children used to crowd with curiosity around the miracle-worker as he ran the movie projector, excitedly gathering up the scraps of celluloid as they fell from his hands.

Thus passed workdays and holidays, days of rain and mud, days of heat and dust, mundane days and great days. Then came November 29, late in the evening. Suddenly there was a knock at the door. Ophir, a seventeen year old youth, stood in the doorway.

"What's up, in the middle of the night?"

"We have a State!" he cried excitedly. "They passed the resolution!"...

The happiness of a dream come true. The whole village came out in pajamas to dance the *hora* to the point of intoxication. Joy passed all bounds, leveled barriers, united us all....

The next day brought a sober awakening: the first battles. The village emptied of its young men. The sound of shooting echoed from the direction of Mishmar ha-'Emeq.... the first bad tidings.... tearful eyes.... bereaved parents bearing their heads up in pride and sorrow.

Ophir fell at Beit Maḥsir, Dov at Radar, Ya'ir at Tel Litvinsky, 'Ami at Nir'am... One after another fresh graves were dug. A new page in the history of the village was written at the foot of the hill overlooking the valley. The State was newborn, but the village had reached maturity and, bearing its scars, sank its roots deeper and raised its vistas higher.

Farms grew and developed, and along with them public institutions were built: a large cultural hall, a swimming pool bursting with activity, an ever growing library, and Ḥankin House...

a museum and botanical garden

It began with the science room of the school. Tools, laboratory equipment, and nature and archaeology collections were gathered together bit by bit, with love and devotion, by a young teacher* and ardent disciple of Yehoshua' Margolin, who inspired children and adults alike with his love and enthusiasm.

Ḥankin House was built by the village in fulfillment of Yehoshua' Ḥankin's last will. The money which Ḥankin bequeathed in his will was eroded through the years and no longer sufficed to build the museum. Therefore the village council took it upon itself to erect the building.

Ḥankin House is further testimony to the capabilities of the individual. Without a budget, almost without help, an institution housing a museum of nature and archaeology, laboratories, a library, an animal corner, and a botanical garden arose. But these are all secondary to the true significance of the edifice which is the educational activity carried on within its walls.

* Menachem Zaharoni, a student of Margolin, taught in Kefar Yehoshua' and later in the A. D. Gordon Teachers' Seminar in Haifa. One of the founders of the Society for the Protection of Nature, he studied the Land of Israel, its history and nature, and attracted many disciples.

1 *Kefar Yehoshua' is built in the shape of the Hebrew letter* yod, *the letter beginning the name of Yehoshua' Ḥankin, redeemer of the land on which the* moshav *was built.*

1

Teachers from all over the Jezreel Valley came week in and week out, by public transportation, to expand their knowledge here. The students of two teachers' seminars, one in Haifa and the other in Nahalal, came to spend a full day here each week, studying nature and agriculture. In the summer teachers came from all over the country, slept in the shed of the storeroom, and studied for an entire month.

Of course Ḥankin House served the pupils of the village school, but thousands of other people have also paid visits to it through the years.

Incredible as it seems, a single person actually served as principal, teacher, laboratory worker, janitor, and caretaker for the plants and animals. One man, Menachem Zaharoni, singlehandedly maintained the educational endeavor and supplied all its needs. His activities and impact extended far beyond the limits of the village and the region, Ḥankin House was the pride of the residents of the village.

As you drive through the Jezreel Valley, turn off to Kefar Yehoshua' and drive through the village. You will be filled with wonder and admiration at the beauty of its streets, its groves, and gardens, and will sense the strength of its economy and the spirit of its members. And, passing the old and picturesque water tower, you will stand in silent respect before the memorial to the sons of the village who fell in battle.

Then turn north to the cemetery. There you may wander among the tombstones and read the history of the village inscribed in the stones. Turn around to look at the village lying beyond; you will know that their work was not in vain.

the days of tower and stockade
1936-1939

Irit Zaharoni

Rising anti-Semitism in eastern and central Europe* and persecution of the Jews on a scale unknown since the Middle Ages spurred tens of thousands of Jews to immigrate to Ereẓ Israel (the Land of Israel).

The British High Commissioner, Sir Arthur Wauchope, was sympathetic towards these persecuted people and, in view of the relative calm in the country and the policy of economic growth, decided to increase the immigration quota. The Jewish Agency's organizational talent and the economic boom in the Jewish community of Ereẓ Israel resulting from capital inflow from Germany led to an unprecedented rise in the number of immigrants. In fewer than three years (1933-1935) over 170,000 Jews entered the country legally. By the time the British hurriedly shut the gates, in response to the Arabs' irate reaction to such large-scale Jewish immigration, the *yishuv* (Jewish community in Ereẓ Israel) numbered over 350,000 people. Immigration in the mid-1930's doubled the Jewish population of the land, bringing the *yishuv* to one third of the land's total population.

On April 19, 1936, attacks on Jewish persons and property erupted in Jaffa and its border with Tel Aviv. Arab rioters descended on the Jews, wounding and murdering them and plundering their property. The death toll was heavy, and in a few days Arab assaults on Jews spread to all parts of the country. The riots of 1936-1939 had begun.* Behind the outburst were extremist Arabs' apprehensions of the rapid growth of the Jewish community. The Arabs demanded an end to Jewish immigration, prohibition of Jewish land acquisition, and establishment of an Arab government in Ereẓ Israel (the Land of Israel). The Arabs of Ereẓ Israel began a general strike that lasted 175 days and was intended to strangle the *yishuv* by cutting off the supply of food and agricultural produce from Arab farms, by closing Jaffa port, the gate to the Jewish population of Ereẓ Israel, etc. Its effect, however, was to make the Jews develop their own economy at an accelerated pace, finding suitable alternatives that helped strengthen and increase the autonomy of the *yishuv*. For example, a Jewish port was established in Tel Aviv in place of the port of Jaffa which had been closed, and Jewish settlements rapidly developed the supply of fresh agricultural produce to the *yishuv*.

Riots and bloodshed lasted three years, exacting a heavy price in lives and money from the Jewish community. The first year eighty Jews were murdered and 400 wounded and thousands of attacks were made on Jews and Jewish property ruined.

Arab gangs attacked Jewish traffic on the roads, set ripe wheat fields ablaze, uprooted fruit trees and forests, and tried to cut off and isolate remote Jewish settlements. They also attacked the British, nor did they refrain from striking at other Arabs (hundreds, perhaps thousands, of moderate Arabs were killed on suspicion of collaborating with Jews, and many were murdered in "settling personal accounts").

The Jewish community mobilized to repulse these attacks, entrusting the matter to the *Haganah*, the *yishuv's* underground defense organization subordinate to the Zionist organs in Ereẓ Israel. They began with passive defense, i.e. protecting what already existed: defense positions were set up, isolated Jewish settlements were fortified and roads between them improved (with the aim of enabling isolated Jewish settlements to withstand Arab attacks on their own), Jews living in Arab areas were relocated in more secure places, and driver's cabins on trucks, and later also on buses, were armored.

The Jewish community and its leadership expected the British Mandatory government to fulfill its duty of protecting the Jewish population against Arab violence. The High Commissioner, afraid of inflaming the situation, in the beginning deliberately held off the army and police from taking firm action against the strike and assaults on the Jewish community and the British.

As the situation deteriorated the Zionist organs demanded that the Mandate authorize Jewish defenders to be placed at vulnerable locations and be armed by the government. Thus the *notrim* (initially called *ghafirs*), temporary Jewish police, were born. This force, called the Jewish Settlement Police, was equipped and trained by the British to answer the burning problem of security in Jewish settlements. In time the *notrim* became a security arm of primary importance for the *yishuv*, many of them essentially being under the command of the *Haganah*.

debate over the policy of restraint

At an early stage of incidents with the Arabs the leadership of the *yishuv* decided on a policy of restraint, not to respond by violent action to Arab violence. As Arab terror increased, voices began to be raised against this policy and in favor of the right to react.

After much wavering the *Haganah* decided to replace the approach of static, passive defense with actively initiated defense. To this end they set up the *nodedet* (roving) unit, which operated beyond the fence of the settlements and attacked the rioters on their bases. Later the *plugot sadeh* (field companies), a nation-wide force that played an important role in defending tower and stockade settlements, was formed.

The British officer Orde Wingate was highly instrumental in imparting knowledge of methods of warfare to the new generation of *Haganah* commanders.

the peel commission

By the end of summer 1936 the situation in the country appeared to be at an impasse; the Arab strike and terrorism continued. In

---

* First conditions for the Jews deteriorated in Poland, where members of the government viewed "one million" of the country's three million Jews as "superfluous," and later conditions worsened in Germany with the rise of the Nazis to power in 1933.

* The Arabs called these riots the Arab Revolt, an uprising aimed simultaneously against the Zionist endeavor and British rule in Ereẓ Israel.

1

2

3

1,2 *Pictures from the movie* Summer in the Galilee, *shot in 1939. The photographer, Ephraim Layish, was a German immigrant.*

1 *Enthusiastically dancing the* horah *near the tower of kibbutz 'Amir, with the snow-capped Mount Ḥermon in the background.*

2 *Kibbutz 'Amir at the foot of the Golan Heights.*

3 *On guard – 1936. Rivka Linkovski, a member of kibbutz Nir David, beside the "stockade."*

The pictures on page 337:

2 *The heliograph – a device for signalling, with the aid of the sun's rays – at Ḥanita.*

3 *The dining room of* Plugot Hakibush *– the advance group that established and consolidated Ḥanita in its early days. Sketches by Menachem Shemi. The artist visited Ḥanita at the time it was founded and was profoundly impressed. These are the first rough sketches he made, which are in the museum at Ḥanita.*

1 *A fence builder at work. The northern border, today still serving as the international boundary between Israel and Lebanon, follows an artificial line devoid of any geographical sense. The borderline was set and marked in 1923 according to an Anglo-French agreement as the boundary between the British Mandate in the Land of Israel and the French Mandate in Lebanon and Syria. This line cuts through and divides the region which we call the Galilee. There is no physical-geographical difference between the regions on either side of this border, nor is there any natural obstruction preventing passage from one side to the other. After the outbreak of the "Arab Revolt," with the rise in penetration of the border by smugglers and members of Arab gangs attacking Jews, and British and Arabs who refused to collaborate, the British decided, in February 1938 to set up the "northern fence" along the border. Jewish laborers and engineers from the construction company* Solel Boneh *were taken on to do the job.*

1

Britain a commission was appointed under Lord William Peel to study the reasons for the riots and make recommendations for restoring order in Ereẓ Israel. The commission began its work in the country in November 1936 and its recommendations were published in July 1937. The principal and most important conclusion reached by the commission was to divide the western part of Ereẓ Israel among the two claimants to the region, establishing two separate national entities.

The region designated for the Jewish state included less than 20 percent of the area of western Ereẓ Israel, primarily along the coastal plain and in the valleys (where, thanks to the Zionist effort, the land became fertile). Jerusalem (with some 80,000 Jews) and its surroundings, the Lod airport and the corridor to the coast around Jaffa were to be a British enclave. The Arab state was to comprise over three quarters of the area of western Ereẓ Israel.

The Arabs rejected the proposal outright, whereas the *yishuv* and the World Zionist movement hotly debated whether to support the proposal or not. In 1938 Britain retreated from the proposals of the Peel Commission.

settlement effort as a counter-attack

In the period of the Arab riots establishment of new Jewish settlements reached a peak, especially in more remote areas. This was the most intensive, forceful and important response of the organized Jewish settlement effort to the Arab attempt to strangle and eliminate it. It was also a response to the trend evinced in the Peel Commission towards restricting the territory of the future Jewish state. The underlying assumption was that the more Jewish communities were established and the more new areas of settlement were opened, the broader the borders of the future Jewish state would be (for the Peel Commission had drawn its proposed borders according to the spread of Jewish settlement as it had developed until the outbreak of the riots).

The danger of new settlements in isolated areas being attacked by Arab gangs required the Jews to find decisive and swift means of operation, involving not only the core group of settlers but also forces of the *Haganah*, the cooperative agricultural settlement movement, and economic bodies of the organized settlement effort.

Defended settlements were established using a method first developed by the settlers who in the summer of 1936 founded *kibbutz* Tel ʿAmal (Nir David). Yehoshua Lurie, a member of the *kibbutz* writes: "The members of Tel ʿAmal sat down to plan how they would stake their claim to the land, notwithstanding the difficult security conditions and knowing that beyond Bet Alfa Arab gangs were lying in wait for us. Various proposals were advanced in the course of lengthy debate over the form our settlement claim should take.... Then the idea came up of erecting a double wall of wood, with gravel fill in between, encompassing an entire courtyard in which we would put up residential huts, a dining hall and kitchen, and a watchtower rising in the center."

The tactic of "tower and stockade," prefabricating

the days of tower and stockade – 1936-1939

1 *The tower of kibbutz Dafna in the northern Ḥula Valley. The settlement was founded May 3, 1939. On that day 76 members of the* kibbutz, *hundreds of members of Kefar Gilʿadi and members of the Haganah from all over the country pitched in to erect the new settlement.*

2 Notrim *(Jewish Settlement Police) and armored cars prior to departure of a convoy of civilian automobiles from Tel Aviv to Jerusalem.*

3 *A tower with a searchlight and huts in a new settlement. Drawn by Aharon Avni.*

4 *Erecting the stockade of kibbutz Tel Yiẓḥaq in the Sharon region, July 25, 1938. The stockade consisted of a double wall of wood with sand from the nearby field between the two walls.*

1

2

transportable buildings for a defended settlement prior to the actual founding, made it possible to establish a new settlement post in a few hours, and to set it up in such a manner that the Arabs would not have the force or means to remove it. Indeed, some such settlements were established in the dark of night, by morning their tower and double stockade, which became the symbol of all Jewish settlement in these years, standing proudly in place.

In these years around 60 new settlements were staked out, their location being determined by strategic and political considerations of a Jewish offensive to lay claim to regions hitherto neglected, establishing a foothold in the area. As an anticipated political decision on the fate of the land became more imminent, possibly partitioning it into a Jewish and an Arab state, settlement became a strategic question of prime importance. New strategic settlement efforts focused on the Bet She'an (Beth-shan) Valley, the Upper Galilee, and the western Galilee. Jewish settlements in these areas were liable to be cut off and isolated. Indeed, some new settlements faced heavy attack by Arab rioters from the moment they were established but managed to repulse them. Not a single Jewish position was destroyed or abandoned. The heroic stand of Ḥanita (on the Lebanese border) and Tirat Zevi (in the southern Bet She'an Valley) came to symbolize determination in the face of danger and hardship, holding on to new settlements under any condition.

aliyah bet – illegal immigration

During the Arab riots the Jews in Ereẓ Israel devoted much effort to continuing the wave of immigration, notwithstanding the British government's decrees and restrictions (the 1936 White Paper, which drastically curtailed the number of immigration certificates issued). Emissaries from Ereẓ Israel organized thousands of persecuted refugees from Germany and Eastern Europe to bring them to Ereẓ Israel, either legally or clandestinely, by boat and over land by way of the northern border. Seventy thousand Jews entered the land legally and 11,000 *ma'apilim* (illegal immigrants), primarily refugees from Germany, Czechoslovakia, and Austria, were brought in without certificates from the Mandate authorities. Some of these immigrants came from pioneering Jewish youth movements and upon their arrival played an important part in establishing new settlements and strengthening existing ones.

From 1936 to 1939, years of emergency and hardship, the very survival of the Zionist endeavor was jeopardized both by Arab aggression and by hostile British policy. During this difficult period the Jewish community in Ereẓ Israel proved its endurance and determination to fight for its survival and its right to continue realization of the Zionist dream.

In the face of rising Arab militancy and the instability which it bred, the Jewish community pursued a pragmatic and restrained policy, which thrived due to an internal democratic regime rich in voluntary activity. The Jewish community grew steadily, both in population and in number of settlements, developed a modern economy and built a strong Jewish defensive force.

Notwithstanding severe attacks on persons and property, the *yishuv* continued to grow, develop its organization, and strengthen itself, working towards the establishment of a Jewish state.

3

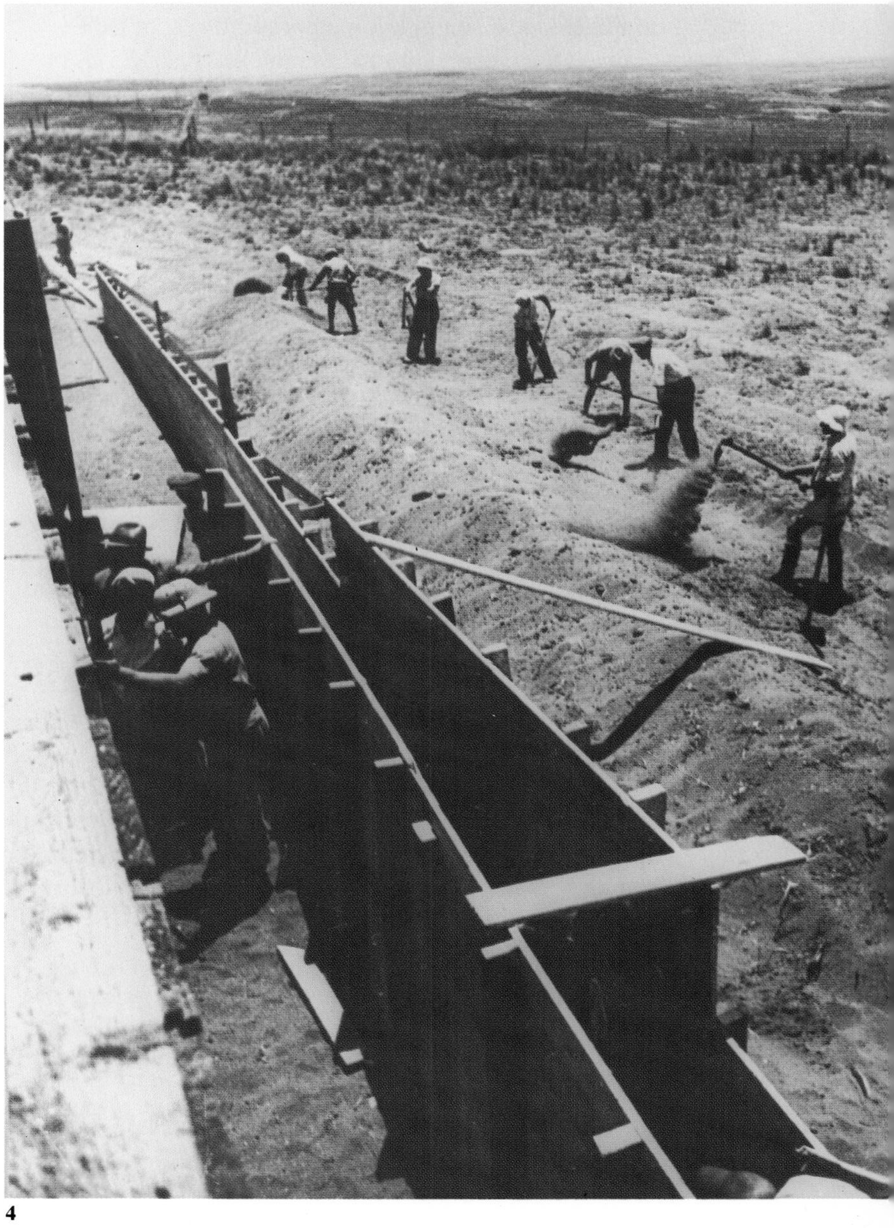

4

in the midst of desolation

Elḥanan Oren

The outbreak of the Arab Revolt inspired the leaders of the *yishuv* (pre-state Jewish community in the Land of Israel) with an unabating determination to settle the Negev, far from existing Jewish settlements. In July 1937, Kefar Menaḥem was founded on a site about ten kilometers east of Be'er Toviyya, at that time the southernmost Jewish settlement. Two weeks later the nucleus of Sha'ar ha-Negev settled on land southeast of Gedera. These settlements, however, still did not extend beyond the limits of Jewish settlement in the region of southern Judea or the partition line proposed by the British Royal Commission of Inquiry headed by Lord Peel.*

In 1939 the British Mandatory Government issued a policy statement drastically reducing the immigration quota for Jews and prohibiting Jewish land purchases in most parts of the country, save for about 7% of its area. Bitterness against this policy statement, known as the White Paper, gave rise to the decision to strike out southwards. Two months later *kibbutz* Negba established itself eight kilometers southwest of Be'er Toviyya. Since the British authorities imposed restrictions on Jewish movement in the region of Gaza that summer, the *Haganah* planned the settlement as a surprise operation, which was executed under the command of Joseph Rokhel (later Major General Avidar).

Further settlement of the southern part of the country was under consideration when the outbreak of World War II in September 1939 temporarily halted this activity. Despite the difficulties involved, the Jews continued to buy land in the south and the Negev through various circuitous means, since purchasing land there had been forbidden by the White Paper. In 1941-1942 several more settlements were founded east and south of Negba: Dorot, Gat, and Gevar'am. After the British victory in the battle of El Alamein and the Anglo-American invasion of North Africa, Nir'am and Be'erot Yiẓḥaq were added to the list. Gevar'am and Nir'am were especially important, for rich sources of water were found in their vicinity. The land was purchased on the advice of the hydraulic engineer Simḥah Blass, in accordance with a plan for irrigating the Negev he had worked out in 1939 at the request of Arthur Ruppin.

Despite the importance of settling south of Negba, its relative weight in the settlement effort was still rather small. Of the 20 settlements which were established throughout the country from the beginning of the war until January, 1943, only five were in the south, and these were actually north of the Negev, in the area known as Sha'ar ha-Negev or the Gateway of the Negev.

In the summer of 1942 the Zionist movement adopted the Biltmore Program, which called for the establishment of a Jewish Commonwealth in the Land of Israel upon the conclusion of the war. After the improvement in Allied fortunes in the battle against the Germans in the winter of 1942-1943, the leadership of the *yishuv* and the Zionist movement began to realize more clearly that with the end of the war the fate of the country would be decided, and that the Jewish position had to be strengthened while there was still time. The Jewish institutions decided to step up the pace of settlement, penetrating boldly into new areas. In April 1943, Kefar 'Eẓyon was founded in the Judean Mountains, and in the same month a joint decision was taken by the Settlement Department of the Jewish Agency, the Jewish National Fund, and the Agricultural Center to establish three observation posts in the Negev, south of Beersheba (Be'er Sheba). This was to be the first penetration of Jews into the area, even beyond the Gaza – Beersheba road.

Joseph Weitz, Director of the Jewish National Fund's Land Development Division, formulated the objective of the observation posts: to serve as testing stations in areas where a block of Jewish settlements would be built after the war. The settlers would be considered employees of the Jewish Agency,

* The Peel Commission was appointed by Britain in response to the Arab riots of 1936-1939, and was charged with finding a way to resolve the unrest in the country. Initially the commission came up with a three-way partition plan: a Jewish state, an Arab state, and an area under international control. The proposed Jewish state was to extend along the coastal plain from Ashdod to Rosh ha-Niqra, and to include the Jezreel Valley, the Bet She'an Valley and the Galilee. The entire area of the proposed Jewish state amounted to less than one quarter of the British Mandate and did not include any of the Negev.

Observation posts in the midst of desolation – Three small groups established a hold in three regions south of Beersheba and made a fait accompli: the Jews live in the remote Negev, as well.

1 *Bet Eshel, the third observation post in the Negev, east of Beersheba, established on October 9, 1943. Planned as a future* moshav. *The settlers of Bet Eshel, including women and children, were besieged by the Egyptians all through the War of Independence, until Beersheba was captured in Operation Yo'av. When the war ended, they abandoned the Bet Eshel observation post and founded* moshav *Ha-Yogev in the Jezreel Valley.*

The observation posts were intended as research stations for studying three regions of the Negev, where blocks of settlements were being planned.

engaged in an experimental project for at least two years. If the experiments justified developing the area, the observation post would be expanded into a settlement. Initially Weitz planned a chain of about ten observation posts, six to be built in the first stage, but it was decided to begin with only four points: Bet Eshel, Gevulot, Revivim, and Ruḥama (the last one, however, was not established until 1944).

three different regions

About a dozen members at each observation post were to research the condition of the soil, climate, flora, and water supply in three different regions of the northern Negev – the coastal region, the plateau of Beersheba, and the vicinity of 'Asluj. Pioneering groups set out southward for a prolonged period of isolated life, leaving behind comrades affiliated with the settlement who explicitly consented to wait in the north until the settlement was sufficiently established for them to join it.

On May 12, 1943, twelve men and women settled on the land of Gevulot, in the western Negev, north of the border with the Sinai Peninsula, about thirty kilometers from the nearest Jewish settlement, Be'erot Yiẓḥaq. In calm times one could reach Gevulot by way of the Gaza – Rafiaḥ road, turning east at Khan Yunis. When the War of Independence broke out, contact with the hinterland was maintained by way of dirt roads and the "Famine Road," the present-day Magen – Ofaqim road, part of which was paved in 1946-1947, during a severe drought, in order to give work to the starving bedouins.

At the time it was feared that the British might try to foil attempts to get a foothold in the Negev. Hence it was decided to establish the settlements without any publicity and to camouflage them under the guise of teams going out to conduct surveys and prolonged experiments. Actually the founders of Gevulot and other observation posts did not encounter any opposition from the authorities.

At the end of July the Revivim post was established thirty kilometers south of Beersheba and, in early October, Bet Eshel, east of Beersheba, on the Negev plateau. Gevulot and Revivim were planned as *kibbutzim* (collective farm settlements) and Bet Eshel as a *moshav* (cooperative smallholders' village). All three settlements were built on loess and sand. Each observation post was to carry out a systematic investigation of the soil and climate and of the flora and water sources in its vicinity. Each region had unique soil and climatic characteristics, but all were thirsty for water. The annual precipitation at the observation posts was infinitesimal, 250-300 mm. at Bet Eshel, 200-250 mm. at Gevulot and no more than 80-100 mm. at Revivim. Here attempts were made to dam up Naḥal Revivim, but the dams could not withstand the force of the flash floods.

David Ben-Gurion, head of the Jewish Agency, viewed the observation posts as opening the way to the great enterprise of conquering the desert. In the fall of 1943 he delivered his "desert address" at a convention of the Jewish National Fund, praised the Negev pioneers, and even cast his glance towards Elat and the kingdom of Solomon whose remains were being uncovered at the time in excavations by the archaeologist Nelson Glueck. At the end of that year, addressing a conference of fishermen, he called on his audience to storm Elat and take over fishing in the Red Sea and wished the fishermen that they might hold their next conference in Elat.

Economic difficulties inherent in opening the Negev to settlement were not long in coming. For example, the cost of supplying water over dirt roads to Gevulot reached 40 Israel pounds per month, a considerable sum in those days.

Those who settled the observation posts needed courage and a pioneering spirit to face the problems of security and the lack of a social life. The settlers took a calculated risk. The posts were extremely remote from the network of Jewish settlements in the region bordering on the Negev, the nearest area to which they could look for aid in time of attack.

The *Haganah** provided special security arrangements to enable the settlers of the observation posts to withstand a prolonged attack under conditions of isolation. Each post was built like a fort: a two-storey security building, a corner tower, and farm sheds were built in a yard surrounded by a stone wall. Much thought was given to building the fort aesthetically, in order to reduce the sense of isolation. The *Haganah* also saw to wireless communications with the remote observation posts, although these had to be maintained clandestinely, since the British did not permit the operation of transmitters.

The settlers were employed in building the forts and, until their completion, lived in temporary quarters. In Revivim they actually lived in a cave. Moving into their homes marked an important moment in the life of the settlement nucleus, as Joseph Weitz put it, giving the members a sense of "getting under way from a new beginning."

Until the end of World War II there were no threats to the security of the observation posts, and their members actually managed to foster neighborly relations with the bedouins, helped to purchase land and to guard land already acquired in the Negev.

1

the burden of solitude

As the days went by, social pressures in the pioneering group mounted. They felt their isolation from the remainder of their group, who were waiting impatiently in the north for the day the entire nucleus could settle down at the post. Work progressed at the posts, and the number of people living there was gradually increased, but by no means to more than 20-25 people at each post. The mood of the times is reflected in the book of Yonat and Alexander Sened*, *Adamah le-lo Ẓel* (Land without Shade), a work which for many people brought to life the feeling of being cut off from society and the feeling of primal creation experienced by the first Jewish settlers in the Negev.

Most of the members of Revivim and Gevulot lived in the camp near Rishon le-Ẓiyyon, and the members of *moshav* Bet Eshel at first lived near Nahalal. The latter group, who suffered from the isolation, transferred their families to Giv'at Micha'el near Nes Ẓiyyona, and later started sneaking single members

* The *Haganah* was founded in 1920, during the Arab riots against the Jews in Jerusalem. It was organized and run by the *Va'ad Le'umi* (National Council), the official representative organ of the Jews in the Land of Israel. Initially it operated clandestinely with respect to the British authorities. Its duty was to protect Jews in Jewish settlements and in Jewish neighborhoods of mixed cities against attack by Arab gangs. The *Haganah* was established in order to provide a foundation for a Jewish armed force, in anticipation of the future establishment of a Jewish state. All factions of the *yishuv* were part of the *Haganah*, although its leaders were primarily from the Labor Movement. The *Haganah* proved its importance and capabilities in the Arab riots of 1936-1939.

* Members of kibbutz Revivim.

2

1 *The Revivim observation post was established on July 29, 1943. The posts were built like forts: a two-storey security building, a corner tower, and a farm shed were built inside a courtyard, enclosed by a stone wall with a single entrance.*

2 *An experimental plantation of palm trees, planted in the early days of the Revivim observation post. The idea remained nothing more than an experiment.*

3 *Land without shade.... The loess soil expands when the rains come, but becomes cracked and parched under the burning summer sun.*

4 Maghura, *a Byzantine cistern hewn in the rock, with a supporting column. This is where the first settlers of Revivim lived. During the siege in the War of Independence the cistern became a place of refuge and station for gathering the wounded. At that time pipes for ventilation (shown in the picture above) were installed.*

into the observation post, until by 1945 there were 65 people living at Bet Eshel on a budget for no more than 25.

While the English did not actually make trouble for the observation posts, they did not view them with favor. The British scholar George Kirk, who subsequently became known as an expert on the Middle East, asserted that they were "nothing more than three front bases of a network for arms smuggling, spread over the Middle East," by volunteers in the British army, and were an indication of the intrigues devised by the Jewish Agency.

From the time the first posts were established until the end of the Second World War in 1945, there were only two new settlements in the south: in December 1943, Yad Mordechai was founded between Majdal and Gaza, and in the spring of 1944 the settlement at Ruḥama was re-established. With these settlements, the number of Jews in the southern and Negev regions reached 1,600, including affiliated members who were still waiting in the "hinterland." The lull in settling the Negev continued through 1945 and during the period of the "struggle" against the British, from the beginning of October 1945 until September 1946. This struggle, initiated by the leaders of the *yishuv* in response to the White Paper, found expression primarily in bringing in "illegal" immigrants and establishing settlements in areas which were officially proscribed. During this

3

4

1

stage of the struggle, 22 new settlements were established in the country, but none in the Negev.

The core groups who were setting up the observation posts pressed the powers that be to move up the date for their settlement, but Joseph Weitz maintained that, despite the progress which had been made in the experiments, it was not yet time to turn the posts into settlements. In September 1945, two full years after their establishment, Weitz submitted a report in which he stated that, although there had been progress, no post was yet ready for permanent settlement. Reliable data had not yet been obtained on agriculture, even with respect to field crops; there was still not enough land, nor was there a reasonable solution to the water problem. Therefore, he maintained, the posts ought to continue in their present form for another three years.

conquering new lands

The fate of the country, however, was in the balance, and the leadership of the *yishuv* sought to bolster Jewish strength in the Negev. In deliberations at the Jewish Agency, Moshe Shertok (Sharett), director of the political division, stressed that establishment of every new settlement would henceforth be discussed in terms of its political-strategic importance, in view of "the political importance of conquering new areas of land during this interim period." On the night of October 5th-6th, 1946, following the Day of Atonement, eleven settlements were established clandestinely throughout the Negev, in the region between Negba and the observation posts and along the route planned for the water pipelines to the Negev. From then on the observation posts were no longer isolated points; they became

2

the boundary markers of the network of settlements spread over the Negev.

Until the War of Independence the boundary of the area settled was marked by a line between the observation posts (save for the *moshav* of Nevatim, which was founded east of Bet Eshel). Thus by 1943 the three observation posts had already delimited the southern and eastern bounds of the area of Jewish settlement in the Negev.

This settled area, and the pipelines laid there in 1947, had a decisive impact on the UN commission which set the borders of the state and, since the commission believed in the Jews' ability to develop the area, included most of the Negev, down to Elat, within those boundaries. Indeed, when the War of Independence broke out, the settlements kept their hold on the northern Negev, even when this region was severed from the rest of the country, and in the end provided the springboard for the campaign southward to Elat.

1 *Irrigating the experimental date palm plantation of Revivim. The three settlements were erected on sand and loess. Each observation post had to make a systematic study of the soil, climate, flora and water sources in its region. Each region had soil and climatic conditions particular to itself, but all thirsted for water. The members of Revivim engaged in agricultural experiments and sought ways to overcome the water shortage for five years. They tried collecting water by damming up Naḥal Revivim, but the dams could not withstand the force of the flash floods; they looked for plants that could tolerate saline water, but none were found....*
"In 1948 hope seemed forlorn in everything concerning agriculture." Today kibbutz Revivim is blossoming; plants suitable to the desert were found and water was brought from the north.

2 *Gevulot, the first observation post in the Negev, was established on May 12, 1943.*

3 *Sowing the barren land of Gevulot.... Hope proved true, for today it is a verdant settlement on a sound economic footing.*

3

the extent of our will shall determine

Ben-Gurion in essays and speeches on the Negev

the negev – the cradle of our nation

The Negev is the cradle of our nation, the vulnerable region of our state, as well as its great hope.

When the patriarch Abraham was commanded to leave his country, his homeland in Mesopotamia, and to go to the destined land, he set out and journeyed towards the Negev. After famine forced him down to Egypt, he returned to the Negev; and after Sodom was overturned, when he parted from Lot, he traveled once more **"toward the land of the South** [the Negev], **and dwelt between Kadesh and Shur; and he sojourned in Gerar"** (Genesis 20:1).

Isaac his son also dwelled in the Negev; and there he met Rebekah, who came from Aram-naharaim.

The reason is clear: this was the uninhabited part of the land, as in our day, and the first immigrant from Iraq found wide latitude in the Negev.

The spies whom Moses sent to explore the land also started in the Negev and proceeded from there to Hebron. The first Canaanite king that the Children of Israel encountered in their journey from south to north was the king of 'Arad, who dwelled in the Negev.

1

Today, as then, the Negev is Israel's large, empty, open area. This area has seen much hardship and many changes since the patriarchs first set foot here; the ruins of cities in the Negev are silent witness to the efforts of generations to settle the wilderness. The Arab conquest reduced these efforts to naught; and today there is no longer any vestige of the numerous cities of the tribes of Simeon and Judah which once existed in the Negev: Kabzeel, Eder, Jagur, Kinah, Dimonah, Adadah, Kedesh, Hazor, Ithnan, Ziph, Telem, Bealoth, Hazor-Hadattah, Kerioth Hezron, Amam, Shema, Moladah, Hazar-shual, Beer-sheba, Baalah, Iim, Ezem, Eltolad, Chesil, Hormah, Ziklag, Madmannah, Sansannah, Lebaoth, Shilhim, Ain, Rimmon (Joshua 15:21-32), Sheba, Balah, Bethul, Beth-marcaboth, Hazar-susah, Sharuhen, Ether, Ashan (*Ibid.,* 19:2-7).

The prophets could never accept the desolation of the Negev. Isaiah prophesied: **"The wilderness and the parched land shall be glad; and the desert shall rejoice, and blossom as the rose... Then shall the lame man leap as a hart, and the tongue of the dumb shall sing; for in the wilderness shall waters break out, and streams in the desert. And the parched land shall become a pool, and the thirsty ground springs of water... And a highway shall be there, and a way, and it shall be called The way of holiness... but the redeemed shall walk there"** (Isaiah 35:1-9).

The courageous spirit and the toil of our pioneers over the past three generations transformed the face of the land while it was yet under foreign rule. The trailblazers – who paved the way to the establishment of the state – dried swamps, made sandy and rocky soil bear fruit, dug wells, planted vineyards and orchards, forested the hills, and built villages and cities; but their work was confined to the northern part of the country where the land is fertile and the rainfall is adequate. The south, the Negev, which is the greater part of the State of Israel, remained desolate until the establishment of the state. Jeremiah's malediction lay over the Negev whilst it was under foreign rule: **"The cities of the South are shut up, and there is none to open them"** (Jeremiah 13:19).

Three kings of the Davidic dynasty, Solomon, Jehoshaphat, and Uzziah, sought to reach the southern end of the land and make Elat a Jewish port at the tip of the Red Sea. The way to Elat, the 'Arava, and the city which lay on the shores of the Red Sea belonged at first to Edom, as we read in the Torah: **"So we passed by from our brethren the children of Esau, that dwell in Seir, from the way of the Arabah, from Elath and from Ezion-geber"** (Deuteronomy 2:8). Under David, Edom was conquered, **"and all the Edomites became servants to David"** (II Samuel 8:14). And Solomon, who directed all his efforts towards increasing the wealth of his realm through peaceful means, appreciated the economic importance of Elat. **"And king Solomon made a navy of ships in Ezion-geber, which is beside Eloth, on the shore of the Red Sea, in the land of Edom"** (I Kings 9:26). The split in the monarchy in the time of Rehoboam led to the loss of Elat. The fourth king after

the extent of our strength

2

Rehoboam, Jehoshaphat son of Asa, had the wisdom to make a treaty with Ahab king of Israel and conquered Elat, but after Ahab's death relations between Jehoshaphat and Ahab's son, King Ahaziah, deteriorated and the Jews lost Elat once more. Four generations later King Amaziah son of Joash defeated Edom in the Valley of Salt and seized Sela (the capital of Edom) in battle, and his son Azariah (or Uzziah), one of the great kings of Judah, perhaps the greatest of them all, **"built Elath, and restored it to Judah"** (II Kings 14:22). This time Elath remained in the hands of the Jews for three generations. When the Kingdom of Israel was destroyed, **"Rezin king of Aram recovered Elath to Aram, and drove the Jews from Elath; and the Edomites came to Elath, and dwelt there, unto this day"** (II Kings 16:6).

In our time, about six years ago (1949), "unto this day" was erased from the pages of history by the Israel Defense Forces, and Elat once more became a Jewish city. Thus for the first time in the history of our people the Jewish state had two exits to the sea: to the Mediterranean in the west, and to the Red Sea in the south, as promised in the Torah: **"And I will set thy border from the Red Sea even unto the sea of the Philistines"** (Exodus 23:31).

Israel is one of the few countries in the world with direct access to the Atlantic Ocean via the Mediterranean Sea and access to the Indian Ocean by way of the Red Sea, and from there on to the Pacific. In terms of global transportation the Negev is like the Suez Canal, serving as a bridge between the world's two major navigational zones, the East and the West.

The Negev is blessed with yet another sea, the Dead Sea, but, being a land-locked body of water, it is of no navigational value. However this sea, more than any other in the world, hides a treasure trove of natural resources in its salty water: vast quantities of phosphates, magnesium chloride, bromine, etc.

Since the plains of the Negev were redeemed by the IDF, the Negev has been studied anew, and the words of the Torah about the iron and copper hidden in the mountains and stones of the land (Deuteronomy 8:9) have been confirmed. Nor are these the only minerals found in the Negev.

The triangle of the Negev is wedged between two enemy lands: Egypt and Ammon (Jordan). The Negev is bounded on the southwest by the Sinai Desert and on the east by the Arabian Desert. The Arabs have turned quite a few countries into deserts, and the desolation does not disturb their existence. The continued existence of the State of Israel cannot suffer a desert in its midst.

If the state does not wipe out the desert, the desert is likely to wipe out the state. The narrow strip between Jaffa and Haifa, which contains the vast majority of the population in Israel, will not survive without extensive settlement of the Negev and the southern expanses of the country. The pressing, vital, and supreme call of our generation is to settle the wilderness and make it bloom. Of all the trials which we have faced and of all the battles which we have yet to face, this is the most difficult and the most blessed.

This challenge requires a prolonged national effort, much material investment, far-sighted planning, great practical capabilities, full utilization of scientific and technological advances, and above all – man's most supreme and valuable gift – the gift of the fulfilling, daring and creative pioneering spirit which neither shrinks from difficulty nor fears danger, the gift which makes man the master both of the forces of nature and of his own fate.

Only by appealing to this spirit in the youth shall we succeed in making the desert bloom, in transforming the broad expanses of the Negev into a source of might and strength, of blessing and wealth, for the State of Israel and the Diaspora.

what exists is not enough

Israel's first Prime Minister, addressing the Defense Committee, February 3, 1948

Our battle is not to defend the existing, for in my opinion there is nothing in the Land of Israel which may be called "existing" in the historical sense of the word. That which exists, if that alone is what we defend, is nothing but a house of cards that can be scattered by the slightest breeze. I cannot accept a proposal not to defend the desert – when we are obliged to provide defense for Tel Aviv. If we do not stand firm on the desert, Tel Aviv will not stand. The existence of the Negev is perhaps more tangible than the existence of Tel Aviv. Historical perspective tells us that nothing Jewish will have lasting existence in this land if we do not guarantee the victory of Zionism. Excluding twelve million dunams of desert land from the account is a non-Zionist calculation; that land defends Zionism, no more and no less. It is a mistake to assume that the Negev "will not run away" – and that it is our duty now to maintain with our own hands that which is in our hands, as certain unnamed individuals present here believe. If we do not take hold of the desert now, not only will the Negev "run away," but I am not sure that even Tel Aviv will remain in our hands. The question is not whether we should abandon or not abandon the Negev, but whether to go to the Negev or not. We are not even present in the Negev yet. The few points which we have in the south are not the Negev, and if we do not send sufficient force there, it means that we are abandoning it. If we are not present there, they will walk off with it for nothing, and we are only deluding ourselves if we believe that later they will give it to us.

In this respect there is no difference between our defense efforts and all our settlement efforts throughout the country. Those who immigrated to Israel did not come here to enjoy what exists. Even now what exists does not suffice, and surely it did not suffice 30 years ago, 40 years ago, and 70 years ago. All of my generation who came to the Land of Israel did not come to enjoy Tel Aviv, for Tel Aviv existed only as a vision. Stampfer and Salomon did not come here to enjoy Petaḥ Tikva, for even that city only existed in their dreams. And this visionary existence, not the actuality, motivated all our pioneers, and also motivates all those defending us. The young men who stand guard night after night to defend the Ha-Tikva quarter are not the ones who founded the neighborhood, nor the ones who built

1

Pictures on the two previous pages:

1 *The desert comes alive. Desert flowers have developed various ways of adapting to their habitat. Some plants wait patiently for sufficient rainfall not only to germinate their seeds but also to complete their full life cycle, through blossoming and the ripening of new seeds. In years of plentiful rainfall the desert suddenly bursts into bloom. In the picture, a sea of* Launaea angustifolia.

2 *In 1953 David Ben-Gurion resigned from the office of prime minister and minister of defense and went to live in kibbutz Sede Boqer in the Negev. Working in the sheep pen there.*

Pictures on this page:

1 Ranunculus asiaticus *blossoming on the Negev highlands. Rainwater accumulates in the shade of stones and in crevices of rocks, providing natural "flower-pots" for magnificent blooming plants.*

2 *Making the desert blossom – peach trees in bloom. "And hath made her wilderness like Eden, and her desert like the garden of the Lord" (Isaiah 51:3).*

On the next two pages:

"Thus your south side shall be from the wilderness of Zin" (Numbers 34:3). The Naḥal Ẓin rift valley, viewed from the Sedeh Boqer campus.

2

it, and more than defending their neighborhood, which is called "The Hope," they are defending hope itself, and the hope of the Negev is no less real a factor in our fighting, pioneering spirit, than the reality of Tel Aviv.

... It has been said here that methods of warfare should be determined by experts. Incontrovertibly, we need experts in all our undertakings, in agriculture, in industry, in education, and in warfare. But no expert shall determine what we shall fight for and what we shall not fight for. I go so far as to maintain: no expert shall determine beforehand what our military capabilities are. This is not a capability which is given, which is allotted beforehand. This capability is undoubtedly limited, but its measure depends greatly on the objective of the war. That which we are fighting for determines the extent of our capabilities. A limited objective limits our capabilities and a broad objective broadens them. What expert can tell us how far the Jewish people is prepared to go in defending its national future? If we wish to bring water to the Negev, experts will tell us how this should be done; but we shall not ask them if it is worthwhile or not worthwhile bringing water there. And I am not prepared to ask any expert if it is worth fighting for the Negev. I am sure that it is within our power to defend all of the Land of Israel, and I know wherein lies the source of our strength. If the expert knows the extent of our strength, he can advise us how to use it most effectively to achieve our goal. The goal itself shall be decided by our Zionist will, and the extent of our will shall determine the extent of our strength!

desolate land is difficult to hold

From David Ben-Gurion's address to a conference of moshav youth at Nahalal, June 11, 1954.

We have at our command two important possessions: a million and a half Jews and the land of the State. Here one might ask: the million and a half people are already in the State of Israel, why need we help them immigrate again? The land is in our hands, why need we redeem it again? What is the reality which we must change here?

A casual glance at the map gives the answer to this question. **The vast majority of our million and a half Jews are concentrated in several urban centers, while the vast majority of our land lies empty and desolate. And both these things harbor grave danger to the million and a half Jews and to the land.** First of all, there is the danger to our security. And there is no greater danger than this, today. I stress, today, for today there is a means of destruction which no one could have imagined a generation earlier. Concentration of the people in a narrow, confined area, in Tel Aviv and its environs, jeopardizes the entire state and our entire future. Today it is easy to wipe out all of Tel Aviv and its environs in a single blow, and if such a thing, God forbid, should happen, the entire state would be lost. Our only protection is population dispersal. In our day there is no such thing as absolute security anywhere in the world, for the era when wars were fought only between armies is gone, past

retrieval. War, in our day, means war by an entire nation and against an entire nation. There is hardly a place which is not vulnerable to the enemy's bombs, and there is no man or woman, young or old, who is out of danger. But there are different degrees of danger. The smaller and more dispersed our settlements, the less the danger. The more concentrated the population in a single place or in a few places, the greater the danger. And security considerations alone, that is, considerations of survival, considerations of life and death for our population, make it incumbent upon us to disperse our one and a half million people over the largest area possible, in many

1 *"The pressing, vital, and supreme call of our generation is to settle the wilderness and make it bloom.... The courageous spirit and the toil of our pioneers ... transformed the face of the land" (from the words of Ben-Gurion).*

settlements which are as far from one another as possible.

Danger also threatens the land which we possess as long as it remains desolate. For centuries the Arab nations have possessed, and still possess, large desert regions; and there is no danger of anyone taking these desert lands out of their hands. For us it is hard to keep hold of a desert in its desolation for long. We based our claim to this land not only on the rights of the Patriarchs, but also on the land being desolate and our being the only people who have the need and the talent to make the wilderness bloom. And it will not be easy to hold on to desolate land for decades, for people are already laying claim to it.

We can still recall the many debates in the United Nations over the Negev and the Galilee. The UN General Assembly did not include all of the Galilee within the borders of the Jewish state. The Negev was also the subject of much debate. And after it was decided to include it within the limits of the Jewish state – only after that – in view of Arab opposition, a resolution was adopted to send an arbitrator to the country, and this arbitrator afterwards lodged an appeal against the Negev having been given to Israel. This region serves as a wedge between the Arab states. And who knows, maybe in time it will become the most important part of the state? For its many mysteries have yet to be revealed...

the phenomenon of mass immigration

Yosef Gorny

The mass immigration of the 1950s was an all-embracing social phenomenon, culturally unique, which had a decisive national impact on the existence of the State of Israel. Nearly forty years have passed since that electrifying, agonizing period when masses of Jews streamed into the land: Holocaust survivors from the Displaced Persons camps of Germany; the "caravan people" from distant Yemen; the mountain people of the Atlas and the residents of the coastal cities of North Africa; the centuries-old Iraqi population that had dwelled along the shores of the Tigris and the Euphrates.

The newcomers encountered a weary community which had just undergone a war of survival – the War of Independence – and which had lost one per cent of its people, including some of its finest sons. The history of this mass immigration, the process by which it struck roots in Ereẓ Israel (the Land of Israel), and the nature of its encounter with the older, settled population have yet to be researched as a comprehensive whole, which could then project a balanced, multi-faceted image of the period. It is, in fact, surprising that this type of research has not yet been undertaken, for the mass immigration and its integration into the country was a uniquely daring social undertaking in the history of Zionist settlement in Ereẓ Israel. Perhaps its absence can be explained by the insufficient passage of time to allow for a more balanced historic perspective, or, alternatively, by the dynamic tempo of events in the State of Israel which offers the researcher more compelling topics in the diplomatic, political and military areas.

The historic basis of immigration to Ereẓ Israel lies in the view of Zionism as an idea that must be realized. The phenomenon of mass immigration could not have occurred were it not for the experience in the organizational, settlement, economic and psychological areas which had accumulated during the preceding sixty years, from the First *Aliyah* until the establishment of the State of Israel.

1

Between the early 1880s and the late 1950s there were six waves of immigration. The first three waves were the formative immigrations, while the last three were the solidifying ones. The three formative waves, during 1882-1923, were decidedly small in scale, especially in comparison with the mass Jewish immigration to the U.S. during the same period. On the other hand, the solidifying immigrations, during 1924-51, were massive in scale, both absolutely and in terms of the short time span in which they occurred.

At the time of the formative immigrations, the world was open to Jewish immigrants, so that masses of East European Jews, forced to emigrate, could choose between immigration to the U.S. and other countries, or *aliyah* to Ereẓ Israel. The main thrust was, indeed, to the U.S. However, from 1924 to the end of World War II and thereafter, in the wake of restrictive U.S. immigration laws, the choice of destination was no longer available. If the early minimal immigrations to Ereẓ Israel were characterized primarily by an ideological, even a messianic, basis, and a pioneering spirit, the later immigrations were triggered primarily by the distress of the Jewish population, which intensified from the mid-twenties onward. This type of differentiation ought not be applied too rigorously, for the impetus of distress was also present during the early immigrations, and the pioneering basis existed in each of the later immigrations as well. Nevertheless, what can be conclusively stated is that the early immigrations molded the new Jewish society in Ereẓ Israel, and that social norms were solidified, unaltered, by the later immigrants up until the establishment of the state. The two qualities – formation and solidification – were complementary, and together accounted for transforming the Zionist endeavor from dream to reality.

The First, Second and Third *Aliyot* – the formative immigrations – comprised some 100,000 immigrants who arrived during 1882-1923. They established the organizational and social structure of the Jewish community which was to serve eventually as a basis for the Jewish state. The First *Aliyah* (1882-1903) built the first *moshavot* (colonies), from Rosh Pinna in the Upper Galilee to Gedera in the southern Judean foothills, which constituted the first foothold on the land in terms of national settlement and agricultural pioneering. Simultaneously, new urban Jewish communities developed in addition to the traditional four holy cities of Jerusalem, Hebron, Tiberias and Safed. For example, a Jewish community of several thousand sprang up in Jaffa. These communities became support bases for the settlement of outlying *moshavot*. The First *Aliyah* also established the basis for Hebrew education, opening schools where the spoken language was Hebrew, indisputably one of Zionism's greatest achievements.

The Second *Aliyah* (1903-14) established several social precedents which were to have long-term implications for the fate

Despite the desperate situation of the masses of Jewish refugees in Europe, and the fact that at the international conference held on this subject in 1938 in Evian, France, no country was willing to accept large numbers of Jews, the British announced their new policy in May 1939, called the White Paper, terminating Jewish immigration to Ereẓ Israel (the Land of Israel). The Jewish people suffered the greatest tragedy in its history during the World War II period – six million of its people were murdered. After the war, the British prevented tens of thousands of Holocaust survivors from reaching Ereẓ Israel. Most of the boats commissioned by the representatives of the Jewish community (Yishuv) *in Ereẓ Israel to bring the exhausted refugees home were caught off the Ereẓ Israel shore, and the "illegal" immigrants were incarcerated in detention camps on the island of Cyprus.*

With the establishment of the State of Israel on May 14, 1948, the gates of the country were thrown open immediately to every Jew who wanted to come.

1 *The last "illegal" Jewish immigrant leaves the detention camp in Cyprus on his way home to Israel, 1949.*

Captions are on the next page.

2

3

4

the phenomenon of mass immigration

of the Jewish community in Ereẓ Israel. The activists among the immigrants of this period were groups of young people who established the Jewish labor movement in the country and laid the foundations for cooperative settlement as symbolized by Deganya. They created a Hebrew defense force – the *Ha-Shomer* society, which would be followed by the *Haganah* and the Israel Defense Forces. Building a network of political parties, unions and a political press, they also laid the foundations for political democracy within the Jewish community of Ereẓ Israel, a tradition which was passed on to the State of Israel. In addition, they created the ethos of the central role of young people in developing the new Jewish society through personal contribution, an ethos later to be passed on to Israel's youth movements.

The organizational, social and political systems of the Jewish community were forged during the Third *Aliyah* period (1919-23) in four main areas: the institutions of the Zionist Organization, which was the body that was granted legal status during the Mandate to represent the Jewish people throughout the world; the domestic representative institutions, or *Knesset Israel*, which turned an unorganized public into an autonomous national body; the labor movement's *Histadrut* (General Federation of Labor in Ereẓ Israel), which became the backbone of the entire political and social structure of Israel; and the *Haganah*, supported by the *Histadrut*, which became the defense force of the Jewish community. During this period, too, the communal settlement movement strengthened its unique structures – the *kibbutz*, the *kevutza* and the *moshav ovedim* (workers' cooperative) – becoming the implementing arm of the Zionist Organization's national policy. This movement made an important contribution not only in its influence on Jewish society in the country, but to a large extent in establishing the State of Israel's physical boundaries in 1948.

The later, solidifying, immigrations – the Fourth *Aliyah* (1924-31), the Fifth *Aliyah* (1932-39) and the Sixth *Aliyah* (1948-52) – were characterized, first and foremost, by their mass nature. Some 80,000 immigrants arrived during the Fourth *Aliyah* – that is, nearly the same number as had immigrated during the three preceding immigrations all together. The Fifth *Aliyah* exceeded the Fourth threefold, while the mass immigration following the establishment of the state was nearly three times again the size of the Fifth *Aliyah*. Its mass character was also more pronounced because it was compressed into a narrow time frame. In 1925 there were 34,000 Jewish immigrants, approximately a third of the Jewish population of the country then. In 1935, some 65,000 Jews arrived, approximately a quarter of the Jewish inhabitants, while during the first four years of the existence of the state, in 1948-52, the Jewish population doubled – from over 600,000 to nearly 1,400,000. This quantity of immigrants, both relatively and absolutely, had broad significance. It transformed the country's Jewish community into a national entity and gave the state a substantial Jewish majority.

The period of mass immigration witnessed expansion in both the rural and the urban sectors. Agricultural settlements became rooted throughout the country, while urban centers developed commerce, industry and services. The Fourth *Aliyah* made a special contribution to the growth of Tel Aviv. The Fifth *Aliyah* brought a large measure of Western culture to the country.

The mass immigrations during the first years of statehood were characterized by the quantity of immigrants and by their social and cultural diversity. These immigrations took place in a very different political and social environment from preceding immigrations. With the establishment of the state, the role of the Zionist movement changed drastically. It was no longer responsible for building the national home, for, with the restoration of Jewish nationhood, Zionism achieved both the longed-for national sovereignty, on the one hand, and strict supervision of all future development by the state, on the other. Whereas during the Mandate period, when Britain ruled the country, the Zionist movement waged a constant struggle with the authorities over immigration quotas and land acquisition, these matters were now controlled by national Jewish bodies. Furthermore, as a consequence of the catastrophe of World War II for the Jewish people, and the establishment of the state, these national bodies now had funds at their disposal, provided primarily by contributions from the Jewish people, restitution payments from Germany and loans from the U.S.

The mass immigration of the early years of statehood was, ultimately, the realization of the Zionist idea in its ingathering of

1

2

3

Pictures on the previous page:

2 *David Ben-Gurion, father of the mass immigration, visits a school in one of the immigrant absorption camps.*

3 *An Iraqi immigrant family in the Sha'ar Ha-Aliyah transit camp near Haifa, 1951.*

4 *The immigration of the remnants of European Jewry, which began in September 1948, brought most of Europe's Displaced Persons camp inmates to Israel, along with the immigrants in the detention camps of Cyprus.*

Pictures on these pages:

1,2 *Some 700,000 immigrants arrived during the period of the mass immigration. The receiving population was small, and the means available to the absorptive bodies meager. Temporary absorption sites* (ma'abarot) *sprang up throughout the country, offering tents or shanties for housing, and wooden huts for schools, clinics, groceries, synagogues and other services. The immigrants were assisted in finding work in the vicinity in order to support themselves. The assumption was that the stay in the* ma'abara *would be short, just until the immigrant could become integrated into Israeli society. Most of the* ma'abara *residents did indeed find permanent housing and employment during a very short period. In the picture: A hard winter in the* ma'abara.

3 *The immigration from the Islamic countries during the early years of the state, 1948–51, was a result of the distress, fear and persecution brought on by the rise of Arab nationalism, as well as yearnings for the return to Zion. The masses of Jewish refugees from the Islamic countries left all their possessions behind and arrived in Israel with little more than the clothes on their backs.*

Picture on the next page:

1 *Teaching in the* ma'abara. *The most pressing cultural need was to teach Hebrew to the masses of immigrants, adults and children alike.*

This article was translated by Judith Krausz.

the phenomenon of mass immigration

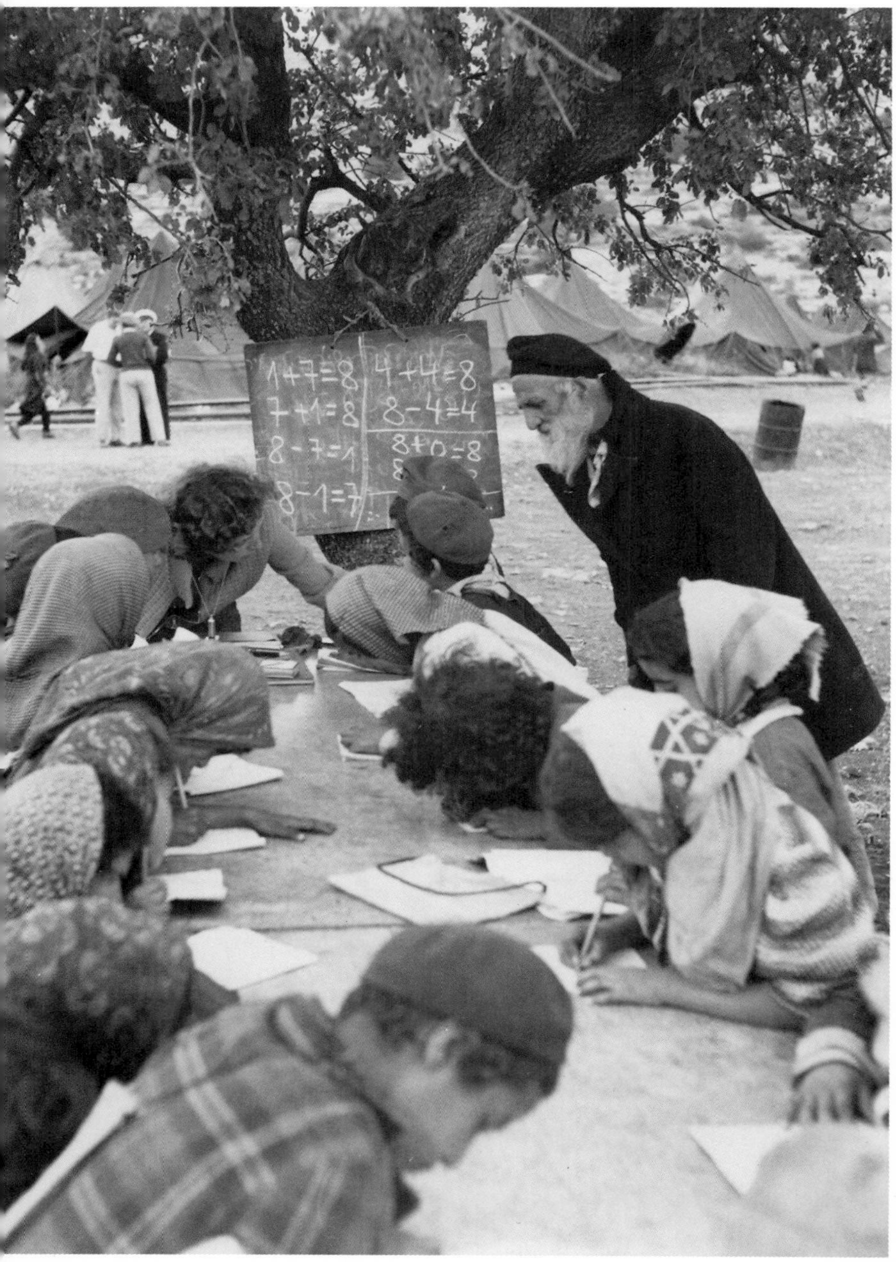

1

exiles and its integration of masses of Jews in distress. For the first time, the Zionist movement could offer a solution to Jewish distress: to Holocaust survivors whom no one wanted; to the Jews of Iraq, fearful of the rising tide of Arab nationalism; to the Jews of North Africa who feared their fate when the French withdrew from that region.

The masses who reached Israel's shores during this period were settled primarily in three different kinds of urban areas: in cities which already had a large Jewish population dating back to the pre-state period, such as the three major cities; in cities whose Arab populations had left; and in development towns which were established as part of the country's continuing settlement program. Some of the development towns were conceived as urban centers that would service surrounding agricultural areas, such as Qiryat Gat in the south and Qiryat Shemona in the north. Others were planned as a spearhead for settlement in unpopulated zones, such as Dimona, Yeroḥam and Elat. The development towns were a new, post-state component of the settlement plan, which heretofore had consisted of *moshavot*, *kibbutzim* and *moshavim*. All of them together served the national interest of settling border areas and filling the hinterland, with the mass immigration making a unique contribution in this area.

For the mass immigration was not exclusively urban; it also contributed to agricultural settlement. Some 300 agricultural communities were founded during the early years of statehood, two-thirds of them *moshavim* consisting of new immigrants. These settlements served too to populate the country's hinterland and secure its borders. In fact, settlement activity during the first four years of statehood equaled all that the Zionist settlement program had achieved during its first 65 years, from 1882 to 1947, in terms of size of population and number of agricultural settlements.

As a result of the mass immigration, the Zionist settlement endeavor became one of the largest and most comprehensive settlement projects in the world at that time. The Jewish community of Ereẓ Israel had undertaken the task of building a brand-new society. First it had to overcome the obstacles placed by the ruling British government in the land; the prolonged armed struggle with the Arab majority; and the constant threat of war after the establishment of the state. In addition to these objective obstacles, there was the difficult and dramatic confrontation between the new immigrants and the older, established community, as well as the cultural confrontation between the many immigrant groups themselves. These problems were exacerbated by shortages of the most basic necessities – employment and proper housing. Tents, shanties and temporary houses became immigrant neighborhoods that spread throughout the country. The immigrants of that period, with their achievements and their struggles, became an inseparable part of Israeli society. They had inherited the burden of suffering, loneliness and even disgrace that had been the lot of preceding generations of immigrants.

The mass immigration was both a marvel and a symbol. It was a marvel in the ingenuity of the immigrants to adjust to strange conditions; in the organizational ability of the receiving population to integrate hundreds of thousands of newcomers; and in the generosity of the Jewish people in the Diaspora in providing the means for building the Jewish society in Israel.

It was a symbol in the unique Jewish historic encounter between different cultures and traditions mixed together into a new reality, forging new communal patterns. It was also a symbol in that this immigrant population, the most socially diverse of all the Zionist immigrations, contributed so greatly to building the new society and made the kind of personal pioneering effort that had heretofore characterized the small elite groups of pioneers. Their pioneering efforts, which they were barely aware of, and which were sometimes the product of necessity, were no less worthy of recognition. These simple people knew little Hebrew and had no Zionist education, but they did have a deep, emotional national consciousness and thus wrote an inspiring page in Israel's history through their ordinary, everyday life-struggles.

transliteration and explanation of hebrew place names

Hebrew place names can be rendered in English in a wide variety of ways. We have chosen, as a general rule, to follow the spelling presented in Carta's Official Guide to Israel, based on the official transliteration system of the Academy of the Hebrew Language. We wished, however, to underscore the connection between biblical stories and their actual setting in Israel's landscape; hence many place names originating from the Bible are given according to their rendition in the Jewish Publication Society's translation of the Bible (for example, Kidron as opposed to Qidron). Other exceptions to Carta's transliteration system include names with an accepted and familiar form in English (for example Acre, Jerusalem, Tiberias, Capernaum) and minor modification of certain Carta transcriptions which were felt to be misleading in terms of pronunciation.

In transcription of proper names the letter Ḥ is pronounced like the guttural consonant in the Scottish "loch", and Ẓ like ts in "bits". Apostrophes, inverted (ʻ) and normal (ʼ) designate the letters "Ayin" and "Aleph" respectively.

Many Hebrew proper names are built of words whose meaning is important to a fuller understanding of the name. We wish to explain several such terms for the benefit of the reader.

Naḥal – a river or stream. The Land of Israel has very few spring-fed rivers that flow all year round; for example, Naḥal Dan. More often the term Naḥal denotes a seasonal watercourse or stream that flows only a short fraction of the year, during the rainy season; for example, Naḥal Kidron.

Wadi – denotes a rocky watercourse, dry except for several days in the rainy season. Wadis in Israel are found mostly in the Negev and the Judean Desert.

Ḥurba – ruins of an ancient settlement that have become covered with earth and vegetation. In Hebrew names it occurs in the construct form Ḥurbat ("ruins of"), as in Ḥurbat Bet Lavih in the Golan, or simply Ḥ, in abbreviation, as in Ḥ. Yavnit in the Galilee. The Arabic term for the same is Khirbe, or Kh. in abbreviation, as in Kh. Jifat, the same as Yodefat of the Great Revolt.

ʻEn – denotes a spring, as in ʻEn Rogel, meaning Spring of Rogel. Its Arabic rendition is ʻEin.

Quotations from the Bible have been taken from "The Holy Scriptures, A New Translation" (Philadelphia: The Jewish Publication Society of America, 1917).

list of maps

picture credits

Listed by page and picture number. Panoramas listed by two consecutive page numbers.

Alon Azaria: **233** – 1, 2; **234** – 1, 2; **235** – 4; **236** – 1; **242** – 1; **246** – 1; **349** – 1; **350-351**

Amit Itzhak: **234** – 3

Arad Shlomo: **16** – 1; **17** – 2; **22-23**; **50** – 1, 2; **53** – 1, 2, 3; **54** – 1; **55** – 2; **57** – 1; **58-59**; **63** – 1, 2; **65** – 1 , 2; **67** – 1; **253** – 1, 2, 3; **255** – 1; **256** – 1; **257** – 2, 3; **258** – 1; **259** – 2; **296** – 1; **297** – 2, 3; **298** – 1; **299** – 3; **311** – 1; **312** – 1; **314** – 1, 2; **316** – 1; **318** – 1; **324** – 1; **325** – 2, 3; **326** – 1; **327** – 4; **329** – 1; **352-353**

Ariel Publishing House: **10** – 1; **12** – 1; **18** – 1; **24** – 1

Bank of Israel Collection: **151** – 2

Bar-Am Micha: **92** – 1; **93** – 2; **94** – 1, 2; **97** – 1; **102** – 1; **124** – 1; **125** – 2; **126** – 1; **128** – 1; **305** – 2; **349** – 2

Bishko Herbert: **35** – 1, 2; **41** – 2, 4; **47** – 2; **182** – 1; **194** – 1; **196** – 1, 2; **197** – 3; **198** – 1; **199** – 2; **200** – 1; **201** – 2; **202** – 1; **205** – 1; **206** – 1, 2, 3; **207** – 4; **208-209**; **210** – 1; **211** – 3, 4; **212** – 1; **213** – 3; **215** – 3; **219** – 1; **245** – 4; **280** – 1; **281** – 2; **282** – 1; **283** – 2, 3; **340** – 1; **342** – 1 , 2; **343** – 4; **344** – 2

Braun Werner: **105** – 1, 2; **236-237**; **321** – 2

Brener Yitzhak: **25** – 2

Brown Ofer: **217** – 1

Darom David: **346** – 1

Deganya Archives: **302** – 1; **304** – 1; **306** – 1; **307** – 2; **309** – 1

Eitan Moshe: **273** – 2

Folberg Neil: **251** – 2

Freedman Dani: **129** – 2

Galili Dror: **285** – 2, 3, 4; **287** – 1, 2

Ginott Shai: **88-99**; **127** – 2; **157** – 2; **183** – 3

Gottesmann Zwi: **229** – 2

Government Press Office: **354** – 1; **355** – 2, 3, 4; **356** – 1; **357** – 2, 3; **358** – 1

Guthmann Hanoch: **76** – 1; **107** – 2; **108** – 1; **109** – 2; **111** – 2, 3; **114** – 1; **115** – 2; **116** – 1; **118** – 1; **119** – 2; **120** – 1; **121** – 3; **221** – 1, 2; **222** – 1; **223** – 2; **225** – 1; **226** – 1; **227** – 2; **228** – 1; **230** – 1; **231** – 2; **289** – 2; **290** – 1; **291** – 2, 3

Ḥadera Historical Archives: **288** – 1; **291** – 4; **294** – 1; **295** – 2

Haganah Historical Archives: **313** – 2; **338** – 1

Hanani Jacky: **271** – 1; **272** – 1; **275** – 3

Ḥankin House, Kefar Yehoshua‘: **327** – 2; **330** – 1

Hay Avraham: **110** – 1; **132** – 1, 2; **135** – 1; **136** – 1; **138** – 1; **139** – 2, 3; **140-141**; **142-143**; **147** – 1 ,2; **190** – 1; **193** – 1

Israel Exploration Society: **26** – 1; **27** – 2; **42** – 1; **134** – 2; **144** – 1; **145** – 2; **148** – 1; **149** – 2; **155** – 4; **203** – 2; **205** – 2; **210** – 2; **212** – 2; **214** – 1, 2; **245** – 3

Kariv Itai: **158** – 1; **160** – 1; **333** – 1

Keren Uzi: **32** – 1; **33** – 2; **36** – 1, 2; **37** – 3; **38** – 1; **39** – 2; **42** – 2; **45** – 1, 2, 3; **46** – 1; **48** – 1; **49** – 2; **91** – 1; **95** – 3; **100** – 1; **101** – 1, 2; **153** – 1; **156** – 1; **158** – 2; **162-163**; **244** – 1; **279** – 1

Krause Family Archives: **276** – 2; **292** – 1; **293** – 2

Laish Ephraim: **335** – 1, 2

Lester Kenny: **99** – 2; **184-185**

Ma‘ariv Archives: **274** – 1; **275** – 2; **301** – 2; **320** – 1

Raban Avner: **106** – 1

Radovan Zev: **176-177**; **178** – 1, 2; **179** – 3; **181** – 2, 3, 4; **187** – 1; **188** – 1; **189** – 2, 3, 4; **190** – 2; **191** – 3; **238** – 1; **249** – 2

Reshef Ora: **73** – 1; **327** – 3; **331** – 1

Revivim Archives: **343** – 3; **344** – 1

Shoob Amikam: **11** – 2, 3, 4; **13** – 2; **14** – 1; **19** – 2, 3, 4; **21** – 2; **29** – 1; **30** – 1; **31** – 2, 3

Tel Ḥai Archives: **315** – 3; **319** – 2

Tsarfati Michael: **250** – 1; **284** – 1; **337** – 2, 3; **339** – 3

Vered Avraham: **239** – 2; **240** – 1; **241** – 2; **243** – 2, 3; **245** – 2; **247** – 2; **248** – 1; **261** – 1, 2 ; **262** – 1; **263** – 2, 3; **264** – 1

Weinberg Moshe: **167** – 2; **168** – 1; **169** – 3, 4; **170** – 1; **172** – 1; **173** – 2; **174** – 1; **175** – 2

Yariv Rafi: **325** – 4

Zaharoni Ilan: **70** – 1; **71** – 2; **73** – 2; **74** – 1, 2, 3; **75** – 4; **77** – 2; **78** – 2; **79** – 1, 3; **80** – 1; **81** – 2, 3; **83** – 2; **84** – 2; **85** – 1, 3; **87** – 1, 2, 3; **120** – 2; **122-123**

Zionist Historical Archives: **265** – 2; **299** – 2, 4; **300** – 1; **322** – 1, 2; **323** – 3; **335** – 3; **336** – 1; **338** – 2; **339** – 4; **345** – 3; **347** – 2